SOCIAL ISSUES, JUSTICE AND STATUS SERIES

YOUTH VIOLENCE AND JUVENILE JUSTICE: CAUSES, INTERVENTION AND TREATMENT PROGRAMS

SOCIAL ISSUES, JUSTICE AND STATUS SERIES

Risk and Social Welfare
Jason L. Powell and Azrini Wahidin (Editors)
2009. ISBN: 978-1-60741-691-3

Risk and Social Welfare
Jason L. Powell and Azrini Wahidin (Editors)
2009. ISBN: 978-1-60876-798-4
(Online Book)

Low Incomes: Social, Health and Educational Impacts
Jacob K. Levine (Editor)
2009. ISBN: 978-1-60741-175-8

Handbook on Social Change
Brooke H. Stroud and Scott E. Corbin (Editors)
2009. ISBN: 978-1-60741-222-9

Handbook on Social Change
Brooke H. Stroud and Scott E. Corbin (Editors)
2009. ISBN: 978-1-60876-776-2
(Online Book)

Social Development
Lynda R. Elling (Editor)
2009. ISBN: 978-1-60741-612-8

Social Development
Lynda R. Elling (Editor)
2009. ISBN: 978-1-60876-688-8
(Online Book)

Handbook of Social Justice
Augustus Kakanowski and Marijus Narusevich (Editors)
2009. ISBN: 978-1-60741-713-2

Doctoring Medical Governance: Medical Self-Regulation in Transition
John M. Chamberlain
2009. ISBN: 978-1-60876-119-7

Who Pays the Price? Foreign Workers, Society, Crime and the Law
Mally Shechory, Sarah Ben-David and Dan Soen (Editors)
2010. ISBN: 978-1-60876-320-7

Social Epileptology: Understanding Social Aspects of Epilepsy
Jaya Pinikahana and Christine Walker (Editors)
2009. ISBN: 978-1-60876-228-6

**Race and Ethnicity: Cultural Roles, Spiritual Practices
and Social Challenges**
Jonathan K. Crennan (Editor)
2010. ISBN: 978-1-60692-099-2

**Race and Ethnicity: Cultural Roles, Spiritual Practices
and Social Challenges**
Jonathan K. Crennan (Editor)
2010. ISBN: 978-1-61668-535-5 (Online Book)

**Youth Violence and Juvenile Justice: Causes,
Intervention and Treatment Programs**
Neil A. Ramsay and Colin R. Morrison (Editors)
2010. ISBN: 978-1-61668-011-4

Issues and Lessons for Incarcerated and Released Parents
Jonathan T. Swift (Editor)
2010. ISBN: 978-1-60692-961-2

Runaway and Homeless Youth
Josiah Hughes and Isiah Wright (Editors)
2010. ISBN: 978-1-60741-521-3

Sexual Harassment around the Globe
Katherine C. Wong
2010. ISBN: 978-1-60876-328-3

Sexual Harassment around the Globe
Katherine C. Wong
2010. ISBN: 978-1-61668-348-1 (Online Book)

Disconnected Youth
Gregory Dublanc (Editor)
2010. ISBN: 978-1-60876-135-7

Counting the Homeless: Unsheltered and Sheltered
Trevor D. Morgan (Editor)
2010. ISBN: 978-1-60876-760-1

Community Oriented Policing: Background and Issues
Jake V. Burke (Editor)
2010. ISBN: 978-1-60876-767-0

Social Policy: Challenges, Developments and Implications
Lara P. Harrison (Editor)
2010. ISBN: 978-1-60876-961-2

Same-Sex Issues
Jason V. Albertson (Editor)
2010. ISBN: 978-1-61668-220-0

SOCIAL ISSUES, JUSTICE AND STATUS SERIES

YOUTH VIOLENCE AND JUVENILE JUSTICE: CAUSES, INTERVENTION AND TREATMENT PROGRAMS

NEIL A. RAMSAY
AND
COLIN R. MORRISON
EDITORS

Nova Science Publishers, Inc.
New York

Copyright © 2010 by Nova Science Publishers, Inc.

All rights reserved. No part of this book may be reproduced, stored in a retrieval system or transmitted in any form or by any means: electronic, electrostatic, magnetic, tape, mechanical photocopying, recording or otherwise without the written permission of the Publisher.

For permission to use material from this book please contact us:
Telephone 631-231-7269; Fax 631-231-8175
Web Site: http://www.novapublishers.com

NOTICE TO THE READER

The Publisher has taken reasonable care in the preparation of this book, but makes no expressed or implied warranty of any kind and assumes no responsibility for any errors or omissions. No liability is assumed for incidental or consequential damages in connection with or arising out of information contained in this book. The Publisher shall not be liable for any special, consequential, or exemplary damages resulting, in whole or in part, from the readers' use of, or reliance upon, this material. Any parts of this book based on government reports are so indicated and copyright is claimed for those parts to the extent applicable to compilations of such works.

Independent verification should be sought for any data, advice or recommendations contained in this book. In addition, no responsibility is assumed by the publisher for any injury and/or damage to persons or property arising from any methods, products, instructions, ideas or otherwise contained in this publication.

This publication is designed to provide accurate and authoritative information with regard to the subject matter covered herein. It is sold with the clear understanding that the Publisher is not engaged in rendering legal or any other professional services. If legal or any other expert assistance is required, the services of a competent person should be sought. FROM A DECLARATION OF PARTICIPANTS JOINTLY ADOPTED BY A COMMITTEE OF THE AMERICAN BAR ASSOCIATION AND A COMMITTEE OF PUBLISHERS.

LIBRARY OF CONGRESS CATALOGING-IN-PUBLICATION DATA
Youth violence and juvenile justice : causes, intervention and treatment
>programs / editors, Neil A. Ramsay and Colin R. Morrison.
>   p. cm.
> Includes index.
> ISBN 978-1-61668-011-4 (hardcover)
> 1. Youth and violence. 2. Youth and violence--Prevention. 3. Juvenile
>delinquency--Prevention. 4. Juvenile justice, Administration of. 5.
>Juvenile delinquents--Rehabilitation. 6. Problem
>youth--Rehabilitation--United States. I. Ramsay, Neil A. II. Morrison,
>Colin R.
> HQ799.2.V56Y655 2010
> 364.36--dc22
>   2009051294

Published by Nova Science Publishers, Inc, ✦ *New York*

CONTENTS

Preface		ix
Chapter 1	Entre Dos Mundos/Between Two Worlds: An Evidence-Based Bicultural Skills Training Program for Acculturating Latino Families	1
	Martica Bacallao and Paul R. Smokowski	
Chapter 2	Evidence-Base Practices for Juvenile Delinquency: Risk and Protective Factors in Treatment Implementation	35
	Katherine L. Montgomery, Amanda N. Barczyk and Sanna J. Thompson	
Chapter 3	Risk and Protective Factors in Youth Violence and Aggression: Promising Family-Based Prevention Models	65
	Amanda N. Barczyk, Katherine Montgomery, Sanna J. Thompson and Sharon Matai	
Chapter 4	Sport as a Cure for Adolescent Aggressive, Antisocial, and Delinquent Behaviors	93
	Amanda J. Visek and Jonathan P. Maxwell	
Chapter 5	Sociometric Status and Bullying: Peer Relationships, Aggressive Behavior, and Victimization	117
	Martica Bacallao and Paul Smokowski	
Chapter 6	Violent and Delinquent Youths: Relationships with Institutional Authorities and Compliance with Social Norms	139
	Estefanía Estévez and Marina Rachitskiy	
Chapter 7	Violence Prevention and Treatment Programmes for Young Offenders	163
	Thomas Ross, Friedemann Pfäfflin, and María Isabel Fontao	

Chapter 8	Bullying and Victimization Experiences at School, the Parent-Child Relationship and Child School Performance: A Longitudinal Investigation *Kostas A. Fanti and Stelios N. Georgiou*	183
Chapter 9	Personal and Interpersonal Mediators Linking Acculturation Stress to Aggressive Behavior in Latino Adolescents *Paul Richard Smokowski, Rachel Lee Buchanan and Martica Bacallao*	205
Chapter 10	Child-Rearing Practices and Delinquency in Children and Adolescents *Stavros P. Kiriakidis*	225
Chapter 11	Sharks & Jets Vs. Bloods & Crips: Socio-Economics, Prevention, and Intervention in Different Eras of Gang Violence *Rosalyn M Bertram and Jennifer Dartt*	243
Chapter 12	The Motivational Influence of Attitude, Subjective Norm, Perceived Behavioral Control and Anticipated Affective Self-Reactions, on Behavioral Decision Making of Re-Offending *Stavros P. Kiriakidis*	259
Chapter 13	Exploring Issues about Youth Gangs in Canada *Lauren D. Eisler*	273
Chapter 14	Risk and Resiliency among Juveniles and Young Adults *Julie E. Sprinkle*	287
Chapter 15	Learning from Success with at Risk Adolescents *Helene S. Wallach and Yafit Levi*	303
Chapter 16	The Influence of Normative Beliefs about Aggression on Behavior in Children *Julie E. Sprinkle*	317
Chapter 17	Public Perceptions of Registry Laws for Juvenile Sex Offenders *Carrie E. Reynolds, Cynthia J. Najdowski, Jessica M. Salerno, Margaret C. Stevenson, Tisha R. A. Wiley and Bette L. Bottoms*	331
Index		335

PREFACE

There are multiple reasons to prevent juveniles from becoming delinquent or continuing to engage in delinquent behavior. The most obvious reason is that delinquency puts youth at risk for substance abuse and delinquency, school drop-out, gang involvement, criminality, and mental health challenges. Youth engaging in delinquent behaviors are also vulnerable to physical injury, early pregnancy, domestic violence and sexual assault. To address issues of juvenile delinquency, this book describes various youth and family risk and protective factors associated with delinquency and provides a description of various family-oriented treatment options for preventing and treating youth violence and aggression. The authors also examine how sociometric status influences childhood bullying, aggressive behavior and victimization. Special attention is given to the affect of sociometric neglect and rejection on child development. In addition, this book summarizes the transformation of youth gangs and violence associated with them, the basis of interventions to reduce youth gang affiliation and aggression in these different eras. To conclude, implications for the prevention and treatment of juvenile crime are presented, as well as recommendations for extinguishing violent and aggressive beliefs and behaviors in children.

Chapter 1- This chapter evaluates the efficacy of two implementation strategies for *Entre Dos Mundos/Between Two Worlds*, a prevention program for Latino adolescents, measured at posttest and 1 year after program completion. Using an experimental research design, 81 Latino families were randomly assigned to 2 program formats that used identical session themes: 56 families attended action-oriented bicultural skills training and 25 attended unstructured support groups. At posttest, program dosage was more important than delivery style. High dosage parents from both action-oriented groups and support groups reported higher levels of bicultural support, bicultural identity integration, and family adaptability along with lower levels of adolescent aggression and oppositional defiant behavior. At one-year follow-up, program delivery method was critical for long-term behavior change. As compared with families that received *Entre Dos Mundos* content through a traditional support group format, parents who attended the action-oriented groups that used psychodrama techniques reported lower rates of parent-adolescent conflict and lower rates of aggression, oppositional defiant behavior, anxious depression, and total problems in their immigrant adolescents. The 1-year follow-up showed that action-oriented groups maintained superior effects as compared to support groups. We discuss implications for practice and future research.

Chapter 2- There are multiple reasons to prevent juveniles from becoming delinquent or continuing to engage in delinquent behavior. The most obvious reason is that delinquency puts youth at risk for substance abuse and dependency, school drop-out, gang involvement, criminality, and mental health challenges. Youth engaging in delinquent behaviors are also vulnerable to physical injury, early pregnancy, domestic violence, and sexual assault.

Due to the complex nature of delinquency, individual youth characteristics and other contributing factors, such as issues in the family, often intersect. The diverse backgrounds and experiences of youth, including difficult family circumstances and exposure to victimization, require services that meet their unique needs. Empirical evidence has shown the importance of the inclusion of the family in treatment of delinquent youth. Services provided to delinquent youth include detention facilities, medical care, case management, independent living skills training, and referrals for high-risk behaviors such as substance abuse. To be effective, however, treatment must address the co-occurring problems of these youth within the context of where they live. As families struggling with a breakdown in communication, trying to control the behavior of an unruly child, or experiencing a crisis often look for outside assistance, employing family-based treatments to address juvenile delinquency holds great promise.

To address issues of juvenile delinquency, this chapter describes various youth and family risk and protective factors associated with delinquency. This discussion is followed by a review of family-based intervention strategies aimed at preventing or ameliorating delinquent behaviors of youth. Reviewing what is known concerning families who engage collaboratively to generate support of the delinquent child can help service providers improve family relationships while decreasing delinquent youth behaviors. Thus, evidence-based, family-centered interventions, such as are multisystemic therapy (MST), brief strategic family therapy (BSFT), multi-dimensional family therapy (MDFT), and solution-focused family therapy (SBFT) will be examined.

Chapter 3- Contrary to what might be concluded from media reports, statistics show that youth aggression and violence is decreasing, particularly in schools. Although multiple victim homicides in schools have increased, schools are among the safest places for children. The issue of youth aggression and violence has been pushed to the forefront with the recognition that prevention is the most effective strategy for reducing youth aggression and violence.

No single risk factor can predict who is likely to engage in violent behavior, but longitudinal studies have established developmental pathways that lead to patterns of aggression and violence. Influences in the school and community also help establish enduring patterns of aggressive and violent behavior. School factors include low school involvement, academic and social failure, lack of clarity and follow-through in rules and policies, poor and/or inconsistent administrative support, and few allowances for individual differences. Attention deficit-hyperactivity disorders, specific learning disabilities, restlessness, risk-taking, poor social skills and certain beliefs and attitudes (e.g., the necessity of retaliation), appear to favor the development of aggressive behavior and violent actions. Conditions in the home--harsh and ineffective parental discipline, lack of parental involvement, family conflict, parental criminality, child abuse and/or neglect, and rejection--also predict early onset and chronic patterns of aggressive behaviors. When these conditions are present, children may be "literally trained to be aggressive during episodes of conflict with family members".

Many youth who are exposed to risk factors do not display aggressive and violent behaviors. Certain protective factors appear to account for this phenomenon. Often, these factors are described in terms of resiliency--the ability to recover strength and spirit under adversity on both internal (self) and external (family, school, community) factors for a positive outcome. Like risk factors, protective factors may be strengthened through interaction with other factors. Individual protective factors include having a more positive view of one's life circumstances and ability to affect those around them, as well as stress-reducing strategies. Family protective factors may include having an attachment to at least one family member who engages in proactive, healthy behaviors with the youth (e.g., high expectations for academic and social performance in and out of school, shared values and morals). Family cohesiveness and positive functioning discourage aggressive and violent behaviors.

Traditionally, schools and communities have responded to aggressive and violent behaviors with reactive strategies that are punitive (e.g., corporal punishment, suspension, expulsion, incarceration). These approaches have had poor results. However, evidence is accumulating that more integrative, proactive approaches that include the family are effective in preventing youth aggression and violence. This chapter describes risk and protective factors found associated with aggression and provides a description of various family-oriented treatment options for preventing youth violence and aggression.

Chapter 4- Hostile and antisocial behavior amongst adolescents is a common problem in many societies. The rehabilitation and support of problem and at-risk youths is a social and moral responsibility that necessitates the development of effective interventions. Sport has often been promoted as a means of developing character, respect, and social responsibility in young people. Thus, many sport-based schemes have been developed that attempt to help problem and at-risk youths develop into socially responsible adults who can make a positive contribution to society, rather than dysfunctional members at risk of involvement in criminal behaviors. Whilst supporters of sport schemes often claim positive results, critics point out that involvement in sport does not guarantee positive effects on the attitudes and behaviors of adolescent participants. In fact, some evidence has been published that demonstrates clear links among sport participation, alcohol consumption, and aggressive behavior. It has been argued that sport should be combined with educational programs that promote positive ways of dealing with negative emotions and thoughts. This chapter reviews the evidence and identifies problems with current research. We conclude by suggesting possible avenues for future research and provide practical advice for using sport as a tool for improving the conduct of adolescents.

Chapter 5- This chapter examines how sociometric status influences childhood bullying, aggressive behavior, and victimization. Sociometric status is associated with bullying dynamics that pose a serious threat to victimized children and damage school climate. Special attention is given to the affect of sociometric neglect and rejection on child development. By using sociometric testing, small group practitioners are able to identify low status children at risk for becoming victims of bullying. Further, practitioners in schools can help prevent and reduce bullying by implementing sociometric interventions such as peer pairing of popular and rejected or neglected children. By working to create classroom and school environments with fluid sociometric roles, we can make strides to promote the safety, security, and growth of all students.

Chapter 6- Society is based on a set of norms and rules, compliance with which ensures the survival of that society. Within psychology, the two main issues of compliance with social norms are exhibition of violent behaviour and cooperation with authorities in order to promote further compliance. Extensive research suggests that among other social and psychological factors, relationships with institutional authorities are one of the most prominent factors of compliance in childhood and adolescence. In this chapter we discuss the research available on the role of authorities and warning signs associated with violence and cooperation with institutional authorities. Finally, we explore theories proposed to explain the relationship between compliance and authorities, as well as their relevance to prevention of non-compliance with social norms. In short, this chapter outlines research and theory suggesting that negative experiences with authorities lead to negative attitudes to authorities and norms regarding compliance. In turn, these attitudes and norms lead to exhibition of violent behaviours and lower cooperation with authorities. As such, we suggest that focusing resources on improving the relationships between authorities and youth will prevent non-compliance with social norms, namely, violence and non-cooperation with authorities.

Chapter 7- Correctional research has shown that young offenders have different treatment and programming needs than adult offenders. A large number of specific treatment and violence prevention programs for young offenders have been developed and applied in many countries. The majority of these programs are of the "cognitive skills type", i.e. they aim at enhancing cognitive and social skills, which are often deficient in young offenders. Modern treatment programs attend to criminogenic needs of offenders, such as impulsivity or poor affect control, empathy deficits, low levels of socio-moral reasoning, substance use and poor problem-solving skills; a style of delivery that young offenders will find interesting and engaging; and flexibility in its administration in order to take into account potentially small custodial sentences. Programs of this type teach young offenders cognitive-behavioral skills that enable them to take their time, i.e. to stop and think before they act, in order to resolve socially complex and potentially "dangerous" situations. Focussing on treatment programs, this chapter provides a brief overview of the history of (young) offender treatment and some of the most common treatment and violence prevention models for young offenders.

Chapter 8- The current investigation examines longitudinal differences between bullies, victims, and bully-victims in terms of the quality of their relationship with their parents and school performance. We also investigate the longitudinal transactional association between the quality of the parent-child relationship and bullying behavior. The sample consisted of 895 mothers and their children who were participants in the NICHD Study of Early Child-Care. According to the findings, the co-occurring bully victim groups were at higher risk to experience continuous conflict with their mothers and to perform worse academically. The findings also offer support for the hypothesized transactional association between bullying and the parent-child relationship. Further, it was found that there might be a positive longitudinal transactional association between victimization and parent-child closeness. Finally, school performance was positively related to victimization.

Chapter 9- This chapter discusses a study that we conducted to examine pathways that lead to aggressive behavior in Latino adolescents. Adolescent mental health, risk-taking, family environment, and friendships with peers were investigated as potential mediators linking acculturation stress to adolescent aggression. Path analyses were conducted using data collected at 3 time points from a sample of 286 adolescents, 66% of whom were born outside of the United States. Our findings indicated that acculturation stressors, rather than assimilation measures, were associated with baseline aggression, Time 2 parent-adolescent conflict, and Time 2 adolescent substance use. We trace mediation pathways through internalizing problems, parent-adolescent conflict, negative friend associations, and adolescent substance use to incidence of aggressive behavior 6 months later. Findings show involvement in Latino culture is an asset positively connected to familism and self-esteem, and ultimately leads to lower levels of adolescent aggression. The discussion includes implications for practice and study limitations.

Chapter 10- The present paper is an overview of studies examining the way family influences the development of delinquency in adolescents. The review focused on published papers dealing with the association of adolescent delinquency and their families. The association between family practices and juvenile delinquency, with potent predictive value is established and bidirectional effects exist. However the influence from parents to adolescents is stronger. In addition indirect evidence, from early intervention studies, supports the causal role of family variables in the development of juvenile delinquency. Effective family functioning, in spite of several social adversities, exerts a buffering influence on children, thus protecting them from delinquent behavioural manifestations. Finally, the assumption that genetic influences are responsible for both poor child-rearing practices by the parents and juvenile delinquency is not well supported by the literature, suggesting that effective parenting exerts an independent influence in the socioemotional functioning of children and adolescents. The evidence suggests that effective child rearing practices is a necessary though not sufficient factor for the psychosocial development of children and adolescents. Educational programmes, of a preventive nature, could be promising in reducing levels of delinquency. The important role of family functioning in protecting children and adolescents from antisocial behaviours is evident from many studies internationally. The protective role of parenting is generally supported. The role of a supportive family environment could be suggested as a protective factor for juvenile delinquency.

Chapter 11- A youth gang is an intimate social group composed of adolescents or young adults who temporarily share common values, identities, symbols, and standards of behavior. Largely an urban phenomenon, gangs may be seen as subcultures whose interests and attitudes are different from, and sometimes even in direct conflict with, those of the larger society. Although some youth violence occurs independent of gang involvement, gang affiliation greatly increases a youth's propensity to commit violent acts. Once comprised of delinquent males who defended neighborhood territory, gangs now include both genders and engage in drug trafficking and other illegal activities. This chapter briefly explores the transformation of youth gangs and violence associated with them, the basis of interventions to reduce youth gang affiliation and aggression in these different eras, as well as factors contributing to and mitigating modern era gang affiliation.

Chapter 12- The paper is an application of an extended version of the theory of planned behavior to behavioral choice of performing illegal behavior. The aim of the study was to examine whether self-sanctions, in terms of affective self-reaction, provide an avenue for extending the theoy of planned behavior and at the same time testing the necessity and the sufficieny of the model. Young people detained for illegal actions participated in the study and they filled in a questionaire assessing the sociocognitve determinants of the theory of planned behavior and a measure of affective self-reaction invoked after the execution of an illegal action. It was found that the model overall afforded accurate prediction of behavioral choice of performing illegal actions in the future, however, affective self-reaction contributed significantly, to the prediction of behavioral choice of performing illegal actions in the future. The theory of planned behavior provides a parsimonious way of predicting behavioral choice of performing illegal actions in the future. However, self-sanctions, in terms of affective self-reaction, could be a variable that expands the model, when it is applied to the prediction of behavioral choice of performing illegal actions in the future.

Chapter 13- In recent years media coverage of youth gangs and youth gang violence has increased substantially across Canada. This increase in coverage my influence and/or reflect a growing public and political perception that youth gangs are becoming a more serious challenge to communities across the country. Political rhetoric and news coverage indicate that the activities of youth gangs in Canada is escalating in frequency and violence and linkages between youth gangs and the drug trade, and organized crime have been considered as an explanation for this increase. This chapter seeks to provide an in-depth overview of the prevalence of youth gangs and youth gang participation in Canada, and employs strain and social disorganization theories to explore factors which are linked to youth participation in gangs. The chapter concludes with a discussion on the types of programs employed to address the problems of youth gangs in Canadian society.

Chapter 14- The Appalachian region of the United States extends from New York to Alabama. However, it is the central and southern Appalachians that seem to garner the most attention in television, magazines, and movies. This attention is often negative, with far-reaching implications for the members of the population. Using standardized risk and resiliency assessment tools, the current study investigates the risk and protective factors juveniles from the southern Appalachian region are exposed to and possess. In addition, comparisons to young adults residing outside of this region are explored to offer a thorough understanding of risk and resiliency among juveniles and young adults. There are numerous risk factors that increase the likelihood of an individual engaging in violent or aggressive acts, performing poorly in school, or falling victim to substance use and abuse. The current investigation also considers resiliency and seeks to examine the factors that allow some juveniles to emerge from neglectful families and drug-infested, poverty stricken neighborhoods without resorting to negative behaviors themselves. To conclude the chapter, implications for the prevention and treatment of juvenile crime both within and outside of Appalachia are presented.

Chapter 15-"I am reborn...and that will help me succeed" this sentence exemplifies the meaning of success among youth at risk. "Learning from success" is a system that advocates learning from clients who succeeded. This chapter reports on research that examined the parameters of success among youth at risk. Interviews were conducted with six youth living at the "House on Haim street" or the apartment belonging to the "Sachlav" project, as well as with the instructors and the manager of the "House". We chose adolescents who were identified as youth that succeeded in improving their condition. When we examined the data to determine what helped them make the change, several categories evolved: 1. Past behavior (anti-social behavior, low self esteem), 2. The change process (helping others without receiving compensation, listening understanding and accepting others, taking responsibility for ones behavior, a change in the social environment and degree of integration into a normative environment), 3. The change point (fear of alternatives, relationship to others). The important factors in the change process were: fear of the alternative such as going to jail or being kicked out of the "House", and the relationship with others in the "House". If these findings are replicated in further studies using additional populations, it will help to shape interventions with youth at risk.

Chapter 16- Beliefs and attitudes have each been shown to exert an indirect influence on behaviors – including but not limited to violent and aggressive behaviors. Beliefs about whether or not the consequences of the behavior outweigh the benefits mediate the relationship. However, positive associations between proviolence attitudes and violent behavior have been documented by several research studies (Tolan, Guerra, & Kendall, 1995). Similar associations have been acknowledged between normative beliefs about aggression and actual violent and aggressive behaviors. While behavioral beliefs are based upon an individual's weighing of the cost versus benefit of an action, normative beliefs are an individual's schema for viewing behaviors as good or bad, right or wrong. The current study investigates the relationship between normative beliefs about aggression and subsequent aggressive behaviors of school-aged children using two standardized instruments. The results of the present study are examined using inter-item correlation analysis. Recommendations for extinguishing violent and aggressive beliefs and behaviors in children are presented.

Chapter 17- The first federal sex offender registry law was established in 1994 with the creation of the Jacob Wetterling Crimes Against Children Sexually Violent Offender Registration Act (1994). This law requires that sex offenders register personal information (e.g., name, address, photograph, etc.) with law enforcement after serving their sentences. Megan's Law amended the Wetterling Act, further requiring that all states have procedures in place to notify communities of local sex offenders.

These laws were created to prevent sex offender recidivism. Specifically, the goals of these laws are to (a) facilitate the quick and efficient apprehension of offenders, (b) deter offenders from re-offending by letting them know that they are being watched, and (c) make the public more aware of offenders living nearby. In 2006, the Sex Offender Registration and Notification Act (SORNA; 42 U.S.C. § 16911), also known as the Adam Walsh Act, extended adult sex offender registry laws to include juveniles convicted in adult court of sex offenses and juveniles 14 years of age and older adjudicated in juvenile court for sex offenses involving aggravating circumstances. SORNA established these minimum registration guidelines for juveniles, but many states have stricter, more inclusive laws. For example, in some states, juveniles as young as 7 years of age can be required to register.

In: Youth Violence and Juvenile Justice: Causes, Intervention…   ISBN: 978-1-61668-011-4
Editor: N. A. Ramsay and C. R. Morrison, pp. 1-33   © 2010 Nova Science Publishers, Inc.

Chapter 1

ENTRE DOS MUNDOS/BETWEEN TWO WORLDS: AN EVIDENCE-BASED BICULTURAL SKILLS TRAINING PROGRAM FOR ACCULTURATING LATINO FAMILIES

Martica Bacallao[1] and Paul R. Smokowski[2]

[1]Department of Social Work, University of North Carolina – Greensboro, NC, USA
[2]School of Social Work, University of North Carolina at Chapel Hill, NC, USA

ABSTRACT

This chapter evaluates the efficacy of two implementation strategies for *Entre Dos Mundos/Between Two Worlds*, a prevention program for Latino adolescents, measured at posttest and 1 year after program completion. Using an experimental research design, 81 Latino families were randomly assigned to 2 program formats that used identical session themes: 56 families attended action-oriented bicultural skills training and 25 attended unstructured support groups. At posttest, program dosage was more important than delivery style. High dosage parents from both action-oriented groups and support groups reported higher levels of bicultural support, bicultural identity integration, and family adaptability along with lower levels of adolescent aggression and oppositional defiant behavior. At one-year follow-up, program delivery method was critical for long-term behavior change. As compared with families that received *Entre Dos Mundos* content through a traditional support group format, parents who attended the action-oriented groups that used psychodrama techniques reported lower rates of parent-adolescent conflict and lower rates of aggression, oppositional defiant behavior, anxious depression, and total problems in their immigrant adolescents. The 1-year follow-up showed that action-oriented groups maintained superior effects as compared to support groups. We discuss implications for practice and future research.

Keywords: Latinos, acculturation, youth violence.

INTRODUCTION

The United States Census Bureau reported that in July 2002, the U.S. Latino population reached 38.8 million individuals, making this the largest minority group in the nation (U.S. Census Bureau, 2003). New immigrants represent a significant proportion of the burgeoning Latino population, and consequently a large segment of the Latino population contains recent arrivals who are adjusting to life in the United States. In 2002, slightly more than 40% of the U.S. Latino population (15 million people) was foreign born (Ramirez & de la Cruz, 2002).

Research data has suggested that, in the absence of prevention and intervention services, many Latino adolescents and adults are at risk for alcohol and drug use, aggressive behavior, and mental health problems (Centers for Disease Control and Prevention, 2004; Gonzales, Knight, Morgan-Lopez, Saenz, & Sirolli, 2002; Rogler, Cortes, & Malgady, 1991; Rounds-Bryant & Staab, 2001; Smokowski, David-Ferdon, & Stroupe, 2009; Vega, Alderete, Kolody, & Aguilar-Gaxiola, 2000). This heightened risk for antisocial behavior and psychopathology has been linked to the acculturation stressors experienced by many Latinos while trying to adapt to life in the United States.

Acculturation is the process through which cultural change results from contact between two autonomous and independent cultural groups (Berry, 1998). This process usually entails interactions between dominant and nondominant groups, and is commonly characterized by a nondominant group taking on the language, laws, religions, norms, and behaviors of the dominant group (Castro, Coe, Gutierres, & Saenz, 1996). *Acculturation stress* results from the daily difficulties, conflicts, and strains experienced when individuals and families are trying to adjust to a new cultural system. Acculturation stress seems to be heightened by negative experiences such as racial/ethnic discrimination and coping with language barriers. Many authors have hypothesized a link between acculturation stress and negative health behaviors (e.g., Al-Issa & Tousignant, 1997; Delgado, 1998; Gil, Vega, & Dimas, 1994; Gonzales et al., 2002; Szapocznik & Kurtines, 1980).

Given the growing immigrant Latino population, there is a clear need for interventions to address the negative effects of acculturation stress. The *Entre Dos Mundos/Between Two Worlds* (Bacallao & Smokowski, 2005) multifamily group intervention was designed to prevent the development of aggression and mental health problems in Latino adolescents by both helping participants cope with acculturation stress and promoting family adaptability and bicultural coping skills.

LITERATURE REVIEW

Assimilation and Acculturation Stress as Risk Factors

Several decades of empirical research have illuminated problematic outcomes of the acculturation process, showing that increasing levels of *assimilation* (i.e., often used interchangeably with acculturation to describe the process of replacing culture-of-origin traditions, beliefs, and behaviors with those of the host culture) are associated with negative health behaviors and mental health difficulties (Miranda, Estrada, & Firpo-Jimenez, 2000).

When compared with less assimilated peers, Latinos who have become more assimilated to U.S. culture display higher levels of alcohol use, more consumption of marijuana and cocaine, more aggressive behavior, and less consumption of balanced healthful meals (Amaro, Whitaker, Coffman, & Heeren, 1990; Marks, Garcia, & Solts, 1990; Smokowski, David-Ferdon et al., 2009; Vega et al., 1998).

In their literature review on acculturation and mental health in Latino youth, Gonzales and her colleagues (2002) identified eight studies that examined the link between adolescent acculturation and externalizing problems. A majority of these investigations (6 of 8), showed that higher levels of assimilation were associated with increased delinquency and stronger relationships with antisocial peers (Buriel, Calzada, & Vasquez, 1982; Fridrich & Flannery, 1995; Samaniego & Gonzales, 1999; Wall, Power, & Arbona, 1993; Vega, Gil, Warheit, Zimmerman, & Apospori, 1993; Vega, Zimmerman, Khoury, Gil, & Warheit, 1995). Consistently across these studies, this association between assimilation and externalizing behavior surfaced even when simple proxy measures of acculturation, such as time since immigration, language use, or nativity, were used as markers for complex acculturation processes (Gonzales et al., 2002). Indeed, most investigations of acculturation and problem behavior have used simple measures of acculturation, such as time since immigration. Comparisons of simple measures and more complex, multidimensional acculturation instruments have shown these approaches to have comparable predictive validity (Fridrich & Flannery, 1995; Smokowski, Buchanan, & Bacallao, 2009). Consequently, we adopted a parsimonious perspective for this evaluation by controlling for time since immigration in our analyses.

Recently, Smokowski, David-Ferdon, and Stroupe (2009) conducted a comprehensive review of studies that examined the relationship of Latino adolescent acculturation and youth violence. The association between acculturation and youth violence outcomes was the focus of 16 studies; the outcome examined in 13 of those investigations was the perpetration of violence, whereas the outcome examined in the other 3 investigations was the fear of being a victim of violence. The results favored a significant positive association between assimilation and youth violence. Nine of the 13 studies that examined perpetration of violence reported higher levels of adolescent assimilation (although defined in different ways, including time in the United States, generational status, language use, or with multidimensional measures) were associated with increased youth violence (Brook , Whiteman, Balka, Win, & Gursen, 1998; Bui & Thongniramol, 2005; Buriel, Calzada, & Vasquez, 1982; Dinh, Roosa, Tein, & Lopez, 2002; Samaniego & Gonzales, 1999; Schwartz, Zamboanga, & Jarvis, 2007; Smokowski & Bacallao, 2006; Sommers Fagan, & Baskin,1993; Vega et al., 1993; Vega et al., 1995).

Children commonly assimilate faster than adults, which can create an acculturation gap between generations that often precipitates family stress (Smokowski, Rose, & Bacallao, 2008; Szapocznik & Kurtines, 1980; Szapocznik, Santisteban, Kurtines, Perez-Vidal, & Hervis, 1984, 1986; Szapocznik & Williams, 2000). Younger family members who are rapidly acculturating may adopt norms and values of the host society that conflict with those held by less acculturated older family members. This rapid acculturation and resulting acculturation gap may create alienation between parents and adolescents that can fuel adolescent rebellion (Bacallao & Smokowski, 2007; Szapocznik & Williams, 2000). Problems in the acculturating family system can erode *familism*, which is a sense of family pride and giving priority to the family over other social relationships. The erosion of familism consequently heightens acculturation strains and negative behavioral outcomes (Gil et al.,

1994). Gil and Vega (1996) reported that adolescent and parent acculturation stress was strongly associated with lower levels of family cohesion and increased parent-child conflicts. More recently, Smokowski and Bacallao (2006) reported that parent-adolescent conflict mediated the impact of acculturation conflicts on adolescent aggression.

Biculturalism as a Protective Factor

A growing number of acculturation researchers believe that *biculturalism*, defined as the ability to competently navigate within and between two cultures, is the optimal endpoint for the process of cultural acquisition (LaFromboise, Coleman, & Gerton, 1993; Gonzales et al., 2002). Because the bicultural individual has skills to handle stressors as well as access to resources from both cultural systems, that individual experiences less stress and anxiety as compared to a person without such skills (Bacallao & Smokowski, 2009; Rashid, 1984). Bicultural individuals maintain a positive relationship with both cultures without having to choose one or the other; they participate in the two different cultures by tailoring their behavior to the situational context (LaFromboise et al., 1993).

Positive outcomes associated with biculturalism were reported by Lang, Munoz, Bernal, and Sorensen (1982), who demonstrated that, as compared to either low- or high-assimilated Latinos, bicultural Latinos obtained higher quality of life levels, affect balance, and psychological adjustment. Miranda and Umhoefer (1998) reported that bicultural individuals had high levels of social interest and low levels of depression. In addition, Gil and colleagues (1994) found bicultural adolescents had the lowest levels of acculturation stress and were less likely to report low family pride when compared with either low- or high-assimilated Latino adolescents. Moreover, several studies have found bilingual youths achieved more than those who spoke only one language (e.g., English-alone or limited-English speakers; Feliciano, 2001; Rumberger & Larson, 1998; Stanton-Salazar & Dornbusch, 1995), and to show fewer emotional or behavioral problems, less delinquency, and lower levels of aggression (Smokowski, Buchanan, et al., 2009; Toppleberg, Medrano, Pena Morgens, & Nieto-Castanon, 2002).

In a study with 315 Hispanic youth, Coatsworth, Maldonado-Molina, Pantin, and Szapocznik (2005) compared acculturation patterns, and found that bicultural youth demonstrated the most adaptive pattern of functioning across a number of different ecological domains. Lending support to these findings, bicultural youth were found to report significantly higher levels of academic competence, peer competence, and parental monitoring.

In summary, assimilation appears to be an important risk factor for immigrant Latino families. Research has found that highly assimilated Latinos tend to engage in negative health behaviors, especially alcohol use and aggressive behavior (Bacallao & Smokowski, 2005; Smokowski & Bacallao, forthcoming). Prevention interventions are critical to lessen acculturation stress and slow the development of problems related to rapid assimilation. However, it is equally important to support the cultural strengths and assets that families bring with them when they immigrate. To this end, a second body of research shifts the focus from thinking of assimilation as a risk factor to considering cultural assets as a factor that promotes positive outcomes. This growing body of literature has suggested that biculturalism is not only a critical mediator of acculturation processes but also an appropriate intervention target. These findings prompted us to create a new training program to promote bicultural skills; we called the program *Entre Dos Mundos/Between Two Worlds*. The goal of the *Entre Dos Mundos* program is to help Latino families adjust to life in the United States and avoid the stress and problems associated with assimilation.

ACCULTURATION-BASED PREVENTION AND INTERVENTION PROGRAMS

Several programs represent important first steps or initiatives for acculturation-based prevention and intervention efforts. In general, these programs have both acknowledged the important role that culture plays in intervention, and attempted to decrease assimilation stress while increasing bicultural social skills. This review is focused on bicultural skills training programs. Bicultural skills training groups have been used with a broad range of groups, including Native American students (Marsiglia, Cross & Mitchell-Enos,1998; LaFramboise & Rowe, 1983; Schinke et al., 1988), foster parents and children (Mullender, 1990), middle-school teenagers (Bilides, 1990), African American adults with alcoholism (Beverly, 1989), Asian American parents (Ying, 1999), preschool children (Arenas, 1978), Latina adolescents (Peeks, 1999), and Latino families (Szapocznik, Santisteban, Kurtines, Perez-Vidal, & Hervis, 1986; Smokowski & Bacallao, 2008; 2009). Our primary concentration is directed toward how the acculturation-based intervention approach has been used with Latino immigrant adolescents and their parents.

Bicultural skills training programs have evolved from three strains of empirical research. Originally introduced as a cultural adaptation to social skills training models, LaFromboise and Rowe (1983) regarded bicultural training as a promising method for teaching assertiveness skills to Native American adults. LaFromboise and Rowe's goals for their bicultural skills training model were to promote communication skills that enhanced self-determination, to teach coping skills that would enable participants to resist the pressure to acculturate, and to help participants develop discretionary skills that would help them determine the appropriateness of assertive behavior in Indian and non-Indian cultures (LaFromboise & Rowe, 1983). In what was the largest evaluation of the LaFromboise and Rowe model, Schinke and his colleagues (1988) used the bicultural training in their work with Native American adolescents at risk for tobacco, alcohol, and substance use. Using an experimental research design, 137 Native American adolescents from the State of Washington were randomly assigned to either a no-intervention comparison condition or to a prevention condition that received 10 sessions of bicultural competence skills training. At posttest and at a 6-month posttreatment follow-up, Schinke and colleagues reported that adolescents in the bicultural skills training prevention group performed significantly better than their counterparts in the no-intervention group when compared on measures of knowledge and attitudes related to substance use. Compared with the control group, the bicultural skills training participants had higher ratings on measures of self-control, assertiveness, and making alternative suggestions to substance use pressure. Equally important, participants who received the bicultural prevention intervention reported lower rates of tobacco, alcohol, and marijuana use at posttest and at the 6-month follow-up.

The second strain of bicultural skills training was developed specifically for Puerto Rican children ages 5 to 8 years living in New York City, using Puerto Rican folktales (*cuentos*) as peer models of adaptive behavior (*Cuento* therapy; Constantino, Malgady, & Rogler, 1986). These researchers later adapted the model for adolescents, replacing the folktales with biographies of heroic Puerto Ricans (Malgady, Rogler, & Constantino, 1990). In this treatment model, the children's mothers attended the sessions and worked with the therapists to present Puerto Rican folktales. Using a randomized experimental design, 210 high-risk Puerto Rican children, ages 5 to 8 years, were assigned to one of four intervention conditions: therapy using an original *cuento* folktale, therapy using an adapted *cuento* folktale, therapy using art/play techniques, and a no-therapy group (Constantino et al., 1986). When compared with children in the two control groups (i.e., art/play therapy and no-therapy group), the children who received the Cuento therapy demonstrated less anxiety, higher scores on the Wechsler Intelligence Scale for Children-Revised and decreased aggression.

In a similar study, Malgady and colleagues (1990) used this therapeutic storytelling approach, substituting biographies of famous Puerto Ricans for the folktales. Called Hero/Heroine modeling, Malgady and colleagues' tested this prevention intervention with 90 Puerto Rican eighth and ninth grade students who were U.S.-born and living in New York City. The goal of the research was to test whether providing ethnic and bicultural role models would help mediate the social and family conflicts experienced by these adolescents. Using random assignment, the adolescents were assigned to either a control group or a culture-based role modeling intervention. Malgady et al. (1990) reported that, as compared with adolescents in the control group, adolescents who received the treatment intervention had significantly lower scores on measures of anxiety, and higher scores on measures of ethnic identity and self-concept. Program effects varied by participants' grade level, gender, and household composition. This ethnic modeling therapy was particularly effective for high-risk Puerto Rican adolescents from single-parent families.

The third strain of bicultural skills training was developed through the research of Szapocznik and his colleagues (Szapocznik et al., 1984, 1986; Szapocznik et al., 1989). The first model, Bicultural Effectiveness Training (BET; Szapocznik et al., 1984, 1986) was a family intervention modality that focused on reducing intercultural and intergenerational conflict among immigrant parents and their adolescent children who were experiencing conduct problems or social maladjustment. Each of the lessons in the psychoeducational curriculum attempted to create a shared worldview among family members and to explore how cultural conflicts affect interactions among family members. Therapists worked with the family to reframe problems by placing blame on the acculturation process rather than any particular family member. In addition, therapists worked to foster intergenerational alliances and increase bicultural coping skills. In a small pilot test with 41 Cuban American families raising an adolescent with behavior problems, Szapocznik and colleagues (1986) found BET was equally effective as brief structural family therapy (BSFT) in improving adolescent problem behaviors and family functioning. At the time of their investigation, this was the only study of bicultural skills training programs that measured changes in participants' bicultural skill levels. The scores on measures of biculturalism increased significantly among the participants in the BET group, whereas the BSFT comparison group did not demonstrate an increase in bicultural skills (Szapocznik et al., 1986).

Building from that research, Szapocznik and colleagues conducted another study in which BET was integrated into a larger intervention package called Family Effectiveness

Training (FET; Szapocznik et al., 1989). FET was compared to a no-treatment control condition in a study of 79 Latino (76% Cuban) families with a preadolescent (6 to 11 years) with emotional or behavioral problems. The results of the study indicated that families in the FET condition displayed significantly greater improvement than did control families on measures of structural family functioning, child behavior problems, and child self-concept.

Subsequently, the acculturation-based family intervention developed by Szapocznik and his colleagues (1984, 1986; Szapocznik et al., 1989) was adapted by Ying (1999) for use with Chinese American families (i.e., Strengthening of Intergenerational/Intercultural Ties in Immigrant Chinese American Families). In a pilot test of 15 immigrant Chinese American parents, statistically significant pre- to posttest changes indicated that parents who received the 8-week parenting program increased their sense of efficacy, sense of coherence, and feeling of responsibility for their child's behavior. The quality of the parent-child relationship also improved from pre- to posttest; however, child self-esteem and parental depression did not change.

Coatsworth, Pantin, and Szapocznik (2002) presented an evolution of the early BET work as an intervention called *Familias Unidas*. Like Szapocznik and colleagues' earlier work, *Familias Unidas* targeted immigrant parents and their adolescent children (12 to 14 year olds) living in Dade County, Florida. Whereas the earlier iterations of BET and FET were interventions designed for a target audience of families experiencing problems and undergoing treatment, *Familias Unidas* was a prevention intervention designed for all immigrant families. Further, *Familias Unidas* was designed to be delivered in a community setting, such as schools. Similar to BET and FET, *Familias Unidas* was a family-centered intervention that had a primary goal of enhancing parental investment in and involvement with adolescent children. The theory underlying *Familias Unidas* held that enhancing parental investment and strengthening parental influence across ecological systems (e.g., with school, with the adolescent's friends) would positively influence the adolescent's self-regulation, social competence, academic achievement, and school bonding (Coatsworth et al., 2002).

Familias Unidas was evaluated in a randomized clinical trial of 167 Latino families with children in sixth and seventh grades (Pantin et al., 2003). Participants were recruited from three middle schools in Miami, Florida. Results from mixed model analyses indicated that, relative to a nonintervention control group, families in the intervention group reported higher rates of parental investment and decreased conduct problems in adolescent children. The intervention did not affect adolescent academic achievement or school bonding.

Current State of Model Development

Bicultural skills training models have shown promising initial results on a variety of outcome measures. Researchers have reported that the results of bicultural skills training programs were better than no-treatment comparison groups and, in some cases, superior to alternative treatments. These training programs appeared to reduce or mediate some of the risks associated with rapid assimilation (e.g., alcohol and substance use, anxiety, conduct problems); however, without a standard set of outcomes, it is difficult to compare the different intervention models.

Evaluation of these programs remains a challenge because only a few studies have used adequate sample sizes and rigorous methodologies that allow for comparison. Current models have been pilot tested in only a single study, and in several cases, the testing has used small numbers of participants (e.g., sample sizes were 17, 31, 79, 110, 117, 137, 167, and 210). Researchers in all three strains of this research changed their intervention models without conducting replication studies (i.e., *Cuento* therapy evolved to Hero/Heroine modeling, BET was integrated into FET). This failure to replicate studies and validate results has kept the progress of model development suspended in Thomas and Rothman's (1994) evaluation and advanced development stage. Whether these earlier models can be generalized to other populations is unknown because none of the tested models has been replicated in diverse field settings. Similarly, no bicultural skills training model has gone through Thomas and Rothman's (1994) dissemination stage to promote widespread use.

Few studies have measured proximal outcomes that might account for the impact of the intervention. Only the original BET study conducted by Szapocznik et al. (1986) measured changes in the participants' bicultural skills. Coatsworth et al. (2002) reported changes in parental investment, which was an important proximal outcome for their *Familias Unidas* intervention model. Although the other studies provided promising information that bicultural skills training models influenced distal outcomes, the research did not illuminate the mechanisms by which the intervention affected outcomes (i.e., the mechanisms that made the program work).

Bicultural skills training deserves further attention. Current models have shown promising results, but require replication and dissemination. Future research in this area would benefit from the use of a standard set of distal outcomes as well as the inclusion of proximal outcomes or pathways that map onto a conceptual model for the program. Inclusion of proximal outcomes, such as parent investment or self- esteem, would allow researchers to go beyond whether or not the programs work and determine *how* the programs work. These proximal outcomes delineate pathways that are used in exerting the programs' effects. For example, a bicultural skills training program might lower parent-adolescent conflict (e.g., the proximal outcome) and in so doing adolescent aggression is subsequently reduced. The next generation of bicultural skills training programs needs to be guided by sophisticated conceptual or logic models that articulate hypothesized pathways for program effects.

Considering this current state of model development, we move forward to describe a new, experiential model for bicultural skills training.

Entre Dos Mundos/Between Two Worlds Bicultural Skills Training

Theoretical background

Entre Dos Mundos (Bacallao & Smokowski, 2005) is based on knowledge gathered through two streams of research: (a) risk and protective factor research with Latino families in North Carolina and Arizona (see Bacallao & Smokowski, 2007; Smokowski & Bacallao, 2006, 2007), and (b) prior acculturation research (for reviews see Gonzales et al., 2002; LaFromboise et al., 1993; Rogler et al., 1991). As illustrated in Figure 1, *Entre Dos Mundos* attempts to mediate the negative impact of acculturation stress by increasing family adaptability and biculturalism in Latino adolescents and their parents. The theoretical background of the intervention hypothesizes that increasing biculturalism and family adaptability in immigrant Latino families will decrease intergenerational cultural conflict between parents and adolescents (Szapocznik et al., 1986). Ultimately, this decrease of intergenerational conflict should lead to decreased levels of adolescent anxiety, depression, and conduct problems.

Entre Dos Mundos Program Design and Description

As described in detail by Bacallao and Smokowski (2005), *Entre Dos Mundos* is an 8-week prevention program that uses a multifamily group format in weekly sessions. Bringing groups of adolescents and parents from 8 to 10 families together to discuss acculturation stressors and challenges provides the opportunity to intervene in problematic parent-adolescent relationship processes. The multifamily group format also builds social support networks among the group members. Each session is devoted to a theme that has been empirically linked to acculturation stress (e.g., handling cultural conflicts in the family, coping with racial discrimination, navigating within U.S. schools). *Entre Dos Mundos* session themes are posed as questions for families to grapple with during the session and as homework between sessions. The session themes are presented in detail in Table 1. In the final session, a graduation ceremony is orchestrated to engender a sense of pride and to provide participants a focal point for their new competencies.

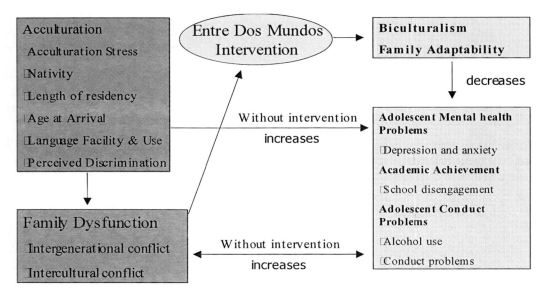

Figure 1. Entre Dos Mundos Conceptual Model.

Table 1. Entre Dos Mundos Curriculum Themes.

Program Week	Session Theme Questions
Week 1	How are we as a family changing as we adapt to life in the United States? How do we as a family balance demands from two different cultures (our culture-of-origin and the U.S. host culture)?
Week 2	What worries do adolescents have for their parents? What worries do parents have for their adolescents? How can we help each other decrease some of these worries? How can we comfort one another?
Week 3	When cultural conflict arises, how can we remain united with each other as a family when we have different perspectives?
Week 4	How can we handle discrimination at school and at work? In what ways can family members support each other during or after these experiences?
Week 5	In what ways do adolescents participate in school? In what ways do adolescents wish to participate in school? (Same two questions posed to parents.)
Week 6	How can we strengthen our relationships with non-Latino Americans (peers, teachers, co-workers) outside of our families?
Week 7	What does our future look like in 10 years? (Developing bicultural identities)
Week 8	Review, integration, evaluation, and closure (graduation ceremony & fiesta!)

In designing a pilot test of *Entre Dos Mundos*, we chose to include eight lessons in the curriculum design to maximize feasibility and retention in the initial program; however, additional lessons could be added for ongoing, established groups. Unlike other bicultural skills training models, the *Entre Dos Mundos* lessons are designed for use in relatively large multifamily groups with at least one parent and one adolescent from each of the 8 to 10 families attending the weekly group sessions. This format has been used to address a range of mental health problems and has been shown as more effective than either individual or single-family therapy (McFarlane, 2002). Adopting the multifamily group format not only maximizes the potential for impacting parent-adolescent communication but also allows multiple family members to practice newly learned skills, and increases the probability of expanding social support networks for the participating families.

Action-oriented groups using psychodrama techniques. An integral concept in the *Entre Dos Mundos* design was that the weekly sessions should be action-oriented groups that fully engage participants of various ages, genders, and levels of acculturation. For example, in the initial testing of *Entre Dos Mundos,* the action-oriented groups used a variety of psychodrama techniques such as role reversal, doubling, mirroring, empty chair, and enactment of critical scenes from personal and social experiences shared by participating families. Session content for each theme was experiential, based on psychodramatic strategies for exploring intrapersonal and interpersonal situations, and encouraged practicing behavioral change in a supportive group environment (Blatner, 2005; Oxford & Weiner, 2003). Structured warm-ups were used to focus the multiple family groups on the week's theme (see Table 1).

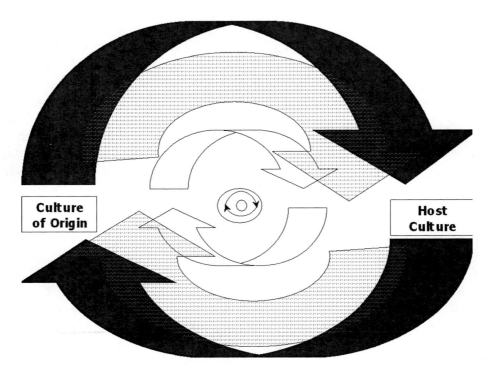

Figure 2. Circular Model of Bicultural Development.

One salient example of a structured warm-up activity central to the *Entre Dos Mundos* curriculum was a variation on a *spectogram* or circular diamond of opposites (Carlson-Sabelli, Sabelli, Patel, & Holm, 1992), which focused on acculturation relationships between culture-of-origin and the host culture. Depicted in Figure 2, the circular model of acculturation is the theoretical and experiential backbone of the *Entre Dos Mundos* prevention program. During each session, a large cutout of this circular model is placed on the floor with "culture-of-origin" on the left side and "dominant culture" on the right. More important, the circular model emphasizes that acculturation is not a linear process, and prompts Latino families to think about movement between cultures as a dynamic process. The visual representation of acculturation reinforces the importance of bicultural skills and this exercise tends to decrease parents' anxieties about losing their children to American assimilation because of linear accommodation to the new culture (Bacallao & Smokowski, 2007).

In addition, the circular model has a developmental focus that underscores the idea that acculturation interventions should facilitate integration of bicultural identity (Benet-Martinez, Leu, Lee, & Morris, 2002; Sanchez-Flores, 2003). Moving back and forth between cultures as called for by the situation and context is encouraged because such movement is the manifestation of bicultural skills. An integrated bicultural identity allows participants to move effectively between cultural contexts, and such integration has been shown to increase socio-cognitive functioning in some immigrant groups (Haritatos & Benet-Martinez, 2002).

After learning U.S. customs, many Latino youth turn back to culture-of-origin values in a circular cycle (Sanchez-Flores, 2003). In other words, bicultural evolution is developmental. Latino adolescents have to navigate the cultural differences between home and school every day. The ease and speed with which Latino youth navigate the circle are indicators of their bicultural development. As such, these stages of development are illustrated in the group as parents and adolescents stand on the acculturation circle and speak to each other about their different positions. In subsequent sessions, movement is tracked as a way to process change. Dialogues between adolescents, parents, and group members, who play roles representing the culture-of-origin or host culture, are facilitated using the circular model as the backdrop for the action.

When *Entre Dos Mundos* has been used with Latino families, activities incorporated into weekly sessions actively have explored the different poles and pulls in the flow of the circular model. Guided by each session theme, the group facilitator identified psychodramatic scenes that the group members enacted with the model as a container for the experiential action. For example, Latino adolescents commonly experience discrimination from Anglo or African American peers as they move from their culture-of-origin to host culture involvement. The group discussion in Session 4 includes a critical example of participants' discrimination experiences, such as the difficulty of walking through school hallways while taunted by peers saying, "Go back to your own country!" Participants first recreate the scene and then explore behavioral options. Doubling, mirroring, role reversal, and other psychodramatic techniques are used to encourage catharsis, promote insight, and engender new skills. The circular model is used to identify where participants are in the process, and where they would like to be, in relation to both their culture-of-origin and the host culture. The circular model is introduced at the beginning of the session and again at the end of each session for closure and to capture intrasession change. Use of these structured activities and psychodramatic techniques characterized the *Entre Dos Mundos* action-oriented sessions.

Testing the Entre Dos Mundos Approach

A primary challenge in intervention research is finding ways to isolate the effect of a program and thereby illuminate the mechanisms by which a program creates a desired effect. The randomized experimental trial is the gold standard for testing the efficacy of a new intervention model. In designing an efficacy evaluation of the Entre Dos Mundos program, we had two main concerns.

1) We wanted to test the effect of our psychodramatic action orientation to the program activities. It was important to assess if the experiential learning activities would be more efficacious for Latino participants than simply letting Latino families address the program themes without such structure. Consequently, we wanted to evaluate different formats for delivering the program. The overall objective of the study was to determine which of two implementation formats would show greater sustained benefit in lowering adolescent problems (i.e., decreasing aggressive behavior and mental health problems) in Latino youth at posttest and one year after *Entre Dos Mundos* program completion. A fundamental assumption of this research was that

prevention program sessions should be active and dynamic. This cornerstone led us to hypothesize the *Entre Dos Mundos* session themes delivered in action-oriented skills training (i.e., using psychodrama techniques to enhance bicultural coping skills) would have sustained benefit for both adolescent problems and parent-adolescent conflict than the identical themes delivered in unstructured support groups (i.e., traditional discussion format aimed at facilitating parent-adolescent communication and interfamily social networking).

Entre Dos Mundos support group families were exposed to the identical session themes listed in Table 1. However, the support groups did not receive the structured activities for exploring the themes and were not introduced to the circular model of acculturation or to psychodramatic techniques in any form. Instead, support group facilitators posed the weekly themes as questions for families to discuss. Family members and facilitators shared their experiences and offered interpersonal support. When the participants concurred that the weekly theme had been adequately addressed, the group members were allowed to redirect the discussion to any topic they wanted to discuss.

2) We also wanted to see if exposure to the program themes was more critical than the style of delivery, and if being exposed to more of the themes had a stronger effect than processing fewer of them. This was a test of program dosage. We hypothesized that commitment to program participation, as indexed by higher attendance rates, would be significantly associated with lower levels of both adolescent problems and parent-adolescent conflict.

RESEARCH METHOD

To distinguish the effect of the *Entre Dos Mundos* action-oriented groups from the effect of *Entre Dos Mundos* delivered in a less active form, we designed a study that offered the intervention two formats. One format used the *Entre Dos Mundos* action-oriented group format as described above with psychodramatic structured activities. The second format offered the identical *Entre Dos Mundos* topics in a traditional support group format. Using an experimental research design, 81 Latino families were randomly assigned to the two formats that used identical session themes: 56 families attended action-oriented bicultural skills training and 25 attended unstructured support groups

Internal Review Board approval for all study methods and measures was obtained from a large university in the Southeast. A Certificate of Confidentiality was also obtained from the United States Centers for Disease Control and Prevention to protect data obtained from study participants.

Research Design

To be eligible to participate in the *Entre Dos Mundos* research project, Latino families had to include a foreign-born adolescent between the ages of 12 and 18 years and have one parent willing to attend program sessions with the adolescent. The classic experimental design was used to test the efficacy of two implementation formats for the *Entre Dos Mundos* prevention program: action-oriented skills training compared to unstructured support groups. Notably, both implementation formats used identical session themes. The program was implemented in agencies, churches, and arts centers serving Latino communities in rural, midsized, and urban settings in North Carolina. Having multiple, diverse settings for the investigation (i.e., rural, urban, and midsized metropolitan sites) added to the external validity of the study by making the sample more representative (Campbell & Stanley, 1963). Latino families that met eligibility criteria were assigned to these two conditions using a randomized experimental design to evaluate changes from pretest to posttest (8 weeks later) and ultimately to one-year post program follow-up. Follow-up data were collected 14 months after pretest data collection, which was equivalent to one year after program completion. Data were also collected at posttest, 3-month, and 6-month follow-up interviews; however, this chapter focuses on examining proximal outcomes at posttest and distal outcomes at one-year follow-up.

An experimental design allows the investigator to observe and measure changes in the dependent variables caused by manipulating the independent variables (i.e., the two *Entre Dos Mundos* group conditions). We selected an experimental design because it is the most rigorous research design for clinical trials, and guards against nearly all intrinsic and extrinsic threats to internal validity such as history, maturation, instrumentation, and testing (Campbell & Stanley, 1963). Further, adherence to an experimental design allows causal inferences to be determined between the antecedent variables and outcome variables (Frankfort-Nachmias & Nachmias, 2000). A true experimental design utilizes random assignment that allows for comparison between two equalized groups of Latino families. Comparisons were made between the experimental and comparison groups to determine the *Entre Dos Mundos* prevention intervention's impact on proximal outcomes at posttest and on four distal outcomes—adolescent oppositional defiant behavior, anxious depression, parent-adolescent conflict, and total adolescent problems—at one year after program completion.

A number of procedures were implemented to reduce threats to internal validity (Bickman, 1992). Staff working in agencies serving Latinos referred potential participants to the study's clinical supervisor, who then screened families to ensure they met the study criteria for inclusion. After eligibility was determined, a program specialist interviewed both potential participants (the parent and adolescent) and invited them to participate in the project. The program specialist explained to the family that they would be randomly assigned to either the action-oriented prevention group or to a support group. Those families unwilling to participate in randomization left the study at this point (i.e., before randomization occurred). Although this voluntary dropout may have influenced external validity by making the results most applicable to willing and cooperative participants, this recruiting step bolstered internal validity by guarding against attrition after random assignment (Bickman, 1992). Random assignment was delayed until pretest data were collected and the groups were ready to begin. Randomization occurred within each of the geographic implementation sites (i.e., rural, urban, and midsize metropolitan locations).

Intervention implementation and fidelity. *Entre Dos Mundos* program sessions were held in community settings (e.g., churches, arts centers) that were convenient for and familiar to the participants. To reduce attrition and encourage participation, the *Entre Dos Mundos* research staff provided participants with transportation (i.e., a university van) to program sessions. Each of the sites also provided child care for younger siblings and refreshments. All groups were closed; that is, after the random assignment to groups, no new members were allowed to join the groups. Each of the eight program sessions lasted 3 hours. Group sessions were videotaped to allow the research team to closely examine implementation fidelity and to guide supervision of group facilitators.

The first author (Bacallao), who is a bicultural, bilingual psychotherapist with clinical experience working with Latino families, facilitated each *Entre Dos Mundos* action-oriented program session. Bacallao has master's degrees in social work and community counseling, a doctorate in social work, and is certified by the American Board of Examiners in psychodrama, sociometry, and group psychotherapy. Skills in psychodramatic action methods were needed to facilitate the action-oriented groups. Two bicultural, bilingual research staff members with master's degrees in social work and clinical experience working with Latino families facilitated *Entre Dos Mundos* support group sessions. Group sessions in both intervention conditions were conducted in Spanish. The second author supervised implementation of each of these intervention conditions separately to maintain intervention fidelity and to avoid the possibility of contamination that can occur when staff members attend group supervision.

Sample

This investigation used a community-based, nonprobability sampling design with some purposive clustering (Frankfort-Nachmias & Nachmias, 2000). For example, rather than recruiting solely in one county or from one agency, our selection of rural, urban, and small metropolitan recruitment sites substantially broadened the possible range of socioeconomic status levels that might be represented by participants. In addition, this design element made the sample representative of urban, small metropolitan, and rural settings, which increases the generalizability of the findings. Each site provided approximately one third of the overall sample.

Table 2 presents the sociodemographic characteristics of the sample. Of the 81 families, 56 were randomized to the *Entre Dos Mundos* action-oriented prevention groups and 25 were randomized to the *Entre Dos Mundos* support groups. A randomization ratio of 2:1 in favor of the action-oriented condition was implemented to parallel our directional hypotheses that participation in action-oriented programming would be more efficacious than support groups.

Overall, adolescents in the sample had lived in the United States for an average of 3.6 years and their parents had been in this country for an average of 5.3 years. All families spoke Spanish in their homes and more than 75% chose Spanish as their preferred language for the research interview assessments. A majority of the families (78%) had emigrated from Mexico. The families' average annual income was approximately $20,000, which was slightly above the federal poverty threshold of $17,000 for a family of four. Participating parents were typically working mothers in their late thirties. Attendance was very good at both the action-oriented prevention program and support groups. On average, parents attended 5.4 sessions and adolescents attended nearly 7 of the 8 sessions offered.

Table 2. Sociodemographic Characteristics by *Entre Dos Mundos* (EDM) Group.

Action	EDM Group	EDM Support	Total
	(n=56)	(n=25)	(N=81)
	M(SD)	M(SD)	M(SD)
Adolescent's Age (years)	14(1.8)	14(1.7)	14(1.8)
Adolescent's Gender (% Female)	55%	52%	54%
Annual Income Reported by Parent	$19,454(8,375)	$20,788(6,839)	$19,857(7,920)
Time Spent Living in U.S.-Adolescent	3.5(2.4)	3.8(2.6)	3.6(2.5)
Time Spent Living in U.S.-Parent	5.2(2.7)	5.5(2.9)	5.3(2.8)
Country of Origin (%)			
Mexico	73%	89%	78%
El Salvador	5%	7%	6%
Colombia	10%	0%	7%
Other	12%	4%	9%
Gender of Participating Parent (% Female)	86%	78%	83%
Parent Age	39 (7.0)	40 (7.0)	39(7.1)
Parent Currently Working (%)	62%	78%	.67(.47)
Parent Education (%)			
No Schooling	7%	4%	6%
Elementary School	52%	41%	48%
Some High School	16%	33%	22%
High School Graduate	14%	14%	14%
More than High School	11%	8%	10%
Parent-Intervention Sessions Attended	5.3(2.7)	5.6(2.6)	5.4(2.7)
Adolescent-Intervention Sessions Attended	6.8(1.9)	6.6(1.2)	6.7(1.7)

Note: No statistically significant difference were found using chi square and T-tests

Attrition. Pretest measures were collected on 81 families (56 attended action-oriented groups and 25 attended support groups). At the one-year follow-up, 62 families (47 had attended action-oriented groups, 15 had attended support group) were available and willing to be reassessed. The study attrition rate was 16% for families who participated in the action-oriented groups and 40% for those who participated in the support groups. These attrition rates are not surprising given that immigrant families are particularly unstable because of employment instability, seasonal employment, risk of deportation, and socioeconomic disadvantage. Indeed, the 84% retention rate in the action-oriented groups may be a sign of their satisfaction with participation in the project.

To assess attrition bias, we examined sociodemographic indicators and pretest measures for potential differences between families available at follow-up and those lost to attrition; we found only one statistically significant difference between families with complete data and those with missing data. Families with data missing at follow-up had attended significantly fewer program sessions. Those with complete data attended an average of six *Entre Dos*

Mundos sessions (standard deviation = 2.2), whereas families lost at follow-up attended an average of four sessions (standard deviation = 3.1, t $_{(80)}$ = 3.37, p < .001). On all other indicators, the families lost at follow-up did not differ significantly from families who continued to participate at follow-up (e.g., adolescents had equivalent levels of problem behaviors; reports of parent-adolescent conflict were equivalent). Consequently, the only bias we detected was that families who were lost to attrition or who declined to be interviewed at follow-up had shown less commitment to their initial participation in the project. Thus, our results may be more characteristic of Latino immigrant families who are more willing to participate in prevention programming.

Measures

Adolescents and parents completed a research interview in their homes at pretest (baseline), posttest, 3-months after posttest, 6-months after posttest, and one year after posttest. The research interview contained a series of psychosocial scales that are used in the program evaluation. Identical psychosocial scales were completed at each assessment. All instruments were available in Spanish or English. Measures were translated and back translated for the study. Common measures, such as the Child Behavior Check List, have well-established Spanish versions with strong psychometric properties that were used in this investigation (see Achenbach & Rescorla, 2001; Vega et al., 1995). More than 75% of adolescents and parents chose to use the Spanish version of the interview, indicating their lower acculturation levels. In order to standardize the research interview administration across a wide range of literacy levels, interviewers read all questions to the adolescent and parent participants. Interviews were conducted separately and simultaneously with adolescents and parents.

Independent Variables. Pretest scores were obtained using standardized measures administered before families began their participation in the *Entre Dos Mundos* program groups. Annual family income was measured by one item that asked parents their family's annual household income. Parent education was measured as the number of years the participant had attended school, and recorded as an ordinal variable with response options 0 for *no schooling*, 1 for *elementary school*, 2 for *some high school*, 3 for *high school graduate*, 4 for *some college*, and 5 for *college graduate or more*. The amount of time the parent had been in the United States was recorded as a continuous variable that measured years since immigration. This variable is a proxy measure controlling for differences in assimilation levels.

A dichotomous variable was used for *Entre Dos Mundos* prevention program participation, with assignment to the action-oriented group coded as 1 and assignment to the support group coded as 0. Parents' attendance at the group sessions, or *program dosage*, was a continuous variable measuring the number of *Entre Dos Mundos* sessions that the parent attended; the score ranged from 0 to 8.

Parent-Reported Proximal Dependent Variables – Measured at Pretest, Posttest, 3-Month, 6-Month, and One-Year Follow-up. The Faces II Family Adaptability scale is a subscale of the Faces II scale (Olson, 1992). The family adaptability subscale consists of 12 items measured on a 5-point Likert scale. Participants mark with what frequency each scale item occurs in their family; choices range from *not at all* (1) to *sometimes* (3) to *all the time* (5). The range of possible scores is 14 to 60, with a higher score indicating a high amount of family adaptability. Items on the scale include "In our family, it is easy for everyone to express his/her opinion," "We shift household responsibilities from person to person," and "Family members are afraid to say what is on their minds." The scale reliability for this sample was .79.

The Bicultural Support Scale is a seven item scale measured using a 5-point Likert scale. It was developed for this study by the research team. Participants mark to what extent they believe each person or group described in the question values the ability to function in different cultures (i.e., to move between cultures). The choices range from *not at all* (1) to *some* (3) to *very much* (5). The range of possible scores is 11 to 55, with a higher score indicating the parent feels a high level of bicultural support. Items on the scale include "How much do you value going between different cultures?", "How much do your Latino friends value going between different cultures?", and "How much do people in your town or city value going between different cultures?" The scale reliability for this sample was .76.

The Bicultural Identity Integration scale (BII; Benet-Martínez & Haritatos, 2005; Benet-Martinez, Leu, Lee, & Morris, 2002) consists of eight items measured on a 4-point Likert scale. An answer of *strongly agree* is coded as 1, *agree* as 2, *disagree* as 3, and *strongly disagree* as 4. The range of possible scores is 8 to 32, with a higher score indicating a highly developed compatible bicultural identity and a lower score indicating a less developed bicultural identity. Items on the scale include "I simply feel like a (COUNTRY OF ORIGIN) person who lives in the United States," "I feel (COUNTRY OF ORIGIN)-American," "I feel like someone moving between two cultures," and "I feel caught between the (COUNTRY OF ORIGIN) and American cultures." The scale reliability was .60.

Parent-Reported Distal Dependent Variables – Measured at Pretest, Posttest, 3-Month, 6-Month, and One-Year Follow-up.

Parent-adolescent conflict was assessed using the Conflict Behavior Questionnaire-20 (CBQ-20; Robin & Foster, 1989). This scale provides an overall measure of negative communication conflict within a parent-adolescent dyad. The CBQ-20 has 20 items that use a *yes-no* response format to assess positive and negative interactions in both routine and argumentative exchanges. This instrument has been used to distinguish distressed from nondistressed families, and has been judged to have good clinical utility as an easily administered intervention and evaluation instrument (Rush & Task Force for the Handbook of Psychiatric Measures, 2000). The internal consistency reliability for the CBQ-20 in this sample was .89.

The Child Behavior Checklist (CBCL; Achenbach & Rescorla, 2001) is a parent-report questionnaire used to record parents' perceptions of their child's behavioral, emotional, and social problems. The CBCL oppositional defiant problems scale consists of five items measured using a 3-point Likert scale (*less than average, average, more than average*). The possible score ranges from 0 to 15, with a higher score indicating a greater number and severity of oppositional defiant problems. Examples of items from the CBCL oppositional defiant problems scale include "Parent's child is disobedient at home," "Parent's child is disobedient at school," and "Parent's child is stubborn, sullen, or irritable." The scale reliability for this sample was .79.

The CBCL attention problems subscale consists of five items measured on a 3-point Likert scale (*less than average, average, more than average*). The possible score ranges from 0 to 15, with a higher score indicating a greater number and severity of attention problems. The CBCL attention problems scale includes the following items: ","Parent's child acts too young for his/her age"; "Parent's child can't sit still, is restless, or hyperactive"; and "Parent's child is impulsive or acts without thinking." The scale reliability for this sample was .70.

The CBCL attention-deficit/hyperactivity problems subscale consists of seven items measured on a 3-point Likert scale (*less than average, average, more than average*). The possible score ranges from 0 to 21, with a higher score indicating a greater number and severity of attention-deficit/hyperactivity problems. Examples of items on the CBCL attention-deficit/hyperactivity problems subscale include the following: "Parent's child fails to finish what he/she starts," "Parent's child can't concentrate or pay attention for a long time," and "Parent's child talks too much." The scale reliability for this sample is .73.

One CBCL scale of particular interest in this study was the anxious-depressed problems scale that consisted of 13 items measured on a 3-point Likert scale (*less than average, average, more than average*). The scores for this scale have a possible range of 0 to 26, with a higher score indicating a greater number and severity of anxious-depressed problems. The CBCL anxious-depressed problems scale asks the parent to assess the characteristics of the child such as "cries a lot," "fears going to school," "feels or complains that no one loves him/her," "high strung, or tense," and "self-conscious or easily embarrassed." The scale reliability for this sample was .84.

The CBCL total problems scale consists of 60 items measured on a 3-point Likert scale (*less than average, average, more than average*). Possible scores range from 0 to 120, with a higher score indicating a greater number and severity of total problems. Items on the CBCL total problems scale include items from externalizing, internalizing, social, thought, and attention problems subscales, among others. The internal consistency reliability for the CBCL total problems scale in this sample was .89.

Data Analyses

Analyses were conducted using SPSS version 14.0, using an Attributes-Treatments-Interactions design (Pedhazur & Pedhazur Schmelkin, 1991). Stepwise multiple regression analyses were performed to examine the percentage of variation explained by attributes (e.g., pretest scores, family income, parent education, age, marital status, and length of parent residency in the United States), intervention condition, attendance, and the interactions between the attributes and intervention. The pretest score for the dependent variable being examined was entered as the first step in a stepwise multiple regression equation. Family income, parent education, age, marital status, and length of parent's U.S. residency were entered in the second through sixth steps, followed by intervention condition in the seventh step, and the number of sessions attended entered in the eighth step. Interaction terms for attendance-by-pretest score and intervention condition-by-pretest score were entered in the final step; these terms were dropped if they did not demonstrate statistical significance. Because interaction terms can introduce problematic levels of multicollinearity into regression equations, creating high variance inflation factors and low tolerances, all of the pretest score variables were centered (e.g., taking the difference between observed scores and the grand mean) before calculating interaction terms (Neter, Kutner, Nachtsheim, & Wasserman, 1996). This centering procedure helped to limit problems with multicollinearity that arise when independent variables and interaction terms are highly correlated. Centering is a standard procedure used when conducting regression analyses with interaction terms (Tabachnick & Fidell, 2001). Moreover, the centering procedure lowered collinearity, thus rendering acceptable variance inflation factors and tolerance diagnostics.

The data were screened to ensure that all of the assumptions for multiple regression analyses were met. Issues concerning linearity, normality, homoscedasticity, multicollinearity, singularity, and independence of residuals were all considered. Missing data were not a problem. Residual outliers greater than three standard deviations from the mean, Mahalnobis Distance scores, and Cook's Distance scores were all examined. Outliers did not influence regression results and were retained in the analyses. Collinearity diagnostics, normal probability plots, and studentized residual by standardized predicted value plots showed no serious problems. Thus, all of the multiple regression assumptions were met.

RESULTS

Our findings from *t*-tests and chi-square comparisons revealed no significant sociodemographic differences between the action-oriented and support groups at pretest (see Table 2). Both format types of *Entre Dos Mundos* groups were well attended. On average, parents in both study arms attended more than 5 of the 8 sessions offered. Similarly, adolescents had high attendance rates: adolescents in the action-oriented groups attended an average of 6.8 of the 8 sessions, and adolescents in the support groups attended an average of 6.6 of the 8 sessions.

Posttest Analyses

Shown in Table 3, multiple regression models confirmed that the number of group sessions attended by parents explained 13% of the variance in bicultural identity integration, 7% of the variance in bicultural support, and 4% of the variance in family adaptability, even when controlling for pretest scores, annual family income, parent education, and time since parent immigration. Each of these proximal outcomes was positively associated with the number of sessions parents attended. Parental attendance also explained variance in three CBCL measures: 10% of the variance in adolescent aggression, 9% in adolescent oppositional defiant behavior, and approximately 5% in attention problems and attention-deficit hyperactivity disorder was explained by parent group attendance. The statistically significant negative regression coefficients in these posttest models indicated substantial reductions in each of these outcomes for parents who came to more group sessions. There were no statistically significant moderation or mediation effects in the posttest multiple regression models.

Entre Dos Mundos/Between Two Worlds: An Evidence-Based Bicultural Skills... 21

Table 3. Multivariate Models for Proximal Outcomes at Posttest.

	Family Adaptability		Bicultural Support		Bicultural Identity Integration		Aggression		ADHD		Oppositional Defiant Behavior		Attention Problems	
	Beta	ΔR^2	Beta	ΔR^2	Beta	ΔR^2	Beta	ΔR^2	Beta	ΔR^2	Beta	ΔR^2	Beta	ΔR^2
Pretest Score	.72***	.48***	.37**	.11**	.23**	.14**	.62***	.37***	.61***	.42***	.45***	.21***	.64***	.43***
Annual Income	-.05	.02	-.05	.02	.26*	.01	-.08	.00	-.13	.00	-.14	.00	-.14	.00
Parent Education	-.07	.00	-.13	.01	.09	.01	.15	.01	.17	.02	.10	.00	.16	.02
Time Parent has been in U.S.	-.14	.01	-.17	.02	-.10	.00	.06	.00	.18	.01	.08	.00	.18	.02
EDM Action-Oriented Group	-.05	.00	.06	.01	-.23*	.04	.00	.00	.12	.01	-.03	.00	.07	.00
Number of Sessions Parent Attended	.21*	.04*	.28*	.07*	.36**	.12**	-.33**	.10***	-.23*	.05*	-.31**	.09**	-.24*	.06*
Model F Adjusted R^2	12.76*** .51		3.08* .16		4.51*** .25		11.74*** .44		10.67*** .47		4.542** .24		10.910*** .48	

* p < .05, ** p < .01, *** p < .001

Table 4. High vs. Low Dosage Participants' Means (SD) at Pretest and Posttest – Parent Data.

	Pretest		Posttest		
	Low Dosage	High Dosage	Low Dosage	High Dosage	
Outcome Measures	M(SD)	M(SD)	M(SD)	M(SD)	Effect Size
Proximal Outcomes					
Bicultural Support	26.47(6.12)	28.55(4.47)	22.00(7.92)	27.29(4.03)***	.89
Bicultural Identity Integration	17.16(3.66)	18.92(4.18)	17.85(3.24)	20.05(3.58)*	.65
Family Adaptability	56.95(6.00)	57.49(8.63)	53.69(7.53)	59.13(7.99)*	.70
Parent-Reported Distal Outcomes					
CBCL Aggression	5.94(5.48)	6.38(5.84)	9.53(6.42)	5.03(4.30)**	.84
CBCL Oppositional Defiant Behavior	2.50(2.60)	2.61(2.35)	3.69(2.93)	2.16(1.91)*	63
CBCL Attention Problems	4.33(3.60)	4.80(4.23)	5.33(3.06)	3.79(3.36)	.48
CBCL ADHD	4.00(2.72)	3.87(3.05)	4.33(3.58)	2.95(2.69)	.44

Notes: Low dosage parents attended less than 4 of the 8 group sessions. High dosage parents attended 4 or more group sessions.

Between-group differences were tested using two-tailed t-tests comparing group means. Effect sizes were calculated as the difference between the group means divided by the pooled standard deviation. * p < .05, ** p < .01, *** p < .001

There were two possible explanations for the significant program dosage effects. These effects could be attributed to the prevention program; that is, due to the experimental design, with all other factors being equal, we could conclude that higher attendance leads to better proximal and distal outcomes. An alternate explanation is that the attendance effects could be due to differential attrition; that is, higher risk families drop out of the program earlier, leaving healthier families with lower outcome scores to persist longer. This alternative hypothesis suggests that the treatment effects were spurious. To explore these rival explanations, we dichotomized the attendance variable into low- and high-dosage groups. Low-dosage parents attended fewer than 4 of the 8 program sessions; they did not participate for even one month of the 2-month program. High-dosage parents participated in four or more sessions, completing at least one month of the 2-month curriculum.

Table 4 shows means and standard deviations for these low- and high-dosage groups. Results of t-tests comparing group differences on pretest and posttest outcome measures showed no significant differences between high- and low-dosage groups at pretest. Specifically, low-dosage participants were not at higher risk at pretest. Indeed, as compared with the high-dosage group, low-dosage participants had lower pretest group means for adolescent aggression, oppositional defiant behavior, and attention problems. This finding stands in opposition to the hypothesis of differential attrition. At posttest comparison with low-dosage parents, parents in the high-dosage group reported significantly higher bicultural support, bicultural identity integration, and family adaptability. The high-dosage group parents-reports of adolescent behavior also indicated significantly lower levels of aggression and oppositional defiant behavior in their adolescents than the parents in low-dosage group. Similarly, parent reports of adolescents' attention problems and attention deficit/hyperactivity problems showed a trend towards significance ($p = .1$), but did not reach the conventional level of statistical significance.

Relative to low-dosage parents, the high-dosage parent group had a large treatment effect size (.6 to .9) for bicultural support, adolescent aggression, family adaptability, bicultural identity integration, and adolescent oppositional defiant behavior. The effect size for adolescent attention problems and attention deficit/hyperactivity problems was moderate (.4 to .5). Overall, this evidence led us to reject the differential attrition hypothesis, and consider differences in outcomes associated with attendance to be attributable to the *Entre Dos Mundos* curriculum.

Analyses of One-Year Follow-Up Data

Table 5 displays pretest and one-year follow-up means and standard deviations of the dependent variables measured for the action-oriented and support group conditions. Standardized coefficients from multiple regression models, shown in Table 6, show the effects of the *Entre Dos Mundos* program conditions. When controlling for variation based on pretest scores, length of parent's U.S. residency, family income, parent education, age, and marital status, the dichotomous variable indicating program format (i.e., action-oriented versus support group) was found to be a statistically significant predictor of adolescent aggression, oppositional defiant behavior, problems with anxious-depression, parent-adolescent conflict, and total adolescent problems—all in favor of action-oriented group delivery. On average at the one-year follow-up, parents who had participated in the action-oriented *Entre Dos Mundos* skills training groups reported significantly less conflict with their adolescents as compared with parents who attended the unstructured support group. Further, parents who had attended the action-oriented group reported significantly fewer mental health problems for their adolescent children than did the parents who attended the support group. The statistically significant negative regression coefficients in these outcome models indicated substantial reductions in each of these outcomes reported by parents who participated in action-oriented *Entre Dos Mundos* groups.

Table 5: Pretest and 1-Year Follow-up Means and Standard Deviations for *Entre Dos Mundos* (EDM) Action-Oriented and Support Groups

	Aggression		Oppositional Defiant Problems		Anxious-Depressed Behavior		Parent-Adolescent Conflict		Total Problems	
	Pretest	1 year	Pretest	1 year	Pretest	1 year	Pretest	1 year	Pretest	1 year
EDM Action Groups	6.5 (5.6)	5.1 (5.1)	2.7 (2.4)	2.1 (2.2)	4.4 (4.2)	3.4 (3.4)	6.0 (5.5)	5.3 (4.9)	31.0 (22.8)	15.6 (12.2)
EDM Support Groups	6.3 (6.7)	6.1 (7.5)	2.6 (2.7)	2.7 (2.9)	3.2 (4.0)	4.0 (4.3)	5.5 (6.3)	6.1 (5.9)	28.0 (27.6)	19.1 (17.1)

Table 6. Standardized Regression Coefficients Predicting Distal Outcome Measures at 1-Year Follow-up.

	Aggression	Oppositional Defiant Behavior	Anxious-Depressed Behavior	Parent-Adolescent Conflict	Total Problems
Pretest	.663***	.664***	.602***	.539***	.528***
Time Parent in United States	.096	.105	.032	.242*	.050
Income	-.138	-.168	-.091	-.198	-.066
Parent Education	.126	-.080	-.032	.031	-.031
Parent Age	.073	.058	.135	,092	.233
Martial Status	.082	.103	.039	.120	.024
EDM intervention (1= action-oriented, 0 = support groups)	-.230*	-.255*	-.319*	-.276*	-.321*
Attendance (Dosage)	-.094	-.089	.040	-.028	-.095
Model F / *Adjusted* R^2	*5.1*** / .40	*5.5*** / .41	*3.8** / .30	*4.1*** / .31	*3.3* / .30
R^2 *Change for Intervention*	*.04*	*.06*	*.09*	*.07*	*.08*
Estimated Effect Size	*.4*	*.5*	*.7*	*.6*	*.6*

* $p < .05$, ** $p < .01$, *** $p < .001$

Participation in action-oriented *Entre Dos Mundos* groups explained 4% of the variance in adolescent aggression, 6% of the variance in oppositional defiant behavior, 9% in anxious-depressed behavior, 7% in parent-adolescent conflict, and 8% of total problems—even when controlling for pretest scores, annual family income, parent education, age, marital status, and time since parent immigration. These percentages of variance explained by the intervention condition translate to an estimated program effect size of .5 for aggression and oppositional defiant behavior, .7 for anxious-depressed problems, .6 for parent-adolescent conflict, and .6 for total problems. These effect sizes for adolescent aggression, oppositional defiant behavior, parent-adolescent conflict, and total problems were clearly moderate (.5 and .6), and the program effect for anxious-depression nearly reached the conventionally accepted threshold considered to mark large effects (.7 whereas .8 is considered large). There were no statistically significant moderation or mediation effects in the multiple regression models.

DISCUSSION

This study compared the sustained effects of two alternative delivery methods for the *Entre Dos Mundos* curriculum; an action-oriented facilitation style characterized by the extensive use of psychodrama techniques versus a traditional support group format characterized by a passive, discussion-oriented delivery. Interestingly, the pattern of effects suggested that program attendance (or dosage) was critical for fostering proximal outcomes at posttest whereas the program delivery format determined the distal outcomes at one-year follow-up.

We hypothesized that commitment to program participation, as indexed by higher attendance rates, would be significantly associated with proximal outcomes such as lower levels of adolescent problems and parent-adolescent conflict. The multiple regression models for posttest data supported this hypothesis; program dosage was the key for proximal outcomes. Parents who attended higher numbers of *Entre Dos Mundos* sessions (i.e., received a higher dosage of the multifamily group program) reported significantly decreased family problems—for both delivery formats—which translated to a moderate to large treatment effect size (.6 to .9) for bicultural support, adolescent aggression, family adaptability, bicultural identity integration, and adolescent oppositional defiant behavior. The effect size for adolescent attention problems and attention deficit/hyperactivity problems at posttest was moderate (.4 to .5). Consequently, we believe these short term-changes were associated with new learning gained from processing acculturation stress issues (e.g., the weekly themes from the *Entre Dos Mundos* curriculum) either in action or through group discussion.

This investigation advanced beyond prior studies by measuring program impacts on both proximal and distal outcomes. Given that only the original BET study (Szapocznik et al., 1986) measured changes in bicultural skills and only Coatsworth et al. (2002) reported changes in parental investment, few prior studies on bicultural skills training programs illuminated the mechanisms that made the programs work. Consequently, the current study is distinguished in its demonstration of program effects on family adaptability, bicultural support, and bicultural identity integration. The *Entre Dos Mundos* research was the first study since Szapocznik and colleagues' (1986) tested BET to show significant changes on variables related to biculturalism based on program participation.

The effect sizes that were associated with differences in parents' program dosage were noteworthy. Few prevention programs for adolescent aggression have rendered effect sizes near .8. The large effect we have reported for *Entre Dos Mundos* may be due to our program design that included parents and adolescents in the same sessions using a multiple family group format. These multiple family groups provided a context for parents and adolescents to communicate in new ways while discussing challenging acculturation topics. Most of the families reported that they did not discuss acculturation issues at home, which left parents and adolescents to cope with these issues on their own. The *Entre Dos Mundos* groups allowed the family members to come together, provided a forum for discussing acculturation, and enhanced parent-adolescent understanding of each other. This heightened understanding, coupled with support from other participating families and gains in bicultural identity, appeared to be key elements in helping these Latino families adapt to acculturation challenges and decrease problematic behaviors in adolescents.

For long-term learning, skills acquisition, and second-order family system change (i.e., foundational change; Nichols & Schwartz, 2007), the one-year follow-up analyses suggested that program implementation style, specifically adopting an action-oriented delivery approach, was more important than simple attendance. One year after program completion, *Entre Dos Mundos* sessions delivered using action-oriented psychodrama techniques to enhance bicultural coping skills showed sustained benefits on adolescent problems and parent-adolescent conflict than did support group facilitation of parent-adolescent communication and between-family social networking. As compared with parents who had participated in the unstructured support group, at the one-year follow-up parents who had participated in the action-oriented *Entre Dos Mundos* groups reported significantly lower adolescent aggression, oppositional defiant behavior, anxious depression, and total problems in their adolescent children as well as less parent-adolescent conflict in their families. The percentages of variance explained by *Entre Dos Mundos* delivery format at one-year follow-up (.5 for aggression and oppositional defiant behavior, .7 for anxious-depressed problems, .6 for parent-adolescent conflict, and .6 for total problems) showed that posttest effects for aggression and oppositional defiant behavior were sustained at one-year follow-up for families that attended action-oriented *Entre Dos Mundos* groups. The moderate posttest effects on attention problems and attention deficit/hyperactivity problems decreased enough at one-year follow-up to lose their statistical significance; however, beneficial sleeper effects for *Entre Dos Mundos* action-oriented delivery families were found for decreases in anxious-depressed problems, parent-adolescent conflict, and total adolescent problems at one-year follow-up that were not significant at posttest. It took additional time beyond the 8-week program to integrate new coping skills in family systems and to create fundamental relationship changes between parents and adolescents.

These positive effects of action-oriented implementation were consistent with earlier evaluations of bicultural skills training packages (Arenas, 1978; Bilides, 1990; Costantino et al., 1986; LaFromboise & Rowe, 1983; Malgady et al., 1990; Marsiglia et al., 1998; Mullender, 1990; Pantin et al., 2003; Schinke et al., 1988; Szapocznik et al., 1986; Ying, 1999), further illustrating the utility of bicultural skills training. Equally important, the research on *Entre Dos Mundos* advanced current knowledge by measuring program impacts one year after program completion. Few prior studies of bicultural skills training programs have evaluated longitudinal data.

In addition, this study contributed to the body of research knowledge supporting the use of psychodramatic methods in prevention and treatment. Psychodrama has been used as a therapeutic modality for more than seven decades. This approach dominated the field of group psychotherapy during the first half of the twentieth century and evolved as a viable alternative to, or complement for, psychoanalytic treatment (Buchanan 1984; Oxford and Weiner, 2003; Blatner 2005). Although psychodrama is one of the oldest forms of psychotherapy, dating back to the 1930s, empirical evidence showing the efficacy of this approach has been somewhat limited (Buchanan, 1984; Kellerman, 1987; Kipper, 1978). Even so, psychodramatic methods are commonly implemented in combination with other adjunctive approaches or used independently for a variety of applications in education, business, social services, and personal development (Blatner, 1999). Kipper and Ritchie (2003) conducted a meta-analysis of 25 experimentally designed studies of psychodramatic techniques such as doubling and role reversal. Their results showed that the large treatment effect size displayed by psychodrama intervention was comparable or superior to other group psychotherapy strategies. Indeed, the overall Cohen's d of .95 compared favorably with many psychosocial and educational interventions that typically fall in the moderate .3 to .6 range. The Kipper and Ritchie analytical results showed no difference between the effectiveness of psychodrama techniques used with clinical versus student populations or between psychodrama techniques used in single versus multiple sessions. The most effective psychodrama interventions were doubling and role reversal. Based on this body of evidence, we felt comfortable integrating action methods such as doubling and role reversal in our Entre Dos Mundos prevention program. Furthermore, the results of this study on Entre Dos Mundos effectiveness are in line with Kipper's meta-analysis of psychodrama treatment in general, confirming the substantial treatment effect sizes for action-oriented programs.

Blatner (1999), one of the most eminent scholars in this area, has suggested studying the efficacy of psychodrama by comparing group or family therapy that integrates action methods with interventions that use a similar therapeutic approach but do not incorporate psychodrama. The current study began to fulfill this mandate by empirically demonstrating that action-oriented psychodramatic groups proved superior to support groups that used the same topical themes. Further research on psychodramatic action methods in prevention and intervention is clearly warranted.

Although this study underscored the promise of action-oriented bicultural skills programs, there were clear limitations. The sample size was small for sophisticated statistical analyses and did not allow us to perform subanalyses on families from different countries of origin (e.g., Mexicans versus Colombians). We focused solely on parent reports, which we considered more objective measures of adolescent mental health problems than adolescent reports. Future studies should integrate data from multiple reporters and include larger samples of Latino families. A distinct strength of the study is that conducting the study in metropolitan, small town, and rural communities, rather than in one or two agencies, enhanced generalizability of the findings. However, caution is warranted in generalizing findings beyond Latino immigrant families living in North Carolina, or beyond Latino immigrant families willing to participate in prevention programs. Although our attrition analyses showed no differences in demographic indicators or mental health measures between families with follow-up data and those lost to attrition, families with follow-up data had attended significantly more program sessions. Consequently, we must limit our discussion of program effects to Latino immigrant families who are committed to program participation. This limitation is common in prevention science.

Finally, the differences between action-oriented and support groups showed that the *Entre Dos Mundos* program was more efficacious when implemented using action-oriented psychodrama techniques with structured warm-up activities. However, program effects may be underestimated because participants in the comparison condition (i.e., support group program) received the same weekly themes from the *Entre Dos Mundos* curriculum. In our next study, we will compare *Entre Dos Mundos* prevention with either a no-service comparison group or a basic case management group to provide a suitable contrast between groups focused on acculturation and groups with no acculturation content. It is possible that comparison to no-service control families could produce even stronger program effects.

CONCLUSION

At posttest, according to parents who received a significant dose of the program, *Entre Dos Mundos* youth violence prevention was efficacious in lowering adolescent aggression, oppositional defiant behavior, attention problems, and attention deficit hyperactivity disorder in acculturating Latino immigrant families. Program participation was also associated with increased family adaptability, bicultural support, and bicultural identity integration. The *Entre Dos Mundos* curriculum was equally efficacious when delivered in action-oriented experiential groups or in unstructured support groups. Having parents commit to attending at least 4 of the 8 program sessions appears to be the critical component related to the enhanced proximal outcomes.

At one-year follow-up, program delivery format became important for long-term change and skills acquisition. *Entre Dos Mundos* prevention, when delivered in action-oriented multifamily groups using psychodrama techniques, was efficacious and resulted in parent reports of lower adolescent aggression, oppositional defiant behavior, anxious depression, parent-adolescent conflict, and total problems in acculturating Latino immigrant adolescents. At the one-year follow-up after program completion, action-oriented experiential groups showed superior effects when compared to support groups focused on the same session themes. Findings were characteristic of Latino immigrant families who participated in more program sessions.

REFERENCES

Achenbach, T. M. & Rescorla, L. A. (2001). *Manual for ASEBA school-age forms and profiles.* Burlington: University of Vermont, Research Center for Children, Youth, & Families.

Al-Issa, I., Tousignant, M. (Eds.). (1997). *Ethnicity, immigration, and psychopathology.* New York, NY: Plenum Press.

Amaro, H., Whitaker, R., Coffman, G. & Heeren, T. (1990). Acculturation and marijuana and cocaine use: Findings from HHANES 1982-1984. *American Journal of Public Health, 80*(Suppl), 54-60.

Arenas, S. (1978). Bilingual/bicultural programs for preschool children. *Children Today, 7(4)*, 2-6.

Bacallao, M. & Smokowski, P. R. (2005). Entre Dos Mundos (Between Two Worlds) bicultural skills training and Latino immigrant families. *Journal of Primary Prevention, 26*, 485-509. doi: 10.1007/s10935-005-0008-6.

Bacallao, M. & Smokowski, P. R. (2007). The costs of getting ahead: Mexican family systems after immigration. *Family Relations, 56*, 52-66.

Bacallao, M. & Smokowski, P. R. (2009). Entre Dos Mundos /Between Two Worlds: Bicultural development in context. *Journal of Primary Prevention, 30*(3/4),421-452. doi: 10.1007/s10935-009-0176-x.

Benet-Martínez, V. & Haritatos, J. (2005). Bicultural Identity Integration (BII): Components and psychosocial antecedents. *Journal of Personality, 73*, 1015-1050.

Benet-Martinez, V., Leu, J., Lee, F. & Morris, M. (2002). Negotiating biculturalism: Cultural frame switching in biculturals with oppositional versus compatible cultural identities. *Journal of Cross-Cultural Psychology, 33*, 492-517. doi:10.1177/0022022102033005005

Berry, J. W. (1998). Acculturation stress. In P. Balls Organista, K. M. Chun, & G. Marin (Eds.), *Readings in ethnic psychology* (117-122). New York, NY: Routledge.

Beverly, C. (1989). Treatment issues for black, alcoholic clients. *Social-Casework, 70(6)*, 370-374.

Bickman, L . (1992). Designing outcome evaluations for children's mental health services: Improving internal validity. *New Directions for Program Evaluation, 54(Summer)*, 57-68.

Bilides, D. G. (1990). Race, color, ethnicity, and class: Issues of biculturalism in school-based adolescent counseling groups. *Social Work With Groups, 13(4)*, 43-58.

Blatner, A. (1999). Psychodramatic methods in psychotherapy. In D. J. Weiner (Ed.) *Beyond talk therapy: Using movement and expressive techniques in clinical practice* (125-143). Washington, DC: American Psychological Association.

Blatner, A. (2005). Psychodrama. In R. J. Corsini, & D. Wedding (Eds.), *Current psychotherapies* (7th ed., 405-438). Belmont, CA: Brooks/Cole.

Brook, J. S., Whiteman, M., Balka, E. B., Win, T. & Gursen, M. D. (1998). African American and Puerto Rican drug use: A longitudinal study. *Journal of the American Academy of Child and Adolescent Psychiatry, 36*, 1260-1268.

Bui, H. & Thongniramol, O. (2005). Immigration and self-reported delinquency: The interplay of immigration, generations, gender, race, and ethnicity. *Journal of Crime and Justice, 28(2)*, 71-80.

Buchanan, D. R. (1984). Psychodrama. In T. B. Karasu (Ed.). *The psychosocial therapies: Part II of the psychiatric therapies* (783-789). Washington, DC: American Psychiatric Association.

Buriel, R., Calzada, S. & Vasquez, R. (1982). The relationship of traditional Mexican American culture to adjustment and delinquency among three generations of Mexican American male adolescents. *Hispanic Journal of Behavioral Sciences, 4(1)*, 41-55.

Carlson-Sabelli, L., Sabelli, H., Patel, M. & Holm, K. (1992). The union of opposites in sociometry. *Journal of Group Psychotherapy, Psychodrama & Sociometry, 44(4)*, 147-171.

Campbell, D. T. & Stanley, J. C. (1963). *Experimental and quasi-experimental designs for research*. Boston, MA: Houghton Mifflin.

Castro, F. G., Coe, K., Gutierres, S. & Saenz, D. (1996). Designing health promotion programs for Latinos. In P. M. Kato, & T. Mann (Eds.), *Handbook of diversity issues in health psychology* (319-346). New York, NY: Plenum.

Centers for Disease Control and Prevention. (2004). *Youth risk behavior surveillance—United States, 2003. Surveillance summaries: May 21, 2004*, MMWR 2004:53(No. SS-2). Retrieved June 25, 2007, from http://www.cdc.gov/mmwr/PDF/SS/SS5302.pdf

Coatsworth, J. D., Maldonido-Molina, M., Pantin, H. & Szapocznik, J. (2005). A person-centered and ecological investigation of acculturation strategies in Hispanic immigrant youth. *Journal of Community Psychology, 33*, 157-174.

Coatsworth, J. D., Pantin, H. & Szapocznik, J. (2002). Familias Unidas: A family-centeredecodevelopmental intervention to reduce risk for problem behavior among Hispanic adolescents. *Clinical Child & Family Psychology Review, 5(2)*, 113-132.

Costantino, G., Malgady, R. G. & Rogler, L. H. (1986). Cuento therapy: A culturally sensitive modality for Puerto Rican children. *Journal of Consulting and Clinical Psychology, 54*, 639-645.

Delgado, M. (Ed.). (1998). *Alcohol use/abuse among Latinos: Issues and examples of culturally competent service*. New York, NY: Haworth Press.

Dinh, K. T., Roosa, M. W., Tein, J. Y. & Lopez, V. A. (2002). The relationship between acculturation and problem behavior proneness in a Hispanic youth sample: A longitudinal mediation model. *Journal of Abnormal Child Psychology, 30*, 295-309.

Feliciano, C. (2001). The benefits of biculturalism: Exposure to immigrant culture and dropping out of school among Asian and Latino youths. *Social Science Quarterly, 82*, 865-879.

Frankfort-Nachmias, C. & Nachmias, D. (2000). *Research methods in the social sciences*. (6th ed.). New York, NY: Worth.

Fridrich, A. H. & Flannery, D. J. (1995). The effects of ethnicity and acculturation on early adolescent delinquency. *Journal of Child and Family Studies, 4*, 69-87.

Gil, A. G. & Vega, W. A. (1996). Two different worlds: Acculturation stress and adaptation among Cuban and Nicaraguan families. *Journal of Social and Personal Relationships, 13*, 435-456. doi: 10.1177/0265407596133008.

Gil, A. G., Vega, W. A. & Dimas, J. M. (1994). Acculturation stress and personal adjustment among Hispanic adolescent boys. *Journal of Community Psychology, 22,* 43-54. doi: 10.1002/1520-6629(199401)22:1<43::AID-JCOP2290220106>3.0.CO;2-T.

Gonzales, N. A., Knight, G. P., Morgan-Lopez, A. A., Saenz, D. & Sirolli, A. (2002). Acculturation and the mental health of Latino youths: An integration and critique of the literature. In J. M. Contreras, K. A. Kerns, & A. M. Neal-Barnett (Eds.), *Latino children and families in the United States*. Westport, CT: Greenwood.

Haritatos, J. & Benet-Martinez, V. (2002). Bicultural identities: The interface of cultural, personality, and socio-cognitive processes. *Journal of Research in Personality, 36*, 598-606.

Kellerman, P. F. (1987). Outcome research in classical psychodrama. *Small Group Research, 18*, 459-469.

Kipper, D. A. (1978). Trends in the research on the effectiveness of psychodrama. *Group Psychotherapy, Psychodrama, and Sociometry, 31*, 5-18.

Kipper, D. A. & Ritchie, T. D. (2003). The effectiveness of psychodramatic techniques: A meta-analysis. *Group Dynamics: Theory, Research, and Practice, Vol 7*(1),13-25.

LaFromboise, T. D., Coleman, H. L. & Gerton, J. (1993). Psychological impact of biculturalism: Evidence and theory. *Psychological Bulletin, 114,* 395-412. doi: 10.1037/0033-2909.114.3.395.

LaFromboise, T. D. & Rowe, W. (1983). Skills training for bicultural competence: Rationale and application. *Journal of Counseling Psychology, 30,* 589-595.

Lang, J. G., Munoz, R., Bernal, G. & Sorensen, J. (1982). Quality of life and psychological well-being in a bicultural Latino community. *Hispanic Journal of Behavioral Sciences, 4,* 433-450. doi:10.1177/07399863820044002.

McFarlane, W. R. (2002). *Multifamily groups in the treatment of severe psychiatric disorders.* New York, NY: Guilford Press.

Malgady, R. G., Rogler, L. H. & Costantino, G. (1990). Culturally sensitive psychotherapy for Puerto Rican children and adolescents: A program of treatment outcome research. *Journal of Consulting and Clinical Psychology, 58,* 704-712. doi: 10.1037/0022-006X.58.6.704.

Marks, G., Garcia, M. & Solts, J. M. (1990). Health risk behaviors of Hispanics in the United States: Findings from the HHANES 1982-1984. *American Journal of Public Health, 80(Suppl.),* 20-26.

Marsiglia, F., Cross, S. & Mitchell-Enos, V. (1998). Culturally grounded group work with adolescent American Indian students. *Social Work with Groups, 21(1-2),* 89-102. doi: 10.1300/J009v21n01_08.

Miranda, A., Estrada, D. & Firpo-Jimenez (2000). Differences in family cohesion, adaptability, and environment among Latino families in dissimilar stages of acculturation. *Family Journal, 8,* 341-350.

Miranda, A. & Umhoefer, D. (1998). Depression and social interest differences between Latinos in dissimilar acculturation stages. *Journal of Mental Health Counseling, 20(2),* 159-171.

Mullender, A. (1990). The Ebony project: Bicultural group work with transracial foster parents. *Social Work with Groups, 13(4),* 23-41.doi: 10.1300/J009v13n04_03.

Neter, J., Kutner, M. H., Nachtsheim, C. J. & Wasserman, W. (1996). *Applied linear regression models* (3rd ed.)*.* Chicago, IL: Irwin.

Nichols, M. & Schwartz, R. C. (2006). *Family therapy: Concepts and methods (7th Edition).* Needham Heights, MA: Allyn and Bacon.

Olson, D. H. (1992). *Family inventories manual.* Minneapolis, MN: Life Innovations.

Oxford, L. K. & Weiner, D. J. (2003). Rescripting family dramas using psychodramatic methods. In D. J. Weiner & L. K. Oxford (Eds.), *Action therapy with families and groups: Using creative arts improvisation in clinical practice.* Washington, DC: American Psychological Association.

Pantin, H., Coatsworth, J. D., Feaster, D. I., Newman, F. L. Briones, E., Prado, G. & Szapocznik, J. (2003). Familias Unidas: The efficacy of an intervention to increase parental investment in Hispanic immigrant families. *Prevention Science, 4(3),* 189-201. doi: 10.1023/A:1024601906942.

Pedhazur, E. J. & Pedhazur Schmelkin, L. (1991). *Measurement, design and analysis: An integrated approach.* Hillsdale, NJ: Lawrence Erlbaum.

Peeks, A. L. (1999). Conducting a social skills group with Latina adolescents. *Journal of Child and Adolescent Group Therapy, 9,* 139-156. doi: 10.1023/A:1022990522081.

Ramirez, R. R. & de la Cruz, G. P. (2002). *The Hispanic population in the United States: March 2002.* Retrieved June 25, 2007, from http://www.census.gov/prod/2003pubs/p20-545.pdf.

Rashid, H. M. (1984). Promoting biculturalism in young African American children. *Young Children, 39,* 13-23.

Robin, A. L. & Foster, S. L. (1989). *Negotiating parent-adolescent conflict: A behavioral-family systems approach.* New York, NY: Guilford.

Rogler, L. H., Cortes, R. S. & Malgady, R. G. (1991). Acculturation and mental health status among Hispanics: Convergence and new directions for research. *American Psychologist, 46,* 585-597. doi: 10.1037/0003-066X.46.6.585.

Rounds-Bryant, J. L. & Staab, J. (2001). Patient characteristics and treatment outcomes for African American, Hispanic, and White adolescents in DATOS-A. *Journal of Adolescent Research, 16,* 624-641.

Rumberger, R. W. & Larson, K. A. (1998). Towards explaining differences in educational achievement among Mexican American language minority students. *Sociology of Education, 71,* 68-92.

Rush, A. J. & Task Force for the Handbook of Psychiatric Measures. (2000). *Handbook of psychiatric measures.* Washington, DC: American Psychiatric Association.

Samaniego, R. Y. & Gonzales, N. A. (1999). Multiple mediators of the effects of acculturation status on delinquency for Mexican American adolescents. *American Journal of Community Psychology, 27,* 189-210.

Sanchez-Flores, H. (2003, November 9). *Teen pregnancy prevention for Latino youth.* Presentation at North Carolina Teen Pregnancy Prevention Conference, Chapel Hill, NC.

Schinke, S. P., Orlandi, M. A., Botvin, G. J., Gilchrist, L. D., Trimble, J. E. & Locklear, V. S. (1988). Preventing substance abuse among American-Indian adolescents: A bicultural competence skills approach. *Journal of Counseling Psychology, 35,* 87-90. doi: 10.1037/0022-0167.35.1.87.

Schwartz, S. J., Zamboanga, B. L. & Jarvis, L. H. (2007). Ethnic identity and acculturation in Hispanic early adolescents: Mediated relationships to academic grades, prosocial behaviors, and externalizing symptoms. *Cultural Diversity and Ethnic Minority Psychology, 13,* 364-373.

Smokowski, P. R. & Bacallao, M. L. (2006). Acculturation and aggression in Latino adolescents: A structural model focusing on cultural risk factors and assets. *Journal of Abnormal Child Psychology, 34,* 657-671.

Smokowski, P. R. & Bacallao, M. L. (2007). Acculturation, internalizing mental health symptoms, and self-esteem: Cultural experiences of Latino adolescents in North Carolina. *Child Psychiatry and Human Development, 37(3),* 273-292.

Smokowski, P. R. & Bacallao, M. L. (2008). Entre Dos Mundos/Between Two Worlds: Youth violence prevention for acculturating Latino families. *Research on Social Work Practice, 19,* 165-178. doi: 10.1177/1049731508315989

Smokowski, P.R. & Bacallao, M.L. (2009). Entre Dos Mundos/Between Two Worlds Youth Violence Prevention for Acculturating Latino Families: A Randomized Trial Comparing Psychodramatic and Support Group Delivery Formats One-Year After Program Participation. *Small Group Research, 40(1),* 3-27.

Smokowski, P. R. & Bacallao, M. L. (forthcoming). *Becoming bicultural: Risk factors and cultural assets for Latino adolescents.* New York University Press.

Smokowski, P. R. & Buchanan, R. L. & Bacallao, M. (2009). Acculturation and adjustment in Latino adolescents: How cultural risk factors and assets influence multiple domains of adolescent mental health. *Journal of Primary Prevention, 30(3/4)*, 371-394.

Smokowski, P. R. David-Ferdon, C. & Stroupe, N. (2009). Acculturation, youth violence, and suicidal behavior in minority adolescents: A review of the empirical literature. *Journal of Primary Prevention, 30(3/4)*, 215-264. 10.1007/s10935-009-0173-0

Smokowski, P. R. Rose, R. & Bacallao, M. L. (2008). Acculturation and Latino family processes: How parent-adolescent acculturation gaps influence family dynamics. *Family Relations, 57(3)*, 295-308.

Smokowski, P. R., Rose, R. & Bacallao, M. L. (2009). Acculturation and aggression in Latino adolescents: Modeling longitudinal trajectories from the Latino acculturation and health project. *Child Psychiatry and Human Development*. Advanced online publication. Retrieved August 1, 2009. doi: 10.1007/s10578-009-0146-9.

Sommers, I., Fagan, J. & Baskin, D. (1993). Sociocultural influences on the explanation of delinquency for Puerto Rican youths. *Hispanic Journal of Behavioral Sciences, 15*, 36-62.

Stanton-Salazar, R. D. & Dornbusch, S. M. (1995). Social capital and the reproduction of inequality: Information networks among Mexican-origin high school students. *Sociology of Education, 68*, 116-135.

Szapocznik, J. & Kurtines, W. (1980). Acculturation, biculturalism and adjustment among Cuban Americans. In A. Padilla (Ed.). *Acculturation: Theory, models, and some new findings* (139-159). Boulder, CO: Praeger.

Szapocznik, J., Santisteban, D., Kurtines, W., Perez-Vidal, A. & Hervis, O. (1984). Bicultural effectiveness training: A treatment intervention for enhancing intercultural adjustment in Cuban American families. *Hispanic Journal of Behavioral Sciences, 6*, 317-344.

Szapocznik, J., Santisteban, D., Kurtines, W., Perez-Vidal, A. & Hervis, O. (1986). Bicultural effectiveness training (BET): An experimental test of an intervention modality for families experiencing intergenerational/intercultural conflict. *Hispanic Journal of Behavioral Sciences, 8*, 303-330.

Szapocznik, J., Santisteban, D., Rio, A., Perez-Vidal, A., Santisteban, D. A. & Kurtines, W. M. (1989). Family effectiveness training: An intervention to prevent problem behavior in Hispanic adolescents. *Hispanic Journal of Behavioral Science, 11(1)*, 4-27.

Szapocznik, J. & Williams, R. A. (2000). Brief strategic family therapy: Twenty-five years of interplay among theory, research, and practice in adolescent behavior problems and drug abuse. *Clinical Child and Family Psychology Review, 3*, 117-134.

Tabachnick, B. G. & Fidell, L. S. (2001). *Using multivariate statistics* (4th ed.). Boston, MA: Allyn & Bacon.

Thomas, E. J. & Rothman, J. (1994). An integrative perspective on intervention research. In J. Rothman, & E. J. Thomas (Eds.), *Intervention research: Design and development for human service* (3-24). New York, NY: Haworth Press.

Toppleberg, C. O., Medrano, L., Pena Morgens, L. & Nieto-Castanon, A. (2002). Bilingual children referred for psychiatric services: Associations of language disorders, language skills, and psychopathology. *Journal of the American Academy of Child and Adolescent Psychiatry, 41*, 712-722.

U.S. Census Bureau. (2003). *Hispanic population reaches all time high of 38.8 million, New Census Bureau estimates show.* Retrieved September 15, 2008, from http://www.census.gov/Press-Release/www/releases/archives/population/011193.html

Vega, W. A., Alderete, E., Kolody, B. & Aguilar-Gaxiola, S. (2000). Adulthood sequela of adolescent heavy drinking among Mexican Americans. *Hispanic Journal of Behavioral Sciences, 22*, 254-266.

Vega, W. A., Gil, A. G., Warheit, G., Zimmerman, R. & Apospori, E. (1993). Acculturation and delinquent behavior among Cuban American adolescents: Toward an empirical model. *American Journal of Community Psychology, 21*, 113-125.

Vega, W., Kolody, B., Aguilar-Gaxiola, S., Alderete, E., Catalano, R. & Caraveo-Anduaga, J. (1998). Lifetime prevalence of *DSM-III-R* psychiatric disorders among urban and rural Mexican Americans in California. *Archives of General Psychiatry, 55*, 771-778.

Vega, W. A., Zimmerman, R., Khoury, E., Gil, A. G. & Warheit, G. (1995). Cultural conflicts and problem behaviors of Latino adolescents in home and school environments. *Journal of Community Psychology, 23*, 167-179.

Wall, J. A., Power, T. G. & Arbona, C. (1993). Susceptibility to antisocial peer pressure and its relation to acculturation in Mexican American adolescents. *Journal of Adolescent Research, 8*, 403-418.

Ying, Y. W. (1999). Strengthening intergenerational/intercultural ties in migrant families: A new intervention for parents. *Journal of Community Psychology, 27*, 89-96.

In: Youth Violence and Juvenile Justice: Causes, Intervention... ISBN: 978-1-61668-011-4
Editor: N. A. Ramsay et al, pp. 35-63 © 2010 Nova Science Publishers, Inc.

Chapter 2

EVIDENCE-BASE PRACTICES FOR JUVENILE DELINQUENCY: RISK AND PROTECTIVE FACTORS IN TREATMENT IMPLEMENTATION

Katherine L. Montgomery, Amanda N. Barczyk and Sanna J. Thompson
University of Texas at Austin, School of Social Work, Austin, Texas, USA

ABSTRACT

There are multiple reasons to prevent juveniles from becoming delinquent or continuing to engage in delinquent behavior. The most obvious reason is that delinquency puts youth at risk for substance abuse and dependency, school drop-out, gang involvement, criminality, and mental health challenges. Youth engaging in delinquent behaviors are also vulnerable to physical injury, early pregnancy, domestic violence, and sexual assault.

Due to the complex nature of delinquency, individual youth characteristics and other contributing factors, such as issues in the family, often intersect. The diverse backgrounds and experiences of youth, including difficult family circumstances and exposure to victimization, require services that meet their unique needs. Empirical evidence has shown the importance of the inclusion of the family in treatment of delinquent youth. Services provided to delinquent youth include detention facilities, medical care, case management, independent living skills training, and referrals for high-risk behaviors such as substance abuse. To be effective, however, treatment must address the co-occurring problems of these youth within the context of where they live. As families struggling with a breakdown in communication, trying to control the behavior of an unruly child, or experiencing a crisis often look for outside assistance, employing family-based treatments to address juvenile delinquency holds great promise.

To address issues of juvenile delinquency, this chapter describes various youth and family risk and protective factors associated with delinquency. This discussion is followed by a review of family-based intervention strategies aimed at preventing or ameliorating delinquent behaviors of youth. Reviewing what is known concerning families who engage collaboratively to generate support of the delinquent child can help service providers improve family relationships while decreasing delinquent youth behaviors. Thus, evidence-based, family-centered interventions, such as are multisystemic therapy (MST), brief strategic family therapy (BSFT), multi-dimensional family therapy (MDFT), and solution-focused family therapy (SBFT) will be examined.

Case Study

Dylan Smith walked into the child and youth unit at the local mental health agency with his mother, Tammy. Tammy was overwhelmed by her son's worsening behavior and outbursts. She felt like she had tried everything to help her son and had become fed up with him. During the intake assessment, Tammy described Dylan's recent behavior to the psychiatrist. "My fiancé and I are trying to plan our wedding and it seems like all of our time is used on dealing with Dylan. I get a phone call almost every day from his teacher-Dylan's either punched a kid on the play ground, cussed someone out, or has been talking back to the teacher." "What is his behavior like at home?" the psychiatrist asked. "Just last week he stole $100 dollars from my purse! He lied to the neighbors and told them he had permission to go with them to the mall. Dylan was missing for 6 hours. I called the police because I thought he had been kidnapped!" "Does he take things that don't belong to him often?" the doctor asked. "Oh yes."Tammy responded. "Yesterday, he came home with an apartment key that he had taken from someone at the pool. And two weeks ago, he got in my purse in the middle of the night and lit up one of my cigarettes in the apartment!"

During the assessment, the psychiatrist was able to get a fairly thorough description of Dylan's history. Dylan was an intelligent, well-spoken 11-year old boy. Tammy reported that Dylan would go for weeks at a "crazy-high speed" and then there would be times when he would cry alone in his room and not want to be around anyone. She also noted that Dylan didn't sleep well; he would get up and eat junk food or he would watch TV all through the night. "He says he has nightmares and is afraid that his father will find him again."

Dylan had been physically and sexually abused by his biological father. The last time Tammy and Dylan saw his father, Dylan was 5 years old. His father kidnapped Tammy and Dylan because he felt that if he couldn't have Dylan and Tammy, no one else could either. After two days, Dylan was able to call 911 from the phone in the home. Tammy thought that Dylan's father had been diagnosed with Bipolar, but she was unsure.

Since that time, Tammy has relocated and is happily engaged to new man. Tammy has tried multiple methods to discipline Dylan--from time-outs, taking things out of this room, to grounding and spanking him. She was feeling hopeless and concerned that her son was headed for a destructive life. The psychiatrist diagnosed Dylan with Post-Traumatic Stress Disorder (PTSD), Conduct Disorder, and Bipolar I Disorder. He explained to Tammy that she has reason to be concerned about her son because he displays many of the risk factors associated with juvenile delinquency. "The good news," the doctor continued, "is that by getting Dylan into treatment at this age, you may be able to prevent him from becoming delinquent. There are many treatments that have been created to address the multiple risk factors Dylan's displays."

INTRODUCTION

The case of Dylan Smith is presented as an example of a child at risk of becoming delinquent during adolescence. The complexity and variation in the factors leading to delinquency creates immense difficulties for parents, service providers and researchers who aim to understand adolescent delinquency. Recognizing the variability of characteristics that might predict delinquent behavior, the task of preventing or treating delinquent behavior is not a simple one. To address these important issues, this chapter defines delinquency, describes several domains of risk and protective factors associated with juvenile delinquency, and reviews family-based intervention strategies aimed at ameliorating risk factors while encouraging protective factors for youth at-risk for delinquency.

Juvenile Delinquency Defined

Juvenile delinquency has been defined as "behavior that is in violation of the criminal code and committed by a youth who has not reached adult age" (Roberts, 2004). The necessity to differentiate the term "juvenile delinquent" from "adult criminal offender" has been recognized by the courts as juveniles are considered to have limited comprehension of elicit behaviors. They are viewed as in need of assistance as much as reprimand and judicial involvement (Seigel & Welsh, 2008). The juvenile court system contains three main distinctions from the adult system. First, terminology differs, such that juveniles are not arrested, they are detained. They are not sentenced, but adjudicated. They do not plead guilty, but plead true or false to accusations. Secondly, juveniles are often mandated to complete treatment programs, enroll in therapy, and engage in systems that aim to treat rather than simply punish. Finally, youth systems differ from adult criminal systems in the additional laws unique to minors, such as status offenses. Despite the clear differences between the juvenile justice system and the adult criminal system, the term "juvenile delinquent" encompasses a variety of meanings.

Juvenile delinquency is a very broad term that ranges from engaging in status offenses to violent and criminal behaviors. A great deal of research examines juvenile delinquent behavior across three broad categories: status offenses (running away, curfew violations, school truancy, drinking alcohol), substance use offenses (use/sale/distribution of illegal substances), property offenses (breaking and entering, burglary), and violent offenses (actions involving human or animal victims). Youth who engage in status offenses likely differ from youths who engage in more extensive criminal activity. Due to the amount of variation in offenses and behaviors associated with juvenile delinquency, professionals working with juvenile delinquents require extensive understanding of the factors that lead to delinquency.

Risk Factors

According to Howell (2003), "risk factors are those elements in an individual's life that increase his or her vulnerability to negative developmental outcomes and also increase the probability of maintenance of a problem condition or digression to a more serious state." (p. 104). Specifically, certain factors can increase ones risk for particular negative outcomes. The "risk-focused approach" posits that bonding with family, peers, and institutions that promote prosocial norms acts as a protection against prevailing risks that may otherwise contribute to problem behaviors. However, when bonds with the family do not develop or are weak, the adolescent ultimately identifies with peers. These relationships often reinforce disruptive and deviant behaviors.

The progressive accumulation of risk factors also plays a role. Herenkohl and colleagues (2000) found that a 10-year old with 6 or more risk factors is ten times more likely to become a juvenile delinquent than an 18-year old presenting with one risk factor. Others have noted that the combination of school failure, criminal involvement and precocious involvement in adult behaviors, such as sex, drug use, and smoking, markedly increase the likelihood for dysfunction (Whitbeck, 1999). Multiple risk behaviors (e.g. substance use, dysfunctional family, and deviant peer interaction) are related to greater problem behaviors, like delinquency (Garbarino, 1991). Thus, accumulated risk processes increase the odds or probability that deviant behaviors will occur (Werner, 1990).

Kraemer and colleagues (1997) have described risk factors by dividing them into three major types: 1) correlates or markers, 2) predictive factors, and 3) causal factors. Correlates are risk factors that exist concurrently with identified problems. For example, being male is often considered a risk factor for engaging in delinquent behaviors. Predictive factors are those that exist prior to emergence of problem behaviors. One possible predictive factor might be parental criminal involvement, as parents' model behaviors that result in their children engaging in forms of the same activity. Finally, causal factors can be directly linked to the problem behavior and can be directly changed through initiating treatment aimed at the specified problem behavior.

Protective Factors

While a great deal of research has focused on developing an understanding of risk factors, less is known about protective factors. Kirby and Fraser (1997) reported that protective factors are internalizing and externalizing factors that assist children and adolescents in guarding against or avoiding risk. It is believed that the more protective factors present, the less likely the adolescent will engage in delinquent behaviors. It is noteworthy that adolescents displaying particular risk factors are not assured to become delinquent, but simply at greater risk of developing delinquent behaviors than those not displaying the specific risk factor. Because some adolescents posses several risk factors and never become involved in the juvenile justice system, researchers have explored explanations as to why this may be the case. Researchers have suggested protective factors are simply the opposite of risk factors; for example, being male is a risk factor while being female is a protective factor for delinquency.

A large body of research has focused on the concept of resilience in the context of protective factors. Resilience is defined as "the remarkable capacity of individuals to withstand considerable hardship, to bounce back in the face of adversity, and to go on to live functional lives with a sense of well-being" (Turner, 2000, p 441). Vaillant (1993) metaphorically emphasizes that resiliency is "the capacity to be bent without breaking and the capacity, once bent, to spring back" (p. 248). Researchers have found that resiliency is a strong protective factor for those potentially at risk of becoming delinquent (Weiner, 2003; Howell, 2008) and vary widely among children and adolescents. Understanding the importance of resiliency and its association with delinquency is important for the concerned friend, family member, or service provider

Table 1. Juvenile Delinquency Risk and Protective Factors.

Domain	Early Onset Risk Factors	Late Onset Risk Factors	Protective Factors
Individual	Substance use Being male Aggression* Hyperactivity Problem (antisocial) behavior Exposure to television violence Low IQ Antisocial attitudes, beliefs Dishonesty* Poor cognitive development	Restlessness Difficulty concentrating* Risk taking Aggression* Being male Physical violence Antisocial attitudes, beliefs Crimes against persons Antisocial behavior Low IQ Substance use	Intolerant attitude toward deviance High IQ Being female Positive social orientation Perceived sanctions for Transgressions Religiosity Resilient temperament Sociability
Peer	Weak social ties Antisocial peers Peer rejection	Weak social ties Antisocial, delinquent peers Gang membership	Friends who engage in conventional behavior
School	Failure to bond to school Poor academic performance Low academic aspirations	Poor attitude towards school Academic failure	Commitment to school Recognition for involvement in pro-social activities
Community	Access to weapons Neighborhood disadvantage Concentration of delinquent groups	Neighborhood crime, drugs Neighborhood disorganization	
Family	Low family socioeconomic status/poverty Antisocial parents Poor parent-child relationship Harsh, lax, or inconsistent discipline Divorce Separation from parents Abusive parents Neglect Teenage parent	Poor parent-child relationship Harsh or lax discipline Poor monitoring, supervision Low parental involvement Antisocial parents Broken home Low family socioeconomic status/poverty Abusive parents Family conflict*	Warm, supportive relationships with parents or other adults Parents' positive evaluation of peers Parental monitoring

Note: * True for males only. Source: Adapted from Shader 2004, Wasserman, et al., 2003, & Office of the Surgeon General, 2001.

RISK AND PROTECTIVE FACTOR DOMAINS

Various frameworks have been employed to understand risk/protective factors and are used to provide additional specification. The most commonly used framework identifies factors across specific domains (Hawkins, Catalano & Miller, 1992). These domains include: 1) individual, 2) peer, 3) school, 4) community, and 5) family. Table 1 illustrates commonly identified juvenile delinquency risk and protective factors that will guide the following discussion. Each domain plays a substantial role in either protecting or placing the adolescent at risk of engaging in delinquent behavior.

INDIVIDUAL RISK FACTORS

There are multiple individual factors that contribute to the protection or risk of youth becoming delinquent. Factors such as substance use, mental illness, low IQ, exposure to violence, and gender have all been shown to contribute to or protect a child from becoming involved with the juvenile justice system (Denning & Homel, 2008). As mentioned previously, a child or adolescent possessing various risk characteristics does not definitively determine that he or she will actually engage in delinquent behaviors. What this list does provide, however, are key factors that are essential in understanding and preventing juvenile delinquency (Shader, 2004).

Substance Use

Of all the factors that will be discussed in this chapter, substance use is one of the most widely cited in connection with juvenile delinquency (Hawkins, Catalano, & Miller, 1992; Jenson, 1997; Williams, Ayers, Abbott, Hawkins, & Catalano, 1999; Rivaux, Springer, Bohman, Wagner, & Gil, 2006). Adolescents in the juvenile justice system are three times as likely to use substances when compared to the general population (Office of Applied Studies, 2003). Williams et al. (1999) notes six factors that predict both juvenile delinquency and substance abuse, including: moral beliefs, peer influence, school attachment and commitment, family relationships, academic achievement, and social skills. Thus, youth who are at high risk of becoming delinquent are often at high risk of abusing substances.

Loeber and colleagues (2000) found that the earlier a child begins to use substances, the greater the likelihood he or she has of becoming involved with the juvenile justice system (Loeber, Green, Lahey, Frick, & McBurnett). According to the most recent national adolescent drug use report from the Monitoring the Future study (Johnston, O'Malley, Bachman, & Schulenberg, 2009), adolescent substance abuse continues to exist at concerning rates. The study revealed that 38% of high school adolescents reported using an illegal substance in 2008, 31% reported smoking cigarettes, and 55% of high school adolescents reported drinking alcohol. Of growing concern, the study revealed the rising rates of prescription drug use for a nonmedical purposes. Results showed that that 15% of twelfth graders had taken one or more of the following in 2008: amphetamines, sedatives/barbiturates, tranquilizers, and opiates other than heroin (Johnston, et. al, 2009).

Mental Illness

Approximately 16.5 percent of all adolescents have a mental health diagnosis (Roberts, Attkisson, & Rosenblatt, 2002). Among juvenile offenders, it is estimated that approximately 52 to 73 percent have a diagnosable mental illness (Garland, Hough, McCabe, Yeh, Wood, & Aarons, 2001; Abrantes, Hoffman, & Anton, 2005). It is has been noted that nearly two-thirds of boys and 75% of girls in juvenile detention have at least one psychiatric disorder (Teplin, Abram, McClelland, Dulcan, & Mericle, (2002). These rates are much lower than the estimated 15% of youth in the general population thought to have a psychiatric illness and places detained teens on par with those considered at highest risk, such as maltreated and runaway youth. Colins, et. al (2009) found that the adolescents presented with a wide range of psychiatric disorders: anxiety disorder (9.1%), major depressive disorder (13.2%), ADHD (11%), oppositional defiant disorder (28.2%), conduct disorder (59.6%), substance abuse disorder (73.5%), and schizophrenia (2.1%).

The specific mental illnesses, as defined by the Diagnostic and Statistical Manual of Mental Disorders (*DSM-IV-TR*, American Psychological Association, 2000) that are most common among juvenile delinquents are oppositional defiant disorder (ODD) and conduct disorder (CD). Additionally, while children and adolescents cannot be diagnosed with antisocial personality disorder (due to age restrictions), a common risk factor for juvenile delinquency is antisocial attitudes, beliefs, or traits. Being able to recognize some of the main symptoms of these mental illnesses is an initial pathway to assist the child or adolescent in receiving services. If there is concern that an adolescent or child might be displaying several of these symptoms, a referral to a psychiatrist or pediatrician is necessary. While a psychiatrist or pediatrician is the professional qualified to diagnose ODD, CD, and antisocial personality traits, family members, friends, teachers, youth pastors, case workers, and/or therapists are often the first to observe these symptoms and make the appropriate referral.

A child or adolescent might be classified with oppositional defiant disorder if they display four or more of the following symptoms: often lose their temper, often argue with adults, often refuses to comply with adults, often purposefully annoys others, often blames others for their mistakes, often easily annoyed, often angry or resentful, and is often spiteful or vindictive (APA, 2000, p.70). Conduct disorder is considered to be more severe than ODD and symptoms are categorized into four domains: aggression towards people or animals, destruction of property, deceitfulness or theft, and serious violation of rules (APA, 2000, p. 68). As previously noted, only those eighteen and older can be diagnosed with antisocial personality disorder; however, to be given the diagnosis, symptoms have to have been present from at least fifteen years of age. Those diagnosable with antisocial personality disorder will display three or more of the following: failure to conform to social norms and laws, repeated lying and deceit, impulsivity, repeatedly engaging in physical fights or assaults, disregard for the safety of self or others, failure to sustain employment or financial responsibilities, and lack of remorse. Often, those with ODD or CD have another co-occurring mental disorder. In a recent study among 245 detained adolescents, Colins and colleagues found that 83.5% had been diagnosed with a psychiatric disorder and that 72.6% had two or more diagnosed mental disorders (Colins, Vermeiren, Schuyten, & Broekaert, 2009).

Other Individual Risk Factors

In addition to substance use and mental illnesses, individual behavioral, genetic, and social factors may place youth at increased risk of delinquency. For example, youth who are impulsive, hyperactive, and prone to risk-taking are more likely to become juvenile delinquents (Shader, 2004). Youth with poor social skills may be more likely to engage in delinquent behaviors and develop antisocial behaviors; males are twice as likely to become a serious juvenile offender as females (Fagan, Van Horn, Hawkins, & Arthur, 2007). Having a lower IQ, vocabulary, verbal reasoning skills and educational achievement are also risk factors for delinquency (Mann & Reynolds, 2006). Adolescents with these difficulties often feel socially isolated and disconnected from their peers and environment. As a result, they have less concern for protecting the relationships and property around them. They may become bored, lonely, feel wronged by others, and are more inclined to seek an outlet of distraction, entertainment, or revenge through engaging in delinquent behavior (Arthur, Hawkins, Pollard, Catalano, & Baglioni, 2002).

INDIVIDUAL PROTECTIVE FACTORS

Some protective factors in the individual domain, high IQ and being female, are opposite of specific risk factors that have been found to protect against delinquency (Shader, 2004). Additional individual protective factors include intolerant attitude toward deviance, positive social orientation, perceived sanctions for transgressions (Shader, 2004), religiosity (youth who engage in organized religious activities), belief in moral order, resilient temperament (as discussed above), and sociability (children and adolescents who are socially outgoing) (Arthur, Hawkins, Pollard, Catalano, & Baglioni, 2002). Many of the individual protective factors coalesce around an adolescent's beliefs and the ways in which they view the world. Central to the process of molding ones belief structure are peers and the family system. The way a child and adolescent views the world is often a reflection of how they are influenced by those around them.

PEER RISK FACTORS

Association with Deviant Peers

It is well documented that association with deviant peers puts children and adolescents are greater risk of engaging in the same deviant behaviors (Dishion & Loeber, 1985; Hawkins, Catalano, & Miller, 1992; Elliott & Menard, 1996; Dishion, 2000; and Leve & Chamberlain, 2005). Youth involved in a gang, having peers with antisocial traits, and associating with peers who use substances increase the risk for delinquent behaviors. Often, one of these risk factors will precipitate engagement in others. For example, youth who join a gang typically find themselves involved in using substances.

Gang association is often associated with multiple risk factors for delinquency among adolescents. In a longitudinal study, Gatti and colleagues observed the differences between the frequency of delinquent behaviors and gang participation (Gatti, Tremblay, Vitaro, & McDuff, 2005). Adolescents involved in a gang engaged in delinquent behavior four times as often as those not involved in a gang. When observing specific crimes between groups, those involved in gang-committed crimes also sold drugs more than four times as often and used drugs about twice as often. The youth who choose to join a gang largely do so based upon the gang experience itself rather than simply engaging in delinquent acts (Gatti, et al., 2005).

Weak Social Ties and Peer Rejection

Weak social ties (Shader, 2004) and peer rejection (Arthur, et. al, 2002) are also considered to be risk factors associated with juvenile delinquency. A child's level of aggression increases dramatically with longer periods of social rejection from normative peers (Dodge, Lansford, Burks, Bates, Pettit, Fontaine, et al., 2003). When children or adolescents experience difficulty in connecting and bonding with pro-social peers, they have a greater likelihood of viewing harm to others as acceptable. Further, after experiencing levels of peer rejection, a cyclical exchange between aggression and normative peer rejection ensues (Dodge, et al., 2003), leading to increased risk of delinquent behavior. One study found a significant relationship between violent delinquency at ages 14-15 and peer rejection at ages 7-9 (Vitaro, Pedersen, & Brendgen, 2007).

It appears that there is a great deal of co-occurrence across juvenile delinquency risk factors. A child with a lower IQ might be rejected by their peers beginning at age seven. As this child begins to socially isolate himself from his peers, aggressive and deviant behavior might seem more normative. As an early teenager, the inclusion felt by joining a gang might lead to substance abuse, truancy, and a diagnosis of conduct disorder. Without appropriate protective factors and intervention, the perpetuating nature of risk factors could render a child quite vulnerable to the juvenile justice system.

PEER PROTECTIVE FACTORS

It is quite normal for adolescents who feel isolated and alone to quickly become willing to compromise their standards at the benefit of friendship and inclusion. While many adolescents befriend peers with non-deviant behaviors (Shader, 2004), those who meet peers engaged in delinquent behavior, may find themselves mimicking and joining in poor choices. Thus, for treatment purposes, it is important that children having difficulty bonding with healthy peers are provided the guidance necessary to do so.

SCHOOL RISK FACTORS

The number of school-related risk factors related to delinquency is largely related to poor attitude and performance concerning education and academic failure (Shader, 2004). Christle and colleagues found that low academic achievement, high suspension rates, and high dropout rates were significantly correlated with higher rates of juvenile delinquency (Christle,

Jolivette, & Nelson, 2005). Further, they found that children coming from a lower socioeconomic background had higher rates of academic failure, suspension and dropout rates. Often, academic failure is merely a symptom of a combination of risk factors from the individual, peer, and family domain. Because symptoms can be remain hidden in a family system, peer culture, and in the community, the school system is often the first to notice concerning risk factors and make necessary referrals. It is important for the school to be equipped with necessary referrals and tools to aid in early prevention. Unfortunately, schools in lower socioeconomic communities lack the resources and staff to provide the needed treatments and referrals.

SCHOOL PROTECTIVE FACTORS

While various risk factors are associated with academic achievement, schools can provide protective factors that reduce the likelihood of delinquency. Youth who are committed to school and receive recognition for involvement in conventional activities may be more resilient and are less likely to engage in delinquent behaviors (Shader, 2004). Within the school environment, characteristics such as supportive leadership and school-wide behavioral management can minimize the risk of delinquency. Having a positive relationship with teachers can also play a role in the development of youth factors that inhibit juvenile delinquency (Simoes, Matos, Batista-Foguet, 2008). Dedicated and collegial staff as well as effective academic instruction (e.g. setting high but achievable expectations, providing a safe learning environment, and facilitating success) have also been noted as characteristics supporting protective factors (Christle, Jolivette, & Nelson, 2005). When school faculty and staff are able to engage students and facilitate an environment where the child or adolescent feels connected, they are more likely to be committed to school. In addition, students who have pro-social opportunities (e.g. assisting in developing classroom activities and rules) and rewarded for good behavior are factors that decrease the risk of delinquency (Fagan, Horn, Hawkins, Arthur, 2007).

COMMUNITY RISK FACTORS

Of the five domains, the area with the least amount of research is the community domain (Farrington, 2000). Shader (2004) notes that neighborhood crime, drug use, and disorganization are the community risk factors. Neighborhood disorganization has been defined as the "inability of a community structure to realize the common values of its residents and maintain effective social control" (Sampson and Groves, 1989, p. 777). As children age, they are more inclined to respond to and be influenced by their environment, resulting in negative outocmes (Howell, 2008). Further, the highest rates of crime can often be centralized to specific areas or communities (Hawkins, 1996). Research has shown that perception of community disorganization and low community attachment is significantly correlated with higher levels of delinquency (Van Horn, Hawkins, Arthur, & Catalano, 2007). While macro-level research and interventions are in their infancy (Thyer, 2008), many agree that children being raised in neighborhoods with high levels of poverty and crime are at serious risk of becoming delinquent (McCord, Widom, & Crowell, 2001).

FAMILY RISK FACTORS

There are several factors associated with the family that effect a child or adolescent's risk of becoming delinquent. Whether it is the stability of the home, neglect and/or abuse, or with whom a child lives, the impact of the family is great (Roe-Sepowitz, 2008). The risk and protective factors associated with the family domain include abuse and neglect, low family socioeconomic status, parent's history of involvement with crime and substance abuse, and parenting style.

Abuse and Neglect

A child or adolescent that has experienced neglect, physical abuse, or sexual abuse within the family system is at greater risk of becoming delinquent (Shader, 2004). Dembo and colleagues explain that abuse in the family effects males and females delinquent behaviors differently (Dembo, Schmeidler, & Childs, 2007). Females respond to abuse by running away in adolescence and begin a life on the streets; they often turning to prostitution and substance abuse to support themselves (Dembo, Williams, & Schmeidler, 1993, 1998). Males, however, are more likely to aggressively act out and repeat the abusive behaviors they observed in the home. When children observe parents being violent or abused by someone else, they often utilize violence in problem-solving (Kim & Kim, 2008).

Children who are abused are almost 4 times more likely to become a persistent and serious juvenile offender than peers who have not been abused (Stouthamer-Loeber, Wei, Homish, & Loeber, 2002).This high prevalence of abuse is of serious concern, as one study found that approximately 45% of detained youth reported being either physically or sexually abused (Dembo, Schmeidler, & Childs, 2007). This rate is most likely higher than what was reported due to the sensitivity and humiliation associated with reporting abuse.

Parents' History

A parent who displays a history of antisocial behavior, criminal involvement, and/or substance use has been shown to increase the likelihood of youth becoming delinquent (Shader, 2004; Arthur et. al, 2003). Li and colleagues (2002) found that adolescents having one or both parents abusing substances predicted youth to be 2 to 3 times more likely to use substances than their peers whose parents didn't abuse substances. In a study of the effects of parent imprisonment on delinquent behavior, Murray and Farrington (2005) found that sons were roughly 5 times more likely to become involved with the juvenile justice system than those whose parents had never been incarcerated. Further, the sons of an incarcerated parent were also 12 times more likely to have antisocial personality disorder by age 18. When children and adolescents grow up seeing their parent make poor social and behavioral choices, it is not uncommon for the child to mimic the behavior.

Parenting Style

According to Shader (2004), there are two extremes of parenting styles that place a child at risk of becoming delinquent: harsh or lax discipline. When a parenting style is too controlling or too harsh, youth often rebel and do not respond favorably. This risk factor is also accompanied by poor parental monitoring or supervision. Parental monitoring refers to a parent being involved in their child's life, having knowledge of and monitoring their child's whereabouts, and providing a consistent, balanced level of discipline (Dishion & McMahon, 1998). DiClemente and colleagues found that adolescents were twice as likely to be arrested if their parents provided poor monitoring and supervision (DiClemente, Wingood, Crosby, Sionean, Cobb, Harrington, et. al, 2001). Further, they found parents providing poor monitoring and supervision had youth who were more likely to engage in sexually risky behavior, substance use, and participate in fights (DiClemente, et. al, 2001). If a parent is struggling with finding the appropriate balance of discipline and supervision, it is important they are connected with the appropriate professionals that can assist in providing necessary training.

Other Family Risk Factors

There are several other risk factors that fall under the family domain. Some coalesce around loss: divorce (Wasserman, et. al, 2003) and separation from parents (Shader, 2004). As divorce rates continue to rise, children continue to take on the stress associated with the changes. Often parents will struggle with guilt when "putting their children through a divorce" and allow structure and consistency to fluctuate. Additionally, factors that cause internal stress within the family system have been cited as risk factors: low family socioeconomic status, family conflict (Shader, 2004) teenage parenthood (Wasserman, et al., 2003). Children do not do well in chaotic, stressful environments. Living in a family with high levels of conflict, lack of structure, and stress will often leave children vulnerable to risky behaviors.

Family Protective Factors

Various characteristics of the parent-child relationship can reduce the likelihood of becoming delinquent. Proper parental monitoring and supervision can serve as a protective factor to children and adolescents (Shader, 2004). Fagan, Horn, Hawkins, and Arthur (2007) found that youth with a positive attachment to their mother or father (e.g. shared thoughts and feelings with their mother or father) were associated with less involvement in serious offending. In addition, when the youth was rewarded for their good behavior they were also found to be associated with less involvement in serious offending. Additional protective factors include warm, supportive relationship with parents or other adults and parents' positive evaluation of peers.

Briefly worth noting is a debate that has emerged in research literature over the past 2 decades. Some researchers believe it is not necessarily the environment and family system from which the adolescent came that contributes to levels of delinquency; rather, it is the genetics passed from a parent to a child that is the main contributor to the family domain risk factors. Other researchers believe, however, that it is a combination of genetics and family system that contribute to an adolescent's risk of delinquency (Beaver & Wright, 2007). If the research regarding the connection between genetics and delinquency is true, it is important to become familiar with the biological parents' history when working with the child or adolescent at risk of becoming delinquent.

FAMILIES AND HIGH-RISK YOUTH

Some have argued that families are key in youth developing emotional and behavioral problems (Paradise et al., 2001). The relationship between vulnerability, risk and resiliency becomes cemented early in life through a series of interactions between parent and child. Poor family management, lack of positive parenting skills, and dysfunctional caregiving have been strongly related to delinquency of youth (Formoso, Gonzales, & Aiken, 2000). Conversely, family support and positive relationships predict positive adjustment in childhood and adolescence; indirect evidence suggests that family support is a protective factor for adolescent conduct problems (Cauce, Reid, Landesman, & Gonzales, 1990; Wills, Vaccaro, & McNamara, 1992).

Given the family's fundamental influence on a child's life, research has consistently suggested the benefits for including families in treatment of high-risk youth. Recent reviews of services for families with youths coping with a wide variety of problems have strongly urged inclusion of families in all service options (Burns & Weisz, 2000). Prevention efforts with delinquent youth suggest that the single most effective form of prevention involves working with the total family system (Kumpfer, Alexander, McDonald, & Olds, 1998). Identification of situations where families may be engaged in services is a potentially beneficial method for addressing problems experienced by youth.

To effectively intervene and address the multiple risk factors juvenile delinquents often posses, utilizing an empirically supported, systems approach is necessary. Family intervention strategies, involving the family system and the adolescent at risk of becoming delinquent, have strong empirical support (Dowden & Andrews, 2003). The following evidence-based family therapies are some of the most effective treatments for juvenile delinquency.

FAMILY-BASED TREATMENT OPTIONS

Many studies have demonstrated that parenting and family interventions are critical to reducing family risk factors associated with problematic youth behaviors (Catalano, Gainey, Fleming, Haggerty, & Johnson, 1999; Spoth, Goldberg, & Redmond, 1999). Family-based therapies developed from two foundational therapies originated in the early 1970s: (1)

Structural Family Therapy developed by Salvador Minuchin, and (2) Strategic Family Therapy, developed by Jay Haley. These therapeutic modalities are built on the assumptions that 1) families are rule-governed systems that can best be understood in context; 2) the presenting problem serves a function within the family; and 3) the concepts of boundaries, coalitions, hierarchy, power, metaphor, family life cycle development and triangles are basic to the development of a "stuck" family (Irvine, Biglan, Smolkowski, Metzler, & Ary, 1999). These therapeutic models are the core theories from which later models developed.

Empirical research has evaluated various treatment modalities targeting adolescents who engage in high-risk behaviors and juvenile delinquency. Many of these studies implement and evaluate structured and manualized family interventions developed during the past two decades. Included among these empirically supported treatments are multisystemic therapy (MST), brief strategic family therapy (BSFT), multi-dimensional family therapy (MDFT), and solution-focused family therapy (SBFT).

MULTISYSTEMIC THERAPY

Multisystemic therapy (MST) treatment views individuals in terms of the complex systems in which they are embedded (Letourneau, Cunningham, & Henggeler, 2002). Individuals restructure their environments while simultaneously being influenced by them. Behavior is best understood when viewed within broader contexts, such as school, family, peers, neighborhood, services, and community institutions (Henggeler, Schoenwald, Borduin, et al., 1998). MST has been extensively evaluated and suggests that antisocial behavior in youth is determined by a variety of correlates. These factors, along with other antisocial behaviors, such as conduct disorder, are relevant for delinquency (Hawkins, et al., 1992) and MST lends itself to these complex issues.

Growing evidence supports the effectiveness of MST for delinquent adolescents. Stanton & Shadish (1997) conducted a meta-analysis of family-based treatments for youths' drug use and found that MST was the most effective of those reviewed. An early MST outcome study (Henggeler, 1986) used a quasi-experimental design to study youth and their families in a delinquency diversion program. Findings showed the MST was more effective than usual community services in terms of client behaviors and family relationships. Subsequently, MST has been substantiated as an evidenced-based treatment for adolescents and their families in randomized clinical trials. It has been effective in reducing out-of-home placements, delinquent behavior, substance use, and psychiatric disorders (Sheidow & Woodford, 2003).

The effects of MST on delinquency have been examined in trials using juvenile offenders as participants (Henggeler, Melton & Smith, 1992; Borduin, Mann, Cone, et al., 1995). In these studies, MST significantly reduced self-reported drug use, criminal activity, violence, incarceration (Henggeler, et al., 1992), incarceration recidivism, aggression with peers, family cohesion (Henggeler, Melton, Smith, et al., 1993), and drug-related and other arrests (Borduin et al., 1995). Henggeler, Pickrel, Brondino, & Crouch (1996) found school attendance increased and maintained successful outcomes at 6-month follow-up (Brown, Henggeler & Schoenwald, 1999). Additionally, it was found that the cost of MST was mitigated by the reduced incarceration costs (Schoenwald, Ward & Henggeler, 1996).

BRIEF STRATEGIC FAMILY THERAPY

Brief Strategic Family Therapy (BSFT) was developed through the integration of theory, research, and practice of structural and strategic methods (Szapocznik & Williams, 2000). BSFT is especially appropriate for treatment of substance use that co-occurs with other behavior problems, including conduct disorders, oppositional behavior, delinquency, associating with antisocial peers, aggressive and violent behavior, and risky sexual behavior (Perrino, Gonzalez-Soldevilla, Pantin & Szapocznik, 2000). Three basic principles typify BSFT: (1) the family is viewed as a system that suggests that family members are interdependent and that individual behaviors affect others in the family; (2) structure or patterns of interactions among family members are habitual, repeat over time and contribute to behavior problems, such as delinquent behaviors; and (3) strategies for intervention relates to the notion that intervention must be practical, deliberate and linked directly to problem behaviors (Szapocznik & Williams, 2000).

BSFT is incorporated into the youth's daily family life and is manualized (Szapocznik, Hervis, & Schwartz, 2001). BSFT is a flexible approach that appeals to cultures that emphasize family and interpersonal relationships. BSFT has been well-established in the treatment of adolescents with problems ranging from substance use to conduct problems, associations with antisocial peers, and impaired family functioning.

In clinical trials, BSFT was effective in reducing emotional and behavior problems and showed continued significant improvement of family functioning at the one-year follow-up (Szapocznik, Santisteban, Rio, et al., 1986). Other studies have shown BSFT effective in reducing behavior problems among 12-18 year old Hispanic adolescents and their families. Adolescents receiving BSFT showed significantly decreased levels of conduct disorder and socialized aggression from pre- to post- treatment, while the control condition showed no change. Another recent study compared BSFT to a group treatment control (Santisteban, Coatsworth, & Perez-Vidal, 2003) and BSFT families showed significant improvement in conduct problems and delinquency, as well as marijuana use and family functioning.

MULTIDIMENSIONAL FAMILY THERAPY (MDFT)

Multidimensional Family Therapy (MDFT) focuses on changing systemic influences that establish and maintain problem behaviors in adolescents. MDFT was first introduced as a weekly, clinic-based intervention (Liddle & Hogue, 2000). A newer version provides a home-based, intensive treatment that incorporates alterations for highly delinquent youth. MDFT is based on the integration of existing therapeutic work in areas such as case management, school interventions, drug counseling methods, use of multimedia, and HIV/AIDS prevention (Rowe, Liddle, & McClintic, 2002).

MDFT is manualized and treatment includes sessions with various combinations of family members. Phone contacts between family members and therapists are frequent and provide opportunities for "mini-sessions." Intervention occurs within five domains: interventions with the adolescent, parent, parent-adolescent relationship, other family members, and systems external to the family (Liddle & Dakof, 1995). Treatment incorporates a collaborative, individualized approach that requires a high degree of engagement by families. Strategies for engagement is employed to capture the interest of the family and assess risk and protective factors within the specific ecological context of the family in order to create a working agenda for addressing youth delinquent behaviors (Becker, Hogue & Liddle, 2002).

MDFT has been empirically supported as a therapy for substance abusing and delinquent teens. Its efficacy has been supported by studies comparing MDFT with alternate therapies in controlled trials (Hogue, Liddle, Becker, Johnson-Leckrone, 2002; Liddle et al., 2001). A prevention study with Multidimensional Family Prevention (MDFP) showed greater gains when compared to controls on mediators of substance use and other high-risk behaviors (Liddle & Hogue, 2000). Domains studied included self-competence, family functioning, school involvement, and peer associations. Preliminary evidence of short-term efficacy indicated strengthened family cohesion, school bonding, and reduced peer delinquency compared to controls (Hogue, et al., 2002).

Solution Focused Family Therapy

Service providers and youth report brief, strengths-based practices delivered in the youths' environments can be effective, more so than "problem-oriented" approaches (Baer, Peterson, & Wells, 2004; Cauce et al., 2000; Kidd, 2003). Delinquent youth respond best to client-centered services that are flexible and encourage them to continually strive to attain goals despite relapses and setbacks (Cauce et al., 1994). Strengths-based approaches focus on the strengths already possessed by the client and those found within their environment. Solution- focused family therapy (SFFT) is a strengths-based model that utilizes a cognitive-behavioral approach to help clients imagine what could be different and what would be required to make changes occur. One study of adolescent offenders in juvenile justice custody demonstrated increased levels of optimism for the future, greater ability to feel empathy, and decreased levels of substance abuse following solution-focused treatment (Gingerich & Eisengart, 2000).

The SFFT approach views the client as the expert on his/her life, and aims to increase client autonomy (Selekman, 1997). Empowerment is emphasized through identifying and amplifying client strengths and resources as tools to use in the reduction of the problem (Green, 2004). Springer (2001) notes the solution-focused techniques are especially useful during the assessment phase to establish rapport and build therapeutic alliance. SFFT's emphasis on strengths and solutions assists in building the expectation that not only is change possible, but likely. Change using the SFFT model is typically achieved in incremental steps, with a basic assumption that small changes elicit larger changes (Selekman, 2005).

SFFT, with its emphasis on the strengths, resiliency, and instilling hope, can facilitate building rapport with youth who are engaged in delinquent behaviors to increase their sense of self-efficacy by assisting them to identify strengths and resources (Springer, 2001). Helping the youth explore solutions and mobilize resources and strengths to attain desired goals increases their sense of control over their lives, a common difficulty among traumatized young people (Ouimette, Brown, & Najavits, 1998). Utilizing a strengths-based approach could assist delinquent youth in looking toward the future with the belief that they have the power to effect positive change in their lives, overcome the challenges associated with abuse, and find alternative behaviors that are pro-social and positively oriented.

CONCLUSIONS

This review of the literature provides evidence for the effectiveness of various family-based interventions in reducing youth delinquent behaviors. Although the findings are somewhat inconclusive concerning the lasting effects, the evidence suggests that the short-term effectiveness of these interventions appear comparable to the effectiveness of individually-based interventions. In light of these findings, understanding the multiple factors associated with delinquency may provide illumination on the vulnerability of Dylan's case. His gender, experimentation with substances, mental health diagnosis, exposure to violence, and antisocial behaviors are risk factors that suggest possible delinquency as he moves into adolescence. His conduct disorder symptoms, bullying, physical cruelty to others, and theft are symptoms that need immediate attention. Risk factors associated with his father's aggressive and criminal history may lead him to not only repeat his father's behavior, but to engage in other delinquent behaviors as well. Utilizing family-based treatment approaches to address the complex needs of Dylan and his family may prevent further behavioral difficulties and allow systemic change in their home. Exploring and harnessing the family strengths, engaging existing support networks, and utilizing community resources will allow Tammy to feel empowered and supported. As Dylan begins to see positive reinforcement, external support from healthy systems, and consistency in his family relationships, it is likely some of his risk factors will naturally decrease.

Youth involved in the juvenile justice system often resemble facets of Dylan's story. Professionals assessing youth's risk for delinquency is a necessary step in the effective implementation of evidence-based treatments aimed to reduce juvenile justice involvement. By understanding the level of risk and resiliency, therapists can implement family-based treatments uniquely targeted to the family system and not simply the problem or "identified child." Involving multiple systems in the change process allows potential shifts in risk and protective factors, resulting in decreased delinquency among youth.

REFERENCES

Abrantes, A. M., Hoffman, N. G. & Anton, R. (2005). Prevalence of co-occurring disorders among juveniles committed to detention centers. *International Journal of Offender Therapy and Comparative Criminology, 49,* 179-193.

Aktan, G. (1995). Organizational framework for a substance use prevention program. *International Journal of Addition, 30,* 185-201.

Aktan, G., Kumpfer, K. L. & Turner, C. (1996). Effectiveness of a family skills training program for substance abuse prevention with inner-city African-American families. *International Journal of Addition, 31,* 158-175.

American Psychiatric Association. (2000). *Desk reference to the diagnostic and statistical manual of mental disorders (4th ed., text revision).* Washington, DC: Author.

Baer, J. S., Peterson, P. L. & Wells, E. A. (2004). Rationale and design of a brief substance use intervention for homeless adolescents. *Addiction Research and Theory, 12(4)*, 317-334.

Beaver, K. M. & Wright, J. P. (2007). A child effects explanation for the association between family and risk and involvement in an antisocial lifestyle. *Journal of Adolescent Research, 22*, 640-664.

Becker, D., Hogue, A. & Liddle, H. A. (2002). Methods of engagement in family-based preventive intervention. *Child & Adolescent Social Work Journal, 19(2),* 163-179.

Borduin, C. M., Mann, B. J., Cone, L. T., Henggeler, S. W., Fucci, B. R., Blaske, D. M. & Williams, R. A. (1995). Multisystemic treatment of serious juvenile offenders: Long-term prevention of criminality and violence. *Journal of Consulting and Clinical Psychology, 63*, 569-578.

Broome, K. M., Joe, G. W. & Simpson, D. D. (2001). Engagement Models for Adolescents in DATOS-A. *Journal of Adolescent Research, 16(6)*, 608-610.

Broome, K. M., Knight, D. K., Knight, K., Hiller, M. L. & Simpson, D. D. (1997). Peer, family, and motivational influences on drug treatment process and recidivism for probationers. *Journal of Clinical Psychology, 53(4)*, 387-397.

Brown, T. L., Henggeler, S. W. & Schoenwald, S. K. (1999). Multisystemic treatment of substance abusing and dependent juvenile delinquents: Effects on school attendance at posttreatment and 6-month follow-up. *Children's Services: Social Policy, Research, and Practice, 2(2)*, 81-93.

Bry, B. H. & Krinsley, K. E. (1992). Booster sessions and long-term effects of behavioral family therapy on adolescent substance use and school performance. *Journal of Behavior Therapy & Experimental Psychiatry, 23(3),* 183-189.

Burns, B. J. & Weisz, J. (2000). *Implementing child services and interventions: At the crossroads*. Rockville, MD: Discussion and Plenary Session, NIMH Challenges for the 21st Century: Mental Health Services Research.

Catalano, R. F., Gainey, R. R., Fleming, C. B., Haggerty, K. P. & Johnson, N. O. (1999). An experimental intervention with families of substance abusers: One-year follow-up of the focus on families project. *Addiction, 94(2)*, 241-255.

Catalano, R. F & Hawkins, J. D. (1996). The social development model: A theory of antisocial behavior. In J. D. Hawkins (Ed.), *Delinquency and crime: Current theories*. New York: Cambridge University Press.

Catalano, R. F., Kosterman, R. & Hawkins, J. D. (1996). Modeling the etiology *Journal of Drug Issues, 26(2),* 429-455.

Cauce, A. M., Morgan, C. J., Wagner, J., Moore, E., Sy, J., Wurzbacher, K., et al. (1994). Effectiveness of intensive case managment for homeless adolescents: Results of a 3-month follow-up. *Journal of Emotional & Behavioral Disorders, 2(4)*, 219-227.

Cauce, A. M., Paradise, M., Ginzler, J. A., Embry, L., Morgan, C. J., Lohr, Y., et al. (2000). The characteristics and mental health of homeless adolescents: Age and gender differences. *Journal of Emotional and Behavioral Disorders, 8(4)*, 230-239.

Cauce, A. M., Reid, M., Landesman, S. & Gonzales, N. A. (1990). Social support in young children: Measurement, structure, and behavioral impact. In B. R. Sarason, I. G. Sarason, & G. R. Pierce (Eds.), *Social support: An interactional view* (64-94). New York: Wiley.

Christle, C., Jolivette, K. & Nelson, C. (2005). Breaking the School to Prison Pipeline: Identifying School Risk and Protective Factors for Youth Delinquency. *Exceptionality, 13*, 69-88.

Coatsworth, J. D., Santisteban, D. A. & McBride, C. K. (2001). Brief strategic family therapy versus community control: Engagement, retention, and an exploration of the moderating role of adolescent symptom severity. *Family Process, 40(3), 313*-332.

Colins, O., Vermeiren, R., Schuyten, G. & Broekaert, E. (2009). Psychiatric disorders in property, violent, and versatile offending detained male adolescents. *American Journal of Orthopsychiatry, 79*, 31-38.

DeLeon, G. (1996). Integrative recovery: A state paradigm. *Substance Abuse, 17*, 51-63.

Denning, R. & Homel, R. (2008). Predicting recidivism in juvenile offenders on community based orders: The impact of risk factors and service delivery. Journal of Offender Rehabilitation, *46*, 189-215.

Dennis, M., Titus, J., Diamond, G., Babor, T., Donaldson, J., Godley, S.H., Tims, F., Webb, C., Liddle, H.A. & Scott, C. (In press). The Cannabis Youth Treatment (CYT) experiment: a multi-site study of five approaches to outpatient treatment for adolescents. *Addiction*.

Dembo, R., Schmeidler, J. & Childs, K. (2007). Correlates of male and female juvenile offender abuse experiences. *Journal of Child Sexual Abuse, 16*, 75-94.

Dembo, R., Williams, L.,& Schmeidler, J. (1993). Gender differences in service needs among youths entering a juvenile detention center. *Journal of Prison & Jail Health, 12*, 73-101.

Dembo, R., Williams, L. & Schmeidler, J. (1998). Key findings of the Tampa longitudinal study of juvenile detainees: Contributions to a theory of drug use and delinquency among high risk youths. In A. R. Roberts (Ed.), *Juvenile justice: Policies, programs and services* (2nd ed., 274-311). Chicago: Nelson-Hall.

DiClemente, R. J., Wingwood, G. M., Crosby, R., Sionean, C., Cobb, B., Harrington, K., et al.(2001). Parental monitoring: Association with adolescents' risk behaviors. *Pediatrics, 107*, 1363-1368.

Dishion, T. J. (2000). Cross-setting consistency in early adolescent psychopathology: Deviant friendships and problem behavior sequelae. *Journal of Personality, 68,* 1109-26.

Dishion, T. J. & Loeber, R. (1985). Male adolescent marijuana and alcohol use: The role of parents and peers revisited. *American Journal of Drug and Alcohol Abuse, 11,* 11-25.

Dishion, T. J. & McMahon, R. J. (1998). Parental monitoring and the prevention of child and adolescent problem behavior: A conceptual and empirical formulation. *Journal of Abnormal Child Psychology, 26*, 53-69.

Dodge, K., Lansford, J., Burks, V., Pettit, G., Price, J., Fontaine, R., et al. (2003). Peer rejection and social information-processing factors in the development of aggressive behavior problems in children. *Child Development, 74*, 374-393.

Dowden,C. & Andrews, D. A. (2003). Does family intervention work for delinquents? Results of a meta-analysis. *Canadian Journal of Criminology and Criminal Justice, 45*, 327-342.

Elliott, D. S. & Menard, S. (1996). Delinquent friends and delinquent behavior: Temporal and developmental patterns. In J. D. Hawkins (Ed.), *Delinquency and crime: Current theories* (28-67). New York: Cambridge University Press.

Fagan, A. A., Van Horn, M. L., Hawkins, J. D. & Arthur, M. W. (2009). Gender similarities and differences in the association between risk and protective factors and self-reported serious delinquency. *Society for Prevention Research, 8*, 115-124.

Farrington, D. P. (2000). Explaining and preventing crime: The globalization of knowledge—The American Society of Criminology 1999 presidential address. *Criminology, 38*, 1-24.

Formoso, D., Gonzales, N. A. & Aiken, L. S. (2000). Family conflict and children's internalizing and externalizing behavior: Protective factors. *American Journal of Community Psychology, 28(2)*, 175-199.

Foxcroft, D. R., Ireland, D. & Lister-Sharp, D. J. (2003). Longer-term primary prevention for alcohol misuse in young people: a systematic review. *Addiction, 98(4)*, 397-411.

Gainey, R. R., Wells, E. A., Hawkins, J. D. & Catalano, R. F. (1993). Predicting treatment retention among cocaine users. *International Journal of the Addictions, 28(6)*, 487-505.

Garbarino, J. (1991). The human ecology of early risk. In S. J. Meisels, & J. Shankoff (Eds.), *Handbook of early childhood intervention.* New York: Cambridge University Press.

Garland, A. F., Hough, R. L., McCabe, K. M., Yeh, M., Wood, P. A. & Aarons, G. A. (2001). Prevalence of psychiatric disorders in youths across five sectors of care. *Journal of the American Academy of Child and Adolescent Psychiatry, 40*, 409-418.

Gatti, U., Tremblay, R., Vitaro, F. & McDuff, P. (2005). Youth gangs, delinquency and drug use: A test of the selection, facilitation, and enhancement hypotheses. *Journal of Child Psychology and Psychiatry, 46*, 1178-1190.

Gingerich, W. J. & Eisengart, S. (2000). Solution-Focused Brief Therapy: A Review of the Outcome Research. *Family Process, 39(4)*, 477-499.

Green, M. R. (2004). Interventions with traumatized adolescents. *Adolescent Psychiatry, 27(special issue)*, 283-305.

Haley, J. (1973). Strategic therapy when a child is presented as the problem. *Journal of the American Academy of Child Psychiatry, 12(4)*, 641-659.

Hawkins, J. D. (1996) *Delinquency and crime: Current theories.* New York: Cambridge University Press.

Hawkins, J. D., Catalano, R. F. & Miller, J. Y. (1992). Risk and protective factors for alcohol and other drug problems in adolescence and early adulthood: Implications for substance abuse prevention. *Psychological Bulletin, 112*, 64-105.

Hawkins, J. D., Catalano, R.F. & Morrison, D. M. (1992). The Seattle In: McCord, Joan (Ed); Tremblay, Richard Ernest (Ed); 1992. *Preventing antisocial behavior: Interventions from birth through adolescence.* New York, NY, US: Guilford Press. 139-161.

Henggler, S. W. (1986). Multisystemic treatment of juvenile offenders: Effects on adolescent behavior and family interaction. *Developmental Psychology, 22(1)*, 132-141.

Henggeler, S. W., Borduin, C. M., Melton, G. B., Mann, B. J., Smith, L., Hall, J. A., Cone, L. & Fucci, B. R. (1991). Effects of multisystemic therapy on drug use and abuse in serious juvenile offenders: A progress report from two outcome studies. *Family Dynamics of Addiction Quarterly, 1*, 40-51.

Henggler, S. W., Clingempeel, W. G., Brondino, M. J. & Pickrel, S. G. (2002). Four year follow-up of multisystemic therapy with substance abusing and dependent juvenile offenders. *Journal of the American Academy of Child and Adolescent Psychiatry, 41*, 868-874.

Henggeler, S. W., Melton, G. B. & Smith, L. A. (1992). Family preservation using multisystemic therapy: An effective alternative to incarcerating serious juvenile offenders. *Journal of Consulting and Clinical Psychology, 60*, 953-961.

Henggeler, S. W., Melton, G. B., Smith, L. A., Schoenwald, S. K. & Hanley, J. H. (1993). Family preservation using multisystemic treatment: Long-term follow-up to a clinical trial with serious juvenile offenders. *Journal of Child and Family Studies, 2*, 283-293.

Henggeler, S. W., Pickrel, S. G. & Brondino, M. J. (1999). Multisystemic treatment of substance abusing and dependent delinquents: Outcomes, treatment fidelity, and transportability. *Mental Health Services Research, 1*, 171-184.

Henggler, S. W., Pickrel, S. G., Brondino, M. J. & Crouch, J. L. (1996). Eliminating (almost) treatment dropout of substance abusing or dependent delinquents through home-based multisystemic therapy. *American Journal of Psychiatry, 153*, 427-428.

Henggeler, S. W., Schoenwald, S. K., Borduin, C. M., Rowland, M. D. & Cunningham, P. B. (1998). *Multisystemic Treatment of Antisocial Behavior in Children and Adolescents.* New York, NY: The Guildford Press.

Hogue, A. & Liddle, H.A. (1999). Family-based preventive intervention: An approach to preventing substance use and antisocial behavior. *American Journal of Orthopsychiatry, 69(3)*, 278-293.

Hogue, A. T., Liddle, H. A., Becker, D. & Johnson-Leckrone, J. (2002). Family-based prevention counseling for high risk young adolescents: immediate outcomes. *Journal of Community Psychology, 30(1)*, 1-22.

Howell, J. C. (2008). Prevention and reducing juvenile delinquency: A comprehensive framework: Second edition. Thousand Oaks, CA: Sage.

Huizinga, D., Loeber, R. & Thornberry, T. P. (1994). *Urban delinquency and substance abuse: Initial findings.* Washington, DC: U.S. Government Printing Office.

Irvine, A. B., Biglan, A., Smolkowski, K., Metzler, C. W. & Ary, D. V. (1999). The effectiveness of a parenting skills program for parents of middle school students in small communities. *Journal of Consulting and Clinical Psychology, 67*, 811-825.

Jenson, J. M. (1997). Juvenile delinquency and drug abuse: Implications for social work practice in the justice system. In C. A. McNeece, & A. R. Roberts (Eds.), *Policy and practice in the justice system* (107-123). Chicago: Nelson-Hall.

Joe, G. W., Simpson, D. D. & Broome, K. M. (1998). Effects of readiness for drug abuse treatment on client retention and assessment of process. *Addiction, 93(8)*, 1177-1190.

Johnston, L. D., O'Malley, P. M. & Bachman, J. G. (2002). *Demographic subgroup trends for various licit and illicit drugs, 1975-2001.* (Monitoring the Future Occasional Paper No. 57). Ann Arbor, MI: Institute for Social Research. Available: http://monitoringthefuture.org.

Johnston, L. D., O'Malley, P. M. & Bachman, J. G. & Schulenberg, J. E. (2009). *Monitoring the future: National survey results on drug use, 1975-2008. Vol. 1: Secondary school students* (NIMH No. 09-7401). Bethesda, MD: National Institute on Drug Abuse.

Kaminski, R. A., Stormshak, E. A., Good, R. H.. & Goodman, M. R. (2002). Prevention of Substance Abuse With Rural Head Start Children and Families: Results of Project STAR. *Psychology of Addictive Behaviors, 16(Suppl4)*, S11-S26.

Kamoeoka, V. A. (1996). *The effects of a family-focused intervention on reducing risk for substance abuse among Asian and Pacific-Island youths and families: Evaluation of the*

Strengthening Hawaii's Families Project. Honolulu: University of Hawaii, Social Welfare Evaluation and Research Unit.

Kidd, S. A. (2003). Street Youth: Coping and interventions. *Child & Adolescent Social Work Journal, 20(4)*, 235-261.

Kim, H. & Kim, H. (2008). The impact of family violence, family functioning, and parental partner dynamics on Korean juvenile delinquency. *Child Psychiatry and Human Development, 39*, 439-453.

Kirby, L. D. & Fraser, M. W. (1997). Risk and resilience in childhood. In M. W. Fraser (Ed.), *Risk and resilience in childhood: An ecological perspective* (10-33). Washington, DC: NASW Press.

Kraemer, H., Kazdin, A., Offord, D. & Kessler, R. (1997). Coming to terms with the terms of risk. *Archives of General Psychiatry, 54*, 337-343.

Kumpfer, K. L. (1998). Selective prevention approaches for drug use prevention: Overview of outcome results from multi-ethnic replications of the Strengthening Families Program. In: R. Ashery, K. L. Kumpfer, & E. Robertson (Eds.), *Drug Abuse Prevention Through Family Interventions.* National Institute on Drug Abuse Research Monograph 177. U.S. Department of Health and Human Services, National Institutes of Health, National Institute on Drug Abuse.

Kumpfer, K. L., Alexander, L. B., McDonald, L. & Olds, D. L. (1998). *Family-focused substance abuse prevention: What has been learned from other fields* (No. Monograph 177). Rockville, MD: National Institute of Drug Abuse.

Kumpfer, K. L. & Alvarado, R. (1995). Strengthening families to prevent drug use in multi-ethnic youth. In G. Botvin, S. Schinke, & M. Orlandi (Eds.), *Drug abuse prevention with multi-ethnic youth* (253-292). Newbury Park, CA: Sage.

Kumpfer, K. L., Alvarado, R. & Smith, P. (2002). Cultural sensitivity and adaptation in family-based prevention interventions. *Prevention Science, 3(3),* 241-246.

Kumpfer, K. L., Alvarado, R. & Tait, C. (2002). Effectiveness of school-based family and children's skills training for substance prevention among 6-8 year-old rural children. *Psychology of Addictive Behaviors, 16*(Suppl4), S65-S71.

Kumpfer, K. L., DeMarsh, J. P. & Child, W. (1989). *Strengthening Families Program: Children's Skills Training Curriculum Manual, Parent Training Manual, Children's Skill Training Manual, and Family Skills Training Manual* (Prevention Services to Children of Substance-Abusing Parents). Salt Lake City: Social Research Institute, Graduate School of Social Work, University of Utah.

Kumpfer, K. L., Molgaard, V. & Spoth, R. (1996). The Strengthening Families Program for prevention of delinquency and drug use in special populations. In R. DeV Peters, & R. J. McMahon (Eds.), *Childhood disorders, substance abuse, and delinquency: Prevention and early intervention approaches.* Newbury Park, CA: Sage.

Kumpfer, K. L. & Turner, C. W. (1990-1991). The social ecology model of adolescent substance abuse: Implications for prevention. *Internal Journal of the Addictions, 25(4-A)*, 435-463.

Kumpfer, K. L., Wamberg, K. & Martinez, D. (1996). *Strengthening Hispanic Families Program.* Paper presented at the Center for Substance Abuse Prevention, High Risk Youth Conference, Washington, DC.

Latimer, W. W., Winters, K. C. & D'Zurilla, T. (2003). Integrated Family and Cognitive-Behavioral Therapy for adolescent substance abusers: A Stage I efficacy study. *Drug & Alcohol Dependence, 71(3),* 303-317.

Letourneau, E. J., Cunningham, P. B. & Henggeler, S. W. (2002) Multisystemic treatment of antisocial behavior In: Hofmann, S.G. & Tompson, M.C. (Eds.). *Treating chronic and severe mental disorders: A handbook of empirically supported interventions.* New York, NY, US: Guilford Press, 364-381.

Leve, L. & Chamberlain, P. (2005). Association with Delinquent Peers: Intervention Effects for Youth in the Juvenile Justice System. *Journal of Abnormal Child Psychology, 33,* 339-347.

Lewis, R. A., Piercy, F. P. & Sprenkle, D. H. (1990). Family-based interventions for helping drug-abusing adolescents *Journal of Adolescent Research, 5(1),* 82-95.

Li, C, Pentz, M. A. & Chou, C. (2002). Parental substance use as a modifier of adolescent substance use risk. *Addiction, 97,* 1537-1550.

Liddle, H. A. & Dakof, G. A. (1995). Efficacy of family therapy for drug abuse: Promising but not definitive. *Journal of Marital & Family Therapy, 21(4),* 511-539.

Liddle, H. A., Dakof, G. A., Parker, K., Diamond, G. S., Barrett, K. & Tejeda, M. (2001). Multidimensional family therapy for adolescent drug abuse: Results of a randomized clinical trial. *American Journal of Drug & Alcohol Abuse, 27(4),* 651-688.

Liddle, H. A., Dakof, G. A., Turner, R. M. & Tejeda, M. (in press). Treating adolescent substance abuse: a comparison of individual and family therapy interventions. *NIDA Monograph on the 2001 CPDD Conference* (paper presented at Adolescent Drug Abuse Treatment Research Symposium [A. Morral & M. Dennis, Chairs], CPDD, June, 2001).

Liddle, H. A. & Hogue, A. (2000). A family-based, developmental-ecological preventive intervention for high-risk adolescents. *Journal of Marital & Family Therapy, 26(3),* 265-279.

Loeber, R., Green, S. M., Lahey, B. B., Frick, P. J. & McBurnett, K. (2000). Findings on disruptive behavior disorders from the first decade of the Developmental Trends Study. *Clinical Child and Family Review, 3,* 37-60.

Lonczak, H. S. (2000). An examination of the long-term effects of the Seattle *Dissertation Abstracts International Section A: Humanities &* Social *Sciences, Vol 60(7-A),* 2371.

Lonczak, H. S., Huang, B. & Catalano, R. F. (2001). The social predictors *Journal of Studies on Alcohol, 62(2),* 179-189.

Lundahl, L. H., Davis, T. M., Adesso, V. J. & Lukas, S. E. (1997). Alcohol expectancies: effects of gender, age, and family history of alcoholism. *Addictive Behaviors, 22(1),* 115-125.

McCord, J., Widom, C. S. & Crowell, N. A., eds. (2001). *Juvenile Crime, Juvenile Justice. Panel on Juvenile Crime: Prevention, Treatment, and Control.* Washington, DC: National Academy Press.

Minuchin, S. (1974). *Families & family therapy.* Oxford, England: Harvard University Press, 268.

Moncher, M. S., Holden, G. W. & Schinke, S. P. (1990). Behavioral family treatment of the substance abusing Hispanic adolescent. In E. L. Feindler, & G. R. Kalfus (Eds.), *Adolescent behavior therapy handbook.* New York, NY: Springer Publishing Co., 329-349.

Murray, J. & Farrington, D. P. (2005). Parental imprisonment: Effects on boys' antisocial behavior and delinquency through the life-course. *Journal of Child Psychology and Psychiatry, 46*, 1269-1278.

Newcomb, M. D. (1992). Understanding the multidimensional nature of drug use and abuse: The role of consumption, risk factors, and protective factors. In: M. D. Glantz, & R. W. Pickens (Eds.), *Vulnerability to drug abuse.* Washington, DC: American Psychological Association.

Newcomb, M. D. & Bentler, P. M. (1989). Substance use and abuse among children and teenagers. *American Psychologist, 44*, 242-248.

Nichols, M. P. & Schwartz, R. C. (1995). *Family Therapy: Concepts and Methods.* Needham Heights, MA: Allyn and Bacon.

Oetting, E. R. (1992). Planning programs for prevention of deviant behavior: A psychosocial model. *Drugs & Society, 6(3-4),* 313-344.

Ouimette, P. C., Brown, P. J. & Najavits, L. M. (1998). Course and treatment of patients with both substance use and posttraumatic stress disorders. *Addictive Behaviors, 23(6),* 785-795.

Paradise, M., Cauce, A. M., Ginzler, J., Wert, S., Wruck, K. & Brooker, M. (2001). The role of relationships in developmental trajectories of homeless and runaway youth. In B. R. Sarason, & S. Duck (Eds.), *Personal relationships: Implications for clinical and community psychology.* New York: John Wiley & Sons.

Perrino, T., Gonzalez-Soldevilla, A., Pantin, H. & Szapocznik, J. (2000). The role of families in adolescent HIV prevention: A review. *Clinical Child and Family Psychology Review, 3(2),* 81-96.

Rahdert, E. & Czechowicz, D. (Eds.). (1995). *Adolescent drug abuse: Clinical assessment and therapeutic interventions.* Washington, DC: NIDA Research Monograph 156. U.S. Government Printing Office.

Randall, J. & Cunningham, P. B. (2003). Multisystemic therapy: A treatment for violent substance-abusing and substance-dependent juvenile offenders. *Addictive Behaviors, 28(9),* 1731-1739.

Randall, J., Henggeler, S. W. & Cunningham, P. B. (2001). Adapting multisystemic therapy to treat adolescent substance abuse more effectively. *Cognitive & Behavioral Practice, 8(4),* 359-366.

Rivaux, S. L., Springer, D. W., Bohman, T., Wagner, E. F. & Gil, A. G. (2006). Differences among substance abusing Latino, Anglo, and African-American juvenile offenders in predictors of recidivism and treatment outcome. *Journal of Social Work Practice in the Addictions, 6*, 5-29.

Robbins, M. S., Mitrani, V. B. & Zarate, M. (2002). Change processes in family therapy with Hispanic adolescents. *Hispanic Journal of Behavioral Sciences, 24(4),* 505-519.

Robbins, M. S., Szapocznik, J. & Santisteban, D. A. (2003). Brief strategic family therapy for Hispanic youth. In A. E. Kazdin (Ed), *Yale University School of Medicine, Child Study Center. Evidence-based psychotherapies for children and adolescents.* New York, NY: Guilford Press, 407-424.

Roberts, A. R. (2004). An overview of juvenile justice and juvenile delinquency. In A. R. Roberts (Ed.) *Juvenile justice sourcebook: Past, present, and future* (5-40). New York: Oxford University Press.

Roberts, R. E., Attkisson, C. C. & Rosenblatt, A. (1998). Prevalence of psychopathology among children and adolescents. *The American Journal of Psychiatry, 155,* 715-725.

Rowe, C., Liddle, H. A. & McClintic, K. (2002). Integrative treatment development: Multidimensional family therapy for adolescent substance abuse. In: F. W. Kaslow (Ed.), *Comprehensive handbook of psychotherapy: Integrative/eclectic.* New York, NY: John Wiley & Sons, Inc. 133-161.

Sampson, R. J. & Groves, W. B., (1989). Community structure and crime: Testing social disorganization theory. *American Journal of Sociology, 94,* 774-802.

Santisteban, D. A., Coatsworth, J. D. & Perez-Vidal, A. (2003). Efficacy of brief strategic family therapy in modifying Hispanic adolescen behavior problems and substance use. *Journal of Family Psychology, 17(1),* 121-133.

Santisteban, D. A., Szapocznik, J., Perez-Vidal, A., Kurtines, W. M., Coatsworth, J. D. & LaPerriere, A. (2000). *The efficacy of brief strategic/structural family therapy in modifying behavior problems and an exploration of the role that family functioning plays in behavior change.* Manuscript in preparation, University of Miami, Center for Family Studies.

Santisteban, D. A., Szapocznik, J., Perez-Vidal, A., Kurtines, W. M., Murray, E. J. & LaPerriere, A. (1996). Efficacy of intervention for engaging youth and families into treatment and some variables that may contribute to differential effectiveness. *Journal of Family Psychology, 10,* 35-44.

Schoenwald, S. K., Halliday-Boykins, C. A. & Henggeler, S. W. (2003). Client-level predictors of adherence to MST in community service settings. *Family Process, 42(3),* 345-359.

Schoenwald, S. K., Ward, D. M. & Henggeler, S. W. (1996). Multisystemic therapy treatment of substance abusing or dependent adolescent offenders: Costs of reducing incarceration, inpatient, and residential placement. *Journal of Child & Family Studies, 5(4),* 431-444.

Siegel, L. J. & Welsh, B. C. (2008). *Juvenile delinquency: Theory, practice, and law, tenth edition.* Florence, KY: Cengage Learning.

Selekman, M. D. (1997). *Solution-focused Therapy with children: Harnessing family strengths for systemic change.* NewYork: The Guilford Press.

Selekman, M. D. (2005). *Pathways to Change: Brief therapy with difficult adolescents* (2nd Ed. ed.). New York: The Guilford Press.

Shader, M. (2004). *Risk factors for delinquency: An overview.* (NCJ 207540). U. S. Department of Justice.

Sheidow, A. J. & Woodford, M. S. (2003). Multisystemic therapy: An empirically supported, home-based family therapy approach. *Family Journal-Counseling & Therapy for Couples & Families, 11(3),* 257-263.

Simoes, C., Matos, M. M. & Batista-Foguet, J. M. (2008). Juvenile delinquency: Analysis of risk and protective factors using quantitative and qualitative methods. *Cognition, Brain, Behavior,* 4, 389-408.

Simpson, D. D. (2001). Modeling treatment process and outcomes. *Addiction, 96(2),* 207-211.

Simpson, D. D., Joe, G. W. & Brown, B. S. (1997). Treatment retention and follow-up outcomes in the Drug Abuse Treatment Outcome Study (DATOS). *Psychology of Addictive Behaviors, 11(4),* 294-307.

Simpson, D. D., Joe, G. W., Rowan-Szal, G. & Greener, J. (1995). Client engagement and change during drug abuse treatment. *Journal of Substance Abuse, 7(1),* 117-134.

Soo-Hoo, T. (1999). Brief strategic family therapy with Chinese Americans. *American Journal of Family Therapy, 27(2),* 163-179.

Spoth, R. (1998). *Results From Iowa Strengthening Families Program for Drug Use.* Paper presented to the Society for Prevention Research Annual Conference, Baltimore, MD.

Spoth, R., Guyll, M. & Chao, W. (2003). Exploratory Study of a Preventive Intervention with General Population African American Families. *Journal of Early Adolescence, 23(4),* 435-468.

Spoth, R. L., Guyll, M. & Day, S. X. (2002). Universal family-focused interventions in alcohol-use disorder prevention: Cost-effectiveness and cost-benefit analyses of two interventions. *Journal of Studies on Alcohol, 63(2),* 219-228.

Spoth, R., Redmond, C. & Lepper, H. (1999). Alcohol initiation outcomes of universal family-focused preventive interventions: One- and two-year follow-ups of a controlled study. *Journal of Studies on Alcohol, supp 13,* 103-111.

Spoth, R., Redmond, C. & Shin, C. (1998). Direct and indirect latent-variable parenting outcomes of two universal family-focused preventive interventions: Extending a public health-oriented research base. *Journal of Consulting & Clinical Psychology, 66(2),* 385-399.

Spoth, R. L., Redmond, C. & Shin, C. (2001). Randomized trial of brief family interventions for general populations: Adolescent substance use outcomes 4 years following baseline. *Journal of Consulting & Clinical Psychology, 69(4),* 627-642.

Spoth, R. L., Redmond, C. & Trudeau, L. (2002). Longitudinal substance initiation outcomes for a universal preventive intervention combining family and school programs. *Psychology of Addictive Behaviors, 16(2),* 129-134.

Spoth, R., Reyes, M. L. & Redmond, C. (1999). Assessing a public health approach to delay onset and progression of adolescent substance use: Latent transition and log-linear analyses of longitudinal family preventive intervention outcomes. *Journal of Consulting & Clinical Psychology, 67(5),* 619-630.

Stanton, M. D. & Shadish, W. R. (1997). Outcomes, attrition, and family-couple treatment for drug abuse: A meta-analysis and review of the controlled, comparative studies. *Psychological Bulletin, 122,* 170-191.

Spoth, R., Goldberg, C. & Redmond, C. (1999). Engaging Families in Longitudinal Preventive Intervention Research : Discrete-Time Survival Analysis of Socioeconomic and Social -Emotional Risk Factors. *Journal of Consulting and Clinical Psychology, 67(1),* 157-163.

Springer, D. W. (2001). Runaway adolescents: Today's Huckleberry Finn crisis. *Brief Treatment & Crisis Intervention, 1(2),* 131-151.

Stanton, M. D. & Shadish, W. R. (1997). Outcomes, attrition, and family-couple treatment for drug abuse: A meta-analysis and review of the controlled, comparative studies. *Psychological Bulletin, 122,* 170-191.

Stouthamer-Loeber, M., Wei, E. H., Homish, D. L. & Loeber, R. (2002). Which family and demographic factors are related to both maltreatment and persistent serious juvenile delinquency? *Children's Services: Social Policy, Research, and Practice, 5,* 261-272.

Szapocznik, J., Hervis, O. & Schwartz, S. (2001). *Brief Strategic Family Therapy Manual [NIDA Treatment Manual Series].* Rockvill, MD: National Institute on Drug Abuse.

Szapocznik, J. & Kurtines, W. M. (1989). *Breakthroughs in family therapy with drug abusing problem youth.* New York: Springer.

Szapocznik, J. & Kurtines, W. M. (1990). Interplay of advances between theory, research, and application in treatment interventions aimed at behavior problem children and adolescents. *Journal of Consulting & Clinical Psychology, 58(6)*, 696-703.

Szapocznik, J., Kurtines, W. M., Foote, F., Perez-Vidal, A. & Hervis, O. E. (1986). Conjoint versus one-person family therapy: Further evidence for the effectiveness of conducting family therapy through one person with drug-abusing adolescents. *Journal of Consulting & Clinical Psychology, 54(3)*, 395-397.

Szapocznik, J., Perez-Vidal, A., Brickman, A., Foote, F. H., Santisteban, D., Hervis, O. E. & Kurtines, W. M. (1988). Engaging adolescent drug abusers and their families into treatment: A strategic structural systems approach. *Journal of Consulting and Clinical Psychology, 56*, 552-557.

Szapocznik, J., Perez-Vidal, A., Hervis, O. E., Brickman, A. E. & Kurtines, W. M. (1989). Innovations in family therapy: Strategies for overcoming resistance to treatment. In R. A. Wells, & V. J. Giannetti (Eds.), *Handbook of brief psychotherapies*. (93-114). New York: Plenum.

Szapocznik, J., Rio, A. & Murray, E. (1989). Structural family versus psychodynamic child therapy for problematic Hispanic boys. *Journal of Consulting & Clinical Psychology, 57(5)*, 571-578.

Szapocznik, J., Santisteban, D., Rio, A., Perez Vidal, A. & Kurtines, W. M. (1986). Family effectiveness training for Hispanic families: Strategic structural systems intervention for the prevention of drug abuse. In H. P. Lefley, & P. B. Pedersen (Eds.), *Cross cultural training for mental health professionals*. (245-261). Springfield, IL: Charles C Thomas.

Szapocznik, J., Santisteban, D., Rio, A., Perez Vidal, A., Kurtines, W. M. & Hervis, O. E. (1986). Bicultural effectiveness training (BET): An intervention modality for families experiencing intergenerational/intercultural conflict. *Hispanic Journal of Behavioral Sciences, 6*, 303-330.

Szapocznik, J. & Williams, R. A. (2000). Brief Strategic Family Therapy: Twenty-five years of interplay among theory, research and practice in adolescent behavior problems and drug abuse. *Clinical Child & Family Psychological Review, 3(2)*, 117-134.

Teplin, L. A., Abram, K. M., McClelland, G. M., Dulcan, M. K. & Mericle, A. A. (2002). Psychiatric disorders in youth in juvenile detention. *Archives of General Psychiatry, 59*, 1133-1143.

Trepper, T. S., Piercy, F. P. & Lewis, R. A. (1993). Family therapy In: O'Farrell, Timothy J. (Ed). *Treating alcohol problems: Marital and* family *interventions*. New York, NY, US: Guilford Press, 261-278.

Thyer, B. A. (2008). Evidence-Based Macro Practice: Addressing the Challenges and Opportunities. *Journal of Evidence-Based Social Work, 5*, 453-472.

Turner, S. G. (2001). Resilience and social work practice: Three case studies. *Families in Society, The Journal of Contemporary Human Services, 82*, 441-448.

Vaillant, G. E. (1993). *The wisdom of the ego*. Cambridge, MA: Harvard University Press. M. Van Horn, J. D. Hawkins, M. Arthur, & R. Catalano (2007). Assessing community effects on adolescent substance use and delinquency. *Journal of Community Psychology, 35*, 925-946.

Vitaro, F., Pedersen, S. & Brendgen, M. (2007). Children's disruptiveness, peer rejection, friends' deviancy, and delinquent behaviors: A process-oriented approach. *Development and Psychopathology, 19*, 433-453.

Waldron, H. B., Slesnick, N. & Brody, J. L. (2001). Treatment outcomes for adolescent substance abuse at 4- and 7-month assessments. *Journal of Consulting & Clinical Psychology, 69(5),* 802-813.

Wasserman, G. A., Keenan, K., Tremblay, R. E., Coie, J., Herrenkohl, T. I., loeber, R., et al. (2003). Risk and protective factors of child delinquency. In *Child Delinquency Bulletin Series* (OJJDP No. 193409). Rockville, MD: Juvenile Justice Clearinghouse.

Weiner, I. B. (2003). *Handbook of psychology.* Hoboken, NJ: John Wiley and Sons.

Werner, E. E. (1990). Protective factors and individual resilience. In J. Meisels, & J. P. Shankoff (Eds.), *Handbook of early childhood intervention.* Cambridge, MA: Cambridge University Press.

Whisman, M. A. (1990). The efficacy of booster maintenance sessions in behavior therapy: Review and methodological critique. *Clinical Psychology Review, 10,* 155-170.

Whitbeck, L. B. (1999). Primary socialization theory: It all begins with the family. *Substance Use & Misuse, 34,* 1025-1032.

Williams, J., Ayers, C., Abbott, R., Hawkins, J. & Catalano, R. (1999). Racial differences in risk factors for delinquency and substance use among adolescents. *Social Work Research,* 23, 241-256.

Wills, T. A. V. & D McNamara, G. (1992). The role of life events, family support, and competence in adolescent substance use: A test of vulnerability and protective factors. *American Journal of Community Psychology, 20(3)*, 349-374.

Winters, K. C. (1999). *Treatment of adolescents with substance use disorders.* (SMA 99-3283). Rockville MD: Center for Substance Abuse Treatment.

Baer, J. S., Peterson, P. L. & Wells, E. A. (2004). Rationale and design of a brief substance use intervention for homeless adolescents. *Addiction Research and Theory, 12(4)*, 317-334.

Catalano, R. F., Gainey, R. R., Fleming, C. B., Haggerty, K. P. & Johnson, N. O. (1999). An experimental intervention with families of substance abusers: One-year follow-up of the focus on families project. *Addiction, 94(2)*, 241-255.

Cauce, A. M., Morgan, C. J., Wagner, J., Moore, E., Sy, J., Wurzbacher, K., et al. (1994). Effectiveness of intensive case managment for homeless adolescents: Results of a 3-month follow-up. *Journal of Emotional & Behavioral Disorders, 2(4)*, 219-227.

Cauce, A. M., Paradise, M., Ginzler, J. A., Embry, L., Morgan, C. J., Lohr, Y., et al. (2000). The characteristics and mental health of homeless adolescents: Age and gender differences. *Journal of Emotional and Behavioral Disorders, 8(4)*, 230-239.

Cauce, A. M., Reid, M., Landesman, S. & Gonzales, N. A. (1990). Social support in young children: Measurement, structure, and behavioral impact. In B. R. Sarason, I. G. Sarason, & G. R. Pierce (Eds.), *Social support: An interactional view* (64-94). New York: Wiley.

Formoso, D., Gonzales, N. A. & Aiken, L. S. (2000). Family conflict and children's internalizing and externalizing behavior: Protective factors. *American Journal of Community Psychology, 28(2)*, 175-199.

Gingerich, W. J. & Eisengart, S. (2000). Solution-Focused Brief Therapy: A Review of the Outcome Research. *Family Process, 39(4)*, 477-499.

Green, M. R. (2004). Interventions with traumatized adolescents. *Adolescent Psychiatry,* 27(special issue), 283-305.

Irvine, A. B., Biglan, A., Smolkowski, K., Metzler, C. W. & Ary, D. V. (1999). The effectiveness of a parenting skills program for parents of middle school students in small communities. *Journal of Consulting and Clinical Psychology, 67*, 811-825.

Kidd, S. A. (2003). Street Youth: Coping and interventions. *Child & Adolescent Social Work Journal, 20(4)*, 235-261.

Kumpfer, K. L., Alexander, L. B., McDonald, L. & Olds, D. L. (1998). *Family-focused substance abuse prevention: What has been learned from other fields* (No. Monograph 177). Rockville, MD: National Institute of Drug Abuse.

Ouimette, P. C., Brown, P. J. & Najavits, L. M. (1998). Course and treatment of patients with both substance use and posttraumatic stress disorders. *Addictive Behaviors, 23(6)*, 785-795.

Paradise, M., Cauce, A. M., Ginzler, J., Wert, S., Wruck, K. & Brooker, M. (2001). The role of relationships in developmental trajectories of homeless and runaway youth. In B. R. Sarason, & S. Duck (Eds.), *Personal relationships: Implications for clinical and community psychology*. New York: John Wiley & Sons.

Selekman, M. D. (1997). *Solution-focused Therapy with children: Harnessing family strengths for systemic change*. NewYork: The Guilford Press.

Selekman, M. D. (2005). *Pathways to Change: Brief therapy with difficult adolescents* (2nd Ed. ed.). New York: The Guilford Press.

Spoth, R., Goldberg, C. & Redmond, C. (1999). Engaging Families in Longitudinal Preventive Intervention Research : Discrete-Time Survival Analysis of Socioeconomic and Social -Emotional Risk Factors. *Journal of Consulting and Clinical Psychology, 67(1)*, 157-163.

Springer, D. W. (2001). Runaway adolescents: Today's Huckleberry Finn crisis. *Brief Treatment & Crisis Intervention, 1(2)*, 131-151.

Wills, T. A., Vaccaro, D. & McNamara, G. (1992). The role of life events, family support, and competence in adolescent substance use: A test of vulnerability and protective factors. *American Journal of Community Psychology, 20(3)*, 349-374.

In: Youth Violence and Juvenile Justice: Causes, Intervention…   ISBN: 978-1-61668-011-4
Editor: Neil A. Ramsay et al., pp. 65-115   © 2010 Nova Science Publishers, Inc.

Chapter 3

RISK AND PROTECTIVE FACTORS IN YOUTH VIOLENCE AND AGGRESSION: PROMISING FAMILY-BASED PREVENTION MODELS

Amanda N. Barczyk, Katherine Montgomery, Sanna J. Thompson and Sharon Matai
University of Texas at Austin, School of Social Work, Austin, Texas, USA

ABSTRACT

Contrary to what might be concluded from media reports, statistics show that youth aggression and violence is decreasing, particularly in schools. Although multiple victim homicides in schools have increased, schools are among the safest places for children. The issue of youth aggression and violence has been pushed to the forefront with the recognition that prevention is the most effective strategy for reducing youth aggression and violence.

No single risk factor can predict who is likely to engage in violent behavior, but longitudinal studies have established developmental pathways that lead to patterns of aggression and violence. Influences in the school and community also help establish enduring patterns of aggressive and violent behavior. School factors include low school involvement, academic and social failure, lack of clarity and follow-through in rules and policies, poor and/or inconsistent administrative support, and few allowances for individual differences. Attention deficit-hyperactivity disorders, specific learning disabilities, restlessness, risk-taking, poor social skills and certain beliefs and attitudes (e.g., the necessity of retaliation), appear to favor the development of aggressive behavior and violent actions. Conditions in the home--harsh and ineffective parental discipline, lack of parental involvement, family conflict, parental criminality, child abuse and/or neglect, and rejection--also predict early onset and chronic patterns of aggressive behaviors. When these conditions are present, children may be "literally trained to be aggressive during episodes of conflict with family members".

Many youth who are exposed to risk factors do not display aggressive and violent behaviors. Certain protective factors appear to account for this phenomenon. Often, these factors are described in terms of resiliency--the ability to recover strength and spirit under adversity on both internal (self) and external (family, school, community) factors for a positive outcome. Like risk factors, protective factors may be strengthened through interaction with other factors. Individual protective factors include having a more positive view of one's life circumstances and ability to affect those around them, as well as stress-reducing strategies. Family protective factors may include having an attachment to at least one family member who engages in proactive, healthy behaviors with the youth (e.g., high expectations for academic and social performance in and out of school, shared values and morals). Family cohesiveness and positive functioning discourage aggressive and violent behaviors.

Traditionally, schools and communities have responded to aggressive and violent behaviors with reactive strategies that are punitive (e.g., corporal punishment, suspension, expulsion, incarceration). These approaches have had poor results. However, evidence is accumulating that more integrative, proactive approaches that include the family are effective in preventing youth aggression and violence. This chapter describes risk and protective factors found associated with aggression and provides a description of various family-oriented treatment options for preventing youth violence and aggression.

INTRODUCTION

Contrary to what might be concluded from media reports, statistics show that youth aggression and violence is decreasing, particularly in schools (Graber, Nichols, Lynne, Brooks-Gunn, & Botvin, 2006). Although multiple victim homicides in schools have increased, schools are among the safest places for children (Youngblade et al., 2007). The issue of youth aggression and violence has been pushed to the forefront with the recognition that prevention is the most effective strategy for reducing youth aggression and violence.

Factors exist that increase and decrease the likelihood of a child or adolescent developing aggressive or violent behaviors. No single factor can predict who is likely to engage or not engage in violent behavior, but longitudinal studies have established developmental pathways leading to patterns of aggression and violence (Temcheff et al., 2008). Influences by the family, peers, school, and community also help establish enduring patterns of aggressive and violent behavior.

Traditionally, schools and communities have responded to aggressive and violent youth behaviors with punitive, reactive strategies (e.g., corporal punishment, suspension, expulsion, incarceration), but with poor results (Mahoney, Donnelly, Lewis, & Maynard, 2000). However, evidence is accumulating that more integrative, proactive approaches are effective in preventing youth aggression and violence, particularly family-based approaches (Tolan, Hanish, McKay, & Dickey, 2002). This chapter describes the risk and protective factors associated with aggression and also provides a description of various family-oriented treatment options for preventing and treating youth violence and aggression.

Aggression and Violence Defined

Aggression describes a range of behaviors varying by the age of onset, the severity of the act, and the opponent or victim harmed by the act (Loeber & Hay, 1997). For the purpose of this chapter we will define aggression as any behavior that causes or threatens the physical or mental harm on another individual (Loeber & Hay, 1997; Loeber & Stouthamer-Loeber, 1998). Bullying, verbal aggression, and physical fighting are all examples of aggression (Loeber & Hay, 1997). Aggression, with its many forms, develops as a child matures and progresses.

Loeber and Hay (1997) reported key issues concerning the development of aggression and violence. As youth move through developmental stages, aggression is manifested differentially. Aggression may appear as early as infancy through signs of rage and frustration. When the infant reaches toddlerhood, temper tantrums and aggression toward adults and peers may be observed. As children begin regularly attending day-care and other organized peer groups, gender differences became more apparent. For example, girls tend to use more verbal, indirect, and relational aggression, while boys express their aggression physically.

A variety of changes in severity and patterns of aggression begin to occur during adolescence and early adulthood. During this later stage of development, there is an increase in the impact of aggression that mirrors individuals' increased physical strength, and some begin to use weapons. Collective forms of violence (e.g. pressuring individuals to do things against their will) become more common in peer groups, particularly in the formation of gangs. In addition, cross-gender aggression increases as dating and intimate relationship develop (Loeber & Hay, 1997).

Violence, a higher-level manifestation of aggression, will be the primary context in which aggression is discussed throughout this chapter (Loeber & Hay, 1997). Here, violence is defined as the aggressive behaviors that cause serious harm to an opponent or victim (e.g. robbery, rape, homicide, and aggravated assault) (Loeber & Stouthamer-Loeber, 1998). Although many individuals displaying violent behavior have been highly aggressive earlier in their life, not all juveniles who become violent have a history of aggression (Loeber & Stouthamer-Loeber, 1998).

Risk Factors

According to Howell (2003), "risk factors are those elements in an individual's life that increase his or her vulnerability to negative developmental outcomes and also increase the probability of maintenance of a problem condition or digression to a more serious state." (p. 104). Specifically, certain factors can increase ones risk for particular negative outcomes. The "risk-focused approach" posits that bonding with family, peers, and institutions that promote prosocial norms acts as a protection against prevailing risks that may otherwise contribute to problem behaviors. However, when bonds with the family do not develop or are weak, the adolescent ultimately identifies with peers. These disruptive relationships often reinforce disruptive and deviant behaviors. Saner & Ellickson (1996) found that adolescents with multiple risk factors are more likely to be involved in violence.

Kraemer and colleagues (1997) have described risk factors by dividing them into three major types: 1) correlates or markers, 2) predictive factors, and 3) causal factors. Correlates are risk factors that exist concurrently with identified problems, such as being male and are often considered a risk factor for engaging in aggressive behaviors. Predictive factors are those that exist prior to emergence of problem behaviors. One possible predictive factor might be parental criminal involvement, as parents' model behaviors that result in their children engaging in forms of the same activity. Finally, causal factors can be linked to the problem behavior and can be directly changed through initiating treatment aimed at the problem behavior.

Protective Factors

While a great deal of research has focused on developing understanding of risk factors, less is known about protective factors. Kirby and Fraser (1997) reported that protective factors are "the internal and external forces that help children (and adolescents) resists or ameliorate risk" (p. 16). It is believed that the more protective factors present, the less likely the adolescent is at risk of engaging in violent behaviors. It is noteworthy that adolescents displaying particular risk factors are not assured to become aggressive and violent, but simply at greater risk of developing aggressive and violent behaviors than those not displaying the specific risk factor. Because some adolescents do posses several risk factors and never become aggressive or violent, researchers have explored explanations as to why this may be the case. A large body of research has focused on the concept of resilience in the context of protective factors.

Resilience is defined as "the remarkable capacity of individuals to withstand considerable hardship, to bounce back in the face of adversity, and to go on to live functional lives with a sense of well-being" (Turner, 2001, p. 441). Vaillant (1993) metaphorically emphasizes that resiliency is "the capacity to be bent without breaking and the capacity, once bent, to spring back" (p. 248). The fact is that some children and adolescents are simply more resilient than others, which suggests that protective factors are evident in the lives of young people. Thus, it is important for the concerned friend, family member, or service provider working with an at-risk children or adolescents to be familiar with risk and protective factors associated with aggression and violence to be able to determine or deliver effective treatment.

Risk and Protective Factor Domains

Various frameworks have been employed to understand risk/protective factors referenced framework and are used to provide additional specification. The most commonly used framework identifies factors across four domains (Hawkins, Catalano, & Miller, 1992). These domains include: individual, peers, school, community, and family. Each domain plays a substantial role in either protecting or placing the child or adolescent at risk of aggressive and violent behavior. These domains will be delineated below.

INDIVIDUAL DOMAIN

In this section various individual risk and protective factors of children with aggressive and violent behavior will be reviewed. A list of individual factors is available in Table 1. Rather than discussing each factor, selected individual factors associated with aggressive and violent behavior will be highlighted, including biological, cognitive, and physiological factors.

Table 1. Risk and Protective Factors of Aggression and Violence by Domain.

Domain	Risk Factors	Protective Factors
Individual	• *Biological* • Genes • Cognitive • Low intelligence • Low achievement • Executive cognitive functioning • Social cognitive deficiencies and sensitivities • Social information-processing deficiencies/distortions • Inflated self-esteem • Difficult temperament • Comorbid ADHD, anxiety, depression, substance abuse, etc. • Hyperactivity, impulsivity, restlessness, and risk taking • Poor social skills • Low guilt, antisocial attitudes and beliefs • *Physiological* • Low cortisol levels • Response of the hypothalamic-pituitary-adrenal axis response to stress • Low cerebrospinal fluid concentration of serotonin metabolite 5-hydroxyindoleacetic acid • High androgen or testosterone • Problems and complications during pregnancy • Low resting heart rate • Male gender • Chronic medical/physical condition	• High IQ • Female gender • Social, emotional, and self-regulation capacities and skills • Positive social orientation • Adaptive social interaction skills • Prosocial Values • Intolerant attitude toward deviance • Concern for others • High self-esteem and self-efficacy • Perceived sanctions for transgressions
Peer	• Affiliation with "deviant" or aggressive peers • Antisocial peer group • Gang involvement • Social isolation/peer rejection	• Association with prosocial peers • Association with friends who engage in conventional behavior
School	• Low educational aspirations • Academic failure or poor performance • School transitions • Over-crowded schools • Low school commitment and bonding • Pro-drug school (i.e. high levels of marijuana/cigarette use) • Ineffective or harmful school responses • Bullying	• Positive relationship with teacher • Attend effective schools • Bond/committment with prosocial school • Opportunities for prosocial school activities • Recognition for involvement in conventional activities
Community	• *Exposure to Violence* • Community violence • Stressful life events • Violent media influences • *Neighborhood Quality* • Neighborhood disorganization/crime • Low neighborhood attachment • Little enforcement of laws against violence	• Safe and organized neighborhoods • Access to effective community services (mental health, social service, etc.) • Prosocial media influences • Higher socioeconomic status • Opportunities for positive community activities • Bond with prosocial community institution

Table 1. (*Continued*)

Domain	Risk Factors	Protective Factors
	• Access to drugs and weapons • Discrimination • *Economics* • Disadvantaged neighborhood/low income/low socioeconomic status • Poor housing	
Family	• *Family Characteristics* • Single parent household • Parent-child separation • Family instability including residential mobility • Parental unemployment/low socioeconomic status/poverty • Poorly educated parent/primary caregiver • Young parent/primary caregiver • Delinquent siblings • Parental criminality • Parental attitudes favorable to substance use and violence • Parental substance abuse • Poor parental supervision/monitoring • *Parental Discipline* • Harsh, lax, or inconsistent disciplinary practices • Maternal depression • Ineffective parenting/low levels of parental involvement • Low parental reinforcement • *Family Interactions* • Poor attachment • Poor parent-child relations • Abuse/neglect/maltreatment • Family violence • Marital aggression/conflict • Sibling conflict • Poor family management practices • Parent-child coercive interactions	• Two parent/caregiver household • Parental monitoring • Infant-mother attachment • Adaptive parent-child interactions • Close relationship with parental figure • Functional family relationships • Functioning parent • Positive family environment • Supportive, warm relationships with parents or other adults • Supportive and authoritative parenting • Parents' positive evaluation of peers

Individual Risk Factors

Biological risk factors

The aspects of aggressive behavior can be linked to biological parameters, genetic vulnerability, and neurological processes. Miles and Carey (1997) conducted a review of the literature on data from 24 genetically informative studies. They found genes and family environment attributed to differences in aggression. The genetic effect was particularly strong and may have accounted for approximately 50% of the differences. While biological factors may not be able to be changed in a child, it is important for practitioners, family members, friends, and the like to understand this process in order to assist in the implementation of effective interventions (Bloomquist & Schnell, 2002).

Cognitive risk factors

Several cognitive features have been shown to be related to the development of aggression and violent behavior in youth. In a literature review conducted by Loeber and Hay (1997), low intelligence, attention problems, and an inflated self-esteem are among the cognitive factors associated with aggression and violence.

Executive cognitive functioning is a cognitive factor that refers to the cognitive processes an individual uses to control their behavioral and emotional responses, restrains inappropriate responses, and maintains attention and effort (Bloomquist & Schnell, 2002). Children displaying aggression often have low scores on neuropsychological tests that measure executive cognitive functioning (Giancola, Martin, Tarter, Pelham, & Moss, 1996; Giancola, Moss, Martin, Kirisci, & Tarter, 1996; Oosterlaan & Sergeant, 1996; Seguin, Pihl, Harden, Tremblay, & Boulerice, 1995). Therefore, these children's ability to filter inappropriate responses and behave appropriately in situations is distorted. Violence prevention and treatment intervention programs should consider including cognitive habilitation in trainings such as abstract reasoning, judgment, attention, learning from experience, attention, and behavioral self-monitoring (Giancola, Martin et al., 1996).

Physiological risk factors

Physiological risk factors associated with aggression also contribute to the individual domain. Emotional health of the mother during the pregnancy, physical problems during pregnancy and delivery, and birth complications (only found in females) are associated with behavioral problems in childhood and adolescence (Allen, Lewinsohn, & Seeley, 1998). Physiological under-activity has been observed in some youth with aggression. For example, low cortisol levels were found to be associated with early onset and persistence of aggression in school-aged boys (McBurnett, Lahey, Rathouz, & Loeber, 2000; Moss, Vanyukov, & Martin, 1995). The level of cortisol may not be the only predictor of violence as one study found the hypothalamic-pituitary-adrenal axis response to stress may also predict disruptive behavior (van Goozen, Matthys, Cohen-Kettenis, Buitelaar, & van Engeland, 2000). In a longitudinal study, Clarke, Murphy, and Constantino (1999) found a modest relationship between low cerebrospinal fluid concentrations of serotonin metabolite 5-hydroxyindoleacetic acid and high levels of acting-out behaviors in young children. Adolescents who had early exposure to androgen self-reported increases in aggression (Berenbaum & Resnick, 1997). Finally, the results on the effect of testosterone on aggression have been mixed (Brooks & Reddon, 1996; Gerra et al., 1998; Olweus, Mattsson, Schalling, & Low, 1988; Tremblay, 1998).

It is important to note that research on youth violence has focused primarily on males (Rappaport & Thomas, 2004). The focus on males is likely due to the higher probability of male adolescents engaging in violence when compared to female adolescents (Ellickson & K. A. McGuigan, 2000). Researchers have shown that aggression may be expressed differently in boys and girls (Crick, 1997; Crick & Grotpeter, 1995). Overt aggression refers to physical and verbal behaviors and is the focus of most literature on aggression and violence (Rappaport & Thomas, 2004). Males have shown to have higher levels of overt aggression and females have been shown to have higher levels of relational aggression (Crick, 1997; Crick & Grotpeter, 1995). Relational aggression refers to an individual manipulating others to obtain control and it is motivated by the intent to be mean and harm another (Rappaport &

Thomas, 2004). Therefore, while many studies focus on males because of the belief that more aggression and violence occurs in this population, it may be that more overt aggression is occurring in this population. The mental harm and anguish that can be caused through manipulation and other forms of relational aggression may be overlooked in the literature. In the past 10 years more empirical studies have been published on aggression in females; however, more in depth work is needed to fully understand the differences in risk and protective factors of aggression and violence in males and females (Rappaport & Thomas, 2004).

Individual Protective Factors

As previously mentioned, biological factors cannot be changed. However, environmental factors have been found to protect against aggression in childhood. While various subsets of environmental protective factors will be discussed in later sections, it is important to highlight a protective factor that specifically relates to characteristics of the child. In a study of children with behavioral problems, researchers found concern for others as a protective factor for the development of aggression and other behavior problems. They concluded that fostering children's concern for others may be a method for improving the developmental trajectory of children with behavioral problems (Hastings, Zahn-Waxler, Robinson, Usher, & Bridges, 2000).

PEER DOMAIN

Given the amount of time children and adolescents spend with their peer groups, it is important to understand the effects these groups can have on children or adolescents. Increasing knowledge about the effects one's peers can have will not only help in the creation of interventions but can also assist parents and teachers assess warning signs of the potential development of aggressive or violent behavior due to their child's/student's association with deviant peers. Research suggests that peer status may differ based on the type of aggression displayed. Poulin and Boivin (1999) found that boys with proactive aggressive behavior (i.e. goal-directed aggression intended to dominate and harm) reported higher satisfaction and quality friendships at the beginning of the school year but their levels of conflict increased over the year. Boys with reactive aggressive behaviors (i.e. aggression that is responding to a perceived provocation or threat) reported more conflict and lower levels of satisfaction at the beginning of the school year that decreased over the year. Proactive aggression has also been found to predict delinquency and conduct problems in mid-adolescence (Vitaro, Gendreau, Tremblay, & Oligny, 1998). As shown in Table 1, numerous peer factors influence youth aggression. This section reviews the influence of deviant peer groups, gang membership, social isolation and rejection on youths' aggressive and violent behavior

Peer Risk Factors

Deviant peer group risk factors

A variety of peer factors may place a child at risk of developing violent and aggressive behavior, including having anti-social peer group or experiencing a high degree of social isolation (Verlinden, Hersen, & Thomas, 2000). Involvement with delinquent peers has shown to be the strongest risk factor of serious violent behavior. It is in these friendships that violence is taught, rewarded, encouraged, reinforced and modeled (Elliott, 1994). During adolescence, the influence of deviant peer behavior on the development of aggressive behavior is most prominent (Rappaport & Thomas, 2004). Research has shown that problematic peer interactions in early adolescence are associated with deviant peer involvement in adolescence for boys and girls (Fergusson, Woodward, & Horwood, 1999).

Various factors may play a role in a child or adolescent choosing to befriend delinquent peers, including aggressive behavior patterns, weak internal and family controls, and exposure to violence (Elliott, 1994). There is an important distinction in the association between peers. While children befriending more aggressive peers result in externalizing behavior problems, children who report being liked by aggressive peers did not necessarily lead to engaging in externalizing or problem behaviors (Mrug, Hoza, & Bukowski, 2004). Therefore, simply being liked by deviant peers does not necessarily mean a child will befriend this peer group and in turn adopt the aggressive and violent behaviors.

Gangs are one subtype of deviant peer groups. Association with delinquent peers and gang membership has been found to contribute to adolescent's delinquency (Herrenkohl et al., 2000). Gangs can be found in all 50 states and in both suburban and inner city areas. While male gang members outnumber female gang members 15 to 1, the gap is narrowing slowly. Only a small percentage of youth become members of delinquent gangs and few gang members engage in violence. However, when looking at the cases of murder and assault committed by youth, in 3 out of 4 cases the perpetrator is likely to be a gang member (American Psychological Association, 2003). Gang members have also reported a higher frequency of fighting (Wright & Fitzpatrick, 2006) and other violent crimes (Battin, Hill, Abbott, & Catalano, 1998).

Gatti and colleagues (2005) found that youths' decision to join a gang was largely based upon the gang experience itself rather than simply engaging in delinquent acts. In a review of the literature by Howell (1998), social, economic, and cultural forces were found to impact an adolescent's decision to join a gang. An adolescent may join a gang to gain social relationships, enhance their status or prestige among peers or to experience excitement through selling drugs and making money. Gang membership may also protect an individual from another gang. Some youth may have virtually no choice and join a gang because of family or neighborhood traditions.

Gang membership is often associated with multiple risk factors for aggressive and violent behaviors among adolescents. In a longitudinal study, Gatti, Tremblay, Vitaro, and McDuff (2005) observed the differences between gang participation and the frequency of delinquent behaviors, including violent and aggressive acts such as beating up someone and using a weapon during a fight. Adolescents involved in a gang engaged in delinquent behavior four times as often as those not involved in a gang. When observing specific crimes between groups, those involved in gang-committed crimes also sold drugs more than four times as often and used drugs twice as often (Gatti et al., 2005). In another study, current and former gang members were compared to non-gang members and found to have higher levels of involvement in aggressive behaviors (e.g. delinquent behaviors, drug use, and perpetration of crimes), higher exposure to violence, higher distress symptoms (e.g. despondency about the future, intrusive thoughts, sense of lack of belongingness), and lower levels of resilience (e.g. social problem-solving skills, family involvement) (Li et al., 2002).

Social isolation risk factors

Some children and adolescents have difficulty forming peer relationships and, after being rejected by their peers, become socially isolated. In one study, French (1988) found approximately half of peer-rejected adolescent boys exhibited aggressive behavior and many were also characterized by their peers as being socially withdrawn. It appears that the peer-rejected boys would have more difficulty associating with peers in the future, even into adulthood and would have less satisfactory adjustment that their nonaggressive rejected counterparts. Aggressive-rejected boys were found to be more argumentative, disruptive, physically aggressive, inattentive, imperceptive, and less prosocial when compared to their nonproblematic classmates (Bierman, Smoot, & Aumiller, 1993).

Aggression and peer-rejection can have significant impacts as children progress developmentally into adolescence. For boys, peer rejection and aggression are strong antecedants of more serious delinquency during the adolescent years. In girls, aggression results in more serious delinquency while peer rejection often leads to engaging in minor assaults during adolescent years (Miller-Johnson, Coie, Maumary-Gremaud, Lochman, & Terry, 1999). Prevention efforts should be made to identify children with social deficits and aggressive tendencies early in their development.

Other research contradicts these findings, however. For example, Farver (1996) found that school-age children and adolescents with aggressive behavior were not rejected by their peers. These children may be choosing to form social cliques and reciprocated friendships with other aggressive children and adolescents. Another study found that aggressive children preferred to be friends with prosocial children who were not aggressive. However, aggressive children were often rejected by their nonaggressive peers and by default the children befriended more aggressive peers (Hektner, August, & Realmuto, 2000).

Peer Protective Factors

Very little research has been conducted to assess protective factors related to violence and aggression in the peer domain. However, with the recognition that the impact of peer relationships on individual's aggression is profound, more researchers have become interested in uncovering the factors that can protect youth from developing violent behavior. Bollmer, Milich, Harris, and Maras (2005) studied the friendship quality of children 10 to 13 years of age. They found that children with lower scores of externalizing behavior were less likely to bully their peers when compared to the children with higher scores. Additionally, the quality of friendships had an effect on the likelihood of a child bullying. Children with higher quality friendships were less likely to bully their peers than those children who had lower quality friendships. Thus, investment in prosocial relationship can protect children from engaging in aggressive behaviors.

Studies have shown that association with prosocial peers and having adaptive social interaction skills serve as protective factors against aggression and conduct problems (Bloomquist & Schnell, 2002). Having friends who engage in conventional behavior has also been shown as a protective factor (Department of Health and Human Services, 2001). Professionals working with youth at risk of becoming violent should make efforts to assist children establishing healthy social skills and creating meaningful, healthy relationships.

SCHOOL DOMAIN

Very few school factors have been recognized as associated with higher levels of aggression and violence. This may be surprising to some since education is such a key component of the development for youth. While the literature in this area is lacking, it is still crucial to understand how the school environment impacts youth's aggressive and violent behavior. A complete list of school factors is available in Table 1.

School Risk Factors

Multiple reviews of the literature have found that academic failure has consistently been shown to predict delinquent behavior in later life (Herrenkohl et al., 2000; Verlinden et al., 2000). In addition, results from a longitudinal self-report survey of 4300 high school seniors and dropouts found that pro-drug middle school environments (i.e. those with high levels of cigarette and marijuana use), poor grades, weak elementary school bonds, and early deviant behavior predicted violent behavior later in life (Ellickson & Kimberly A. McGuigan, 2000).

School Protective Factors

In a study of 1319 adolescents 11 to 16 years of age, the classroom environment was the strongest protective factors for adolescent aggression in boys. It also impacted girls' aggressive behavior, but not as strongly (Lopez, Perez, Ochoa, & Ruiz, 2008). When looking at the aspects of the classroom environment, the teacher can make the greatest impact on a student. Hughes, Cavell, and Jackson (1999) studied 61 second and third grade students whose teachers rated them as aggressive. Results showed that students who had a positive relationship with their teacher were rated by their teachers as less aggressive the following year. In addition, students who had a positive relationship with their teacher in years one and two predicted less peer-rated aggression in year three. While it is obvious that the student's relationship to the classroom and teacher are critical, the relationship with their school is also important. In a review of the literature, Verlinden et al. (2000) found that a strong bond/commitment to school is an important protective factor against violence. More research is necessary to develop strategies to increasing student's commitment to their school.

COMMUNITY DOMAIN

The community in which children and adolescents live substantially impacts their development. Some neighborhoods expose youth to violence, fostering disruptive cognition favorable to aggressive behaviors. Youth exposed to illegal markets, gangs, drug trafficking and other violent activities often model problematic norms and are rewarded for such activities. Unfortunately, these are often disadvantaged neighborhoods that increase the likelihood of a variety of other risk factors for violence and aggression. For example, disadvantaged neighborhoods typically have an increase in rates of adolescent pregnancy, dropout, substance abuse, school violence, unemployment, single parent families, and ineffective parenting (Elliott, 1994). This section will explore risk and protective factors in the community domain including the impact of exposure to violence, neighborhood quality, and economics.

Community Risk Factors

Exposure to violence has been widely reported as having various negative effects on children, including increased levels of traumatic stress, depression, anxiety, bullying by peers, social rejection, aggression and lowered their self-esteem (Fitzpatrick, 1997; Gorman–Smith & Tolan, 1998; Lynch & Cicchetti, 1998; Schwartz & Proctor, 2000). Halliday-Boykins and Gram (2001) interviewed incarcerated adolescent males and found that those exposed to higher levels of community violence engaged in higher levels of violent behavior. In addition, reflecting overlap with the peer domain, these adolescents associated with more deviant peers. Fitzpatrick (1997) studied low-income African-American youth and found that when compared to nonaggressive peers, those who were aggressive were not only more often witnesses, but were also frequently victims of violence. Often children exposed to such violence, may develop stress; moreover, the stress associated with neighborhood violence has been found to be another predictor of aggression among urban children (Guerra, Huesmann, Tolan, Van Acker, & Eron, 1995).

Serving as a predictor of violence in youth, communities can also expose children and adolescents to additional negative activities, such as drugs use and crime (Herrenkohl et al., 2000). All of these negative community factors (e.g. violence, drugs, and crime) impact the quality of a neighborhood. Low quality neighborhoods are associated with an increase in problematic and acting out behaviors in youth (Greenberg, Lengua, Coie, & Pinderhughes, 1999). The quality of the neighborhood may not just refer to a neighborhood's negative factors, but may also be a reflection of what is lacking. For example, disorganized communities often have a greater level of youth violence (Herrenkohl et al., 2000). It is not surprising that in such communities, members will have low attachment to their neighborhood. Young people who have difficulty bonding to their community is an additional risk factor for aggressive and violent behavior (Herrenkohl et al., 2000).

Financial factors in disadvantaged neighborhoods have been shown to place youth at risk of displaying violent behavior (Halliday-Boykins & Graham, 2001). In fact, teacher reports and peer nominations suggest that low income inner-city elementary school children have higher levels of aggressive behavior when compared to children in less disadvantaged samples. Aggression in these children may be fostered from school environments, especially for boys, as their aggression increased during the beginning of their school career (Guerra et al., 1995). Studies have also found that residing in underclass (Peeples & Loeber, 1994) and socioeconomic disadvantage (Dodge, Pettit, & Bates, 1994) communities are predictors of delinquency and youth aggressive behaviors. Overall, these studies demonstrate the powerful impact of economics. One study found persistent economic hardship predicted externalizing behavior problems in youth (Bolger, Patterson, Thompson, & Kupersmidt, 1995). While the economic state of a community may be difficult to reverse, strategies must be found that can protect children and adolescents from aggressive and violent behavior.

Community Protective Factors

As is evident from the above discussion, communities have a strong influence on the development of aggressive and violent behavior. When communities are disadvantaged and disorganized, these factors can increase the likelihood of violence. However, factors can protect a child from becoming violent and aggressive. Living in an organized, safe community with opportunities for positive activities and access to effective community services (e.g. mental health, social, etc.) are all protective factors (Bloomquist & Schnell, 2002).

Additionally, one study of 1,271 children grades second through fifth, found that residing in a middle-socioeconomic status neighborhood was a protective factor of aggressive behavior. Specifically, it was found to be a protective factor among African American children from low-income, single-parent households. These results suggest that communities with resources can protect children who are exposed to various risk factors from developing aggressive behavior (Kupersmidt, Griesler, DeRosier, Patterson, & Davis, 1995).

FAMILY DOMAIN

The impact of the family environment is a highly influential factor in the initiation of aggression (Miles & Carey, 1997) and is one of the most widely studied (Bloomquist & Schnell, 2002). As shown in Table 1, there are a variety of risk and protective factors. This section will focus on the characteristics of family members, parental monitoring/supervision, parenting discipline styles and family interactions as they relate to aggressive and violent behaviors of adolescents.

Family Risk Factors

Various characteristics of one's family can place a child at risk of developing aggressive and violent behaviors such as parental occupation (Greenberg et al., 1999), maternal depression (Greenberg et al., 1999; Webster-Stratton & Hammond, 1988) and fathers who abuse substances (Moss, Mezzich, Yao, Gavaler, & Martin, 1995). Family instability may also place a child at risk. Family instability is defined by the number of moves a family makes, recent negative life events, the number of persons moving in and out of a home, the number of relationships the primary caretaker has been involved in, and other factors related to the stability of the home environment (Ackerman, Kogos, Youngstrom, Schoff, & Izard, 1999; Bloomquist & Schnell, 2002).

Residing in a single parent household is another family characteristic that has been shown to increase a child's risk of developing aggressive behaviors. In a study of fourth grade elementary school students, children of single-mother families displayed more aggressive behavior than families with a father or male partner in the household (Vaden-Kiernan, Ialongo, Pearson, & Kellam, 1995). However, in another study of urban, public school boys, single-parent status and poverty/welfare were not related to aggressive behavior (Peeples & Loeber, 1994). Single motherhood has been hypothesized to place the parent at a disadvantage for providing adequate parenting when compared to dual parent households (Bloomquist & Schnell, 2002). It is likely much more difficult to properly supervise children when there is only one adult in charge of supervising.

Parental supervision, commonly referred to in the literature as parental monitoring, has been found as one of the strongest factors associated with delinquency and aggressive behavior (Peeples & Loeber, 1994). Parental monitoring is defined as a parent's involvement in their child's life, knowledge of their child's whereabouts and with whom their child is spending time, and level of discipline provided (Dishion & McMahon, 1998). DiClemente and colleagues (2001) found that youth who had parents providing poor monitoring were more likely to engage in sexually risky behavior, substance use, and participate in fights.

Parents' monitoring of their children is also related to their parenting style. Parenting styles have been shown to be associated with aggression and other conduct problems (Stormshak, Bierman, McMahon, & Lengua, 2000). Parental discipline is a large component of parenting styles and has been found to predict conduct problems (Kilgore, Snyder, & Lentz, 2000). Harsh physical discipline is a risk factor for future externalizing behavior problems. However, one study has found that warm parent-child relationships may buffer this effect (Deater-Deckard & Dodge, 1997). Spanking has also been linked to childhood aggression (Bloomquist & Schnell, 2002; Stormshak et al., 2000).

In addition to the way in which a parent disciplines their child, the way a parent interacts with their child can have a strong impact on their development. Coercive parent-child interactions are present in families of children with aggression (Dumas, LaFreniere, & Serketich, 1995). Coercive interactions are defined by reciprocal negative child and parent behaviors. Parental negative behaviors include negative verbalizations directed at the child, harsh and inconsistent discipline, little warmth/nourishment, and poor parental monitoring. In these situations, a child often responds aggressively or is noncompliant. A central feature of these interactions is that when the parent and child have a confrontation, the other withdraws and gives in to the aggression (Bloomquist & Schnell, 2002).

One of the most extreme forms of coercive parent-child interactions is physical abuse which studies have found to be associated with aggressive and violent behaviors (Bloomquist & Schnell, 2002). Abuse, neglect and maltreatment have all been shown to increase a child's risk of conduct problems (Lynch & Cicchetti, 1998; Shields & Cicchetti, 1998; Widom, 1989). Family violence and marital aggression are also predictors of conduct problems in children (Bloomquist & Schnell, 2002; Jouriles, Murphy, & O'Leary, 1989).

Other, less severe, family interactions may also predict conduct problems such as aggression and violence in youth. Family stress and conflict has been found to be associated with the propensity for violent behavior (Paschall & Hubbard, 1998). For example, marital arguments have been related to conduct problems in children, especially for low SES families (Jouriles, Bourg, & Farris, 1991). In addition, marital disagreements about childrearing have been found to be related to externalizing behavioral problems in children (Mahoney, Jouriles, & Scavone, 1997). Aside from the interactions observed by the child, their interactions with siblings may also place them at risk. In a study of low income families, sibling conflict was related to the development of conduct problems and aggressive behavior in boys (Garcia, Shaw, Winslow, & Yaggi, 2000).

Family Protective Factors

While there are a large amount of familial risk factors, there are ways in which a child can be protected against developing aggressive and violent behavior. Some of the protective factors are characterized as a lack of a risk factor. For example, as mentioned above, single-parent households have been shown to be a risk factor for aggression in children whereas residing in a household where a mother and father or mother and male partner are present is a suggested protective factor (Vaden-Kiernan et al., 1995). In addition, while the above section discussed the detriments to having negative interactions with family members, adaptive parent child interactions can protect a child from developing aggressive behaviors (Bloomquist & Schnell, 2002).

Having an overall positive family environment may also be a protective factor. One study of 1319 adolescents 11 to 16 years of age found that a positive family environment consisting of expressiveness, cohesion, and low levels of conflict was the strongest protective factor for adolescent aggression in girls. It also played an important role in boys aggressive behavior but was not as strong (Lopez et al., 2008).

Protective factors can start as early as infancy. Infant-mother attachment is another protective factor against the development of aggressive behaviors, particularly in the classroom (Dallaire & Weinraub, 2007). Attachment refers to the quality of the relationship between a parent and child from the standpoint of the child. Attachment relates to how available and responsive a parent is to the child's needs (Bloomquist & Schnell, 2002). While protective factors can be present as early as infancy, parents who have a child displaying aggressive and violent behaviors can utilize various forms of treatments to combat these behaviors.

FAMILIES AND AGGRESSIVE YOUTH

Some have argued that families are key in youth developing emotional and behavioral problems (Paradise et al., 2001). The relationship between vulnerability, risk and resiliency becomes cemented early in life through a series of interactions between parent and child. Poor family management, lack of positive parenting skills, and dysfunctional caregiving have been strongly related to delinquency and aggressive behaviors among youth (Formoso, Gonzales, & Aiken, 2000). Conversely, family support and positive relationships predict positive adjustment in childhood and adolescence; indirect evidence suggests that family support is a protective factor for adolescent conduct problems (Cauce, Reid, Landesman, & Gonzales, 1990; Wills, Vaccaro, & McNamara, 1992).

Given the family's fundamental influence on a child's life, research has consistently suggested the benefits for including families in treatment of high-risk youth. Recent reviews of services for families with youths coping with a wide variety of problems have strongly urged inclusion of families in all service options (Burns & Weisz, 2000). Prevention efforts with delinquent youth suggest that the single most effective form of prevention involves working with the total family system (Kumpfer, Alexander, McDonald, & Olds, 1998). Identification of situations where families may be engaged in services is a potentially beneficial method for addressing aggression and violent behaviors experienced by youth.

Family-Based Treatment Options

Many studies have demonstrated that parenting and family interventions are critical to reducing family risk factors associated with problematic youth behaviors (Catalano, Gainey, Fleming, Haggerty, & Johnson, 1999; Spoth, Goldberg, & Redmond, 1999). Family-based therapies developed from two foundational therapies originated in the early 1970s: (1) Structural Family Therapy developed by Salvador Minuchin, and (2) Strategic Family Therapy, developed by Jay Haley. These therapeutic modalities are built on the assumptions that 1) families are rule-governed systems that can best be understood in context; 2) the presenting problem serves a function within the family; and 3) the concepts of boundaries, coalitions, hierarchy, power, metaphor, family life cycle development and triangles are basic to the development of a "stuck" family (Irvine, Biglan, Smolkowski, Metzler, & Ary, 1999). These therapeutic models are the core theories from which later models developed.

Empirical research has evaluated various treatment modalities targeting adolescents who engage in high-risk behaviors and juvenile delinquency. Many of these studies implement and evaluate structured and manualized family interventions developed during the past two decades. Included among these empirically supported treatments are multisystemic therapy (MST), brief strategic family therapy (BSFT), multi-dimensional family therapy (MDFT), and solution-focused family therapy (SBFT).

MULTISYSTEMIC THERAPY

Multisystemic therapy (MST) treatment views individuals in terms of the complex systems in which they are embedded. Individuals restructure their environments while simultaneously being influenced by them. Behavior is best understood when viewed within broader contexts, such as school, family, peers, neighborhood, services, and community institutions (Henggeler, Schoenwald, Borduin, Rowland, & Cunningham, 1998). MST has been extensively evaluated and suggests that antisocial behavior in youth is determined by a variety of correlates. These factors, along with other antisocial behaviors, such as conduct disorder, are relevant for treating issues of aggression and violent behaviors (Hawkins, Catalano & Miller, 1992).

Growing evidence supports the effectiveness of MST for aggressive adolescents. Researchers conducted a meta-analysis of family-based treatments for youths' drug use and found that MST was the most effective of those reviewed (Stanton & Shadish, 1997). An early MST outcome study (Henggeler, 1986) used a quasi-experimental design to study youth and their families in a delinquency diversion program. Findings showed the MST was more effective than usual community services in terms of client behaviors and family relationships. Subsequently, MST has been substantiated as an evidenced-based treatment for adolescents and their families in randomized clinical trials. It has been effective in reducing out-of-home placements, aggressive behavior, substance use, and psychiatric disorders (Sheidow & Woodford, 2003).

The effects of MST on aggression have been examined in trials using juvenile offenders as participants (Borduin, Cavell, & Malcolm, 2007; Henggeler, Melton, Smith, & Schoenwald, 1993). In these studies, MST significantly reduced self-reported drug use, criminal activity, violence, incarceration, recidivism, aggression with peers, family cohesion and drug-related and other arrests. In addition, others found school attendance increased and maintained successful outcomes at 6-month follow-up (Henggeler, Pickrel, Brondino, & Crouch, 1996) and the cost of MST was mitigated by the reduced incarceration costs (Schoenwald, Henggeler, Brondino, & Rowland, 2000).

Brief strategic family therapy

Brief Strategic Family Therapy (BSFT) was developed through the integration of theory, research, and practice of structural and strategic methods (Szapocznik & Williams, 2000). BSFT is especially appropriate for treatment of substance use that co-occurs with other behavior problems, including conduct disorders, oppositional behavior, delinquency, associating with antisocial peers, aggressive and violent behavior, and risky sexual behavior (Perrino, Coatsworth, Briones, Pantin, & Szapocznik, 2001). Three basic principles typify BSFT: (1) the family is viewed as a system that suggests that family members are interdependent and that individual behaviors affect others in the family; (2) structure or patterns of interactions among family members are habitual, repeat over time and contribute to behavior problems, such as aggressive behaviors; and (3) strategies for intervention relates to the notion that intervention must be practical, deliberate and linked directly to problem behaviors (Szapocznik & Williams, 2000).

BSFT is incorporated into the youth's daily family life and is manualized. BSFT is a flexible approach that appeals to cultures that emphasize family and interpersonal relationships. BSFT has been well-established in the treatment of adolescents with problems ranging from substance use to aggressive and violent behaviors, associations with antisocial peers, and impaired family functioning.

In clinical trials, BSFT was effective in reducing emotional and behavior problems and showed continued significant improvement of family functioning at the one-year follow-up (Szapocznik et al., 1989). Other studies have shown BSFT effective in reducing behavior problems among 12-18 year old Hispanic adolescents and their families. Adolescents receiving BSFT showed significantly decreased levels of conduct disorder and socialized aggression from pre- to post- treatment, while the control condition showed no change. Another recent study compared BSFT to a group treatment control (Coatsworth, Santisteban, McBride, & Szapocznik, 2001) and youth in BSFT families showed significant improvement in conduct problems and aggressive behaviors, as well as marijuana use and family functioning.

MULTIDIMENSIONAL FAMILY THERAPY (MDFT)

Multidimensional Family Therapy (MDFT) focuses on changing systemic influences that establish and maintain problem behaviors in adolescents. MDFT was first introduced as a weekly, clinic-based intervention (Liddle & Hogue, 2000). A newer version provides a home-based, intensive treatment that incorporates alterations for highly delinquent and aggressive youth. MDFT is based on the integration of existing therapeutic work in areas such as case management, school interventions, drug counseling methods, use of multimedia, and HIV/AIDS prevention (Rowe, Liddle, McClintic, Quille, & Kaslow, 2002).

MDFT is manualized and treatment includes sessions with various combinations of family members. Phone contacts between family members and therapists are frequent and provide opportunities for "mini-sessions." Intervention occurs within five domains: interventions with the adolescent, parent, parent-adolescent relationship, other family members, and systems external to the family. Treatment incorporates a collaborative, individualized approach that requires a high degree of engagement by families. Strategies for engagement is employed to capture the interest of the family and assess risk and protective factors within the specific ecological context of the family in order to create a working agenda for addressing youth aggressive behaviors (Liddle & Hogue, 2000).

MDFT has been empirically supported as a therapy for substance abusing and delinquent teens. Its efficacy has been supported by studies comparing MDFT with alternate therapies in controlled trials. A prevention study with Multidimensional Family Prevention (MDFP) showed greater gains when compared to controls on mediators of substance use and other high-risk behaviors (Liddle & Hogue, 2000). Domains studied included self-competence, family functioning, school involvement, and peer associations. Preliminary evidence of short-term efficacy indicated strengthened family cohesion, school bonding, and reduced peer delinquency compared to controls (Hogue, Liddle, Singer, & Leckrone, 2005).

Solution focused family therapy

Service providers and youth report brief, strengths-based practices delivered in the youths' environments can be effective, even more than "problem-oriented" approaches (Baer, Peterson, & Wells, 2004; Cauce et al., 2000; Kidd, 2003). Aggressive youth respond best to client-centered services that are flexible and encourage them to continually strive to attain goals despite relapses and setbacks (Cauce et al., 1994). Strengths-based approaches focus on the strengths already possessed by the client and those found within their environment. Solution- focused family therapy (SFFT) is a strengths-based model that utilizes a cognitive-behavioral approach to help clients imagine what could be different and what would be required to make changes occur. One study of adolescent offenders in juvenile justice custody demonstrated increased levels of optimism for the future, greater ability to feel empathy, and decreased levels of substance abuse following solution-focused treatment (Gingerich & Eisengart, 2000).

The SFFT approach views the client as the expert on his/her life, and aims to increase client autonomy (Selekman, 1997). Empowerment is emphasized through identifying and amplifying client strengths and resources as tools to use in the reduction of the problem (Green, 2004). Springer (2001) notes the solution-focused techniques are especially useful during the assessment phase to establish rapport and build therapeutic alliance. SFFT's emphasis on strengths and solutions assists in building the expectation that not only is change possible, but likely. Change using the SFFT model is typically achieved in incremental steps, with a basic assumption that small changes elicit larger changes (Selekman, 2005).

SFFT, with its emphasis on the strengths, resiliency, and instilling hope, can facilitate building rapport with youth who are engaged in aggressive behaviors to increase their sense of self-efficacy by assisting them to identify strengths and resources (Springer, 2001). Helping the youth explore solutions and mobilize resources and strengths to attain desired goals increases their sense of control over their lives, a common difficulty among traumatized young people (Ouimette, Brown, & Najavits, 1998). Utilizing a strengths-based approach could assist aggressive youth to look toward the future with the belief that they have the power to effect positive change in their lives, overcome the challenges associated with abuse, and find alternative behaviors that are pro-social and positively oriented.

CONCLUSIONS

This review of the literature provides evidence for the effectiveness of various family-based interventions in reducing youth aggressive behaviors. Although the findings are somewhat inconclusive concerning the lasting effects, the evidence suggests that the short-term effectiveness of these interventions appear comparable to the effectiveness of individually-based interventions. Professionals assessing youth's risk for aggressive and violent behavior is a necessary step in the effective implementation of evidence-based treatments aimed to reduce juvenile justice involvement. By understanding the level of risk and resiliency, therapists can implement family-based treatments uniquely targeted to the family system and not simply the problem or "identified child." Involving multiple systems in the change process allows potential shifts in risk and protective factors, improving the chances of decreased aggressive and violent behaviors among youth.

REFERENCES

Ackerman, B. P., Kogos, J., Youngstrom, E., Schoff, K. & Izard, C. (1999). Family instability and the problem behaviors of children from economically disadvantaged families. *Developmental Psychology, 35(1)*, 258.

Allen, N. B., Lewinsohn, P. M. & Seeley, J. R. (1998). Prenatal and perinatal influences on risk for psychopathology in childhood and adolescence. *Development and Psychopathology, 10(03)*, 513-529.

American Psychological Association. (2003). *Is Youth Violence Just Another Fact of Life?* Washington, District of Columbia, US: American Psychological Association, Public Interest Directorate.

Baer, J. S., Peterson, P. L. & Wells, E. A. (2004). Rationale and design of a brief substance use intervention for homeless adolescents. *Addiction Research and Theory, 12(4)*, 317-334.

Battin, S. R., Hill, K. G., Abbott, R. D. & Catalano, R. F. (1998). The contribution of gang membership to delinquency beyond delinquent friends. *Criminology, 36(1)*, 93-115.

Berenbaum, S. A. & Resnick, S. M. (1997). Early androgen effects on aggression in children and adults with congenital adrenal hyperplasia. *Psychoneuroendocrinology, 22(7)*, 505-515.

Bierman, K. L., Smoot, D. L. & Aumiller, K. (1993). Characteristics of aggressive-rejected, aggressive (nonrejected), and rejected (nonaggressive) boys. *Child development*, 139-151.

Bloomquist, M. L. & Schnell, S. V. (2002). *Helping children with aggression and conduct problems: Best practices for intervention.*

Bolger, K. E., Patterson, C. J., Thompson, W. W. & Kupersmidt, J. B. (1995). Psychosocial adjustment among children experiencing persistent and intermittent family economic hardship. *Child development*, 1107-1129.

Bollmer, J. M., Milich, R., Harris, M. J. & Maras, M. A. (2005). A friend in need: the role of friendship quality as a protective factor in peer victimization and bullying. *Journal of interpersonal violence, 20(6)*, 701.

Borduin, C. M., Cavell, T. A. & Malcolm, K. T. (2007). Multisystemic treatment of violent youth and their families. In *Anger, aggression and interventions for interpersonal violence.* (239-265). Mahwah, NJ US: Lawrence Erlbaum Associates Publishers.

Brooks, J. H. & Reddon, J. R. (1996). Serum testosterone in violent and nonviolent young offenders. *Journal of clinical psychology, 52(4)*, 475-483.

Catalano, R. F., Gainey, R. R., Fleming, C. B., Haggerty, K. P. & Johnson, N. O. (1999). An experimental intervention with families of substance abusers: One-year follow-up of the focus on families project. [Article]. *Addiction, 94(2)*, 241-255.

Cauce, A. M., Morgan, C. J., Wagner, J., Moore, E., Sy, J., Wurzbacher, K., et al. (1994). Effectiveness of intensive case managment for homeless adolescents: Results of a 3-month follow-up. *Journal of Emotional & Behavioral Disorders, 2(4)*, 219-227.

Cauce, A. M., Paradise, M., Ginzler, J. A., Embry, L., Morgan, C. J., Lohr, Y., et al. (2000). The characteristics and mental health of homeless adolescents: Age and gender differences. *Journal of Emotional and Behavioral Disorders, 8(4)*, 230-239.

Cauce, A. M., Reid, M., Landesman, S. & Gonzales, N. A. (1990). Social support in young children: Measurement, structure, and behavioral impact. In B. R. Sarason, I. G. Sarason, & G. R. Pierce (Eds.), *Social support: An interactional view* (64-94). New York: Wiley.

Clarke, R. A., Murphy, D. L. & Constantino, J. N. (1999). Serotonin and externalizing behavior in young children. *Psychiatry research, 86(1)*, 29-40.

Coatsworth, J. D., Santisteban, D. A., McBride, C. K. & Szapocznik, J. (2001). Brief strategic family therapy versus community control: Engagement, retention, and an exploration of the moderating role of adolescent symptom severity. [Article]. *Family Process, 40(3)*, 313-327.

Crick, N. R. (1997). Engagement in gender normative versus nonnormative forms of aggression: Links to social-psychological adjustment. *Developmental Psychology, 33(4)*, 610-617.

Crick, N. R. & Grotpeter, J. K. (1995). Relational aggression, gender, and social-psychological adjustment. *Child Development*, 710-722.

Dallaire, D. H. & Weinraub, M. (2007). Infant–mother attachment security and children's anxiety and aggression at first grade. *Journal of Applied Developmental Psychology, 28*(5-6), 477-492.

Deater-Deckard, K. & Dodge, K. A. (1997). Externalizing behavior problems and discipline revisited: Nonlinear effects and variation by culture, context, and gender. *Psychological Inquiry, 8(3)*, 161-175.

Department of Health and Human Services (2001). Youth violence: A report of the Surgeon General. *Journal*. Retrieved from http://www.surgeongeneral.gov/library/youthviolence/report.html

DiClemente, R. J., Wingood, G. M., Crosby, R., Sionean, C., Cobb, B. K., Harrington, K., et al. (2001). Parental monitoring: association with adolescents' risk behaviors. *Pediatrics, 107(6)*, 1363-1368.

Dodge, K. A., Pettit, G. S. & Bates, J. E. (1994). Socialization mediators of the relation between socioeconomic status and child conduct problems. *Child development*, 649-665.

Dumas, J. E., LaFreniere, P. J. & Serketich, W. J. (1995). " Balance of power": a transactional analysis of control in mother-child dyads involving socially competent, aggressive, and anxious children. *Journal of Abnormal Psychology, 104(1)*, 104.

Ellickson, P. L. & McGuigan, K. A. (2000). Early predictors of adolescent violence. *American Journal of Public Health, 90(4)*, 566-572.

Ellickson, P. L. & McGuigan, K. A. (2000). Early predictors of adolescent violence. *90(4)*, 566-572.

Elliott, D. S. (1994). *Youth violence: An overview.* Paper presented at the The Aspen Institute's Children's Policy Forum "Children and Violence Conference", Queenstown, MD.

Farrington, D. P. (1998). Predictors, causes, and correlates of male youth violence. *Crime and justice*, 421-475.

Farver, J. A. M. (1996). Aggressive behavior in preschoolers' social networks: Do birds of a feather flock together? *Early Childhood Research Quarterly, 11(3)*, 333-350.

Fergusson, D. M., Woodward, L. J. & Horwood, L. J. (1999). Childhood peer relationship problems and young people's involvement with deviant peers in adolescence. *Journal of Abnormal Child Psychology, 27(5)*, 357-369.

Fitzpatrick, K. M. (1997). Aggression and environmental risk among low-income African-American youth. *The Journal of adolescent health: official publication of the Society for Adolescent Medicine, 21(3)*, 172.

Formoso, D., Gonzales, N. A. & Aiken, L. S. (2000). Family conflict and children's internalizing and externalizing behavior: Protective factors. *American Journal of Community Psychology, 28(2)*, 175-199.

French, D. C. (1988). Heterogeneity of peer-rejected boys: Aggressive and nonaggressive subtypes. *Child development*, 976-985.

Garcia, M. M., Shaw, D. S., Winslow, E. B. & Yaggi, K. E. (2000). Destructive sibling conflict and the development of conduct problems in young boys. *Developmental Psychology, 36(1)*, 44.

Gatti, U., Tremblay, R. E., Vitaro, F. & McDuff, P. (2005). Youth gangs, delinquency and drug use: A test of the selection, facilitation, and enhancement hypotheses. *Journal of Child Psychology and Psychiatry, 46(11)*, 1178-1190.

Gerra, G., Zaimovic, A., Giucastro, G., Folli, F., Maestri, D., Tessoni, A., et al. (1998). Neurotransmitter-hormonal responses to psychological stress in peripubertal subjects: relationship to aggressive behavior. *Life Sciences, 62(7)*, 617-625.

Giancola, P. R., Martin, C. S., Tarter, R. E., Pelham, W. E. & Moss, H. B. (1996). Executive cognitive functioning and aggressive behavior in preadolescent boys at high risk for substance abuse/dependence. *Journal of Studies on Alcohol, 57(4)*, 352-359.

Giancola, P. R., Moss, H. B., Martin, C. S., Kirisci, L. & Tarter, R. E. (1996). Executive cognitive functioning predicts reactive aggression in boys at high risk for substance abuse: A prospective study. *Alcoholism: Clinical and Experimental Research, 20(4)*, 740-744.

Gingerich, W. J. & Eisengart, S. (2000). Solution-Focused Brief Therapy: A Review of the Outcome Research. *Family Process, 39(4)*, 477-499.

Gorman–Smith, D. & Tolan, P. (1998). The role of exposure to community violence and developmental problems among inner-city youth. *Development and Psychopathology, 10(01)*, 101-116.

Graber, J. A., Nichols, T., Lynne, S. D., Brooks-Gunn, J. & Botvin, G. J. (2006). A Longitudinal Examination of Family, Friend, and Media Influences on Competent Versus Problem Behaviors Among Urban Minority Youth. *Applied Developmental Science, 10(2)*, 75-85.

Green, M. R. (2004). Interventions with traumatized adolescents. *Adolescent Psychiatry, 27*(special issue), 283-305.

Greenberg, M. T., Lengua, L. J., Coie, J. D. & Pinderhughes, E. E. (1999). Predicting developmental outcomes at school entry using a multiple-risk model: Four American communities. *Development and Psychopathology, 35(2)*, 403-417.

Guerra, N. G., Huesmann, L. R., Tolan, P. H., Van Acker, R. & Eron, L. D. (1995). Stressful events and individual belief as correlates of economic disadvantage and aggression among urban children: Prediction and prevnetion of child and adolescent antisocial behavior. *Journal of Consulting and Clinical Psychology, 63(4)*, 518-528.

Halliday-Boykins, C. A. & Graham, S. (2001). At both ends of the gun: Testing the relationship between community violence exposure and youth violent behavior. *Journal of Abnormal Child Psychology, 29(5)*, 383-402.

Hastings, P. D., Zahn-Waxler, C., Robinson, J., Usher, B. & Bridges, D. (2000). The development of concern for others in children with behavior problems. *Developmental Psychology, 36(5)*, 531-545.

Hawkins, J., Catalano, R. & Miller, J. (1992). Risk and protective factors for alcohol and other drug problems in adolescence and early adulthood: Implications for substance abuse prevention. *Psychological Bulletin, 112(1)*, 64-105.

Hawkins, J. D., Catalano, R. F. & Miller, J. Y. (1992). Risk and protective factors for alcohol and other drug problems in adolescence and early adulthood: Implications for substance abuse prevention. *Psychological Bulletin, 112(1)*, 64-105.

Hawkins, J. D., Herrenkohl, T. I., Farrington, D. P., Brewer, D., Catalano, R. F., Harachi, T. W., et al. (2000). *Predictors of Youth Violence*. Washington, District of Columbia, US:

US Department of Justice, Office of Justice Programs; Office of Juvenile Justice and Delinquency Prevention.

Hektner, J. M., August, G. J. & Realmuto, G. M. (2000). Patterns and temporal changes in peer affiliation among aggressive and nonaggressive children participating in a summer school program. *Journal of Clinical Child & Adolescent Psychology, 29(4)*, 603-614.

Henggeler, S., Pickrel, S., Brondino, M. & Crouch, J. (1996). Eliminating (almost) treatment dropout of substance abusing or dependent delinquents through home-based multisystemic therapy. *Am J Psychiatry, 153(3)*, 427-428.

Henggeler, S. W. (1986). Multisystemic treatment of juvenile offenders: effects on adolescent behavior and family interaction. *Developmental Psychology, 22(1)*, 132-142.

Henggeler, S. W., Melton, G. B., Smith, L. A. & Schoenwald, S. K. (1993). Family preservation using multisystemic treatment: Long-term follow-up to a clinical trial with serious juvenile offenders. *Journal of Child & Family Studies, 2(4)*, 283-293.

Henggeler, S. W., Schoenwald, S. K., Borduin, C. M., Rowland, M. & Cunningham, P. B. (1998). *Multisystemic treatment of antisocial behavior in child and adolescents*. New York: Guilford Press.

Herrenkohl, T. I., Maguin, E., Hill, K. G., Hawkins, J. D., Abbott, R. D. & Catalano, R. F. (2000). Developmental risk factors for youth violence. *The Journal of adolescent health: official publication of the Society for Adolescent Medicine, 26(3)*, 176.

Hogue, A., Liddle, H. A., Singer, A. & Leckrone, J. (2005). Intervention fidelity in family-based prevention counseling for adolescent problem behaviors. *Journal of Community Psychology, 33(2)*, 191-211.

Howell, J. C. (1998). Youth gangs: An overview. *Bulletin. Washington, DC: US Department of Justice, Office of Justice Programs, Office of Juvenile Justice and Delinquency Prevention*.

Howell, J. C. (2003). *Preventing & reducing juvenile delinquency: A comprehensive framework*. Thousand Oaks, CA: Sage.

Hughes, J. N., Cavell, T. A. & Jackson, T. (1999). Influence of the teacher-student relationship on childhood conduct problems: A prospective study. *Journal of Clinical Child & Adolescent Psychology, 28(2)*, 173-184.

Irvine, A. B., Biglan, A., Smolkowski, K., Metzler, C. W. & Ary, D. V. (1999). The effectiveness of a parenting skills program for parents of middle school students in small communities. *Journal of Consulting and Clinical Psychology, 67*, 811-825.

Jouriles, E. N., Bourg, W. J. & Farris, A. M. (1991). Marital adjustment and child conduct problems: A comparison of the correlation across subsamples. *Journal of Consulting and Clinical Psychology, 59(2)*, 354-357.

Jouriles, E. N., Murphy, C. M. & O'Leary, K. D. (1989). Interspousal aggression, marital discord, and child problems. *Journal of Consulting and Clinical Psychology, 57(3)*, 453-455.

Kidd, S. A. (2003). Street Youth: Coping and interventions. *Child & Adolescent Social Work Journal, 20(4)*, 235-261.

Kilgore, K., Snyder, J. & Lentz, C. (2000). The contribution of parental discipline, parental monitoring, and school risk to early-onset conduct problems in African American boys and girls. *Developmental Psychology, 36(6)*, 835-845.

Kirby, L. D. & Fraser, M. W. (1997). Risk and resilience in childhood: An ecological perspective In M. W. Fraser (Ed.), *Risk and resilience in childhood*. Washington, DC: NASW Press.

Kraemer, H. C., Kazdin, A. E., Offord, D. R., Kessler, R. C., Jensen, P. S. & Kupfer, D. J. (1997). Coming to terms with the terms of risk. *Archives of General Psychiatry, 54(4)*, 337-343.

Kumpfer, K. L., Alexander, L. B., McDonald, L. & Olds, D. L. (1998). *Family-focused substance abuse prevention: What has been learned from other fields* (No. Monograph 177). Rockville, MD: National Institute of Drug Abuse.

Kupersmidt, J. B., Griesler, P. C., DeRosier, M. E., Patterson, C. J. & Davis, P. W. (1995). Childhood aggression and peer relations in the context of family and neighborhood factors. *Child development, 66(2)*, 360-375.

Li, X., Stanton, B., Pack, R., Harris, C., Cottrell, L. & Burns, J. (2002). Risk and protective factors associated with gang involvement among urban African American adolescents. *Youth & Society, 34(2)*, 172-194.

Liddle, H. A. & Hogue, A. (2000). A family-based, developmental-ecological preventive intervention for high-risk adolescents. *Journal of Marital & Family Therapy, 26(3)*, 265-279.

Loeber, R. & Hay, D. (1997). Key issues in the development of aggression and violence from childhood to early adulthood. *Annual Review of Psychology, 48(1)*, 371.

Loeber, R. & Stouthamer-Loeber, M. (1998). Development of juvenile aggression and violence: Some common misconceptions and controversies. *American Psychologist, 53(2)*, 242-259.

Lopez, E. E., Perez, S. M., Ochoa, G. M. & Ruiz, D. M. (2008). Adolescent aggression: Effects of gender and family and school enrinments. *Journal of Adolescence, 31(4)*, 433-450.

Lynch, M. & Cicchetti, D. (1998). An ecological-transactional analysis of children and contexts: The longitudinal interplay among child maltreatment, community violence, and children's symptomatology. *Development and Psychopathology, 10(02)*, 235-257.

Mahoney, A., Donnelly, W. O., Lewis, T. & Maynard, C. (2000). Mother and Father Self-Reports of Corporal Punishment and Severe Physical Aggression Toward Clinic-Referred Youth. *Journal of Clinical Child Psychology, 29(2)*, 266-281.

Mahoney, A., Jouriles, E. N. & Scavone, J. (1997). Marital adjustment, marital discord over childrearing, and child behavior problems: Moderating effects of child age. *Journal of Clinical Child & Adolescent Psychology, 26(4)*, 415-423.

McBurnett, K., Lahey, B. B., Rathouz, P. J. & Loeber, R. (2000). Low salivary cortisol and persistent aggression in boys referred for disruptive behavior. *57(1)*, 38-43.

Miles, D. R. & Carey, G. (1997). Genetic and environmental architecture of human aggression. *Journal of Personality and Social Psychology, 72(1)*, 207-217.

Miller-Johnson, S., Coie, J. D., Maumary-Gremaud, A., Lochman, J. & Terry, R. (1999). Relationship between childhood peer rejection and aggression and adolescent delinquency severity and type among African American youth. *Journal of Emotional and Behavioral Disorders, 7(3)*, 137-146.

Moss, H. B., Mezzich, A., Yao, J. K., Gavaler, J. & Martin, C. S. (1995). Aggressivity among sons of substance-abusing fathers: Association with psychiatric disorder in the father and son, paternal personality, pubertal development, and socioeconomic status. *The American journal of drug and alcohol abuse, 21(2)*, 195-208.

Moss, H. B., Vanyukov, M. M. & Martin, C. S. (1995). Salivary cortisol responses and the risk for substance abuse in prepubertal boys. *Biological psychiatry, 38(8)*, 547-555.

Mrug, S., Hoza, B. & Bukowski, W. M. (2004). Choosing or being chosen by aggressive–disruptive peers: Do they contribute to children's externalizing and internalizing problems? *Journal of Abnormal Child Psychology, 32(1)*, 53-65.

Olweus, D., Mattsson, A., Schalling, D. & Low, H. (1988). Circulating testosterone levels and aggression in adolescent males: A causal analysis. *Psychosomatic Medicine, 50(3)*, 261-272.

Oosterlaan, J. & Sergeant, J. A. (1996). Inhibition in ADHD, aggressive, and anxious children: A biologically based model of child psychopathology. *Journal of Abnormal Child Psychology, 24(1)*, 19-36.

Ouimette, P. C., Brown, P. J. & Najavits, L. M. (1998). Course and treatment of patients with both substance use and posttraumatic stress disorders. *Addictive Behaviors, 23(6)*, 785-795.

Paradise, M., Cauce, A. M., Ginzler, J., Wert, S., Wruck, K. & Brooker, M. (2001). The role of relationships in developmental trajectories of homeless and runaway youth. In B. R. Sarason, & S. Duck (Eds.), *Personal relationships: Implications for clinical and community psychology*. New York: John Wiley & Sons.

Paschall, M. J. & Hubbard, M. L. (1998). Effects of neighborhood and family stressors on African American male adolescents' self-worth and propensity for violent behavior. *Journal of Consulting and Clinical Psychology, 66(5)*, 825-831.

Peeples, F. & Loeber, R. (1994). Do individual factors and neighborhood context explain ethnic differences in juvenile delinquency? *Journal of Quantitative Criminology, 10(2)*, 141-157.

Perrino, T., Coatsworth, J. D., Briones, E., Pantin, H. & Szapocznik, J. (2001). Initial Engagement in Parent-Centered Preventive Interventions: A Family Systems Perspective. *The Journal of Primary Prevention, 22(1)*, 21-44.

Poulin, F. & Boivin, M. (1999). Proactive and reactive aggression and boys' friendship quality in mainstream classrooms. *Journal of Emotional and Behavioral Disorders, 7(3)*, 168-177.

Rappaport, N. & Thomas, C. (2004). Recent research findings on aggressive and violent behavior in youth: Implications for clinical assessment and intervention. *Journal of Adolescent Health, 35(4)*, 260-277.

Rowe, C., Liddle, H. A., McClintic, K., Quille, T. J. & Kaslow, F. W. (2002). Integrative treatment development: Multidimensional family therapy for adolescent substance abuse. In *Comprehensive handbook of psychotherapy: Integrative/eclectic, Vol. 4.* (133-161): John Wiley & Sons, Inc.

Saner, H. & Ellickson, P. (1996). Concurrent risk factors for adolescent violence. *Journal of Adolescent Health, 19(2)*, 94-103.

Schoenwald, S. K., Henggeler, S. W., Brondino, M. J. & Rowland, M. D. (2000). Multisystemic Therapy: Monitoring Treatment Fidelity. [Article]. *Family Process Family Process J1- Family Process, 39(1)*, 83.

Schwartz, D. & Proctor, L. J. (2000). Community violence exposure and children's social adjustment in the school peer group: the mediating roles of emotion regulation and social cognition. *Journal of Consulting and Clinical Psychology, 68(4)*, 670.

Seguin, J. R., Pihl, R. O., Harden, P. W., Tremblay, R. E. & Boulerice, B. (1995). Cognitive and neuropsychological characteristics of physically aggressive boys. *Journal of Abnormal Psychology, 104(4)*, 614-624.

Selekman, M. D. (1997). *Solution-focused Therapy with children: Harnessing family strengths for systemic change.* NewYork: The Guilford Press.

Selekman, M. D. (2005). *Pathways to Change: Brief therapy with difficult adolescents* (2nd Ed. ed.). New York: The Guilford Press.

Shields, A. & Cicchetti, D. (1998). Reactive aggression among maltreated children: The contributions of attention and emotion dysregulation. *Journal of Clinical Child & Adolescent Psychology, 27(4)*, 381-395.

Spoth, R., Goldberg, C. & Redmond, C. (1999). Engaging Families in Longitudinal Preventive Intervention Research : Discrete-Time Survival Analysis of Socioeconomic and Social -Emotional Risk Factors. *Journal of Consulting and Clinical Psychology, 67(1)*, 157-163.

Springer, D. W. (2001). Runaway adolescents: Today's Huckleberry Finn crisis. *Brief Treatment & Crisis Intervention, 1(2)*, 131-151.

Stanton, M. D. & Shadish, W. R. (1997). Outcome, attrition, and family-couples treatment for drug abuse: A meta-analysis and review of the controlled, comparative studies. *Psychological Bulletin, 122(2)*, 170-191.

Stormshak, E. A., Bierman, K. L., McMahon, R. J. & Lengua, L. J. (2000). Parenting practices and child disruptive behavior problems in early elementary school. *Journal of Clinical Child & Adolescent Psychology, 29(1)*, 17-29.

Szapocznik, J., Rio, A., Murray, E., Cohen, R., Scopetta, M., Rivas-Vazquez, A., et al. (1989). Structural family versus psychodynamic child therapy for problematic Hispanic boys. *Journal of Consulting & Clinical Psychology, 57(5)*, 571-578.

Szapocznik, J. & Williams, R. A. (2000). Brief Strategic Family Therapy: Twenty-Five Years of Interplay Among Theory, Research and Practice in Adolescent Behavior Problems and Drug Abuse. [Article]. *Clinical Child & Family Psychology Review Clinical Child & Family Psychology Review J1 - Clinical Child & Family Psychology Review, 3(2)*, 117-134.

Temcheff, C., Serbin, L., Martin-Storey, A., Stack, D., Hodgins, S., Ledingham, J., et al. (2008). Continuity and Pathways from Aggression in Childhood to Family Violence in Adulthood: A 30-year Longitudinal Study. *Journal of Family Violence, 23(4)*, 231-242.

Tolan, P. H., Hanish, L. D., McKay, M. M. & Dickey, M. H. (2002). Evaluating process in child and family interventions : Aggression prevention as an example. *Journal of Family Psychology, 16(2)*, 220-236.

Tremblay, R. E. (1998). Testosterone, physical aggression, dominance, and physical development in early adolescence. *International Journal of Behavioral Development, 22(4)*, 753-777.

Turner, S. G. (2001). Resilience and social work practice: Three case studies. *Families in Society, 82(5)*, 441-448.

Vaden-Kiernan, N., Ialongo, N. S., Pearson, J. & Kellam, S. (1995). Household family structure and children's aggressive behavior: A longitudinal study of urban elementary school children. *Journal of Abnormal Child Psychology, 23(5)*, 553-568.

Valliant, G. E. (1993). The wisdom of the ego: Cambridge, MA: Harvard University Press.

van der Merwe, A. & Dawes, A. (2007). Youth violence: A review of risk factors, causal pathways and effective intervention. *Journal of Child and Adolescent Mental Health, 19(2)*, 95-113.

van Goozen, S. H., Matthys, W., Cohen-Kettenis, P. T., Buitelaar, J. K. & van Engeland, H. (2000). Hypothalamic-pituitary-adrenal axis and autonomic nervous system activity in disruptive children and matched controls. *Journal of The American Academy of Child and Adolescent Psychiatry, 39(11)*, 1438-1445.

Verlinden, S., Hersen, M. & Thomas, J. (2000). Risk factors in school shootings. *Clinical Psychology Review, 20(1)*, 3-56.

Vitaro, F., Gendreau, P. L., Tremblay, R. E. & Oligny, P. (1998). Reactive and proactive aggression differentially predict later conduct problems. *The Journal of Child Psychology and Psychiatry and Allied Disciplines, 39(3)*, 377-385.

Webster-Stratton, C. & Hammond, M. (1988). Maternal depression and its relationship to life stress, perceptions of child behavior problems, parenting behaviors, and child conduct problems. *Journal of Abnormal Child Psychology, 16(3)*, 299-315.

Widom, C. S. (1989). The cycle of violence. *Science, 244*(4901), 160-166.

Wills, T. A., Vaccaro, D. & McNamara, G. (1992). The role of life events, family support, and competence in adolescent substance use: A test of vulnerability and protective factors. *American Journal of Community Psychology, 20(3)*, 349-374.

Wright, D. R. & Fitzpatrick, K. M. (2006). Violence and minority youth: The effects of risk and asses factors on fighting among african american children and adolescents. *Adolescence, 41(162)*, 251-262.

Youngblade, L. M., Theokas, C., Schulenberg, J., Curry, L., Huang, I. C. & Novak, M. (2007). Risk and Promotive Factors in Families, Schools, and Communities: A Contextual Model of Positive Youth Development in Adolescence. *Pediatrics, 119*, S47-S53.

In: Youth Violence and Juvenile Justice: Causes, Intervention...   ISBN: 978-1-61668-011-4
Editor: Neil A. Ramsay et al., pp. 117-139   © 2010 Nova Science Publishers, Inc.

Chapter 4

SPORT AS A CURE FOR ADOLESCENT AGGRESSIVE, ANTISOCIAL, AND DELINQUENT BEHAVIORS

Amanda J. Visek[1] and Jonathan P. Maxwell[2]*
[1]The George Washington University, Washington DC, USA
[2]The University of Hong Kong, Hong Kong, China

ABSTRACT

Hostile and antisocial behavior amongst adolescents is a common problem in many societies. The rehabilitation and support of problem and at-risk youths is a social and moral responsibility that necessitates the development of effective interventions. Sport has often been promoted as a means of developing character, respect, and social responsibility in young people. Thus, many sport-based schemes have been developed that attempt to help problem and at-risk youths develop into socially responsible adults who can make a positive contribution to society, rather than dysfunctional members at risk of involvement in criminal behaviors. Whilst supporters of sport schemes often claim positive results, critics point out that involvement in sport does not guarantee positive effects on the attitudes and behaviors of adolescent participants. In fact, some evidence has been published that demonstrates clear links among sport participation, alcohol consumption, and aggressive behavior. It has been argued that sport should be combined with educational programs that promote positive ways of dealing with negative emotions and thoughts. This chapter reviews the evidence and identifies problems with current research. We conclude by suggesting possible avenues for future research and provide practical advice for using sport as a tool for improving the conduct of adolescents.

---

*Corresponding author: The George Washington University, School of Public Health and Health Services, Department of Exercise Science, 817 23rd St., NW, Washington, D.C. 20052. E-mail: avisek@gwu.edu. Phone: 202.994.3997, Fax: 202.994.1420.

INTRODUCTION

Juvenile delinquency refers to criminal acts committed by individuals who are not classed as adults (i.e., usually under the age of 18 years). Delinquent acts include interpersonal aggression or violence (including sexual aggression/violence), property damage, and theft. In all parts of the world the incidence of juvenile delinquency is increasing (United Nations, 2003) with the possible exception of the United States (Snyder, 2006). Delinquent behavior reaches its prevalence and incidence peaks between the ages of 15 and 17 years with boys displaying higher rates than girls (Quinsey, Skilling, Lalumière, & Craig, 2004) and is linked to criminal behavior in later life and to substance abuse. In addition, delinquency has a negative impact on youths who are not delinquent, but are victims (for a comprehensive examination of the delinquency literature see Quinsey et al., 2004).

Aggressive, delinquent, and hostile children tend to exhibit poor peer relations (Dodge & Pettit, 2003; Fraser, et al., 2005), weak emotional control skills (Bierman, 2004), poor social decision making skills (Arsenio & Lemerise, 2001; Dodge, 2003), and aggressive attribution biases (Crick, Grotpeter, & Bigbee, 2002). Wright (2006) points out that these youths also tend to spend little time at school (Hinshaw, 1992) or with families, are rarely open to constructive relationship with adults, and are often from low socioeconomic status families. with parents who may also engage in criminal behavior (see Rowe & Farrington, 1997). They are also likely to associate with other delinquent peers; and, negative peer relations reinforce problem behaviors and attitudes (Andrews, 1995; Beinart, Anderson, Lee, & Utting, 2002; Paetsch & Bertrand, 1997; Thornberry & Krohn, 1997), whereas positive peer relations deter such behaviors (Simpkins, Eccles, & Becnel, 2008).

Unfortunately, delinquency and violent behavior in youths has been linked to substance use, criminal behavior, unemployment, health problems, and poor interpersonal relationships in adulthood (e.g., Booth, Farrell, & Varano, 2008; Bourduin & Schaeffer, 1998; Campbell, 1995; Dodge, 1993; Dunlap et al., 2006; Fite, Colder, Lochman, & Wells, 2007; Sampson & Laub, 1990). In addition, delinquent youths seem to be involved in a wide range, rather than a specific type of crimes (Quincy, et al., 2004). Thus, considerable effort has been expended in the search for intervention programs that have a positive impact on delinquent youths (for a review of recent programs, such as Boot Camps and Wrap-Around Community-Based Care, see Flash, 2003). However, as Flash points out, their effectiveness in eliminating recidivism seems limited at worst and under analyzed at best.

Some school based (e.g., Durlak et al., 2007; Fraser et al. 2005; Fraser, Day, Galinsky, Hodges, & Smokowski, 2004; Fraser, Nash, Galinsky, & Darwin, 2000; Paone, Packman, Maddux, & Rothman, 2008) and after-school programs (e.g., Tebes et al., 2007) have found positive effects on levels of hostility and delinquency; however, they may fail to influence the most delinquent youths who tend to skip school in favour of other activities (Wright, 2006). It is important, therefore, that schemes aimed at these youths are appealing and encourage attendance. The idea that sport may fill this role and prove to be a useful instrument for the rehabilitation of young offenders, and as a deterrent from delinquent or unlawful behaviors for at-risk youths, has been repeatedly suggested (e.g., Andrews & Andrews, 2003; Caldwell & Smith, 2006; Colthart, 1996; Fraser-Thomas, Cote, & Deakin, 2005; Hartmann, 2001).

Positive Effects of Sport Participation

Some consider sport a positive reflection of human society, the epitome of human endeavor and highly valued (e.g., Caldwell & Smith, 2006; Coakley, 2001, 2002; Ewing, Gano-Overway, Branta, & Seefeldt, 2002; Gardner & Janelle, 2002; Hemery, 1986). It has been claimed that important life skills, such as cooperation, competition, determination, and stress management, can be acquired through participation in sport (Estrada, Geltand, & Hartmann, 1988; Smith & Smoll, 1991). Many parents believe that sport participation is an essential childhood activity that promotes personal, moral, and social growth (Dunn, Kinney, & Hofferth, 2003; Kremer-Sadlik & Kim, 2007). In addition, attributes or skills learned through sport are thought to generalise to other aspects of life (e.g., academic achievement; Jeziorski, 1994). The perceived benefits of sport are so pervasive that they have become important instruments in political attempts at social engineering (Faulkner et al., 2007; Krouwel, Boonstra, Duyvendak, & Velboer, 2006). The European Commission, for example, has recently produced a white paper on sport as a tool for social integration (European Commission, 2008).

In fact, empirical investigations supporting a number of positive consequences of sport participation (or regular exercise) have been reported in the sport sciences literature. Ewing, et al. (2002) note that benefits from regular exercise and sport participation are not isolated to physical or psychomotor health, but have been found for psychological health (Bartholomew & Linder, 1998; Donaldson & Ronan, 2006; Landers & Arent, 2007; Norris, Carroll, & Cochran, 1992; Pelham, Campagna, Ritvo, & Birnie, 1993), socialization (Donaldson & Ronan, 2006; Weiss & Duncan, 1992), self-esteem (Ekeland, Heian, & Hagen, 2005; Faulkner et al., 2007; Nelson & Gordon-Larsen, 2006; Smith, Smoll, & Curtis, 1979), and moral development (Shields & Bredemeier, 1995).

In a sample of British 16 year-old adolescents, Steptoe and Butler (1996) found that sport participation was positively correlated with emotional well-being (although some activities were associated with poorer psychological health). Similar results have been reported for younger adolescents. Donaldson and Ronan (2006) examined a range of social, psychological, and emotional problems in New Zealand youths aged between 11 and 14 years old. They found that length (i.e., number of years) of formal sport participation was negatively correlated with externalizing, aggression, and delinquency problems (r's ranged from -.19 to -.25) as measured by the behavioral problems section of Achenbach's (1991) Youth Self-Report Scale (YSR). Also, a recent study by Findlay and Coplan (2008) found that sport participation over a period of twelve months helped to ease anxiety in shy Canadian children.

Trulson (1986) found a beneficial effect of traditional martial art training (Taekwondo) on decreasing aggressiveness, whereas modern martial art training (that did not stress philosophical aspects of the art) tended to increase aggressiveness. Similar results have been reported by other authors (e.g., Bjørkvist & Varhama, 2001; Daniels & Thornton, 1990; Lamarre & Nosanchuck, 1999; Nosanchuk, 1981; Nosanchuk & MacNeil, 1989; Palermo et al., 2006; Reynes & Lorant, 2004; Skelton, Glynn, & Berta, 1991). However, most of these studies were cross-sectional, based on small sample sizes, had no long-term follow-up, and did not control for attrition (Endresen & Olweus, 2005). One exception, conducted by Palermo et al. (2006), examined the effects of karate training on children (aged 8-10 years) with oppositional defiant disorder (ODD). ODD is characterised by aggressiveness, defiant behavior, disobedience, hostility, and temper tantrums (American Psychiatric Association,

2000). In addition, ODD is thought to be an antecedent of behavioral problems later in life (Hämäläinen & Pulkkinen, 1996; Lahey, McBurnett, & Loeber, 2000; Loeber, Burke, Lahey, Winters, & Zera, 2000; Mash & Barkley, 1998). Children with ODD who practiced karate (n = 8) for a period of 10 months showed significant improvements in their ability to control the intensity of their negative reactions, became more adaptable to varying situations, and improved mood (i.e., fewer instances of unpleasant behavior), relative to a group of children with ODD (n = 8) who did not receive karate training.

However, positive effects of sport participation on aggression have not always been found. Endresen and Olweus (2005) conducted a longitudinal study of fight (i.e., boxing, martial arts, and wrestling) or strength (i.e., weightlifting) sport participation and involvement in aggressive or antisocial activities. They found that participation in power or strength sports was associated with a relative enhancement of aggressive and antisocial activities. However, martial arts tended to have the smallest effect consistent with the idea that the philosophical approach taken by some instructors might ameliorate enhancement of aggressive tendencies (e.g., Palermo et al., 2006). In addition, Endresen and Olweus found no evidence for a selection effect; in other words, aggressive and antisocial youths did not preferentially select sports sometimes associated with aggressive behavior. Thus, empirical evidence for and against positive effects of sport participation on the aggressive behaviors of adolescents is mixed at best. Clearly, further research is required before strong conclusions can be drawn.

SPORT AS A CURE FOR HOSTILE AND ANTISOCIAL BEHAVIORS

Despite conflicting evidence from the sport and social science literatures, several sport-based programs have been established with the intention of combating juvenile delinquency. In the context of treating delinquent and/or hostile youths, sport is viewed as either a deterrent or as a rehabilitation exercise for aggression. For example, active participation in sport removes children from the streets and prevents them from engaging in delinquent behaviors (Langbein & Bess, 2002; Osgood, Wilson, O'Malley, Bachman, & Johnston, 1996). Also, sport has been found to teach valuable social lessons, such as respect for others, cooperation, and determination, which encourage the development of skills that can be applied to life in general (Andrews & Andrews, 2003; Coakley, 2002; Coalter, 2000). Additionally, sport provides an opportunity for social maturation through the development of social bonds (Hirschi, 1969; Sage, 1990).

Programmatic Initiatives

Caldwell's (2005) TimeWise program, although targeting leisure time rather than sport participation *per se*, was designed to help deter substance use by teaching youths to develop leisure skills and take control of their free time in a positive manner. Some evidence for the efficacy of this approach was provided in the form of slightly lower frequency of property damage in youths who received the program compared to those who did not (Caldwell & Smith, 2006). However, further research is required to identify exactly what sort of leisure activity is important and whether the program reduces the tendency to engage in other negative behaviors.

More recently, Wright (2006) describes boxing programs in New York and San Francisco that target delinquent youths at-risk of gang membership. Wright argues that boxing is of particular value to delinquent youths because it is seen as a respectable, yet "tough" sport and attendance tends to be high as a result. Other sports, such as golf (Brunelle, Danish, & Forneris, 2007), soccer, and volleyball (Papacharisis, Goudas, Danish, & Theodorakis, 2005) have also shown positive effects on prosocial behavior, particularly when integrated with community-based activities (Brunelle, et al., 2007).

Similar programs have been conducted in several countries, such as Canada (Taylor, Scott, & Danish, in press), Hong Kong (Joe Laidler, Li, & Tang, 2005), the United States (O'Hearn & Gatz, 2002), New Zealand (Hodge, Cresswell, Sherburn, & Dugdale, 1999) and the United Kingdom (Crabbe, 2000). Crabbe describes several soccer-based programs that develop within small communities and are often led by individuals who organize groups of youths into small teams. These programs often develop into larger organisations, but often fall apart due to a lack of funding, facilities, or management. Crabbe describes one team that dissolved because one or two members began to abuse drugs and other members either lost heart or followed suit. These problems highlight the need for proper management, oversight, and support, often across multiple service providers (e.g., social services, probation services, police authorities) if such schemes are to succeed.

In Hong Kong, "Operation Breakthrough" is a charitable organisation that provides sport programs for children who have been recommended by social services or directly from various police authorities, normally for relatively minor problems (e.g., theft, fighting, or social drug use). The project, initiated in 1996 by a group of Hong Kong police officers, began with three objectives: (1) to create positive relationships between at risk youth and authorities, (2) to encourage self discipline and control, and (3) to provide a support network to keep at risk youth from pursuing delinquent activities. In a small scale study (Joe Laidler, et al., 2005), 30 youths were given a self report questionnaire to document attitudes and behaviors towards school, family, peers, authorities and the law, leisure activities, and self reported delinquency. The same questionnaire was administered seven months later to assess changes in attitudes and behaviors, along with follow-up semi-structured questions regarding their views on the program. In general, there were increases in positive attitudes and participation in school and with family members. Peer relationships remained constant. Participants reported being slightly less involved in risky and delinquent behaviors. Finally, participants reported increased interest and commitment to rugby or boxing, improved their English skills, developed new friendship networks, and improved physical and mental health.

While the potential for the lessons learned in sport to transfer to other life domains is evident, it is important to recognize that this transfer will not necessarily occur (Coakley, 2002; Danish, 2002; Ewing et al., 2002). Some view sport as a negative aspect of human society because it fosters competitive rather than cooperative ideals (Kohn, 1986), teaches individuals to use physical force as a weapon of choice (e.g., Endresen & Olweus, 2005; Forbes, Adams-Curtis, Pakalka, & White, 2006; Koss & Gaines, 1993; Melnick, 1992; Nixon, 1997), encourage aggression and delinquency (e.g., Begg, Langley, Moffitt, & Marshall, 1996; Burton & Marshall, 2005; Miller, Melnick, Barnes, Sabo, & Farrell, 2007), replicates social problems (Krouwel, et al. 2006), encourages substance use (Aaron, et al., 1995; Eccles & Barber, 1999; Faulkner & Slaterry, 1990; Garry & Morrissey, 2000; Lorente, Souville,

Griffet, & Grélot, 2004; Maxwell, 2008; Moore & Werch, 2005; Peck, Vida, & Eccles, 2008; Peretti-Watel, Beck, & Legleye, 2002; Rainey, McKeown, Sargent, & Valois, 1996; Tao et al., 2007), and supports a male hegemony that debases and objectifies women, and encourages sexual aggression against them (e.g., Benedict, 1997; Koss, 1988; Messner & Sabo, 1990; Strauss, Gelles, & Steinmetz, 1980). Additionally, current data suggests that involvement in sport may have, at best, only short term effects on behavior and emotional health (e.g., Coakley, 2002; Jones & Offord, 1989).

In their early theoretical examination, Sugden and Yiannakis (1982) counselled against the use of traditional sports for the rehabilitation of delinquent youths. They argued that sports are simply a small scale replication of the wider social context with peer norms, control, and conformity playing key roles; therefore, traditional sports are unlikely to appeal to delinquent youths. Instead, Sugden and Yiannakis suggested that Outward Bound courses might be a better alternative because challenges are individualized, exciting, informal, free from rules (other than those pertaining to minimal safety requirements), demonstrate physical prowess and courage, and can be group or individual based. Sugden and Yiannakis further argued that these attributes more accurately represent the delinquent sub-culture and identity norms.

Although leaders of sport and adventure education programs often claim a certain degree of success, the evidence has been mixed (Mason & Wilson, 1988). What appears to be crucial to the success of adventure or sport programs is the way in which they are delivered (Rutton, et al. 2008). In a now famous example of this effect, Sherrif, Harvey, Hood, and Sherif (1987) reported that involvement in competitive sports increased occurrences of negative behaviors in groups of adolescents involved in an adventure education program. Only when the researchers intervened by introducing group goals were positive effects on behavior witnessed. Similarly, in the context of athletics Rutton et al., demonstrated that relational support from a coach, team attitudes towards fair play, and high levels of moral reasoning in sport were positively associated with both on-field and off-field prosocial behaviors. Thus, both contextual and individual factors contribute to potential benefits from sport participation. These benefits have also been said to extend beyond the playing field and into every day life.

Previously, Danish (2002a, 2002b; Danish & Nellen, 1997) stated that sport can be an effective context in which to teach life skills. Indeed, he argued that physical skills are similar to life skills in that they are most often learned through demonstration (i.e., modeling) and practice (Danish & Hale, 1981). Also, Danish, Fazio, Nellen, and Owens (2002,) argued that "many of the skills learned in sport - including performing under pressure, solving problems, meeting deadlines and challenges, setting goals, communicating, handling both success and failure, working with a team and within a system, and receiving feedback and benefiting from it - are transferable to other life domains" (p. 274-275).

In an attempt to utilize sport for the teaching of life skills, Danish and colleagues developed the Going for the Goal (GOAL; Danish, 1996; 2002a) and Sports United to Promote Education and Recreation (SUPER; Danish, 2002c) programs. In both programs, peers are trained as mentors to deliver the goal setting program. Participants are taught the importance of goals and how to achieve them. The SUPER program, for example, involves a series of 18 thirty-minute workshops focussed on teaching goal setting. Danish et al. (2002) notes that the workshops are designed to teach seven essential skills, including: (a) the identification of positive life goals, (b) the importance of focusing on the process (not the outcome) of goal attainment, (c) the use of a general problem-solving model, (d) the identification of health-compromising behaviors that can impede goal attainment, (e) the identification of health-promoting behaviors that can facilitate goal attainment, (f) the importance of seeking and creating social support, and (g) ways to transfer these skills from one life situation to another.

The effectiveness of the GOAL and SUPER programs has been evaluated in a handful of studies (Brunelle, et al., 2007; Forneris, Danish, & Scott, 2007; Goudas & Giannoudis, in press; Papacharisis, et al., 2005). In all cases, positive effects of combining sport with the life skills training program were found. For example, Forneris et al. utilized the GOAL program with twenty adolescents (ages ranged from 14 to 16 years) from a Canadian high school. Half the adolescents received the goal setting intervention whilst the other half acted as controls. Following the 10-week program, participants were interviewed about their knowledge of goal setting, problem solving, and social support. Perhaps unsurprisingly, the adolescents who had taken part in the GOAL program were better able to describe: goal setting strategies, appropriate problem solving techniques, and how to seek appropriate support. In an examination of the influence of the SUPER program on prosocial values, Brunelle et al. found similar positive effects. Thus, the available evidence provides preliminary support for the use of the GOAL and SUPER programs as a means for improving the life skills of young people.

Hellison's (1978; 1995; 2000; 2003) Responsibility Model offers guidelines, which are similar to those promoted by Danish and colleagues, for the use of physical activity for positive youth development. The Responsibility Model seeks to develop goal setting, inter-personal, and decision making skills through a caring approach to each individual. These skills are introduced over five "levels" with the final level focusing on transferring new skills to situations encountered outside physical activity. Support for the efficacy of Hellison's Caring Program, grounded in the Responsibility Model, has been provided in a study of 9 to 17 year old youths from disadvantaged backgrounds. More recently, Newton et al. (2007) found that outcomes using the caring approach with regard to physical activity were superior to programs that solely focused on physical activity.

LIMITATIONS OF PAST RESEARCH AND GOALS FOR THE FUTURE

It is possible that programs that are designed to teach life skills through sport participation may be useful in the rehabilitation of delinquent adolescents. Unfortunately, programs like GOAL, SUPER, and the Caring Program have not been evaluated with respect to delinquent or at-risk youths. The lack of evaluation of program outcomes has been a major problem in this field of research (e.g., Crabbe, 2000; Flash, 2003; Mason & Wilson, 1988). Whilst short term benefits have been reported (e.g., Joe Laidler et al., 2005; Wright, 2007) long-term benefits, particularly for recidivism, are largely unknown (Endresen & Olweus, 2005; Mason & Wilson, 1988; McKenney & Dattilo, 2001; United Nations Office for Drug Control and Prevention, 2002). Additionally, no objective measures of benefits outside the programs have been collected. It is important, therefore, for future research to evaluate the long-term impact of such programs with delinquent adolescents to ensure that the intended positive outcomes are apparent and that unintended negative outcomes are not (Quinsey et al., 2004).

The vast majority of research involving sport-based intervention programs has failed to adopt appropriate control conditions to isolate intervention effects from developmental or placebo effects. Whilst non-delinquent and occasionally delinquent control groups have been used, the placebo effect has rarely (i.e., to the authors' knowledge never) been seriously evaluated within the context of sport. Coupled with the lack of long-term follow-up data, this is a major problem that should be overcome by future research. Short-term placebo effects may give the false impression that an ineffective program is beneficial and may even mask long-term negative effects.

Quinsey et al., (2004) identify three major types of juvenile delinquents: (a) early-starting neurologically vulnerable, (b) early-starting neurologically normal, and (c) adolescent-limited delinquents. Individuals from the first two groups tend to be life-long offenders with the former having some neurological disorder (e.g., brain damage caused by birth complications). The third group normally consists of individuals who start offending in early adolescence, typically around puberty, and desist as they reach early adulthood. Studies of sport interventions rarely take these individual differences into account. For example, it is possible that the three types might display differential outcomes from sport participation or have differential adherence rates. Further, few studies mention drop-out rates or the characteristics of those who drop-out relative to those who do not. It is possible that the most serious or multiple offenders (i.e., early-onset) do not adhere to programs and that youth guilty of only a few and/or minor crimes (i.e., adolescent-limited or late-starters) gain benefits from participation in sport interventions.

Another important issue is the possibility that delinquent youths are often grouped together in sport interventions allowing for the possibility of negative peer modeling (Dishion, Eddy, Haas, Li, & Spracklen, 1997; Dishion, McCord, & Poulin, 1999; Tremblay, Pagani-Kurtz, Vitaro, Masse, & Pihl, 1995). According to Social Learning Theory (Bandura, 1973, 1983), children quickly learn aggressive and delinquent behaviors from peers and are likely to adopt these behaviors. For example, Brendgen, Vitaro, & Bukowski (2000) found that even short-term contact with delinquent peers was sufficient to increase delinquent behavior. In other words, interventions may act as a delinquency school, rather than rehabilitation setting, with individuals sharing criminal techniques and experiences or modeling delinquent behavior. It may be advisable, therefore, to mix groups so that non-delinquent youths are in the minority and that the behavior of group leaders is consistent and exemplary. Tremblay et al., (1995) provided evidence that mixed groups have a beneficial effect on delinquents without negative effects for non-delinquents. It is probable, in the group context, that non-delinquent children are less likely to be led astray by the misbehavior of delinquent juveniles; although, further evidence for this assertion in the context of sport (particularly sports of an aggressive nature typified by contact and collision) is required.

A final and major problem with many sport intervention programs is their lack of theoretical motivation. There is sufficient evidence to dismiss the notion that, even with the best intentions, sport involvement will have positive effects on delinquent youths. Therefore, it is imperative that theoretical considerations are incorporated into the design of future schemes and that empirical evidence is generated in support of the most effective interventions. For example, Social Bond Theory (Hirschi, 1969) argues that the development of close family relationships and social ties help to protect youths against the temptation to engage in delinquent behaviors. Sports schemes should be designed, therefore, to encourage group membership and establish a non-delinquent identity in participants. Team sports may be particularly amenable to this manipulation. Again, however, the efficacy of such manipulations requires empirical verification.

WORKING WITH DELINQUENT AND NON-DELINQUENT ADOLESCENTS

It is important that adolescent delinquents are treated appropriately and that their personal experiences and environmental circumstances are taken into account during program design and implementation. Hellison (2000, 2003) argues for positive attitudes towards youths from troubled backgrounds rather than focusing on "fixing" them. Traditional programs often fail (Flash, 2003) because delinquent youth are treated as aberrations of the social norm, rather than individuals with a difficult background who may have alternative ideas about what is right and wrong (Riner & Saywell, 2002; Wright, 2006) due to the social and societal norms and culture in which they have been faced. These youths may be unable to gain self-esteem through conventional avenues (e.g., academic achievement) and therefore turn to delinquent acts as an alternative (Donnellan, Trzesniewski, Robins, Moffitt, & Caspi, 2005; Hirschi, 1969), which·may be an alternative means to acceptance and self-esteem amongst one's peers. For example, delinquent youths may feel a sense of esteem ("street cred") if they are shot, get tattooed, or physically scarred in some way (Wright, 2006). These youths often identify with gang culture and often idolize older gang members. Wounds sustained in acting out these roles reinforce their gang identity and serve as a mark of respect solidifying their in-group membership. Sport may provide an alternative identity, but only if it commands the same sort of respect from significant peers. For example, Wright describes the possession of the boxer identity by at-risk youths in San Francisco. In gang or street culture, boxing is viewed as a credible pursuit that can function as an alternative to gang membership or involvement in crime. It is likely that many other sports (e.g., tennis, track and field) would not be viewed so favorably. Therefore, it is important that sport-related interventions take into account the prevailing culture and offer sports that are more likely to be viewed with respect.

In a similar vein, Caldwell and Smith (2006) found a positive relationship between motivation to engage in leisure-time activity and property damage, implying that some youths view property damage as a leisure-time activity. This is likely true of many delinquent activities and re-emphasizes the importance of replacing these activities with something that is equally appealing (Galloway, 2006), yet legal and productive societal behavior. The recent fad of "Happy Slapping" that has escalated in many European countries, particularly the United Kingdom, provides further evidence of delinquents' use of violent behavior in the pursuit of entertainment (Akwagyiram, 2005). Happy slapping involves filming, often using the video function of mobile phones, the reactions of victims receiving a surprise slap. The original fad was seen as relatively harmless; however, the severity of assaults seems to be escalating as delinquent youth find ever more elaborate ways of attacking their victims (Gibb, 2008).

It is possible that sport may provide an environment in which youths may perceive that they have more control over their lives and future. The sport environment is relatively safe compared to life on the street, so youths are free from the fear of victimization from neighbourhood gangs, criminal involvement, and harassment from law enforcement officers.

The routes available for success may also be relatively transparent, relative to academic or vocational success, thereby promoting greater commitment and less cynicism. These youths may also regard themselves as more capable of achieving athletic success; however, the tendency to promote sport as a mobility escalator and means of increasing their socio-economic status by pursuing professional sport opportunities (Eitzen & Sage, 2003) should be tempered with realistic evaluations of athletic potential and protection from unscrupulous promoters.

It is well known that one of the best predictors of delinquent behavior is having reference-others (i.e., any person(s) or group who directly influence an individual's perceptions or actions (Morra & Smith, 1995; Smith 1979) who are also delinquent (e.g., Andrews, Tildesley, Hops, & Li, 2002; Haynie, 2001). It is important, therefore, that delinquent role models are replaced with more acceptable, and possibly athletic, individuals who command a high degree of respect. Support from respected adults has been shown to impact positively on the behaviors and attitudes of adolescents (DuBois, Hooloway, Valentine, & Cooper, 2002). The relationship between young athletes and their coach is also an important variable when considering the ability of sport programs to deal with delinquency. Rutten et al. (2007) found that adolescents who have a good relationship with their coach tend to exhibit more prosocial behaviors and less antisocial behavior, relative to adolescents who not have a good relationship. Coaches provide models for their athletes and, therefore, have a duty to exhibit high levels of moral reasoning, prosocial behavior, fairness, and encouragement. However, coaches who display negative attitudes and behaviors are more likely to breed aggressive and delinquent athletes (Loughead & Leith, 2001; Luxbacher, 1986; Smith, 1979, Vaz, 1982).

Parental involvement also influences the potential for sport to have a positive effect on youths. In a longitudinal study of almost 12,000 adolescents, Nelson and Gordon-Larsen (2006) found that high overall sport participation and playing sports with parents were indicative of positive health outcomes, such as lower levels of delinquency, substance use, and sexual behavior, and increased self-esteem. These adolescents were also more successful in their academic endeavors and were also more helpful at home. It is possible therefore, that parental involvement may improve the quality and outcomes of youth sport programs; although, some parents might be detrimental to the success of the program if they adopt overly competitive attitudes or if they are hostile and/or abusive (Clark, Vaz, Vetere, & Ward, 1978; Smith, 1975, 1979, 1980). Thus, parents might also be encouraged to train as group leaders through parent education programs. One such program designed to educate parents about prosocial behaviors (e.g., encouragement, positive modeling, respectful sideline behavior) and bring awareness to their roles and responsibilities and how they can be a positive and integral factor in their children's sport experiences and enjoyment is the Parent's Association for Youth Sport (PAYS), which is an educational program of the National Alliance for Youth Sport (NAYS, 2008). Unfortunately, systematic research examining the effectiveness of parent education programs such as PAYS and the role of parents in the implementation of youth sport programs and their effects on desirable outcomes has been largely neglected as a topic of research and thus warrants scientific attention in the quest to validate intervention programs empirically.

Another important consideration when dealing with youths in a sport program is the prevention of drop-out or reduced motivation to participate. If youths feel that they are not gaining benefits from their participation, they are unlikely to continue their involvement.

Research has demonstrated that adolescents need not be proficient (as judged by an independent observer and relative to other children) at sport in order to gain psychological benefits. Donaldson and Ronan (2006) found that youths who simply thought themselves competent at sport were more likely to display high levels of emotional and psychological health (e.g., anxiety, depression, internalizing problems, and somatic complaints). They were also less likely to have attentional or social problems. Thus, it is important to build youths' self-efficacy and maintain their perceptions that they are skilled at a particular sport by ensuring that they achieve ability specific goals, regardless of their ability relative to other adolescents. In this context, the importance of competition and winning at all costs should be deemphasised (Kohn, 1986) in favor of the accomplishment of personal goals.

Many of the studies described in this review have concentrated on younger adolescents (12 – 16 years old), but it is well known that older at-risk youths are the most challenging to reach, engage, and retain (Calhoun, Glaser, & Bartolomucci, 2001). Most of these youths have well developed delinquent careers and are fully immersed in gang culture. It is also plausible that they may have experienced several benefits from such behavior (e.g., money earned through selling drugs or gained through violent crime) thus reinforcing its continuance. Some may even have family responsibilities that encourage criminal behavior in the absence of legal employment. Again, these variables have yet to be examined by researchers.

Delinquency has been linked to executive (i.e., working memory), sensory, motor, and perceptual deficits that contribute to learning problems (e.g., Brickman, McManus, Grapentine, & Alessi, 1984; Lawson & Sanet, 1992; Wolff, Waber, Bauermeister, Cohen, & Ferber, 1982), which may result in poorer reading and comprehension skills than their non-delinquent counterparts (Sobotowicz, Evans, & Laughlin, 1987; Wolff et al., 1982). It is plausible that these deficits severely hamper the development of positive social and reasoning skills leading to problems when interacting with other children. Coupled with negative role models (possibly parents or peers), these children may resort to hostile behaviors in an attempt to assert their identity. Social rejection may follow and the severity of acts may increase as a consequence of the child's increasing efforts to attract attention and gain approval. Previous longitudinal research has confirmed a reduction in recidivism, as well as improved reading skills, in young offenders who receive an intervention designed to remedy visual and perceptual problems (Dzik, 1975; Kaseno, 1985 as cited in Quinsey et al., 2004). Therefore, a combination of sporting, life skills, and academic programs (designed to remedy some of these deficits or to teach more appropriate coping skills) may be worthwhile.

It must also be borne in mind that delinquent children who present with attentional or executive problems (Sobotowicz, et al., 1987; Wolff et al., 1982;) may also have co-morbid movement problems. Recent research has suggested that deficits in academic performance and the capacity and/or efficiency of working memory resources may be linked to poor motor skills (Alloway, 2007; Alloway & Archibald, 2008; Alloway, Gathercole, Willis, & Adams, 2005; Alloway & Temple, 2007; Pickering & Gathercole, 2004). Thus, these children may be particularly poor at sport and may require additional help with such movement skills (e.g., Maxwell, Masters, & Hammond, in press). If such help is not forthcoming they are likely to face failure frequently with a concomitant loss in movement specific self-efficacy and possibly general self-confidence (Bandura, 1977); and, lowered self-esteem is unlikely to promote adherence to the program (Steptoe & Butler, 1996).

Finally, it is customary in sport to counsel against the treatment of adolescents as "mini-adults" from a physical, psychological, emotional, and social perspective (Visek, Harris, & Blom, 2009). However, it is likely that many delinquent juveniles would have a considerable amount of "life experience" that ages them beyond their years and non-delinquent counterparts. Delinquent youths may have experienced several traumatic events, have abusive parents, endure low socioeconomic status, be prone to violence, have an unstable home history, be suspicious of adults' motivations, demand respect, and are unlikely in many cases to tolerate being treated like "children". Some delinquents may even have been involved in violent or even sexual crimes. It is important, therefore, that interventions consider the needs of both the individual and the group. This requirement demands a high degree of flexibility in service provision and may work against precise empirical investigation. Perhaps, however, it is precisely this lack of flexibility that has led to the demise of many a well-intentioned program.

CONCLUSIONS

Sport has often been put forward as a candidate treatment in the battle against juvenile delinquency. Adherents claim that sport promotes a number of desirable qualities including competitiveness, good character, leadership, and social responsibility. Three levels of intervention have been described for the implementation of preventative strategies (such as sport) targeting delinquency (Caplan, 1964; Mrazek & Haggerty, 1994; Quinsey, et al., 2004): primary, secondary, and tertiary. Primary intervention involves younger children and is broad in its application. Primary intervention may be more concerned with target behaviors rather than a specific target group. It would appear that sport is ideally suited to this level of intervention, but very little (if any) empirical data is available to support this claim (but for a potential application see Trulson, 1986). Secondary intervention is more focused in its application. At-risk (e.g., aggressive children) are introduced to a broad intervention strategy designed to combat a wider range of behaviors (e.g., prosocial attitudes etc.). Although several sports interventions have been conducted at this level (e.g., Joe Laidler et al., 2005), their long-term impact on delinquent behavior is essentially unknown. Tertiary intervention targets individuals with specific behavioral problems such as delinquency. Tertiary intervention has received the most empirical interest in the context of sport (e.g., Palermo et al., 2006; Wright, 2007).

It is important to note that the majority of juvenile crimes are committed by a small number of delinquents and only a small percentage of these individuals engage in violent crimes (Elliot, Dunford, & Huizinga, 1987). In turn, only a small percentage of delinquent youths are arrested and prosecuted for their crimes. Thus, the policy of using predominantly tertiary prevention strategies, therefore, becomes questionable because the majority of delinquents will not be reached. It is important to develop primary and secondary prevention strategies that target minor delinquent and anti-social behaviors before they have a chance to develop into chronic criminality. Whilst some have proffered a damning opinion of its effectiveness (e.g., Leitenberg, 1987), sport may offer a unique arena in which to deliver such interventions because most youths are exposed to some form of physical activity and sport early in their development.

In addition, sport can be relatively inexpensive compared to more intensive intervention strategies. However, it is clear that simple involvement in sport is unlikely to be sufficient. Life skills and other educational programs should be integrated with sport provision and should be grounded theoretically and based on carefully considered outcomes, rather than goodwill or moral imperatives. Wright (2006), for example, argued that a correctly implemented boxing program (or for that matter any sport) should promote ten specific attributes: (a) adoption of a new (athletic) identity, (b) safety, (c) discipline, (d) physical and psychological defence, (e) impulse control and patience, (f) ability to focus, (g) commitment, (h) respect, (i) stress relief, and (j) mutual aid. It is also important that long-term intervention strategies are introduced as early as possible because behaviors are easier to treat at early stages of development (Tremblay & Craig, 1995). In this respect, it is important that future research also examine potential risk factors so that targeted interventions can be developed. Finally, researchers should subject intervention programs to rigorous evaluation that includes measures of recidivism, social function, and individual development.

REFERENCES

Aaron, D. J., Dearwater, S. R., Anderson, R., Olsen, T., Kriska, A. M. & Laporte, R. E. (1995). Physical activity and the initiation of high-risk health behaviors in adolescents. *Medicine and Science in Sport and Exercise, 27,* 1639-1645.

Achenbach, T. M. (1991). *Manual for the Youth Self-Report and 1991 Profile.* Burlington: University of Vermont Department of Psychiatry.

Akwagyiram, A. (2005, May 12). Does *"happy slapping"* exist? Retrieved December 18, 2008, from http://news.bbc.co.uk/2/hi/uk_news/4539913.stm.

Alloway, T. P. (2007). Working memory, literacy and numeracy in children with developmental coordination disorder. *Journal of Experimental Child Psychology, 96,* 20-36.

Alloway, T. P. & Archibald, L. (2008). Working memory and learning in children with developmental coordination disorder and specific language impairment. *Journal of Learning Disabilities, 41,* 251-262.

Alloway, T. P., Gathercole, S. E., Willis, C. & Adams, A. M. (2005). Working memory and special educational needs. *Educational and Child Psychology, 22,* 56-67.

Alloway, T. P. & Temple, K. J. (2007). A comparison of working memory skills and learning in children with developmental coordination disorder and moderate learning difficulties. *Applied Cognitive Psychology, 21,* 473-487.

American Psychiatric Association. (2000). *Diagnostic and statistical manual of mental disorders* (3rd ed.). Washington, D. C.: American Psychiatric Association.

Andrews, D. (1995). The psychology of criminal conduct and effective treatment. In J. McGuire (Ed.), *What works? Reducing reoffending* (35-62). Chichester: Wiley.

Andrews, J. P. & Andrews, G. J. (2003). Life in a secure unit: The rehabilitation of young people through the use of sport. *Social Science and Medicine, 56,* 531-550.

Andrews, J. A., Tildesley, E., Hops, H. & Li, F. (2002). The influence of peers on young adult substance use. *Health Psychology, 21,* 349-357.

Arsenio, W. F. & Lemerise, E. A. (2001). Varieties of childhood bullying: Values, emotion processes, and social competence. *Social Development, 10,* 59-73.

Bandura, A. (1973). *Aggression: A social learning analysis.* Englewood Cliffs, NJ: Prentice-Hall.

Bandura, A. (1977). Self-efficacy: Toward a unifying theory of personality change. *Psychological Review, 84,* 191-215.

Bandura, A. (1983). Psychological mechanisms of aggression. In R. G. Geen, & E. I. Donnerstein (Eds.), *Aggression: Theoretical and empirical reviews* (Vol. 1, 1-40). New York: Academic Press.

Bartholomew, J. B. & Linder, D. E. (1998). State anxiety following resistance exercise: The role of gender and exercise intensity. *Journal of Behavioral Medicine, 21,* 205-219.

Begg, D. J., Langley, J. D., Moffitt, T. & Marshall, S. W. (1996). Sport and delinquency: An examination of the deterrence hypothesis in a longitudinal study. *British Journal of Sports Medicine, 30,* 335-341.

Benedict, J. R. (1997). *Public heroes, private felons: Athletes and crimes against women.* Boston: Northeastern University Press.

Beinart, S., Anderson, B., Lee, S. & Utting, D. (2002). *Youth at risk? A national survey of risk factors, protective factors, and problem behavior among young people in England, Scotland, and Wales.* London: Communities that Care.

Bierman, K. L. (2004). *Peer rejection: Developmental processes and intervention strategies.* New York: Guilford.

Bjørkvist, K. & Varhama, L. (2001). Attitudes towards violent conflict resolution among male and female karateka in comparison with practitioners of other sports. *Perceptual and Motor Skills, 92,* 586-588.

Booth, J. A., Farrell, A. & Varano, S. P., (2008). Social control, serious delinquency, and risky behavior: A gendered analysis. *Crime & Delinquency, 54,* 423-456.

Bourduin, C. & Schaeffer, C. (1998). Violent offending in adolescence: Epidemiology, correlates, outcomes and treatment. In T. Gullota, G. Adams, & R. Montemayor (Eds.), *Delinquent violent youth: Theory and interventions,* (144-174). Thousand Oaks, CA: Sage.

Brickman, A. S., McManus, M. M., Grapentine, W. & Alessi, N. (1984). Neurological assessment of seriously delinquent adolescents. *Journal of the Academy of Child Psychiatry, 23,* 453-457.

Brunelle, J., Danish, S. J. & Forneris, T. (2007). The impact of a sport-based life skill program on adolescent prosocial values. *Applied Developmental Science, 11,* 43-55.

Burton, J. M. & Marshall, L. A. (2005). Protective factors for youth considered at risk of criminal behavior: Does participation in extracurricular activities help? *Criminal Behavior and Mental Health, 15,* 46-64.

Caldwell, L. L. (2005). *TimeWise: Taking charge of leisure time.* Scotts Valley, CA: ETR Associates.

Caldwell, L. L. & Smith, E. A., (2006). Leisure as a context for youth development and delinquency prevention. *The Australian and New Zealand Journal of Criminology, 39,* 398-418.

Calhoun, G., Glaser, B. & Bartolomucci, C. (2001). Counseling the juvenile offender. In A. Horne, & M. Kiselica (Eds.), *Handbook of counselling boys and adolescent males* (25-34). Thousand Oaks, CA: Sage Publications.

Campbell, S. B. (1995). Behavior problems in preschool children: A review of recent research. *Journal of Child Psychology and Psychiatry, 36,* 113-149.

Caplan, G. (1964). *Principals of preventative psychiatry.* New York: Basic Books.

Clark, W. J., Vaz, E., Vetere, V. & Ward, T. A. (1978). Illegal aggression in minor league hockey: A causal model. In F. Landry, & W. Orban (Eds.), *Ice hockey research, development and new concepts* (81-88). Miami, FL: Symposium Specialists.

Coakley, J. (2001). *Sport in society: Issues and controversies.* New York: McGraw-Hill.

Coakley, J. (2002). Using sports to control deviance and violence among youths: Let's be critical and cautious. In M. Gatz, M. A. Messner, & S. J. Ball-Rokeach (Eds.), *Paradoxes of youth and sport,* (13-30). Albany, NY: State University of New York Press.

Coalter, F. (2000). *The role of sport in regenerating deprived urban areas.* The Scottish Office, Edinburgh.

Crabbe, T. (2000). A sporting chance? Using sport to tackle drug use and crime. *Drugs: Education, Prevention, and Policy, 7,* 381-391.

Crick, N. R., Grotpeter, J. K. & Bigbee, M. A. (2002). Relationally and physically aggressive children's intent attributions and feelings of distress for relational and instrumental peer provocations. *Child Development, 73,* 1134-1142.

Daniels, K. & Thornton, E. W. (1990). An analysis of the relationship between hostility and training in the martial arts. *Journal of Sports Sciences, 8,* 95-101.

Danish, S. J. (1996). Interventions for enhancing adolescents' life skills. *The Humanistic Psychologist, 24,* 365-381.

Danish, S. J. (2002a). *Going for the goal: Leader manual and student activity book* (4th ed.). Richmond, VA: Life Skills Center, Virginia Commonwealth University.

Danish, S. J. (2002b). Teaching life skills through sport. In M. Gatz, M. A. Messner, & S. J. Ball-Rokeach, (Eds.), *Paradoxes of youth and sport,* (49-60). Albany, NY: State University of New York Press.

Danish, S. J. (2002c). *SUPER (Sports United to Promote Education and Recreation) program: Leader manual* (3rd Ed.) Richmond: Life Skills Centre, Virginia Commonwealth University.

Danish, S. J., Fazio, R. J., Nellen, V. C. & Owens, S. S. (2002). Teaching life skills through sport: Community-based programs to enhance adolescent development. In J. L. Van Raalte, & B. W. Brewer (Eds.), *Exploring sport and exercise psychology* (2nd ed., 269-288). Washington, D.C.: American Psychological Association.

Danish, S. J. & Hale, B. D. (1981). Toward an understanding of the practice of sport psychology. *Journal of Sport Psychology, 3(2),* 90-99.

Danish, S. J. & Nellen, V. C. (1997). New roles for sport psychologists: Teaching life skills through sport to at-risk youth. *Quest, 49,* 100-113.

Dishion, T. J., Eddy, J. M., Haas, E., Li, F. & Spracklen, K. (1997). Friendships and violent behavior during adolescence. *Social Development, 6,* 207-223.

Dishion, T. J., McCord, J. & Poulin, F. (1999). When interventions harm: Peer groups and problem behavior. *American Psychologist, 54,* 755-764.

Durlak, J. A., Taylor, R. D., Kawashima, K., Pachan, M. K., DuPre, E. P., Celio, C. I., Berger, S. R., Dymnicki, A. B. & Weissberg, R. P. (2007). Effects of positive youth development programs on school, family, and community systems. *American Journal of Community Psychology, 39,* 269-286.

Dodge, K. (1993). The future of research on conduct disorder. *Development and Psychopathology, 5,* 311-320.

Dodge, K. A. (2003). Do social information-processing patterns mediate aggressive behavior? In B. B. Lahey, T. E. Moffitt, & A. Caspi (Eds.), *Causes of conduct disorder and juvenile delinquency* (pp. 254-274). New York: Guilford Press.

Dodge, K. A. & Pettit, G. S. (2003). A biopsychosocial model of the development of chronic conduct problems in adolescence. *Developmental Psychology, 39,* 349-371.

Donaldson, S. J. & Ronan, K. R. (2006). The effects of sports participation on young adolescents' emotional well-being. *Adolescence, 41,* 369-389.

Donnellan, M. B., Trzesniewski, K. H., Robins, R. W., Moffitt, T. E. & Caspi, A. (2005). Low self-esteem is related to aggression, antisocial behavior, and delinquency. *Psychological Science, 16,* 328-335.

DuBois, D. L., Hooloway, B. E., Valentine, J. C. & Cooper, H. (2002). Effectiveness of monitoring programs for youth: A meta-analytic review. *American Journal of Community Psychology, 30,* 157-197.

Dunlap, G., Strain, P. S., Fox, L., Carta, J. J., Conroy, M., Smith, B. J., Kern, L., Hemmeter, M. L., Timm, M. A., McCart, A., Sailor, W., Markey, U., Markey, D. J., Lardeiri, S. & Sowell, C. (2006). Prevention and intervention with young children's challenging behavior: Perspectives regarding current knowledge. *Behavioral Disorders, 32,* 29-45.

Dunn, J. S., Kinney, D. A. & Hofferth, S. L., (2003). Parental ideologies and children's after school activities. *American Behavioral Scientist, 46,* 1359-1386.

Dzik, D. (1975). Optometric intervention in the control of juvenile delinquents. *Journal of the American Optometric Association, 46,* 629-634.

Eccles, J. S. & Barber, B. L. (1999). Student council, volunteering, basketball, or marching band: What kind of extracurricular involvement matters? *Journal of Adolescent Research, 14,* 10-43.

Eitzen, D. S. & Sage, G. H. (2003). Intercollegiate sport. *Sociology of North American sport* (110-128). New York, NY: McGraw-Hill.

Ekeland, E., Heian, F. & Hagen, K. B. (2005). Can exercise improve self-esteem in children and young people? A systematic review of randomized controlled trials. *British Journal of Sports Medicine, 39,* 792-798.

Elliot, D. S., Dunford, F. W. & Huizinga, D. (1987). The identification and prediction of career offenders utilizing self-reported and official data. In J. D. Burchard, & S. N. Burchard (Eds.), *Prevention of delinquent behavior* (90-121). Newbury Park, CA: Sage.

Endresen, I. M. & Olweus, D. (2005). Participation in power sports and antisocial involvement in preadolescent and adolescent boys. *Journal of Child Psychology and Psychiatry, 46,* 468-478.

Estrada, A. M., Geltand, D. M. & Hartmann, D. P. (1988). Children's sport and development of social behaviors. In F. Smoll, R. Magill, & M. Ash (Eds.), *Children in sport* (3rd ed.). Champaign, IL: Human Kinetics.

European Commission (2008). White paper on sport. Available online at http://ec.europa.eu/sport/white-paper/index_en.htm.

Ewing, M. E., Gano-Overway, L. A., Branta, C. F. & Seefeldt, V. D. (2002). The role of sports in youth development. In M. Gatz, M. A. Messner, & S. J. Ball-Rokeach (Eds.), *Paradoxes of youth and sport* (31-47). Albany, NY: State University of New York Press.

Faulkner, G. E. J., Adlaf, E. M., Irving, H. M., Allison, K. R., Dwyer, J. J. M. & Goodman, J. (2007). The relationship between vigorous physical activity and juvenile delinquency: A mediating role for self-esteem? *Journal of Behavioral Medicine, 30,* 155-163.

Faulkner, R. A. & Slaterry, C. M. (1990). The relationship of physical activity to alcohol consumption in youth, 15-16 year old. *Canadian Journal of Public Health, 100,* 172-180.

Findlay, L. C. & Coplan, R. J. (2008). Come out and play: Shyness in childhood and the benefits of organized sports participation. *Canadian Journal of Behavioral Science, 40,* 153-161.

Fite, P. J., Colder, C. R., Lochman, J. E. & Wells, K. C. (2007). Pathways from proactive and reactive aggression to substance use. *Psychology of Addictive Behaviors, 21,* 355-364.

Flash, K. (2003). Treatment strategies for juvenile delinquency: Alternative solutions. *Child and Adolescent Social Work Journal, 20,* 509-527.

Forbes, G. B., Adams-Curtis, L. E., Pakalka, A. H. & White, K. B. (2006). Dating aggression, sexual coercion, and aggression-supporting attitudes among college men as a function of participation in aggressive high school sports. *Violence Against Women, 12,* 441-455.

Fraser, M. W., Day, S. H., Galinsky, M. J., Hodges, V. G. & Smokowski, P. R. (2004). Conduct problems and peer rejection in childhood: A randomized trial of the making Choices and Strong Families programs. *Research on Social Work Practice, 14,* 313-324.

Fraser, M. W., Galinsky, M. J., Smokowski, P. R., Day, S. H., Terzian, M. A., Rose, R. A. & Guo, S. (2005). Social information-processing skills training to promote social competence and prevent aggressive behavior in the third grade. *Journal of Consulting and Clinical Psychology, 73,* 1045-1055.

Fraser, M. W., Nash, J. K., Galinsky, M. J. & Darwin, K. M. (2000). *Making Choices: Social problem-solving skills for children.* Washington, D.C.: NASW Press.

Fraser-Thomas, J. L., Cote, J. & Deakin, J. (2005). Youth sport programs: An avenue to foster positive youth development. *Physical Education, Sport, and Pedagogy, 10,* 19-40.

Forneris, T., Danish, S. J. & Scott, D. L. (2007). Setting goals, solving problems, and seeking social support: Developing adolescents' abilities through a life skills program. *Adolescence, 42,* 103-114.

Galloway, S. (2006). Adventure education reconceived: Positive forms of deviant leisure. *Leisure/Loisir, 30,* 219-232.

Gardner, R. E. & Janelle, C. M. (2002). Legitimacy judgments of perceived aggression and assertion by contact and non-contact sport participants. *International Journal of Sport Psychology, 33,* 290-306.

Garry, J. P. & Morrissey, S. L. (2000). Team sports participation and risk-taking behaviors among a biracial middle school population. *Clinical Journal of Sports Medicine, 10,* 185-190.

Gibb, F. (2008, Feb. 15). Girl faces jail for 'happy slap' pictures. Retrieved December 18, 2008, from http://www.timesonline.co.uk/tol/news/uk/crime/article3372199.ece.

Goudas, M. & Giannoudis, G. (In press). A team-sports-based life-skills program in a physical education context. *Learning and Instruction.*

Hämäläinen, M. & Pulkkinen, L. (1996). Problem behavior as a precursor of male criminality. *Development and psychopathology, 8,* 443-445.

Hartmann, D. (2001). Notes on Midnight Basketball and the cultural politics of recreation, race, and at-risk urban youth. *Journal of Sport and Social Issues, 25,* 339-372.

Haynie, D. L. (2001). Delinquent peers revisited: Does network structure matter? *American Journal of Sociology, 106*, 1151-1178.

Hellison, D. (1978). *Beyond bats and balls: Alienated (and other) youth in the gym.* Washington, D.C.: AAHPERD.

Hellison, D. (1995). *Teaching responsibility through physical activity.* Champaign, IL: Human Kinetics.

Hellison, D. (2000). Physical activity programs for underserved youth. *Journal of Science and Medicine in Sport, 3*, 238–242.

Hellison, D. (2003). *Teaching responsibility through physical activity.* (2nd Ed.). Champaign, IL: Human Kinetics.

Hemery, D. (1986). *The pursuit of sporting excellence: A study of sport's highest achievers.* London: Willow Books.

Hinshaw, S. P. (1992). Externalizing behavior problems and academic under-achievement in childhood and adolescence: Causal relationships and underlying mechanisms. *Psychological Bulletin, 111*, 127-155.

Hirschi, T. (1969). *Causes of delinquency.* Berkeley, CA: University of California Press.

Hodge, K., Cresswell, S., Sherburn, D. & Dugdale, J. (1999). Physical activity-based life skills programs: Part II, example programmes. *Physical Education New Zealand Journal, 32*, 12-15.

Jeziorski, R. M. (1994). *The importance of school sports in American education and socialization.* New York: University Press of America.

Joe Laidler, K., Li, N. & Tang, T. (2005). An Evaluation of Operation Breakthrough (2004-2005). *Final Report on Hong Kong Police Programme.* HKU: Centre for Criminology.

Jones, M. B. & Offord, D. R. (1989). Reduction of antisocial behavior in poor children by non-school skill-development. *Journal of Child Psychology and Psychiatry, 30*, 737-750.

Kaseno, S. L. (1985). The visual anatomy of the juvenile delinquent. *Academic Therapy, 21*, 99-105.

Kohn, A. (1986). *No contest: The case against competition.* Boston, MA: Houghton, Mifflin, & Company.

Koss, M. P. (1988). Hidden rape: Sexual aggression and victimization in a national sample of students in higher education. In A. W. Burgess (Ed.), *Rape and sexual assault: II* (3-25). New York: Garland.

Koss, M. P. & Gaines, J. (1993). The prediction of sexual aggression by alcohol use, athletic participation and fraternity affiliation. *Journal of Interpersonal Violence, 8*, 94-108.

Kremer-Sadlik, T. & Kim, J. L. (2007). Lessons from sports: Children's socialization to values through family interaction during sports activities. *Discourse & Society, 18*, 35-52.

Krouwel, A., Boonstra, N., Duyvendak, J. W. & Velboer, L. (2006). A good sport? Research into the capacity of recreational sport to integrate Dutch minorities. *International Review for the Sociology of Sport, 41*, 165-180.

Lahey, B. B., McBurnett, K. & Loeber, R. (2000). Are attention-deficit hyperactivity disorder and oppositional defiant disorder development precursors of conduct disorder? In A. Semeroff, M. Lewis, & S. Miller (Eds.), *Handbook of developmental psychopathology* (431-446). New York: Plenum.

Lamarre, B. W. & Nosanchuck, T. A. (1999). Judo-the gentle way: A replication of studies on martial arts and aggression. *Perceptual & Motor Skills, 88*, 992-996.

Landers, D. M. & Arent, S. M. (2007). Physical activity and mental health. In G. Tenenbaum, & R. C. Eklund (Eds.), *Handbook of sport psychology* (3rd Ed.), (469-491). Hoboken, New Jersey: John Wiley & Sons, Inc.

Langbein, L. & Bess, R. (2002). Sports in school: Source of amity or antipathy? *Social Science Quarterly, 83,* 436-454.

Lawson, A. W. & Sanet, R. (1992). Vision problems, juvenile delinquency, and drug abuse. In G. W. Lawson, & A. W. Lawson (Eds.), *Adolescent substance abuse: Etiology, treatment, and prevention* (337-350). Gaithersburg, MD: Aspen.

Leitenberg, H. (1987). Primary prevention of delinquency. In J. D. Burchard, & S. N. Burchard (Eds.), *Prevention of delinquent behavior* (312-330). Newbury Park, CA: Sage.

Loeber, R., Burke, J. D., Lahey, B. B., Winters, A. & Zera, M. (2000). Oppositional defiant and conduct disorder: A review of the past 10 years, part I. *Journal of the American Academy of Child and Adolescent Psychiatry, 39,* 1468-1484.

Loeber, R., Farrington, D. P. & Petechuk, D. (2003). Child Delinquency: Early intervention and prevention. Child Delinquency Bulletin Series, Office of Juvenile Justice and Delinquency Prevention. Retrieved on 27th December 2008, from http://www.ojjdp.ncjrs.org/.

Lorente, F. O., Souville, M., Griffet, J. & Grélot, L. (2004). Participation in sports and alcohol consumption among French adolescents. *Addictive behaviors, 29,* 941-946.

Loughead, T. M. & Leith, L. M. (2001). Hockey coaches' and players' perceptions of aggression and the aggressive behavior of players. *Journal of Sport Behavior, 24,* 394-407.

Luxbacher, J. (1986). Violence in sports: An examination of the theories of aggression and how the coach can influence the degree of violence displayed in sport. *Coaching Review, 9,* 14-17.

Mash, E. J. & Barkley, R. A. (Eds.) (1998). Treatment of child disorders (2nd ed.). New York: Guilford.

Mason, G. & Wilson, P. (1988). *Sport, recreation, and juvenile crime.* Canberra, Australia: Australian Institute of Criminology.

Maxwell, J. P. (2008). Alcohol use, alcohol-related problems, psychological health, and sport participation in Hong Kong Chinese adolescents. *3rd International Conference on Child and Adolescent Psychopathology, July 14 - 15, Roehampton, UK.*

Maxwell, J. P., Masters, R. S. W. & Hammond, J. (In press). The implicit benefits of learning without errors: Interactions with fundamental movement ability in children. *Journal of Experimental Child Psychology.*

McKenny, A. & Dattilo, J. (2001). Effects of an intervention within a sport context on the prosocial behavior and antisocial behavior of adolescents with disruptive behavior disorders. *Therapeutic Recreation Journal, 35,* 123-140.

Melnick, M. (1992). Male athletes and sexual assault. *Journal of Physical Education, Recreation, and Dance, 63,* 32-35.

Messner, M. A. & Sabo, D. F. (1990). *Sport, men, and the gender order.* Champaign, IL: Human Kinetics Books.

Miller, K. E., Melnick, M. J., Barnes, G. M., Sabo, D. & Farrell, M. P. (2007). Athletic involvement and adolescent delinquency. *Journal of Youth and Adolescence, 36,* 711-723.

Moore, M. J. & Werch, C. E. (2005). Sport and physical activity participation and substance use among adolescents. *Journal of Adolescent Health, 36,* 486-493.

Morra, N. & Smith, M. D. (1995). Interpersonal sources of violence in hockey: The influence of the media, parents, coaches and game officials. *Children and youth in sport: A biopsychosocial perspective* (142-155). Madison: Brown & Benchmark.

Mrazek, P. J. & Haggerty, R. J. (Eds.) (1994). *Reducing the risks for mental disorders: Frontiers for preventative intervention research.* Washington, D.C.: National Academy Press.

National Alliance for Youth Sport. (2008). Overview – parents association for youth sport. Retrieved January 26, 2009, from http://www.nays.org/Parents/index.cfm.

Nelson, M. C. & Gordon-Larsen, P. (2006). Physical activity and sedentary behavior patterns are associated with selected adolescent health risk behaviors. *Pediatrics, 117,* 1281-1290.

Newton, M., Watson, D. L., Gano-Overway, L., Fry, M., Kim, M. S. & Magyar, M. (2007). The role of a caring-based intervention in a physical activity setting. *The Urban Review, 39,* 281-299.

Nixon, H. L. II (1997). Gender, sport, and aggressive behavior outside sport. *Journal of Sport and Social Issues, 21,* 379-391.

Norris, R., Carroll, D. & Cochran, R. (1992). The effects of physical activity and exercise training on psychological stress and well-being in an adolescent population. *Journal of Psychosomatic Research, 36,* 55-65.

Nosanchuk, T. A. (1981). The way of the warrior: The effects of traditional martial arts training on aggressiveness. *Human Relations, 34,* 435-444.

Nosanchuk, T. A. & MacNeil, M. L. C. (1989). Examination of the effects of traditional and modern martial arts training on aggressiveness. *Aggressive Behavior, 15,* 153-159.

O'Hearn, T. C. & Gatz, M. (2002). Going for the goal: Improving youth problem solving skills through a school based intervention. *Journal of Community Psychology, 30,* 281-303.

Osgood, W. D., Wilson, J. K., O'Malley, P. M., Bachman, J. G. & Johnston, L. D. (1996). Routine activities and individual deviant behavior. *Sociological Review, 61,* 635-656.

Paetsch, J. J. & Bertrand, L. D. (1997). The relationship between peer, social, and school factors, and delinquency among youth. *Journal of School Health, 67,* 27-32.

Palermo, M. T., Di Luigi, M., Dal Forno, G., Dominici, C., Vicomandi, D., Sambucioni, A., Proietti, L. & Pasqualetti, P. (2006). Externalizing and oppositional behaviors and Karate-do: The *Way* of crime prevention. *International Journal of Offender Therapy and Comparative Criminology, 50,* 654-660.

Paone, T. R., Packman, J., Maddux, C. & Rothman, T. (2008). A school-based group activity therapy intervention with at-risk high school students as it relates to their moral reasoning. *International Journal of Play Therapy, 17,* 122-137.

Papacharisis, V., Goudas, M., Danish, S. J. & Theodorakis, Y. (2005). The effectiveness of teaching a life skills program in a sport context. *Journal of Applied Sport Psychology, 17,* 247-254.

Peck, S. C., Vida, M. & Eccles, J. S. (2008). Adolescent pathways to adult drinking: Sport involvement is not necessarily risky or protective. *Addiction, 103,* 69-83.

Pelham, T. W., Campagna, P. D., Ritvo, P. G. & Birnie, W. A. (1993). The effects of exercise therapy on clients in a psychiatric rehabilitation program. *Psychosocial Rehabilitation Journal, 16,* 75-84.

Perreti-Watel, P., Beck, F. & Legleye, S. (2002). Beyond the U-curve: The relationship between sport and alcohol, cigarette, and cannabis use in adolescents. *Addiction, 97,* 707-716.

Pickering, S. J. & Gathercole, S. E., (2004). Distinctive working memory profiles in children with varying special education needs. *Educational Psychology, 24,* 393-408.

Quinsey, V. L., Skilling, T. A., Lalumière, M. L. & Craig, W. M. (2004). *Juvenile delinquency: Understanding the origins of individual differences.* Washington D.C.: American Psychological Association.

Rainey, C. J., McKeown, R. E., Sargent, R. C. & Valois, R. F. (1996). Patterns of tobacco and alcohol use among sedentary, exercising, non-athletic, and athletic youths. *Journal of School Health, 66,* 27-32.

Reynes, E. & Lorant, J. (2004). Competitive martial arts and aggressiveness: A 2-year longitudinal study among young boys. *Perceptual and Motor Skills, 98,* 103-115.

Riner, M. E. & Saywell, R. M. (2002). Development of the social ecology model of adolescent interpersonal violence prevention (SEMAIVP). *Journal of School Health, 72,* 65-70.

Rowe, D. C. & Farrington, D. P. (1997). The familial transmissions of criminal convictions. *Criminology, 35,* 177-201.

Rutton, E. A., Deković, M., Stams, G. J. J. M., Schuengel, C., Hoeksma, J. B. & Biesta, G. J. J. (2008). On-and off-field antisocial and prosocial behavior in adolescent soccer players: A multilevel study. *Journal of Adolescence, 31,* 371-387.

Sage, G. H. (1990). *Power and ideology in American sport.* Leeds: Human Kinetics Publishers.

Sampson, R. J. & Laub, J. H. (1990). Crime and deviance over the life course: The salience of adult social bonds. *American Sociological Review, 55,* 609-627.

Sherif, O. J., Harvey, B., Hood, W. R. & Sherif, C. W. (1987). *Intergroup conflict and cooperation: The robbers cave experiment.* Middletown, CN: Wesleyan University.

Shields, D. L. L. & Bredemeier, B. J. L. (1995). *Character development and physical activity.* Champaign, IL: Human Kinetics.

Simpkins, S. D., Eccles, J. S. & Becnel, J. N. (2008). The meditational role of adolescents' friends in relations between activity breadth and adjustment. *Developmental Psychology, 44,* 1081-1094.

Skelton, D. L., Glynn, M. A. & Berta, S. M. (1991). Aggressive behavior as a function of taekwondo ranking. *Perceptual and Motor Skills, 72,* 179-182.

Smith, M. D. (1975). The legitimation of violence: Hockey players' perception of their reference groups' sanctions for assault. *Canadian Review of Sociology and Anthropology, 12,* 72-80.

Smith, M. D. (1979). Towards an explanation of hockey violence: A reference other approach. *Canadian Journal of Sociology, 4,* 105-124.

Smith, M. D. (1980). Hockey violence: Interring some myths. *Sport psychology: An analysis of athlete behavior* (141-146). Ithaca, NY: Mouvement Publications.

Smith, R. E. & Smoll, F. L., (1991). Behavioral research and intervention in youth sports. *Behavior Therapy, 22,* 329-344.

Smith, R. E., Smoll, F. L. & Curtis, B. (1979). Coach effectiveness training: A cognitive-behavioral approach to enhancing relationship skills in youth sport coaches. *Journal of Sport Psychology, 1,* 59-75.

Snyder, H. N. (2006). *Juvenile arrests 2006.* Retrieved 27th December 2008 from http://www.ojp.usdoj.gov/ojjdp.

Sobotowicz, W., Evans, J. R. & Laughlin, J. (1987). Neuropsychological function and social support in delinquency and learning disability. *International Journal of Clinical Neuropsychology, 9,* 178-186.

Steptoe, A. & Butler, N. (1996). Sport participation and emotional well-being in adolescents. *Lancet, 347,* 1789-1792.

Strauss, M. A., Gelles, R. J. & Steinmetz, S. K. (1980). *Behind closed doors.* Garden City, NJ: Anchor Press.

Sugden, J. & Yiannakis, A. (1982). Sport and juvenile delinquency: A theoretical base. *Journal of Sport and Social Issues, 6,* 22-30.

Tao, F. B., Xu, M. L., Kim, S. D., Sun, Y., Su, P. Y. & Huang, K. (2007). Physical activity might not be the protective factor for health risk behaviors and psychopathological symptoms in adolescents. *Journal of Paediatrics and Child Health, 43,* 762-767.

Taylor, T., Scott, D. L. & Danish, S. J. (In press). Developing adolescents' goal setting, problem solving and seeking social support skills through a life skills program. *Adolescence.*

Tebes, J. K., Feinn, R., Vanderploeg, J. J., Chinman, M. J., Shepard, J., Brabham, T., Genovese, M. & Connell, C. (2007). Impact of a positive youth development program in urban after-school settings on the prevention of adolescent substance use. *Journal of Adolescent Health, 41,* 239-247.

Thornberry, T. P. & Krohn, M. D. (1997). Peers, drug use, and delinquency. In D. Skoff, J. Breiling, & J. D. Maser (Eds.), *Handbook of antisocial behavior* (218-233). New York: Wiley.

Tremblay, R. E. & Craig, W. (1995). Developmental crime prevention. In M. Tonry, & D. P. Farrington (Eds.), *Building a safer society: Strategic approaches to crime prevention* (151-236). Chicago: University of Chicago Press.

Tremblay, R. E., Pagani-Kurtz, L., Vitaro, F., Masse, L. C. & Pihl, R. O. (1995). A bimodal prevention intervention for disruptive kindergarten boys: Its impact through mid-adolescence. *Journal of Consulting and Clinical Psychology, 63,* 560-568.

Trulson, M. E. (1986). Martial arts training: A novel 'cure' for juvenile delinquency. *Human Relations, 39,* 1131-1140.

United Nations (2003). *World Youth Report.* New York: United Nations Publication.

United Nations Office for Drug Control and Prevention (2002). Sport: Using sport for drug abuse prevention. New York: United Nations Publication.

Vaz, E. W. (1982). *The professionalization of young hockey players.* Lincoln: University of Nebraska Press.

Visek, A. J., Harris, B. S. & Blom, L. C. (2006). Youth athletes are NOT miniature adults: A comprehensive guide to performance enhancement with youth sports. In *Association for the Advancement of Applied Sport Psychology Conference Proceedings* (111). Madison, WI: AAASP.

Visek, A. J., Harris, B. S. & Blom, L. C. (2009). Doing sport psychology: A youth sport consulting model for practitioners. *The Sport Psychologist, 23,* 271-291.

Weiss, M. R. & Duncan, S. C. (1992). The relation between physical competence and peer acceptance in the context of children's sport participation. *Journal of Sport and Exercise Psychology, 14,* 177-191.

Wollf, P. H., Waber, D, Bauermeister, M., Cohen. C. & Ferber, (1982). The neuropsychological status of adolescent delinquent boys. *Journal of Child Psychology and Psychiatry, 23,* 267-279.

Wright, W. (2006). Keep it in the ring: Using boxing in social group work with high-risk and offender youth to reduce violence. *Social Work with Groups, 29,* 149-174.

In: Youth Violence and Juvenile Justice: Causes, Intervention... ISBN: 978-1-61668-011-4
Editor: Neil A. Ramsay et al., pp. 141-162 © 2010 Nova Science Publishers, Inc.

Chapter 5

SOCIOMETRIC STATUS AND BULLYING: PEER RELATIONSHIPS, AGGRESSIVE BEHAVIOR, AND VICTIMIZATION

[1]Martica Bacallao and [2]Paul Smokowski[*]
[1]University of North Carolina – Greensboro, NC, USA
[2]University of North Carolina at Chapel Hill, NC, USA

ABSTRACT

This chapter examines how sociometric status influences childhood bullying, aggressive behavior, and victimization. Sociometric status is associated with bullying dynamics that pose a serious threat to victimized children and damage school climate. Special attention is given to the affect of sociometric neglect and rejection on child development. By using sociometric testing, small group practitioners are able to identify low status children at risk for becoming victims of bullying. Further, practitioners in schools can help prevent and reduce bullying by implementing sociometric interventions such as peer pairing of popular and rejected or neglected children. By working to create classroom and school environments with fluid sociometric roles, we can make strides to promote the safety, security, and growth of all students.

Keywords: Sociometry, Bullying, Childhood Peer Relations.

INTRODUCTION

Sociometry has a long and distinguished history dating to the 1920s. Bronfenbrenner (1943) defined sociometry as "a method for discovering, describing, and evaluating social

---

[*] Corresponding author: Associate Professor, University of North Carolina at Chapel Hill, School of Social Work, CB# 3550, 325 Pittsboro St., Chapel Hill, NC 27599-3550, by phone 919-843-8281, or by E-mail: smokowsk@email.unc.edu

status, structure, and development through measuring the extent of acceptance or rejection between individuals in groups" (p. 364). Moreno's (1934) pioneering publication, *Who Shall Survive? A New Approach to the Problem of Human Interrelations,* offered a comprehensive account of sociometric theory and practice. In the 1950s, social psychologists became interested in sociometry, and sociometric research was conducted in a variety of settings. Today, sociometric testing is widely used by developmental psychologists as a measure of childhood adjustment because the testing methods are clear-cut, easy to administer, reliable, can be predictive of adaptive and maladaptive outcomes in both social (Parker, Rubin, Erath, Wojslawwowicz, & Buskirk, 2006) and academic domains (Poulin & Dishion, 2008; Véronneau & Vitaro, 2007; Williams & Gilmour, 1994). In this chapter, we review the modern application of sociometric research and practice with elementary and middle-school children. Specifically, we examine the role of sociometric status in childhood bullying and victimization. Special attention is given to the impact of sociometric isolation on child development.

Sociometry in the Classroom

Most sociometric studies have been conducted in schools because schools are not only the environment in which children spend substantial time but also the context in which children are exposed to a stable peer group. During their elementary school years, children are assigned to stable or fixed classrooms; they interact with the same classmates for several hours each weekday for the entire school year. Considering the importance of this context in children's social life, it is not surprising that most of the research using sociometric nominations has been school based.

Sociometry has provided both theory and method for examining peer relationships and group processes (Poulin & Dishion, 2008). Sociometric testing usually involved one of two methods. The most commonly used method is *peer nomination* in which students nominate three classmates whom they like and three whom they dislike. The wording of the sociometric question or criterion is important; it can be either general (e.g., "Who do you like most?") or specific (e.g., "Who would you choose to sit next to on the bus?"). In studies conducted among preadolescents and adolescents, general nominations are appropriate and parsimonious because youth generally understand the concept of *liking* and *disliking* (Poulin & Dishion, 2008). However, younger children may need prompts to enhance clarity. Even so, a meta-analysis conducted by Jiang and Cillessen (2005) showed that the wording of the sociometric questions did not affect the stability of sociometric scores.

The next step in the sociometric testing is to tally the peer nominations to form groups of students based on the number of positive and negative connections within the group. These aggregate scores can be used to create sociometric categories (e.g., rejected, popular, controversial, neglected, and average) or a continuous index of peer status (e.g., acceptance, rejection, social preference). If sociometric ratings are going to be used in advanced statistical techniques such as structural equation modeling, continuous indexes are more stable and are easier to handle as compared to categorical data (Cillessen & Mayeux, 2004; Jiang & Cillessen, 2005). The social preference index, which is calculated by subtracting the number of rejection nominations from the number of acceptance nominations an individual received, is generally used to summarize youth's peer status (Coie, Dodge, & Coppotelli, 1982; Newcomb & Bukowski, 1983; Poulin & Dishion, 2008). Moreover, the sociometric scores and categories are often useful to teachers, school social workers, and psychologists. The peer nominations can also be used as the bases for creating experiential activities and diagrams of social dynamics. For example, relationships from the nominations may be drawn using positive and negative lines to form a *social atom* or map of interrelationships (Hale, 1974).

A second sociometric measurement strategy of *peer rating* is similar to peer nomination but is more comprehensive. Whereas peer nomination considers only the three most preferred and the three least preferred classmates, the peer rating method asks students to provide a rating for each of their classmates. In this strategy, students use a Likert scale to give their responses to specific criteria such as how much they like to "spend time with" or "work with" each child in the class. Categorization is based on two dimensions: social preference and social impact. Preference ratings are determined by the extent to which the child was liked or disliked by peers, and impact ratings describe the child's social salience or visibility (Coie et al., 1982). Preference and impact scores can be calculated using the nomination totals, and children categorized into a sociometric status group based on those scores.

Many studies have documented the relationships between sociometric status and adolescents' antisocial behavior and academic achievement (Cillessen & Mayeux, 2004; Véronneau & Vitaro, 2007). One commonly accepted classification system assigns a child to one of six sociometric status groups: popular, rejected, neglected, controversial, average, and other (Coie et al., 1982). We use this classification system as a guide to review existing knowledge on sociometric status and bullying. As shown in Table 1, we have defined these groups and delineated risk and protective factors inherent in each classification. Children classified as popular were liked by many and received few, if any, negative nominations. Popular children tended to demonstrate prosocial behavior, were helpful and considerate, respected authority and rules, and actively engaged in interactions with their peers (Coie & Kupersmidt, 1983; Coie, Dodge, & Kupersmidt, 1990). Further, the popularity of some students appears to be based on their athletic or academic competence (Dunn, Dunn, & Bayduza, 2007; Newcomb, Bukowski, & Pattee, 1993). Researchers have found a positive relationship between a child's intelligence and popularity among peers (Czeschlik & Rost, 1995). Popular status children tended to have adult support from both teachers and parents.

In contrast, children classified as rejected status received few, if any, positive nominations and many negative nominations. These children are distinguished from those in the neglected group in that rejected children are actively disliked by their peers. However, despite rejected children's lack of popularity and general acceptance, researchers have indicated that these children are seldom entirely friendless or completely isolated (Cadwallader, 2000/2001). Further, the rejected category typically contains two subgroups: children who are rejected for being overly aggressive and children who are rejected for being withdrawn or immature. However, most peers express a dislike for both subgroups. In addition, researchers have suggested that peer rejection was negatively related to intelligence and that rejected children are likely to be at risk for later adjustment difficulties (Asher & Coie, 1990; Asher & Parker, 1989; Czeschlik & Rost, 1995; Kupersmidt, Coie, & Dodge, 1990; Putallaz, 1983).

Children classified as controversial received both positive and negative nominations from peers, but may also be aggressive or disruptive in the classroom. Despite this behavior, controversial children seem to possess social and leadership skills, which gain them popularity with some children. In a study that investigated the sociometric status of adopted children in the Netherlands, Juffer, Stams, and van IJzendoorn (2004) reported that adopted children identified by peer report as controversial or rejected had significantly higher scores on externalizing problems than did adopted children whose peer reports classified them as popular, average, or neglected.

In contrast to the other classifications, neglected children are categorized as such because they receive few nominations at all. Peers tend to label these children as shy, and some research has shown that they often preferred to play by themselves (Coie et al., 1982). Although neglected children may have a few friends (French & Waas, 1985), overall this group was generally ignored by peers rather than actively liked or disliked.

Children with average status generally received some positive and negative nominations and tended to be viewed as neither highly popular nor unpopular. Average status children often served as the reference point for other groups (Williams & Gilmour, 1994). The final classification of children as "other status" comprises those who receive a mix of nomination types that do not fit clearly into any of these other five categories.

Researchers have indicated that the rejected status group may be more stable than the others. However, some investigators have argued that—even though some movement between groups may occur over time—within a consistent social environment, children tend to remain perceived in broadly the same terms by their peers (Williams & Gilmour, 1994). Although sociometry can be used to measure a child's relationships within his or her peer group, researchers caution that a child's status within a particular group is not necessarily reflective of their overall status (Williams & Gilmour, 1994; Cadwallader, 2000/2001). For example, a child may have been popular among his or her neighborhood friends and family members, but neglected by peer groups at school.

Sociometry has been useful in providing professionals with an easy-to-use method for examining peer relationships and in helping to determine which children might be at risk for later adjustment difficulties or emotional disturbance (Poulin & Dishion, 2008; Williams & Gilmour, 1994). Further, sociometric testing has allowed professionals to determine whether children were at risk for becoming bullies or for being victimized by their peers. In turn, this knowledge has been used to guide sociometric interventions aimed at preventing aggression, victimization, and long-term adjustment difficulties. For school personnel to take a proactive approach to prevention, it was important for educators and administrators to understand the dynamics of childhood sociometry and how the six classification categories (Table 1) have been linked to aggression and victimization. Children who are classified as neglected, rejected, or controversial may have the most difficulties. The next section focuses on neglected and rejected status children, delineating the risk factors they face.

Neglected Social Status

Researchers investigating the sociometric status of children have reported that neglected status children tended to play alone and were often characterized as withdrawn (Bergin, 1986; Williams & Gilmour, 1994). This group of children seemed to be low in approach motivation, yet did not seem to be necessarily low in avoidance motivation (Asendorpf, 1990; Harrist, Zaia, Bates, Dodge, & Pettit, 1997). Thus, even though these children had the social competence to interact with other children, they often preferred to play alone (Harrist et al., 1997). This dynamic may be due to the neglected child's inability to initiate interactions with other children or a lack of confidence regarding their ability to engage with their peers. Once the difficulties of engagement were surmounted, neglected children interacted appropriately with others. However, some research has indicated that deficits in social competence (rather than lack of confidence) were the cause of neglected girls being ignored by peers (Feldman & Dodge, 1987). Overall, neglected children tended to be less socially active and less aggressive than other children when they interacted with their peers (Bergin, 1986; Coie et al., 1990). Therefore, it appears that what distinguished neglected children from average children was that neglected children were not well known by their peers and lacked visibility within the peer group (Newcomb & Bukowski, 1983).

Table 1. Sociometric Classifications and Bullying.

Sociometric Category	Definition	Risk Factors	Protective Factors	Relationship to Bullying
Popular	Many peers like & few dislike the child; the child displays high visibility & preference in the group.	Few. These children may feel the need to protect their high status. May use status in negative ways (e.g. to exclude others).	Prosocial behavior, respect for authority & rules, helpfulness, engagement in interactions with peers, intelligence, adult protection. High levels of social skills.	Witnesses to bullying. Under stress, popular children may engage in relational aggression.
Average	Some peers like and some dislike the child; the child displays mid-range visibility & preference in the group.	Few. These children may feel the need to protect the relationships they have. They may seek more popularity and fear becoming controversial, neglected, or rejected.	Peer support from the friends they have, moderate level of social skills.	Witnesses to bullying. These children may not intervene because they fear becoming the next victim.
Controversial	Many peers both like and dislike the child; High visibility; mid-range preference. Child may take risks or speak out in unconventional ways.	Disruptive, aggressive behavior, the child's friends may also be controversial.	Possess leadership skills, may have friends. May have resilience and rebellious spirit.	May become Bully/victims. When victimized by bullies, the child may seek other children to bully. May engage in relational aggression.
Neglected	Few peers like or dislike the child; low visibility. Child may withdraw or hide during group interactions. He or she may want to interact, but does not know how.	Unsociable, prefer solitary play, engage in fewer verbal interactions with peers, ignored by peers. Low levels of social support and social skills.	May or may not be lonely, may have one or two reliable friends. Child may be sensitive, creative, and unconventional. May have dynamic inner life to compensate for interpersonal difficulties.	At high risk for becoming victims. Easy targets with little capacity for retaliation.
Rejected	Few children like & many dislike the child; high visibility & low preference in the group; lack popularity, but may not be entirely friendless or isolated. Two subgroups identified – Rejected/Withdrawn and Rejected/Aggressive.	Lack of social skills, inappropriate behavior, anxiety, aggression, immaturity, hyperactivity, impulsivity, having a disability, less intelligent, underlying disturbance.	Rejected/Withdrawn children may cope by hiding, may have dynamic inner life. Rejected/Aggressive children may have some friends. These friends may be older and engaged in delinquent or deviant behavior.	Rejected/ Withdrawn - Worry about being victimized and/or humiliated, are easy targets, are often victims Rejected/ Aggressive- Tend to be bullies.

Researchers have also found differences in the parenting styles of the parents of neglected status children as compared with parents of children in the other categories. The parents of neglected status children tended to engage in fewer overall interactions with their children than did parents of other children (Franz & Gross, 2001). In addition, parents of neglected status children were inclined to use an authoritarian parenting style, which was characterized by criticism, excessive disciplinary control, and little praise or affection (Franz & Gross, 2001).

In terms of status stability, neglected children showed less continuity than rejected children and were more likely to improve their status over time (Coie & Dodge, 1983). In addition, research has suggested that neglected children were not at risk for later adjustment difficulties or disorders (Williams & Gilmour, 1994). In fact, one study found that neglected children did not exhibit greater numbers or severity of problem behaviors than popular or average children and were less deviant than rejected children (French & Waas, 1985).

Rejected Social Status

In contrast to neglected children who were ignored by peers, rejected children, who were disliked by peers, were found to be at risk for becoming victims of bullying. However, rejected children also tended to become bullies if they were physically larger than other children and relied on aggressive behavior to respond to social situations. Rejected status children seemed to be a heterogeneous group usually divided into rejected/aggressive and rejected/withdrawn subgroups (Parkhurst & Asher, 1992). Nearly half of rejected children (40-50%) were perceived by their peers as aggressive, whereas 10-20% of rejected children were perceived by their peers as socially withdrawn (Cillessen, van IJzendoorn, van Lieshout, & Hartup, 1992). The rejected/aggressive group was described as "impulsive, disruptive, dishonest, hypersensitive, and non-cooperative" (Cillessen et al., 1992, p. 902). In contrast, children in the rejected/withdrawn group were active-isolates, rather immature and socially unskilled children who wanted to play with others, but were usually unable to find willing partners (Harrist et al., 1997). These children often became withdrawn as a result of their rejection.

However, in the research conducted to date, these two rejected subtypes have applied more to rejected boys than to rejected girls. Moreover, in examining peer-rejected girls, French (1990) found that two further subgroups emerged based on deviant behavior. The more deviant group was characterized by withdrawal, anxiety, and low academic functioning whereas the less deviant group was distinguished by behavior disorders, aggression, and self-control deficits relative to popular girls (French, 1990). Therefore, although aggression appeared to be the most common reason for rejection among boys, withdrawal distinguished rejected girls. In addition, the presence of aggression differentiated the subgroups of rejected boys whereas the presence of internalizing disorders seemed to differentiate the subgroups of rejected girls (French, 1990).

On the whole, however, rejected children tended to be less sociable than average children (Newcomb et al., 1993). In addition, those in the rejected status tended to be perceived by peers as lacking positive qualities to balance unfavorable reputations and were viewed as lacking friendships (Newcomb et al., 1993). Compared to popular children, rejected children reported significantly higher feelings of loneliness and lower levels of athletic ability (Dunn et al., 2007) Despite this characterization, rejected children were not entirely alone (Cairns, Cairns, Neckerman, Gest, & Gariepy, 1988). Some research has suggested that although rejected children have a social network, they engaged in lower levels of social participation as compared with average children (Newcomb et al., 1993). Other researchers have offered an alternate scenario in which rejected children commonly formed subgroups, banding together in a counterculture with the covert message "If I'm not 'good enough,' then I can be 'bad enough.'" In terms of family, rejected children, similar to neglected children, tend to have parents who rely on authoritarian parenting styles (Franz & Gross, 2001).

A growing body of research has established a link between childhood aggression and peer rejection (Cillessen & Mayeux, 2004; Véronneau & Vitaro, 2007). Children who were rejected by their peers, were also more likely than other children to use aggression to achieve social goals (Bierman, Smoot, & Aumiller, 1993; Miller-Johnson, Coie, Maumary-Gremaud, Bierman, & Conduct Problems Prevention Research Group, 2002). Moreover, rejected children were more likely to escalate their aggressive behavior if they were the targets of harassing acts such as teasing or taunting. Rejected children were quick to fight and slow to employ negotiation, bargaining, and other forms of problem solving. Although fighting back may be perceived as self-defense in some circumstances, the result was often increased rejection and marginalization by other children (Hanish & Guerra, 2002). One rare longitudinal study conducted by Nelson and Dishion (2004) has demonstrated the relation of childhood sociometric status of 200 fourth-grade boys to their outcomes as young adults. Nelson and Dishion found that when young men were compared on measures of antisocial behavior and work /school engagement as young adults (ages 23-24 years), those who had been rejected and isolated boys differed from those who had been amiable and popular boys, even when these behaviors were accounted for at earlier time points.

Similar to Nelson and Dishion, a substantial body of evidence has shown that childhood sociometric status has implications that persist beyond the classroom. Neglected and rejected children are at increased risk of problems in their schools and communities because they lack connections with prosocial peer groups (Coie, Lochman, Terry, & Hyman, 1992; Hawkins & Weis, 1985; Kaplow, Curran, Dodge, & Conduct Problems Prevention Research Group, 2002; Kupersmidt et al., 1990; Rieffe, Villanueva, & Meerum Terwogt, 2005). Rejection by prosocial peers heightened the probability of a rejected child associating with delinquent peers, which is an important risk factor for subsequent crime and substance use (Cairns & Cairns, 1994; Fergusson, Swain-Campbell, & Horwood, 2002; Hanish & Guerra, 2002). Consequently, rejection by peers is one of the most commonly cited factors in a risk sequence associated with poor developmental outcomes (see Cillessen & Mayeux, 2004; Fraser, Kirby, & Smokowski, 2004; Hanish & Guerra, 2002; Kaplow et al., 2002; Lonczak et al., 2001; Miller-Johnson et al., 2002; Miller-Johnson, Coie, Maumary-Gremaud, Lochman, & Terry, 1999; Véronneau & Vitaro, 2007).

Both neglected and rejected status children experienced low acceptance from their peers. This low acceptance may lead to victimization; Olweus (1978) has argued that many victims of bullying have low sociometric status. Thus, professionals working with children may be able to use sociometric testing to identify potential victims of bullying. Specifically, neglected and rejected/withdrawn children were found to be at greatest risk for bullying because they were not accepted by their peers and did not have friends to support them. Therefore, it is critical that professionals be able to not only identify potential victims, such as neglected and rejected status children, but also have an understanding of the dynamics and consequences of bullying. The following section provides a brief overview of bullying.

BULLYING

Over the past 30 years, clinicians and researchers have come to understand that bullying is a serious threat to healthy child development and a potential cause of school violence (Olweus, 1978). Bullying has usually been defined as a form of aggression in which one or more children act with intention to harm or disturb a child who is perceived as being unable to defend himself or herself (Glew, Rivara, & Feudtner, 2000). Typically, a power imbalance exists between the bully and the victim, with the bully either physically or psychologically more powerful (Nansel et al., 2001). Often, the perpetrator uses bullying as a means to establish dominance or maintain status (Pellegrini, Bartini, & Brooks, 1999; Roberts, 2000). In addition, the perpetrators tend to repeat the bullying behaviors over time (Nansel et al., 2001).

Bullying represents a significant problem in schools (Glew, Fan, Katon, & Rivara, 2008). The National School Safety Center has labeled bullying the most enduring and underrated problem in U.S. schools (Beale, 2001). In a recent study, nearly 30% of students reported being involved in bullying in the current term, either as a perpetrator or a victim (Nansel et al., 2001). Bullying is a common problem among elementary, middle-, and high-school settings, and thus is an issue that deserves greater attention.

Types of Bullying

In the bully/victim relationship, bullies are the aggressors or perpetrators of harm. Although boys have been identified as bullies more often than girls, both genders engage in bullying behaviors (Olweus, 1993; Pellegrini, 1998). Direct bullying is characterized by physical assault whereas indirect bullying tactics cause the victim to be socially isolated (Beale, 2001). Generally, researchers have identified four types of bullies: *physical, verbal, relational, and reactive bullies* (Argenbright & Edgell, 1999; Beale, 2001). Well-known in schools, physical bullies tend to be action-oriented and use direct bullying behaviors such as hitting and kicking. In contrast, verbal bullies tend to use words to hurt or humiliate their victims. In the third type of bullying, the relational bully uses words and actions to convince his or her peers to exclude certain children. Research has shown girls use relational bullying most often. Indeed, some researchers have suggested that popular status children, particularly popular girls, used relational bullying as a way to maintain their own status (McDonald, Putallaz, Grimes, Kupersmidt, & Coie, 2007). The final type of bullying is reactive. Often characterized by impulsivity, reactive bullies tend to taunt other bullies into fighting with them. Once a physical encounter was provoked, the reactive bullies fought back, claiming self-defense. Because it was often difficult for their peers to determine who was the victim in this type of encounter, peers often reported mixed feelings about reactive bullies. Thus, sociometrically, reactive bullies are most often considered by their peers as controversial (i.e., both liked and disliked).

Characteristics of Bullies

Even though bullies differ in the type of aggression they use, most bullies share common characteristics. Research has shown that most bullies were classified as rejected/aggressive status children, and they tended to be hot-tempered, impulsive, and had a low tolerance for frustration (Olweus, 1993). In addition, most bullies had a positive attitude towards violence, particularly as a means to solve problems or get what they want (Glew et al., 2000; Carney & Merrell, 2001). Further, researchers found that bullies were more likely to be involved with other problem behaviors such as drinking and smoking (Nansel et al., 2001).

Ongoing controversy exists regarding the relation of bullying and the perpetrator's level of self-esteem. Some researchers have suggested that children who became bullies suffered from low self-esteem (O'Moore & Kirkham, 2001) whereas others have contended that bullies displayed average or above average levels of self-esteem (Glew et al., 2000).

Short- and Long-Term Effects of Being a Bully

Some research has reported that many bullies have experienced mental health difficulties including attention deficit disorder, depression, and oppositional/conduct disorder (Kumpulainen, Rasanen, & Puura, 2001). In addition, researchers have found that relative to their victims, bullies are more likely to engage in frequent, excessive alcohol and substance use (Kaltiala-Heino, Rimpela, & Rimpela, 2000). When followed up as adults, bullies displayed externalizing behaviors, hyperactivity, and antisocial characteristics (Kumpulainen & Rasanen, 2000; Olweus, 1993). Further, research has indicated that by the age of 30 years, bullies were likely to have more criminal convictions and traffic violations than their less aggressive peers (Roberts, 2000). In fact, a 1991 study found that 60% of boys who were labeled as bullies in Grades 6 to 9 had at least one criminal conviction by the age of 24 years, and approximately 40% of these boys had three or more convictions by that age (Glew et al., 2000; Olweus, 1995). As adults, these boy bullies were also more likely to have displayed aggression towards their spouses and were more likely to use severe physical punishment on their children (Roberts, 2000).

Characteristics of Victims

Just as there are various types of bullies, there are various types of victims. The vast majority of victims of bullying are passive or submissive, making rejected/withdrawn and neglected status children potential targets for bullying. As compared with their peers who were bullies, victims tend to be less robust physically; victims in one study tended to be small in stature, weak, frail, and, therefore, often unable to protect themselves from abuse (McNamara & McNamara, 1997). Victims also tend to be characterized as being more quiet, cautious, anxious, insecure, and sensitive than most other children, in addition to having poor communication and problem-solving skills (Glew et al., 2000; McClure & Shirataki, 1989). Thus, many victims are described as having been abandoned by other children, having few friends, and are often found alone on the playground or at lunchtime (Olweus, 1993). Some research has shown that victims tended to suffer from poor self-esteem, which lead them to either incorrectly blame themselves for the bullying or caused them to be unwilling to report the bullying (Carney & Merrell, 2001; O'Moore & Kirkham, 2001). Victims performed average or better in elementary school, but usually tended to be less successful than other children in middle school when bullying was most prevalent (Olweus, 1993).

Short- and Long-Term Effects of Victimization

As a result of being bullied, victims experience many detrimental short- and long-term effects. Most victims developed a negative view of themselves and their lives. Studies have suggested that victimization is correlated with several disorders such as anxiety, depression, and eating disorders in adolescence (Kaltiala-Heino et al., 2000). Further, one study found that attention deficit disorder was common among victims (Kumpulainen et al., 2001). Researchers have found that victims of bullying often suffered from chronic absenteeism, reduced academic performance, increased apprehension, loneliness, and abandonment by peers (Beale, 2001; Roberts & Coursol, 1996). Bullying often results in physical harm, with victims commonly reporting being injured, cut, bruised, or scratched by bullies. Physical altercations with bullies often result in victims who report torn clothing and damaged property.

The consequences and repercussions of bullying are far reaching. At night, victims have reported experiencing difficulty sleeping and patterns of disturbing nightmares (McNamara & McNamara, 1997). Moreover, as evidenced by an increasing number of school shootings, victims are more likely than nonvictims to bring weapons to school, whether to feel safe or to retaliate (Carney & Merrell, 2001) However, it appears that it is more common for victims to internalize their responses to bullying. Unfortunately, some victims have felt hopeless and attempted suicide (Olweus, 1993).

When assessed as adults, former victims had lower levels of achievement than their nonvictimized peers (McNamara & McNamara, 1997). As compared with nonvictimized young adults, former victims tended to have lower self-esteem, more depressive symptoms, and experienced greater psychosocial difficulties during adulthood, such as having problems in sexual relationships (Carney & Merrell, 2001; Gilmartin, 1987; Hazler, 1996; Olweus, 1993). Although a minority among former victims, as adults some former victims have carried out acts of retribution, including murder, against former bullies (Carney & Merrell, 2001).

Characteristics of Bully/Victims

A third category of children involved in bullying situations has been labeled *bully/victims*, also called reactive bullies or provocative victims. These children both bully others and are themselves bullied. In studies of classroom behavior, bully/victims were characterized by both anxious and aggressive behavior (Olweus, 1995); they tended to annoy other students and regularly caused aggravation (Carney & Merrell, 2001). However, bully/victims usually had poor self-esteem, were often hyperactive, and had difficulties with concentration and problem solving (Andreou, 2001). As a result, bully/victims tended to externalize their problems, displaying neurotic and psychotic behavior (Mynard & Joseph, 1997). For example, one study that examined pure bullies and bully/victims found that bully/victims viewed themselves as more troublesome, having lower intellectual and school status, less physically attractive, more anxious, less popular, and unhappier than pure bullies (O'Moore & Kirkham, 2001). Thus, the bully/victims' own negative self-perceptions strained relationships with their peers.

In terms of sociometry, bully/victims were most likely to be classified as controversial status children. Although bully/victims had high visibility upon their peers because of their disruptive, hyperactive behavior, they tended to receive both positive and negative sociometric nominations. It may be that peers viewed bully/victims as class clowns, with some children liking them and others being annoyed by their behavior. Coie and colleagues (1990) concluded that controversial status children were highly active, aggressive, and provoked peer group anger. In addition, the disruptive activities of controversial status children both entertained the peer group and attracted teacher reprimand (Coie et al., 1990). Thus, controversial status children caused mixed feelings within the classroom, particularly when these children were involved in bullying behaviors.

Short- and Long-Term Effects of Being Both a Bully and a Victim

Research has shown that most bully/victims have suffered from low self-esteem and have a negative self-perception. In addition to later adjustment problems, their involvement with bullying impacted their mental health as adolescents (Batsche, 1997). In one study, 21.5% of bully/victims had oppositional/conduct disorder, 17.7% had depression, and 17.7% had attention deficit disorder (Kumpulainen et al., 2001). Another study examined the three categories of children typically involved in bullying situations (i.e., victims, bullies, and bully/victims) and found that bully/victims had the greatest risk for depressive symptoms, anxiety, psychosomatic symptoms, and eating disorders (Kaltiala-Heino et al., 2000). In addition, Kaltiala-Heino and colleagues also found that bully/victims were at significant risk for drinking and substance use as adolescents.

BULLYING USING RELATIONAL AGGRESSION

The discussion thus far has primarily focused on direct, or physical, bullying. However in recent years, indirect bullying, commonly referred to as relational or social aggression, has received increasing attention (McDonald et al., Coie, 2007). Whereas bullies and victims commonly remained neglected or rejected on the periphery of the group's sociometric structure, relationally aggressive children may have been quite popular, highly chosen, and situated at the core of the class's sociometry. Relationally aggressive children typically use interpersonal schemes (e.g., gossip, rumors, slandering) to shift sociometry so as to ostracize children who are their victims (Crick & Grotpeter, 1996). For example, a common goal of a relational bully might be to deprive a girl of her best girlfriend or to have a targeted girl listen on the telephone as two other girls discussed how much they hate her. These strategies may use new technology such as text messaging and Internet chat rooms to harass victims (David-Ferdon & Feldman-Hertz, 2007; Ybarra, Diener-West, & Leaf, 2007). Popular girls use relationally aggressive tactics to ward off threats to their cliques; to keep average, rejected, and neglected peers from gaining social status; to keep homeostasis in the peer group's sociometric structure; or simply for sport out of boredom or maliciousness.

THE SILENT MAJORITY

Bullying generally occurs in the presence of witnesses. Although little research has been done on the silent majority of children who witness, but do not participate in bullying, we can speculate that witnesses most likely tend to be children in the popular and average status groups. During a bullying episode, witnesses may be quiet and may not take any sort of action. The reasons for inaction and silence may largely depend on sociometric status. Popular children commonly have the most capacity to intervene because they have substantial influence with peers and adults. Even so, popular children may fear losing their status if they defend a peer of lower status. Average children also have reason to fear losing their status and becoming rejected; realizing that such a loss might place them at risk of being victimized, they may feel powerless to act. Moreover, when a group witnesses bullying, the sense of responsibility to intervene may become diffused through the group, leaving average status children waiting for their higher status and more influential peers to act. Although further research is needed to confirm these speculative relationships, sociometry processes are likely to inform and infuse the latent and manifest dynamics inherent in bullying and victimization, making it essential for school personnel to understand group dynamics and sociometric structure.

IMPLICATIONS AND INTERVENTIONS FOR PRACTICE

School social workers and other clinicians can use sociometric testing to target children at risk of victimization as well as to identify those children who may be abusing their status of higher peer acceptance. Based on findings from those tests, school social workers and counselors can then implement sociometric interventions designed to prevent victimization and to improve peer relations. However, the first step is assessment. The school social worker or counselor should conduct sociometric testing within classrooms using either the peer-rating or peer-nomination method. The peer-rating method has some advantages over the peer nomination method. For instance, some researchers have argued that the peer-rating method is kinder in that it does not force children to make active dislike nominations. In addition, some researchers prefer the peer-rating method because it provides an idea of how a child feels about every peer in the class, instead of only six children as in the peer-nomination method (Williams & Gilmour, 1994). Despite these advantages, some researchers have cautioned that the peer-rating method may not be equally effective as the peer-nomination method in determining neglected status children (Asher & Dodge; 1986; Ollendick, Greene, Francis, & Baum, 1991). Regardless of the method chosen, conducting an assessment of peer relations is a critical first step toward identifying social dynamics and targeting certain behaviors.

Once testing is completed, the school social worker or counselor can focus on potential victims, specifically those children classified as having neglected or rejected status. In working with these children, especially those with rejected status, the social worker or counselor can explore ways in which these children might become more socially competent or enhance their social skills such as learning to initiate conversation or play with peers, to interact cooperatively (i.e., turn taking), and to resolve problems or conflicts. Social skills training may be an effective approach for some rejected children to overcome social deficits. By becoming socially competent, these children may be able to establish friendships with peers.

Neglected status children pose a greater challenge because most already possess adequate social skills but they prefer to be alone. However, their tendency to self-isolate places these children at increased risk for victimization by bullies. A promising approach is for the school social worker to find structured avenues that encourage neglected status children to engage more with their peers. For example, pairing a low-status child with a higher-status buddy not only secures at least one source of social support for the low-status child but also provides a model of prosocial skills for neglected and rejected children. This pairing needs to be structured so that the students meet on a regular basis for buddy time. There are potential worthwhile benefits for both children in this new buddy relationship. For neglected status children, this relationship provides a safe place for practicing social skills and feeling accepted. For the higher-status buddy, this relationship may engender feelings of compassion or increased self-esteem through the positive experience of helping others. From interacting with neglected children, high status children may also gain new insight into what it is like to be in a different sociommetric role. Ultimately, both children may benefit from having a new relationship which may not have formed outside of the pairing intervention.

Sociometric Interventions in Empirical Research

The research literature has reported two examples of sociometric interventions designed to address the needs of rejected and neglected children. Morris, Messer, and Gross (1995) sought to test the utility of a peer-pairing intervention that aimed to improve the sociometric status and social interaction of neglected children. The study used a sample of 229 first- and second-grade children from a public school in the Southern United States. The sample was almost evenly divided among Caucasians (49.3%) and African Americans (48%), with only 2.7% reporting other race/ethnicity. Approximately 50.8% of the sample was female, and the average age was 7.63 years old. This study used the peer-nomination method, with the children asked to nominate the three classmates they most liked to play with and the three classmates least liked as playmates. The research team devised sociometric groups based on the number of positive and negative nominations received by each child. Neglected status children were the focus of the intervention: popular status children served as peer partners, and average status children provided a normative comparison for social interaction. The research team identified 24 neglected status children and paired each with a popular partner; peer pairs were also matched on gender. After the pairing procedure, the peer pairs were randomly assigned to either the treatment or the control group. The researchers made behavioral observations of the peer pairs' social interactions during recess; these observations were made during pretreatment, posttreatment, and one-month follow-up.

The treatment in this intervention consisted of 12 peer-pairing sessions, each of which was 15 minutes, conducted during recess over a 4-week.period. During the sessions, the peer pair worked together to complete an activity.

The peer-nomination sociometric testing was repeated at posttreatment and at the one-month follow-up. Results indicated that as compared to children in the control group (i.e., average status) more than 4 times as many treatment children (i.e., neglected status) had increased their sociometric status (Morris et al., 1995). In addition, children in the treatment group demonstrated increased rates of prosocial interaction, and these improvements remained stable through follow-up. Future research might examine the mechanisms through which peer pairing facilitates change.

In the second example of sociometric intervention, Lochman, Coie, Underwood, and Terry (1993) examined the effects of a comprehensive social relations intervention for aggressive-rejected and rejected-only African American children. The intervention combined social skills training with cognitive-behavioral elements.

Using the peer-nomination method, 602 third-graders in an inner-city school were asked to indicate the three peers they liked most, the three peers they liked least, and who started fights. From these nominations, the researchers identified 86 children as rejected status; consent to participate in the research was obtained from the parents of 52 of these children. The sample was nearly evenly divided by gender, with 27 boys and 25 girls. The children were stratified into groups based on their rejection and aggression scores and then randomly assigned to treatment or control groups. The four groups were aggressive–rejected intervention, rejected–only intervention, aggressive–rejected control, and rejected–only control. In addition to peer nomination screening, a self-concept scale was administered to participants and teachers were asked to complete a behavior checklist for participants. Peer nominations, self-concept scale, and teacher ratings of behavior were collected again at posttest and one-year follow-up.

The treatment intervention consisted of 34 thirty-minute sessions; participants were seen individually by female graduate students in psychology for the first 26 sessions, and then participated in eight small group sessions. The treatment used a manualized intervention that focused on four main components or modules: social problem solving, positive play training, group-entry skills training, and dealing effectively with negative feelings (Lochman et al., 1993). The first module consisted of seven sessions and focused on helping the children identify problem situations, define goals, decrease impulsivity, and consider alternative solutions and consequences. The second module consisted of nine sessions and focused on improving social skills for playing and maintaining relationships. The third module included 14 sessions and helped the children learn how to join groups. The last module of the intervention focused on coping with anger, curtailing impulsivity, and using self-statements to regulate behavior. The sessions used training aids such as videotapes and role-plays to engage the students.

Results of the posttest measures showed that, as compared with the aggressive–rejected control group, the aggressive–rejected intervention group had significant decreases in aggression and social rejection and improvements in prosocial behavior (Lochman et al., 1993). Future research should continue to explore subtypes of rejected children, particularly in relation to different interventions. This intervention, though promising, was only tested

Example of a Sociometric Test and Action Methods Intervention

The interventions tested by Lochman et al. (1993) and Morris et al. (1995) used structured treatment manuals and elaborate research protocols. However, it is likely that there will be numerous times when a school social worker or counselor may need to direct a brief, spontaneous intervention toward bullying behavior and peer dynamics. In one example of a brief intervention approach, a school social worker used a simplified version of the classic sociometric test (Hale, 1981) to explore bullying dynamics in a small after-school program group. In the brief approach, the sociometric data collection was immediately followed by working with the group to process the information by using a psychodramatic action intervention (Blatner, 2000).

The social worker asked 12 third-grade children to think about two questions (e.g., the sociometric criteria); "Who in this class teases, taunts, or bullies others?" and "Who in this class is teased, taunted, or bullied by others?" Although sociometric criteria are usually action oriented and phrased in the future tense (e.g., "Who in this group would you go for a walk with through the woods?"), the social worker fashioned these criteria specifically to make current and past bullying dynamics overt. Children were given a roster that listed all of the class members by name in one column and were asked to answer positive (+), negative (-), or neutral (e.g., don't know or no opinion = N) if each child was a bully or victim. Tabulated data appear in Table 2; to protect the identity of the participants, the table and text use fictitious names.

The sociometric data clearly showed that Tauche and Taylor were the "negative stars," who were identified by the majority of their peers as bullies. Jose was identified as the primary victim. Devonte was classified as having controversial status because he had high numbers of both positive and negative nominations. James turned out to be a bully/victim with positive nominations in both of those categories. Rachel was new to the group and was a neglected isolate, receiving few positive or negative nominations. Interestingly, bullying dynamics also surfaced among the girls. In discussing the data with the group, it came out that Megan had formed a clique with Ashley to ostracize Claire. The girls had used relational aggression, such as not inviting Claire to birthday parties and loudly insulting her clothes and hair during lunch. If Ashley did not participate in the bullying along with Megan, she became Megan's victim.

Discussing the data "warmed up" the group until the school social worker thought they were ready to explore the issue using action oriented techniques. She asked Tauche and Taylor to stand to the side, effectively putting them in the mirror position. She then directed Jose to pretend he was Tauche and to enact a scene when bullying occurred. Cesar was cast in the role of the victim, Jose. The school social worker chose Cesar to play the victim because he was a positive star in the group, did not engage in bullying, and was not victimized. She thought that putting a highly valued group member in the victim role would engender sympathy for victims. As conflict came out in the scene, the role-playing was done in slow motion. When the bully went to push down his victim, the school social worker froze the action and invited "doubles" from the audience to go behind Cesar (the victim) and to express what they thought he might be feeling. After several children had taken turns as a double, Tauche and Taylor doubled for the victim, and both expressed anger and humiliation. As a next step, the children were invited to double the bully by saying what they imagined the person in this role might be thinking and feeling. Next, the school social worker asked the group for alternative endings to the scene, and members of the group role-played the different strategies suggested for handling bullying situations. Finally, the school social worker thanked the actors and asked the group to share what the drama meant to each of them.

Table 2. Example Sociometric Test for Exploring Bullying Dynamics in School.

Sociometric Criterion 1: Who in this class teases, taunts, or bullies others?			
Name	Positive	Negative	Neutral
James	+++	- - - - - -	N N N
Taylor	+++++++++	-	N N
John		- - -	N N N N N N N N
Tauche	+++++++++++	-	
Cesar		- - - - - - -	N N N N N
Devonte	+++++	- - - - - - -	
Jose		- - - - - - - - - - -	N
Claire		- - - - - - - -	N N N N
Megan	+++	- - - - - - -	N N
Melanie		- - - - - - - - - -	N
Ashley	+	- - - - - -	N N N N N
Rachel		- -	N N N N N N N N N N
Sociometric Criterion 2: Who in this class is teased, taunted, or bullied by others?			
James	++++	- - - - - -	N N
Taylor	+	- - - - - - - - - -	N
John		- - - -	N N N N N N N
Tauche		- - - - -	N N N N N N
Cesar		- - - - - - - - - -	N
Devonte	++	- - -	N N N N N N
Jose	+++++++++		N N N
Claire	++++	- - - - - -	N N
Megan		- - - - - - - - -	N N N
Melanie		- - - - - - - -	N N N N
Ashley	+ +	- - -	N N N N N N
Rachel		- -	N N N N N N N N N

This example illustrated several important points about using sociometric testing and action methods in addressing bullying in schools. Sociometric testing was useful in making latent group dynamics overt and in identifying roles and sociometric status for group members. This information was then used to process bullying issues directly with the group. Action methods were used to effectively intervene in group processes in several ways. Among the role-play activities, role reversal was particularly useful in allowing the children to gain a different perspective on the bullying situation by experiencing new roles. To use role reversal effectively, popular and average status children should be cast in the roles of neglected and rejected characters whereas low sociometric status children should play popular or powerful roles. The mirror technique prompted bullies to critique their actions, develop empathy for others, and consider alternatives. Bullying scenes were played in slow motion and frozen at critical times to solicit ideas from all children in the class. Doubling helped the group, including the bullies, to express empathy for the victim. The action sequence allowed group members to brainstorm alternate endings. Finally, an honest dialogue about bullying experiences was held during sharing. Overall, these activities emphasized consequences for bullies, encouraged empathy for victims, and provided an outlet for expression.

Often, group leaders try to work with just the bully and the victim to reach a truce that will allow the group to function. However, in this example it was important that the whole group was involved in processing the issue and finding resolutions because the presence of bullying in the group had affected all members in some way. Thus, leaders must emphasize how bullying behavior affects the whole classroom or group environment. Finally, peer mediation might be used between classmates of different sociometric status. Peer mediation sessions can also benefit from using action techniques, especially role reversal. Regardless of the intervention, the school social worker or counselor must carefully identify and target students who may need assistance in negotiating peer relations. Sociometry and action methods are helpful tools in addressing the seriousness of bullying and in intervening early to avoid deleterious long-term consequences of these behaviors for bullies and victims.

CONCLUSION

Sociometry has a long, distinguished history and can be effectively integrated into classroom assessment and intervention. Sociometric classifications (popular, rejected, neglected, controversial, and average) are associated with bullying dynamics that pose a serious threat to victimized children and damage the school environment. Average, neglected, and rejected students may not feel safe at school and this, in turn, may negatively impact their learning process. Sociometric testing enables school professionals to identify low-status children who are at risk for becoming victims of bullying. Furthermore, school social workers can help prevent and reduce bullying by implementing sociometric interventions such as peer pairing of popular students with those with rejected/neglected status. By working to create classroom and school environments where sociometric roles are fluid rather than fixed, we can make strides to promote the safety, security, and well-being of all students.

REFERENCES

Andreou, E. (2001). Bully/victim problems and their association with coping behaviour in conflictual peer interactions among school-age children. *Educational Psychology, 21,* 59-66.

Argenbright, G. C. & Edgell, L. A. (1999). *Taking a stand against bullying behavior: Helping to make our schools safer for all children.* Unpublished manuscript, Chesterfield County Public Schools, Richmond, VA.

Asendorpf, J. (1990). Beyond social withdrawal: Shyness, unsociability, and peer avoidance. *Human Development, 33,* 250-259.

Asher, S. & Coie, J. (1990). *Peer rejection in childhood.* New York, NY: Cambridge University Press.

Asher, S. & Dodge, K. (1986). Identifying children who are rejected by their peers. *Developmental Psychology, 22,* 444-449.

Asher, S. & Parker, J. (1989). Significance of peer relationship problems in childhood. In B. H. Schneider, G. Attili, J. Nadel, & R. P. Weissberg (Eds.), *Social competence in developmental perspective* (5-23). NATO Advanced Science Institute series. Series D: Behavioral and social sciences, Vol. 51. Dordrecht, Netherlands: Kluwer Academic.

Batsche, G. M. (1997). Bullying. In G. G. Bear, K. M. Minke, & A. Thomas (Eds.) *Children's needs II: Development, problems, and alternatives.* Bethesda, IN: National Association of School Psychologists.

Beale, A. V. (2001). Bullybusters: Using drama to empower students to take a stand against bullying behavior. *Professional School Counseling, 4,* 300-306.

Bergin, G. (1986). Sociometric status and social interaction: Are the neglected children socially less active? *Perceptual and Motor Skills, 63,* 823-830.

Bierman, K., Smoot, D. & Aumiller, K. (1993) Characteristics of aggressive-rejected, aggressive-nonrejected, and rejected-nonaggressive boys. *Child Development, 64,* 139-151.

Blatner, A. (2000). *Foundations of psychodrama: History, theory, and practice* (4th ed.). New York, NY: Springer.

Bronfenbrenner, U. (1943). A constant frame of reference for sociometric research. Sociometry, *6,* 363-397.

Cadwallader, T. (2000/2001). Sociometry reconsidered: The social context of peer rejection in childhood. *International Journal of Action Methods, 53*(3/4), 99-118.

Cairns, R. B. & Cairns, B. D. (1994). *Lifelines and risks: Pathways of youth in our time.* New York, NY: Cambridge University Press.

Cairns, R., Cairns, B., Neckerman, H., Gest, S. & Gariepy, J-L. (1988). Social networks and aggressive behavior: Peer support or peer rejection. *Developmental Psychology, 24,* 815-823.

Carney, A. G. & Merrell, K. W. (2001). Bullying in schools: Perspectives on understanding and preventing an international problem. *School Psychology International, 22,* 364-382.

Cillessen, A. H. & Mayeux, L. (2004). From censure to reinforcement: Developmental changes in the association between aggression and social status. *Child Development, 75,* 147-163.

Cillessen, A., van IJzendoorn, H., van Lieshout, C. & Hartup, W. (1992). Heterogeneity among peer-rejected boys: Subtypes and stabilities. *Child Development, 63,* 893-905.

Coie, J. & Dodge, K. (1983). Continuities and changes in children's social status: A five- year longitudinal study. *Merrill-Palmer Quarterly, 29,* 261-282.

Coie, J., Dodge, K. & Coppotelli, H. (1982). Dimensions and types of social status: A cross-age perspective. *Developmental Psychology, 18,* 557-570.

Coie, J., Dodge, K. & Kupersmidt, J. (1990). Peer group behavior and social status. In S. R. Asher, & J. D. Coie (Eds.), *Peer rejection in childhood* (pp.17-59). Cambridge, UK: Cambridge University Press.

Coie, J. & Kupersmidt, J. (1983). A behavioral analysis of emerging social status in boys' groups. *Child Development, 54*, 1400-1416.

Coie, J. D., Lochman, J. E., Terry, R. & Hyman, C. (1992). Predicting early adolescent disorder from childhood aggression and peer rejection. *Journal of Consulting and Clinical Psychology, 60*, 783-792.

Crick, N. & Grotpeter, J. (1996). Children's treatment by peers: Victims of relational and overt aggression. *Development and Psychopathology, 8,* 367-380.

Czeschlik, T. & Rost, D. (1995). Sociometric types and children's intelligence. *British Journal of Developmental Psychology, 13*, 177-189.

David-Ferdon, C. & Feldman-Hertz, M. F. (2007). Electronic media, violence, and adolescents: An emerging public health problem. *Journal of Adolescent Health, 41*(6,Suppl), S1-S5.

Dunn, J.C., Dunn, J.G.H. & Bayduza, A. (2007). Perceived athletic competence, sociometric status, and loneliness in elementary school children. *Journal of Sport Behavior, 30(3)*, 249-269.

Feldman, E. & Dodge, K. (1987). Social information processing and sociometric status: Sex, age, and situational effects. *Journal of Abnormal Child Psychology, 15*, 211-217.

Fergusson, D. M., Swain-Campbell, N. R. & Horwood, L. J. (2002). Deviant peer affiliations, crime and substance use: A fixed effects regression analysis. *Journal of Abnormal Child Psychology, 30*, 419-430.

Franz, D. & Gross, A. (2001). Child sociometric status and parent behaviors: An observational study. *Behavior Modification, 25*, 3-20.

Fraser, M. W., Kirby, L. D. & Smokowski, P. R. (2004). Risk and resilience in childhood. In M. W. Fraser (Ed.), *Risk and resilience in childhood: An ecological perspective* (2nd ed., 13-66). Washington DC: NASW Press.

French, D. (1990). Heterogeneity among peer-rejected girls. *Child Development, 61,* 2028-2031.

French, D. & Waas, G. (1985). Behavior problems of peer-neglected and peer-rejected elementary age children: Parent and teacher perspectives. *Child Development, 56,* 246-252.

Gilmartin, B. G. (1987). Peer group antecedents of severe love-shyness in males. *Journal of Personality, 55*, 467-489.

Glew, G., Fan, M.Y., Katon, W. & Rivara, F.P. (2008). Bullying and school safety. *Journal of Pediatrics, 152*, 123-128.

Glew, G., Rivara, F. & Feudtner, C. (2000). Bullying: Children hurting children. *Pediatrics in Review, 21*, 183-190.

Hale, A. (1974). Warm-up to a sociometric exploration. *Group Psychotherapy and Psychodrama, 27,* 157-172.

Hale, A. (1981). *Conducting clinical sociometric explorations: A manual for psychodramatists and sociometrists.* Roanoke, VA: Royal.

Hanish, L. D. & Guerra, N. G. (2002). A longitudinal analysis of patterns of adjustment following peer victimization. *Development and Psychopathology, 14,* 69-89.

Harrist, A., Zaia, A., Bates, J., Dodge, K. & Petit, G. (1997). Subtypes of social withdrawal in early childhood: Sociometric status and social-cognitive differences across four years. *Child Development, 68*, 278-294.

Hawkins, J. D. & Weis, J. G. (1985). The social development model: An integrated approach to delinquency prevention. *Journal of Primary Prevention, 6*(2), 73-97.

Hazler, R. J. (1996). *Breaking the cycle of violence: Interventions for bullying and victimization.* Washington, DC: Accelerated Development.

Jiang, X. L. & Cillessen, A.H.N. (2005). Stability of continuous measures of sociometric status: A meta-analysis. *Developmental Review, 25*, 1-25.

Juffer, F., Stams, G. J. M. & van IJzendoorn, M. H. (2004). Adopted children's problem behavior is significantly related to their ego resiliency, ego control, and sociometric status. *Journal of Child Psychology and Psychiatry, 45*, 697-706.

Kaltiala-Heino, R., Rimpela, P. R. & Rimpela, A. (2000). Bullying at school: An indicator of adolescents at risk for mental disorders. *Journal of Adolescence, 23*, 661-674.

Kaplow, J. B., Curran, P. J. & Dodge, K. A. (2002). the Conduct Problems Prevention Research Group. Child, parent, and peer predictors of early-onset substance use: A multisite longitudinal study. *Journal of Abnormal Child Psychology, 30*, 199-216.

Kumpulainen, K. & Rasanen, E. (2000). Children involved in bullying at elementary and school age: Their psychiatric symptoms and deviance in adolescence. *Child Abuse and Neglect, 24*, 1567-1577.

Kumpulainen, K., Rasanen, E. & Puura, K. (2001). Psychiatric disorders and the use of mental health services among children involved in bullying. *Aggressive Behavior, 27*, 102-110.

Kupersmidt, J., Coie, J. & Dodge, K. (1990). The role of poor peer relationships in the development of disorder. In S. R. Asher, & J. D. Coie (Eds.), *Peer rejection in childhood.* Cambridge, UK: Cambridge University Press.

Lochman, J., Coie, J., Underwood, M. & Terry, R. (1993). Effectiveness of a social relations intervention program for aggressive and nonaggressive, rejected children. *Journal of Consulting and Clinical Psychology, 61*, 1053-1058.

Lonczak, H. S., Huang, B., Catalano, R. F., Hawkins, J. D., Hill, K. G., Abbott, R. D. &. Kosterman, R. (2001). The social predictors of adolescent alcohol misuse: A test of the social development model. *Journal of Studies on Alcohol, 62*, 179-189.

McClure, M. & Shirataki, S. (1989). Child psychiatry in Japan. *Journal of the American Academy of Child and Adolescent Psychiatry, 28*, 488-493.

McDonald, K. L., Putallaz, M., Grimes, C. L., Kupersmidt, J. B. & Coie, J. D. (2007). Girl talk: Gossip, friendship, and sociometric status. *Merrill-Palmer Quarterly, 53(3)*, 381-411.

McNamara, B. E. & McNamara, F. J. (1997). *Keys to dealing with bullies.* Hauppauge, NY: Barron's.

Miller-Johnson, S., Coie, J. D., Maumary-Gremaud, A. & Bierman, K. (2002). the Conduct Problems Prevention Research Group. (2002). Peer rejection and aggression and early starter models of conduct disorder. *Journal of Abnormal Child Psychology, 30*, 217-230.

Miller-Johnson, S., Coie, J. D., Maumary-Gremaud, A., Lochman, J. & Terry, R. (1999). Peer rejection and aggression in childhood and severity and type of delinquency during adolescence among African American youth. *Journal of Emotional and Behavioral Disorders, 7*, 137-146.

Moreno, J. L. (1934). *Who shall survive? A new approach to the problem of human interrelations.* Washington, DC: Nervous and Mental Disease Publishing.

Morris, T., Messer, S. & Gross, A. (1995). Enhancement of the social interaction and status of neglected children: A peer-pairing approach. *Journal of Clinical Child Psychology, 24,* 11-20.

Mynard, H. & Joseph, S. (1997). Bully victim problems and their association with Eysenck's personality dimensions in 8 to 13 year-olds. *British Journal of Educational Psychology, 67,* 51-54.

Nansel, T. R., Overpeck, M., Pilla, R. S., Ruan, W. J., Simons-Morton, B. & Scheidt, P. (2001). Bullying behaviors among US youth: Prevalence and association with psycho-social adjustment. *Journal of the American Medical Association, 285,* 2094-2110.

Nelson, S. E. & Dishion, T. J. (2004). From boys to men: Predicting adult adaptation from middle childhood sociometric status. *Development and Psychopathology, 16*(2), 441-459.

Newcomb, A. & Bukowski, W. (1983). Social impact and social preference as determinants of children's peer group status. *Developmental Psychology, 19,* 856-867.

Newcomb, A., Bukowski, W. & Pattee, L. (1993). Children's peer relations: A Meta- analytic review of popular, rejected, neglected, controversial, and average sociometric status. *Psychological Bulletin, 113,* 99-128.

Ollendick, T. H., Greene, R. W., Francis, G. & Baum, C. G. (1991). Sociometric status: Its stability and validity among neglected, rejected and popular children. *Journal of Child Psychology and Psychiatry, 32,* 525-34.

Olweus, D. (1978). *Aggression in the schools: Bullies and whipping boys.* London, UK: Hemisphere.

Olweus, D. (1993). *Bullying at school: What we know and what we can do.* Cambridge, MA: Blackwell.

Olweus, D. (1995). Bullying or peer abuse in school: Fact and intervention. *Current Directions in Psychological Science, 4,* 196-200.

O'Moore, M. & Kirkham, C. (2001). Self-esteem and its relationship to bullying behavior. *Aggressive Behavior, 27,* 269-283.

Parker, J. G., Rubin, K. H., Erath, S. A., Wojslawwowicz, J. C. & Buskirk, A. R. (2006). Peer relationships, child development, and adjustment: A developmental psychopathology perspective. In D. Cicchetti, & D. J. Cohen (Eds.), *Developmental psychopathology* (2nd ed., 419-493). Hoboken, NJ: John Wiley & Sons.

Parkhurst, J. & Asher, S. (1992). Peer rejection in middle school: Subgroups differences in behavior, loneliness, and interpersonal concerns. *Developmental Psychology, 28,* 231-241.

Pellegrini, A. D. (1998). Bullies and victims in school: A review and call for research. *Journal of Applied Developmental Psychology, 19,* 165-176.

Pellegrini, A. D., Bartini, M. & Brooks, F. (1999). School bullies, victims, and aggressive victims: Factors relating to group affiliation and victimization in early adolescence. *Journal of Educational Psychology, 91,* 216-224.

Poulin, F. & Dishion, T. J. (2008). Methodological issues in the use of peer sociometric nominations with middle school youth. *Social Development, 17,* 908-921.

Putallaz, M. (1983). Predicting children's sociometric status from their behavior. *Child Development, 54,* 1417-1426.

Rieffe, C., Villanueva, L. & Meerum Terwogt, M. (2005). Use of trait information in the attribution of intentions by popular, average, and rejected children. *Infant and Child Development, 14*, 1-10.

Roberts, W. B. (2000). The bully as victim. *Professional School Counseling, 4*, 148-156.

Roberts, W. & Coursol, D. (1996). Strategies for intervention with childhood and adolescent victims of bullying, teasing, and intimidation in school setting. *Elementary School Guidance and Counseling, 30*, 204-212.

Véronneau, M.-H. & Vitaro, F. (2007). Social experience with peers and high school graduation: A review of theoretical and empirical research. *Educational Psychology, 27*, 419-445.

Williams, B. & Gilmour, J. (1994). Sociometry and peer relationships. *Journal of Child Psychology and Psychiatry and Allied Disciplines, 35*, 997-1013.

Ybarra, M. L., Diener-West, M. & Leaf, P. J. (2007). Examining the overlap in internet harassment and school bullying: Implications for school intervention. *Journal of Adolescent Health, 41(6,Suppl)*, S42-S50.

In: Youth Violence and Juvenile Justice: Causes, Intervention…   ISBN: 978-1-61668-011-4
Editor: Neil A. Ramsay et al., pp. 163-186   © 2010 Nova Science Publishers, Inc.

Chapter 6

VIOLENT AND DELINQUENT YOUTHS: RELATIONSHIPS WITH INSTITUTIONAL AUTHORITIES AND COMPLIANCE WITH SOCIAL NORMS

Estefanía Estévez[1] and Marina Rachitskiy[2]

[1]Universidad Miguel Hernández, Elche, Alicante, Spain., Departamento de Psicología de la Salud, Edificio Altamira, Facultad de Ciencias Sociales y Jurídicas de Elche, Avenida Universidad, s/n, 03202, Elche (Alicante), Spain.
[2]University of Surrey, Department of Psychology, Guildford, United Kingdom, GU2 7XH.

ABSTRACT

Society is based on a set of norms and rules, compliance with which ensures the survival of that society. Within psychology, the two main issues of compliance with social norms are exhibition of violent behaviour and cooperation with authorities in order to promote further compliance. Extensive research suggests that among other social and psychological factors, relationships with institutional authorities are one of the most prominent factors of compliance in childhood and adolescence. In this chapter we discuss the research available on the role of authorities and warning signs associated with violence and cooperation with institutional authorities. Finally, we explore theories proposed to explain the relationship between compliance and authorities, as well as their relevance to prevention of non-compliance with social norms. In short, this chapter outlines research and theory suggesting that negative experiences with authorities lead to negative attitudes to authorities and norms regarding compliance. In turn, these attitudes and norms lead to exhibition of violent behaviours and lower cooperation with authorities. As such, we suggest that focusing resources on improving the relationships between authorities and youth will prevent non-compliance with social norms, namely, violence and non-cooperation with authorities.

INTRODUCTION

Society is based on a set of norms and rules, compliance with which ensures the survival of that society. Compliance with social norms has been a topic of interest for many centuries, starting from ancient Greek philosophers, such as Socrates and Aristotle who explored the nature of good life and the role of the common good, and continues in the current research within forensic and social psychology (e.g. Emler, 2009; Tyler, 2006). Within psychology, the two main issues of compliance with social norms are exhibition of violent behaviour and cooperation with authorities in order to promote further compliance. Extensive research suggests that among other social and psychological factors, relationships with institutional authorities are one of the most prominent factors of compliance in childhood and adolescence. In this chapter we will discuss the research available on the role of authorities and warning signs associated with violence and cooperation with institutional authorities. Finally, we will explore theories proposed to explain the relationship between compliance and authorities, as well as their relevance to prevention of non-compliance with social norms.

I. INSTITUTIONAL AUTHORITIES

Institutional authority figures play a significant role in the lives of children and youth. They are one of the primary sources of care, protection, and knowledge in the lives of adolescents. Consequently, children become highly dependant on the authority figures in their lives, most prominent of which are educational authorities, such as teachers, and legal authorities, such as police. From birth, parents socialize the children and introduce them to the world. They shape the norms and morals of their children and model behaviours (Durkin, 2002; Howes & James, 2004; Murray & Thompson, 1985; Smetana, 1988). However, later, as the children start attending school, teachers are the ones who shape their minds and advance their understanding of the world (Emler, 1992; Ladd, Buhs & Troop, 2004; Molinari, 2001; Murray & Thompson, 1985; Smetana & Bitz, 1996; Verkuyten, 2002). Finally, coming into contact with the police and other institutional authorities outside the home and school solidifies the youths' perception of the world and their role in it (Molinari, 2001; Murray & Thompson, 1985). Authority figures provide children with the concept and function of social norms, as well as the consequences of non-compliance with these norms. As such, the role of authorities is to introduce the younger generation to how the world functions and socialize them so that they may function better within that world.

The role of authorities as socializing agents is primarily fulfilled through caring and protecting the youth, as well as modelling and teaching. All authority figures have a *duty of care* to youth. Being young and inexperienced in the world, children look to institutional authority figures to protect them from threat or harm. By providing this service, youth develop an idea of a fair world, where those that cause harm are punished and those that do good are rewarded (Durkin, 2002). Furthermore, youth look to authority figures to educate them of the social norms practiced within their society, to set an example of how to comply with these norms, and to enforce these norms by punishing those that do not comply and protecting those affected by the non-compliers. However, authorities may have difficulty in fulfilling these roles and in some circumstances the effect of authorities may result in a more anti-social behaviour. Emler and colleagues (Emler, 2009; Emler & Reicher, 1987; 1995; 2005) suggest that when authority figures fail to protect the children from harm, some children may turn to violence in order to protect themselves, believing that victimizers can not be victims. As such, experiences with authorities in performing, or not performing, these roles may affect youth and children's compliance with social norms. The following two sections present an overview of research exploring the relationship between compliance with social norms and experiences with authorities, and attitudes to authorities.

Experiences with Institutional Authorities

Institutional authorities are one the primary drivers of youths' social development, which shapes the child into well adjusted contributing members of society. Being treated with dignity, trust, fairness, and attentiveness by the authorities, commonly known as *procedural justice,* may affect individuals' future compliance with authorities (Goldsmith, 2005; Watson & Angell, 2007). Seron, Pereira and Kovath (2004) found, in a sample of New York citizens, that seriousness of misconduct was based on both legal and extralegal factors, and that Black citizens rated police misconduct as significantly more serious than White citizens. Furthermore, a recent study found that evaluation of officers performance was highly associated with acting professional, competent, attentive, and helpful (Wells, 2007). Goldsmith (2005) suggests that police-community relations can be improved through the police acting fairly, respectfully, and with limited use of force, suggesting that improving the experiences that individuals have with authorities will improve their relationships with authorities. An evaluation of British youth found that adolescents expect teachers to impart knowledge and advice to prepare them for life, and police to be tough but also compassionate (Murray & Thompson, 1985). Since authority figures are expected to exhibit model behaviour, it is reasonable to expect that experience with authorities living up to these expectations would be a crucial factor in compliance with social norms. In fact, extensive research suggests that experiences with authorities are strongly associated with both violence and intention to cooperate with authorities.

Experience with Authorities and Cooperation with Authorities

Although cooperation with authorities among youth has been widely neglected, cooperation among adults has recently received some attention from the academic community (see Table 1). Cooperation with authorities commonly refers to compliance with laws and instructions set out by institutional authorities. With the new interest in compliance with laws (cooperation), rather than violation of laws (aggression), experiences with authorities has become a topic of interest for many researchers (Goldsmith, 2005), with Tom R. Tyler heading the most prominent contributions. Experience with authorities commonly refers to the conditions under which an individual had contact with an authority figure and the level of satisfaction that the individual experiences with that contact, as well as the overall positive or negative feelings regarding the climate and the context of the contact.

Sunshine and Tyler (2003a) evaluated cooperation with authorities among American adults and found that moral solidarity with the authority figures was strongly associated with cooperation. Further, they suggested that moral solidarity of the authority figures is reflected through procedural justice. Although Sunshine and Tyler (2003a) did not directly evaluate the relationship between procedural justice and support of legal authorities, they do suggest that such relationship exists (Sunshine & Tyler, 2003a; 2003b; Tyler, 2006). A later research by De Cremer and Tyler (2007) reports three studies supporting the relationship between experience with authorities and cooperation with legal authorities. Furthermore, they found no gender, ethnicity or age effects on cooperation and experiences of procedural justice (De Cremer & Tyler, 2007). A recent study by Murphy and Tyler (2008) reports similar findings in relation to legal and work authorities. These findings were further confirmed by Reisig, Bratton and Gertz (2007).

Similar results were found among British adults. Eller, Viki, Imara and Peerbux (2007) evaluated 105 university students in England and found a strong relationship between quality of experiences with police and intentions to cooperate with police. Furthermore, they found that race had a significant effect on both experiences and intentions to cooperate with authorities, with Blacks reporting more negative experiences and intentions (Eller et al., 2007). These findings were later confirmed by Viki, Culmer, Eller and Abrams (2006) in their evaluation of 120 English university students.

Research among youth, although somewhat limited, suggests a similar pattern to adults. Woolard, Harvell and Graham (2008) evaluated 1393 adolescents from the community, detention centres, and jails in America. They found that cooperation with legal authorities was highly associated with increased justice experience, younger age, and being female. Further, they found that ethnic minorities, especially those without justice experience, anticipated less fair treatment from legal authorities.

The findings of the studies mentioned above are summarised in Table 1. The studies are consistent in their findings that there is a strong relationship between positive experiences with authorities and increased cooperation with them, with somewhat mixed results regarding race, gender, and age effects. Although the cited studies present compelling evidence to the presence of the relationship, majority of these studies have focused on cooperation with only legal authorities and only two of them have focused on youth. There is a great gap in the literature regarding cooperation of adolescents with the different types of authorities.

Experience with Authorities and Violence

The relationship between violence and experiences with authorities has received more attention within the academic community than cooperation. Clark and Wenning (1967) performed one of the earliest evaluations of the relationship. Although, they do not suggest a causal relationship, Clark and Wenning (1964) point out the possible importance of quality and quantity of contact with the legal system in shaping the opinions the youth hold regarding that system and violent behaviour. Over five decades of research have confirmed these findings among British, American and Spanish youth (see Table 2).

Table 1. Empirical Study of Cooperation and Experience with Authority.

Study	Sample	Results
Watson & Angell (2007)		Previous experiences of procedural justice shape future cooperation with authorities
Woolard, Harvell & Graham (2008)	1,393 US adolescents aged 11-13	Compliance with legal authority related to increased justice experience ($\beta = -.12$, $p < .001$), being female ($\beta = -.18$, $p < .001$), and younger ($\beta = .21$, $p < .001$)
Viki, Culmer, Eller & Abrams (2006)	120 UK university students aged 19-50	Experience with police related to intention to cooperate with legal authorities ($r = .46$). Black participants had lower intentions to cooperate ($r = .21$) and more negative experiences ($r = .24$)
De Cremer & Tyler (2007)	Study 1: 70 US undergraduate students; Study 2: 80 US undergraduate students; Study 3: 1656 US citizens	Study 1 and 2: Procedural fairness related to cooperation with authorities (Study 1: $F(1, 66) = 29.70$, $p < .001$, $\eta^2 = .31$; Study 2: $F(1, 76) = 6.82$, $p < .001$, $\eta^2 = .08$). Study 3: procedural fairness related to cooperation with legal authorities ($r = .77$, $p < .001$). Age, gender, and ethnicity had no effect on cooperation ($r = .13$, $-.04$, $.15$ respectively, $p > .05$) or procedural fairness ($r = .13$, $-.05$, $.16$ respectively, $p > .05$)
Eller, Abrams, Viki, Imara & Peerbux (2007)	105 UK university students	Positive contact with police related to higher intentions to cooperate with police ($r = .26$). Blacks reported more negative quality of contact and lower intentions to cooperate
Sunshine & Tyler (2003a)	589 US citizens aged 19-88	Cooperation with legal authorities related to moral solidarity (reflected through procedural justice; $\beta = .16$, $p < .01$). Minority respondents were more likely to cooperate
Sunshine & Tyler (2003b)	483 US citizens aged 19-88	Cooperation with legal authorities was related to higher legitimacy ($\beta = .30$, $p < .001$). Legitimacy was determined primarily by procedural justice ($\beta = .62$, $p < .001$)
Reisig, Bratton & Gertz (2007)	432 US adults	Positive experience with legal authorities related to cooperation ($B = .15$, $SE = .05$)
Wells (2007)	3,719 US citizens	Procedural justice and outcome-oriented behaviour of officers related to more positive ratings of their performance ($\beta = 1.45$, $SE = .07$, $p < .05$)
Murphy & Tyler (2008)	652 US tax payers	Procedural justice related to cooperation with legal authority ($r = .11$)

Table 2. Empirical Study of Violence and Experience with Authority.

Study	Sample	Results
Liska & Reed (1985)	2,213 US boys	Negative experiences with teachers (attachment) related to delinquency ($\chi2 >$ 1209, p > .05)
Smetana & Bitz (1996)	120 US students from 5th, 7th, 9th, and 11th grades	Misbehaviour in school related to negative evaluation of school context (r = .17) No gender effects (r = .08) Older students reported more misbehaviour (r = -.22)
Herrero, Estévez & Musitu (2006).	973 Spanish students aged 11–16	Violence related to negative experience with teachers (r = .16)
Estévez, Murgui, Moreno & Musitu (2007)	1049 Spanish students aged 11-16	Violent behaviour in school related to negative experience with teachers (r = .20) No gender effect ($\chi2(23) = 34.38$, p > .05)
Musitu, Estévez & Emler (2007)	1068 Spanish students aged 11 to 16	Violence related to negative experience with teachers (r = .20)
Estévez, Murgui, Musitu & Moreno (2008)	1319 Spanish secondary school students	Higher violence related to negative experiences with teachers (r = .13)

A qualitative study of British youth found that many students held teachers responsible for their disruptive behaviour (Verkuyten, 2002). Furthermore, students expected teachers to keep order, be fair, and teach effectively. In an American evaluation of adolescent misbehaviour, Smetana and Bitz (1996) found that experience with school authorities was highly associated with misbehaviour in school. Furthermore, an earlier study by Liska and Reed (1985) reported that negative attachment to teachers was highly associated with delinquency. Spanish studies have found similar results. In their studies, the Valencia team (Estévez, Murgui, Moreno & Musitu, 2007; Estévez, Murgui, Musitu & Moreno, 2008; Herrero, Estévez & Musitu, 2006; Musitu, Estévez & Emler, 2007) found that negative experiences with teachers were significantly associated with violence.

The studies (Table 2) are fairly consistent in their findings that experiences with authorities are highly associated with aggression among adolescents. Specifically, the studies suggest that experiences of fairness, high communication with, and positive attachment to teachers and police are highly predictive of lower levels of violent behaviours. The results regarding gender are somewhat mixed, although it seems that boys and older students tend to exhibit higher levels of aggression.

Experiences with Institutional Authorities Summary

When evaluating experiences, adolescents place great emphasis on fairness of treatment, communication/expressiveness, and the authority's ability to keep order and perform their roles effectively. Despite the fact that there is a great gap in the literature regarding adolescent compliance, the empirical evaluation of the role of experiences in compliance with social norms is fairly consistent in its findings that the relationship exists. In fact, numerous studies confirm that negative experiences with authorities are associated with higher non-compliance with social norms. Although the gender effects are mixed, it is commonly expressed that boys and older youth tend to have higher levels of non-compliance. However, many researchers suggest that the relationship between experiences and violence is not a direct one (e.g. Emler, 2009). As will be discussed shortly, some academics suggest that attitudes to authorities is a stronger predictor of violent behaviour and mediate the relationship between experiences with authorities and violence.

ATTITUDES TO AUTHORITY

There is a large body of research suggesting a strong link between *attitudes to authority* and compliance with social norms. Although many operational definitions exist, in general *attitudes to authority* refer to how individuals feel regarding a particular authority. Specifically, it refers to whether they feel positively toward the authority and approve of its conduct, commonly labelled as legitimacy of authority. Emler et al. (Emler, 2009; Emler & Reicher, 1987; 1995; 2005) suggest that experiencing authority's inadequacy in performing their expected roles will shape attitudes to those authorities and consequently the choice in complying with social norms. Smetana et al. (Smetana, 1988; Smetana & Bitz, 1996) suggest that adolescence is a transitional period when perceptions and attitudes of authorities change. Research in the area of attitudes to authority has primarily been focused on its relationship to violent behaviour with little attention to cooperation with the authorities.

Attitude to Authorities and Cooperation with Authorities

Although only few direct evaluations of intention to cooperate with authorities have been conducted with adolescents, there are a number of studies suggesting that positive attitudes to authority are strongly associated with compliance with authorities. Brown (1974) evaluated 216 students attending Wisconsin junior schools on their attitudes to law and the police, and their obedience with specific laws and rules. He found that negative attitudes to legal authorities were strongly associated with less obedience with these authorities. Furthermore, he found that males and older students reported more acts of disobedience (Brown, 1974). Similar results were found by Rigby, Schofield, and Slee (1987) who concluded that attitudes to authority became more negative with age. Furthermore, contrary to previous findings (Burwen & Campbell, 1957), they found a high degree of similarity between attitudes to the different types of authorities (Rigby, Schofield & Slee, 1987), suggesting that negative attitudes to one authority may affect non-compliance with other authority figures. These findings are consistent with studies conducted on adults (e.g. Eller at al., 2007; Murphy & Tyler, 2008; Reisig et al., 2007; Sunshine & Tyler, 2003b). These early evaluations of compliance, summarised in Table 3, suggest that attitudes to authority is a strong factor in cooperation with police.

Table 3. Empirical Study of Cooperation with Authorities and Attitudes to Authorities.

Study	Sample	Results
Brown (1974)	216 US junior school students	Compliance related to positive orientation to legal authorities ($r = .47$) Boys and older students reported more non-compliance
Rigby, Schofield & Slee (1987)	327 Australian secondary school students	Authority salient behaviour related to positive attitudes to authority ($r = .38$) No gender effects (all z $<\pm1.26$, p>.05) Younger students had more positive attitudes to authority
Eller, Abrams, Viki, Imara & Peerbux (2007)	130 UK university students	Quality of contact with police related to attitudes to police ($r = .34$). Blacks reported more negative quality of contact and view of police
Sunshine & Tyler (2003b)	483 US citizens aged 19-88	Cooperation with legal authorities was related to legitimacy ($\beta = .30, p < .001$)
Reisig, Bratton & Gertz (2007)	432 US adults	Positive experience with legal authorities related to cooperation ($B = .15, SE = .05$)
Murphy & Tyler (2008)	652 US tax payers	Cooperation with authorities related to positive emotions to legal authority ($r = .22$)

Although the above studies suggest a strong relationship between attitudes to authority and cooperation with them, the studies on youth are few and primarily focus on only one type of authority, the police and law. With teachers being the primary institutional authority figures in a youth's life, further investigation of cooperation with these authorities may shed more light on the causes of violent behaviour among youth.

Attitudes to Authorities and Violence

Unlike cooperation with authorities, the relationship between violence and attitudes to authority has received greater academic attention. Although early research suggests mixed results (Johnson & Stanley, 1955), the relationship has been demonstrated as early as the 1960s. Shore, Massimo and Mack (1965) found that psychotherapy provided to adolescent delinquents improved attitudes to authority and was associated with improved academic achievement and reduction in violent behaviour. These findings were further confirmed by later research, with the most prominent contributions by Nicholas P. Emler.

Emler and colleagues (e.g. Emler & Reicher, 1987; 1995; 2005; Tarry & Emler, 2007) have dedicated their research to evaluate the relationship between violence and attitudes to authority among youth. Over the years they have confirmed the presence of a very strong association between negative attitudes to authority and antisocial behaviour (e.g. Emler & Reicher, 1987; Tarry & Emler, 2007). Their studies suggest that overall youth hold a fairly positive attitude to institutional authorities, especially among females (Emler & Reicher, 1995). These findings are consistent with further research conducted in Britain (Murray & Thompson, 1985), Australia (Rigby, Mak & Slee, 1989; Rigby & Rump, 1981; Rigby, Schofield, & Slee, 1987), Spain (Cava, Musitu & Murgui, 2006; Estévez et al., 2007; Gouveaia-Pereira, Vala, Palmonari & Rubini, 2003; Musitu, Estévez & Emler, 2007) and America (Amoroso & Ware, 1986; Johnson & Stanley, 1955; Reisig et al., 2007; Shore et al., 1965; Tyler, 2006), although no gender differences were found among the Australian youth (Rigby et al., 1987; 1989). A later Australian study by Levy (2001) has evaluated students attending regular secondary schools and institutions for delinquent youth. Although the students held fairly positive attitudes to authority in general, the study found that non-delinquents showed more positive attitudes to authorities than institutionalized and non-institutionalized delinquents. Further, non-institutionalized delinquents had more positive attitudes to police and law, and more negative attitudes to teachers than institutional (Levi, 2001). It is possible that the more positive attitudes of non-institutionalized delinquents to police and law may be the result of these youth having only limited experiences with the police and law compared to institutionalized delinquents.

Table 4 summarises some of the empirical evaluations of the effect of attitudes to authorities on violent behaviour among adolescents. As is evident from the table, studies are fairly consistent in their findings that negative attitudes to authority are strongly associated with higher level of violence. Further, the studies suggest that youth generally have a positive attitude to authorities. Finally, there are mixed results regarding gender and age effect.

Attitudes to Authorities and Experiences with Authorities

Over the years, studies have confirmed the existence of the relationship between experiences with authorities and attitudes to authorities. Carr, Napolitano and Keating (2007) conducted a qualitative evaluation of 147 adolescents in Philadelphia and found that their negative disposition toward the police was grounded in their negative encounters with police. While the presence of the relationship among adolescents is still being explored, it has been well established among adult populations (Eller et al., 2007; Hinds & Murphy, 2007; Jackson & Sunshine, 2007; Murphy & Tyler, 2008; Reisig et al., 2007; Sunshine & Tyler, 2003b; Tyler, 2006; Wells, 2007).

One of the earliest evaluations of the relationship between experiences and attitudes has been conducted by Giordano (1976) among American adolescents. She found that greater contact with legal agencies was associated with more negative opinions regarding the effectiveness of the agencies. Similar results were found, among American youth, in relation to school authorities (Smetana & Bitz, 1996) and police (Hurst & Frank, 2000; Leiber, Nalla & Farnworth, 1998). Hurst and Frank (2000) found that negative attitudes to police were significantly associated with both direct and indirect quality of previous contact with police. Direct contact was specifically associated with negative attitudes when it was initiated by police and was negative in quality. Positive attitudes were associated with citizen initiated positive contact. The significance of both direct and indirect experiences in relation to attitudes was also confirmed in adult samples (Weitzer, 2002). These studies suggest that both direct and indirect negative experience with authorities can have detrimental effects on the attitudes youth hold regarding authorities.

Table 4. Empirical Study of Violence and Attitudes to Authority.

Study	Sample	Results
Johnson & Stanley (1955)	40 US boys aged 10-12.	Hostile and non-hostile youth showed similar attitudes to authorities ($F(1, 38) = 2.932$, $p>.05$).
Shore, Massimo & Mack (1965)	20 US boys aged 15-17	Treatment focusing on attitudes to authority reduced antisocial behaviour
Rigby & Rump (1981)	157 Australian youth aged 13-17	Older students reported more positive attitudes to institutional authority ($F(2,149) = 6.25$, $p < .01$)
Murray & Thompson (1985)	2060 UK students attending 1st, 3rd, and 5th years	Overall positive attitude to authorities (62% favourable of teachers, and 67% of police) Girls and younger students exhibit more positive attitudes to authority
Emler & Reicher (1987)	231 UK students aged 12 to 25	Higher violence related to negative attitudes to institutional authorities ($r = .65$ for police and law; $r = .68$ for teachers and school) Boys reported more negative attitudes to authorities
Rigby, Mak & Slee (1989)	115 Australian youth aged 13-15	Negative attitudes to authorities (police, teachers) were related to increased violence ($r = .26$) No gender effects on attitudes ($t(94) = .35$, $p>.05$) Boys reported more delinquent acts ($t(75) = 4.19$, $p<.001$)
Levy (2001)	365 Australian secondary school students in delinquent institutions	Non-delinquents had more positive attitudes to authorities (teachers, police, law) than institutionalized and non-institutionalized delinquents ($F(2, 362) = 73.49$, $p<.01$) No gender effects
Cava, Musitu & Murgui (2006)	665 Spanish youth aged 12-16	Violence related to negative attitudes to school ($r =.29$) Boys showed higher levels of violence
Estévez, Murgui, Moreno & Musitu (2007)	1049 Spanish students aged 11-16	Violent behaviour in school related to negative attitudes to institutional authority ($r = .34$)
Musitu, Estévez & Emler (2007)	1068 Spanish students aged 11-16	Violence related to negative attitudes to teachers and police ($r = .34$)

Table 4. (*Continued*)

Study	Sample	Results
Tarry & Emler (2007)	789 UK boys aged 12-15	Delinquency related to negative attitudes to institutional authority ($r = .51$)
Estévez, Murgui, Musitu & Moreno (2008)	1319 Spanish secondary school students	Higher violence related to negative attitudes to institutional authority ($r = .35$)
Reisig, Bratton & Gertz (2007)	432 US adults	Legitimacy related to lower illegal activity ($B = .12$, $SE = .04$)
Tyler (2006)	1,575 US adults	Legitimacy (attitudes to legal authority) related to illegal activity ($r = .22$) Female ($r = .28$) and older ($r = .38$) participant reported less illegal activity Older participants reported higher legitimacy of authorities ($r = .23$)

The largest number of studies evaluating the relationship between experiences and attitudes of authorities has been conducted in Spain and Portugal. Gouveaia-Pereira et al. (Gouveaia-Pereira, Vala, Palmonari & Rubini, 2003) evaluated the direct relationship between attitudes to authority and experiences with authorities. The study was conducted on 448 Portuguese adolescents and focused on only one type of authority, teachers. Gouveaia-Pereira et al. (2003) evaluated the youth on their perceived justice of teacher behaviour (fairness of treatment and marking overall and compared to others), school experience (rules, performance, and relationship with classmates) and attitude to authorities (teachers, judicial, legal). They found that positive school experience was associated with more positive attitudes to authorities. However, they suggest that the perceived justice of the teacher behaviour was a better predictor of legitimacy granted to authority. These findings were confirmed by later Spanish studies (Estévez et al., 2007; Estévez et al., 2008; Musitu et al, 2007).

Although only few studies have been conducted outside Spain and America, similar results were found in Singapore (Khoo & Oakes, 2000) and Australia (1981). A qualitative evaluation by Dobash, Dobash, Ballintyne and Schumann (1990) sheds some further light on the relationship between experiences and authorities in Europe. Dobash et al. (1990) compared the experiences of Scottish and German youth with police. They found that in both samples, those who had contact with police (as a suspect, witness, or victim) had significantly lower evaluation of the police. Although, the study indicated that youth had overall positive attitudes towards the police, youth did object to how the police perform their duties. Specifically, many youth report the police being discourteous, impolite, malicious, brusque, and aggressive. Furthermore, the majority of the youth felt that they would have been treated differently had they been older (Dobash et al., 1990). Research is fairly consistent in its findings that experiences with authorities are a contributing factor in attitudes to authority (see Table 5). However, this research is primarily focused on adults.

Table 5. Empirical Study of Experiences and Attitudes to Authority.

Study	Sample	Results
Giordano (1976)	119 US youth aged 14-18	Negative experiences with authorities related to negative attitudes to authorities ($r = .23$)
Smetana & Bitz (1996)	120 US students from 5th, 7th, 9th, and 11th grades	Legitimacy of school authorities related to positive evaluation of school context ($r = .17$)
Leiber, Nalla & Farnworth (1998)	337 US juvenile delinquent boys	Experience with police related to attitudes to authority (fairness $R^2 = .19$; respect $R^2 = .15$; discrimination $R^2 = .05$)
Hurst & Frank (2000)	852 US secondary school students	Negative experience with police related to negative attitudes to police ($r = .15$) No age, race, or gender effects
Khoo & Oakes (2000)	117 Singapore inmates aged 13-16	Negative experiences with authorities (public reprimand) related to negative attitudes to authorities, especially among males ($F(1, 108) = 6.38, p < .05$).
Gouveaia-Pereira, Vala, Palmonari & Rubini (2003)	448 Spanish students aged 15-18	Attitudes to institutional authorities related to perceived justice in school context ($r = .38$)
Eller, Abrams, Viki, Imara & Peerbux (2007)	130 UK university students	Quality of contact with police related to attitudes to police ($r = .34$). Blacks reported more negative quality of contact and view of police
Estévez, Murgui, Moreno & Musitu (2007)	1049 Spanish students aged 11-16	Negative attitudes to authority related to negative experience with teachers ($r = .21$)
Hinds & Murphy (2007)	2611 Australians aged 16-94	Experiences with police related to positive attitudes to authority ($r = .37$)
Musitu, Estévez & Emler (2007)	1068 Spanish students aged 11 to 16	Negative attitudes to school authority related to negative experiences with teachers ($r = .21$)
Estévez, Murgui, Musitu & Moreno (2008)	1319 Spanish secondary school students	Negative attitudes to authority related to negative experiences with teachers ($r = .12$)
Sunshine & Tyler (2003b)	483 US citizens aged 19-88	Legitimacy of legal authorities was determined by procedural justice ($\beta = .62, p < .001$)
Tyler (2006)	1,575 US adults	Positive experience with authorities related to higher legitimacy ($R^2 = .15$) Older participants reported higher legitimacy of ($r = .23$) and experience with legal authorities ($r = .09$)
Jackson & Sunshine (2007)	1,023 UK citizens aged over 16	Procedural justice related to attitudes to police ($\beta = .35, p < .05$) Younger participants reported more negative attitudes to authority
Reisig, Bratton & Gertz (2007)	432 US adults	Experience with legal authorities related to legitimacy ($r = .63$)
Wells (2007)	3,719 US citizens	Procedural justice related to more positive ratings of officer performance ($\beta = 1.45, SE = .07, p < .05$)
Murphy & Tyler (2008)	652 US tax payers	Procedural justice related to positive emotions to legal authority ($r = .25$)

Attitudes to Authority Summary

The term *attitudes to authority* is commonly used to describe the emotions and perceptions that individuals hold regarding particular authority figures. These include the perceived legitimacy of an authority, acceptance of their power, and approval of their behaviour. Overall, the research is consistent in its findings that positive attitudes to authority have a strong relationship to compliance with social norms and positive experiences with police. However, the research was primary conducted among adults and only in relation to legal authorities. Further exploration of the role of attitudes to authorities in compliance with social norms, especially cooperation with authorities, is necessary to shed light on the nature of the compliance.

Summary of the Effects of Institutional Authority

Authorities are one of the primary socializing agents in youths' lives. Their role is to care, provide, and protect children, as well as inform them of the social norms of their community and model accepted behaviour. Authorities are expected to perform all these behaviours at all times. However, some authority figures may fall short of that responsibility, which may affect the youths understanding of the world and thus lead them toward exhibiting less pro-social behaviour.

Research suggests that experience with authorities performing their respective roles has a strong relationship with compliance with social norms. Youth commonly evaluate their experiences with authorities in light of fairness of treatment, communication/expressiveness, and the authority's ability to keep order and perform their roles effectively. Negative experiences with individual institutional authority figures have been associated with higher violence and lower intentions to cooperate with police. Although, the link has been empirically established, the studies are few, primarily focused on violence, and show mixed results regarding the effects of gender, ethnicity, and age.

Experiences with authorities have been further linked to attitudes to authorities. Attitudes to authorities are commonly defined as feelings and perceptions one holds regarding the authority, including legitimacy, trust, and approval of the authority's actions. Extensive research suggests that negative attitudes to authority are highly associated with negative experiences with the authorities, increased violence, and lower intention to cooperate with authorities. However, again majority of the studies are conducted on adults and few focus on school authorities.

There are many theories attempting to explain the relationship between the role of authorities and compliance with social norms. Some of the more prominent theories will be discussed later in this chapter. However, in order to attain a more complete understanding of compliance with social norms, warning signs must be explored first.

II. Warning Signs

As the above section outlines, authority figures play a significant role in the lives of youth. Research and theory identify a number of warning signs that can be used to predict compliance with social norms. The following are factors that we believe are essential in the understanding of compliant behaviour: the fact of having been victimized, the level of empathy, the desired reputation among peers, and the general satisfaction with life.

Victimization

The relationship between victimization and compliance has been widely investigated and discussed in the academic community. The previous section discussed the effect of negative experiences with authorities, which can be viewed as a form of victimization, on compliance. However, victimization by peers and other non-authority figures, such as bullying or other types of physical aggression, verbal threats, or social exclusion from the group, can also have a significant effect on compliance. In fact, Emler and colleagues (Emler, 2009; Emler & Reicher, 1987; 1995; 2005) suggest that peer victimization drives youth to act antisocially as a way to protect themselves when the authority figures fall short of that role. The link between victimization and violence has been reported among British (e.g. Deadman & MacDonals, 2004; Sampson & Lauritsen, 1990; Smith & Ecob, 2007), North American (e.g. Regoeczi, 2000; Shaffer & Ruback, 2002; for a review see Siegfried, Ko, & Kelley, 2004), and Spanish (e.g. Herrero et al., 2006) youth.

However, the relationship between victimization and intention to cooperate with authorities has been widely neglected. In light of the theory proposed by Emler and colleagues it is reasonable to expect that victimized individuals would be less likely to cooperate with authorities as they feel alienated from them due to the fact that authorities are unable to protect them from the victimization. However, a direct evaluation of the relationship between victimization and compliance with social norms is required in order to accept Emler's explanation. Some of the research exploring the relationship between victimization and compliance is summarised in Table 6.

Empathy

Within the academic community the link between empathy and compliance is widely supported. Empathy is commonly defined as the ability to understand and share the emotions of others. It is the ability to take perspective and anticipate the consequences of one's behaviour. Over the years, a large number of studies have found that low empathy is highly associated with violence (for a review see Jolliffe & Farrington, 2004; Lovett & Sheffield, 2007; and Varker, Devilly, Ward & Beech, 2008). Recent studies further confirmed this relationship among British (e.g. Dolan & Rennie, 2007; Whattaker, Brown, Beckett & Gerhold, 2006), North American (e.g. Laible, 2007), Australian (e.g. Varker & Devilly, 2007), and Spanish (e.g. Estévez et al., 2008) youth.

Violent and Delinquent Youths: Relationships with Institutional Authorities... 153

Table 6. Empirical Study of Victimization and Compliance.

Study	Sample	Results
Regoeczi (2000)	319 Canadian homicide victims aged 12-17	43.7% of victims used substances 25.7% of victims were killed while committing an antisocial act. 32.6% of victims had a previous criminal record
Shaffer & Ruback (2002)	5,003 US students aged 11-17	Violent victimization predicted violent offending ($B = .86$, $SE = .11$, OR $= 2.36$)
Herrero, Estévez & Musitu (2006).	973 Spanish students aged 11–16	Violence related to victimization ($r = .33$)
Smith & Ecob (2007)	4,300 UK secondary school students	Victimization related to offending behaviour (r $= .39$) and bullying ($r = .37$) Being bullied related to offending ($r = .10$) and bullying ($r = .17$)
Deadman & MacDonals (2004)	4,848 UK citizens aged 12-30	Victimization related to offending behaviour (violent $\beta = .50$, $t = 5.48$; non-violent $\beta = .23$, $t = 2.74$
Sampson & Lauritsen (1990)	10,905 UK citizens aged over 16	Victimization related to self reported violence ($B = .25$, $SE = 4.58$, $p < .001$)

The relationship between empathy and cooperation with authorities has received only limited attention. Only one evaluation of the relationship exists. Laibel (2007) evaluated 170 US university students and found a significant positive relationship between high empathy and cooperation. Although the relationship between empathy and violence is well established, the relationship of empathy with cooperation must be further explored before conclusions could be made with certainty. Table 7 summarises some of the research findings evaluating the relationship between empathy and compliance.

Table 7. Empirical Study of Empathy and Compliance.

Study	Sample	Results
Whattaker, Brown, Beckett & Gerhold (2006)	276 UK males adolescents	Sex offender reported lower empathy scores than non-offenders ($t(140.75) = 4.02$, $p < .001$)
Dolan & Rennie (2007)	115 UK males aged 13-18	Psychopathic youth displayed lower empathy than non-psychopathic youth ($t = -1.86$, $p < .05$)
Varker & Devilly (2007)	32 Australians aged 13-20	Sex offenders showed lower empathy than non-offenders ($Z = -2.53$, $p < .05$)
Estévez, Murgui, Musitu & Moreno (2008)	1319 Spanish secondary school students	Higher violence related to lower empathy ($r = .24$)
Laible (2007)	170 US university students	Low empathy related to high violence ($r = .54$) and low pro-social behaviour ($r = .33$)

Reputation

Reputation has recently received some attention in the academic community. Reputation can be defined as the social representation a group has in relation to a particular person, consequently it refers to how an individual is perceived by others. Emler and colleagues (Emler, 2009; Emler & Reicher, 1987; 1995; 2005) suggest that in order for youth to protect themselves from victimization, they attempt to establish a tough and dangerous reputation by behaving antisocially. As such, it is reasonable to expect that the desire for more non-conforming reputation would be associated with higher non-compliance. This hypothesis has been confirmed among Australian (Carroll, Hattie, Durkin & Houghton, 2001; Carroll, Houghton, Hattie & Durkin, 1999), Spanish (Buelga, Musitu, Murgui & Pons, 2008; Estévez et al., 2008), and American (Kerpelman & Smith-Adcock, 2005) youth. Although the studies are few and conducted only in relation to violence (Table 8), they nonetheless point out the important contribution of non-conforming reputation in understanding compliance with social norms.

Satisfaction with Life

Although it may be intuitive that satisfaction with life may have a relationship with compliance with social norms, there are only few studies addressing that relationship. Satisfaction in life is commonly assessed through low psychological distress, such as depression, and high happiness with one's overall life conditions. Herrero, Estévez and Musitu (2006) evaluated 973 Spanish adolescents and found that violence was associated with higher psychological distress. These findings were further confirmed by Buelga, Musitu, Murgui & Pons (2008). Similarly, Hosser and Bosold (2006) found that sexually offending adolescents in Germany had lower psychological well being. Similar findings were reported within an American population (Rose & Swenson, 2009). There is an obvious disparity of research in the area of compliance and satisfaction with life. Nonetheless, the studies point out that satisfaction with life may be a contributing factor in understanding compliance (Table 9).

Table 8. Empirical Study of Reputation and Compliance.

Study	Sample	Results
Carroll, Houghton, Hattie & Durkin (1999)	230 Australians aged 12-16	Delinquents reported higher non-conforming reputation (all $F > .11.15, p < .01$)
Carroll, Hattie, Durkin & Houghton (2001)	260 Australians aged 12-18	Delinquents reported higher non-conforming reputation (all $F (14, 484) = 6.67, p < .001$)
Kerpelman & Smith-Adcock (2005)	188 US girls from grades 7-11	Violence related to more non-conforming reputation ($r = .40$)
Buelga, Musitu, Murgui & Pons (2008)	1,319 Spanish students aged 11-16	High violence related to non-conforming reputation ($r = .18$)
Estévez, Murgui, Musitu & Moreno (2008)	1319 Spanish secondary school students	Higher violence related to lower pro-social reputation ($r = .37$)

Table 9. Empirical Study of Satisfaction with Life and Compliance.

Study	Sample	Results
Hosser & Bosold (2006)	105 German youth prisoners aged 17-24	Psychological adjustment problems predicted sexual offending (B = -1.56, $p < .05$)
Herrero, Estévez & Musitu (2006).	973 Spanish students aged 11–16	High violence related to psychological distress (r = .13)
Buelga, Musitu, Murgui & Pons (2008)	1,319 Spanish students aged 11-16	High violence related to lower satisfaction with life (r = .17)
Rose & Swenson (2009)	439 US 7th & 9th grade students	High violence related to psychological distress (r = .16)

Summary of Warning Signs

Over the years, research on compliance with social norms has identified numerous risk factors contributing to the understanding of compliance, especially violence. Some of the most prominent warning signs of maladaptive tendencies are high victimization, low empathy, desired non-conforming reputation, and low satisfaction with life. However, research conducted on these factors in light of compliance is limited in number and has been primarily conducted in relation to violence. Further evaluations of these warning signs in relation to cooperation with authorities is required.

III. UNDERSTANDING COMPLIANCE: A THEORETICAL APPROACH

This chapter outlined factors identified through research and theory that can possibly shed light on the nature of adolescent compliance with social norms. Specifically, the chapter described the research findings regarding the effects of authorities, victimization, empathy, reputation, and satisfaction with life on exhibition of violent behaviour and intentions to cooperate with authorities. Over the years, academics proposed theories explaining the relationship between each individual factor and compliance. However, one prominent theory, proposed by Emler and colleages, offers insight into how these factors interact together to explain compliance with social norms.

Emler and colleagues (1987, 2005, 2009) advance a theory to explain how relationships with institutional authorities relate to compliance with social norms. These authors suggest that the role of institutional authorities, such as teachers and police, is the protection of individual rights and freedoms through laws and the use of their power. Through socialization by the authorities, children learn to believe and expect authorities to perform that role. However, over time and through direct experience of victimization and authority hostility, some youth come to understand that authorities can not always live up to that expectation. This results in the youth feeling resentment to and alienation from authorities and their protection. Thus, resulting in a lower satisfaction with life and negative attitudes to authorities. This feeling of alienation from formal protection and the social order leads some youth to re-evaluate their beliefs and norms, and find the antisocial minority group as more appealing. Youth start believing that while formal authority may lack the capacity or desire to protect them, antisocial groups offer easy protection and support outside of the social order.

Consequently, this feeling of alienation from formal protection and appeal of the antisocial group leads some youth to act violently, not comply with social norms, and desire to develop a non-conforming reputation in order to fit in within that antisocial group. As such, Emler and colleagues propose that victimization and experience with authorities affect youths' satisfaction with life and desire for non-conforming reputation. These in turn affect their attitudes to authorities, which lead to compliance or non-compliance with social norms. Figure 1 summarises the proposed model of the relationships between the mentioned variables of interest, in light of the literature. A number of empirical evaluations (see Table 10) have already suggested some validity of this model. Furthermore, a direct evaluation of the validity of this model is currently being carried out in the United Kingdom.

IV. CONCLUSIONS AND IMPLICATIONS FOR PREVENTION AND INTERVENTION

Research and theory suggests that authorities play a significant role in the lives of youth. Their role is to shape youth into well functioning members of society. As such, relationships between youth and authorities are highly important in preventing non-compliance with social norms, namely, violence and non-cooperation with authorities. The exhibition of desired non-conforming reputation, low satisfaction with life, and low empathy are warning signs that a youth may be experiencing victimization and/or negative relationships with authorities, which may lead in turn the youth to develop and/or maintain negative attitudes towards formal figures and institutions and refuse compliance. As such, in order to prevent non-compliance attention must be focused on exploring the warning signs exhibited by the at-risk youth and addressing their relationships with authorities.

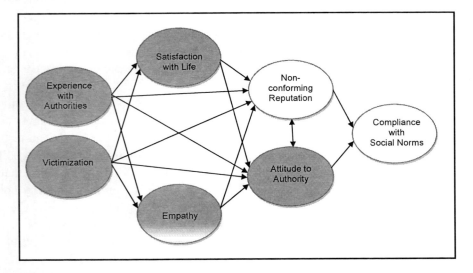

Figure 1. Hypothesised Model of Relationships between the Variables of Interest.

Table 10. Empirical Study of Paths to Compliance.

Study	Sample	Results
Liska & Reed (1985)	2,213 US boys	Experience with parents led to delinquency, delinquency led to school experience, and school experience fed back into parental experience The model did not fit Blacks well
Kerpelman, & Smith-Adcock (2005)	188 US girls from grades 7-11	Experience with police affected reputation, and the two combined affected delinquency (GFI = .98, RMSEA = .02)
Cava, Musitu & Murgui (2006)	665 Spanish youth aged 12-16	Attitudes to authority mediated the relationship between aggression and experience with parents (NNFI = .98; RMSEA = .049)
Estévez, Murgui, Moreno & Musitu (2007)	1,049 Spanish students aged 11-16	Negative attitudes to authority mediated the relationship between negative experience with authorities and violence (NNFI= .97; RMSEA= .04)
Musitu, Estévez & Emler (2007)	1,068 Spanish students aged 11-16	Negative attitude to authority mediated the relationship between negative experiences with authorities and violence (NNFI = .97; RMSEA =.04)
Estévez, Murgui, Musitu & Moreno (2008)	1,319 Spanish secondary school students	Attitudes to authorities, empathy, and reputation mediated the relationship between experience and aggression (NNFI > .96; RMSEA <.04) Model was more salient for boys.
Laible (2007)	170 US university students	Empathy mediated the relationship between experiences and compliance
Sunshine & Tyler (2003b)	483 US citizens aged 19-88	Legitimacy mediated the relationship between procedural justice and cooperation (IFI = 0.90, RMSEA = 0.06).
Viki, Culmer, Eller & Abrams (2006)	120 UK students aged 19-50	Norms mediated the relationship between experiences with police and intentions to cooperate with legal authorities (NNFI=.99, RMSEA<.1)
Murphy & Tyler (2008)	3,018 US tax payers	Positive attitudes to authority mediated the relationship between procedural justice and compliance.

As research discussed in this chapter indicates, youth expect authorities to perform their role as socializing agents, role models, and protectors, as well as treat others with dignity and respect. Consequently, institutional authorities must continue fulfilling these expectations in order to encourage compliance with social norms. Intervention programs must be aimed at addressing how authority figures interact with adolescents. Specifically, mandatory training programs must be made available to teachers and the police, which will educate authority figures in the expectations and needs of adolescents, as well as provide them with information regarding the appropriate methods of communication and conflict resolution with young people. Since authority figures are expected to be role models and treat others with dignity and respect, particular attention should be placed on the behaviours that the youth observe authorities performing. Intervention programs focusing on the direct behaviour of institutional authority figures with adolescents will produce more positive experiences with authorities, and consequently higher compliance with social norms.

Programs focused on improving school and learning environment in general will further encourage adolescents to trust in authorities and comply with social norms. Continuing the campaign against bullying and victimization will give youth confidence that institutional authorities are attempting to fulfil their role as protectors and, consequently, encourage trust in the authorities. Smaller classes and greater availability of teachers and police for support and interaction will help the authority figures to identify youth in need and address their concerns prior to the youth turning to violence as coping strategy for their problems. Overall, providing the youth with more positive learning environment will encourage the development of more positive relationships between the authorities and adolescents, thus making it easier for the authorities to fulfil their roles as socializing agents, role models, and protectors.

Finally, separate intervention programs should focus specifically on the perceptions and experiences of youth. For those youth who already possess negative attitudes to authorities due to their previous experiences, intervention programs must be made available to address those attitudes. Continued availability of programs offering support and assistance for victimized youth, as well as behaviour modification programs to teach them of better coping strategies will provide adolescents with more socially accepted forms of coping with their negative life experiences. In addition, providing the youth with opportunities for more positive experiences with authorities will encourage some of them to change their attitudes regarding authorities.

Overall, institutional authorities play a significant role in the lives of adolescents and relationships with these authorities can shape adolescent compliance with social norms. Negative relationships with authorities may lead some youth to turn to violence and lack of cooperation with the authorities. Intervention programs that target the learning environment as a whole, the behaviour of the authority figures, and the perceptions and experiences of adolescents will prevent some and encourage other youth to trust authorities, thus, promoting compliance with social norms. Most importantly, the continued commitment of teachers and police in trying to improve their relationships with adolescents is essential for breaking down the barriers of previous negative experience.

REFERENCES

Ajzen, I. (1991). The theory of planned behaviour. *Organizational Behaviour and Human Decision Process, 50*, 179-211.

Amoroso, D. M. & Ware, E. E. (1986). Adolescents' perception of aspects of the home environment and their attitudes towards parents, self, and external authority. *Adolescence, 21*, 191-204.

Brown, D. W. (1974). Adolescent attitudes and lawful behavior. *Public Opinion Quarterly, 38*, 98-106.

Buelga, S., Musitu, G., Murgui, S. & Pons, J. (2008). Reputation, loneliness, satisfaction with life and aggressive behaviour in adolescence. *The Spanish Journal of Psychology, 11*, 192-200.

Burwen, L. S. & Campbell, D. T. (1957). The generality of attitudes toward authority and nonauthority figures. *The Journal of Abnormal and Social Psychology, 54*, 24-31.

Carroll, A., Houghton, S., Hattie, J. & Durkin, K., (1999). Adolescent reputation enhancement: Differentiating delinquent, nondelinquent, and at-risk youth. *Journal of Child Psychology and Psychiatry, 40*, 593-606.

Carroll, A., Hattie, J., Durkin, K. & Houghton, S. (2001). Goal-setting and reputation enhancement: Behavioural choice among delinquent, at-risk and not at-risk adolescents. *Legal and Criminological Psychology, 6,* 165-184.

Carr, P. J., Napolitano, L. & Keating, J. (2007). We never call hr cops and here is why: A qualitative examination of legal cynicism in three Philadelphia neighborhoods. *Criminology, 45,* 445-480.

Cava, M. J., Musitu, G. & Murgui, S. (2006). Familia y violencia escolar: el rol mediador de la autoestima y la actitud hacia la autoridad institucional/Family and school violence: the mediator role of self-esteem and attitudes towards institutional authority. *Psicothema, 18,* 367-373.

Deadman, D. & MacDonald, Z. (2004). Offenders as victims of crime? An investigation into the relationship between criminal behaviour and victimization. *Journal of Royal Statistical Society, 167,* 53-67.

De Cremer, D. & Tyler, T. R. (2007). The effects of trust in authority and procedural fairness on cooperation. *Journal of Applied Psychology, 92,* 639-649.

Dobash, R. P., Dobash, R. E., Ballintyne, S. & Schumann, K. (1990). Ignorance and suspicion: Young people and criminal justice in Scotland and Germany. *British Journal of Criminology, 30,* 306-320.

Dolan, M. C. & Rennie, C. E. (2007). The relationship between psychopathic traits measured by the Youth Psychopathy trait Inventory and psychopathology in UK sample of conduct disordered boys. *Journal of Adolescence, 30,* 601-611.

Durkin, K. (2002). *Developmental social psychology.* Oxford, UK: Blackwell Publishers Ltd.

Eller, A., Abrams, D., Viki, G. T., Imara, D. A. & Peerbux, S. (2007). Stay cool, hang loose, admit nothing: Race, intergroup contact, and public-police relations. *Basic and Applied Social Psychology, 29,* 213-224.

Emler, N. (1992). Childhood origins of beliefs about institutional authority. In H. Haste (Ed.). *Development of political understanding: A new perspective* (65-77). CA, US: Jossey-Bass Publishers.

Emler, N. (2009). Delinquents as a minority group: Accidental tourists in forbidden territory or voluntary émigrés? In F. Butera, & J. Levine (Eds.). *Coping with minority status: Responses to exclusion and inclusion.* US: Cambridge University Press.

Emler, N. & Reicher, S. (1987). Orientations to institutional authority in adolescence. *Journal of Moral Education, 16,* 108-116.

Emler, N. & Reicher, S. (1995). *Adolescence and delinquency.* Oxford, UK: Blackwell Publishers Ltd.

Emler, N. & Reicher, S. (2005). Delinquency: Cause or consequence of social exclusion? In D. Abrams, M. A. Hogg, & J. M. Marques (Eds.), *The Social Psychology of Inclusion and Exclusion.* New York: Psychology Press.

Estévez, E., Murgui, S., Moreno, D. & Musitu, G. (2007). Family communication styles, attitude towards institutional authority and adolescents' violent behaviour at school. *Psicothema, 19,* 108-113.

Estévez, E., Murgui, S., Musitu, G. & Moreno, D. (2008). Adolescent aggression: Effects of gender and family and school environments. *Journal of Adolescence, 31,* 433-450.

Giordano, P. (1976). The sense of injustice? An analysis of juveniles' reactions to the justice system. *Criminology, 14,* 93-111.

Goldsmith, A. (2005). Police reform and the problem of trust. *Theoretical Criminology, 9,* 443-470.

Gouveaia-Pereira, M., Vala, J., Palmonari, A. & Rubini, M. (2003). School Experience, relational justice and legitimation of institutional [authority]. *European Journal of Psychology of Education, 18,* 309-325.

Hinds, L. & Murphy, K. (2007). Public satisfaction with police: Using procedural justice to improve police legitimacy. *The Australian and New Zealand Journal of Criminology, 40,* 27-42.

Herrero, J., Estévez, E. & Musitu, G. (2006). The relationships of adolescent school-related deviant behaviour and victimization with psychological distress: testing a general model of the mediational role of parents and teachers across groups of gender and age. *Journal of Adolescence, 29,* 671-690.

Hosser, D. & Bosold, C. (2006). A comparison of sexual and violent offenders in a German youth prison. *The Howard Journal, 45,* 159-170.

Howes, C. & James, J. (2004). Children's social development within the socialization context of childcare and early childhood education. In P. K. Smith, & C. H. Heart (Eds.), *Blackwell handbook of childhood social development* (pp. 137-155). Oxford, UK: Blackwell Publishing Ltd.

Jackson, J. & Sunshine, J. (2007). Public confidence in police: A neo-Durkheimian perspective. *The British Journal of Criminology, 47,* 214-33.

Johnson, O.G. & Stanley, J.C. (1955). Attitudes toward authority of delinquent and nondelinquent boys. *The Journal of Abnormal and Social Psychology, 51,* 712-716.

Jolliffe, D. & Farrington, D.P. (2004). Empathy and offending: A systematic review and meta-analysis. *Aggression and Violent Behavior, 9,* 441-476.

Jones-Brown, D. D. (2000). Debunking the myth of officer friendly: How African American males experience community policing. *Journal of Contemporary Criminal Justice, 16,* 209-229.

Kerpelman, J.L. & Smith-Adcock, S. (2005). Female adolescents' delinquent activity: The intersection of bonds to parents and reputation enhancements. *Youth Society, 37,* 176-200.

Khoo, A.C.E, & Oakes, P.J. (2000). The variability of the delinquent self: Anti-authority attitudes and endorsement of neutralization techniques among incarcerated delinquents in Singapore. *Asian Journal of Social Psychology, 3,* 125-132.

Ladd, G.W., Buhs, E.S, & Troop, W. (2004). Children's interpersonal skills and relationships in school settings: Adaptive significance and implications for school-based prevention and intervention programs. In P. K. Smith, & C. H. Heart (Eds.), *Blackwell handbook of childhood social development* (394-416). Oxford, UK: Blackwell Publishing Ltd.

Laible, D. (2007). Attachment with parents and peers in late adolescence: Links with emotional competence and social behavior. *Personality and Individual Differences, 43,* 1185-1197.

Leiber, M., Nalla, M. & Farnworth, M. (1998). Explaining juveniles' attitudes toward the police. *Justice Quarterly, 15,* 151-173.

Levy, K. S. (2001). The relationship between adolescent attitudes towards authority, self-concept, and delinquency. *Adolescence, 36,* 333-346.

Liska, A. E. & Reed, M. D. (1985). Ties to conventional institutions and delinquency: Estimating reciprocal effects. *American Sociological Review, 50,* 547-560.

Lovett, B. J. & Sheffield, R. A. (2007). Affective empathy deificits in aggressive children and adolescents: A critical review. *Clinical Psychology Review, 27,* 1-13.

Molinari, L. (2001). Social representations of children's rights: The point of view of adolescents. *Swiss Journal of Psychology, 60,* 231-243.

Murphy, K. & Tyler, T. (2008). Procedural justice and compliance behaviour: the mediating role of emotions. *European Journal of Social Psychology, 38,* 652-668.

Murray, C. & Thompson, F. (1985). The representation of authority: An adolescent viewpoint. *Journal of Adolescence, 8,* 217-229.

Musitu, G., Estévez, E. & Emler, N. P. (2007). Adjustment problems in the family and school contexts, attitudes towards authority, and violent behaviour at school in adolescence. *Adolescence, 42,* 779-794.

Reisig, M. D., Bratton, J. & Gertz, M. G. (2007). The construct validity and refinement of process-based policing measures. *Criminal Justice and Behavior, 34,* 1005-1028.

Rigby, K., Mak, A. S. & Slee, P. T. (1989). Notes and short communications: Impulsiveness, orientation to institutional authority, and gender as factors in self-reported delinquency among Australian adolescents. *Personality and Individual Differences, 6,* 689-692.

Rigby, R. & Rump, J. (1981). Attitudes towards parents and institutional authorities during adolescence. *Journal of Psychology,* 109, 109-118.

Rigby, K., Schofield, P. & Slee, P. T. (1987). The similarly of attitudes towards personal and impersonal types of Authority among adolescent schoolchildren. *Journal of Adolescence, 10,* 241-253.

Regoeczi, W. C. (2000). Adolescent violent victimization and offending: Assessing the extent of the link. *Canadian Journal of Criminology, 24,* 493-505.

Rose, A. J. & Swenson, L. P. (2009). Do perceived popular adolescents who aggress against others experience emotional adjustment problems themselves? *Developmental Psychology, 45,* 868-872.

Sampson, R. J. & Lauritsen, J. L. (1990). Deviant lifestyle, proximity to crime, and the offend-victim link in personal violence. *Journal of Research in Crime and Delinquency, 27,* 110-139.

Seron, C., Pereira, J. & Kovath, J. (2004). Judging police misconduct: "Street-level" versus professional policing. *Law and Society Review, 38,* 665-710.

Shore, M. F., Massimo, J. L. & Mack, R. (1965). Changes in the perceptions of interpersonal relationships in successfully treated adolescent delinquent boys. *Journal of Consulting Psychology, 29,* 213-217.

Shaffer, J. N. & Ruback, R. B. (2002). Violent victimization as a risk factor for violent offending among juveniles. *Juvenile Justice Bulletin, December 2002.*

Siegfried, C. B., Ko, S. J. & Kelley, A. (2004). *Victimization and juvenile offending.* US: The National Child Traumatic Stress Network.

Smetana, J. G. (1988). Adolescents' and parents' conceptions of parental authority. *Child Development, 59,* 321-335.

Smetana, J. G. & Bitz, B. (1996). Adolescents' conceptions of teachers' authority and their relations to rule violations in school. *Child Development, 67,* 1153-1172.

Smith, D. J. & Ecob, R. (2007). An investigation into causal inks between victimization and offending in adolescents. *British Journal of Sociology, 58,* 633-659.

Sunshine, J. & Tyler, T. (2003a). Moral Solidarity, Identification with the Community, and the Importance of Procedural Justice: The Police as Prototypical Representatives of a Group's Moral Values. *Social Psychology Quarterly, 66*, 153-165.

Sunshine, J. & Tyler, T. R. (2003b). The role of procedural justice and legitimacy in shaping public support for policing. *Law & Society Review, 37*, 513-547.

Tarry, H. & Emler, N. (2007). Attitudes, values and moral reasoning as predictors of delinquency. *British Journal of Developmental Psychology, 25*, 169-183.

Tyler, T. R. (2006). *Why people obey the law.* Princeton, NJ: Princeton University Press.

Varker, T. & Devilly, G. J. (2007). Types of empathy and adolescent sexual offenders. *Journal of Sexual Aggression, 13*, 139-149.

Varker, T., Devilly, G. J., Ward, T. & Beech, A. R. (2008). Empathy and adolescent sexual offenders: A review of the literature. *Aggression and Violent Behavior, 13*, 251-260.

Verkuyten, M. (2002). Making teachers accountable for students' disruptive classroom behaviour. *British Journal of Sociology of Education, 23*, 107-122.

Viki, G. T., Culmer, M. J., Eller, A. & Abrams, D. (2006). Race and willingness to co-operate with the police: The role of quality of contact, attitudes towards the behaviour and subjective norms. *British Journal of Social Psychology, 45*, 285-302.

Watson, A. C. & Angell, B. (2007). Applying Procedural Justice Theory to law enforcement's response to persons with mental illness. *Psychiatric Services, 58*, 787-793.

Weitzer, R. (2002). Incidents of police misconduct and public opinion. *Journal of Criminal Justice, 30*, 397-408.

Wells, W. (2007). Type of contact and evaluations of police officers: The effects of procedural justice across three types of police-citizen contacts. *Journal of Criminal Justice, 35*, 612-621.

Whattaker, M. K., Brown, J., Beckett, R. & Gerhold, C. (2006). Sexual knowledge and empathy: A comparison of adolescent child molesters and non-offending adolescents. *Journal of Sexual Aggression, 12*, 143-154.

Woolard, J. L., Harvell, S. & Graham, S. (2008). Anticipatory injustice among adolescents: Age and racial/ethnic differences in perceived unfairness of the justice system. *Behavioral Sciences and the Law, 26*, 207-226.

In: Youth Violence and Juvenile Justice: Causes, Intervention...   ISBN: 978-1-61668-011-4
Editor: Neil A. Ramsay et al., pp. 187-206   © 2010 Nova Science Publishers, Inc.

Chapter 7

VIOLENCE PREVENTION AND TREATMENT PROGRAMMES FOR YOUNG OFFENDERS

Thomas Ross, Friedemann Pfäfflin, and María Isabel Fontao
Forensic Psychotherapy, University Hospital Ulm, Germany

ABSTRACT

Correctional research has shown that young offenders have different treatment and programming needs than adult offenders. A large number of specific treatment and violence prevention programs for young offenders have been developed and applied in many countries. The majority of these programs are of the "cognitive skills type", i.e. they aim at enhancing cognitive and social skills, which are often deficient in young offenders. Modern treatment programs attend to criminogenic needs of offenders, such as impulsivity or poor affect control, empathy deficits, low levels of socio-moral reasoning, substance use and poor problem-solving skills; a style of delivery that young offenders will find interesting and engaging; and flexibility in its administration in order to take into account potentially small custodial sentences. Programs of this type teach young offenders cognitive-behavioral skills that enable them to take their time, i.e. to stop and think before they act, in order to resolve socially complex and potentially "dangerous" situations. Focussing on treatment programs, this chapter provides a brief overview of the history of (young) offender treatment and some of the most common treatment and violence prevention models for young offenders.

DEFINING JUVENILE DELINQUENCY

Whether or not a young person is legally judged as a young or youthful offender depends on the legal definition of the terms related to the young age of the offender, i.e. children, juveniles, or adolescents. Due to the differences of legal systems and jurisdictions in different countries and sometimes even federal states within countries, a general definition is impossible to provide. General agreement may be assumed, however, on that a person´s age when he or she committed an act that is regarded to be a crime, is the most compelling and decisive factor as to whether this person can legally be treated as an adult, as an adolescent, or as a youth. In addition to age, the need of supervision, treatment, or confinement of that person may also be taken into account for the legal classification of a person. The age frame for a person legally to be considered as a juvenile varies between a minimum of seven (this is, for example, the case in some US jurisdictions) and a maximum of twenty-one years (true in Germany for exceptional cases). In the literature, the most common terms for non-adults who break the law are the following: Youthful offender, juvenile delinquent, juvenile offender, young offender, and adolescent offender. The terms juvenile offender, juvenile delinquent, and adolescent offender are typically used as a sub-category of the higher order categories denoted by the terms young offender or youthful offender. For the purpose of this chapter, it should be sufficient to note that most treatment and prevention models aimed at the prevention or reduction of criminal offences committed by young offenders address offender groups between 10 and 18 years of age.

THE ROOTS OF JUVENILE AND ADULT OFFENDER TREATMENT

The Austrian psychiatrist August Aichhorn was the first seriously to concern himself with the treatment of young delinquent individuals (Aichhorn, 1925). Working with delinquent youth at the city borders of Vienna about 100 years ago, he developed an influential treatment concept which has later been described as the *corrective emotional experience* (Alexander & French, 1946), now an indispensable terminus technicus in psychoanalytical treatment (Cordess & Cox, 1998; Welldon & van Velsen, 1997). From a theoretical point of view, he proposed a dual deficit model. He posited a failure of progression from the pleasure principle to the reality principle in conjunction with a malformation of the superego in his developmental account of the disorder. This basically accounts for lack of impulse control in delinquent individuals, as a tendency for immediate gratification persists and remains unchallenged. Excessive strictness and overindulgence were both seen as causes of the child´s or youth's failure to renounce the pleasure principle. He saw psychosocial deprivation as the primary reason for impeding the renunciation of the pleasure principle and for disrupting the internalisation of parental norms. This and the internalisation of poor parental norms in delinquent families were put forward as explanations of superego dysfunction (Cordess & Cox, 1998). Before the "cognitive revolution" in the 1950s brought about a different theoretical view about the antecedents of delinquent and violent behavior, British, Dutch, and many German forensic psychiatric and social therapeutic facilities had worked in correspondence with the ideas laid out above. Aichhorn´s approach to treatment included a phase of getting the patient involved in the treatment process. Instead of re-enacting punishment, he would frustrate the patients´ wishes for punishment later in the process, i.e. in the case of recidivism, he tried to understand what the delinquent act actually meant for the individual, and what it stood for in the individual´s mind. Aichhorn believed that in order to renounce their narcissistic position and give up the pleasure principle in favour of the reality principle, delinquent individuals had to establish an idealizing relationship with their therapist. To establish a relationship stable enough to make positive treatment effects possible, the therapist had to be able to indulge the patient and compromise traditional views on psychoanalytic treatment techniques.

Drawing on Aichhorn's early work, Kurt Eissler, a US-American psychoanalyst of Austrian origin, suggested that delinquents, due to their narcissistic position, are not able to establish positive transference with their therapists (Eissler, 1953). He described the technical difficulties in treating a delinquent as a consequence of his lack of desire to change. Delinquents have no need or motive to tell the therapist what is going on in them, and their symptoms are painful not to them but to others in their environment. Furthermore, he postulated that delinquents will not be able to differentiate sources of external and internal danger, and to consciously experience and cope with anxiety stemming from these sources. Instead, in order to cope with anxiety, they tend to engage in destructive acting-out. In order to reduce anxiety, the attitude of the therapist should be characterized by qualities such as warmth, firmness, and high expectations of the person combined with clear guidance. Implicit in this notion is the therapist's positive regard for the delinquent, his or her own sense of integrity and authority and belief in the possibility of change. Furthermore, he stressed the importance of capturing the imagination and curiosity of the resistant patient. Instead of applying classical psychoanalytic technique such as analysis and interpretation of thought and behavior, he stated that from time to time, real gratification should be granted. Eissler was convinced that a basic treatment of this sort is a necessary condition for aggression to translate in anxiety, and the fruitful application of psychoanalytic technique on offender patients.

Modern psychodynamic offender treatment highlights the need for establishing well structured therapeutic regimes that can support the patient's needs to overcome resistance. This is also true for the psychodynamic treatment of young offenders. Good staff management, support and consultation are empathized; the patients need an empathetic, encouraging, and challenging therapeutic relationship and a therapeutic team that is able to convey (psychological) security. The latter is seen to be important in order to help a patient recognize and cope with his conflicts and eventually to facilitate effective prosocial conflict resolution. Recent work informed by attachment theory and its application to the treatment of offenders has generally empirically supported the notions laid out above (e.g. Fonagy, 2003; 2004).

Historically, there was a second approach to offender treatment, derived from behavior therapy. In the 1960s, behavioral researchers began to aversively condition unwanted sexual fantasies, reactions, and behaviors in adults, i.e. they tried to extinguish these by means of well recognized learning mechanisms such as classical conditioning. Electric shocks or aversive olfactory stimuli were applied, for example, for the reconditioning of sexual deviant arousal. Aversion therapy was reported to be effective, at first, but scientific enthusiasm for these approaches faded quickly in the light of new findings that were more promising. Today, there is scientific consensus that, in the long run, aversive reconditioning aggravate rather than extinguish deviant sexual preferences, i.e. patients tend to get worse (Hall, 1995). This is not to say that general learning principles do not work in offender populations. The principle of positive reinforcement, for example, is unquestioned as an important means of enhancing prosocial behaviors in virtually all psychotherapeutic approaches to treatment, including treatments of young patients. It is important to note, however, that classical approaches to positive reinforcement such as "token economies", i.e. the simple gratification of "correct" behavioral responses, have been abandoned in recent years. This is true for both adult and young offender groups. A detailed account of the history of cognitive-behavioral approaches

THE UPSURGE OF MANUALIZED TREATMENT PROGRAMS

Beginning in the early 1970s, and in the tradition of early behavioral therapy for offenders and especially sexual offenders, scientists in Canada and the United States started to develop more complex programs aiming at the enhancement of more prosocial attitudes and skills in order to counteract antisocial behaviors. These programs replaced older ones which had mainly focussed on symptom reduction as a means of relapse prevention. In order to be effective, treatment interventions had to shift towards cognitive processes facilitating delinquent behavior and/or recidivism, i.e. denial and minimization, prosocial norm building, victim empathy, self-regulation, splitting, and the enhancement of self assertiveness. Therefore, modern offender treatment programs address a range of cognitive and social elements often found in offender populations: cognitive distortions, social skills, and low self-esteem, lack of empathy, and, especially but not exclusively in the case of sexual offenders, intimacy deficits and deviant sexuality (e.g. Marshall, 1998; Hollin, 2004).

Today, numerous programs exist worldwide, and many of them are manualized, albeit not all to the same degree. By the time this paper was written in September 2009, the United States alone had several repositories of model programs and systematic reviews on the Internet, e.g. published by the US National Registry of Effective Programs and Practice (SAMHSA's National Registry of Evidence-based Programs and Practices [NREPP] at http://nrepp.samhsa.gov; a model programs guide, published by the US Office of Juvenile Justice and Delinquency Prevention (OJJDP Model Program guide -Developmental Services group at www.dsgonline.com/mpg2.5/mpg_index.htm; or a web page with valuable information on blueprint programs for violence prevention (Blueprints: Center for the study and prevention of violence at http://www.colorado.edu/cspv/blueprints/modelprograms.html). Individual programs comprise different types of intervention for different offender types aiming at a range of life domains among various settings: Program types are prevention, intervention, and suppression programs; Settings can be structured along a continuum of institutionalisation: Correctional (highly institutionalised) programs; mental health programs, and non-institutionalised community programs. Offender types are grouped by age, risk (violent/non-violent), and degree of offender organisation, i.e. programs primarily devised for individuals or gang-related programs; school and after-school programs, and specialized interventions on individual, family, and peer group levels.

THE DEVELOPMENTAL PERSPECTIVE OF YOUTH DELINQUENCY AND CRIME

Age Related Risk Factors

Age related risk factors for violence and delinquency in youth have been investigated according to a developmental model of crime. The developmental perspective focuses on two areas, namely within-individual changes in offending over time and the risk factors that explain changes in offending patterns over time. Modern developmental studies use longitudinal designs with repeated measurements on the same person to examine within-individual changes in offending over time. Thus, the developmental point of view entails a life-course perspective of crime as it relates to individual developmental processes. Some of the most important developmental theories which have spurred much scientific research about juvenile offender careers and age-related risk factors for violence and crime were formulated by Moffit, who distinguished life-course persistent and adolescent-limited offenders (Moffit, 1993), Thornberry (Developmental and Interactional Theory, Thornberry & Krohn, 2001; Thornberry & Krohn, 2005), and Loeber and colleagues (Three Pathway Model; e.g. Loeber, 1988; Loeber, Slot & Stouthamer-Loeber, 2007). While these theories are described in detail elsewhere, some of the research that has been conducted against the background of the developmental perspective is highly significant for risk-needs analyses that need to be done in order to adequately assign youth to programs. For example, Loeber and Farrington (1998; 2001) suggested four distinct developmental stages in the pathway to delinquency: preschool, school entry, childhood, and adolescence. Each of these four stages can be assigned to a number of risk factors that correlate substantially with later delinquency. Individual risk factors are usually tied to factors stemming from different areas influencing a person´s behavior; individual or idiosyncratic factors (of the child), family and community characteristics interact and may produce aggressive and disruptive behavioral patterns by the time of school entry (e.g. Loeber & Farrington, 2001; Thornberry & Krohn, 2001, Farrington, 2003). Among child related risk factors for later behavioral problems count prenatal and delivery complications, (difficult) temperament, hyperactivity, impulsivity, and attention problems at an early age (Farrington, 2003; 2007; 2009). Having a teenage mother, alcohol, drug, and tobacco use problems during pregnancy, parental substance abuse in general, parental discord, poor communication skills in the family, and poverty or low socio-economic status are typical family problems associated with juvenile criminal conduct. Among these, poor parental supervision in childhood is the best predictor of violent and property crimes up to age 45, and a cold, rejecting parenting style is related to delinquent behavior in children. While the above risk factors were described for very young children up to approximately five years of age, other age related risk factors might add on later.

Lipsey and Derson (1998) were among the first to organize risk factors and outcomes into different developmental time frames. At ages 6-11, the best predictors of subsequent serious or violent offences at ages 15-25 are involvement in delinquency and drug use. The second strongest predictor group of predictors are being a male, living in a poor family, and having antisocial parents. A history of aggression and ethnicity are in the third strongest group of predictors. For the 12-14 age group, lacking social ties and having antisocial peers are the strongest predictors for serious and violent crime at ages 15-25. Involvement in general delinquency comes second, and a history of aggression, school attitude and performance, mental health, parent-adolescent relations, and a history of violence rank third.

The significance of antisocial peers and substance abuse is reversed at these two age groups. Whereas having antisocial peers is a weak predictor for the 6-11 age group, it is one of the strongest predictors in the 12-14 age group. Conversely, in the 6-11 age group, substance abuse is one of the strongest predictors, whereas it is only a weak predictor a few years later, i.e. in the 12-14 age group.

The implications of these findings are obviously important for defining prevention and treatment programming priorities. Early intervention with young children should target early delinquent behaviors associated with individual risk factors (i.e. hyperactivity, impulsivity, and attention problems), drug use, aggressive behavior, family poverty, and effective parenting with antisocial parents. Interventions for adolescents should aim towards loosening offender's affiliation to antisocial peers; one focus should lie on the reduction of general involvement in delinquency, another one on the avoidance of physical violence. Pro-social ties should be strengthened at this time, improvement of mental health and relationships with parents are other issues to be taken into account. From a programmatic point of view, programs for adolescents must be systemic and multi-topic, i.e. they should comprise specific interventions on the individual, family, school, peer, and, where possible, on community level (e.g. Lipsey, 2006).

Offender Types

Risk analyses prior to treatment allocation should take into account the *type of juvenile offender* which is best characterized by their offence history. Developmental trajectories of criminal and violent behavior suggest that there are several types of young offenders, some of whom will need intensive treatment (i.e. persistent chronic offenders), less intensive treatment (e.g. transitional offenders, or late starters), or no treatment at all, because it is likely that their criminal activity will soon fade out (i.e. low level opportunistic offenders).

One of the most compelling studies ever made on juvenile offender careers employed a birth cohort of all people born from 1962 through 1977 who were referred to the juvenile court in Maricopa County, Arizona for an offence prior to their 18th birthday (Snyder, 1998). The analysis comprised 16 annual birth cohorts who turned 18 between 1980 and 1995. Thus, a sample of over 150.000 court careers was generated. Roughly two thirds of juvenile court careers were non-chronic, i.e. there were fewer than four referrals, and did not include any serious or violent offences. Eighteen per cent of all careers had serious non-violent offences including burglary, arson, weapon offences, motor vehicle theft, and drug trafficking, 8% had violent offences, and 3% had serious, violent, and chronic offences, including murder, manslaughter, kidnapping, violent sexual assault, robbery, and aggravated assault. Treatment need is associated with the seriousness of offences. It is obvious from this analysis that it is a very small fraction of youth who commit the most serious crimes. It is precisely this group of offenders who most needs treatment. Another very informative study about juvenile offender careers was conducted by Thornberry and colleagues (Thornberry et al., 2003; see also Thornberry and Krohn, 2003, for a general overview of longitudinal studies on this matter). In their Rochester New York Youth Development Study they investigated offender careers on a subgroup of N=647 males and found that (1) offending is ubiquitous in juveniles (94% of the sample self-reported some involvement in unlawful behavior by their early 20s, (2) that persistent, violent, and chronic offending is rare (6,9% of the sample were rated in this group), and (3) that offender careers can be more variable than suggested by Moffit and colleagues who divided patterns of offending in two dominant groups, i.e. life-course persistent and adolescence-limited offenders (e.g. Moffit 1993). The Thornberry study suggests that there are at least eight trajectory groups, with clearly differing ages of onset (low-level offenders [29.7%], intermittent offenders [10.8%], mid-adolescent offenders [7.9%], gradual-uptake offenders [12.6%], low-level desistors [12.4%], transitional offenders [10.4%], late bloomers [9.4%], and persistent high-level offenders [6.9%]). The members of the low-level offender group have the latest age of onset (M=15.1 years), and only 17% of this group began before age 13. The mean age of persistent high-risk offenders, in contrast, averaged 9.4 years, with 84% of them beginning before age 13. The average onsets of the other groups rank between these two extremes.

An impressive European study is currently being conducted by Farrington and colleagues, who in their Cambridge study of delinquent development have data on a forty-year follow-up on 411 delinquent males from the South London area (Farrington, 2003). Interviews were made from age 8 to age 48, and criminal records analysed from age 10 to age 50, with accompanying information from parents, teachers, peers and female partners. Violence was measured at different ages, and childhood risk factors described for different kinds of violence at different ages. Furthermore, violent offenders were traced and interviewed at ages 18, 32, and 48. Key findings that are relevant to treatment issues comprise the following: Criminal careers: 21% were convicted as juveniles (age 10-16), 41% were convicted up to age 50. The peak age of increase in offending was 14, and the peak age of decrease 23, with average onset of criminal behaviors at age 19, and average age of desistance at 28. Juvenile offenders tended to extend their criminal careers more into adulthood (73%) than juvenile non-offenders (16%, i.e. those, who first offended in adult age). Out of a total of 411 subjects, 28 (6.8%) were chronic offenders. These seven percent of males committed 52% of all crimes (10 or more crimes each). Furthermore, many childhood risk factors predict different types of violence in adulthood (view Farrington, 2003, for details). Other important longitudinal studies on the causes and correlates of delinquency comprise the Pittsburgh Youth Study (the entire issue 2, volume 12, 2002 of the journal Criminal Behavior and Mental Health is dedicated to this study; see also Loeber et al., 2003; Loeber et al., 2008), the Denver Youth Survey (e.g. Huizinga et al., 2003), and the Dunedin Multidisciplinary Health and Development Study. The latter study is not primarily designed to test for causes and correlates of delinquency, but it has produced about 1000 publications so far, some of them clearly relating to youth delinquency (e.g. Odgers et al., 2008; Arseneault et al., 2003; Broidy et al., 2003).

PRINCIPLES OF EFFECTIVE (CORRECTIONAL) INTERVENTION

Drawing on the intensive research conducted predominantly by Andrews and colleagues since the beginning of the 1990s, a number of principles of effective correctional intervention have been formulated (e.g., Andrews et al., 1990; Andrews, 2006; Andrews & Dowden, 2006). (1) Correctional intervention should make use of structured and validated risk-assessment. The implementation of a complete system of continuous offender risk screening and need assessments is better than the application of isolated instruments or procedures. Assessing offenders in a reliable and valid manner is regarded as a prerequisite for effective treatment, management and supervision of offenders. Furthermore, assessments should be made by staff who are well trained in the administration of tools and instruments; and there should be written accounts or protocols of the procedures that are applied. (2) Clients should be assigned to treatment according to the risk principle, i.e. intensive services should be reserved for moderate and high risk cases, and never for low risk cases. Treatment targets must be strongly related to the criminogenic needs of the target group (need principle). (3) Cognitive behavioral interventions are the methods of choice, if they are administered in a way that matches the intellectual and emotional skills of their clients (responsivity principle). (4) Managers and supervisors should attend to the relationship and structural skills of service delivery staff. (5) Reinforcement of relationship and structural skills on a regular basis will help maintain primary treatment effects. (6) The dosage of service delivery must be sufficiently high. For example, high risk offenders need significantly more initial structure and services than low-risk offenders. This claim is especially true for the management of day time activities, which should be occupied with delineated routine (employment, education, therapy) and other appropriated services (physical exercise, etc.). (7) Treatment will work better if the management policy is supportive. Monitoring, feedback, and corrective action routine should be active ingredients of the management strategy in correctional services. (8) Staff should relate to offenders in interpersonally sensitive and constructive ways to enhance intrinsic motivation because lasting behavioral change will not occur if intrinsic motivation for change is low. In recent years, motivational interviewing has been described as a technique to help clients enhance motivation for treatment. Feelings of ambivalence which usually accompany both phases of the decision process that eventually results in adherence to treatment and treatment itself, can be explored by motivational interviews. Essentially, methods of communication (e.g. Socratic questioning) are used to help clients think about why they feel that treatment is not what they want. There is reason to assume that motivational interviewing serves its purpose, i.e. helps effectively enhance motivation for initiating and maintaining self-referential processes that might eventually lead to more pro-treatment attitudes (e.g. Miller & Rollnick, 2002). (9) The probability for change to occur is strongly influenced by the quality of relationship experiences an offender is making in his present environment, i.e. with probation officers, treatment providers, and institution staff. Therefore, ongoing positive reinforcement of perceived behavioral change both in correctional institutions and natural communities is regarded as a cornerstone of the maintenance and improvement of treatment effects coming from different sources, i.e. cognitive behavioral therapy, individual and/or counselling and therapy, or interpersonal skills training.

It is not far-fetched to say that there is a general rule to potential effectiveness of intervention programs. The outcome of intervention depends on the degree to which individual risk factors for violence match with the treatment components offered by the program. Treatment effects are additive. For example, programs taking into account two Andrews principles tend to have better outcomes than those focussing on one, and those who focused on three principles were better than others focussing on only two (see, for example, Landenberger & Lipsey, 2005; Lipsey, 2006, Hanson et al., 2009). Thus, there is a statistical relationship in the number of risk factors under treatment and the potential outcome of the program. Furthermore, the effectiveness of treatment programs depends on the quality of the program itself (evidence based treatment with well trained mental health personnel), the availability of supplemental services (e.g. individual psychotherapeutic treatment), the optimal service amount (50 or more contact hours), appropriate clients (selected according to risk-needs analyses). In comparison with untreated controls with average recidivism rates of 40%, Lipsey and co-workers (Lipsey, 2006; Lipsey & Cullen, 2007) expect roughly 20%

recidivism for youth under the best available treatment conditions. In other words, if all relevant known factors are taken into consideration, and optimal treatment can be delivered, recidivism may be reduced by approximately 50%.

CORE ELEMENTS OF BEST PRACTICE PROGRAMS

The vast majority of treatment programs for young offenders to date is of a cognitive-behavioral type. In a meta-analysis of 509 juvenile justice programs, Lipsey (2007) identified five main features of effective juvenile delinquency prevention and treatment programs. (1) *The primary service*, i.e. the therapeutic element in it is effective, independent of its use with another intervention. In other words, the therapeutic program used must be effective for the target group. (2) *Supplementary services*: Adding another service component to primary service often increases the effectiveness of the intervention. (3) *Treatment amount*: The amount of service frequency must be sufficient, as indicated by service frequency, program duration, and program quality. (4) *Treatment quality*: Service quality and the quality of implementation influence effectiveness. (5) *Youth risk level:* Programs are generally more effective with high-risk offenders than for low-risk offenders.

Lipsey's work also makes clear that the configurations of programs have a considerable impact on their effectiveness. Since many juvenile delinquency prevention and treatment programs are not large-scale and multi-systemic including a combination of effective individual, family, educational and vocational interventions, they programs will be less effective, even if they use single components which are typically regarded as adequate treatments for young offenders.

There are three major program effectiveness criteria: Type of program, fidelity of program implementation, and risk level. About 40% of the variation in recidivism is associated with the type of program, another 40% of the total value of a program is associated with the quality of program implementation, which is measured in terms of frequency and duration of the program (25%), and quality of service (15%). Risk levels account for roughly 20% of the variation, i.e. programs addressing high-risk subjects are usually more effective than those addressing youth with low risk of delinquency and/or violence.

Based on his meta-analyses of programs for general delinquents, Lipsey grouped programs according to their relative effectiveness for prevention subjects, juvenile offenders on probation, and institutionalised offenders. For example, for juvenile probationers, he divided his database into three main categories, on the basis of their average effects: above-average effects, average effects, and below-average effects. Among the services with above average effects count cognitive-behavioral therapy, group counselling, vocational training, mentoring, and some forms of sex offender treatment and drug abuse treatment. Average effects are associated with family counselling or therapy, individual counselling or therapy, life skills enhancement, multi-systemic therapy, and educational intervention. Below average effects score all programs with recreation components, challenge programs, intensive supervision, and restitution. Finally, there is a number of interventions that will at best render no rehabilitative effects at all, or make things even worse. Among these count punishment regimes for juvenile offenders, scared straight programs, boot camps, large custodial facilities, long terms of confinement, curfew laws, and restrictive out of home placement for mental health treatment, psychiatric hospitalisation, and placements in residential treatment centres (Howell, 2009).

BEST PRACTICE PROGRAMS FOR YOUTH AND ADULTS

While adult and young offender treatment including cognitive-behavioral treatment approaches using manualized programs have the same roots, different developmental paths have been pursued especially after Andrews published his principles of effective correctional intervention in the early 1990s (Andrews et al., 1990). It has since been clear that young offenders have somewhat different treatment and programming needs than adult offenders. As both juvenile and adult offender programs draw on essentially the same knowledge base in criminology and forensic psychology, similarities prevail, especially as far as the structural makeup of best practice programs is concerned. For example, key structural components of cognitive-behavioral programs for both adults and young offenders include a shared set of criminogenic needs, such as impulsivity or poor affect control, empathy deficits, low levels of socio-moral reasoning, substance use and poor problem-solving skills. A style of delivery that participants will find interesting and engaging is not only important for young offenders, because offender groups tend to suffer from boredom, especially when they are in custody. However, owing to the ground breaking conceptual work of Andrews and co-workers (Andrews et al., 1990; Andrews, 2006; Andrews & Dowden, 2006), the application of meta-analysis as a method for the comparison of large samples of treatment studies (e.g. Durlak & Lipsey, 1991), and the pioneering scientific work of key researchers in the field it has recently been possible to describe an array of age-related risk factors for violence and general delinquency in youth (see the paragraphs above, for relevant literature). These risk factors must be met if a program is to operate effectively. Therefore, programs aiming at the prevention and reduction of crime and violence in juveniles must be broader than those of adult offenders, using several structural elements related to the current developmental stage of the young person. In youth, parallel, where possible multi-systemic interventions on individual, vocational, peer group, community and family levels are indicated. In adult offenders, some target areas of intervention will inevitably differ from those aimed at juveniles, i.e. family (especially parents) and peer group interventions, and schooling or vocational training. Furthermore, the level of legal sanctioning is generally higher with adults than with youth, and offender careers are more visible. Adults will therefore spend more time in correctional facilities with less chances to participate in effective community programs.

THE REASONING AND REHABILITATION PROGRAMME: AN EXAMPLE FOR A MANUALIZED BEST PRACTICE TREATMENT PROGRAM

The Reasoning and Rehabilitation Program (R & R; Ross, Fabiano & Ross, 1986) is a multifaceted, cognitive-behavioral program designed to teach juvenile and adult offenders cognitive skills and values that are essential for prosocial competence. The program was devised about 30 years ago and continuously updated with research findings. It is based on more than 100 studies that have yielded substantial reductions of re-offending. To date, the program has been delivered to more than forty thousand offenders world-wide. It has its roots in Canada, where about 8000 serious offenders in 47 penitentiaries have participated in the program. R&R has been applied across the spectrum of offender types: children in schools deemed at risk for offending; chronically recidivistic adult offenders; alcohol and drug-abusing offenders; violent offenders; property offenders; car thieves; child and spouse abusers; sex offenders, and white collar criminals. R&R is now being conducted in secure forensic psychiatric facilities all over the English speaking world, Germany, Spain, the Netherlands, and the Baltic States.

The program consists of nine interrelated modules: problem solving, social skills, values enhancement, critical reasoning, negotiation skills, creative thinking, the management of emotions, cognitive exercises, and skills in review. Program targets are: (1) The enhancement of self-control: offenders are taught to stop and think before they act; to consider all the consequences before making decisions; to formulate (future) plans; to use thinking techniques to control their emotions and their behavior; (2) Meta-cognition: Offenders are encouraged to critically assess their own thinking; to realize that how they think determines what they think, how they feel and how they behave. Thinking strategies are taught as a means of self-regulating their behavior; (3) Critical reasoning: Offenders are instructed how to think logically, objectively, and rationally without distorting the facts or externalising the blame; (4) Social skills: Utilizing a modification of a structured learning therapy program (Goldstein et al., 1980), skills are taught which will help offenders achieve positive reinforcement rather than rejection in social situations (e.g. responding to criticism or negotiating instead of demanding); (5) Interpersonal cognitive problem solving skills: offenders are taught how to analyse and to understand the emotional content of interpersonal problems, how to consider other people´s values, behavior and feelings, and how to recognize how their behavior affects other people and why others respond to them as they do; (6) Creative thinking: offenders often have a rather rigid thinking style (conceptual rigidity). They are thus taught alternative thinking, i.e. how to consider alternative, prosocial rather than antisocial ways of responding to the problems they experience: (7) Social perspective taking: the emphasis is on other people´s views, feelings, and thoughts, i.e. the development of empathy; (8) Values enhancement: group discussion techniques are used and a number of commercially available games to teach values. The aim is to move the offender from a rather egocentric world view to a consideration of the needs of others; (9) Emotional management: Anger management techniques were adapted to help offenders down-regulate excessive emotional arousal. The focus is on control of negative and the build-up of positive emotions.

The content of R&R is taught in 35 group sessions of two hours duration, the frequency is between two to four sessions a week. Some sessions require preparation on behalf of the participants. The encouragement of group activities based on a great variety of working materials is a core technique to promote behavioral change: role-playing, thinking games, learning exercises with and without video-feedback, and related cognitive exercises.

There is a considerable body of empirical evidence for the effectiveness of the R&R program. As an example of the most compelling evidence of its effectiveness, Tong & Farrington (2006) provided a meta-analysis of sixteen evaluations in four countries, involving 26 separate comparisons in which experimental and control groups were compared. Overall, there was a 14% reduction of recidivism for program participants compared with controls. The program was effective in community and institutional settings, and for both relatively low-risk and high-risk offenders.

PROGRAMS BASED ON OTHER THAN COGNITIVE-BEHAVIORAL THEORY

The vast majority of anglo-american research on psychological treatment programs of juvenile and adult offenders encompass programs devised and delivered in the cognitive-behavioral tradition. This is not surprising given the fact that cognitive-behavioral research and treatment have been stimulating an impressive bulk of data on treatment effectiveness. Research on programs with other theoretical underpinnings, including the psychodynamic group approach, has been lagging behind. There are good reasons for this, as we will demonstrate on the example of psychodynamically oriented treatment. Personal factors of potential program tutors might play a role. Psychodynamic as compared to cognitive-behavioral therapists are on average less research oriented. Issues related to the scientific integrity of the research process have been mentioned in this context, i.e. there has been an ongoing debate about adequate operationalizations of psychodynamic concepts. Furthermore, there might be a bias toward the publication of large-scale quantitative studies which have typically been conducted by cognitive-behavioral research personnel as compared to small qualitative individual case studies which are often preferred by psychodynamic researchers and therapists. During the last 20 years, however, psychodynamically oriented research groups have developed both individual (e.g. Transference Focused Psychotherapy; Clarkin, Yeomans, & Kernberg, 1999; Clarkin et al., 2007) and group treatments for patient groups with personality disorders who are usually regarded as difficult to treat, i.e. patients with borderline and antisocial personality disorders. The group treatment with probably the highest propensity to be effective with juvenile offender samples is mentalization based treatment (MBT; Bateman & Fonagy, 2004).

Mentalization Based Treatment (MBT; Bateman & Fonagy, 2004)

MBT is a manualized psychodynamic group and individual treatment program for patients with borderline personality disorder, developed by Fonagy and Bateman (Bateman & Fonagy, 2004; Fonagy & Bateman, 2006). The core concept of this treatment is mentalization, i.e. the capacity of humans to interpret actions of oneself and others on the basis of intentional states such as beliefs, goals, purposes, reasons, feelings, or desires. Due to disorganized attachment representations, which are often found in patients with borderline personality disorder, they tend to have limited mentalization capacity. This is also thought to be true for most offender patients. The aim of treatment is to increase mentalization in order to improve affect regulation, interpersonal functioning, and the ability to pursue life goals. The therapeutic focus is on the patient's current present state rather than the past. During sessions the therapist seeks to activate the patients' attachment systems, and to encourage them to create and to emotionally experience safe bonds with both the therapist and the other group members. If these processes are made accessible for conscious reflection, a psychological basis for the formation of a secure attachment relationship is provided. Thus, it will be safe for the patient to explore the mind of the other, to confront negative affect, and to understand the intentional nature of interpersonal relationships. According to mentalization theory, the improvement of mentalization capacity of offender patients will help them perceive others as intentional psychological beings who do not pose a threat to their psychological integrity. Mentalization is also thought help them reflect the destructive nature of their violence on the mind of others. Thus, MBT will eventually enhance empathy and impede offenders from engaging in violence as a means of interpersonal conflict resolution, or from acting out negative mental states otherwise. Fonagy and co-workers have conducted extensive outcome research on MBT for borderline personality disorder. Compared to treatment as usual, MBT is clearly superior (Bateman & Fonagy, 2008a). Furthermore, MBT is without doubt a promising approach to the prevention of violence and the treatment of offender groups, including juvenile offenders (e.g. Twemlow, Fonagy, & Sacco, 2001; 2004; Twemlow & Fonagy, 2006; Bateman & Fonagy, 2008b).

TREATMENT EFFECTS

The effectiveness of treatment for the reduction of recidivism has been shown in hundreds if not thousands of studies, and the magnitude of effects at least equals those of many other treatments in somatic medical science (McGuire, 2002; Marshall & McGuire, 2003). The average effect size of all approaches to offender treatment is approximately $r = .10$, i.e. a reduction of recidivism in treated offenders of 10% as compared to untreated offenders (Andrews et al., 1990; Lipsey, 1992; Lipsey & Wilson, 1993; Lösel, 1995; Hall, 1995; Redondo, Sanchez-Meca, & Garrido, 1999; Egg et al., 2001; Hanson et al., 2002). Although this effect size is rather moderate compared to the average effect of psychotherapy with other in- and outpatient groups (approximately $r = .80$, Lambert, 2004), it is highly significant with respect to the avoidance of serious harm otherwise inflicted upon victims and societies at large. Furthermore, treatment is cost-effective. For example, Welsh and Farrington's (2000) study on the cost-benefit ratio of offender treatment reported a ratio of 1 to 1.13 - 7.14 in favour of the treatment condition. Offender treatment programs that take into account the principles of risk, need, and responsivity (e.g. Andrews et al., 1990) usually do better than other approaches, approximating average effect sizes of $r = .30$ (e.g. Pearson et al., 2002; Dowden, Antonowicz & Andrews, 2003; Walker et al., 2004; Lösel & Schmucker, 2005; Landenberger & Lipsey, 2005; Lipsey, 2007). Sexual offender treatment is probably even more effective than the treatment of other (violent) offenders. For example, the meta-analysis of Lösel & Schmucker (2005) included 69 studies on $N = 22181$ sexual offenders and reported a reduction of recidivism in sexual delinquency of roughly 40% in treated compared to untreated individuals. There is good reason to assume that treatment of offenders is most effective when they are treated as youth, regardless of the type of index crime they have committed (see for example Lipsey & Cullen, 2007, and Sherman et al., 2006, for overviews). Recent research on the treatment of juvenile delinquents show high average effect sizes between $r = .30$ (Pearson et al., 2002), $r = .37$ (Walker et al., 2004), and $r = .43$ (Reitzel & Carbonell, 2006). Effect sizes under the best theoretically available treatment conditions approximate $r = .50$ (see Lipsey, 2007).

LIMITATIONS

Although there can be no doubt that the cognitive-behavioral group program approach to the prevention and treatment of juvenile offenders has been effective, there are several limitations to this approach. For example, programs tend to focus on the reduction and elimination of dynamic risk factors by teaching offenders how to avoid recidivism (avoidance goals). They usually do not focus on the flipside of the same coin, namely on the positive human goals or goods all humans seek in order to live satisfying and good lives (approach goals; Ward and co-workers have conceptualised this idea in a theory emphasising goal-directed behavior and they have put forward ten primary human goods, sought by all humans and needed for psychological well-being; for details on this theory see Ward & Brown, 2004; Ward & Gannon, 2006). The inclusion of such approach goals in existing best practice programs might help open up new perspectives on improving manualized treatments for young and adult offenders.

We also know that some (early) intervention programs could not maintain initial positive effects in the long run. One reason for this was that they tended to be repetitious and boring, with too many predefined manualized elements to be complied with and too little space for spontaneous individual input. Although modern program makers have learned from these problems and have therefore introduced systematic elements to keep participants interested, some of these problems remain. Furthermore, programs are better when implemented from and monitored by researchers rather than practitioners (Lipsey, 2006; 2007; Lipsey & Cullen, 2007). It is obvious, however, that for financial and practical reasons not all programs can be accompanied by research personnel.

Rather than a critique of manualized cognitive-behavioral programs as such, we see a current limitation to the effective development of potential alternative treatment strategies for young and adult offenders. Although conceptual work in treatments of other than the cognitive-behavioral type is quite elaborate and well advanced, these approaches are still underrepresented in the modern treatment literature. For example, case research in psychodynamically oriented forensic psychotherapy has produced more than spurious evidence that psychodynamic approaches can under some circumstances be equally as effective as cognitive-behavioral programs (see Cordess & Cox, 1998, for a systematic overview of psychodynamically oriented offender therapy, and the section on MBT for a recent empirical and evidence-based approach to psychodynamic offender treatment).

FINAL REMARKS

In order to make offender treatment programs even more effective than they are, the following main options should be taken into account. First, research on the selective effectiveness of individual program components should be intensified. If new programs are designed, they should be tested based on the intervention components that are significantly associated with effect sizes across studies. We know that not all program components are equally effective. For example, Landenberger & Lipsey (2005) reported that in order to be effective, (cognitive-behavioral) programs must contain modules teaching interpersonal problem solving skills and anger control techniques, whereas unsuccessful programs employed activities aimed at getting offenders to consider the impact of their behavior on their victims (victim impact) and simple reward and penalty schemes designed to reinforce appropriate behavior (behavior modification).

Second, if adequately adapted for the needs of young offender treatment, and implemented in a supplementary and innovative way, programs might profit from the findings of general psychological science (see Ross, 2008, for a discussion of some supplementary elements that might be useful as an addition to existing cognitive-behavioral program modules).

Third, program makers should also take a look on potential protective factors for delinquency. For example, Loeber and colleagues have conceptualised factors that reduce delinquency onset and also promote desistance. In their latest analyses, they demonstrate how protective factors have main effects in essentially the same way as risk factors, i.e. the presence of protective factors can counter-balance risk factors. In a study about common risk and protective factors in successful prevention programs, Durlak (1998) reviewed a total of 1.200 prevention studies. Among the most important protective factors for behavior problems, school failure, physical health, physical injury and abuse and adolescent pregnancy count personal and social skills and self-efficacy (individual level), general (pro-social) support, high social norms and effective social policies (community level), good parent-child relationship (family level), high quality schools (school level), and positive role-models (peer level).

Forth, it should be borne in mind, that treatment effects accumulate with the inclusion of individual treatments, and other supplemental services are a necessary condition for maintaining long term effects of offender treatment. In addition to sound psychological in-patient treatment, an elaborated model of after-care after release from prison or from forensic psychiatry is indispensable.

Finally, effective comprehensive strategies on preventing crime and treating juvenile offenders need to be supported by scientists and further developed. Best practice programs will not be as effective as they could possibly be if they are not embedded in a well functioning and benevolent network of care-takers on different levels of intervention. Therefore, a strong involvement of scientists and practitioners in the development and application of social prevention and treatment policies is needed.

REFERENCES

Aichhorn, A. (1925). Verwahrloste Jugend; Die Psychoanalyse in der Fürsorgeerziehung: 10 Vorträge zur ersten Einführung (11. ed., 2005). Bern: Huber.

Alexander, F. & French, T. M. (1946). *Psychoanalytic therapy: Principles and application.* New York: Ronald Press.

Andrews, D. A. (2006). Enhancing adherence to risk-need-responsivity. *Criminology and Public Policy, 5,* 595-602.

Andrews D. A. & Dowden, C. (2006). Risk principle of case classification in correctional treatment: A meta-analytic investigation. *International Journal of Offender Therapy and Comparative Criminology, 50,* 88-100.

Andrews, D., Zinger, I., Hoge, R. D., Bonta, J., Gendreau, P. & Cullen, F. T. (1990). Does correctional treatment work? A clinically relevant and psychologically informed meta-analysis. *Criminology*, *28*, 369-404.

Arseneault, L., Cannon, M., Murray, R. M., Poulton, R., Caspi, A., Moffitt, T. E. (2003). Childhood origins of violent behaviour in adults with schizophreniform disorder. *British Journal of Psychiatry*, *183*, 520-525.

Bateman, A. W. & Fonagy, P. (2004). Mentalization-based treatment of BPD. *Journal of Personality Disorders*, *18*, 36-51.

Bateman, A. W. & Fonagy, P. (2008a). 8-Year follow-up of patients reated for borderline personality disorder: Mentalization-based treatment versus treatment as usual. *American Journal of Psychiatry*, *165*, 631-638.

Bateman, A. W. & Fonagy, P. (2008b). Comorbid antisocial and borderline personality disorders: mentalization-based treatment. *Journal of Clinical Psychology*, *64*, 181-194.

Broidy, L. M., Nagin, D. S., Tremblay, R. E., Brame, R., Dodge, K., Fergusson, D. M., Horwood, L. J., Loeber, R., Laird, R., Lynam, D. R. & Moffitt, T. E. (2003). Developmental trajectories of childhood disruptive behavior disorders and adolescent delinquency: A cross-national replication. *Developmental Psychology*, *39*, 222-245.

Clarkin, J. F., Yeomans, F. E. & Kernberg, O. F. (1999). *Psychotherapy for Borderline Personality*. New York: John Wiley and Sons.

Clarkin, J. F., Levy, K. N., Lenzenweger, M. F. & Kernberg, O. F. (2007). Evaluating Three Treatments for Borderline Personality Disorder: A Multiwave Study. *American Journal of Psychiatry*, *164*, 922-928.

Cordess, C. & Cox, M. (Eds.). (1998). Forensic psychotherapy. *Crime, psychodynamics and the offender patient*. (Vol. I and II). London, Philadelphia: Jessica Kingsley.

Dowden, C., Antonowicz, D. & Andrews, D.A. (2003). The effectiveness of relapse prevention with offenders: a meta-analysis. *International Journal of Offender Therapy and Comparative Criminology*, *47*, 516-528.

Durlak, J. A. (1998). Common risk and protective factors in successful prevention programs. *American Journal of Orthopsychiatry*, *68*, 512-520.

Durlak, J. A. & Lipsey, M. W. (1991). A practitioner's guide to meta-analysis. American *Journal of Community Psychology*, *19*, 291-332.

Egg, R., Pearson, F. S., Cleland, C. M. & Lipton, D. S. (2001). Evaluation von Straftäterbehandlungsprogrammen in Deutschland: Überblick und Meta-Analyse. In G. Rehn, B. Wischka, F. Lösel, & M. Walter (Eds.). Behandlung gefährlicher Straftäter. Grundlagen, Konzepte, Ergebnisse (321-347). Herbolzheim: Centaurus.

Eissler, R. (1953). The effect of the structure of the ego on psychoanalytic technique. *Journal of the American Psycho-analytic Association*, *1*, 104-143.

Farrington, D. P. (2003). Key results from the first 40 years of the Cambridge Study in Delinquent Development. In T. P. Thornberry, & M. D. Krohn (Eds.), *Taking stock of Delinquency: an overview of findings from contemporary longitudinal studies* (137-184). New York: Kluwer/Plenum.

Farrington, D. P. (2007). Origins of violent behaviour over the life span. In D. J. Flannery, A. T. Vazsonyi, & I. D. Waldman. (Eds.), *The Cambridge Handbook of Violent Behaviour and Aggression* (19-48). Cambridge: Cambridge University Press.

Farrington, D. P. (2009). Conduct disorder, aggression, and delinquency. In R. M. Lerner, & L. Steinberg (Eds.), *Handbook of Adolescent Psychology* (3rd edition) (683-722). Hoboken, NJ: Wiley.

Fonagy, P. (2003). Towards a developmental understanding of violence. *British Journal of Psychiatry, 183*, 190-192.

Fonagy, P. (2004). The developmental roots of violence in the failure of mentalization. In: F. Pfäfflin, & G. Adshead (Eds.). A matter of security. *The application of attachment theory to forensic psychiatry and psychotherapy* (13-56). London, Bristol: Jessica Kingsley.

Fonagy, P. & Bateman, A. W. (2006). Mechanisms of change in mentalization-based treatment of BPD. *Journal of Clinical Psychology, 62*, 411-430.

Goldstein, A. P., Sprafkin, R., Gershaw, N. J. & Klein, P. (1980). Skillstreaming the adolescent. Champaign: Research Press.

Hall, G. N. (1995). Sexual offender recidivism revisited: a meta-analysis of recent treatment studies. *Journal of Consulting and Clinical Psychology, 63*, 802-809.

Hanson, R. K., Bourgon, G., Helmus, L. & Hodgson, S. (2009). A meta-analysis of the effectiveness of treatment for sexual offenders: Risk, need, and responsivity. Corrections Research User Report No. 2009-01. Ottawa: Public Safety Canada.

Hanson, R. K. & Bussiere, M. T. (1998). Predicting relapse: A meta-analysis of sexual offender recidivism studies. *Journal of Consulting and Clinical Psychology, 66*, 348-362.

Hanson, R. K., Gordon, A., Harris, A. J., Marques, J. K., Murphy, W., Quinsey, V. L. & Seto, M. C. (2002). First report of the collaborative outcome data project on the effectiveness of psychological treatment for sex offenders. *Sexual Abuse: Journal of Research & Treatment, 14*, 169-194.

Hollin, C. (Ed.). (2004). The essential handbook of offender treatment and assessment. Chichester: John Wiley & Sons.

Howell, J. C. (2009). Preventing and reducing juvenile delinquency: A comprehensive framework (2nd ed.). Thousand Oaks, CA: Sage.

Huizinga, D., Weiher, A. W., Espiritu, R. & Esbensen, F. (2003). Delinquency and crime. Some highlights from the Denver Youth Survey. In T. P. Thornberry, & M. D. Krohn (Eds.), Taking stock of delinquency: An overview of findings from contemporary longitudinal studies (47-91). New York: Kluwer/Plenum.

Lambert, M. (Ed.). (2004). *Bergin and Garfield's Handbook of psychotherapy and behavior change*. New York: John Wiley & Sons.

Landenberger, N. A. & Lipsey, M. W. (2005). The positive effects of cognitive-behavioral programs for offenders: A meta-analysis of factors associated with effective treatment. *Journal of Experimental Criminology, 1*, 451-476.

Laws, D. R. & Marshall, W. L. (2003). A brief history of behavioral and cognitive behavioral approaches to sexual offenders: Part 1. Early developments. Sexual Abuse: *A Journal of Research and Treatment, 15*, 75-92.

Lipsey, M. W. (1992). The effect of treatment on juvenile delinquents: Results from meta-analysis. In F. Lösel, D. Bender, & T. Bliesener (Eds.), *Psychology and Law*. International Perspectives (131-143). Berlin: De Gruyter.

Lipsey, M. W. (2006). The evidence base for effective juvenile programs as a source for best practice guidelines. Nashville, TN: Vanderbilt University, *Center for Evaluation Research and Methodology*.

Lipsey, M. W. (2007). A standardized program evaluation protocol for programs serving juvenile probationers. Nashville, TN: Vanderbilt University. *Center for Evaluation Research and Methodology.*

Lipsey, M. W. & Cullen, F. T. (2007). The effectiveness of correctional rehabilitation: A review of systematic reviews. *Annual Review of Law and Social Science, 3*, 297-320.

Lipsey, M. W. & Derson, J. H. (1998). Predictors of violent or serious delinquency in adolescence and early adulthood: A synthesis of longitudinal research. In R. Loeber, & D. P. Farrington (Eds.), Serious and violent juvenile offenders: Risk factors and successful interventions (86-105). Thousand Oaks, Ca: Sage.

Lipsey, M. W. & Wilson, D. B. (1993). The efficacy of psychological, educational, and behavioural treatment. *American Psychologist, 48*, 1181-1209.

Loeber, R. (1988). Natural histories of juvenile conduct problems, delinquency, and associated substance abuse: Evidence for developmental progressions. In B. B. Lahey, & A. E. Kazdin (Eds.), *Advances in clinical child psychology (Vol. 11*, 73-124). New York: Plenum.

Loeber, R. & Farrington, D. P. (Eds.). (1998). Serious and violent juvenile offenders: Risk factors and successful interventions. Thousand Oaks, Ca: Sage.

Loeber, R. & Farrington, D. P. (Eds.). (2001). Child delinquents. Development, Intervention, and service needs. Thousand Oaks, CA: Sage.

Loeber, R., Farrington, D. P., Stouthamer-Loeber, M., Moffitt, T. E., Caspi, A., White, H. R., et al. (2003). The development of male offending. Key findings from fourteen years of the Pittsburgh Youth Study. In T. P. Thornberry, & M. D. Krohn (Eds.), Taking stock of delinquency: An overview of findings from contemporary longitudinal studies (93-136). New York: Kluwer/Plenum.

Loeber, R., Farrington, D. P., Stouthamer-Loeber, M. & White, H. R. (2008). Violence and serious theft: Development and prediction from childhood to adulthood. New York: Routledge.

Loeber, R., Slot, W. & Stouthamer-Loeber, M. (2007). A cumulative, three-dimensional developmental model of serious delinquency. In P. O. Wikstrom, & R. Sampson (Eds.), The explanation of crime: Context, mechanisms and development series (153-194). Cambridge: *Cambridge University Press.*

Lösel, F. (1995). The efficacy of correctional treatment: A review and synthesis of meta-evaluations. In J. McGuire (Ed.), What works: Reducing re-offending: Guidelines from research and practice (79-111). John Wiley & Sons, Chichester.

Lösel, F. & Schmucker, M. (2005). The effectiveness of treatment for sexual offenders: A comprehensive meta-analysis. *Journal of Experimental Criminology, 1*, 117-146.

Marshall, W. L., Fernandez, Y., Hudson, S. & Ward, T. (Eds.). (1998). *Sourcebook of treatment programs for sexual offenders.* New York, London: Plenum Press.

Marshall, W. L. & Laws, D. R. (2003). A brief history of behavioral and cognitive behavioral approaches to sexual offender treatment: Part 2: The modern era. Sexual Abuse: A *Journal of Research and Treatment, 15*, 93-120.

Marshall, W. L. & McGuire, J. (2003). Effect sizes in the treatment of sexual offenders. *International Journal of Offender Therapy and Comparative Criminology, 47*, 653-663.

McGuire, J. (2002). Criminal sanctions versus psychologically based interventions with offenders: a comparative empirical analysis. Psychology, *Crime & Law, 8*, 183-208.

Miller, W. R. & Rollnick, S. (2002). Motivational Interviewing: preparing people for change (2nd ed.). New York: Guilford.

Moffitt, T. E. (1993). Adolescence-limited and life-course persistent antisocial behavior: A developmental taxonomy. *Psychological Review, 100*, 674-701.

Odgers, C. L., Caspi, A., Poulton, R., Harrington, H. L., Thomson, W. M., Broadbent, J. M., Hancox, R. J., Dickson, N., Paul, C., Moffitt, T. E. (2008). Female and male antisocial trajectories: From childhood origins to adult outcomes. *Development and Psychopathology, 20*, 673-716.

Pearson, F. S., Lipton, D. S., Cleland, C. M. & Yee, D. S. (2002). The effects of behavioural/cognitive behavioural programs on recidivism. *Crime and Delinquency, 48*, 476-496.

Redondo, S., Sanchez-Meca, J. & Garrido, V. (1999). The influence of treatment programmes on the recidivism of juvenile and adult offenders: A European meta-analytic review. *Psychology, Crime & Law, 5*, 251-278.

Reitzel, L. R. & Carbonell, J. L. (2006). The effectiveness of sexual offender treatment for juveniles as measured by recidivism: A meta-analysis. *Sexual Abuse: Journal of Research and Treatment, 18*, 401-421.

Ross, R. R., Fabiano, E. A. & Ross, R. D. (1986). *Reasoning and Rehabilitation: A handbook for teaching cognitive skills.* Ottawa: Centre for Cognitive Development.

Ross, T. (2008). Current issues in self regulation research and their significance for therapeutic intervention in offender groups. *International Journal of Behavioral Consultation and Therapy, 4*, 68-81.

Sherman, L. W., Farrington, D. P., MacKenzie, D. L. & Welsh, B. C. (2006). Evidence based crime prevention. New York: Routledge.

Snyder, H. N. (1998). Serious, violent, and chronic juvenile offenders: An assessment of the extent of and trends in officially recognized serious criminal behavior in a delinquent population. In R., Loeber, & D. P. Farrington (Eds.), Serious and violent juvenile offenders: Risk factors and successful interventions (428-444). Thousand Oaks, CA: Sage.

Thornberry, T. P. & Krohn, M. D. (2001). The development of delinquency: An interactional perspective. In S. O. White (Ed.), *Handbook of Youth and Justice* (289-305). New York: Plenum.

Thornberry, T. P. & Krohn, M. D. (2003). Taking stock of delinquency: An overview of findings from contemporary longitudinal studies. New York: Kluwer/Plenum.

Thornberry, T. P. & Krohn, M. D. (2005). Applying interactional theory to the explanation of continuity and change in antisocial behavior. In D. P. Farrington (Ed.), *Integrated development and life-course theories of offending* (183-210). New Brunswick, NJ: Transaction.

Thornberry, T. P., Lizotte, A., J., Krohn, M. D., Smith, C. A. & Porter, P. K. (2003). Causes and consequences of delinquency: Findings from the Rochester Youth Development Study. In T. P. Thornberry, & M. D. Krohn (Eds.), *Taking stock of delinquency: An overview of findings from contemporary longitudinal studies* (11-46). New York: Kluwer/Plenum.

Tong, L. S. Y. & Farrington, D. P. (2006). How effective is the "Reasoning and Rehabilitation" programme in reducing reoffending? A meta-analysis of evaluations in four countries. *Psychology, Crime & Law, 12*, 3-24.

Twemlow, S. W. & Fonagy, P. (2006). Transforming violent social systems into non-violent mentalizing systems: an experiment in schools. In J. G., Allen, & P. Fonagy (Eds.), *The handbook of mentalization-based treatment* (289-306). Hoboken: John Wiley & Sons.

Twemlow, S. W., Fonagy, P. & Sacco, F. C. (2001). An innovative psychodynamically influenced approach to reduce school violence. *Journal of the American Academy of Child & Adolescent Psychiatry*, *40*, 377-379.

Twemlow, S. W., Fonagy, P. & Sacco, F. C. (2004). The role of the bystander in the social architecture of bullying and violence in schools and communities. In J. Devine, J. Gilligan, K. A., Miczek, R. Shaikh, & D. Pfaff (Eds.), *Youth violence: scientific approaches to prevention* (215-232) New York: New York Academy of Sciences.

Walker, D. F., McGovern, S. K., Poey, E. L. & Otis, K. E. (2004). Treatment effectiveness for male adolescent sexual offenders: a meta-analysis and review. *Journal of Child Sexual Abuse*, *13*, 281-293.

Ward, T. & Brown, M. (2004). The Good Lives Model and conceptual issues in offender rehabilitation. Psychology, *Crime, & Law*, *10*, 243-257.

Ward, T. & Gannon, T. A. (2006). Rehabilitation, etiology, and self-regulation: the comprehensive good lives model of treatment for sexual offenders. *Aggression & Violent Behavior*, *11*, 77-94.

Welldon, E. & van Velsen, C. (Eds.). (1997). *A practical guide to forensic psychotherapy.* London, Bristol: Jessica Kingsley.

Welsh, B. C. & Farrington, D. P. (2000). Correctional intervention programs and cost benefit analysis. *Criminal Justice and Behavior*, *27*, 115-133.

In: Youth Violence and Juvenile Justice: Causes, Intervention... ISBN: 978-1-61668-011-4
Editor: Neil A. Ramsay et al., pp. 207-227 © 2010 Nova Science Publishers, Inc.

Chapter 8

BULLYING AND VICTIMIZATION EXPERIENCES AT SCHOOL, THE PARENT-CHILD RELATIONSHIP AND CHILD SCHOOL PERFORMANCE: A LONGITUDINAL INVESTIGATION

Kostas A. Fanti[*] and Stelios N. Georgiou
University of Cyprus, Cyprus

ABSTRACT

The current investigation examines longitudinal differences between bullies, victims, and bully-victims in terms of the quality of their relationship with their parents and school performance. We also investigate the longitudinal transactional association between the quality of the parent-child relationship and bullying behavior. The sample consisted of 895 mothers and their children who were participants in the NICHD Study of Early Child-Care. According to the findings, the co-occurring bully victim groups were at higher risk to experience continuous conflict with their mothers and to perform worse academically. The findings also offer support for the hypothesized transactional association between bullying and the parent-child relationship. Further, it was found that there might be a positive longitudinal transactional association between victimization and parent-child closeness. Finally, school performance was positively related to victimization.

INTRODUCTION

Bullying at school is a disturbing phenomenon with serious short-term and long-term consequences for both the victim and the perpetrator (e.g. Headley, 2004; Olweus, 1984; Seals & Young, 2003). As such, it deserves to be empirically examined so that its parameters

---

[*] Corresponding author: Department of Psychology, University of Cyprus, P.O. Box 20537, CY 1678, Nicosia, Cyprus, via email to kfanti@ucy.ac.cy, or phone +357.22892067

can be identified. According to Olweus (1993), bullying is defined as a physical, verbal or psychological attack or intimidation that is intended to cause fear, distress or harm to the victim. To be considered as bullying, an aggressive act must meet three criteria: (1) it must be intentional, (2) it must be systematic and (3) it must be characterized by an imbalance of power (Farrington 1993; Rigby 2002). Victims of this painful experience are usually students who are perceived as vulnerable, submissive or different (Naylor, Cowie, & del Rey, 2001; Tanaka, 2001) by peers who are in a dominant role, either by virtue of their own strength or by virtue of being associated with a powerful group (Kaltiala-Heino, Rimpelä, Rantanen & Rimpelä, 2000).

In addition to the bully and passive victim groups, a group of children exhibiting bullying behavior but who are also the victims of bullying has been identified. This group, named the bully-victim or the aggressive victim group, has been linked to greater individual and contextual problems (Bowers, Smith & Brinney, 1992; Fanti, Frick & Georgiou, 2009; Kokkinos & Panayiotou, 2004; Stevens, Bourdeaudhuij & Van Oost, 2002). Based on these findings, the initial purpose of the current investigation is to identify groups of children exhibiting only bullying behavior, experiencing only victimization, and exhibiting co-occurring bullying and victimization from grade 3 to grade 6. An additional goal is to longitudinally examine for differences between the identified groups in terms of the quality of their relationship with their parents and school performance from grade 1 to grade 6.

A number of studies investigated the association between school performance and bullying and victimization, and the majority of these studies suggested that victims of bullying are more likely to have low school achievement compared to bullies and not-involved children (Beran, Hughes, & Lupart, 2008; Berthhold & Hoover, 2000; Glew et al., 2005; Ma, 2002; Woods & Wolke, 2004). Moreover, some studies that took into account the co-occurrence between bullying and victimization suggested that victims and bully-victims were more likely to have low school achievement compared to bullies and not-involved children, while other studies suggest that the bully-victim group might be at higher risk to experience lower school performance (Glew et al., 2005; Schwartz, 2000; Toblin, Schwartz, Gorman & Abou-ezzeddine, 2005). The present study proposes to investigate differences in academic achievement from the beginning to the end of elementary school. Based on previous findings, we expect that not-involved children and bullies will perform better at school from grade 1 to grade 6 compared to passive victims and aggressive victims. Finding that victims and bully-victims do not perform well academically from the beginning of elementary school, might suggest that academic underachievement might not be a consequence of being bullied, but a result of other circumstances related to these children.

The bullying literature has also provided sufficient evidence linking the parent-child relationship to both bullies and victims. For example, Baldry and Farrington (2000) have shown that bullies compared to non-bullies tend to disagree more with their parents. Additionally, Bowers et al. (1992) found that families of bullies and bully-victims were less cohesive, characterized by lower warmth and higher hostility, compared to non-bullies, although families of victims were characterized by high levels of cohesion. Stevens et al. (2002) presented similar evidence in that bullies and bully-victims perceived their families as less cohesive and expressive and characterized by higher conflict as compared to victims and noninvolved children, although victims did not differ from noninvolved children in terms of conflict or cohesion. According to these studies families of both bullies and bully-victims seem to be characterized by high conflict and low connectedness. However, Schwartz, Dodge,

Pettit and Bates (1997) provided evidence that the bully-victim group was at higher risk to experience more hostility by their mothers compared to bullies, victims and non-involved children, suggesting that the bully/victim group is a higher risk group. Moreover, Schwartz et al. (1997) did not find any evidence suggesting that groups of children exhibiting pure or combined levels of bullying and victimization differed in terms of maternal warmth. Even though there are some inconsistencies in the literature investigating differences between bullies, victims and bully-victims, most of the studies suggest that victims, just as non-involved children, experience a positive parent-child relationship, characterized by high closeness and warmth and low conflict. The goal of the present study is to replicate these cross-sectional findings using longitudinal data, and identify differences between bullies, victims, and bully victims in terms of their relationship with their parents beginning at age 7. Based on previous cross-sectional research, we expect that bullies and bully-victims experience a negative parent-child relationship, high conflict and low closeness, from the beginning to the end of the elementary school (grade 1 to grade 6). In contrast , we expect that victims and not-involved children experience a positive parent-child relationship across time.

Finding differences between bullies, victims, and bully-victims is important because the identified differences might suggest a connection between the parent-child relationship and bullying and victimization experiences in school. However, the direction of this association is not specified. For example, we can assume that parental practices characterized by absence of a warm relationship with the child, coldness, indifference or even hostility and conflict are especially harmful and lead to bullying behavior. On the other hand, we can also assume that bullying behavior, which is related to opposition, defiance and aggression towards parents (Olweus, 1993), might elicit a negative parent-child relationship. There are a number of studies providing evidence that parenting characteristics influence bullying behavior (Baldry & Farrington, 2000; Espelage, Bosworth & Simon, 2000; Flouri & Buchanan, 2003; Georgiou, 2008a, 2008b; Olweus, 1980), although there are also stuides suggesting that bullying, aggressive, and antisocial behavior is negatively related to the quality of the parent-child relationship and to decreases in nurturing parental behavior and involvement (Fanti, Henrich, Brookmeyer, & Kuperminc, 2008; Kokkinos & Panayiotou, 2007; Reitz, Dekovic, & Meijer, 2006; Scaramella, Conger, Spoth, & Simons, 2002).

According to the above mentioned studies, we can assume that the parent-child relationship might lead to bullying, and bullying might alter the parent-child relationship. Therefore, it is important to take into account the reciprocal influence between the parent-child relationship and bullying behavior in order to empirically examine this possible bidirectional association. Based on these concerns, the second purpose of the current investigation was to investigate the transactional association between the quality of the parent-child relationship and bullying behavior. According to Sameroff and MacKenzie (2003) the transactional model can be conceptualized as the continuous bidirectional or reciprocal influences between the child and the child's context. Following the transactional model, we conceptualize the development of bullying behavior at school as a product of the continuous reciprocal influences between children and their relationship with their parents. Therefore, we expect that children's experiences with their parents at home will influence their own bullying behavior at school, but also that this bullying behavior will alter the parent-child relationship.

Even though there are a number of transactionally oriented studies investigating the association between parenting variables and child behavioral problems (e.g. Beaver &

Wright, 2007; Buist, Dekovic, Meeus, & Van Aken, 2004; Burt, McGue, Krueger, & Iacono, 2005; Fanti et al., 2008; Huh, Tristan, Wade & Stice, 2006; Jang & Smith, 1997; Laird, Pettit, Bates, & Dodge, 2003; Vuchinich, Bank, & Patterson, 1992), very little is known about the transactional association between parenting and bullying. A study investigating a transactional model has the power to provide evidence that links bullying to parenting, but also provide evidence of the directionality of the effects. Do parents influence bullying, do children influence parenting, or is there a cycle of coercive processes in which both negative parenting and negative child behaviors exacerbate each other, as Patterson (1982) suggested? Furthermore, bullying and victimization problems tend to be comorbid among children (Fanti et al., 2009; Kokkinos & Panayiotou, 2004; Stevens, Bourdeaudhuij & Van Oost, 2002), and inclusion of both in the same model can clarify the unique transactional effects of bullying and victimization problems over time. The present study uses a longitudinal cross-lag model over three waves of measurement (grade 3, 5, and 6) to investigate the reciprocal link between children's relationships with their parents and bullying and victimization. Longitudinal cross-lag models are advantageous because they control for the association between the variables at each time point of measurement, and because of that the co-occurrence between bullying and victimization experiences is taken into account.

Moreover, as previously mentioned, a number of studies have linked bullying and victimization to the child's academic achievement or school performance. To control for the potential covariation of these variables we included academic performance as another covariate in the transactional model under investigation. However, the transactional association between academic achievement and bullying and victimization experiences is also of interest. Previous studies suggested that low school performance and poor grades are not the reason behind student's bullying behavior, and bullies might not necessarily have problems with their school performance (Ma, 2002; Olweus, 1993; Rigby & Slee, 1991). However, being victimized might be negatively related to school adjustment because of the anxiety and the lower concentration to school work associated with being bullied (Sharp, 1995; Slee, 1994). On the other hand, students who perform well at school might be more likely to be victimized (Ma, 2002). Therefore, we expect a transactional association between academic achievement and victimization, but not between academic achievement and bullying.

In addition, we control for gender in our cross-lag analyses because boys are at higher risk for developing aggressive tendencies than girls (e.g. Offord, Boyle, & Racine, 1991; Youngstrom, Findling, & Calabrese, 2003). In general, studies report that compared to girls more boys tend to engage in bullying behavior, although no gender differences in the prevalence rates of victimization have been reported (Schwartz, Proctor, & Chicn, 2001; Seals & Young, 2003; Solberg, Olweus, & Endresen, 2007). Also, girls experience higher-quality relationships with their parents (e.g. Hay & Ashman, 2003; Kenny, 1994) and perform better academically compared to boys (Herbert & Yeung, 1998). According to these findings, there are mean level differences between boys and girls in a number of variables, providing evidence for the need to control for gender.

In sum, we hypothesize that there are different groups of children exhibiting pure bullying, pure victimization, and co-occurring bullying and victimization from grade 3 to grade 6. Additionally, the bully and the bully-victim group are expected to experience more conflict with their mothers and less closeness compared to victims and not-involved children. Victims and bully-victims are expected to do worse academically compared to bullies and non-involved children. We also hypothesize an overall transactional model in which bullying problems are negatively related to the quality of children's relationships with their mothers. In turn, the quality of these relationships is expected to be negatively associated with bullying problems. Even though victims of bullying tend to experience a positive parent-child relationship, we included victimization in the transactional model to control for the comorbidity between bullying and victimization. Furthermore, the students' school performance is also included in the transactional model to control for its potential covariation with bullying and victimization. Finally, we expect to identify a reciprocal model between school performance and victimization.

METHOD

Participants

The present study used data from the longitudinal Study of Early Child-Care, conducted by the National Institute of Child Health and Human Development (NICHD). This study was supported by NICHD through a cooperative agreement that calls for scientific collaboration between the grantees and the NICHD staff. Participants were recruited from different hospitals across ten locations in the United States. A total of 8,986 women gave birth during the sampling period (i.e. between January of 1991 and November of 1991) across the different locations. Of those women 1,364 completed the home interview when the infant was one month old, and comprised the final sample of the study. Recruitment and selection procedures are described elsewhere (http://secc.rti.org). This data set was acquired and handled following all the legal and ethical standards of research practice.

The analyses for the present study were based on 895 participants who had completed reports on the bullying and victimization measures during grade 3 (age 9), grade 5 (age 11), and grade 6 (age 12). Similarly to the NICHD final sample, the sample used for the current study was diverse in terms of gender (50.1% male), ethnicity (76.5% White, 6.1% Hispanic, 12.1% African American, 1.3% Asian, 4% other minority groups), parental educational level and marital status (9.3% of the mothers had not completed high school and 21.7% were single). According to chi-square analyses, the sample used for the current study did not differ in any of the demographics when compared to the children who were excluded from the analyses due to missing data.

Measures

Perceived victimization and the engagement in physical and direct and indirect verbal bullying behaviors with school classmates were based on *The Perception of Peer Support Scale* (PPSS; Kochenderfer & Ladd, 1997; Ladd, Kochenderfer, & Coleman, 1996). In the present study the scale was administered three times, in grades 3, 5 and 6. Participating children responded by choosing a number from 1 to 5 (Never, Hardly ever, Sometimes, Most of the time, and Always). There are two sub-scales, one measuring perceived victimization and the other measuring engagement in bullying behavior. The perceived victimization subscale asks children to report the extent to which they had experienced peer aggression in their class at school using the following questions: Does anyone in your class ever: (1) pick on you at school?, (2) say mean things to you at school?, (3) say bad things about you to other kids at school?, (4) hit you at school? An overall victimization score was calculated by summing the four items with good internal reliability during grade 3 ($\alpha = .76$), grade 5 ($\alpha = .81$) and grade 6 ($\alpha = .85$). The engagement in bullying behaviors sub-scale asks children to report whether they ever exhibited the following behaviors in their school: (1) pick on other kids, (2) hit kids that are weaker than them, (3) say mean things to other kids , (4) do name-calling with other kids at school. An overall bullying score was calculated by summing the four items with good internal reliability during grade 3 ($\alpha = .77$), grade 5 ($\alpha = .78$), and grade 6 ($\alpha = .83$).

School Performance. The children's school performance from grade 1 to grade 6 was measured by means of the Mock Report Card (Pierce, Hamm, & Vandell, 1999). Teacher's rated their students' school performance on a 5-point scale (1 = below grade level, 5 = excellent) in six subjects: Reading, Oral Language, Written Language, Math, Social Studies, and Science. The mean of the 6 subjects was used to indicate the students' School Performance. Cronbach's alpha was consistently high across the six waves of measurement (from .93 to .95).

Closeness and Conflict between the mother and the child during grades 1, 3, 4, 5 and 6 were measured by means of the *Child-Parent Relationship Scale* (CPRS, Pianta, 1992). The items in the CPRS were derived from attachment theory, and the measure enabled mothers to report the child's attachment behaviors at home. The items involved the mother's feelings and beliefs about her relationship with the child, and about the child's behavior toward the parent. The CPRS asks parents to rate items on a 5-point, Likert-type scale, ranged from 1 = "Definitely does not apply" to 5 = "Definitely applies". The conflict score was computed as the sum of 7 items, e.g. "My child easily becomes angry at me," with higher scores indicating more conflict between the mother and the child. Cronbach's alpha ranged from .81 to .87 for the five measurement waves. The closeness score was computed as the sum of 8 items, e.g. "I share an affectionate and warm relationship with my child," with higher scores indicating more closeness between the mother and the child. Cronbach's alpha ranged from .65 to .76 for the five measurement waves.

Data Analysis

We conducted latent growth curve modeling to investigate how school performance, and the parent-child closeness and conflict changed across time using the Mplus 5.1 software package (Muthén & Muthén, 1998-2007). The use of growth curve modeling enabled the identification of the average intercept and growth terms for school performance, and the parent-child closeness and conflict. The residual growth factors were used to suggest whether there is variability in terms of the initial levels of the variables and in terms of change over time. Latent growth curve modeling uses a polynomial function to model the relationship between an attribute, in this case school performance, and the parent-child closeness and conflict, and time (Muthén & Muthén, 1998-2007). For example, in the case that we identify a curvilinear pattern of change, the function takes the form (Singer & Willett, 2003):

$$y_{tt} = \beta_o + \beta_1 grade_{tt} + \beta_2 grade^2_{tt} + \varepsilon$$

where y_{tt} is a latent variable which characterizes the level of conflict or closeness between the mother and the child, or the child's school performance. Grade $_{tt}$ refers to the grade level of participant ι at time t, grade $^2_{tt}$ is the square of the participant ι's grade level at time t, and ε is a disturbance assumed to be normally distributed with zero mean and constant variance. The model's coefficients, β_o, β_1, and β_2, determine the average shape of the trajectory. Three standard fit indexes were used in addition to the Chi-square statistic to evaluate model fit: The Root Mean-square Error of Approximation (RMSEA), Standardized Root Mean Residual (SRMR), and the Comparative Fit Index (CFI). Values less than .06 for the RMSEA and less than .09 for the SRMR are considered a close fit, and a value higher than .90 for CFI is considered acceptable (Hu & Bentler, 1998; Kline, 1998).

In the case that variability was identified in the average intercept or growth terms, we proceeded to investigate for differences between different groups of children, not-involved, bullies, victims, and bully-victims with the use of multiple group mixture modeling in Mplus 5.1. Multiple group mixture modeling is used when there is one categorical variable (i.e., different groups of children based on their engagement in bullying behavior) for which class membership is known and equal to the groups identified in the sample (i.e., not-involved, bullies, victims, and bully-victims). Therefore, this approach investigates how identified categorical groups in the sample changed over time. Similarly to hierarchical and latent growth curve modeling, multiple group mixture modeling uses a polynomial function to model the relationship between an attribute, in this case parent-child relationship quality or school performance, and time (Muthén & Muthén, 1998-2007). The function takes the form:

$$y_{tt}^j = \beta^j_o + \beta^j_1 grade_{tt} + \beta^j_2 grade^2_{tt} + \varepsilon$$

where y_{tt}^j is a latent variable which characterizes the level of externalizing or internalizing problems for participant ι at time t given membership in class j. Grade$_{tt}$ refers to the grade level of participant ι at time t, grade $^2_{tt}$ is the square of the participant ι's grade level at time t, and ε is a disturbance assumed to be normally distributed with zero mean and constant variance. The model's coefficients, β^j_o, β^j_1, and β^j_2, determine the shape of the trajectory. The coefficients are superscripted by j to denote that the groups identified in the sample vary across different levels of the categorical variable (different groups in terms of engagement in bullying or victimization), which allows for cross-group differences in the shape of the trajectories.

Finally, in order to investigate the transactional association between the parent-child relationship and bullying and victimization experiences at school we performed cross-lagged path analysis in Mplus 5.1. This model allowed us to test whether the parent-child relationship, school performance, and bullying and victimization were cross-related over time. The use of a cross-lag model allows testing causal predominance by investigating whether a parent effect model, a child effect model, or a bidirectional model is in effect. After testing the basic model (Figure 3), non-significant paths were dropped from the model and the model was tested again. As with the latent class growth analysis, the RMSEA, SRMR, and the CFI were used as model fit indexes for the path analyses.

RESULTS

Descriptive Statistics

Table 1 shows the means and standard deviations for bullying and victimization. According to pair wise t-test analyses, children reported higher bullying at grade 6 compared to grade 5 (t(895) = 4.94, p < .001), and at grade 5 compared to grade 3 (t(895) = 4.84, p < .001). Victimization decreased form grade 5 to grade 6 (t(895) = 2.26, p < .05), although there were no statistically significant differences between grade 3 and grade 5 (t(895) = -1. 34, p = .15).

To classify individuals in the non-involved, bully only, victim only, and bully-victim groups we used the Means and Standard Deviations (Table 1) of bullying and victimization at grades 3, 5, and 6. To classify individuals in the higher risk groups we chose a cut-off score corresponding to one Standard Deviation (SD) above the mean for bullying and victimization, as done by previous research (e.g. Fanti et al., 2009). During each time point, all individuals scoring below the cut-off score on both bullying and victimization were classified in the non-involved group, individuals scoring 1 SD above the mean on both bullying and victimization were classified in the bully-victim group, individuals scoring 1 SD above the mean on bullying but below the cut-off score on victimization were classified in the bully only group, and individuals scoring below the cut-off score on bullying but 1 SD above the mean on victimization were classified in the victim only group. During grade 3, 79.2% (n = 709) of the sample comprised the low group, 8.7% (n = 78) the victim only group, 7.5% (n = 67) the bullying only group, and 4.6% (n = 41) the bully-victim group. During grade 5, 72.3% (n = 647) of the sample comprised the low group, 7.9% (n = 71) the victim only group, 13.2% (n = 118) the bullying only group, and 6.6% (n = 59) the bully-victim group. During grade 6, 74.2% (n = 664) of the sample comprised the low group, 12.4% (n = 111) the victim only group, 9.2% (n = 82) the bullying only group, and 4.2% (n = 38) the bully-victim group.

Table 1. Mean (and Standard Deviation) Scores on each Measured Variable.

Measured variable:	Grade 3	Grade 5	Grade 6
Bullying	4.82 (1.67)	5.15 (1.81)	5.46 (2.04)
Victimization	7.32 (3.17)	7.16 (3.08)	6.94 (2.79)

Note. Values not enclosed in parenthesis represent the mean of each variable and the values enclosed in parenthesis represent the standard deviation.

We then use a cross-tab analysis in SPSS to classify children as not-involved, bullies only, victims only, and bully-victims across different points at the three waves of measurement. According to our findings, 54% (n = 483) of the students remained uninvolved across time. 14.9% (n = 133) of the children exhibited pure bullying at some point either on grade 3, 5, or 6, and only 1.3% ($n = 11$) exhibited continues high bullying behavior. 13.9% ($n = 124$) of the children were the victims of bullying at some point either on grade 3, 5, or 6, and only 1.2% ($n = 11$) experienced victimization continually. 4.4% ($n = 39$) of the children exhibited co-occurring bullying and victimization at some point either on grade 3, 5, or 6, and only 0.4% ($n = 4$) experienced continues co-occurring bullying and victimization. An additional group of students (9.9%, $n = 89$) exhibited bullying or victimization or both at different time points. Thus, this final group of children was inconsistent in terms of which behavior they exhibited across time, and they might were bullies during one time, and victims or bully-victims during another time point. Because the children exhibiting continuous bullying, or victimization, or both represented a minority of the sample, we decided to collapse these groups with the children exhibiting pure bullying or victimization or both at some point during the 3 chronological periods. Therefore, 54% of the children remained uninvolved across time, 15.1% of the children experienced only victimization, 16.2 % exhibited pure bullying behavior, and 4.8% exhibited co-occurring bullying and victimization. Finally, 9.9% exhibited either bullying, victimization or both at different time points, and this group will be referred to as the occasional bully or victim group. These five groups comprised the final groups to be used in the analyses.

Growth Modeling

To investigate the average trajectories of participants' school performance across time, a latent growth curve model was initially estimated. The growth model fit the data well, $\chi^2_{(12, N = 895)} = 49.81$, $RMSEA = .060$ (RMSEA CI: . 043|.077), $SRMR = .022$, $CFI = .989$. The unstandardized intercept (i = 3.431, SE = .039, p < .001) was significant, although the linear slope (s = -.009, SE = .022, p = .67), and the quadratic acceleration term (q = .002, SE = .003, p = .59) were not significant, suggesting that on average students final school performance did not change from their initial school performance across time (figure 1). In addition, the unstandardized residual intercept (i = .642, SE = .091, p < .001), the residual linear slope (s = .104, SE = .028, p = < .001), and the quadratic acceleration term (q = .002, SE = .001, p < .001) were significant indicating significant variability between-subjects in terms of initial levels of school performance, and in terms of change over time. We then employed multiple group mixture growth modeling to investigate for differences between the identified groups. Figure 1 shows the mixed quadratic growth model resulting from the mixture growth model analyses, and Table 2 shows the unstandardized intercept, linear and quadratic terms for the different groups. According to Figure 1, only the uninvolved children scored above average on academic achievement. The bullies did not differ much from the victims in terms of school performance, and both of these groups scored better in comparison to children who exhibited some combination of bullying and victimization. The occasional bullies or victims had the worse school performance over time, although initially this group's school performance was similar to the bully-victim group.

As with previous analyses, to investigate the average trajectories of students' closeness with their mothers across time, a latent growth curve model was initially estimated. The

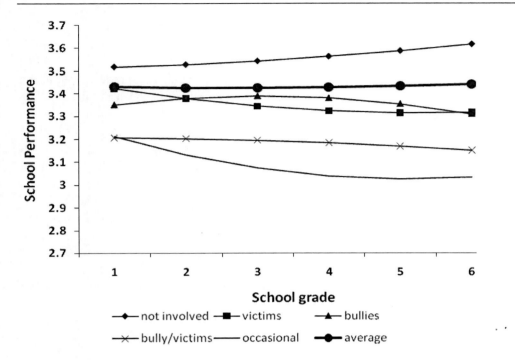

Figure 1. Mixture group growth model examining differences between groups in terms of school performance.

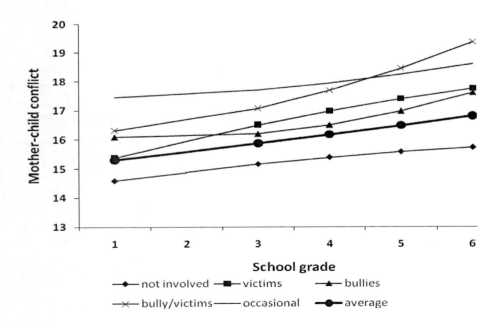

Figure 2. Mixture group growth model examining differences between groups in terms of mother-child conflict.

Bullying and Victimization Experiences at School, the Parent-Child Relationship... 193

growth model fit the data well, $\chi^2_{(6, N = 895)} = 24.67$, *RMSEA* = .059 (RMSEA CI: . 036|.084), *SRMR* = .153, *CFI* = .990. The unstandardized intercept (i = 38.260, SE = .129, p < .001), and the linear slope (s = -.350, SE = .085, p < .001) were significant, although the quadratic acceleration term (q = -.002, SE = .012, p = .87) was not significant, suggesting that on average the students closeness with their mother decreased linearly across time. However, the unstandardized residual intercept (i = -.538, SE = 2.319, p = .81) and the residual linear slope (s = .828, SE = .588, p = .159) were not significant, and only the quadratic acceleration term (q = .027, SE = .009, p = .004) was significant indicating that there was no significant variability between-subjects in terms of initial levels of mother-child closeness and in terms of linear change over time. Additional analysis used multiple group mixture growth modeling to investigate for differences between groups by holding the intercept and linear terms constant and investigating for differences between the groups in terms of curvilinear change. However, an inspection of the graph did not indicate any curvilinear differences between the groups under investigation, and the quadratic acceleration terms were not significant. Based on these findings, we concluded that closeness between mother and children decreased across time in a similar fashion for all children in the sample.

Finally, we investigated the average trajectories of students' conflict with their mothers. The growth model fit the data well, $\chi^2_{(6, N = 895)} = 20.11$, *RMSEA* = .051 (RMSEA CI: . 028|.077), *SRMR* = .018, *CFI* = .995. The unstandardized intercept (i = 15.307, SE = .269, p < .001), and the linear slope (s = .260, SE = .142, p < .05) were significant, although the quadratic term (q = .005, SE = .020, p = .78) was not significant, suggesting that the mother-child conflict increased linearly across time (Figure 2). In addition, the unstandardized residual intercept (i =25 .119, SE = 7.637, p < .001), the residual linear slope (s = 3.890, SE = 1.733, p < .05), and the quadratic acceleration term (q = .089, SE = .026, p < .001) were significant, indicating significant variability between-subjects in terms of initial levels of mother-child conflict and in terms of change over time. Additional analysis used multiple group mixture growth modeling to investigate for differences between groups. Figure 2 shows the mixed quadratic growth model resulting from the multiple group mixture growth model analyses, and Table 2 shows the unstandardized intercept, linear and quadratic terms for the

Table 2. Growth Factor Parameter Estimates.

Groups	Intercept(SE)	Linear Slope(SE)	Quadratic Term(SE)
School performance:			
Uninvolved	3.518(.053)**	.003(.029)	.002(.004)
Victim only	3.424(.098)**	-.064 (.057)	.006(.008)
Bullying only	3.350(.095)**	.056(.055)	-.009(.007)
Bully-victim	3.207(.200)**	.001(.108)	-.002(.014)
Occasional	3.211(.135)**	-.113(.079)	.011(.011)
Mother-child conflict:			
Uninvolved	14.583(.357)**	.363(.189)*	-.019(.026)
Victim only	15.384(.677)**	.672(.349)*	-.028(.048)
Bullying only	16.087(.638)**	-.284(.339)	.084(.047)
Bully-victim	16.314(1.429)**	.059(.892)	.079(.131)
Occasional	17.433(.919)**	-.006(.454)	.035(.066)

Note. * p < .05, ** p < .01

different groups. According to Figure 2, only the uninvolved children scored below average on mother-child conflict. The bully-victim group and the occasional bully-victim group experienced more conflict with their mothers in comparison to the other groups. Bully-victims experienced less conflict with their mothers from grade 1 to grade 4 in comparison to the occasional bully-victim group, although they experienced more conflict with their mothers during grades 5 and 6. Bullies and victims did not differ much in terms of the conflict they experienced, and these two groups were in between the lower risk and the higher risk groups. The uninvolved and the victim only group exhibited significant linear increase from grade 1 to grade 6 in terms of conflict with their mothers.

Cross-Lagged Path Analysis

The model under investigation is illustrated in Figure 3. The hypothesized model fit the data well based on the SRMR and the CFI, $\chi^2_{(25, N = 895)} = 280.57$, $RMSEA = .107$ (RMSEA CI: .096|.118), $SRMR = .029$, $CFI = .95$. The full model (Figure 3) was compared to a nested one with all non-significant paths removed (Figure 4). The reduced model fit the data well based on all of the fit indexes, $\chi^2_{(52, N = 895)} = 311.28$, $RMSEA = .075$ (RMSEA CI: .067|.083), $SRMR = .039$, $CFI = .95$, and fit the data equally as well as the full model, $\Delta\chi^2_{(29, N = 895)} = 30.71$, $p = .38$. Therefore, we decided to proceed with the more parsimonious, reduced model. Not shown in Figure 4 are the correlations between the variables at each time point, and these correlations are presented in Table 3. According to Table 3, bullying was positively correlated with victimization and conflict across time, and it was negatively related to grade 5 closeness and grade 3 school performance. Victimization was positively related to grade 3 and grade 6 conflict, and negatively to grade 3 school performance. Closeness was negatively related to conflict across time, and positively to school performance at grade 3. School performance was negatively related to grade 3 and grade 6 conflict.

As previously mentioned we also controlled for gender (coded with 1 for boys and 2 for girls), and based on the findings gender was significantly related to grade 5 bullying, $\beta = -.07$, $SE = .03$, $p < .05$, indicating that boys were more likely to exhibit bullying behavior in school, to grade 5 closeness, $\beta = .06$, $SE = .03$, $p < .05$, indicating that girls were closer to their mothers, and to grade 5 school performance, $\beta = .10$, $SE = .02$, $p < .001$, indicating that girls performed better at school than boys. Additionally, the autoregressive paths between (1)

Table 3. Path model correlations (N = 895).

	Grade 3				Grade 5				Grade 6			
	Bully	Victim	Conflict	Closen	Bully	Victim	Conflict	Closen.	Bully	Victim	Conflict	Closen.
Victimization	.42**				.36**				.27**			
Conflict	.08*	.15**			.08*	.05			.09**	.07*		
Closeness	-.05	-.05	-.33**		-.07*	-.02	-.26**		-.02	-.04	-.32**	
School perform.	-.07*	-.18**	-.14**	.13**	-.06	-.02	-.05	-.03	.01	-.02	-.11**	.06

Note. $* p < .05$, $** p < .01$

grade 3 and grade 5 bullying, $\beta = .30$, $SE = .03$, $p < .001$, victimization, $\beta = .42$, $SE = .03$, $p < .001$, closeness, $\beta = .54$, $SE = .02$, $p < .001$, conflict, $\beta = .68$, $SE = .02$, $p < .001$, and school performance, $\beta = .72$, $SE = .02$, $p < .001$, and (2) grade 5 and grade 6 bullying, $\beta = .50$, $SE = .02$, $p < .001$, victimization, $\beta = .51$, $SE = .02$, $p < .001$, closeness, $\beta = .60$, $SE = .02$, $p < .001$, conflict, $\beta = .68$, $SE = .02$, $p < .001$, and school performance, $\beta = .75$, $SE = .02$, $p < .001$ were all significant indicating substantial stability across time for all the variables under investigation.

As shown in Figure 4, bullying at grade 3 predicted closeness at grade 5, $\beta = -.08$, $SE = .03$, $p < .01$, and grade 3 closeness predicted bullying at grade 5, $\beta = -.07$ $SE = .03$, $p < .05$, suggesting a negative bidirectional association between these two variables. Grade 3 victimization was positively related to grade 5 closeness, $\beta = .08$, $SE = .03$, $p < .05$, and bullying, $\beta = .11$, $SE = .03$, $p < .001$. Grade 3 conflict was negatively related to grade 5 closeness, $\beta = -.08$, $SE = .03$, $p < .01$. Bullying at grade 5 predicted closeness at grade 6, $\beta = -.06$, $SE = .02$, $p < .05$. Grade 5 conflict was positively related to grade 6 bullying, $\beta = .07$, $SE = .03$, $p < .05$, and victimization, $\beta = .08$, $SE = .03$, $p < .01$. Grade 5 school performance was negatively related to grade 6 conflict, $\beta = -.06$, $SE = .02$, $p < .01$, and positively to grade 6 victimization, $\beta = .06$, $SE = .03$, $p < .05$. Closeness at grade 5 was positively related to victimization at grade 6, $\beta = .06$, $SE = .03$, $p < .05$. Finally, grade 5 conflict was negatively related to grade 6 closeness, $\beta = -.07$, $SE = .02$, $p < .05$, and grade 5 closeness was negatively related to grade 6 conflict, $\beta = -.08$, $SE = .02$, $p < .01$, suggesting a negative bidirectional association between these two variables.

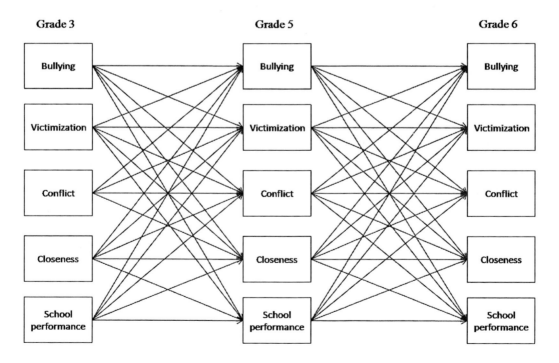

Figure 3. Initial path model.
Note. Not shown in the figure are the correlations between the variables at each time point.

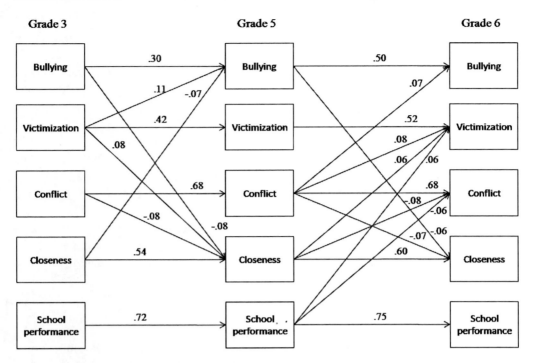

Figure 4. Final path model controlling for gender.
Note. All paths significant at the .05 level. Not shown in the figure are the correlations between the variables at each time point.

DISCUSSION

The present study contributes to prior research by longitudinally identifying different groups of children based on their reports on bullying and victimization, and then comparing these groups on their academic achievement and the relationship with their parents from grade 1 to grade 6. Additionally, the present study investigated a longitudinal transactional model between school performance, the parent-child relationship and child bullying and victimization experiences over a period of four years.

The current study, with the use of a longitudinal design, supports the idea that bullying and victimization can co-occur across time, and complements previous studies that identified groups of children exhibiting pure bullying and victimization problems and co-occurring bullying and victimization problems (Bowers et al., 1992; Stevens et al., 2002; Fanti et al., 2009; Kokkinos & Panayiotou, 2004). However, the present study also provides evidence for an additional group of children who exhibit either bullying, victimization or both during different time points, labeled as the occasional bully-victim group. It is argued that previous cross-sectional studies might provide misleading evidence when comparing groups of children exhibiting bullying, victimization, or both by not taking the occasional bully-victim group into account. Additionally, we support the findings of previous studies suggesting that the group of children exhibiting co-occurring bullying and victimization are at higher risk when compared to children who were uninvolved, bullies only, and victims only, in terms of academic achievement, and parent-child conflict (Glew et al., 2005; Schwartz, 2000; Schwartz et al., 1997; Stevens et al., 2002; Toblin et al., 2005). However, our findings also suggest that the occasional bully-victim group scored lower on school performance compared to the bully-victim group, and the two groups were at similar risk to experience high conflict with their mothers. There are a number of studies which claim that the bully-victim group is a higher risk group, and our study suggests that there is another high risk subgroup of children that needs to be taken into account by future research. Therefore, the comorbidity between bullying and victimization might occur at a specific point in time or across time, with children being bullies or victims at different time points.

Moreover, the current findings contradict evidence that bullies are at higher risk to experience a more conflictual relationship with their mothers in comparison to victims (Stevens et al., 2002). These contradicting evidence might be due to our longitudinal design, since children who are identified in the current investigation as occasional bully-victim might have been classified as bullies or victims by prior cross-sectional studies, which might have inflated their findings. In terms of closeness, our results support previous research that found no differences in the mother-child closeness between bullies, victims, and bully-victims (Schwartz et al., 1997), suggesting that the mother-child relationship becomes more negative for all children across time. Another conclusion that we can draw by examining differences between the groups under investigation from the beginning to the end of elementary school, is that bullies, victims, bully-victims, and occasional bullies or victims start school at higher risk when compared to the uninvolved children on school performance and mother-child conflict. Therefore, a negative home environment and low school achievement might characterize these higher risk groups from the beginning to the end of elementary school, although children in the bully-victim and the occasional bully-victim groups are at higher risk to perform worse academically and experience more conflict with their mothers across time.

Transactional Findings

Our findings provide support of the hypothesized transactional model between bullying and the parent-child relationship, and between victimization experiences and the parent-child relationship. The results suggested that the variables associated with the parent-child relationship, either closeness or conflict, contributed to bullying behavior and that bullying behavior influenced the closeness between parents and children, providing evidence of a transactional association between these variables. Therefore, as Patterson (1982) suggested, the child's problematic behavior might be the result of the dynamic processes that unfold within the household between parents and children. More specifically, there was a negative bidirectional association between closeness and bullying from grade 3 to grade 5, in which bullying behavior decreased the closeness between mothers and children and in turn closeness decreased the child's bullying behavior. Grade 5 bullying was also negatively associated to closeness at grade 6, and at grade 5 conflict increased the likelihood of bullying behavior at grade 6. Therefore, bullying does not necessarily influence the conflict between parents and children, but it affects the parent-child relationship through the negative effects it has on the closeness between parents and children. Moreover, it seems that the conflict between parents and children starts to have its negative effects on the parent-child relationship during early adolescence, which might be due to the transformation in the parent-child relationship during this developmental period characterized by increased conflict and decreases in closeness (Collins & Laursen, 2004; Paikoff & Brooks-Gunn, 1991). Our data also support this inverse growth over time with conflict increasing across time and closeness decreasing across time. We should also mention that these transactional findings were obtained despite controlling for the relatively strong stability of all five constructs over time, and the pattern of findings should be interpreted with the strong autoregressive paths in mind, but also the correlations between the variables during each time point of measurement.

There was also some support for a transactional association between victimization and the parent-child relationship. In contrast to bullying, grade 3 victimization seemed to be positively related to closeness during grade 5, suggesting that parents might adapt their parenting in a positive way because of their child's experiences as a victim. Moreover, both closeness and conflict during grade 5 seemed to influence the likelihood that a child will experience victimization at grade 6. According to these findings, there might be a positive longitudinal transactional association between victimization and parent-child closeness, in which victimization increases closeness, although this increase in closeness might place the child at higher risk for experiencing victimization. This finding is in line with earlier claims that over-involved or over-protective mothers, which might be indicated in the current study by higher closeness, is one factor related to victimization by peers (Georgiou, 2008b; Olweus, 1980; Perren & Hornung, 2005; Stevens, et al., 2002).

Additionally, school performance does not seem to influence the transactional association between the parent-child relationship and bullying and victimization problems. Contrary to our prediction, a transactional association between academic achievement and victimization was not found. As suggested by prior research school performance might not be one of the reasons associated with bullying behavior (Ma, 2002; Olweus, 1993; Rigby & Slee, 1991), although students who are performing well at school might be more likely to be targeted for victimization as our findings and previous findings suggested (Ma, 2002). We add to these findings in that school performance might not be related to victimization during middle childhood (grades 3 to 5 of the elementary school), but it might start to have an effect during the transition to adolescence.

There were a number of gender differences in the mean levels of this study's constructs. In line with previous research, males scored higher on bullying than females (e.g. Seals & Young, 2003). Moreover, mothers reported greater involvement with their daughters as compared to their sons, in accordance with work that finds adolescent females experiencing higher-quality relationships with their parents than male adolescents (e.g. Hay & Ashman, 2003; Kenny, 1994). Finally, we found that girls perform better academically compared to boys, as suggested by prior research (Herbert & Yeung, 1998).

Strengths, Limitations, and Future Directions

Strengths of this investigation included a large sample of children, which enabled us to run a structural equation model and identify children at risk for pure and co-occurring bullying and victimization across time. Furthermore, the data were collected longitudinally, and we were able to test our hypotheses using a longitudinal model, thus enhancing the reliability and flexibility of our analyses (Singer & Willett, 2003). However, data on conflict and closeness were based only on maternal-reports, and would be further enhanced with the use of multiple informants and multiple methods, for example structured observations of children interacting with their parents (Allen, McElhaney, Kuperminc, & Jodl, 2004).

This study builds on existing relevant knowledge by examining the unique effects and contributions of bullying and victimization experiences at school on parenting characteristics over time. Future avenues of research could include mediational models between bullying and victimization experiences and parenting variables, such as the children's personality, motivation, and self perceptions. Such models would enable further understanding of the mechanisms of effects reported in the present study. In addition, because children are embedded within multiple contexts simultaneously (Bronfenbrenner, 1988; Cicchetti & Lynch, 1993; Henrich, Brookmeyer, Shrier, & Shahar, 2006), other social contexts, such as relationships with peers and other important adults, may impact on the dynamics of the parent-child relationship and the development of bullying and victimization experiences.

In conclusion, the current study presents evidence of the existence of different pure and co-occurring groups of children in terms of bullying and victimization, and identifies the group at higher risk for social and individual adversity. This information is important for school interventions, and suggests that both the child's academic achievement and the child's relationship with his/her parents need to be taken into account for future intervention efforts as early as the first grade of school. Furthermore, the present study has contributed to the literature by developing and testing a transactional model, based on longitudinal data, capable to describe the interrelation between mother-child relationship and child bullying and victimization experiences. A transactional relationship was supported between the parent-child relationship quality and bullying and victimization. The transactional findings of the current investigation support earlier claims (Lollis & Kuczynski, 1997; Sameroff, 1975; Sameroff & MacKenzie, 2003) that children and their mothers are intertwined in a cycle of reciprocal associations. The empirical evidence provided contributes to a better understanding of the ongoing dynamics between parents, children, and children behavior across development, particularly regarding bullying and victimization experiences at school. As Dodge and Petit (2003) point out, in symbiotic models of development, like the one between parent and child, influences tend to become reciprocal over time.

REFERENCES

Allen, J. P., McElhaney, K. B., Kuperminc, G. P. & Jodl, K. M. (2004). Stability and change in attachment security across adolescence. *Child Development, 75(6)*, 1792-1805.

Baldry, A. C. & Farrington, D. P. (2000). Bullies and Delinquents: Personal Characteristics and Parental Styles. *Journal of Community & Applied Social Psychology, 10*, 17-31.

Beaver, K. M. & Wright, J. P. (2007). A child effects explanation for the association between family risk and involvement in antisocial lifestyle. *Journal of Adolescent Research, 22(6)*, 640-664.

Beran, T. N., Hughes, G. & Lupart, J. (2008). A model of achievement and bullying: Analyses of the Canadian national longitudinal survey of children and youth data. *Educational research, 50(1)*, 25-39.

Berthhold, K. A. & Hoover, J. H. (2000). Correlated of bullying and victimization among intermediate students in the Midwestern USA. *School Psychology International, 21(1)*, 65-78.

Bowers, L., Smith, P. K. & Brinney, V. (1992). Cohesion and power in the families of children involved in bully/victim problems at school. *Journal of Family Therapy, 14*, 371-387.

Bronfenbrenner (1988). Interacting systems in human development. Research paradigms: Present and future. In N. Bolger, A. Caspi, G. Downey, & M. Moorehouse (Eds.), *Persons in context: Developmental processes* (25-49). New York: Cambridge University Press.

Buist, K. L., Dekovic, M., Meeus, W. & Van Aken, M. A. G. (2004). The reciprocal relationship between early adolescent attachment and internalizing and externalizing problem behavior. *Journal of Adolescence, 27*, 251-266.

Burt, A. S., McGue, M., Krueger, R. F. & Iacono, W. G. (2005). How are parent-child conflict and childhood externalizing symptoms related over time? Results from a genetically informative cross-lagged study. *Development and Psychopathology, 17*, 145-165.

Cicchetti, D. & Lynch, M. (1993). Toward an ecological/transactional model of community violence and child maltreatment: Consequences for children's development. *Psychiatry: Interpersonal and Biological Processes, 56(1)*, 96-118.

Collins,W. A. & Laursen, B. (2004). Parent–adolescent relationships and influences. In R. M. Lerner, & L. Steinberg (Eds.), *Handbook of Adolescent Psychology* (2nd ed., 331-361). New York: Wiley.

Dodge, K. & Pettit, G. S. (2003). A biopsychosocial model of the development of chronic conduct problems in adolescence. *Developmental Psychology, 39(2)*, 349-371.

Espelage, D. L., Bosworth, K. & Simon, T. R. (2000). Examining the social context of bullying behaviors in early adolescence. *Journal of Counselling and Development, 78*, 326-333.

Fanti, K. A., Frick, P. J. & Georgiou, St. (2009). Linking callous-unemotional traits to instrumental and non-instrumental forms of aggression. *Journal of Psychopathology and Behavioral Assessment, 31*, 285-298.

Fanti, K. A., Henrich, C. C., Brookmeyer, K. A. & Kuperminc, G. P. (2008). Toward a transactional model of parent-adolescent relationship quality and adolescent psychological adjustment. *Journal of Early Adolescence, 28(2)*, 252-276.

Farrington, D. P. (1993). Understanding and preventing bullying. In M.Tonry, & N. Morris (Eds.). *Crime and Justice*, (381-458). Chicago: Chicago University press.

Flouri, E. & Buchanan, A. (2003). The Role of Mother Involvement and Father Involvement in Adolescence Bullying Behaviour. *Journal of Interpersonal Violence, 18(6)*, 634-644.

Georgiou, St. (2008a). Bullying and victimization at school: the role of mothers. *British Journal of Educational Psychology, 78,* 109-125.

Georgiou, St. (2008b). Parental style and child bullying and victimization experiences at school. *Social Psychology of Education, 11*, 213-227.

Glew, G. M., Ming-Yu, F., Katon, W., Rivara, F. P. & Kernic, M. A. (2005). Bullying, psychosocial adjustment, and academic performance in elementary school. *Archives of Pediatric Adolescence Medicine, 159*, 1026-1031.

Hay, I. & Ashman, A. F. (2003). The development of adolescents' emotional stability and general self-concept: The interplay of parents, peers, and gender. *International Journal of Disability, Development and Education, 50(1),* 77-91.

Hay, D. F., Vespo, J. E. & Zahn-Waxler, C. (1998). Young children's quarrels with their siblings and mothers: Links with maternal depression and bipolar illness. *British Journal of Developmental Psychology, 16(4),* 519-538.

Headley, S. (2004). Bullying and violence. *Youth studies in Australia, 23(2),* 60-69.

Henrich, C. C., Brookmeyer, K. A., Shrier, L. A. & Shahar, G. (2006). Supportive relationships and sexual risk behavior in adolescence: An ecological-transactional approach. *Journal of Pediatric Psychology, 31(3),* 286-297.

Herbert, H. W. & Yeung, A. S. (1998). Longitudinal structural equation models of academic self-concept and achievement: Gender differences in the development of math and English constructs. *American Educational Research Journal, 35(4),* 705-738.

Hu, L. & Bentler, P. M. (1998). Fit indices in covariance structure modeling: Sensitivity to underparametrized model misspecification. *Psychological Methods, 3,* 424-453.

Huh, D., Tristan, J., Wade, E. & Stice, E. (2006). Does problem behavior elicit poor parenting? A prospective study of adolescent girls. *Journal of Adolescent Research, 21,* 185-204.

Jang, S. J. & Smith, C. A. (1997). A test of reciprocal causal relationships among parental supervision, affective ties, and delinquency. *Journal of Research in Crime and Delinquency, 34,* 307-336.

Kaltiala-Heino, R., Rimpelä, M., Rantanen, P. & Rimpelä A. (2000). Bullying at school – an indicator of adolescents at risk for mental disorders. *Journal of Adolescence, 23,* 661-674.

Kenny, D. A. (1994). *Interpersonal perception: A social relations analysis.* New York: Guilford.

Kline, R. B. (1998). *Principles and practice of structural equation modeling.* New York:The Guilford Press.

Kochenderfer, B. J. & Ladd, G. W. (1997). Victimized children's responses to peers' aggression: Behaviors associated with reduced versus continued victimization. *Development & Psychopathology, 9,* 59-73.

Kokkinos, C. M. & Panayiotou, G. (2004). Predicting bullying and victimization among early adolescents: Associations with disruptive behavior disorders. *Aggressive Behavior, 30,* 520-533.

Kokkinos, C. M. & Panayiotou, G. (2007). Parental discipline practices and locus of control: relationship to bullying and victimization experiences of elementary school students. *Social Psychology of Education, 10,* 281-301.

Ladd, G. W., Kochenderfer, B. J. & Coleman, C. C. (1996). Friendship quality as a predictor of young children's early school adjustment. *Child Development, 67,* 1103-1118.

Laird, R. D., Pettit, G. S., Bates, J. E. & Dodge, K. A. (2003). Parents' monitoring-relevant knowledge and adolescents' delinquent behavior: Evidence of correlated developmental changes and reciprocal influences. *Child Development, 74(3),* 752-768.

Laursen, B. (2005). Conflict between mothers and adolescents in single-mother, blended, and two-biological-parent families. *Parneitng: Science and Practice, 5(4),* 347-370.

Lollis, S. & Kuczynski, L. (1997). Beyond one hand clapping: Seeing bidirectionality in parent–child relations. *Journal of Social and Personal Relationships, 14(4),* 441-461.

Ma, X. (2002). Bullying in middle school: Individual and school characteristics of victims and offenders. *School Effectiveness and School Improvement, 13(1)*, 63-89.

Muthén, L. K. & Muthén, B. (1998-2007). Mplus User's Guide. Los Angeles, CA: Muthén & Muthén.

Naylor, P., Cowie, H. & del Rey, R. (2001). Coping strategies of secondary school children in response to being bullied. *Child Psychology and Psychiatry Review, 6*, 114-120.

Offord, D. R., Boyle, M. H. & Racine, Y. A. (1991). The epidemiology of antisocial behavior in childhood and adolescence. In D. J. Pepler, & K. H. Rubin (Eds.), *The development and treatment of childhood aggression* (31-54). Hillsdale, NJ: Erlbaum.

Olweus, D. (1980). Familial and Temperamental Determinants of Aggressive Behavior in Adolescent Boys: A Causal Analysis. *Developmental Psychology, 16(6)*, 644-660.

Olweus, D. (1984). Aggressors and their victims: Bullying at school. In Frude, N., and Gault, H. (eds.), *Disruptive Behavior in Schools.* Wiley, New York, 57-76.

Olweus, D. (1993). *Bullying at School: What we Know and What We Can Do.* Oxford:Blackwell.

Paikoff, R. L. & Brooks-Gunn, J. (1991). Do parent-child relationships change during puberty? *Psychological Bulletin, 110(1)*, 47-66.

Patterson, G. R. (1982). *Coercive family process: A social learning approach.* Eugene, Oregon: Castalia.

Perren, S. & Hornung, R. (2005). Bulling and Delinquency in Adolescence: Victim's and Perpetrators' Family and Peer Relations. *Swiss Journal of Psychology, 64(1)*, 51-64.

Pianta, R. (1992). Student-Teacher Relationship Scale. Charlottesville, VA: University of Virginia.

Pierce, K. M., Hamm, J. V. & Vandell, D. L. (1999). Experiences in after-school programs and children's adjustment in first-grade classrooms. *Child Development, 70*, 756-767.

Reitz, E., Dekovic, M. & Meijer, A. M. (2006). Relations between parenting and externalizing and internalizing problem behavior in early adolescence: Child behavior as moderator and predictor. *Journal of Adolescence, 29(3)*, 419-436.

Rigby, K. (2002). *New perspective on bullying.* London: Jessica Kingsley.

Rigby, K. & Slee, P. T. (1991). Bullying among Australian school children: Reported behavior and attitudes toward victims. *Journal of Social Psychology, 131*, 615-627.

Sameroff, A. J. (1975). Transactional models in early social relations. *Human Development, 18*, 65-79.

Sameroff, A. J. & MacKenzie, M. J. (2003). Research strategies for capturing transactional models of development: The limits of the possible. *Development & Psychopathology, 15(3)*, 613-640.

Scaramella, L. V., Conger, R. D., Spoth, R. & Simons, R. L. (2002). Evaluation of a social contextual model of delinquency: A cross study replication. *Child Development, 73(1)*, 175-195.

Schwartz, D. (2000). Subtypes of victims and aggressors in children's peer groups. *Journal of Abnormal Child Psychology, 28(2)*, 181-192.

Schwartz, D., Dodge, K. A., Pettit, G. S. & Bates, J. E. (1997). The early scoailization of aggressive victims of bullying. *Child Development, 68(4)*, 665-675.

Schwartz, D., Proctor, L. J. & Chicn, D. H. (2001). The aggressive victim of bullying: Emotional and behavioral dysregulation as a pathway to victimization by peers,

In J. Juvonen, & S. Graham (Eds.), *Peer harassment in school The plight of the vulnerable and victimized* (147-174). New York/London: The Guilford Press.

Seals, D. & Young, J., (2003). Bullying and victimization: prevalence and relationship to gender, grade level, ethnicity, self-esteem and depression. *Adolescence, 38(152)*, 735-747.

Sharp, S. (1995). How much does bullying hurt? *Educational Child Psychology, 12*, 81-88.

Singer, J. D. & Willett, J. B. (2003). *Applied longitudinal data analysis: Modeling change and event occurrence.* Oxford, NY: Oxford University Press.

Solberg, M. E., Olweus, D. & Endresen, I. M. (2007). Bullies and victims at school: Are they the same pupils? *British Journal of Educational Psychology, 77*, 441-464.

Slee, P. T. (1994). Situational and interpersonal correlates of anxiety associated with peer victimization. *Child Psychology and Human Development, 25*, 97-107.

Stevens, V., De Bourdeaudhuij, I. & Van Oost, P. (2002). Relationship of the Family Environment to Children's Involvement in Bully/Victims Problems at School. *Journal of Youth and Adolescence, 31(6)*, 419-428.

Toblin, R. L., Schwartz, D., Gorman, A. H. & Abou-ezzeddine, T. (2005). Social-cognitive and behavioral attributes of aggressive victims of bullying. *Applied Developmental Psychology, 26*, 329-346.

Youngstrom, E., Findling, R. & Calabrese, J. (2003). Who are the comorbid adolescents? Agreement between psychiatric diagnosis, youth, parent, and teacher report. *Journal of Abnormal Child Psychology, 31(3)*, 231-245.

Vuchinich, S., Bank, L. & Patterson, G. R. (1992). Parenting, peers *Developmental Psychology, 28(3)*, 510-521.

Woods, S. & Wolke, D. (2004). Direct and relational bullying among primary school children and academic achievement. *Journal of School Psychology, 42*, 135-155.

In: Youth Violence and Juvenile Justice: Causes, Intervention...   ISBN: 978-1-61668-011-4
Editor: Neil A. Ramsay et al., pp. 229-248   © 2010 Nova Science Publishers, Inc.

Chapter 9

PERSONAL AND INTERPERSONAL MEDIATORS LINKING ACCULTURATION STRESS TO AGGRESSIVE BEHAVIOR IN LATINO ADOLESCENTS

*Paul Richard Smokowski[1], Rachel Lee Buchanan[2] and Martica Bacallao[*3]*
[1]University of North Carolina at Chapel Hill, NC, USA
[2]Salisbury University, MD, USA
[3]University of North Carolina – Greensboro, NC, USA

ABSTRACT

This chapter discusses a study that we conducted to examine pathways that lead to aggressive behavior in Latino adolescents. Adolescent mental health, risk-taking, family environment, and friendships with peers were investigated as potential mediators linking acculturation stress to adolescent aggression. Path analyses were conducted using data collected at 3 time points from a sample of 286 adolescents, 66% of whom were born outside of the United States. Our findings indicated that acculturation stressors, rather than assimilation measures, were associated with baseline aggression, Time 2 parent-adolescent conflict, and Time 2 adolescent substance use. We trace mediation pathways through internalizing problems, parent-adolescent conflict, negative friend associations, and adolescent substance use to incidence of aggressive behavior 6 months later. Findings show involvement in Latino culture is an asset positively connected to familism and self-esteem, and ultimately leads to lower levels of adolescent aggression. The discussion includes implications for practice and study limitations.

Keywords: Latinos, internalizing problems, depression, immigrants, acculturation, culture.

---

* Corresponding author: University of North Carolina at Chapel Hill, 325 Pittsboro Street, CB 3550, Chapel Hill, NC 27599-3550, telephone 919-843-8281 or E-mail: smokowsk@email.unc.edu

INTRODUCTION

Acculturation is a sociological process in which cultural change results from contact between two autonomous and independent cultural groups (Redfield, Linton, & Herskovits, 1936). Usually, the nondominant group is strongly influenced to take on the norms, values, and behaviors espoused by the dominant group (Berry, 1998). For those who are trying to adjust to a different cultural system, the sociological process of acculturation has important links to both individual behavior and family relationships. Many researchers have hypothesized and tested links between acculturation levels and social maladjustment, psychopathology, and substance use. In comparison to less-acculturated peers, researchers have reported that more-acculturated Latinos displayed higher levels of alcohol, marijuana, and cocaine use, and increased levels of youth violence (Carvajal, Photiades, Evans, & Nash, 1997; Gil, Vega, & Dimas, 1994; Gonzales, Knight, Morgan-Lopez, Saenz, & Sirolli, 2002; Martinez, 2006; Rogler, Cortes, & Malgady, 1991; Smokowski, David-Ferdon, & Stroupe, 2009).

Acculturation and Youth Violence

The relation of Latino adolescent acculturation with youth violence outcomes has been examined in 14 studies, which were reviewed in a recent research synthesis (see Smokowski et al., 2009). Although the various studies have defined acculturation in numerous ways—some have used the terms *assimilation, acculturation,* or *acculturation stress* interchangeably—the majority (10 of 14) of these empirical investigations have reported that higher levels of acculturation among Latino adolescents were positively associated with increased incidence of youth violence (Brook, Whiteman, Balka, Win, & Gursen, 1998; Bui & Thongniramol, 2005; Buriel, Calzada, & Vasquez, 1982; Dinh, Roosa, Tein, & Lopez, 2002; Samaniego & Gonzales, 1999; Smokowski & Bacallao, 2007; Schwartz, Zamboanga, & Hernandez Jarvis, 2007; Sommers, Fagan, & Baskin, 1993; Vega, Gil, Warheit, Zimmerman, & Apospori, 1993; Vega, Khoury, Zimmerman, Gil, & Warheit, 1995). In fact, this association between acculturation and youth violence surfaced even when simple proxy measures, such as generational status, language use, time in the United States, or nativity, were used to index complex cultural processes (Gonzales et al., 2002; Smokowski et al., 2009).

Bui and Thongniramol's (2005) study provided a useful example of how straightforward indicators (e.g., generational status, nativity, or language spoken) could be used to index acculturation processes. These researchers examined data from a nationally representative subsample of 18,097 students from the National Longitudinal Study of Adolescent Health using logistic regression models and odds ratio statistics. Their findings showed that second- or third-generation Hispanic youth were 60% and 88% (respectively) more likely to report violent delinquency compared to their first-generation counterparts. Despite criticism aimed at simplistic items used to measure acculturation (Cabassa, 2003; Hunt, Schneider, & Comer, 2004), the majority of existing investigations have provided credible evidence establishing a positive cross-sectional relationship between Latino adolescent assimilation and youth violence.

Other research efforts have focused on stress precipitated by adapting to a new cultural system. *Acculturation stress*, defined by Berry (2006) as, "a response by people to life events that are rooted in intercultural contact" (p. 43), has been linked to several negative outcomes for Latino youth including mental health difficulties (Gil et al., 1994); suicidal ideation (Hovey & King, 1996); delinquent behavior (Samaniego & Gonzales, 1999); and behavior problems (Vega et al., 1995). These researchers have consistently demonstrated the links between specific acculturation stressors (e.g., language conflicts, perceived discrimination, parent-adolescent culture conflicts, and acculturation gaps between parents and children) and negative youth outcomes, especially aggression and violence.

Equally important, four studies failed to find significant associations between acculturation variables and youth violence perpetration. Two studies conducted by Bird and his colleagues (Bird, Canino, et al., 2006; Bird, Davies, & Duarte, 2006) reported that the level of assimilation, parent-child acculturation gaps, and acculturation stress were not associated with disruptive behavior disorders in their probability samples of 2,491 Puerto Rican youth ages 5 to 13 years living in either San Juan or New York City. Similarly, Gonzales, Deardorff, Formoso, Barr, and Barrera (2006) found no significant association between family linguistic acculturation and adolescent conduct problems in their sample of 175 Mexican youth and their mothers living in the Southwest United States; however, these researchers found an indirect relationship was mediated through family conflict. Last, Carvajal, Hanson, Romero, and Coyle's (2002) study of 1,119 sixth- and seventh-grade U.S. Latino and non-Latino White students in Northern California found no significant association between acculturation and any violence measures.

Despite these four studies, the larger body of emerging evidence has demonstrated an association between Latino adolescent acculturation and youth violence; however, important questions remain unanswered. The studies detailed above have all used cross-sectional data, leaving a critical need for longitudinal assessments. Previous to the current study, Dinh and her colleagues' (2002) assessment of 330 Latino youth was the only longitudinal study on Latino adolescent acculturation and youth violence. Dinh and colleagues found higher levels of youth acculturation significantly predicted lower level of parent investment, which was also related to follow-up reports one year later of higher levels of youth-reported proneness for problem behavior (i.e., gang involvement, peer delinquency, conduct problems). However, more longitudinal data is needed to adequately evaluate the sustained effect of Latino adolescent acculturation variables on youth violence outcomes and to evaluate different factors that mediate this relationship.

Cultural Risk Factors, Assets, and Mediation Pathways

Self-esteem and internalizing problems. Two investigations with Mexican American adolescents have shown as many as a third of the sampled youth had reported serious levels of depression and suicidal ideation (Hovey & King, 1996; Katragadda & Tidwell, 1998). Both research teams found acculturation stress was positively related to depression and suicidal ideation among the adolescents. In fact, Hovey and King (1996) identified both perceived family dysfunction and negative expectations for the future as significant predictors of acculturation stress and depression.

Other researchers have identified language conflicts and racial discrimination as significant acculturation stressors. In a study of 5,264 multiethnic Latino high-school students, Rumbaut (1995) concluded that English-language competence was associated with lower rates of depression. Romero and Roberts (2003) reported that lower self-esteem and higher numbers of stressors, including various types of discrimination, predicted depressive symptoms among their sample of 881 middle-school students of Mexican descent. In addition, another investigation that used a sample of 1,843 Cuban adolescents reported a significant correlation between acculturation conflicts and self-derogation (Vega, Gil, Warheit, Zimmerman, et al., 1993). Most recently in a study with a sample of 347 Hispanic youth, Schwartz et al. (2007) reported finding a strong inverse relationship between acculturation stress and self-esteem. Further, these researchers found that self-esteem mediated the effect of ethnic identity on externalizing problems. Moreover, Schwartz et al. (2007) found that acculturation stress was associated with lower self-esteem, and that self-esteem was an important mediator between acculturation variables and behavioral outcomes.

Parent-adolescent conflict. Along with longitudinal analyses, the next generation of research studies in this area must specify mechanisms or pathways that potentiate the relationship between acculturation and youth violence. Mediators between acculturation and youth violence have received some attention, and evidence has emerged that underscored the importance of family processes in mediating the relationship between acculturation and adolescent behavior. Gonzales and colleagues (2006) reported that family conflict was an important mediator that linked acculturation to increased youth externalizing symptoms. The direct relationship between family linguistic acculturation and adolescent conduct problems was not significant. However, linguistic acculturation was associated with heightened family conflict that, in turn, was related to increased adolescent conduct problems. Similarly, Dinh and colleagues' (2002) longitudinal study showed that the relationship between acculturation and youth proneness to problem behavior was mediated by parental investment. In their analyses, when Dinh and colleagues controlled for Time 1 problem behavior proneness, Time 1 acculturation was shown inversely related to Time 1 parental investment, which was negatively associated with Time 2 problem behavior proneness. Related findings were reported by Smokowski and Bacallao (2007) who explored family mediation pathways in a sample of 481 adolescents living in either North Carolina or Arizona. Smokowski and Bacallao found that adolescents' U.S. cultural involvement and acculturation conflicts did not have significant direct effects on youth aggression. However, these researchers reported that family processes mediated the effects of acculturation conflicts on adolescent aggression. Moreover, Smokowski and Bacallao demonstrated that the risk pathway led from acculturation conflicts to increased parent–adolescent conflicts to higher levels of adolescent aggression.

Negative peer relationships. Associating with friends who endorse negative behaviors appears to increase the likelihood that an adolescent will also engage in negative behaviors (Prinstein & Wang, 2005). This proneness to negative behavior may be the result of increased opportunities to participate in the behavior or the result of perceived peer pressure to participate in certain behaviors. Although scant research has been conducted on the relationship between associating with negative friends and aggressive behavior in Latino adolescents, emerging evidence supports that such friendships affect Latino youths' mental health and problem behaviors (Eamon & Mulder, 2005; Frauenglass, Routh, Pantin, & Mason, 1997). Research on resistance to peer pressure among Latino adolescents has shown the adolescents who are least able to resist peer pressure share two characteristics: their families have been in the United States for longer periods, and the adolescents had greater autonomy from their parents (Bámaca & Umaña-Taylor, 2006).

Substance use. Research on the links between acculturation and substance use for Latino adolescents has provided inconsistent results. Some studies have reported that high levels of acculturation were predictive of substance use (Dinh et al., 2002), whereas other researchers have found the reverse (Carvajal et al., 1997; for reviews see, De La Rosa, 2002; Gonzales et al., 2002). Studies of the general adolescent population have indicated that high levels of externalizing problems were related to increased levels of substance use (Helstrom, Bryan, Hutchison, Riggs, & Blechman, 2004; King, Iacono, & McGue, 2004).

Cultural assets: Familism and culture-of-origin involvement. Latino adolescents often possess cultural assets that offset the negative effects of acculturation risk factors and stressors. Culture-of-origin involvement (i.e., ethnic identity) and *familism* (i.e., the focus on family systems as being paramount in an individual's life) are two of the most commonly explored cultural assets. Smokowski and Bacallao (2007) reported that adolescents' levels of both culture-of-origin involvement and familism were inversely associated with adolescent aggression. These researchers demonstrated that familism not only buffered the affects of acculturation conflicts but also was associated with decreased levels of adolescent aggression. Similarly, findings from Taylor, Biafora, Warheit, and Gil's (1997) examination of a multicultural sample of adolescents in Miami underscored the importance of family in the lives of Latino youth. In addition, Taylor and colleagues' findings showed that adolescent culture-of-origin involvement and familism were inversely associated with adolescent aggression.

The study we present in this chapter attempted to contribute to the emerging body of literature on Latino adolescent acculturation and aggression in several ways. We examined how multiple indicators of adolescent acculturation and acculturation stress were related to adolescent aggression. Our sample included adolescents living in rural, small town, and metropolitan areas located in two geographically separated states. We have extended the research knowledge from the cross-sectional studies reviewed above by exploring longitudinal pathways linking acculturation to adolescent aggression. We delineated ecological mediators based on the adolescents' mental health (e.g., internalizing problems, self-esteem, substance use), family relationships (parent-adolescent conflict, familism), and friendships (negative peer relationships). Based on the existing research, we formulated three hypotheses:

1. The assimilation hypothesis, which held that Latino adolescents' time spent in the United States would be positively related to adolescent aggression.
2. As found in previous research, acculturation stress will have a positive cross-sectional relationship with adolescent aggressive behavior at Time 1.
3. The relationships between Latino adolescents' acculturation risk factors and assets at Time 1 and adolescent aggressive behavior at Time 3 will be mediated by Time 2

parent-adolescent conflict, familism, self-esteem, internalizing problems, substance use, and negative peer associations.

4. Time 2 personal and interpersonal mediators will predict adolescent aggression at Time 3, which was 12 months after baseline and 6 months after Time 2.

METHOD

Data Collection

This study was part of the larger Latino Acculturation and Health Project, a longitudinal investigation of acculturation in Latino families in North Carolina and Arizona (Smokowski & Bacallao, 2006, 2007). In-depth, community-based interviews were conducted with Latino adolescents and their parents. Families were recruited from churches, English as a Second Language programs, and at Latino community events. To increase sampling generalizability, special efforts were made to recruit near equal proportions of Latino families from metropolitan (30%); small town (35%); and rural areas (35%). Two thirds of the interviews were conducted in central North Carolina and the remainder was conducted in areas surrounding Phoenix, Arizona. Potential participants were told the purpose of the study was to help discover how Latino adolescents and their parents adjust to life in the United States. Quantitative interviews were conducted in participants' homes, and lasted approximately two hours for each family. Interviewers worked in pairs, with one interviewer working with the adolescent while the other interviewer worked separately with the parents.

The quantitative interview protocol consisted of well-established psychosocial measures that inquire about cultural involvement, discrimination, familism, parent-adolescent conflict, and a range of adolescent mental health issues (e.g., aggression, depression, anxiety, suicide ideation). Bilingual research staff members translated the measures from English to Spanish and then back-translated the measures to English. Both Spanish and English versions of the interview protocols were available, and interviews were conducted in person using the participants' preferred language. All interviewers were graduate students in social work or public health who were bilingual and had spent time abroad in Central and South America. These students received extensive training in interviewing skills to supplement their substantial field experience. Weekly supervision sessions were held to ensure that the protocol was appropriately administered. All consent forms and interview protocols were read to participants to minimize missing data and to standardize administration across a range of literacy levels. Participants were compensated $20 for their time.

Sample

The sample for this study consisted of 286 Latino adolescents (average age 15 years), of which 66% were born outside of the United States. The majority (52%) of the foreign-born adolescents had emigrated from Mexico. Females comprised 54% of the sample. The average length of time in the United States for the adolescents was 8.49 years ($SD=5.55$).

Measures

Assimilation. Data for the variable *time in the United States* was measured by one item that asked "How long have you lived in the U.S.?" Because the parents sometimes emigrate before their children, we recorded the number reported by the adolescent. Adolescents' answers were verified with responses from parents.

Acculturation stress. This study included three measures of acculturation stress: acculturation conflict, language conflict, and perceived discrimination. These measures are consistent with those used by Vega et al. (1995). Acculturation conflict was measured using four items that asked about the frequency of parent-adolescent conflict around acculturation issues. Questions included "How often have you had problems with your family because you prefer American customs?" and "How often do you feel uncomfortable having to choose between non-Latin and Latin ways of doing things?" Responses were given using a 5-point scale that ranged from 1 (*not at all*) to 5 (*frequently*). Lower scores reflected lower levels of acculturation conflict. Cronbach alpha reliability for this scale was 0.72. Language conflict was measured using two items that asked about academic and social difficulties that were the result of problems with understanding or speaking English. Responses were given using a 5-point Likert scale (e.g., 1, *not at all;* 3, *sometimes;* 5, *frequently*). Higher scores indicated more frequent language conflicts. Cronbach alpha reliability was 0.76. Perceived discrimination was measured using three items. One item asked, "How often do people dislike you because you are Latino?" The other two items asked adolescents about unfair treatment they or their friends had experienced because they were Latino. Responses for all three items were given using a 5-point Likert scale (e.g., 1, *not at all;* 3, *sometimes;* 5, *frequently*). Higher scores indicated greater perceptions of discrimination. Cronbach alpha reliability was 0.75.

Latino cultural involvement. This measure of ethnic activity and identity used the Involvement in Latino Culture subscale of the Bicultural Involvement Questionnaire (BIQ; Szapocznik, Kurtines, & Fernandez, 1980). The subscale consists of 20 items designed to measure cultural preferences related to language, entertainment, food, activities, and celebrations. Responses were given using a 5-point Likert scale with higher scores indicating higher levels of involvement in Latino culture. Cronbach alpha reliability for this scale was 0.86.

Family relationships. The status of family relationships was assessed using measures of familism and parent-adolescent conflict. The familism measure included seven items assessed on a 4-point Likert scale ranging from 1 (*strongly agree*) to 4 (*strongly disagree*); the items were consistent with those used by Gil, Wagner, and Vega (2000). This measure included statements such as, "You share similar values and beliefs as a family" and "You really do trust and confide in each other." High scores indicated high level of familism. The Cronbach alpha reliability for this scale was 0.90. Parent-adolescent conflict was measured using a 15-item scale that was a modified version of the Conflict Behavior Questionnarie-20 (Robin & Foster, 1989). Statements in the scale included, "My parent(s) don't understand me" and "I enjoy spending time with my parent(s)." Respondents indicated whether the statement was true for them. A low score indicated lower levels of parent-child conflict. Cronbach alpha reliability for this scale was 0.89.

Self-esteem. The Rosenberg Self-Esteem Scale (SES; Rosenberg, 1989) was selected to measure adolescents' self-esteem. This study retained 7 of the 10 items in the original SES, which were scored using a 4-point Likert scale ranging from 1 (*strongly agree*) to 4 (*strongly disagree*). The three deleted items were "I wish I could have more respect for myself," "At times, I think I am no good at all," and "I am able to do things as well as most other people." These items were dropped by the research team midway through data collection because they did not have significant factor loadings when factor analyses were conducted, and scale reliability was enhanced when they were deleted. In addition, these items had complicated interpretations when answered by undocumented immigrants, making the scale clearer when they were deleted. Higher scores indicated greater self-esteem. Cronbach alpha reliability for this scale was 0.84.

Internalizing problems. An adolescent's tendency to internalize problems was measured using the Internalizing Problems subscale of the Youth Self-Report (YSR; Achenbach & Rescorla, 2001). The YSR consists of 112 items with 16 subscales that measure a range of mental health problems. Items are scored on a 3-point scale (*not true, somewhat or sometimes true,* and *very true or often true*). The internalizing problems subscale consists of 24 items taken from various subscales (i.e., Affective Problems, Anxiety Problems, Anxious-Depressed Problems, Withdrawn-Depressed Problems, and Somatic Complaints subscales). Higher scores indicated greater tendency to internalize problems. Cronbach alpha reliability for this scale was 0.88.

Peer influence. The influence of negative friend associations was measured using a nine-item scale adapted from the Friend Support and Friend Behavior scales of the School Success Profile (see Bowen, Rose, & Bowen, 2005). Statements from this scale included, "My friends use drugs" and "My friends get in trouble at school," and asked for dichotomous *true/false* responses. Four of the items were recoded so that higher scores were indicative of an adolescent having a greater number of negative friend associations. Cronbach alpha reliability for this scale was 0.70.

The substance use measure consisted of seven items concerning the frequency of the adolescent's substance use. The items mirror those questions asked in the Youth Risk Behavior Surveillance (Centers for Disease Control and Prevention, 2008). Examples of items include "During the past 30 days, on how many days did you have 5 or more drinks of alcohol in a row, that is, within a couple of hours?" "How many times have you smoked cigarettes in the last 30 days," and "How many times have you smoked marijuana in your lifetime?" All items are scored on a 7-point scale with the type of responses being matched to the specific question (i.e., 0=0 days, 1=1 day, 2=2 days, 3=3-5 days, 4=6-9 days, 5=10-19 days, and 6=20 or more days; 0=0 times, 1=1-2 times, 2=3-5 times, 3=6-9 times, 4=10-19 times, 5=20-39 times, and 6=40 or more times). The seven substance use items were summed to provide a substance use scale. Higher scores indicate more frequent and higher amounts of substance use. Cronbach alpha reliability for this scale was 0.79.

Dependent variable. This study also used the YSR (Achenbach & Rescorla, 2001) to measure adolescents' aggressive behavior. The YSR aggression scale consists of 17 items measured using a 3-point Likert scale (*not true, sometimes true, often true*). Items included statements such as, "I argue a lot," "I destroy my own things," and "I get in many fights." Higher scores indicated higher levels of aggressive behavior. Cronbach alpha reliability for the aggressive behavior scale was 0.85 at Time 1 and .86 at Time 3.

Data Analysis

Data collected at three time points were used for this analysis: Time 1 data were baseline data collected at study enrollment, Time 2 data were collected 6 months after study enrollment, and Time 3 data were collected 12 months after baseline data. Using Amos 7.0, we conducted path analysis to test the mediating effects of seven variables (i.e., internalizing problems, self-esteem, parent-adolescent conflict, familism, negative friend associations, baseline aggressive behavior, and substance use) between Time 1 acculturation stress and aggressive behavior measured at Time 3. We selected path analysis over general structural equation modeling given the excessive number of indicator variables that the latter modeling approach requires for inclusion in the measurement model.

We used fit statistics to determine the goodness of fit of the final model to the data. Model chi square, normed chi square, comparative fit index (CFI), and root mean square error of approximation (RMSEA) with a 90% confidence interval (CI) were used. Ideally, the chi-square statistic should not be significant; however, it is widely recognized that this statistic is sensitive to large sample sizes (i.e., greater than 200), and therefore it is not always a reliable indicator of model fit (Kline, 2005). The normed chi-square statistic does not share this sensitivity, and a value less than 5.0 indicates a good model fit. The ideal cut off value for the CFI is 0.90, and the ideal value for the RMSEA is less than 0.06 with the upper limit of the 90% CI under 0.08 (Hu & Bentler, 1999).

In addition, we chose to use the full information maximum likelihood method of estimation for this analysis because this approach uses all available data for parameter estimation and eliminates the need for imputation or deletion of incomplete cases (Enders, 2001). In addition, full information maximum likelihood has been determined as more effective than other estimation approaches when dealing with missing data in structural equation models (Enders & Bandalos, 2001). Following testing of the hypothesized model, all nonsignificant paths were deleted, resulting in the final model. Further analysis was completed to test mediating effects using the Sobel test (Kline, 2005).

RESULTS

Table 1 presents the correlations, scale means, and standard deviations for the study variables. The sample had a mean score of 6.86 (*SD*=5.15) on the YSR aggressive behavior scale, with scores ranging from 0 to 24. Bivariate correlations between the study variables showed no correlations high enough for multicollinearity to be a concern (i.e., greater than .85; Kline, 2005). The variable pairs that showed the strongest correlation were language conflict and perceived discrimination (r = .80, p <.01); self-esteem and parent-adolescent conflict behavior (r = -.67, p < .01); time in the United States and language conflict (r = -.59, p < .01); and parent-adolescent conflict behavior and familism (r = -.57, p < .01). The remaining variables were either moderately correlated or not significantly correlated with one another.

Path Analysis

See Figure 1 for the analytical model. The analytical model displayed a good fit to the data, χ^2 (df = 45, N = 288) = 81.20, p = .001, Normed χ^2 = 1.80, CFI = .96, RMSEA = .053, 90% CI (.034-.071).

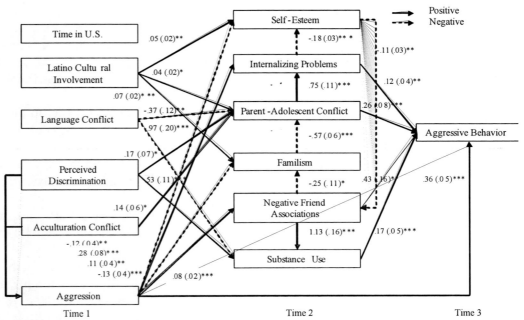

Note: Chi Square = 81.202, 45 df, p =.001; Normed Chi Square=1.804; CFI=.964; RMSEA=.053 (.034-.071)

Figure 1. Final analysis model of pathways from acculturation stress to adolescent aggression.

Direct Effects Unstandardized path estimates and their standard errors for the analytical model are shown in Figure 1. Several of the hypothesized direct paths between the indicators of acculturation stress, family processes, and aggressive behavior at Time 3 were significant. Aggressive behavior at Time 1 had a direct effect on aggressive behavior measured at Time 3. As we had hypothesized, Latino cultural involvement at Time 1 had significant direct effects on Time 2 measurements of self-esteem, parent-adolescent conflict behavior, and familism; however, the effects were small. In addition, as we had predicted, higher levels of parent-child conflict, substance use, and negative friend associations were directly associated with Time 3 measurement of aggressive behavior. One path that was not hypothesized but found to be significant was the path between Time 2 internalizing problems and aggressive behavior at Time 3.

Table 1. Correlations, Means, and Standard Deviations of Study Variables.

	1	2	3	4	5	6	7	8	9	10	11	12	13
1	-												
2	-.18**	-											
3	-.35**	.20**	-										
4	.01	-.26**	.14*	-									
5	-.59**	.21**	.80**	.10	-								
6	.05	-.01	.29**	.19*	.13*	-							
7	-.10	.15*	-.13	-.06	-.06	-.29**	-						
8	.08	-.003	.16*	.11	.07	.33**	-.45**	-					
9	.17**	-.02	.15*	.22**	-.02	.34**	-.67**	.47**	-				
10	-.13*	.23**	-.08	-.18**	-.001	-.25**	.45**	-.31**	-.57**	-			
11	.06	-.12	.10	.10	.10	.29**	-.30**	.24**	.25**	-.24**	-		
12	.20**	-.04	.10	.09	-.08	.26**	-.24**	.24**	.31**	-.18**	.38**	-	
13	.12	-.13	.17*	.16*	.05	.57**	-.30**	.42**	.45**	-.35**	.41**	.42**	-
Mean	8.41	75.16	11.46	7.65	4.54	8.01	23.63	10	2.79	20.3	1.57	2.86	6.86
SD	5.53	11.68	4.38	3.21	2.43	5.32	3.28	6.94	3.62	3.31	1.77	5.21	5.15

$*p < .05, **p < .01, ***p < .001$

1= Time in the U.S.; 2= Latino Cultural Involvement; 3= Perceived Discrimination; 4= Acculturation Conflict; 5= Language Conflict; 6= Aggressive Behavior (Time 1); 7= Self-Esteem; 8= Internalizing Problems; 9= Parent-Adolescent Conflict; 10= Familism; 11= Negative Friend Associations; 12= Substance Use; 13= Aggressive Behavior (Time 3)

Mediation Effects. We examined mediation effects to determine which variables mediated the effects of the acculturation stress indicators on aggressive behavior at Time 3. Table 3 contains information on the full decomposition of effects for the analytical model. Aggressive behavior at Time 1 and substance use both mediated the effect of perceived discrimination on aggressive behavior at Time 3 (aggressive behavior at Time 1: $Z = 3.81$, $p < .001$; substance use: $Z = 2.73$, $p < .01$). Of the total effect of perceived discrimination on aggressive behavior at Time 3, 57% was mediated through aggressive behavior at Time 1 (.12/.21) and 43% was mediated through substance use (.09/.21).

Parent-adolescent conflict and substance use mediated the effect of language conflict on aggressive behavior at Time 3 (parent-adolescent conflict: $Z = -2.22$, $p < .05$; substance use: $Z = -2.76$, $p < .01$). Substance use accounted for 62% of the total effect (-.16/-.26) whereas parent-adolescent conflict accounted for 38% of the total effect (-.10/-.26).

The path from aggressive behavior at Time 1 to aggressive behavior at Time 3 was partially mediated by internalizing problems, parent-adolescent conflict, and negative friend associations (internalizing problems: $Z = 2.28$, $p < .05$; parent-adolescent conflict: $Z = 2.10$, $p < .05$; negative friend associations: $Z = 2.23$, $p < .05$). Each of the mediators accounted for 33% of the indirect effect from aggressive behavior at Time 1 to Time 3.

Finally, aggressive behavior at Time 1 mediated the effect of acculturation conflict on aggressive behavior at Time 3 ($Z = 2.41$, $p < .05$). These findings all supported our hypotheses that substance use, parent-child conflict, and baseline aggressive behavior significantly mediated the associations between indicators of baseline acculturation stress and aggressive behavior at Time 3.

Table 2. Decomposition of Mediation Effects.

Indirect Effect	A	S.E.$_a$	B	S.E.$_b$	ab	S.E.$_{ab}$	Z
Acculturation Conflict → Aggressive Behavior T1 → Aggressive Behavior T3	.26	.10	.36	.05	.10	.04	2.41
Acculturation Conflict → Aggressive Behavior T1 → Negative Friend Associations	.26	.10	.08	.02	.02	.01	2.19
Acculturation Conflict → Aggressive Behavior T1 → Familism	.26	.10	-.13	.04	-.04	.02	-2.07
Acculturation Conflict → Aggressive Behavior T1 → Internalizing Problems	.26	.10	.28	.08	.07	.03	2.11
Acculturation Conflict → Aggressive Behavior T1 → Self-Esteem	.26	.10	-.12	.04	-.03	.02	-2.00
Acculturation Conflict → Parent-Adolescent Conflict → Internalizing Problems	.14	.06	.75	.11	.11	.05	2.27
Perceived Discrimination → Parent-Adolescent Conflict → Internalizing Problems	.17	.07	.75	.11	.13	.06	2.28
Perceived Discrimination → Substance use → Aggressive Behavior T3	.53	.11	.17	.05	.09	.03	2.73
Perceived Discrimination → Aggressive Behavior T1 → Aggressive Behavior T3	.34	.08	.36	.05	.12	.03	3.81
Perceived Discrimination → Aggressive Behavior T1 → Negative Friend Associations	.34	.08	.08	.02	.03	.01	3.09
Perceived Discrimination → Aggressive Behavior T1 → Familism	.34	.08	-.13	.04	-.05	.02	-2.77
Perceived Discrimination → Aggressive Behavior T1 → Parent-Adolescent Conflict	.34	.08	.11	.04	.04	.02	2.50
Perceived Discrimination → Aggressive Behavior T1 → Internalizing Problems	.34	.08	.28	.08	.09	.03	2.86
Perceived Discrimination → Aggressive Behavior T1 → Self-Esteem	.34	.08	-.12	.04	-.04	.02	-2.61
Language Conflict → Parent-Adolescent Conflict → Internalizing Problems	-.37	.12	.75	.11	-.28	.10	-2.73
Language Conflict → Parent-Adolescent Conflict → Aggressive Behavior T3	-.37	.12	.26	.08	-.10	.04	-2.22
Language Conflict → Substance use → Aggressive Behavior T3	-.97	.20	.17	.05	-.16	.06	-2.76
BIQ Latino → Self-esteem → Negative Friend Associations	.05	.02	-.11	.03	-.01	.00	-2.14
BIQ Latino → Parent-Adolescent Conflict → Internalizing Problems	.04	.02	.75	.11	.03	.01	2.21
BIQ Latino → Familism → Parent-Adolescent Conflict	.07	.02	-.57	.06	-.04	.01	-3.59
Self-Esteem → Negative Friend Associations → Aggressive Behavior T3	-.11	.03	.43	.16	-.05	.02	-2.09
Self-Esteem → Negative Friend Associations → Substance use	-.11	.03	1.13	.16	-.12	.04	-2.98

Table 2. (*Continued*)

Indirect Effect	A	S.E.$_a$	B	S.E.$_b$	ab	S.E.$_{ab}$	Z
Familism → Parent-Adolescent Conflict → Internalizing Problems	-.57	.06	.75	.11	-.43	.07	-5.77
Parent-Adolescent Conflict → Internalizing Problems → Self-Esteem	.75	.11	-.18	.03	-.13	.03	-4.79
Parent-Adolescent Conflict → Internalizing Problems → Aggressive Behavior T3	.75	.11	.12	.04	.09	.03	2.70
Familism → Parent-Adolescent Conflict → Aggressive Behavior T3	-.57	.06	.26	.08	-.15	.05	-3.17
Negative Friend Associations → Substance use → Aggressive Behavior T3	1.13	.16	.17	.05	.19	.06	3.05
Negative Friend Associations → Familism → Parent-Adolescent Conflict	-.25	.11	-.57	.06	.14	.07	2.18
Aggressive Behavior T1 → Internalizing Problems → Aggressive Behavior T3	.28	.08	.12	.04	.03	.02	2.28
Aggressive Behavior T1 → Parent-Adolescent Conflict → Aggressive Behavior T3	.11	.04	.24	.08	.03	.01	2.10
Aggressive Behavior T1 → Negative Friend Associations → Aggressive Behavior T3	.08	.02	.43	.16	.03	.02	2.23
Aggressive Behavior T1 → Self-Esteem → Negative Friend Associations	-.12	.04	-.11	.03	.01	.01	2.32
Aggressive Behavior T1 → Internalizing Problems → Self-Esteem	.28	.08	-.18	.03	-.05	.02	-3.02
Aggressive Behavior T1 → Parent-Adolescent Conflict → Internalizing Problems	.11	.04	.75	.11	.08	.03	2.55
Aggressive Behavior T1 → Familism → Parent-Adolescent Conflict	-.13	.04	-.57	.06	.07	.02	3.08
Aggressive Behavior T1 → Negative Friend Associations → Familism	.08	.02	-.25	.11	-.02	.01	-1.98

Notes: Z-values are computed using Sobel's Test for indirect effects. ± 1.96 are the critical values for $p < .05$.
A=path coefficient from initial variable to mediator, B=path coefficient from mediator to final variable, ab=indirect coefficient, S.E.=standard error, S.E.$_{ab}=\sqrt{(b^2 \times \text{S.E.}_a^2) + (a^2 \times \text{S.E.}_b^2)}$. The square root is taken for the entire term. Z=ab/S.E.$_{ab}$.

Multiple Mediation Pathways. Our analysis revealed multiple mediation paths. Although there is no standard statistical test for multiple mediation effects, the accepted practice holds that if every link in the mediation chain is significant, then the entire effect is significant (Kline, 2005); this is the case for the majority of the effects found in this study. Given the numerous multiple mediation effects we found in this study, only a few examples are presented (see Table 2 for additional significant mediation chains). The four most important examples of mediation pathways are given below.

1. Acculturation conflict and perceived discrimination predicted higher aggressive behavior at Time 1 (baseline). Higher aggressive behavior at baseline was positively associated with internalizing problems, parent-adolescent conflict, and negative friend associations, and inversely associated with self-esteem and familism 6 months

later at Time 2. In turn, internalizing problems, parent-adolescent conflict, and negative friend associations predicted high adolescent aggression at Time 3.

2. Acculturation conflict and perceived discrimination were mediated by parent-adolescent conflict, which was connected to internalizing problems, and ultimately to aggression at Time 3.

3. Aggressive behavior at Time 1 predicted negative friend associations that were associated with substance use at Time 2, and which ultimately led to aggressive behavior at Time 3.

4. On a positive note, Latino cultural involvement predicted higher self-esteem that was connected to fewer negative friend associations, less substance use, and less aggressive behavior measured at Time 3.

DISCUSSION

This investigation joins Dinh and colleagues' (2002) investigation as the only longitudinal studies available on acculturation and adolescent aggression. It further contributed to the literature by positing a personal and interpersonal mediation model of adolescent aggressive behavior development that includes individual mental health, family system, peer relationship, and cultural variables. Our analysis delineated multiple paths leading from acculturation stressors to later adolescent aggression.

Acculturation and Aggression

Assimilation versus acculturation stress. Based on available research, we hypothesized that adolescents' time spent in the United States would be positively related to adolescent aggression; however, this hypothesis was not supported. Time spent in the United States displayed no relationship to adolescent aggression or to any of the salient mediators. This finding contradicts the prevailing evidence linking assimilation to adolescent aggression (Gonzales et al., 2002; Smokowski et al., 2009). We interpreted this lack of support for our first hypothesis as an indication that assimilation played little or no role in the development of aggression among the Latino adolescents in our sample. In contrast to the basic premise of assimilation theory (LaFromboise, Coleman, & Gerton, 1993; Rogler et al., 1991), the adolescents in our sample did not appear to increase their levels of aggressive behavior to adjust to norms, values, and behaviors held by the host culture. Instead, our findings strongly suggested that Latino adolescents' aggression was largely a maladaptive coping response to personal and environmental risk factors precipitated by acculturation stress.

Acculturation stressors, such as perceived discrimination, language conflicts, and acculturation conflicts, demonstrated significant direct effects on baseline aggression as well as Time 2 measurements of parent-adolescent conflict and adolescent substance use. This finding supports hypothesis 2 on the cross-sectional link to aggression, as well as previous studies that examined these variables (Smokowski & Bacallao, 2006; Vega, Gil, Warheit, Zimmerman, et al., 1993; Vega, Gil, Warheit, Apospori, & Zimmerman, 1993; Vega et al., 1995). As noted by Smokowski and his colleagues (2009), the majority of prior research studies on adolescent acculturation and aggression have focused on assimilation. However, based on our findings, future investigations would be well served to focus on acculturation stress. Further, it is difficult to fully assess what is actually measured by acculturation markers such as time in the United States, generational status, or language use (Cabassa, 2003; Hunt et al., 2004). The effects for these variables could be easily attributed to acculturation stress rather than to assimilation or acculturation processes. Indeed, the few investigations that have directly compared acculturation stress variables to cultural involvement scales or markers (e.g., time spent in the United States) have clearly shown that acculturation stress variables displayed stronger effects (Smokowski & Bacallao, 2006, 2007). Thus, additional research on acculturation stressors is warranted.

Mediation pathways. Our third and fourth hypotheses were largely supported. We found the effects of acculturation stressors and cultural assets were mediated from Time 1 to Time 2 measurements by parent-adolescent conflict, familism, self-esteem, internalizing problems, substance use, and negative peer associations. Ecological mediators at Time 2, in turn, predicted adolescent aggression 6 months later at Time 3. Our structural equation model showed that acculturation stressors had a cross-sectional relationship that predicted baseline aggression, supporting hypothesis two. Baseline aggression had a wide-ranging impact on Time 2 measurements of self-esteem, internalizing problems, parent-adolescent conflict, familism, and negative friend associations. Finally, internalizing problems, parent-adolescent conflict, negative peer associations, and substance use served as gateways that linked acculturation stressors to Time 3 adolescent aggression.

This path model is significantly more complex than models presented in past research; however, it is not unprecedented. In the only other longitudinal study available, Dinh and colleagues (2002) reported that in a sample of 220 Latino adolescents the effect of Time 1 acculturation on Time 2 proneness to problem behavior was mediated by Time 1 parental investment. Similarly, Gonzales et al. (2006) showed that in a sample of 175 Latino families, family conflict mediated the cross-sectional relationship between family linguistic acculturation and adolescent conduct problems. Further, a third study demonstrated that parent-adolescent conflict and familism mediated the effects of acculturation conflicts and perceived discrimination on adolescent aggression (Smokowski & Bacallao, 2007). Finally, in the ecological model closest to our model, Samaniego and Gonzales (1999) showed that negative peer interaction (defined as *hassles*); family conflict; inconsistent discipline; and parental monitoring mediated the cross-sectional effect of adolescents' acculturation status on delinquency. Our key mediators, especially parent-adolescent conflict and negative friend associations, were reminiscent of the mediators in the Samaniego and Gonzales study. However, we enlarged the set of personal and interpersonal mediators by including variables for adolescent mental health and risk-taking (e.g., internalizing problems and substance use) as alternative mediators and by testing longitudinal relationships.

The mediation pathways showed that acculturation stress led to several personal and interpersonal risk factors. Stress researchers may turn to theories of maladaptive coping to explain the pathway that runs from acculturation stressors to mediation risk factors to aggressive behavior. According to various research studies conducted by Vega and colleagues, individuals who experienced high levels of acculturation stress often exhibited low self-esteem, increased acculturation conflicts, and were typically cut-off from the benefits of their culture-of-origin (Vega, Gil, Warheit, Zimmerman, et al., 1993; Vega, Gil, Warheit,

Aspospori, et al.,1993; Vega et al., 1995). In addition, individuals who have experienced high acculturation stress often lack the resources and skills to successfully navigate within their environment and, consequently experience greater difficulties with negative stereotypes and perceived discrimination (Rogler et al., 1991). In reacting to acculturation stress, Latino adolescents might perceive a need to defend themselves physically or to affiliate with gangs for safety (Bacallao & Smokowski, in press). These youth often vent their frustrations in arguments with their parents, become depressed, or turn to substance use for escape. All of these maladaptive coping strategies can heighten the risk for subsequent aggressive behavior.

We also identified mediation chains of cultural assets that functioned to decrease the chances of adolescent aggression. Latino cultural involvement, an important aspect of ethnic identity (Phinney, 1989), was positively associated with adolescent self-esteem and familism. In one asset path, Latino cultural involvement was associated with higher familism, and higher familism was related to lower parent-adolescent conflict. In turn, the result of decreased parent-adolescent conflict was less adolescent aggression. In an alternate route, Latino cultural involvement predicted higher self-esteem that was related to having fewer negative friend associations, which ultimately led to lower adolescent aggression.

The positive paths associated with Latino cultural involvement have been established in past research. Researchers have consistently found a positive relationship between Latino cultural involvement (i.e., ethnic identity) and self-esteem (Gonzales et al., 2002; Martinez & Dukes, 1997). One investigation with 669 Latino, African American, and White U.S.-born high school students identified ethnic identity as a cultural asset that predicted increased self-esteem for all three ethnic groups (Phinney, Cantu, & Kurtz, 1997). The asset paths in our mediation model extend this research and show how Latino cultural involvement can combine with other promotive factors to decrease the probability of adolescent aggression.

Implications for Practice

The mediation pathways in our model provide rich implications for prevention programming. Decreasing adolescent acculturation stress is an appropriate target for prevention program development because such efforts have the potential to lower key factors associated with adolescent aggression including parent-adolescent conflict, the likelihood of internalizing problems, negative friend associations, and incidence of adolescent substance use. Multifaceted programs that attend to adolescent mental health, coping skills for stress reduction, family dynamics, and peer relationships are particularly warranted (Bacallao & Smokowski, 2005; Coatsworth, Pantin, & Szapocznik, 2002).

Limitations

Our analyses were based on a nonrandom, community-based sample of Latino families living in either North Carolina or Arizona; therefore, caution is warranted in generalizing results to Latino communities outside of these areas. Although our structural equation model was theoretically sound, rooted in past research, and satisfactorily validated by a number of indicators of fit to the data, it is important to note that a large number of alternate models can be generated. No structural equation model can be accepted with absolute certainty without replication.

CONCLUSION

Adolescent mental health, family environment, and friendships with peers were delineated as mediators that linked acculturation stress to adolescent aggression. Acculturation stressors, especially perceived discrimination and acculturation conflicts, were associated with baseline aggression, Time 2 parent-adolescent conflict, and Time 2 adolescent substance use. Using data collected at three time points, mediation pathways were traced through internalizing problems, parent-adolescent conflict, negative friend associations, and adolescent substance use to aggressive behavior. Latino cultural involvement was a cultural asset positively connected to familism and self-esteem that ultimately led to lower levels of adolescent aggression.

REFERENCES

Achenbach, T. M. & Rescorla, L. A. (2001). *Manual for ASEBA school-age forms and profiles.* Burlington: University of Vermont, Research Center for Children, Youth, & Families.

Bacallao, M. L. & Smokowski, P. R. (2005). *Entre dos mundos* (between two worlds) Bicultural skills training and Latino immigrant families. *Journal of Primary Prevention. 26*, 485-509.

Bacallao, M. L. & Smokowski, P. R. (in press). Obstacles to getting ahead: How assimilation mechanisms impact Mexican immigrant families. Social Work in Public Health.

Bámaca, M. Y. & Umaña-Taylor, A. J. (2006). Testing a model of resistance to peer pressure among Mexican-origin adolescents. *Journal of Youth and Adolescence, 35,* 631-645.

Berry, J. W. (1998). Acculturation stress. In P. Balls Organista, K. M. Chun, & G. Marin. (Eds.), *Readings in ethnic psychology* (117-122). New York, NY: Routledge.

Berry, J. W. (2006). Stress perspectives on acculturation. In D. L. Sam, & J. W. Berry (Eds.) *The Cambridge handbook of acculturation psychology* (43-57). New York, NY: Cambridge University Press.

Bird, H. R., Canino, G. J., Davies, M., Duarte, C. S., Febo, V., Ramirez, R. & Loeber, R. (2006). A study of disruptive behavior disorders in Puerto Rican youth: I. Background, design, and survey methods. *Journal of the American Academy of Child and Adolescent Psychiatry, 45*, 1032-1041.

Bird, H. R., Davies, M. & Duarte, C. S. (2006). A study of disruptive behavior disorders in Puerto Rican youth: II. Baseline prevalence, comorbidity, and correlates in two sites. *Journal of the American Academy of Child & Adolescent Psychiatry, 45*, 1042-1053

Bowen, G., Rose, R. & Bowen, N. (2005). *The reliability and validity of the School Success Profile.* Philadelphia, PA: Xlibris.

Brook, J. S., Whiteman, M., Balka, E. B., Win, T. & Gursen, M. D. (1998). African American and Puerto Rican drug use: A longitudinal study. *Journal of the American Academy of Child and Adolescent Psychiatry, 36*, 1260-1268.

Bui, H. & Thongniramol, O. (2005). Immigration and self-reported delinquency: The interplay of immigration, generations, gender, race, and ethnicity. *Journal of Crime and Justice, 28(2)*, 71-80.

Buriel, R., Calzada, S. & Vasquez, R. (1982). The relationship of traditional Mexican American culture to adjustment and delinquency among three generations of Mexican American male adolescents. *Hispanic Journal of Behavioral Sciences, 4*, 41-55.

Cabassa, L. (2003). Measuring acculturation: Where we are and where we need to go. *Hispanic Journal of Behavioral Sciences, 25,* 127-146.

Carvajal, S. C., Hanson, C. E., Romero, A. J. & Coyle, K. K. (2002). Behavioural risk factors and protective factors in adolescents: A comparison of Latino and non-Latino Whites. *Ethnicity & Health, 7(3)*, 181-193.

Carvajal, S. C., Photiades, J. R., Evans, R. I. & Nash, S. G. (1997). Relating a social influence model to the role of acculturation in substance use among Latino adolescents. *Journal of Applied Social Psychology, 27,* 1617-1628.

Centers for Disease Control and Prevention. (2008). *Youth Risk Behavior Surveillance— United States, 2007, Surveillance Summaries*, MMWR 2008; 57(SS-4). Retrieved August 31, 2009, from http://www.cdc.gov/HealthyYouth/yrbs/pdf/yrbss07_mmwr.pdf

Coatsworth, J. D., Pantin, H. & Szapocznik, J. (2002). Familias Unidas: A family-centered ecodevelopmental intervention to reduce risk for problem behavior among Hispanic adolescents. *Clinical Child & Family Psychology Review, 5*, 113-132.

De La Rosa, M. (2002). Acculturation and Latino adolescents' substance use: A research agenda for the future. *Substance Use & Misuse, 37,* 429-456.

Dinh, K. T., Roosa, M. W., Tein, J. Y. & Lopez, V. A. (2002). The relationship between acculturation and problem behavior proneness in a Hispanic youth sample: A longitudinal mediation model. *Journal of Abnormal Child Psychology, 30*, 295-309.

Eamon, M. K. & Mulder, C. (2005). Predicting antisocial behavior among Latino young adolescents: An ecological systems analysis. *American Journal of Orthopsychiatry, 75,* 117-127.

Enders, C. K. (2001). A primer on maximum likelihood algorithms available for use with missing data. *Structural Equation Modeling, 8,* 128-141.

Enders, C. K. & Bandalos, D. L. (2001). The relative performance of full information maximum likelihood estimation for missing data in structural equation models. *Structural Equation Modeling, 8,* 430-457.

Frauenglass, S., Routh, D. K., Pantin, H. M. & Mason, C. A. (1997). Family support decreases influence of deviant peers on Hispanic adolescents' substance use. *Journal of Clinical Child Psychology, 26,* 15-23.

Gil, A. G., Vega, W. A. & Dimas, J. M. (1994). Acculturative stress and personal adjustment among Hispanic adolescent boys. *Journal of Community Psychology, 22*, 43-54.

Gil, A. G., Wagner, E. F. & Vega, W. A. (2000). Acculturation, familism, and alcohol use among Latino adolescent males: Longitudinal relations. *Journal of Community Psychology, 28,* 443-458.

Gonzales, N. A., Deardorff, J., Formoso, D., Barr, A. & Barrera, M. (2006). Family mediators of the relation between acculturation and adolescent mental health. *Family Relations, 55*, 318-330.

Gonzales, N. A., Knight, G. P., Morgan-Lopez, A., Saenz, D. & Sirolli, A. (2002). Acculturation and the mental health of Latino youths: An integration and critique of the literature. In J. M. Contreras, K. A. Kerns, & A. M. Neal-Barnett (Eds.), *Latino children and families in the United States.* Westport, CT: Greenwood.

Helstrom, A., Bryan, A., Hutchison, K. E., Riggs, P. D. & Blechman, E. A. (2004). Tobacco and alcohol use as an explanation for the association between externalizing behavior and illicit drug use among delinquent adolescents. *Prevention Science, 5,* 267-277.

Hovey, J. D. & King, C. A. (1996). Acculturative stress, depression, and suicidal ideation among immigrant and second-generation Latino adolescents. *Journal of the American Academy of Child and Adolescent Psychiatry, 35,* 1183-1192.

Hu, L. T. & Bentler, P. M. (1999). Cutoff criteria for fit indexes in covariance structure analysis: Conventional criteria versus new alternatives, *Structural Equation Modeling, 6,* 1-55.

Hunt, L. M., Schneider, S. & Comer, B. (2004). Should "acculturation" be a variable in health research? A critical review of research on US Hispanics. *Social Science & Medicine, 59,* 973-986.

Katragadda, C. P. & Tidwell, R. (1998). Rural Hispanic adolescents at risk for depressive symptoms. *Journal of Applied Social Psychology, 28,* 1916-1930.

King, S. M., Iacono, W. G. & McGue, M. (2004). Childhood externalizing and internalizing psychopathology in the prediction of early substance use. *Addiction, 99,* 1548-1559.

Kline, R. B. (2005). Principles and practice of structural equation modeling (2nd ed.). New York, NY: Guilford Press.

LaFromboise, T., Coleman, H. L. & Gerton, J. (1993). Psychological impact of biculturalism: Evidence and theory. *Psychological Bulletin, 114,* 395-412.

Martinez, C. R. (2006). Effects of differential family acculturation on Latino adolescent substance use. *Family Relations, 55,* 306-317.

Martinez, R. O. & Dukes, R. L. (1997). The effects of ethnic identity, ethnicity, and gender on adolescent well-being. *Journal of Youth and Adolescence, 26,* 503-516.

Phinney, J. (1989). Stages of ethnic identity development in minority group adolescents. *Journal of Early Adolescence. 9,* 34-49.

Phinney, J. S., Cantu, C. L. & Kurtz, D. A. (1997). Ethnic and American identity as predictors of self-esteem among African-American, Latino, and White adolescents. *Journal of Youth and Adolescence, 26,* 165-185.

Prinstein, M. J. & Wang, S. S. (2005). False consensus and adolescent peer contagion: Examining discrepancies between perceptions and actual reported levels of friends' deviant and health risk behaviors. *Journal of Abnormal Child Psychology, 33,* 293-306.

Redfield, R., Linton, R. & Herskovits, M. (1936). Memorandum for the study of acculturation. *American Anthropologist, 38,* 149-152.

Robin, A. L. & Foster, S. L. (1989). *Negotiating parent-adolescent conflict: A behavioral-family systems approach.* New York, NY: Guilford Press.

Rogler, L. H., Cortes, R. S. & Malgady, R. G. (1991). Acculturation and mental health status among Hispanics. *American Psychologist, 46,* 585-597.

Rosenberg, M. (1989). *Society and the adolescent self-image. Revised edition.* Middletown, CT: Wesleyan University Press.

Rumbaut, R. G. (1995). The new Californians: Comparative research findings on the educational progress of immigrant children. In R.G. Rumbaut, & W. A. Cornelius (Eds.), *California's immigrant children: Theory, research, and implications for educational policy* (17-69). San Diego, CA: Center for U.S.-Mexican Studies.

Romero, A. J. & Roberts, R. E. (2003). Stress within a bicultural context for adolescents of Mexican descent. *Cultural Diversity & Ethnic Minority Psychology, 9,* 171-184.

Samaniego, R. Y. & Gonzales, N. A. (1999). Multiple mediators of the effects of acculturation status on delinquency for Mexican American adolescents. *American Journal of Community Psychology, 27,* 189-210.

Schwartz, S. J., Zamboanga, B. L. & Hernandez Jarvis, L. (2007). Ethnic identity and acculturation in Hispanic early adolescents: Mediating relationship to academic grades, prosocial behaviors, and externalizing symptoms. *Cultural Diversity and Ethnic Minority Psychology, 13,* 364-373.

Smokowski, P. R. & Bacallao, M. L. (2006). Acculturation and aggression in Latino adolescents: A structural model focusing on cultural risk factors and assets. *Journal of Abnormal Child Psychology, 34,* 657-671.

Smokowski, P. R. & Bacallao, M. L. (2007). Acculturation, internalizing mental health symptoms, and self-esteem: Cultural experiences of Latino adolescents in North Carolina. *Child Psychiatry and Human Development, 37,* 273-292.

Smokowski, P. R., David- Ferdon, C. & Stroupe, N. (2009). Acculturation, youth violence, and suicidal behavior in minority adolescents: A review of the empirical literature. *Journal of Primary Prevention.* 30(3/4), 215-264.

Sommers, I., Fagan, J. & Baskin, D. (1993). Sociocultural influences on the explanation of delinquency for Puerto Rican youths. *Hispanic Journal of Behavioral Sciences, 15,* 36-62.

Szapocznik, J., Kurtines, W. & Fernandez, T. (1980). Biculturalism involvement and adjustment in Hispanic-American youths. *International Journal of Intercultural Relations, 4,* 353-365.

Taylor, D. L., Biafora, F. A., Warheit, G. & Gil, A. (1997). Family factors, theft, vandalism, and major deviance among a multiracial/multiethnic sample of adolescent girls. *Journal of Social Distress and the Homeless, 6,* 71-97.

Vega, W. A., Gil, A. G., Warheit, G., Apospori, E. & Zimmerman, R. (1993). The relationship of drug use to suicide ideation and attempts among African American, Hispanic, and White non-Hispanic male adolescents. *Suicide and Life Threatening Behavior, 23,* 110-119.

Vega, W. A., Gil, A. G., Warheit, G., Zimmerman, R. & Apospori, E. (1993). Acculturation and delinquent behavior among Cuban American adolescents: Toward an empirical model. *American Journal of Community Psychology, 21,* 113-125.

Vega, W. A., Khoury, E., Zimmerman, R., Gil, A. G. & Warheit, G. (1995). Cultural conflicts and problem behaviors of Latino adolescents in home and school environments. *Journal of Community Psychology, 23,* 167-179.

In: Youth Violence and Juvenile Justice: Causes, Intervention...   ISBN: 978-1-61668-011-4
Editor: Neil A. Ramsay et al., pp. 251-267   © 2010 Nova Science Publishers, Inc.

Chapter 10

CHILD-REARING PRACTICES AND DELINQUENCY IN CHILDREN AND ADOLESCENTS

Stavros P. Kiriakidis[1]

University of Macedonia, Department of Social & Educational Policy, Greece

ABSTRACT

The present paper is an overview of studies examining the way family influences the development of delinquency in adolescents. The review focused on published papers dealing with the association of adolescent delinquency and their families. The association between family practices and juvenile delinquency, with potent predictive value is established and bidirectional effects exist. However the influence from parents to adolescents is stronger. In addition indirect evidence, from early intervention studies, supports the causal role of family variables in the development of juvenile delinquency. Effective family functioning, in spite of several social adversities, exerts a buffering influence on children, thus protecting them from delinquent behavioural manifestations. Finally, the assumption that genetic influences are responsible for both poor child-rearing practices by the parents and juvenile delinquency is not well supported by the literature, suggesting that effective parenting exerts an independent influence in the socioemotional functioning of children and adolescents. The evidence suggests that effective child rearing practices is a necessary though not sufficient factor for the psychosocial development of children and adolescents. Educational programmes, of a preventive nature, could be promising in reducing levels of delinquency. The important role of family functioning in protecting children and adolescents from antisocial behaviours is evident from many studies internationally. The protective role of parenting is generally supported. The role of a supportive family environment could be suggested as a protective factor for juvenile delinquency.

Keywords: Family; Child-Rearing Practices; Delinquency; Adolescence.

---

[1] Corresponding author: 173 42, Ag. Dimitrios, Greece, (E-mail: skyriak@syros.aegean.gr , kiriaks@yahoo.gr). TEL/FAX: 0030-2109828455.

INTRODUCTION

Neglect in the family has been considered a risk factor for multiple problematic outcomes in adolescence. Parenting has been consistently found to be related and predictive of juvenile delinquency; thus, it is considered a general risk factor for juvenile delinquency and general socio-emotional functioning (Loeber & Farrington, 1998; Pedersen, 1994). Research has followed a variable-oriented strategy, and family functioning has been viewed as a single attribute responsible for many adverse outcomes, including delinquency and substance abuse among others, following the principle of multifinality (Thornberry, Ireland, & Smith, 2001). On the other hand, regarding adolescent delinquency, it has been proposed (Rutter, 1994; Rutter et al., 1997; Rutter, Giller, & Hagell, 1998) that the causes of antisocial and offending behaviour are not easily captured under one causal factor –rather, many factors are operating in adolescents' and young adults' offending behaviour, consistent with the principle of equifinality (Thornberry et al., 2001). A combination of various risk factors with either additive or interactional effects has been proposed (Farrington, 1995).

LONGITUDINAL STUDIES PREDICTING JUVENILE DELINQUENCY FROM CHILD-REARING PRACTICES

McCord (1979), reviewed files of 201 boys, participating in a treatment program of delinquency prevention between 1939 and 1945, who were reared by their natural mothers. The files contained information about their home environment and compared them with court reports thirty years later to obtain an index of offending. This methodological procedure had the advantage that "measures of home atmosphere were uncontaminated by retrospective biases and measures of subsequent behavior were uncontaminated by knowledge of home background" (McCord, 1979). These two sources of data were independent, not coded by the same individuals and they were oblivious of the other source of data. Results from the study indicated that more than a third of the variance in both number of convictions for property offenses and offenses against persons could be predicted from six variables reflecting the child's home environment.

In addition, the most potent predictors were related to child-rearing namely supervision, maternal affect and parental conflict. Furthermore, 75% of the sample could be classified as ever criminal or non-criminal, as youngsters, while a higher 80% could be classified as criminal or non-criminal as adults, that is, after the age of 18, better than chance. The results are limited to the population from which the sample was selected. However they provide support for the possible detrimental effects of poor parenting on the development of juvenile and adult delinquency. Additionally clearly identify home environment, and more specifically, parental child-rearing practices, as potent predictors of juvenile and adult criminality.

Farrington (1995), identified poor parental child-rearing behavior as among the most important independent predictors of juvenile delinquency, based on the results from the Cambridge Study In Delinquent Development, "...a prospective longitudinal survey of the development of delinquency and antisocial behavior in 411 South London boys". A main focus of this study was on "continuity or discontinuity in behavioral development, on the effects of life events on development, and on predicting future behavior" (Farrington, 1995: 930). He noted that strict, controlling discipline, lack of supervision, intermarital conflict and separation from parents constituted the basic elements featuring family functioning that had the most detrimental effects on juvenile male development and the development of delinquent behavior. Farrington (1995), further argued that juvenile delinquents differed significantly from unconvicted juveniles (the measurement of delinquency based either on official convictions or self-reported delinquency, both of which provided similar results), at age eight to ten before anyone in the sample was convicted. On several aspects of their familiar environment, "They tended to be receiving poor parental child-rearing behavior, characterised by harsh or erratic parental discipline, cruel, passive, or neglecting parental attitude, and parental conflict. The parents tended to supervise them poorly, being lax in enforcing rules or under-vigilant" (p. 939). Furthermore, potential juvenile delinquents were more likely to have experienced separation from their parents and their parents tended to have authoritarian child-rearing attitudes.

Moreover, at age 14, those boys who later became delinquents, showed the same pattern of characteristics with regard to their family environment as at age eight to ten, suggesting a continuity of those family characteristics that are related to delinquent behavior over time, and their pervasive influence on child and adolescent psychosocial development. Although the predictive efficiency of poor parenting behaviour, independently of other predictors, was established, it was not possible, as Farrington (1995) argued, to distinguish the possible influence that genetic factors might have played. The study did not include a behavior genetic design, examining twin brothers and/or adopted children. If this was done they could have partialled out the influence of biologiacal factors and the environment on delinquent behavor. Thus genetic influences could account for both poor parenting and juvenile delinquent behavior.

Henry, Moffitt, Robbins, Earls and Silva (1993), in a prospective longitudinal study, attempted to examine the predictive utility of family related variables with children and adolescent antisocial behavior. This was measured from different sources of information, self-reported, official and parents', teachers' and peer ratings. Certain aspects of family functioning were related to general psychosocial child and adolescent functioning, being associated with both externalizing (delinquent behavior) and internalizing (anxiety/ depression/ withdrawal symptoms). The study supported the suggestion that dimensions of the relationship between parents and children could be regarded as general nonspecific risk factors for the psychosocial development of children and adolescents. The study also compared adolescents who showed delinquent behavior and those with other disorders, mainly internalizing symptoms, in an attempt to identify those familial variables that are exclusively related and predictive of different and distinct psychosocial problems in adolescence, with the aim to identify factors possibly uniquely and causally related to delinquency as opposed and compared to internalized psychosocial problems. The results revealed that the two most important predictors of antisocial behavior at age 11, measured by times of police contact, was parental disagreement on discipline when the child was five years old and the number of parent changes experienced in childhood. Cumulative summation of the number of parent changes to age 13 was the most important predictor of the number of police contacts by that age, suggesting a possible causal role of family stability in early adolescent delinquent behavior. Although the percentage of variance explained was quite modest, it provided evidence for unique predictors of antisocial behavior in late childhood and early adolescence.

As Henry et al (1993) noted, several other characteristics could also have been measured, for example, paternal characteristics and family criminality, which could account for higher percentage of variance in delinquent behavior. Moreover, delinquent behavior could have been operationalised as a continuous variable. If this was done, a higher proportion of the variance could have been accounted for by the predictor variables. Yet the approach of group membership provided more confidence in identifying unique correlates and predictors of delinquent behavior, especially stable and pervasive antisocial behavior. It is worth noting that the socio-economic status of the family and pre-school behavior problems, were controlled. This was done, to statistically partial out the possibility that social adversities and early temperamentally difficult children could tax the skills and patience of parents and influence the stability and the quality of the parent-child relationship. Thus, it was possible to assess the relative contribution of other aspects of the family life in the prediction of adolescent delinquency. The two aforementioned variables were identified as possible confounding variables of other correlates of adolescent delinquency. The procedure followed permitted, statistically and to a certain degree, to estimate the relative contribution of variables of a more dynamic psychological nature, as opposed to static social class and biological determinants.

Kolvin, Miller, Fleeting and Kolvin (1988), report similar results from the analysis of the data of the Newcastle Thousand Family Study. The study was a birth cohort longitudinal study of one thousand one hundrend and forty two infants, boys and girls. The aim of the sudy was to investigate the relative contribution of several indices of deprivation in the prediction of delinquency, and the possible transmission of deprivation and delinquency across generations. There were included indices reflecting social deprivation, and ratings about marital instability, poor physical care of the children and poor mothering ability. It was found that poor physical care of the child and the home by the mother emerged as the most significant factor associated with general delinquent behavior. It was also consistently related with different types of delinquent behavior such as violent offenses, theft, fraud, criminal damage, drinking and motor offenses. Additionally, male offenders tended to have parents who were rated as ineffective in their parental role and more aggressive fathers. They concluded that although the operative mechanisms linking deprivation to delinquency are not clear, "taken together, the findings again emphasize the importance of poor supervision, direction, and guidance of children in the genesis of delinquency" (p. 89).

In support for the role of poor child-rearing practices in the prediction of juvenile delinquency comes from a review of the most potent predictors of male delinquency, by Loeber and Dishion (1983). According to the evaluation of several studies measuring parental skills and child-rearing practices to predict future delinquent behavior, parental family management techniques emerged among the most potent ones in predicting male adolescence delinquent behavior. The authors stressed the importance of family related variables both for prediction purposes and preventive actions against the development of delinquency, as family dysfunction can be measured early in the life of children and proper intervention applied. Furthermore, the research showed that children and adolescents from families employing poor family management techniques accounted for approximately half of the offences committed, although they represented a small proportion of the children (approximately 11% to 16%). This finding revealed that offending was gathered within families. The authors suggested that some families were more at risk of delinquency than others, and child-rearing practices could be responsible for that discrimination. A similar pattern emerged from the Cambridge Study In Delinquent Development, where "five percent of the families accounted for half of all the convictions of all family members" (Farrington, 1995: 939), providing extra support for the assertion that environmental factors, expressed by family environment, might be encouraging juvenile delinquency.

In terms of prediction and according to many longitudinal studies (Farrington, 1995; Henry et al, 1993; McCord, 1979), child-rearing practices, operationalised in different ways, consistently predict antisocial behavior and contacts with the law during adolescence. The measurement of child-rearing practices was made at a time when the children were at a young age and prior to any manifestation of antisocial behavior by the children it seems likely that parental management is a probable antecedent of juvenile delinquency and antisocial behaviour.

INTERVENTION STUDIES SUGGESTING A CAUSAL ROLE OF CHILD-REARING PRACTICES IN ANTISOCIAL BEHAVIOUR

Larzelere and Patterson (1990) and Patterson (1986) reported that interventions aimed at parental education and training to deal with delinquent and antisocial behavioral manifestations in children and adolescents, resulted in reductions in the antisocial conduct of the adolescents. Patterson and Reid (1973), replicating an earlier study of parental education on monitoring and effective use of behavioral principles for reducing antisocial behavioral manifestation of their children, reported that nine out of eleven families showed "reductions of greater than 30 per cent (targeted deviant behaviour) from baseline" (Patterson & Reid, 1973: 390). Although the results of the study aimed at changing different kinds of antisocial behavior in general and aggression in particular, they, however, provide support for the proposition that parental management is determining, to a high degree, the antisocial and aggressive behavior of children. Additional indirect evidence of the causal status of parenting in the development and maintenance of antisocial behavior across the life span comes from early intervention programs targeting those risk factors that have been consistently associated and predictive of antisocial conduct.

Yoshikawa (1994) reviewed the programs that had been designed to provide early family support and education to children and their families who were under the influence of risk criminogenic factors. The interventions were intensive during the children's first five years and were designed with a clear research orientation and assessment of progress in view. They included control groups and random assignment to intervention with extensive follow-ups that enabled the researchers to assess possible "sleeper" effects and stability of gains over time. The studies actually postulated two pathways in the development of resiliency against delinquency, one through the effects of cognitive development and school achievement and the other through the enhancement of parenting for buffering socio-emotional dysfunction. The interventions were designed to facilitate the general development of children and functioning of the families.

Yoshikawa (1994), had noticed sustained improvements in the socio-emotional functioning of the children, which included school attainment, reduction in delinquency and antisocial behavior and less chronic delinquency rates in comparison to the controls. Although these results are helpful in estimating the efficiency of early intervention programs, the evidence for the effects of parenting in the general socio-emotional functioning in children, including delinquency, over time can only be inferred indirectly, as the components of the programs targeted many risk factors. However, mainly family support and children education (Danos, 2003; Kavoura, 2001) with those targeting both achieving better results than those that targeted either of them, may be mainly due to their cumulative or interaction effects. Despite the difficulty inherent in the studies, to assess the relative contribution of improved parenting on the delinquent behavior of the children, it seems that effective parenting is a necessary, while not sufficient, factor for the normal development of children and the inhibition of antisocial behavior and delinquency in childhood and adolescence.

Reciprocal Parent-Child Effects in the Development of Antisocial Behaviour

Although the association between parental rejection and persistent juvenile offending seems supported, it is not evident that parental rejection causes delinquency and persistent offending. It is equally plausible to assume that delinquency induces parental rejection or there is a bi-directional relationship (Borduin and Schaeffer, 1998). Liska and Reed (1985) examined the reciprocal effects of ties to conventional institutions and juvenile delinquency, and the results from family studies, measuring parental attachment, supported the idea that low attachment precedes delinquency. They noted that parental attachment is implied by many theories of juvenile delinquency as a causal antecedent of delinquency, although they may disagree on the underlying processes that account for the association. By examining two main institutions that have been consistently associated with juvenile delinquency, family and school, they hypothesized that the effects might be reciprocal. Lower family and school attachment to influence juvenile delinquency and delinquent behavior had an effect on family and school ties by inducing reprimanding and rejecting behavioral responses by parents, teachers and classmates. They reanalyzed the data from the Youth in Transition study (Bachman, 1975 cited in Liska and Reed, 1985) a four-wave, multistage, national probability sample of 1,886 boys to test their hypotheses.

Liska and Reed (1985) concluded "most of the observed negative relationship between parental attachment and delinquency comes about because of the effect of parental attachment on delinquency" (p. 557). In general it was supported that parental rejection has a direct effect on adolescent delinquent behavior and that the relationship between the two was bi-directional is what?. In addition a variability of intervening processes for that relationship has been proposed.

Similar results are reported by Simons, Robertson and Downs (1989). In a two wave panel data of adolescents aged between 13 and 17 years it was found that the path coefficient for the effect of parental rejection on delinquency was significant, whereas the reciprocal path, that is, from delinquent behavior to parental rejection, was not. The results suggest that parental rejection has a possible causal effect on adolescent delinquency and that reciprocal effects are not probable, noting the importance of the quality of the parent - child relationship in the development of antisocial behavior in the adolescent. Evidence, however, for reciprocal, transactional effects between children and parents, for the development and expression of conduct disorder in children and adolescents, has been reviewed by Lytton (1990). Despite the evidence reviewed, it was recognized that family factors, and especially maternal affection, could act as a buffering factor for the expression of conduct disorder.

Rutter et al (1998), in evaluating research about parents-children effects in the relation of coercion and hostility with antisocial behavior, reported that, although children effects on the behavior of their parents exist and the relationship seems to be bi-directional, this cannot be the principal explanation. Family circumstances have been shown to be predictive of adolescent criminality even from the preschool years. The authors concluded that a reciprocal dynamic process can be suggested which is more evident in younger children than adolescents and that the relative strength of each part of the bi-directional relationship remains to be established.

PATTERSON'S COERCION MODEL OF RECIPROCAL PARENT-CHILD EFFECTS IN THE DEVELOPMENT OF ANTISOCIAL BEHAVIOUR

The recognition of reciprocal parent-child effects in the development of antisocial behavior in children and adolescents has been incorporated in performance models advanced by Patterson (1986) and ; Patterson, Dishion and Bank, (1984) for antisocial boys. The first of the models deals with the learning of antisocial behavior in the home, within a social-interactional perspective. "The assumption central to the general model is failure by parents to effectively punish garden variety, coercive behaviors sets into motion interaction sequences that are the basis for training in aggression. The process set into motion involves family members in patterned exchanges of aversive behaviors; the exchanges are such that both members train each other to become increasingly aversive. This process is labeled *coercion.*" (Patterson, 1986: 436). The central and important parental determinant of aggressive patterns in the boys is suggested as being ineffective discipline by parents. Analysis of interaction sequences at the micro social level within the family of antisocial children, revealed that parents respond to disciplinary confrontations with verbal aggressive responses. Some of these include, threats, nagging and lecturing, while they fail to follow their verbal warnings with concrete punishment, in terms of withdrawal of privileges, time out, etc. On the contrary, infrequent, sudden explosions from parents with physical punishment were often observed.

In general, Patterson (1986) and Patterson, Dishion and Bank (1984) suggested that a vicious cycle of coercive exchanges within the family provide a training of coercive patterns to both children and parents. These patterns can potentially escalate to aggressive behavior and generalize to other settings where children function, such as, school and peer groups. Thus coercive patterns substitute for social skills in every day social exchanges.The consequences from the coercive behavioral pattern of the children in these settings, include rejection by peers, low academic attainment and low self-esteem. Furthermore, Patterson (1986) suggested that this process would be more detrimental for children when a combination of poor parental skills and difficult temperament of the child is evident. The presence of other stressors such as substance abuse is expected to exert a negative influence on parenting, thus initiating, maintaining and escalating the coercive exchanges of parents and children within the family. Within the coercion theory the reciprocal effects of parent-child bi-directional relationship have been most accurately described and incorporated into a model of development of antisocial behavior in children and adolescents.

In line with the theoretical model proposed by Patterson (1986), Stice and Barrera (1995), examined the reciprocal relations between parenting and adolescent substance abuse and externalizing behavior. Utilizing data from a two-wave study with an one year interval, and employing structural equation modeling techniques, the authors reported that "full prospective reciprocal relations were found between perceived parenting and adolescent substance use, such that deficits in both parental support and control prospectively predicted adolescent substance use, and adolescent substance use was prospectively related to lower levels of parental support and control". In addition "regarding externalizing symptoms, the prospective effects of adolescent externalizing behavior on parenting practices are consistent only with that aspect of the reciprocal effects model that allows for child influences on parenting practices" (Stice and Barrera, 1995:330).

While the results by Stice and Barrera (1995) suggest a two-way transactional relationship between parent and adolescent behavior, externalizing symptoms are usually manifest earlier in childhood and, by adolescence, they may have been stabilized and the influence of parenting on adolescents' behaviour may not be observable, while adolescents' behavior effect on parental support and control would be easier to trace. Consistent with the view that the association between parenting and antisocial behavior may change over time, adolescence, as a distinct developmental period, might not be very informative for the study of parental effects in the initiation of externalizing symptoms, as they are more likely to exert an influence earlier in the child's life.

Moreover, it is equally plausible to assume that, parental influences in the initial learning of externalizing and antisocial behaviors are prominent in childhood. However, during life span development, other factors and agents, such as deviant peers and school failure, become more prominent in the maintenance, further development, escalation and generalisability of those behavioral patterns. This makes the study of the parental influences on the manifestation of externalizing symptoms difficult to reveal in adolescence.

GENETIC MEDIATION OF CHILD-REARING EFFECTS ON JUVENILE DELINQUENCY

The recognition of reciprocal parent-child effects in the expression of antisocial and delinquent effects is evident mainly in childhood. Interventions aiming at changing child-rearing practices resulted in reductions in children's antisocial behavior. Parental child-rearing practices showed predictive efficiency accounting for both self-reported and official reported delinquency. The probable primary effects of parents on children and adolescents in the expression of antisocial and delinquent behaviour seems supported. However this does not mean that these could be the main sources of delinquent adolescent behavior. It is equally plausible to assume that both, harsh, rejecting and coercive parenting, and, delinquent behavior of children, in addition to the fact that many young offenders have parents that show antisocial behavior themselves, including convictions (Farrington, 1995) are both manifestations of the same tendency for antisocial and delinquent behavior. That is genetically transmitted from parents to their offspring, thus accounting for the relationship of poor parenting and adolescent delinquent behavior (Rutter et al, 1998).

Rutter et al (1998), in reviewing studies, mainly adoptee and twin studies, deals with the genetic influences in the development of antisocial and delinquent behavior. He concluded that there is a rather strong genetic influence in the case of hyperactivity and that of liability which "overlaps greatly with that of antisocial behavior when the two are associated" (Rutter et al, 1998). While there is a stronger environmental influence in the case of self-reported antisocial behavior, which is not, associated with hyperactivity and peer relationships problems. For delinquency the genetic influence is much weaker, in contrast to aggressive or general antisocial behavior. In addition the genetic influence appears to be influential in the case of early onset and persistence into adulthood than in adolescent limited delinquency. Rutter et al (1990a) argues that different genetic research designs have different methodological limitations. Furthermore, multiple methodology should be employed so that the strengths of one method cancel out the disadvantages of the other. Despite any methodological deficiencies in either adoption and twin studies, and their variants, when results tend to be replicated with different methods and are consistent with different methodological designs and operationalisations, the results should be viewed with greater confidence.

Rutter et al (1990a) argued that twin designs assuming that the family environments for monozygotic and dizygotic twins are comparable. Monozygotic twins are more likely to be treated in the same way in comparison to dizygotic twins. Being a member of an identical twin pair may influence development in a unique way, and having an unusually close relationship with an identical twin sibling, are likely to be factors that make monozygotic twins show more behavioural similarities in comparison to dizygotic twins. Rutter et al (1990a) argued that these environmental factors, not captured in the twin designs, are likely to overestimate the genetic influence on behavioural manifestations of monozygotic twins in comparison to dizygotic twins. Rutter et al (1990a) further argued that the disentaglement of genetic and environmental forces in shaping behaviour is better achieved by adoption studies. In such studies the behaviour under investigation is examined in the biological parents and the adopted-away children. Adoption studies are often characterised by a lack of data on the biological father and they cannot easily estimate gene-environment interactions and biases that may arise from the difficulties of being an adopted child. Rutter et al (1990a) noted that while the rate for psychiatric disorders in adoptees is higher than the general population norms, rates of criminality are not and this finding is suggesting that the rate of psychiatric disorders in adoptees is likely to, at least partially, derive from the stresses associated with being an adopted child.

However, regarding the genetic influences in antisocial behaviour that have been argued by adoption studies Stoolmiller (1999) suggested that they should be interpreted with caution. The author suggested that the relatively less influence of family environment found in adoptee studies could be attributed to the restricted range of family environments sampled in such studies. This is possible since the families finally participating in the studies are subject to several selection processes. Such processes are the criteria of adoption agencies for placing children, self-selection by future adoptive parents and volunteering in a study. Stoolmiller (1999), argued that those selection processes are likely to provide an adoption study with a sample characterised by a restricted range of family environment as all the selection processes are highly likely to result in families with good family environment and child-rearing practices, with limited within group variability, thus almost rendering child-rearing practices into a constant. The same degree of restriction in the values of other family characteristics like socio-economic status or intelligence is not likely to occur to the same degree. This is possible only to the extent that they are correlated with the criteria of the selection processes. This means that studies including adoption families appear, at the first glance, to be representative of a general population, and in fact to be on many socio-demographic characteristics. However they can still be restricted to those family characteristics that are more important and more proximally related with children's behavioral outcomes.

Stoolmiller (1999) further continued by arguing that the same range restriction of family environment could account for the high correlations of twins who have been adopted by different families. It was assumed that range restriction of family environment was not regarded as an inherent problem in twin designs. However this assumption may be premature as the restriction of family environment in the sample of those studies could still be operative through volunteer bias. That is families providing a generally supportive environment for their children to participate in the studies.

Stoolmiller (1999) concluded that, possible genetic influences in the development of antisocial and delinquent behavior are likely to operate. However the application of adoption and twin design in examining those issues, is likely to be limited by a restricted range of variability in child-rearing practices used by the families. This makes any associations of child-rearing practices with children's behavioral manifestations difficult to reveal.

Child-rearing Practices as Mediators of the Relationship between Social Disadvantage and Family Structural Variables and Juvenile Delinquency

However, as the experience of adverse family environment does not lead everyone to experience of poor psychosocial functioning, a within-person approach has been followed for the identification of pathways or mediational mechanisms that translate experience of family functioning into developmental problems in adolescence (Bolger & Patterson, 2001; Cicchetti & Rogosch, 1996; Kiriakidis, 2006; 2000). The mediational role of family functioning is more evident in the relation between social disadvantage and delinquency.

Several researchers (Barrera et al., 2002; Conger et al., 2002; Farmer & Farmer, 2001; Wadsworth & Compass, 2002) considered child-rearing practices as mediators of the relationship between social disadvantage and family structural variables and juvenile delinquency. Such an assumption is consistent with the ecological systems theory (Bronfenbrenner, 1979) that problematic behaviour of children and adolescents could not be examined outside the contexts they live in. Such an assumption has been advaced by Rutter (2005) that adverse environmental experiences are a critical factor of psychosocial poor adjustment. Rutter (2005) argued that the development of poor psychosocial functioning, including antisocial and delinquent behaviour, is actually mediated through several processes. He argued that adverse experience has a long term effect on psychosocial functioning through cognitive and/or affective working models, representation of the self, interpersonal interaction and several environmental and social experiences and interactions. Among the most important factors exerting a significant influence on the development of adolescent behaviour is the family environment they are living in. Neglect has been repeatedly related with: 1) antisocial and delinquent behaviour (Stouthamer-Loeber, Loeber, Homish, & Wie, 2001), 2) the development of psychological problems in the general population (Cohen, Brown, & Smailes, 2001), 3) dysfuctions in the neuroendocrine operation (Cicchetti & Rogosch, 2001), 4) the development of multiple dysfuctional behaviours in adolescence (McGee, Wolfe, & Olson,

Child-Rearing Practices and Delinquency in Children and Adolescents   235

2001), and 5) reduced resilience in the face of several stressors during adolescence and adulthood (McGloin & Widom, 2001).

Wilson (1980) reported that child-rearing practices and, especially parental supervision, in deprived inner city areas, exerted a buffering influence on juvenile delinquency by imposing strict rules limiting children's mobility, and examined the possible effects of parental supervision in variable settings representing different levels of social handicap. Overall she reports that juvenile delinquency was significantly higher in families employing less supervision practices and that, in areas with high delinquency rates, the effects of parental supervision were more important than the effects of social handicap. She further argues that the effects of strict parenting in socially handicapped areas restrict children's involvement with delinquent peers, as their parents have expressed their disapproval towards offending behavior and those peers who express the behaviour. Those messages are internalized and turned into self-control, therefore inhibiting mixing with antisocial peers. It is evident that the author implied a process linking parental supervision with juvenile delinquent behaviour, where involvement with antisocial peers is a key mediating variable. However the explanation process remains at a narrative level and is not directly empirically tested.

The role of parental factors as correlates and predictors of delinquency in young people and adulthood were examined by Glueck and Glueck (1950 cited in Laub and Sampson, 1988) in Unraveling Juvenile Delinquency. Laub and Sampson (1988), provided an assessment of the longitudinal study and commented that the data base collected by Glueck and Glueck (1950 cited in Laub and Sampson, 1988) provided a unique source of information that could be very informative about potential correlates and predictors of delinquency. They noted that their work has been criticized on methodological, statistical and ideological grounds. They recognized that their ideological perspective of biological influences in delinquent behavior and their finding that mesomorphy was a predictor of delinquency resulted in their work being severely criticized, mainly from scholars working within the social criminological perspective, and while their statistical analysis was not optimal, they suggested that criticisms about their methodological design were overstated. In fact, Laub and Sampson (1988), believed that the methodological design of the Glueck and Glueck (1950) study, was very strong and they report that it involved the comparison of 500 delinquent males and 500 non-delinquents matched, case by case, on age, race/ethnicity, general intelligence and low-income residence "all criminological variables thought to influence both delinquency and official reaction" (p. 356). In addition, the samples were followed up when the participants were aged approximately 25 and 31 years old. Laub and Sampson (1988), concluded that "[u]sing multiple sources of information, the Gluecks collected data on a variety of interesting and important indicators relevant to understanding the causes of serious, persistent delinquency. Indeed, the Gluecks' data, in all likelihood, are superior to many of the current longitudinal data sets in criminology" (p. 376).

Recognizing the possibility that re-analysis of the data set could be informative of the possible correlates of delinquency and the identification of intervening family variables between structural factors and delinquent behavior. The authors re-examined the data of the study with the aim to examine closely, and with the use of multivariate data analysis techniques, the potential predictive role of family functioning on delinquent behavior. Erratic discipline by mother and father, poor maternal supervision, parental rejection of the boy and parental attachment were found to be significantly related to delinquency. Background factors such as paternal and maternal criminality, parental alcohol abuse, home overcrowding, economic dependence of the family on social welfare and absence of parents during childhood were related both to family functioning and delinquency. More interestingly, the effects of those background structural factors on delinquency were almost totally mediated by family functioning variables, and their effects on delinquency behavior were minimized when family functioning variables were taken into consideration. The only variable that continued to exert a direct effect, although considerably minimized, on delinquency was the number of family relocations. The results are even more supportive of the proposed mediating family processes, since the samples were matched on age, race/ethnicity, general intelligence and low - income residence. The role of family supervision and attachment as potent predictors of delinquency is supported. In addition the hypothesis of the authors that the effects of social structure on delinquency, in a considerable way are, mediated by parental rejection, harsh discipline and poor supervision are further supported as well. These hypotheses are supported by the data, even when other, generally static correlates of delinquency are held constant. The authors concluded, " This model has considerable significance for future research in that it explains *how* key background factors influence delinquency. A concern with only direct effects conceals such relationships and leads to erroneous conclusions" (p. 375).

Larzelere and Patterson (1990), who hypothesized that the effects of socio-economic status on delinquency are mediated by parental management, have reported similar results. They noted that socio-economic status was a central construct of most sociological theories of crime, although the theories differed in the way they conceptualized the impact of social class on delinquency. They reported that while Merton's (1957) anomie-strain theory proposed that greater frustration of lower social class juveniles led them to crime, Sutherland's (1947) differential association theory suggested that lower social class youths would probably be exposed to and influenced by criminal elements of society. Hirschi's (1969) social control theory held that lower social class youths were not sharing and were not committed to the same familial, vocational and scholastic values common to middle class youths, thus making them more prone to delinquent behavior. The common element in all these theories, Larzelere and Patterson (1990) noted, was the direct effects of socio-economic status on delinquency, while these effects seemed to be rather weak and inconsistent, especially when the individual was the unit of analysis.

The authors further hypothesized that parental management would mediated any effects of socio-economic class on delinquent behavior, as child-rearing practices have been associated with juvenile delinquency and have actually been potent predictors of delinquency. The hypothesis is derived from the coercion theory (Patterson, 1986). "The coercion model emphasizes the central role of the family and peer group in providing the positive and negative contingencies that maintain the performance of both prosocial and deviant child behaviors" (Larzelere and Patterson, 1990: 305). This was examined in the longitudinal Oregon Youth Study of 206 boys coming from schools within an area with the highest police arrest rate per capita. The study measured parental discipline and monitoring, with different methods, resulting into multiple indicators, in order to minimize any bias resulting from one measuring method. They concentrated on these two aspects of parental management as mediators of the effects of socio-economic disadvantage on delinquency. The boys in the study were followed up from the fourth to the seventh grade at school. The authors reported that parental management, a combination of measures of parental discipline and monitoring, fully accounted for the relation between socio-economic status at fourth grade and self-reported delinquency at seventh grade, supporting the hypothesis of a mediational role of family child-rearing practices between the link of socio-economic disadvantage and delinquent behavior. The results, however, are informative of the possible role of parental management in early adolescent delinquency behavior, while socio-economic disadvantage could exert an independent influence on later adolescent delinquent behavior, as the authors noted.

The results of the study are in accord with McLoyd (1998), who stated "the link between socio-economic disadvantage and children's socio-emotional functioning appears to be mediated partly by harsh, inconsistent parenting and elevated exposure to acute and chronic stressors" (p. 185). Reviewing the literature on the effects of socio-economic disadvantage on the general socio-emotional functioning of children, McLoyd (1998) reported that there was enough evidence to support the hypothesis. That is, prolonged economic stress, combined with subsequent negative life events and chronic adversities, results in parental dysphoria. This is expressed in the form of anger, irritability and/or depression. This in turn increases the parents' tendency to use harsh, punitive, arbitrary and inconsistent ways of discipline for their children and ignore their dependency needs by withdrawal from their children. The author continues that such a pattern results in a range of, both externalizing and internalizing, socio-emotional problems of the children. These problems include anxiety, depression, temper tantrums, irritability, negativism and delinquency.

McLoyd (1998) provides complementary evidence of the role of parenting in the psychosocial development of children that comes from studies actually in search of protective factors that buffer possible effects of deprivation, disadvantage and chronic stressors on children's development and which instill in to them a sense of resilience. The author reviewed studies of children exposed to a high number of chronic adversities and negative events and tried to distinguish stress resilient children from those affected by stress. The factors that generally characterised resilient children were "no separation of child and primary caregiver during infancy; positive parent-child relations during the preschool years; a strong sense of parenting efficacy by the primary caregivers; and parental use of reasoned, age-appropriate, consistent disciplinary practices" (p. 197). The author stated that effective parenting or the existence of non-parental adults in the children's environment, providing positive role models or having the role of a "mentor" for the child, seemed to be factors that could buffer any negative, effects which adversities and hardships, could have on the psychosocial development of children faced with them.

Similar conclusions were reached by Yoshikawa (1994), by reviewing effects of family support on chronic delinquency. From several studies reviewed, he argued that there is evidence for a mediation role of family variables such as parental discipline and maternal affection between juvenile delinquency and socio-economic disadvantage. In any case he warned that the link between socio-economic disadvantage and delinquency is more evident when the former is measured as a community-wide characteristic, thus the link at the individual level of analysis appears to be prone to the ecological fallacy and any inferences for the individual should be made with extreme caution and only after the link is replicated with the two levels of analysis.

From the literature reviewed it could be argued that the role of the family in the prevention of delinquent behavioural manifestations by children and adolescents is an important one. It seems that effective parenting exerts an influence for the general socioemotional functioning of children and adolescents (Kiriakidis, 2007). From the theoretical studies point of view, the initiation of programmes teaching effective parenting to adolescents and young adults, especially those facing several adversities and in risk of delinquency themselves, could be helpful. They could be helpful in both reducing the risk of delinquency of their children and empower them. In that way they could enjoy a normative and satisfactory psychosocial development (Bitsani & Panagou, 2002).

DISCUSSION

The protective role of parenting is generally supported and a supportive family environment could be suggested as a protective factor for juvenile delinquency. The evidence reviewed suggests that effective family functioning is a necessary although not sufficient factor for the normal socioemotional development and functioning of children and adolescents. This argument is in line with the assumption that delinquency is an international phenomenon. It could be attributed to several factors, postulated and actually identified, to be related to delinquency (Kiriakidis, 2007; 2008). From this point of view, any programmes of educational nature initiated at teaching properly and effective child rearing practises, targeted at youngsters at risk facing several adversities, shouldn't be viewed as the only solution to the problem of delinquency and there should be realistic expectations of their results. However, another reason is the fact that delinquency has been associated with several factors, most of which are mainly static and not readily amenable to change, or even if they are, their change relies to a considerable degree to substantial social and political change that is not always possible or desirable. For the professional who deals with problems of social instability in general and issues of delinquency and its prevention, the improvement of parenting skills in the community appears as an interesting, satisfactory cost-effective and efficient alternative, especially within the line of research suggesting that improvement in parenting skills is associated with improved general socioemotional functioning of children and adolescents and reduced rates of delinquency in particular.

Theoretical Implications

The protective role of parenting is generally supported. The role of a supportive family environment could be suggested as a protective factor for juvenile delinquency. Bowlby (1977) argued that a secure attachment of the children to their primary caregiver results in children that are more able to explore and in that respect refine and employ their skills and talents in a constructive way. Belsky and Cassidy (1994), argued that the concept of attachment has been employed as a domain specific model as well as a broad general model that "depicts attachment security as foundational to a variety of features of development. Thus, sensitivity to attachment signals promotes attachment security, which fosters development in a wide variety of domains" (Belsky and Cassidy, 1994: 382-383). This argument reflects Rutter's (2005) proposition that multiple psychological outcomes might be related and be due to general underlying factors influencing multiple developmental problems. From this general perspective the results of the review seem not surprising. Children and adolescents who perceived their parents as less supportive seem not to be able to function adaptively and to regulate their lives in constructive ways, both for them and society. The results of the review show that inadequate parenting is related with many psychosocial problems including delinquency.

REFERENCES

Barrera, M., Prelow, H. M., Dumka, L. E., Gonzales, N. A., Knight, G. P. & Michaels, M. L. (2002). Pathways from family economic conditions to adolescents' distress: Supportive parenting, stressors outside the family, and deviant peers. *Journal of Community Psychology, 30,* 1-18.

Belsky & Cassidy (1994) Attachment: Theory and evidence. In Rutter, & Hay (Eds.), *Development Through Life.* Oxford: Blackwell Science Ltd.

Bitsani, E. & Panagou, B. (2002). Europe and culture: issues of policies. *Applied Research Review, 1,* 83-111.

Bolger, K. E. & Patterson, C. J. (2001). Pathways from child maltreatment to internalising problems: Perceptions of control as mediators and moderators. *Development and Psychopathology, 13,* 913-940.

Borduin, C. M. & Schaeffer, C. M. (1998). Violent Offending in Adolescence: Epidemiology, Correlates, Outcomes, and Treatment. In T. P. Gullotta, G. R. Adams, & R. Montemayor (Eds.), *Delinquent Violent Youth: Theory, and Interventions.* London: Sage Publications.

Bowlby, J. (1977). The making and breaking of affectional bonds II: Aetiology and psychopathology in the light of attachment theory. *British Journal of Psychiatry, 130,* 201-210.

Bronfenbrenner, U. (1979). Contexts of child rearing: Problems and prospects. *American Psychologist, 34,* 844-850.

Cicchetti, D. & Rogosch, A. F. (2001). The impact of child maltreatment and psychopathology on neuroendocrine functioning. *Development and Psychopathology, 13,* 783-804.

Cohen, P., Brown, J. & Smailes, E. (2001). Child abuse and neglect and the development of mental disorders in the general population. *Development and Psychopathology, 13,* 981-999.

Conger, R. D., Wallace, L. E., Sun, Y., Simons, R. L., McLoyd, V. C. & Brody, G. H. (2002). Economic pressure in African American families: A replication and extension of the family stress model. *Development and Psychopathology, 38,* 179-193.

Danos, A. (2003). The semantic approach of organizational structure in educational organizations. *Applied Research Review, 1,* 155-163.

Farmer, T. W. & Farmer, E. M. Z. (2001). Developmental science, systems of care and prevention of emotional and behavioral problems in youth. *American Journal of Orthopsychiatry, 7,* 171-181.

Farrington, D. P. (1995). The Twelfth Jack Tizard Memorial Lecture. The Development of Offending and Antisocial Behaviour from Childhood: Key Findings from the Cambridge Study in Delinquent Development. *Journal of Child Psychology and Psychiatry, 360, 929-964.*

Henry, B., Moffitt, E. T., Robins, L., Earls, F. & Silva, P. (1993). Early Family Predictors of Child and Adolescent Antisocial Behaviour: Who are the Mothers of Delinquents. *Criminal Behaviour and Mental Health, 3, 97-118.*

Hirschi, T. (1969). *Causes of Delinquency.* Berkeley: University of California Press.

Kavoura A. (2001). Educational programmes and active participation approach of cultural heritage. *Proceedings of the 8th International Conference of Greek Psychological Associations.* Alexandroulopis, 24-27 May 2001.

Kiriakidis S. (2008). Perceived Quality of Parenting and it's Relations with Frequency of Offending and Indeces of Psychosocial Functioning among Institutionalised Adolescents. *Hellenic Journal of Psychology, 5, 199-224.*

Kiriakidis, S. (2007). Chronic adolescents and young offenders: An overview of research findings. *Epidemiologia E Psichiatria Sociale-An International Journal For Epidemiology And Psychiatric Sciences,16(3),* 238-250.

Kiriakidis, S. (2006). Perceived parental care and supervision: Relations with cognitive representations of future offending in a sample of young offenders. *International Journal of Offender Therapy and Comparative Criminology, 50(2),* 187-203.

Kiriakidis, S. (2000). *Psychosocial correlates of juvenile delinquency,* Unpublished doctoral dissertation, University of Stirling.

Kolvin, I., Miller, F. J. W., Fleeting, M. & Kolvin, P. A. (1988). Social and Parenting Factors Affecting Criminal-Offence Rates: Findings from the Newcastle Thousand Family Study (1947-1980). *British Journal of Psychiatry, 152, 80-90.*

Larzelere, R. E. & Patterson, G. R. (1990). Parental Management: Mediator of the Effect of Socioeconomic Status on Early Delinquency. *Criminology, 28, 301-324.*

Laub, J. H. & Sampson, R. J. (1988). Unraveling Families and Delinquency: A Reanalysis of the Gluecks' Data. *Criminology, 26, 355-380.*

Liska, A. E. & Reed, M. D. (1985). Ties to Conventional Institutions and Delinquency: Estimating Reciprocal Effects. *American Sociological Review, 50, 547-560.*

Loeber, R. & Farrington, D. P. (1998). Serious and violent juvenile offenders: Risk factors and successful interventions. Thousand Oaks, CA: Sage.

Loeber, R. & Dishion, T. (1983). Early Predictors of Male Delinquency: A Review. *Psychological Bulletin, 94, 68-99.*

Lytton, H. (1990). Child and Parent Effects in Boys' Conduct Disorder: A Reinterpretation. *Development and Psychology, 26, 683-697.*

McCord, J. (1979). Some Child-Rearing Antecedents of Criminal Behaviour in Adult Men. *Journal of Personality and Social Psychology, 37, 1477-1486.*

McGee, R., Wolfe, D. & Olson, J. (2001). Multiple maltreatment, attribution of blame, and adjustment among adolescents. *Development and Psychopathology, 13,* 827-846.

McGloin, J. M. & Widom, C. S. (2001). Resilience among abused and neglected children grown up. *Development and Psychopathology, 13,* 1021-1038.

McLoyd, V. C. (1998). Socioeconomic Disadvantage and Child Development. *American Psychologist, 53, 185-204.*

Merton, R. K. (1957). *Social Theory and Social Structure.* Glencoe: Free Press.

Patterson, G. R. (1986). Performance models for antisocial boys. *American Psychologist, 41, 432-444.*

Patterson, G. R., Dishion, T. J. & Bank, L. (1984). Family Interaction: A Process Model of Deviancy Training. *Aggressive Behavior, 10, 253-267.*

Patterson, G. R. & Reid, J. B. (1973). Intervention for Families of Aggressive Boys: A Replication Study. *Behavior Research and Therapy, 11, 383-394.*

Pedersen, W. (1994). Parental relations, mental health, and delinquency in adolescents. *Adolescence, 29,* 975-990.

Rutter, M. (2005). Multiple meanings of a developmental perspective on psychopathology. *European Journal of Developmental Psychology, 2(3),* 221-252.

Rutter, M. (1994). Family discord and conduct disorder: Cause, consequence, or correlate? *Journal of Family Psychology, 8,* 170-186.

Rutter, M., Giller, H. & Hagell, A. (1998). *Antisocial Behaviour by Young People.* New York: Cambridge University Press.

Rutter, M., Maughan, B., Meyer, J., Pickles, A., Silberg, J., Simonoff, E. & Taylor, E. (1997). Heterogeneity of antisocial behaviour: Causes, continuities and consequences. In D. W. Osgood (Ed.), *Nebraska Symposium on Motivation: Motivation and delinquency (Vol. 44,* 45-118), Lincoln, NE: University of Nebraska Press.

Rutter, M., Bolton, P., Harrington, R., Couteur, A. L., Macdonald, H. & Simonoff, E. (1990a). Genetic Factors in Child Psychiatric Disorders-I. A Review of Research Strategies. *Journal of Child Psychology and Psychiatry, 31, 3-37.*

Simons, R. L., Robertson, J. F. & Downs, W. R. (1989). The Nature of the Association Between Parental Rejection and Delinquent Behavior. *Journal of Youth and Adolescence, 18, 297-310.*

Stice, E. & Barrera, M. (1995). A Longitudinal Examination of the Reciprocal Relations between Perceived Parenting and Adolescents' Substance Use and Externalising Behaviours. *Developmental Psychology, 31, 322-334.*

Stoolmiller, M. (1999). Implications of the Restricted Range of Family Environments for Estimates of Heritability and Nonshared Environment in Behavior-Genetic Adoption Studies. *Psychological Bulletin, 125, 392-409.*

Stouthamer-Loeber, M., Loeber, R., Homish, D. L. & Wie, E. (2001). Maltreatment of boys and the development of disruptive and delinquent behavior. *Development and Psychopathology, 13,* 941-955.

Sutherland, E. H. (1947). *Principles of criminology (4th ed.).* Philadelphia: Lippincott

Thornberry, T. P., Ireland, T. O. & Smith, C. A. (2001). The importance of timing: The varying impact of childhood and adolescent maltreatment on multiple problem outcomes. *Development and Psychopathology, 13,* 957-979.

Wadsworth, M. E. & Compas, B. E. (2002). Coping with family and economic strain: The adolescent perspective. *Journal of Research on Adolescence, 12,* 243-274.

Wilson, H. (1980). Parental Supervision: A Neglected Aspect of Delinquency. *The British Journal of Criminology, 20, 203-235.*

Yoshikawa, H. (1994). Prevention as Cumulative Protection: Effects of Early Family Support and Education on Chronic Delinquency and Its Risks. *Psychological Bulletin, 115, 28-54.*

In: Youth Violence and Juvenile Justice: Causes, Intervention... ISBN: 978-1-61668-011-4
Editor: Neil A. Ramsay et al., pp. 269-285 © 2010 Nova Science Publishers, Inc.

Chapter 11

SHARKS & JETS VS. BLOODS & CRIPS: SOCIO-ECONOMICS, PREVENTION, AND INTERVENTION IN DIFFERENT ERAS OF GANG VIOLENCE

Rosalyn M Bertram and Jennifer Dartt
University of Missouri-Kansas City, Missouri,USA

ABSTRACT

A youth gang is an intimate social group composed of adolescents or young adults who temporarily share common values, identities, symbols, and standards of behavior. Largely an urban phenomenon, gangs may be seen as subcultures whose interests and attitudes are different from, and sometimes even in direct conflict with, those of the larger society. Although some youth violence occurs independent of gang involvement, gang affiliation greatly increases a youth's propensity to commit violent acts. Once comprised of delinquent males who defended neighborhood territory, gangs now include both genders and engage in drug trafficking and other illegal activities. This chapter briefly explores the transformation of youth gangs and violence associated with them, the basis of interventions to reduce youth gang affiliation and aggression in these different eras, as well as factors contributing to and mitigating modern era gang affiliation.

INTRODUCTION

Rif: "We gotta stand up to them Doc; it's important."
Doc: "Fighting over a little piece of street is so important?"
Action: "To us it is!"
Doc: "To hoodlums it is! War councils? Rumbles? When I was your age..."
Action: "When you was my age? When my old man was my age, when my brother was my age... You was never my age, none of ya! And the sooner you creeps get hip to that, the sooner you'll dig us! A gang that don't own the street is nothin'!" (*West Side Story*, 1961)

The gangs of the 1950s through the early 1970s were territorial, comprised of tightly knit and somewhat stable youth networks. Intra- and inter-group conflicts were commonly organized into planned rumbles to protect the group's turf against perceived threats or disrespect from rival neighborhood gangs or hostile authority figures. These rumbles mainly entailed hand-to-hand combat or the use of weapons such as baseball bats and knives. Gunfire or hurting innocent bystanders, common today, were then rare occurrences. Territorial gangs provided social support for minority, underclass adolescents that countered conflict with their immigrant parents and prejudicial communities. They served as surrogate families that supported individuation from one's biological family while affirming anti-social group bonds (Scheidlinger, 1994). These gangs of territory and identity were perhaps most memorably exemplified in the academy award winning film of 1961, *West Side Story*, in which the Puerto Rican Sharks battled the lower class Euro-American Jets.

> "When you're a Jet you're a Jet all the way from your first cigarette to your last dyin' day. When you're a Jet let them do what they can, little boy you got friends you're a family man" (*West Side Story*, 1961).

During the late 1970s and early 1980s, in major urban areas such as Chicago, Los Angeles and New York, territorial street gangs began to transform into modern era gangs less defined by ethnicity or preference for surrogate family. Instead, modern era gangs were much more driven by necessity to survive in the midst of a severe economic transformation and the consequent, increasingly violent environments of drug trafficking. Many of this era's most prominent gangs such as the Bloods, Crips, and La Familia, developed around drug networks, and gang warfare became increasingly lethal with firearms serving as the most common means for commission of violent crimes (Cummings & Monti, 1993). *West Side Story's* popularized image of a group of kids whose aggressive and rebellious members who though pained, were somehow appealing, has been replaced by today's scavenger gangs comprised of troubling, loosely organized youth whose unpredictable aggression and seemingly random violence around drug trafficking differs drastically from the turf and social identity battles of the Sharks and Jets.

ECONOMICS AND DRUG MARKETS

In our review of the literature, before the late 1970s there was little mention of gang drug trafficking. However, the early to middle 1980s witnessed a rapid growth in the crack cocaine market, and by the late 1980s, there was considerable involvement in this market by both youth and adult gang members (Howell & Decker, 1999). During this period, a drastic decline in manufacturing jobs and a related increase in unemployment and underemployment spawned a growing underclass population in minority and disadvantaged communities. Economic and social policies were altering fundamentals of the U.S. economy, transforming the flow of wealth and opportunity, creating more threatening urban environments where protective mechanisms and alternative means to generate income were necessary. Gangs quickly began to fill this role (Phillips, 1990; Rosenfeld, Bray, & Egley, 1999). The crack cocaine market provided a means of income for many unemployed males, who in turn offered youth with uncertain futures similar paths toward financial gain. By the late 1980s, the Bloods and the Crips controlled 30% of the United States crack cocaine market. These two prominent Los Angeles street gangs emerged during the late 1970s, and within a decade, spread to 46 other states with established cocaine trafficking operations (Howell, 1997; Howell & Decker, 1999).

As the size and stakes of this cocaine economy grew, territorial gang wars morphed into the modern era's gang drug wars. Violence associated with the crack cocaine market was linked to fierce competition to expand markets and profits as well as to retaliation against market participants who violated norms of transaction (Howell & Decker, 1999). This violence captured the attention of popular media.

> The Old Man: "Ain't nobody from outside bringing down the property value. It's these folk, shootin' each other and sellin' that crack rock."

> Furious Styles: "Well, how you think the crack rock gets into the country? We don't own any planes. We don't own no ships. We are not the people who are flyin' and floatin' that shit in here. I know every time you turn on the TV that's what you see. Black People pushing the rock, selling the rock...that's what you see. But see that wasn't a problem as long as it was here [*referring to Compton, Watts, other African American ghettos*]. It wasn't a problem until it was in Iowa or on Wall Street where there are hardly any black people." (*Boyz 'n the Hood*, 1991)

MODERN ERA GANG VIOLENCE

Modern era gang affiliation significantly increases the likelihood and frequency of aggressive, violent youth behavior. As youth are exposed to more risky situations, gangs are more able to motivate and promote youth to participate in violence. The emotionally driven violence between rival gangs is easily contagious to an impressionable young person, while group norms constrain individual choice and inhibit rational reason and judgment in youth who were previously not prone to aggressive, anti-social behaviors (Howell & Decker, 1999; Rosenfeld et al., 1999; Scheidlinger, 1994). A recent study found that 40.4% of gang members reported participating in a drive-by shooting compared to 2% of non-gang members, while 72.3% of gang members reported assaulting rivals compared to 16.3% nongang members (Johnson & Mulhausen, 2005).

Rates of gang affiliation and serious youth violence increased dramatically during the final decades of the 20th century, a period in which American cities reported 800% more gang problems (Jenson, Potter, & Howard, 2001; Johnson & Mulhausen, 2005; Rosenfeld, et al, 1999). Between the late 1980s and mid 1990s, handguns were involved in two to three times more homicides than other weapons. More specifically, during the major American crime surge between 1985 and 1993, firearm homicides increased by 53%. While non-gun homicides actually decreased, gun-related homicide arrests of juveniles quadrupled, and similar arrests tripled among young adults ages 18 to 24 (Travis & Waul, 2002).

Two cities that have had pervasive youth gang problems, Chicago and Los Angeles, demonstrate the extent to which the availability and use of guns has transformed the typology of youth violence. In Chicago, from 1987 to 1990, virtually all of the increase in gang-related homicides involved high-caliber, automatic or semiautomatic weapons. In Los Angeles, gang-related homicides involving firearms increased from 71% in 1979 to 95% in 1994 (Juvenile Justice Bulletin, 1998). This trend is now nationwide and prevalent. Deaths from gunfire in the United States have increased since 2000, while the rate of all other homicides has remained relatively stable (Johnson & Mulhausen, 2005).

Casualties from these gun battles on America's urban streets are staggering when compared to casualties in the current Iraq war. For example, the Children's Defense Fund reported that in 2002, 3,365 youth died from gunshot wounds. In that same year, 13,000 to 16,000 urban youth sustained nonfatal injuries. (Hamrin, Jonker, & Scahill, 2004). These single year urban youth casualties offer striking comparison with US military casualties of 4,334 dead and 31,156 wounded in more than six years of the current Iraq war (iCasualties.org, 2009). Annual urban youth casualty rates have been remarkably consistent, and violence continues to be the leading cause of death for African American adolescents and the second leading cause of death for adolescents overall (Daane, 2003).

In addition to the proliferation of firearm usage, youth gang crimes have become more violent and more random. In the Sharks and Jets era, casualties from gang crime were usually restricted to other gang members or authorities that directly threatened the gang. Today, caution to avoid civilian victims has diminished. Gang activity now often occurs in residential as well as public areas, and offenders are less likely to know their victims (Rosenfeld et al., 1999). As gangs morphed from defenders of territory and identity to drug traffickers expanding and defending their markets, they became less connected to their communities. Gang members are now more likely to inflict casualties upon innocent bystanders and do so without remorse (Cummings & Monti, 1993). In one study, young gang members reported feeling less emotional, empathetic and responsible for accidental, random street violence, responding with remorseless statements such as "tough luck" and "no one looked out for me when I got hit." (Scheidlinger, 1994, p. 9)

CAREGIVERS AND THE SOCIO-ECONOMICS OF GANG AFFILIATION

Why do some youth more readily turn toward gang affiliation and aggression, while others from the same community do not? Answers to this key question reside within each youth's family, and especially within how caregivers enact their role and how well they are able to fulfill their responsibilities. Caregivers walk a fine line with adolescents. It is normative and necessary for parents to relax some controls while still monitoring many aspects of an adolescent's life. With warm guidance, this allows the youth to make decisions, succeed or fail, and learn to develop more complex relationships than those of their childhood. Over time, caregiver roles in direct facilitation and monitoring of youth interaction with peers shift, allowing school and work activities to also influence and increase the youth's opportunity for engagement with peers and other adult role models in their community. Nevertheless, parents must maintain sufficient awareness and appropriate guidance of the youth's activities to ensure that the youth is engaged with pro-social peers and activities (Carter & McGoldrick, 2005).

However, a multitude of challenges and events may compromise parental monitoring and the manner in which they influence their adolescent, and this is especially true in impoverished areas. Daily living conditions in impoverished communities are frequently characterized by lack of food and privacy, unpredictable events, and inadequate support that can slowly diminish a sense of stability and coping abilities. Similar to a war zone, the poor living conditions and absence of resources in these communities decrease individual opportunity and contribute to social disorder and community decline (Feerick & Silverman, 2006). A fundamental feature of a war zone environment is exposure to unpredictable, potentially harmful events. The inability to prevent these occurrences produces a sense of helplessness and requires a sustained, elevated anxiety level to manage the pervasive threat to life and limb (Friedman, 2006; Litz & Orsillo, 2004). Lack of safety permeating everyday life in impoverished urban communities requires that parents and their children maintain persistent caution amidst elevated feelings of helplessness and anxiety (Garbarino, Kostelny, & Dubrow, 1991). They are repeatedly made aware of victimized or murdered peers, and may sense an inevitably similar fate. The frequency of these events "confronts people with the stark reality that their community's capacity to offer safety and support may be shattered by violence and death at any time," (Horowitz, Weine, & Jekel, 1995, p. 1358).

In addition to a withering of social support and increased danger for both caregivers and youth, significant events may challenge and compromise parental response to their adolescent. For example, following separation or divorces, single parents with one or more jobs, may have limited time to supervise their children, especially during out-of-school hours. Poor supervision and lack of opportunity for youth engagement in pro-social peer activities is a recipe for trouble. Youth living in single-parent homes were 2.4 times more likely to be involved in a gang than those from two-parent homes, and juvenile crime peaks during the after-school and weekend hours, as well as during the summer months (Fox & Swatt, 2008; Johnson & Muhlhausen, 2005). When this inter-related structure of community supports and caregiver influence is compromised, when there is need for protection in a violent, crime-ridden community, and when youth see no other options for the future, the probability of anti-social peer group affiliation is enhanced. For youth whose home and school interactions with adults are unsupportive or antagonistic, anti-social peer groups may supply the value models and definitions for thought and behavior (Cummings & Monti, 1993). Adolescents more readily turn to violence when raised in areas of poverty and economic disadvantage in which role models from the legitimate work force are lacking or are unable to provide sufficient support and guidance (Parker & Reckdenwald, 2008).

Although boredom and peer pressure rank high on the list of motivations for youth gang affiliation, the number one justification for gang involvement is protection. Impoverished urban communities are breeding grounds for violence, and an adolescent without the protection that accompanies strong familial and social support is at high risk of being considered fair game (Scheidlinger, 1994). Members of gangs support and protect each other from violence at the hands of outsiders. As youth seek protection from streetwise, experienced peers, they begin to mimic them. Modern era gangs participate in "missions," actively seeking out rivals as targets for violence. Carrying out these missions can heighten a youth's sense of individual power, self-worth, solidarity and status among the peer group. By committing violent acts against "outsiders," feelings of economic and social ineptitude are temporarily substituted with feelings of power and control. Participation in such violence demonstrates their toughness and proves their worth in the eyes of their peers (Cummings & Monti, 1993).

Ultimately, youth raised in impoverished neighborhoods may simply not envision a crime-free lifestyle. Without the presence of tangible opportunities, legitimate employment may seem unrealistic to youth surrounded by perpetually unemployed underclass adults who have turned to criminal activities in order to get by. In this context, crime and gang affiliation can seem a rational method of obtaining life's necessities.

"If a community's economy is not based solidly on wages and salaries, other economies will begin to develop. Welfare, bartering, informal economic arrangements, and illegal economies become substitutes – simply because people must find a way to live. Young people growing up in such communities have little good to anticipate," (Cummings & Monti, 1993, p. 41).

CONTRIBUTING AND MITIGATING FACTORS

Parenting Style, Youth Social Skills, and Academic Performance

The explosion of youth violence during the 1980s spawned several important examinations of its contributing factors. Despite differences in risk noted for gender, race, and stage of adolescence, these studies found remarkably similar results. Anti-social youth behavior was not only determined by factors within the youth, but across important systems that included family, peers, school and neighborhood. Multisystem mediating and contributing factors that influence whether or not youth affiliate with anti-social peers include parenting style, relationships with peers and adults in the school and in the community, and school performance (Elliott, 1994; Loeber, Farrington, Stouthamer-Loeber, & Van Kammen, 1998; Thornberry & Krohn, 2003).

Caregiver roles include provision of nurturance, guidance and discipline for children while providing financial support and organizing household responsibilities (Carter & McGoldrick, 2005). These responsibilities are addressed through dimensions of affect and control that shape parent-child relations (Maccoby & Martin 1983; Seaburn, Landau-Stanton, & Horowitz, 1996). Caregiver warmth affirms emotional bonds. It maintains a positive mood during interactions that teaches the child empathy and to value interactions with others. Low levels of positive affection (emotional neglect) or high levels of negative affection (emotional rejection) place a child at risk for emotional or behavioral disorders. Children raised in this manner may lack social skills necessary to establish and maintain positive interactions with peers and adults. Caregiver methods of guidance and discipline directly control child behavior and range from permissive to restrictive patterns of interaction. Caregiver controls define what behavior is acceptable including cooperation, tolerance and respect for others and for authority, and use of non-aggresive means to resolve differences (Henggeler, Schoenwald, Borduin, Rowland, & Cunningham, 2009).

Thus, caregiver-child relations may be assessed in a continuum of configurations of affect and control, ranging from authoritative to neglectful. Authoritative parents offer their children high warmth and high control. They make developmentally appropriate demands for child behavior with clear, well-defined expectations and rules regarding family relations, peer relations, respect for elders and authority, and for academic and work performance, all while responding to reasonable needs of their child. Authoritarian caregivers offer their children high control with low warmth in the manner in which they provide guidance, nurturance and discipline. They tend to require unquestioning obedience to direct orders and may be highly directive or controlling in a developmentally inappropriate manner as the child enters adolescence. This style offers the youth little participation in decision-making, while punishment for transgressions may be severe and even physical. Permissive parents engage in high warmth and low control interactions with their children, often providing little structure and discipline with few demands for appropriately mature behavior, and may even tolerate impulsive anti-social behavior. Simply put, they are warm and responsive but not demanding. Neglectful caregivers provide low warmth and low control in interactions with their children. Discipline and affection are limited, and they may even appear disinterested in parenting. They are not attentive to the needs of their children and place few expectations, with little consequence or reward, for pro-social behavior (Baumrind, 2005).

It is important to remember that these parenting styles are not necessarily nor solely manifestations of personality, nor even of previous parenting. Caregiver work schedules, the economic necessity of working more than one job, responsibilities in caring for disabled or aging relatives, and responsibilities in raising younger children who demand more attention can all influence parenting style. Furthermore, the dangers and demands of raising children in unsafe, impoverished communities often necessitate an authoritarian parenting style (Henggeler et al., 2009). Nevertheless, parenting style may be either a contributing or a mitigating factor in the youth's development of pro-social or anti-social peer group affiliation and must be considered in primary, secondary, or tertiary prevention efforts to quell anti-social peer affiliation and youth violence.

Parenting styles and parent-child interactions shape development of youth social skills, values, attitudes and behavior. These factors in turn guide the manner in which youth relate to their peers. The ability to have empathy for others, to have perspective on situations and ones own behavior, as well as to initiate, reciprocate, and collaborate in interactions with peers, are important social skills that establish and maintain positive peer relations (Bukowski, Newcomb, & Harrup, 1996). Neglected youth are less able to initiate and reciprocate interactions with peers, while rejected youth may act in an aggressive or obnoxious manner of initiating or responding to peer interactions. Youth that have problematic peer relations, those who associate with anti-social peers, and those with poor social skills are at risk for school delinquency or failure and for aggressive anti-social behavior (Dodge, Dishon, & Lansford, 2006).

Caregivers also directly influence youth interaction with peers by facilitating (e.g. driving to activities, providing bus fare, etc.), by monitoring contacts with peers (e.g. evaluating who they are, having the phone numbers of peers' parents, etc.), and by providing guidance on youth interaction with peers. Parents who use harsh or inconsistent discipline, who do not or can not facilitate opportunities for pro-social peer interaction, or who do not or can not adequately monitor youth peer relations (i.e., authoritarian and neglectful parenting styles) are often associated with youth affiliation with anti-social peers (Kim, Hetherington, & Reiss, 1999; Reid, Patterson, & Snyder, 2002; Vitaro, Brendgen, & Tremblay, 2000).

As children mature to and through adolescence, the school and neighborhood assume greater roles as arenas for development and testing of social skills and behavior (Carter &

McGoldrick, 2005). In impoverished urban communities, the substandard quality and lack of safety of both school and neighborhood may contribute to anti-social peer affiliation and aggressive youth behavior. Adult role models in both school and neighborhood may mitigate or enhance the influence of parenting styles on the development of youth social skills and academic abilities. Thus, a complex web of the youth's relationships with teachers, coaches, and administrators from the school, with key adults in the community, and with the youth's caregivers can mitigate or contribute to youth affiliation with aggressive, anti-social peers (Henggeler et al., 2009)

Youth academic performance is an important factor that is often overlooked in designing interventions to diminish the likelihood of anti-social peer affiliation. Students who are truant or who have poor academic performance are more likely to associate with delinquent peer groups (Henggeler et al., 2009). Dating back to 1915, Healy and Burt identified a strong relationship between poor school performance and delinquent behaviors (LeBlanc, Vallieres, & McDuff, 1993) with more recent research validating a direct correlation between the two. Dishion, Nelson, and Yasui (2005) identified both academic failure and the accompanying peer rejection as factors contributing to youth seeking out peer groups that uphold more deviant value systems. Their study concluded that sixth grade students with poor grades and negative peer interactions were more likely to be involved in a youth gang by the eighth grade. School environments with high rates of failure and peer conflict can serve as breeding grounds for anti-social peer groups and gang affiliation.

SOCIAL INTERVENTIONS TO AVERT ANTI-SOCIAL PEER AFFILIATION

Since the 1950s, efforts to reduce youth affiliation with anti-social aggressive peers have reflected predominant theories of each time period. During the 1950s through late 1970s, the era of gangs of territory and identity, individual and group psychodynamic theories were most often the basis for conceptualizing the nature of youth development and affiliation with anti-social peer groups. One approach shaped by these theories originated in Chicago, where social workers were assigned to specific gangs to develop self-improvement campaigns and recreational activities that encouraged gang members to engage in pro-social activities (Johnson & Mulhausen, 2005). In the 1960s and 1970s, this model was adopted in many major cities, as outreach social workers infiltrated street gangs to gain trust and guide youth towards more contructive behaviors, while at the same time maintaining cohesiveness of the group. Because these were gangs of territory and identity, predominant psychodynamic theories suggested that the gang affiliation served the youth's developmental needs for belonging and peer support, and breaking up the gangs was viewed as counterproductive (Scheidlinger, 1994). However, this psychodynamic, sociological strategy achieved little success and produced unexpected and undesirable results. The complex social and economic contributors to gang affiliation were then not well understood, and in some cases this outreach actually contributed to greater cohesiveness of some gangs (Johnson & Mulhausen, 2005; Scheidlinger, 1994).

In Los Angeles, the nadir of modern era gang activity, two opposing, socio-economic, non-clinical models of intervention emerged in the 1980s. One program began hiring gang members who would attempt to mediate and reduce violence within their own gangs. At first, this approach seemed to make a positive impact, but ultimately it too proved insufficient and unreliable as social and economic policies and the crack cocaine market fueled greater violence in the growing impoverished communities (Cummings & Monti, 1993). In response to the drugs and violence, the Los Angeles Police Department asserted a strict law enforcement approach in the 1980s, conducting "gang roundups," in which they swept entire urban areas, apprehending anyone assumed to be gang-related. This police tactic ignored any clinical intervention or rehabilitation efforts, yet only 60 were arrested from the 1400 individuals remanded to custody (Johnson & Mulhausen, 2005). Nevertheless, as national politics shifted to the right, advocates of tough law enforcement in a so-called "war on drugs" gained traction. For the next decade, states increased the age for permissible school dropout and toughened penalties for gang-related crimes (Johnson & Mulhausen, 2005).

Each of these uni-dimensional methods were inadequate. However, in the mid 1990s, Boston devised a more comprehensive approach that engaged prosecutors, parole and probation officers with community leaders, local clergy and social services. All branches of law enforcement communicated information about specific gang members to social workers and clergy who walked the streets during time periods of high violence to demonstrate support for the police and courts and to increase communication between youth and community residents. This multi-faceted, highly visible united front, provided pro-social support while challenging anti-social behavior and Boston experienced a 25% drop in gun assaults and a 63% drop in monthly youth homicides (Johnson & Mulhausen, 2005).

Boston's attempt to merge law enforcement with clergy, community leaders, and social services was an innovative, successful approach in a time period that produced limited research on best practices for prevention of youth violence. Between 1980 and 1999 there were significantly fewer research articles published on the prevention and treatment of violent youth than there were on the description and assessment of this phenomenon (Acosta, Albus, Reynolds, Spriggs, & Weist, 2001). In other words, although much work was done to identify that youth affiliation with aggressive anti-social peer groups was in fact a problem, little was done to learn how to successfully address it.

EMERGENCE OF A THEORY OF SOCIAL ECOLOGY AND MULTISYSTEMIC INTERVENTIONS

A notable exception to this paucity of research on intervention was the development of Multisystemic Therapy (Henggeler et al., 2009) that built its model for addressing youth anti-social peer affiliation and associated aggression on a systemic theory of families and their social ecology. The struggle for civil rights in the 1960s had heightened awareness of the experience of the poor and disenfranchised. Salvador Minuchin, Braulio Montalvo, Harry Aponte, and other systems theorists and clinicians gravitated toward working with poor families from impoverished urban communities (Minuchin, Montalvo, Guerney, Rosman, & Schumer, 1967). They rejected the individual pathology focus of psychodynamic theory as irrelevant or non-pragmatic for this population, and instead merged systems theory with the communications theory of Bateson to develop a behavioral and structurally transformative family systems theory that emphasized the context and organization of human interaction (Minuchin, 1974). Throughout the 1970s, family systems theory blossomed into multiple applications that explored the many assessment and treatment implications of a fully systemic understanding of behavior, and Bronfenbrenner (1979) culminated this decade of theory development with his articulation of a systemic theory of social ecology that incorporated the influence of simultaneous and multiple contexts.

Building upon this articulation and testing of systemic, contextual theory, Scott Henggeler and Charles Borduin painstakingly created Multisystemic Therapy (MST) during the very time period in which the modern era gangs emerged. Beginning with Henggeler's efficacy trials at Memphis State University in the late 1970s, and progressing through initial randomized clinical trials with serious juvenile offenders conducted by Borduin through the University of Missouri-Columbia in the late 1980s and early 1990s, this ecological systems theory-based model was tested and refined in a program of continuous research that continues to this day. MST has been proven effective and efficient in randomized trials with differing populations. This intervention model simultaneously addresses interrelated problems of juvenile offenders and their families and produces clear evidence that it is effective in improving parenting, family functioning, youth social and academic skills, and peer relations (Curtis, Ronan, & Borduin, 2004).

As the randomized trials moved from controlled university settings into the difficult terrain of program implementation in the community, MST increased its emphasis on structured, model pertinent consultation, supervision, and staff development with a potent focus upon model fidelity and enhanced outcomes. With relative consistency MST randomized trials demonstrate cost effectiveness and reduced rates of criminal offenses, reduced rates of costly out of home placements, decreased substance use, behavior, and mental health problems, and improved family functioning when compared with usual mental health and juvenile justice services. MST's success with aggressive, anti-social youth and their families is derived from an empirically tested theory of change that recognizes and works with empirically derived knowledge that adolescent anti-social behavior is multi-determined, that families must be empowered to address youth problem behavior, that the negative influence of anti-social peers must be directly addressed, that school or vocational performance must be enhanced, and that an indigenous social support system must be developed to help the youth and family sustain treatment gains (Henggeler et al, 2009).

CRIME AND PUNISHMENT

> Ensemble to Juvenile Court Judge: "The trouble is he's lazy. The trouble is he drinks. The trouble is he's crazy. The trouble is he stinks. The trouble is he's growing. The trouble is he's grown. Krupke we got troubles of our own! (*West Side Story*, 1961)

In the 1950s and 1960s, juvenile courts attempted to guide youth away from future trouble (Butts & Harrell, 1998) rather than punish them for past mistakes. Treatment of the youth and community protection took prevalence over punishment (Ogino, 2005). Juvenile courts referred youth to services that were believed to help youth make better future choices. However, in the 1960s, juvenile courts became slightly more formalized and reflective of adult criminal courts. In response to charges that juvenile courts were inconsistent and that judges had too much subjective power to decide what they felt was the best punishment, the

Supreme Court formalized and constrained juvenile court procedures through a series of decisions between 1966 and 1975 (Butts & Harrell, 1998).

As the modern gang era emerged in the late 1970s and early 1980s, state and federal policies increased severity of punishment for youth crimes, further constrained discretion of juvenile court judges, and transferred a growing number of juveniles to adult courts (Butts & Harrell, 1998; Jenson et al., 2001). These policies reflected the nation's political turn to the right as many states passed punitive laws that included mandatory sentencing and automatic waivers to adult courts. This punitive focus continued during the 1990s, as clinical interventions were de-emphasized in favor of stricter sanctions and mandatory incarceration (Jenson et al., 2001). Since 1992, 47 states have toughened their juvenile justice system response by reducing confidentiality protections and/or trying more juveniles as adults (Dorfman & Schiraldi, 2001).

However, incarceration does nothing to address contributing factors to youth aggression and anti-social peer affiliation. It simply removes juvenile offenders from their families and communities, places youth with other deviant peers, and brands them as delinquents or criminals, a stigma difficult to overcome. Furthermore, as the clamor for punishment increased, economic and social policies diminished available resources for juvenile court judges to utilize (Butts & Harrell, 1998). In the last two decades youth incarceration has provided a false solution to juvenile delinquency (Center for Juvenile and Criminal Justice, n.d.). Critics of recent policy trends note that the transfer of youth to the adult criminal court system, or attempts to make juvenile court proceedings like those of adult courts, have stripped the juvenile justice system of the flexibility and focus on individual rehabilitation that once characterized these courts (Butts & Harrell, 1998).

Today's juvenile justice debate weighs two options. One side calls for more juvenile prisons and seeks to punish juveniles as adults. The other questions the effectiveness of incarceration, and promotes well-studied intervention and prevention to keep high-risk youth from entering the system in the first place (Parry, 2009). These approaches need not be politicized as mutually exclusive options. Youth and their families need well-conceptualized programs like MST that promote responsibility and accountability, while at the same time identifying ways to enhance personal, familial and community protective factors that support pro-social means of meeting needs. The power of the courts can complement such programs. However, courts that sanction anti-social behavior and programs that promote pro-social activities will always be like Sisyphus rolling his rock up the mountain only to have it roll down again if the economic and social policies that fueled modern era gang activities are not addressed (Johnson & Mulhausen, 2005).

PRIMARY PREVENTION AND ECONOMICS

Riff: "See Officer Krupke we're very upset, we never had the love that every child ought to get. We ain't no delinquents we're misunderstood. Deep down inside us there is good."
Action: [*pretending to be a psychiatrist*] "Juvenile delinquency is purely a social disease. "
Riff: "Hey! I got a social disease!" (*West Side Story*, 1961)

While MST offers the most promise for effective and efficient secondary and tertiary interventions to challenge youth aggression and affiliation with anti-social peers, the question of primary prevention requires more than well-conceptualized, tested intervention models and the power of the courts to encourage participation in these programs. Economic and social conditions, the collapse of communities and social support, are both context and fuel for youth anti-social peer affiliation and aggression. Both gang and non-gang homicide rates are significantly higher in impoverished communities (Rosenfeld et al., 1999). However, this poverty that breeds violence is an avoidable product of policies that unevenly attenuate the distribution of wealth and opportunity (Lindsey, 2004).

Successful economies develop and nourish an affluent middle class with pathways of upward mobility offering hope to those below. A healthy middle class ensures a stable population and provides purchasing power necessary to sustain economic growth. During the era of gangs of territory and identity, the United States' economy was more inclusive. The middle class was stable, and with proper support, lower class families could achieve middle class status. However, in the final decades of the 20th century, the American middle class has markedly deteriorated, with distribution of wealth and opportunity severely skewed towards the upper class. In fact, economic policies of the 1980s so adversely affected America that by 1990, the combined income of the wealthiest one percent nearly equaled the combined income of the poorest 40%. This skew continues to unfold with the top 10% of American families now owning twice as much wealth as the remaining 90% (Lindsey, 2004). This drastic shift of American wealth decreased the size and ability of the middle class to regulate the economy, and expanded the American underclass and its impoverished communities that contribute to increased crime, gang violence, child abuse, homicides among children, as well as drug abuse and dependency. These communities produce children born into generations of poverty, with little means or hope of escape (Cummings & Monti, 1993; Garbarino et al., 1991; Phillips, 1990, 2002).

This dramatic shift of wealth and opportunity has been striking. In the1960s, President Johnson's so-called war on poverty lowered the percentage of children in poverty and demonstrated that federal social programs could succeed. However, attacks on these social programs begun during the Nixon administration, were exponentially amplified as the so-called Reagonomic social and economic policies of the 1980's reversed the direction of the flow of wealth and cut supports for greater opportunity for those of lesser means (Lindsey, 2004; Phillips, 1990, 2002). Between 1968 and 1987, the population of children under age six remained stable, but the number of children in this age group living below the poverty line increased by 35 percent (Lindsey, 2004). In stark contrast, from 1977 to 1990, the United States' economy supported a 25% expansion of income in the top 10 % of American families while in this same time period, the income of the bottom 20% of families actually fell by 11%. Economic and social policies in the 1980s contributed to a precipitous decline in the quality of life of America's poorest families. For example, though housing is one of the major financial expenses for the poor, funding for public housing was reduced by 80% (Lindsey, 2004).

As previously noted, arrest rates for violent juvenile crime began to rise at alarming rates during the mid-1980s through the early 1990s as rates of arrest for murder, rape, and assault swelled (Pollard, Hawkins, & Arthur, 1999). This steep increase in youth violent crime peaked in 1994, then declined for six years, with juvenile arrests for murder decreasing by an astonishing 68 percent (Butts & Travis, 2002). Although youth crime rates were still much higher in 2000 than they were before the spike in the mid-1980s, violent crime rates among all age groups fell during these six years, with the most significant decrease occurring among youth. Not surprisingly, this coincided with a change of social and economic policies during the Clinton administration (1993-2001) that increased family income and lowered unemployment and poverty rates, especially among single mothers, African-Americans and the elderly. However, this economic growth was fueled by relaxed controls on financial and commodity markets and increased printing of dollars by the Federal Reserve that created bubble economies in the internet, oil, metals, and housing markets, each of which burst even as the United States initiated costly wars in Iraq and Afghanistan (Phillips 2007). These policies and events were amplified during the recent Bush administration (2001-2009) as spending on social and educational programs to support youth were drastically reduced which contributed to another spike in youth violence (Fox and Swatt, 2008). For example, the Bush administration cut spending for Clinton administration initiatives such as after school programs and funding for more police officers and for juvenile justice and prevention programs, some of which were reduced by as much as fifty percent (Butterfield, 2004; Fox & Swatt, 2008).

CONCLUSION

Inter-related factors from the family and its community, to state and national social and economic policies may contribute to or mitigate youth affiliation with anti-social peers and youth aggression. Economic decline contributes to unemployment, under-employment, to development of shadow economies such as illegal drug markets, as well as to diminished community resources and a breakdown of family structure and social support. Crime rates, particularly among youth, mirror the ups and downs of annual U.S. unemployment rates (Butts & Travis, 2002; Parker & Reckdenwald, 2008). It should be obvious that macro social and economic factors and their effects upon families and communities cannot be ignored if we wish to prevent youth affiliation with antisocial peers and its associated violence.

Some avoid addressing these macro influences and assert that regardless of risk factors, it is more important to build upon youth resilience in a strengths-based approach that enables youth to overcome obstacles no matter how oppressive and constraining the environment (Benard, 1993; Benson, 1997). Others criticize this approach because it minimizes how adverse social and economic contexts inhibit the opportunity for initial development and cultivation of assets or resiliency (Tolan, 1996). In this debate, in much the same manner as the debate between punishment and intervention, these positions have been politicized and falsely presented as dichotomous.

We believe the facts are quite clear. When raised in communities impoverished for generations, with compromised parental and adult role models and with limited opportunities, youth are far more likely to affiliate with anti-social peers and to engage in aggressive and violent behavior. A belief that the inherent resiliency of youth can flourish in any environment is not only idealistic but naïve. Efforts to prevent and to reduce youth violence must therefore be multifaceted. Interventions focused upon a single system or symptom will not succeed. Well-conceptualized and tested models like MST that develop preventative social support for families while directly addressing contributing family, school, peer group and community factors must be integrated with flexible and resourceful juvenile justice and law enforcement efforts. However, without viable jobs, opportunity, and social support, families in impoverished or declining communities will have limited success in guiding youth to embrace the limited pro-social opportunities. Like Sisyphus and his rock, we will continue to make a few steps forward only to fall further as our communities decline.

REFERENCES

Acosta, O., Albus, K., Reynolds, M., Spriggs, D. & Weist, M. (2001). Assessing the status of research on violence-related problems among youth. *Journal of Clinical Child Psychology, 30(1)*, 152-160.

Baumrind, D. (2005). Patterns of parental authority and adolescent autonomy. In J. Smetana (Ed.), *New directions for child development: Changes in parental authority during adolescence* (61-69). San Francisco: Jossey-Bass.

Benard, B. (1993, September). *Resiliency paradigm validates craft knowledge*. Western Center News, 6-7.

Benson, P. L. (1997). *All kids are our kids: What communities must do to raise caring and responsible children and adolescents*. San Francisco: Jossey-Bass.

Bronfenbrenner, U. (1979). *The ecology of human development: Experiments by nature and design*. Cambridge: Harvard University Press.

Bukowski, W. M., Newcomb, A. F. & Harrup, W. W. (1996). *The company they keep: Friendship in childhood and adolescence*. New York: Cambridge University Press.

Butterfield, F. (2004, October 12). Triple murder in Boston amid a grim statistic: Killings on the rise. New York Times. Retrieved from http://www.nytimes.com.

Butts, J. & Harrell, A. (1998). *Delinquents or criminals? Policy options for young offenders*. Washington DC: The Urban Institute.

Butts, J. & Travis, J. (2002). *The rise and fall of American youth violence: 1980 to 2000*. Washington, DC: The Urban Institute, Justice Policy Center.

Carter, B. & McGoldrick, M., (Eds.). (2005). *The expanded family life cycle: Individual, family, and social perspectives*. Needham Heights, MA: Allyn & Bacon.

Center of Juvenile and Criminal Justice. (n.d.). *Juvenile Justice History*. Retrieved May 28, 2009, from http://www.cjcj.org/juvenile/justice/juvenile/justice/history/0

Cummings, S. & Monti, D. (Eds.). (1993). *Gangs: The origins and impact of contemporary youth gangs in the United States*. Albany, NY: New York Press.

Curtis, N. M., Ronan, K. R. & Borduin, C. M. (2004). Multisystemic treatment: A meta-analysis of outcome studies. *Journal of Family Psychology, 18(3)*, 411-419.

Daane, D. (2003). Child and adolescent violence. *Orthopedic Nursing, 22*, 22-33.

Dishion, T., Nelson, S. & Yasui, M. (2005). Predicting early adolescent gang involvement from middle school adaptation. *Journal of Clinical Child and Adolescent Psychology, 34(1)*, 62-73.

Dodge, K. A., Dishion, T. J. & Lansford, J. E. (Eds.). (2006). *Deviant peer influences in programs for youth*. New York: Guilford Press.

Dorfman, L. & Schiraldi, V. (2001). *Off balance: Youth, race and crime in the news*. Washington, DC: Building Blocks for Youth.

Elliot, D. S. (1994). *Youth violence: An overview*. Boulder, CO: University of Colorado, Center for the Study and Prevention of Violence, Institute of Behavioral Science.

Feerick, M. & Silverman, G. (Eds.). (2006). *Children exposed to violence.* Baltimore: Paul H. Brooks.

Fox, J. & Swatt, M. (2008). *The recent surge in homicides involving young black males and guns: Time to reinvest in prevention and crime control.* Boston: Northeastern University.

Friedman, M. (2006). Posttraumatic stress disorder among military returnees from Afghanistan and Iraq. *The American Journal of Psychiatry, 163,* 586-593.

Garbarino, J., Kostelny, K. & Dubrow, N. (1991). *No place to be a child: Growing up in a war zone.* Lexington, MA: Lexington Books.

Hamrin, V., Jonker, B. & Scahill, L. (2004). Acute stress disorder symptoms in gunshot-injured youth. *Journal of Child and Adolescent Psychiatric Nursing, 17,* 161-172.

Henggeler, S. W., Schoenwald, S. K., Borduin, C. M., Rowland, M. D. & Cunningham, P. B. (2009). *Multisystemic therapy for anti-social behavior in children and adolescents (2ⁿᵈ ed.).* New York: Guilford Press.

Horowitz, K., Weine, S. & Jekel, J. (1995). PTSD symptoms in urban adolescent girls: Compounded community trauma. *Journal of the American Academy of Child and Adolescent Psychiatry, 43,* 1353-1361.

Howell, J. (1997). Youth gang drug trafficking and homicide: Policy and program implications [Electronic version]. *Juvenile Justice, 4(2).*

Howell, J. (August 1998). Youth gangs and violence. *Juvenile Justice Bulletin.* Washington DC: Office of Juvenile Justice and Delinquency Prevention, U.S. Department of Justice.

Howell, J. & Decker, S. (January 1999). The youth gangs, drugs and violence connection. *Juvenile Justice Bulletin,* Washington DC: Office of Juvenile Justice and

Delinquency Prevention, U.S. Department of Justice. iCasualties.org. (2009). *Iraq coalition casualty count.* Retrieved August, *23,* 2009 from icasualties.org/oif

Johnson, S. & Mulhausen, D. (2005). North American transnational youth gangs: Breaking the chain of violence. *Trends in Organized Crime, 9(1),* 38-54.

Jenson, J., Potter, C. & Howard, M. (2001). American juvenile justice: Recent trends and issues in youth offending. *Social Policy & Administration, 35(1),* 48-68.

Kim, J. E., Hetherington, E. M. & Reiss, D. (1999). Associations among family relationships, antisocial peers, and adolescents' externalizing behavior : Gender and family type differences. *Child Development, 70,* 1209-1230.

LeBlanc, M., Vallieres, E. & McDuff, P. (1993). The prediction of males' adolescent and adult offending from school experience. *Canadian Journal of Criminology,* October, 459-478.

Lindsey, D. (2004). *The welfare of children* (2ⁿᵈ ed.). New York: Oxford University Press.

Litz, B. & Orsillo, S. (2004). The returning veteran of the Iraq War: Background issues and assessment guidelines [Electronic version]. *Iraq War Clinician Guide* (2ⁿᵈ ed.). 21-33.

Loeber, R., Farrington, D. P., Stouthamer-Loeber, M. & Van Kammen, W. B. (1998). *Antisocial behavior and mental health problems: Explanatory factors in childhood and adolescence.* Mahwah, N. J., Erlbaum.

Macoby, E. E. & Martin, J. A. (1983). Socialization in the context of the family: Parent-child interactions. In E. M. Hetherington (Ed.), P. H. Mussen (Series Ed.), *Handbook of child psychology, Vol. 4: Socialization, personality, and social development* (1-101). New York, Wiley.

Marcus, R. (2005). Youth violence in everyday life. *Journal of Interpersonal Violence, 20(4),* 442-447.

Minuchin, S., Montalvo, B., Guerney, B. G., Rosman, B. L. & Schumer, F. (1967). *Families of the slums: An exploration of their structure and their treatment*. New York; Basic Books.

Minuchin, S. (1974). *Families and family therapy*. Cambridge: Harvard University Press.

Nicolaides, S. (Producer), & Singleton, J. (Writer/Director). (1991). *Boyz n the Hood* [Motion picture]. United States: Columbia Pictures.

Ogino, T. (2005). *Prevention of juvenile crime in the United States and Japan,* (USJP Occasional Paper 05-11). Cambridge, MA: Harvard University, Program on U.S. Japan Relations.

Parker, K. & Reckdenwald, A. (2008). Concentrated disadvantage, traditional male role models, and African-American juvenile violence. *American Society of Criminlogy, 46(3)*.

Parry, B. (2009, February). Corrections must lead the fight against youth gangs. *Corrections Today*.

Phillips, K. (1990). *The politics of rich and poor: Wealth and the American electorate in the Reagan aftermath*. New York: HarperCollins.

Phillips, K. (2002). *Wealth and democracy: A political history of the American rich*. New York: Broadway Books, Random House.

Philips, K. (2007). *Bad money: Reckless finance, failed politics, and the global crisis of American capitalism.* New York: Penguin.

Pollard, J., Hawkins, D. & Arthur, M. (1999). Risk and protection: Are both necessary to understand diverse behavioral outcomes in adolescence? *Social Work Research, 23(3)*, 145-158.

Reid, J. B., Patterson, G. R. & Snyder, J. (Eds.). (2002). *Antisocial behavior in children and adolescents: A developmental analysis and model for intervention.* Washington, D. C., American Psychological Association.

Rosenfeld, R., Bray, T. & Egley, A. (1999). Facilitating violence: A comparison of gang-motivated, gang-affiliated, and nongang youth homicides. *Journal of Quantitative Criminology, 15(4)*, 495-516.

Scheidlinger, S. (1994). A commentary on adolescent group violence. *Child Psychiatry and Human Development, 25(1)*, 3-11.

Seaburn, D., Landau-Stanton, J. & Horowitz, S. (1996). Core techniques in family therapy. In R. H., Mikesall, D. Lusterman, & S. H. McDaniel (Eds.), *Integrating family therapy: Handbook of family psychology and systems theory.* Washington, D.C.: American Psychological Association.

Thornberry, T. P. & Krohn, M. D. (Eds.). (2003) *Taking stock of delinquency. An overview of findings from contemporary longitudinal studies*. New York: Kluwest/Plenum.

Tolan, P. H. (1996). How resilient is the concept of resilience? *Community Psychologist, 29*, 12-15.

Travis, J. & Waul, M. (2002). *Reflections on the crime decline: Lessons for the future?* Washington DC: The Urban Institute, Justice Policy Center.

Vitarro, F., Brendgen, M. & Tremblay, R. E. (2000). Influence of deviant friends on delinquency: Searching for moderator variables. *Journal of Abnormal Child Psychology, 28*, 313-325.

Wise, R. (Producer), & Robbins, J. & Wise, R. (Directors). (1961). *West Side Story* [Motion picture]. United States: United Artists.

In: Youth Violence and Juvenile Justice: Causes, Intervention...   ISBN: 978-1-61668-011-4
Editor: Neil A. Ramsay et al., pp. 287-299   © 2010 Nova Science Publishers, Inc.

Chapter 12

THE MOTIVATIONAL INFLUENCE OF ATTITUDE, SUBJECTIVE NORM, PERCEIVED BEHAVIORAL CONTROL AND ANTICIPATED AFFECTIVE SELF-REACTIONS, ON BEHAVIORAL DECISION MAKING OF RE-OFFENDING

Stavros P. Kiriakidis[1]
University of Macedonia, Department of Educational and Social Policy, Greece.

ABSTRACT

The paper is an application of an extended version of the theory of planned behavior to behavioral choice of performing illegal behavior. The aim of the study was to examine whether self-sanctions, in terms of affective self-reaction, provide an avenue for extending the theoy of planned behavior and at the same time testing the necessity and the sufficieny of the model. Young people detained for illegal actions participated in the study and they filled in a questionaire assessing the sociocognitve determinants of the theory of planned behavior and a measure of affective self-reaction invoked after the execution of an illegal action. It was found that the model overall afforded accurate prediction of behavioral choice of performing illegal actions in the future, however, affective self-reaction contributed significantly, to the prediction of behavioral choice of performing illegal actions in the future. The theory of planned behavior provides a parsimonious way of predicting behavioral choice of performing illegal actions in the future. However, self-sanctions, in terms of affective self-reaction, could be a variable that expands the model, when it is applied to the prediction of behavioral choice of performing illegal actions in the future.

Keywords: Behavioral choice; affective self-reaction; self-sanctions; attitude; subjective norm; perceived behavioral control.

---

[1] Corresponding author: Kapetanaki 29, 173 42, Athens, Tel/Fax 210 9828455, E-mail: skyriak@syros.aegean.gr, kiriaks@yahoo.gr.

INTRODUCTION

The Theory of Planned Behavior

The Theory of Planned Behavior (TPB) (Ajzen, 1985) is an extension of the Theory of Reasoned Action (TRA) (Fishbein and Ajzen, 1975). The TRA (Fishbein and Ajzen, 1975; Fishbein, 1967) proposed, as a central concept for the prediction of behavior in any defined social situation, the intention of performing that behavior.

The original TRA (Ajzen and Fishbein, 1970) postulated that intentions are the most immediate antecedents of any behavior that is under voluntary control and are assumed to capture the motivational influences on behavior. Fishbein (1967) provided a new perspective in the conceptualisation and definition of attitude. He reported that the main conclusion for the definition of an attitude is that, an attitude is "a learned predisposition to respond to an object or class of objects in a consistently favourable or unfavourable way" (p. 477). This definition stressed the unidimensionality of the concept and Fishbein (1967) highlighted this unidimensionality as the main problem in the failure of accurate behavioral prediction as an overall attitude towards any object could be the same among individuals, while these individuals may not feel the same degree of favourableness or unfavourableness towards features of the object. Fishbein (1967) further argued that this qualitative differentiation cannot be captured by unidimensional measures of attitudes and this is a reason that attitudes measured in such a way do not predict behavior. Fishbein (1967) argued that for the prediction of behavior, it is not sufficient only to know the attitude of a person but his/her behavioral response must be known as well (e.g. intention). These are treated as different entities, subject, both of them, to the rewards and punishments of the environment which may be differentially reinforced, so that people with the same learned attitude could have different behavioral responses as a result of differential reinforcement of the last. This point was received as stressing the multidimensional composition of the attitude as, if the conative component of attitude is different then the attitude is different as well.

Fishbein (1967) argues for a unidimensional concept of attitude, reflecting the "amount of affect for or against a psychological object" (Fishbein, 1967: 478) while beliefs and behavioral intentions are viewed as separate concepts related to attitudes as antecedents of attitudes and not as part of them. This distinction is based on the actual measurement of attitudes in the literature, which reflects the measurement of affect, and the inability of a single score to accurately reflect this proposed multidimensionality. In addition, in line with an expectancy-value position, Fishbein (1967) proposed that beliefs about a behavior in terms of the value of the behavior and the perceived probability that these outcomes are multiplied and transformed into an evaluative dimension of the behavior, termed attitude towards the behavior (Liska, 1984).

Intentions are in turn determined by attitudes towards the behavior[2], a personal factor, and a social factor, subjective norms, perceived social pressures from significant referents to

---

[2] Fishbein and Ajzen (1975) argued that the general inconsistency reported in the literature for the low correlations between attitudes as behavioral dispositions and behavior, was partly due to the fact that several researchers tried to predict behaviors from attitudes towards objects of the behavior and not towards the behavior per se. The authors proposed that the measurement of the attitude towards the behavior will be a better predictor of the behavior.

perform the behavior and the actors' motivation to comply with the referents[3]. Attitudes and subjective norms are in turn determined by the salient beliefs people hold about the behavior.

Attitudes are formulated by beliefs about the outcomes of performing any behavior and the perceived importance of that outcome for the actor. So, attitudes towards any behavior are a function of the strength that a behavior will result in an outcome and the evaluation of that outcome. In a similar manner, subjective norms depend on views important others, in people's lives have, and their motivation to comply with them. The TPB extends the TRA by including a third determinant of intentions and behavior, perceived behavioral control (PBC), which is assumed to reflect past experience with the performance of the behavior and anticipated obstacles that could inhibit behavior. Ajzen (1985) argued that any behavior is rarely under complete volitional control and identifies, in relation to the individual, many external and internal factors that can potentially inhibit the intended execution of any behavior. He continued that the predictive role of PBC would depend on the degree to which the behavior is under volitional control and the potential role of external and internal factors to interfere with the behavior. The greater the behavior depends on these factors being enacted the greater the predictive and explanatory role of the PBC. Ajzen (1985) postulated that PBC would determine behavior both directly and indirectly. Directly through its influence to account for variations in behavior by taking into account possible obstacles which must be overcome for the successful performance of the behavior. Indirectly by its influence to intentions, as any person intending to perform a behavior takes into account the possible obstacles and whether he/she is able to effectively deal with them. Beliefs are supposed to be the single most important structural units of attitudes, norms and PBC. The contribution of each of these factors to the prediction of behavioral intentions is relative and it depends on the behavior under consideration or/and the person. It is possible that in certain instances either one, or a combination of these determinants will influence intentions. The degree of influence of each one of them in the prediction of intention is provided by empirically obtained standardised regression coefficients (Ajzen and Fishbein, 1973).

The TPB is a dispositional approach to cognitive self-regulation and provides a conceptual and methodological advance in the prediction of behavior and the attitudes behavior consistency (Liska, 1984). According to Ajzen (1991, 1988), the TPB, which deals with the information processing of the individual whose behavior is guided by rational decisions, provides a parsimonious way of predicting intentions, which are regarded as the immediate antecedent of behavior, by selecting attitudes, subjective norms and, recently, PBC as the mediators between several biological and environmental factors and intentions of executing the behavior. Any other variable could have an indirect effect on intentions only by influencing attitudes, subjective norms or PBC.

Early conceptualisations and operationalisations of broad behavioral dispositions, such as traits and attitudes, failed to accurately predict behavior (Fishbein and Ajzen, 1975). In contrast to these early concepts, the TRA and the TPB identify salient beliefs that operate as a function for the formation of attitudes, perceived norms and behavioral control. This feature indicates a degree of specificity for the behavior of interest, with reference to which, the beliefs determining the constructs of the theory are operationalised. Another methodological advance is the specification of the behavior to be predicted in terms of target, time, context

---

[3] Trafimow and Fishbein (1995) challenged the distinction between behavioral and normative beliefs, as both beliefs refer to perceived consequences. This view, however, was not empirically supported.

and action and the corresponding operationalisation of the relevant constructs in this fashion, so that a specific and detailed matching is attained. Ajzen and Fishbein (1980) argued that not all behaviors to be predicted from the constructs of the theory should be specifically defined in terms of target, time, context and action, rather, the operationalisation of both the constructs of the theory and the behavior of interest should correspond, either in specificity or generality. The TPB provides a parsimonious framework for identifying the immediate antecedents of any behavior with many practical advantages in terms of prediction and potential intervention. In addition, it allows for detailed and in-depth analysis of the specific beliefs that are influencing intentions and behavior. Given that any of the determinants of intentions are found related with behavioral intentions, the beliefs underlying the related global factors can be analysed for a more detailed analysis of the beliefs underlying them so that a greater insight is gained regarding the possible determinants of behavior at a more basic level. Any distal factors related to the behavior of interest are supposed to have an indirect effect on the behavior by formulating the attitudes, the perceived social norms and the PBC individuals have towards the behavior or their weights (Ajzen, 1991).

The predictive efficiency of both the TRA and the TPB across numerous behavioral domains is evident from many meta-analytic studies (Godin and Kok, 1996; Randall and Wolff, 1994; Sheppard, Hartwick and Warshaw, 1988). Despite the successful performance of the theory in predicting and explaining behavioral intentions and accounting for a considerable amount of the variance in actual behavior, there are certain issues of the theory that have been subject to criticism.

Franzoi (2000) and Eagly and Chaiken (1998, 1993) pointed to the fact that the models do not account for actions performed spontaneously and suddenly and they cannot explain behaviors that are of a habitual nature, that is, mainly daily performed behaviors that used to be under conscious control, but which through repetition have became more "automatic" and are less governed by rational planning (Wegner and Bargh, 1998).

Eagly and Chaiken (1993), argued that the TPB was unlikely to be perceived as a "complete description of the causes of behavior" (p. 173) as it does not deal with more general characteristics that have been found related with a particular behavior to which the theory is applied to predict. With regard to any behavioral domain to which the theory is applied, every other variable that has been found associated with the specific behavior is treated as an external to the model variable. That is, these variables can exert an influence on the behavior under study, only through their influence on the constructs of the theory or the weights of the constructs in predicting intentions and behavior. Eagly and Chaiken (1993), noted that the theory does not propose any theoretical specifications of those variables and it does not identify the ways that these variables, that are regarded as external to the model, influence the beliefs underlying the constructs of the theory. It can be argued that the TPB identifies the most proximal cognitive antecedents of behavior. A similar conclusion was reached by Petraitis, Flay and Miller (1995), who reviewed the literature of the theories of adolescent substance abuse. They argued that the TRA and the TPB, by assessing behavior specific beliefs, are able to identify very potent predictors of adolescent substance abuse. However, they do not explain the long-term causes of the behavior, they "focus on the effects of substance-specific cognitions but not on their causes" (ibid: 70). The authors concluded that those two theories have been developed as general models of behavior that concentrate on the immediate causes of behavior and while identifying those constructs which proximally influence behavior, they provide a fruitful way of integrating the more distal variables specifically related to any behavioral domain of interest emphasised by other theories.

Eagly and Chaiken (1993), also questioned the proposition of the theories that people actually engage in such a complex scrutiny and evaluation of their beliefs each time they are about to behave in any way. They however concluded that this could not really be the case; it is plausible to assume that the beliefs people hold determine their attitude, subjective norm and PBC. Once those determinants are formed, when faced with a behavioral decision, people retrieve only those determinants, either attitude, subjective norm, behavioral control, intention or a combination of them, that will guide their behavior. However, Eagly and Chaiken (1993) noted that within the theoretical propositions of the theories it is not clear which processes are activated prior to behavior.

Franzoi (2000), argued that a fundamental assumption of the TPB is that individuals' behaviors are guided by rational decisions which, at the most basic level of the determinants of the theory, are captured by their beliefs towards any behavior (Fishbein and Ajzen, 1975), which are regarded as the single structural units of the theory laying at its foundations. By taking this perspective (Ajzen and Fishbein, 1980; Ajzen and Fishbein, 1977) of the inherent rationality of human behavior, their models do not account for the possibility that certain behaviors can be influenced by irrational causes, that are not processed by cognitive informational processing. Fazio and Roskos-Ewoldsen (1994) argued that when people are motivated enough and they have the opportunity to engage in extensive cognitive reasoning, the process described by the TPB could be sufficient to account for the antecedents of behavior. However, when these two requirements are lacking at any given time they proposed that human behavior would be influenced directly by attitudes towards the object, leading to an evaluative definition of the event as bad or good. Definition of the event depends on the perceptions of the object and the definition of the situation, that is, behaviors that are deemed as appropriate in the particular situation. They further continued that if attitudes towards the objects are to exert any influence on behavior, the attitude should be readily accessible from memory, and by that mode of operating attitudes towards objects seem to have a clear functional significance for human behavior by providing people with a simple, efficient, non-time-consuming and energy demanding way to deal effectively with every day life behavioral decisions. It could be argued that no single model can effectively deal with the complexity of human behavior and juvenile offending in particular, and while the TPB cannot be regarded as dealing with the sum of psychological processes that guide human behavior, it was thought that it provides a fruitful theoretical framework for organising the study of the young offenders' beliefs and evaluations of their future offending behavior, and it was, thus, employed as a way to guide the identification, assessment and description of the young offenders' cognitive representations of their future offending behavior.

Fishbein and Ajzen (1975) and Ajzen and Fishbein (1973) proposed that the relative contribution of attitudes and subjective norms to the prediction of intentions are mainly an empirical issue that needs to be established for any behavioral domain the model is applied as "[t]hese empirical weights are expected to vary with the kind of behavior that is predicted, with the conditions under which the behavior is to be performed, and with the person who is to perform the behavior" (Ajzen and Fishbein, 1973: 44). This assumption was challenged by Liska (1984) who argued that this assumption is a conceptual problem and not an empirical one, and that if the weights of the model are expected to vary according to the conditions specified above, then the model becomes increasingly idiosyncratic with limited theoretical specification of the models' variables and constants. This point was also advanced by Bagozzi (1992), who argued that both the TRA and the TPB, do not specify the conditions under which the components of the theories apply or not, as they are thought to function in all contexts. While this seems a justified criticism, it can be argued that for purposes of prediction and practical application, in the sense of informing the content of various intervention programmes for any kind of behavior, the models, which are parsimonious, can be very useful and informative, especially when the underlying beliefs of the constructs of the theory, which lay at the roots of behavior, are assessed in detail

Affective Self-Reactions

Attempts at extending the TPB have concentrated on another construct, namely, anticipated affective reactions resulting from the performance of the behavior. Ajzen (1991) states that the TPB deals with "cognitive self-regulation in the context of a dispositional approach to the prediction of behavior" (Ajzen, 1991: 180) and that individuals make decisions rationally, according to the information available to them. The model derives from the expectancy-value perspective and a calculation of the costs and benefits of any behavior are supposed to be taken into account in the planning of the final performance of it. Richard, van der Pligh and de Vries (1995) argued that the rational decision making, postulated by the model, may not be sufficient in the prediction of behaviors heavily influenced by emotions, as these emotions might have an effect on the process of decision making. They argued that anticipated affective reactions might have a motivational influence, by means of a deterrent effect, on the execution of sexual behaviors that could lead to AIDS prevention.

In a study of a representative sample of 822 adolescents, aged from 15 to 19 years of age, Richard et al (1995) tested the enhancement of prediction of behavioral expectations in three sexual situations, by the addition of anticipated affective reactions. They concluded that the prediction of behavioral expectations in the sexual domain, could be increased by the incorporation of affective reactions to the TPB. The independent increase in the multiple correlation of behavioral expectations was significant and consistent for both behavioral expectations examined: namely refraining from sexual intercourse and using a condom. They further argued that the results of their study replicated previous findings, supporting the idea of including a measure of anticipated affective reactions in the TPB in predicting behavioral expectations, at least, in sexual behaviors. It has to be noted, however, that, although the motivational influences of anticipated affective reactions were supported in this study, whether these effects on behavior are totally mediated by intentions, or exert a direct effect on behavior, has not been examined.

Parker, Manstead and Stradling (1995), report similar results. Anticipated regret substantially improved the prediction of intentions to commit driving violations. It has to be noted, however, that Parker et al (1995) conceptualised anticipated regret and moral norm as different aspects of an individual's personal norm and report the combined effects of these two variables on the prediction of intentions. Conner and Armitage (1998) reviewed studies that examined the role of anticipated regret in the performance of the behavior within the TPB. They noted that a role of anticipated affect across behaviors is generally supported, while they report that interventions, aimed at increasing the salience of anticipated affect, were more successful than interventions targeting change in the other components of the TPB. They also noted a variability of the operationalisation of the construct across studies, similar to the direct measurement of attitudes or as behavioral beliefs. The authors suggested that the later way is preferable as it does not confuse the assessment of anticipated affective reactions with attitudes and provides a way to examine the dimensionality of attitudes, "as the extent to which affective beliefs underlie affective attitudes and instrumental beliefs underlie instrumental attitudes" (Conner and Armitage, 1998: 1448), employing more specific affective reactions than general positive or negative reactions.

Affective self-reactions as a possible way to improve prediction of behavioral intentions, seems promising in behavioral domains that the commitment of the behavior is likely to induce feelings of guilt and shame, as is evident from studies about commitment of driving violations (e.g. Parker et al, 1995). However, its predictive utility in accounting for variance in behavioral intentions of more serious law violations by adolescent males has not been investigated, and the current study attempted to examine this issue in a sample of incarcerated young offenders, whose offences were serious enough to justify sentence to custody.

Purpose of the Study

The study will partially apply the TPB to examine the postulated antecedents of the young offenders intentions to re-offend. Thus, it will concentrate on the proximal cognitive representations serving as motivations for their future offending behavior. The study focuses on young offenders' intentions of future offending as a proximal antecedent of their future offending behavior (Cimler & Beach, 1981), as it has been shown in the literature and in many meta-analytic studies, that intention is a rather potent predictor of actual behavior (Ajzen, 1991).

At the same time, the study will examine the necessity of the inclusion of the components of the model, that is, attitude, subjective norm and PBC of future offending, in predicting intentions of re-offending. It will also assess the relative contribution that each of them makes by determining empirically based weights of the constructs.

According to Ajzen (1991), any other external to the model variable could have an indirect effect on intentions only by influencing attitude, subjective norm or PBC. This line of argument also sets the boundaries of testing the sufficiency of the theory. Having the relevant constructs measured accurately, the components of the theory should predict intentions to the limit of error variance and no other significant contribution should be made to the amount of variance predicted by external to the model variables (Ajzen, 1991). The present study provides an opportunity for testing that assertion, with regard to, personal self-sanctions in terms of affective self-reaction following the execution of offending behavior.

METHOD

Participants

The study included one hundrend and fifty-two male young offenders currently incarcerated in one young offenders' intitution in U.K. The age of the sample ranged from 16 to 21, m=18.9, (s.d.=1.3) The length of their sentences ranged from 2 to 96 months (m=26.4, s.d.= 20.3). Fifty-three percent of the participants were currently incarcerated for a violent offence (i.e offences against a person). They had been in custody m=2.5, (s.d.=2.2) and had been remanded m=4.8, (s.d.=5.4) times. They had 11.1, (s.d.= 13.8) previous sentences and stayed in custody for an average of 6.9 months, (s.d.=7.1) at the time of the interview. The total time they had spent in custody was 19.6 months, (s.d.=16.4). The self reported age of their first offence was 12.3 years, (s.d.=2.6), first arrest 14 years, (s.d.=2.4) and first time in custody 16.8 years, (s.d.=1.5). They had tried alcohol at 12.7, (s.d=1.9) and drugs at 12.8, (s.d=1.7). From the institution approximately one-third of the young offenders from each hall, was selected and interviewed.

Questionnaire

Attitude. An attitude measure was obtained by asking the subjects to evaluate, with reference to them, their offending behavior in the future on a set of 8 seven-point semantic differential items according to Osgood, Suci and Tannenbaum (1957). In half of the items the positive pole was presented first and in the other half the negative pole, so as to control response bias (e.g. rewarding-punishing, boring-interesting, safe-unsafe, useless-useful, good-bad, harmful-beneficial, dull-exciting, wise-foolish).). The average over all 8 scales served as a general measure of direct attitude towards offending. Cronbach's α for this measure is .75.

Subjective norm. Three seven-point rating scales were used to assess perceived subjective norm towards offending behavior as has been operationalised in the literature (Ajzen, 1991; Parker et al, 1995). (1) Most people who are important to me think I should stop offending in the future (Unlikely-Likely), (2) Most people who are important to me approve of my offending in the future (Disapprove-Approve), (3) Most people I know would like me to stop offending in the future (Unlikely-Likely). Summating responses to the three scales gave a direct measure of subjective norm. Cronbach's α for this measure is .46.

Perceived behavioral control. Three seven-point rating scales were used to obtain a measure of PBC according to operationalisations in the literature (Terry & O'Leary, 1995; Sparks et al, 1997). (1) How much control do you have whether you stop offending in the future? (Very little control - Complete control). (2) For me to stop offending in the future is (Easy-Difficult). (3) If I wanted to, I could easily stop offending in the future (Extremely unlikely- Extremely likely). Average responses to the three scales provided a direct measure of PBC to stop offending in the future. Cronbach's α for this measure is .82.

Intentions. Two 7-point semantic-differential items elicited intentions to offend in the future. The items were formulated for offending behavior in the future without precise specification of target and context. (1) I intend to offend in the future (Extremely likely-Extremely unlikely). (2) Will you offend in the future (Definitely plan not to-Definitely plan to). Cronbach's α for this measure is .79.

Affective self-reaction: Three seven-point rating scales supplied a measure of affective self-reaction. (1) After committing an offence I usually feel sorry for doing it (Extremely unlikely-Extremely likely), (2) After committing an offence I feel guilty most of the times (Extremely unlikely-Extremely likely) and (3) I sometimes feel ashamed after committing an offence (True-False). An overall score for affective self-reaction was calculated by averaging the scores of the three scales. Cronbach's α for this measure is .93.

The operationalization and the wording of the items measuring the constructs of the TPB were made according to the way the constructs are operationalised in the literature, applying the TPB in a variety of behavioral domains.

RESULTS

Almost all of the measures of the components of the TPB and the measure of affective self-reaction, show acceptable to very satisfying internal consistencies. These results provide further confidence that the questions were relatively well understood by the population of young offenders and kept ambiguity of meaning across subjects to a minimum. However, the measure of subjective norm is an exception, with an alpha reliability coefficient of .46.

Pearson's correlations between the measured variables of the TPB are displayed in Table 1. From the correlation matrix, it can be observed that all the variables were significantly correlated with behavioral intentions of future offending. Almost all the interrelationships between the variables, were significant and many of them were substantial. It is interesting to note that affective self-reaction correlated substantially with attitude.

Table 1. Intercorrelations of Intention, Affective Self-Reaction, Attitude, Subjective Norm, and Perceived Behavioral Control (N=152).

	Intention	Attitude	Subjective Norm	Perceived Behavioral Control
Attitude	.43**			
Subjective Norm	.28**	.14		
Perceived Behavioral Control	-.48**	-.36**	-.18*	
Affective self-reaction	-.44**	-.47**	-.20*	.29**

**p<.01, *p<.05

Table 2. Hierarchical Regression of Intentions to Re-offend in the Future on Attitude, Subjective Norm, Perceived Behavioral Control and Affective Self-Reaction (N=152).

Predictors	R	Adjusted R^2	Increment to R^2	F	Final b
Attitude	.427	.177	.182	33.43***	.180*
Subjective Norm	.480	.221	.049	9.41**	.148*
Perceived Behavioral Control	.579	.322	.104	23.18***	-.322***
Affective Self-Reaction	.614	.359	.041	9.77**	-.235**

Note: * p< .05,**p< .01, ***p< .001

The fact that the relationships between the variables are significant and substantial, supported the need for performing a regression analysis of intentions on the several predictors so that the unique contribution of each predictor to account for a percentage of the variance of behavioral intentions to offending in the future can be assessed.

Table 2 shows the results of the hierarchical regression of intentions on attitude, subjective norm, behavioral control and affective self-reaction. The results, overall, support the TPB and the prediction of intentions. It can be seen that all the predictors made significant and independent contributions to the prediction of the young offenders' intentions to re-offend.

Behavioral control emerged as the most important determinant of intentions as is evident by the values of b in table 2. The important role of PBC in determining intentions of future re-offending suggests that offending behavior is not totally under volitional control. There appear to be many obstacles, which the young offenders need to overcome, and several resources, they need to acquire, in order to change or discontinue their offending pattern in the future.

Interestingly enough, the second most important predictor of intentions was affective self-reaction, a belief that offending invokes personal affective sanctions. The young offenders who intend to re-offend in the future, tend to perceive that their offending behavior does not invoke personal affective sanctions.

Attitude emerged as the third most important predictor of intentions to re-offend. This is in line with previous research and theoretical propositions of the predictive role of attitude to intentions (Ajzen 1991). Those who acknowledge that they can attain positive and valued consequences from their offending tend to intend to re-offend in the future. It has been suggested that sometimes the material benefits of offending, especially drug dealing, can be so satisfying that a period of incarceration seems a relatively acceptable risk to take. The implications from such accounts are several and important.

Subjective norm, however, was the last predictor to remain in the regression equation. The relatively less important role subjective norm might have in the prediction of intention, has received support from previous studies (Godin & Kok, 1996).

DISCUSSION

The aim of the present research was to investigate the social psychological factors underlying decisions of choice of performing illegal actions in the future by testing the effectiveness of a revised theory of planned behavior model in this context. The results of the study demonstrate the utility of the theory of planned behavior as a conceptual framework for predicting choice of performing illegal actions in the future. Attitude, subjective norm and perceived behavioral control were found to influence young offenders' intentions to perform illegal actions in the future and all significantly predicted intentions to perform illegal actions in the future providing support for the original TPB model. That is, young offenders with positive attitude toward the behavior, who believed that important others would approve of the behavior and who believed they had not control over carrying out the behavior were more likely to intend to offend in the future. This is in line with many studies that report similar findings and which generally support the important motivational influence of perceived control, attitude and subjective norm in the prediction of intentions in diverse behavioral domains (Kimiecik 1992; Dennison & Shepherd, 1995; Ajzen, 1991; 2001).

Overall support was found for the revised TPB model, the inclusion of self sanctions in terms of affective self-reaction significantly increased the predictive potency of the model. That is individuals who reported that are feeling sorry, ashamed and guilty after performing an illegal act were less likely to intend to offend in the future. As predicted, the inclusion of an additional affective self-reaction component improved the prediction of behavioral intention. Thus in line with past research (Richard et al, 1995; Parker, Manstead and Stradling, 1995; Conner and Armitage, 1998; Conner & Abraham, 2001) the present findings support the inclusion of affective self-reaction in the TPB, particularly in the prediction of intentions of performing illegal actions. Affective self-reaction was an independent predictor of intentions of performing illegal actions, and indeed accounted for substantial variance in intentions, emerging as the second more potent predictor of intentions after perceived behavioral control. This understanding is important in furthering knowledge of the processes by which cognitive and affective factors inform behavioral decisions of executing illegal actions (van der Pligt, Zeelenberg, van Dijk, de Vries & Richard, 1997).

One potential limitation of the present study is that the actual performance of illegal behavior was not measured. However, such measurement calls for the collection of longitudinal data which is difficult and expensive procedure. Another reason that longitudinal data could not be available is that the respondents participated anonymously in the study, thus, making their identification in the community not possible. In addition, most of the participants in the study are expected to live rather chaotic lives, further complicating their identification in the community.

The results of the current study are potentially informative for the content of cognitive-behavioral interventions, that is, the beliefs and attitudes that need to be challenged. Further the view that there should be an increase of the salience of post behavioral affective reactions such as regret, guilt and shame is generally supported. This is in line with the fact that has been demonstrated that this increased salience of affective factors has an impact on both behavioral intentions and behavior (van der Pligt, Zeelenberg, van Dijk, de Vries & Richard, 1997). Such interventions should be initiated within the correctional settings of Young Offenders' Institutions.

In addition, the TPB is a theoretical framework that provides a useful model of assessing the relevant needs of the offenders and the factors that the young offenders themselves think that are important and need to be changed in order to avoid future re-offending. It seems that the assessment of the subjectively perceived criminogenic factors is an important issue in the delivery of correctional treatment. Not only because it is the subjective interpretation of factors involved in a decision to commit an antisocial act that is important (Rutter et al, 1997), but, at the same time, provides a means of matching the needs that are identified with the delivery of the program. However, whether the findings of the present study could provide a useful guide for informing the content of any intervention programs, aiming at both cognitive and affective processes, (van der Pligt, Zeelenberg, van Dijk, de Vries & Richard, 1997) within the young offenders' institutions that could be sucessful in reducing the rates of recidivism, has to be established through longitudinal follow-up studies and controlled randomized experimental trials.

REFERENCES

Ajzen, I. (2001). Nature and Operation of Attitudes. *Annual Review of Psychology, 52, 27-58.*

Ajzen, I. (1991). The Theory of Planned Behavior. *Organizational Behavior and Human Decision Processes, 50, 179-211.*

Ajzen, I. (1988). *Attitudes, Personality and Behavior.* Homewood: Dorsey Press.

Ajzen, I. (1985). From Intentions to Actions: A Theory of Planned Behavior. In J. Kuhl, & J. Beckmann, (Eds). *Action Control: From Cognition to Behavior.* Heidelberg: Springer.·

Ajzen, I. & Fishbein, M. (1973). Attitudinal and Normative Variables as Predictors of Specific Behaviors. *Journal of Personality and Social Psychology, 27, 41-57.*

Ajzen, I. & Fishbein, M. (1970). The Prediction of Behavior from Attitudinal and Normative Variables. *Journal of Experimental Social Psychology,6, 466-487.*

Bagozzi, R. P. (1992). The Self-Regulation of Attitudes, Intentions and Behaviour. *Social Psychology Quarterly, 55, 178-204.*

Cimler, E. & Beach, L. R. (1981). Factors Involved in Juveniles' Decisions about Crime. *Criminal Justice and Behavior, 8, 275-286.*

Conner, M. & Abraham, C. (2001). Conscientiousness and the Theory of Planned Behavior: Toward a More Complete Model of the Antecedents of Intentions and Behavior. *Personality and Social Psychology Bulletin, 27(11), 1547-1561.*

Conner, M. & Armitage, C. (1998). Extending the Theory of Planned Behavior: A Review and Avenues for Further Research. *Journal of Applied Social Psychology, 28, 1429-1464.*

Dennison, C. M. & Shepherd, R. (1995). Adolescent food choice: an application of the Theory of Planned Behavior. *Journal of Human Nutrition and Dietetics, 8, 9-23.*

Eagly, A. H. & Chaiken, S. (1998). Attitude Structure and Function. In D. T., Gilbert, S. T. Fiske, & G. Lindzey (Eds.), *The Handbook of Social Psychology (Vol: 1).* New York: Oxford University Press.

Eagly, A. H. & Chaiken, S. (1993). *The Psychology of Attitudes.* Orlando: Harcout Brace Jovanovich, Inc.

Fazio, R. H. & Roskos-Ewoldsen, D. R. (1994). Acting as we Feel: When and How Attitudes Guide Behaviour? In S. Sharon, & B. Timothy (Eds.), *Persuasion: Psychological Insights and Perspectives.* Needham Heights, MA, US: Allyn and Bacon, Inc.

Franzoi, S. L. (2000). *Social Psychology.* New York: McGraw-Hill.

Fishbein, M. (1967). Attitude and Prediction of Behaviour. In Fishbein, M. (Ed) *Readings in Attitude Theory and Measurement.* New York: Wiley.

Fishbein, M. & Ajzen, I. (1975). *Belief, Attitude, Intention and Behavior: An Introduction to Theory and Research.* Reading: Addison Wesley.

Godin, G. & Kok, G. (1996). The Theory of Planned Behavior: A Review of Its Applications to Health-related Behaviors. *American Journal of Health Promotion, 11, 87-98.*

Kimiecik, J. (1992). Predicting Vigorous Physical Activity of Corporate Employees: Comparing the Theories of Reasoned Action and Planned Behavior. *Journal of Sport and Exercise Psychology, 14, 192-206.*

Osgood, C. E., Suci, G. J. & Tannenbaum, P. H. (1957). *The Measurement of Meaning.* Urbana: University of Illinois Press.

Parker, D., Manstead, A. S. R. & Stradling, S. G. (1995). Extending the theory of planned behavior: The role of personal norm. *British Journal of Social Psychology, 34, 127-137.*

Petraitis, J., Flay, B. R. & Miller, T. Q. (1995). Reviewing Theories of Adolescent Substance Use: Organising Pieces in the Puzzle. *Psychological Bulletin, 117, 67-86.*

Richard, R., van der Pligt, J. & de Vries, N. (1995). Anticipated affective reactions and prevention of AIDS. *British Journal of Social Psychology, 34, 9-21.*

Rutter, M., Maughan, B., Meyer, J., Pickles, A., Silberg, J., Simonoff, E. & Taylor, E. (1997). Heterogeneity of Antisocial Behavior: Causes, Continuities and Consequences. In D. W. Osgood (Ed.), *Nebraska Symposium on Motivation: Motivation and Delinquency, (Vol, 44),* (Dienstbier, R.A.) (Gen. Ed.), Lincoln: University of Nebraska Press.

Sparks, P., Guthrie, C. & Shepherd, R. (1997). The Dimensional Structure of the Perceived Behavioral Control Construct. *Journal of Applied Social Psychology, 27, 418-438.*

Terry, D. J. & O'Leary, J. E. (1995). The theory of planned behavior: The effects of perceived behavioral control and self-efficacy. *British Journal of Social Psychology, 34, 199-220.*

Trafimow, D. & Fisbein, M. (1995). Do People Really Distinguish Between Behavioral and Normative Beliefs? *British Journal of Social Psychology, 34, 257-266.*

van der Pligt, J., Zeelenberg, M., van Dijk, W. W, de Vries, N. K. & Richard, R. (1997). Affect, Attitudes and Decisions: Let's Be More Specific. *European Review of Social Psychology, 8.*

Wegner, D. M. & Bargh, J. A. (1998). Control and Automaticity in Social Life. In D. T. Gilbert, S. T. Fiske, & G. Lindzey (Eds.), *The Handbook of Social Psychology (Vol: 1).* New York: Oxford University Press.

In: Youth Violence and Juvenile Justice: Causes, Intervention...   ISBN: 978-1-61668-011-4
Editor: Neil A. Ramsay et al., pp. 301-314   © 2010 Nova Science Publishers, Inc.

Chapter 13

EXPLORING ISSUES ABOUT YOUTH GANGS IN CANADA

Lauren D. Eisler[*]
Department of Criminology, Wilfrid Laurier University, Brantford Campus., Canada

ABSTRACT

In recent years media coverage of youth gangs and youth gang violence has increased substantially across Canada. This increase in coverage my influence and/or reflect a growing public and political perception that youth gangs are becoming a more serious challenge to communities across the country. Political rhetoric and news coverage indicate that the activities of youth gangs in Canada is escalating in frequency and violence and linkages between youth gangs and the drug trade, and organized crime have been considered as an explanation for this increase. This chapter seeks to provide an in-depth overview of the prevalence of youth gangs and youth gang participation in Canada, and employs strain and social disorganization theories to explore factors which are linked to youth participation in gangs. The chapter concludes with a discussion on the types of programs employed to address the problems of youth gangs in Canadian society.

INTRODUCTION

In recent years, media coverage of youth gangs and youth gang violence has increased substantially across Canada. This increase in coverage may influence and/or reflect a growing public and political perception that youth gangs are becoming a more serious challenge to communities across Canada. Political rhetoric and news coverage indicate that the activities of youth gangs across Canada is escalating in frequency and violence and linkages between youth gangs and the drug trade and organized crime have been considered (Clark, 2005; Scott, 2005; McLaren, 2004; Woods, 2004). This chapter explores the issues associated with Canadian youth gangs, including the challenges of defining youth gangs, youth gang

274 Lauren D. Eisler

prevalence in Canada, factors which are linked to youth participation in youth gangs, and measures employed to address the problems of youth gangs in Canadian society.

DEFINING YOUTH GANGS

Perhaps one of the most challenging issues when studying youth gang participation and activity is simply one of definition. What is meant by the word 'gang'? There fails to be one consistent definition accepted and utilized by individuals and organizations throughout Canada. This inconsistency occurs in part because different regions have gang issues that are unique to their jurisdiction and which may involve different types of member participation and activities. Further muddying the waters are inconsistent and inappropriate labels of youth social groups as 'gangs' by outsiders such as media, law enforcement agencies and the public (Mellor, MacRae, Paul, & Hornick, 2005).

For example, Herbert, Hamel, and Savoie reviewed American and Canadian literature on a number of gang-based topics and provided commentary on six different types of identified gangs based, in part, on structure and the use of violence (1997). They identified the first three types as less structured groups who typically do not engage in violence. The other three other gang types were more organized and had a higher tendency to engage in violence. Gordon and Foley (1998) conducted The Greater Vancouver Gang Study which resulted in six classifications regarding youth group involvement. Street gangs were defined as "groups of young people and young adults who band together to form a semi-structured organization primarily to engage in planned and profitable criminal behavior or organized violence against rival street gangs (43)."

The Canadian Police Survey on Youth Gangs, conducted in 2002 by the Astwood Strategy Corporation, was the first Canadian research project that surveyed police departments about the extent and characteristics of youth gangs in Canada. The researchers acknowledged the lack of a common accepted definition of a youth crime and provided their own. For the purpose of the study a youth gang was defined as "a group of youth or young adults under the age of 21, that the respondent or other responsible persons in their agency or community was willing to identify or classify as a gang (2004:4)." Respondents were asked to exclude motorcycle gangs, hate or ideology groups, prison gangs, and other exclusively adult gangs. In comparison several Canadian police departments utilize a definition of 'gang' drafted at a 2005 joint meeting of Chiefs of Police. Their definition is "Three or more persons, formally or informally organized, engaged in a pattern of criminal behavior creating an atmosphere of fear and intimidation within any community, who may have a common name or identifying sign or symbol which may constitute a criminal organization as defined by the Criminal Code of Canada (Department of Justice Canada, 2004).

More recently, Mellor, MacRae, Paul, and Hornick conducted a project meant, in part, to develop a multidimensional conceptual framework for youth gang participation in Canada. Their research focused on five different categories of youth gangs or groups based on organization, recruitment, activities, and exit strategies. One gang type identified by Mellor, MacRae, Paul, and Hornick was "Youth Street Gangs" and was described as:

---

[*] Corresponding author: leisler@wlu.ca

typically organized to carry out money-making criminal activity or organized violence against other gangs. Members can be identified through gang-specific clothing, tattoos, or jewellery and mark their territory with gang graffiti. Activities tend to be planned and organized (2005: 8).

The above mentioned examples provide evidence of the lack of consensus on how to define youth gangs within Canada. As Mathews (1993) states "There is no theory or definition that can account for the pluralistic or heterogeneous gang/group phenomenon in contemporary Canadian society" (4). However, it appears that there are common elements found within each definition. Youth gangs are typically groups of young people who self-identify as a group, are perceived by others to be a distinct group, and who are involved in delinquent and/or criminal activities that consistently produce negative responses from law enforcement agencies and/or the community (R.C.M.P., 2006).

PREVELANCE OF YOUTH GANGS IN CANADA

While there is an abundance of research on the prevalence and makeup of youth gangs in the United States, the same can not be claimed in Canada. The first Canadian work on youth gangs occurred in 1945 when Rogers studied juveniles in street gangs in Toronto. Since then work by Chettleburgh, 2008; Fasilio & Leckie, 1993; Gorden, 1995, 1998, 2000; Hebert, Hamel, & Savoie, 1997; Joe & Robinson, 1980; Kelly & Caputo, 2005; Mathews, 1993, 2005; Mellor, MacRae, Paul, & Hornick, 2005; Young, 1993) have expanded Canadian-based understandings on the development, prevalence, and activities of youth gangs. Grekul and LaBoucane-Benson posit that these studies "establish the fact that gangs are not new to Canada, and that the current concern expressed by communities, governments, law enforcement agencies, and criminal justice system personnel is symptomatic of the latest in a wave of gang concern" (2008: 2).

Recent and comprehensive information available in Canada on the prevalence of youth gangs throughout Canada may be found in the 2002 Canadian Police Survey on Youth Gangs. The Astwood Strategy Corporation, under contract with the Department of the Solicitor General Canada surveyed 264 law enforcement agencies throughout Canada. The goal of the project was to "assess the extent and characteristics of the youth gang problem in communities throughout Canada, as reported by law enforcement agencies (Astwood, 2003: iii). The findings indicate that there are estimated to exist 434 youth gangs with 7,071 members in communities across Canada. The largest concentration of gangs are located in Ontario with 216 gangs and 3,320 members, followed by Saskatchewan with 28 gangs and 1,315 members, British Columbia with 102 gangs and 1,027 members, and Quebec with 25 gangs and 533 members[1] . The provinces of Nova Scotia reports 6 gangs with 37 members, Manitoba reports 15 gangs with 171 members, while no gang activity was reported in the

---

[1] It is important to note however, that only four agencies with the province of Quebec participated in this project. The province of Quebec did not participate in the project as it was conducting its own research project under the supervision of the Ministere de la Securite Publique du Quebec in collaboration with the Service de police de la ville de Montreal. However, it is important to note, the data presented here on the number of youth gangs and membership across Canada does incorporate the findings of the Quebec survey in order to provide the reader with a clear understanding of where gangs are operating and the size of the membership.

three Canadian Territories or in Prince Edward Island, New Brunswick, or Newfoundland/Labrador.

YOUTH GANG DEMOGRAPHICS

Findings of the 2002 Canadian Police Survey on Youth Gangs indicate that the vast majority of gang members are male (94%), but that there is a strong representation of female gang membership in the Western Provinces of British Columbia (12%), Manitoba (10%), and Saskatchewan (9%). Almost one half of the gang members are under the age of 18 (48%) and the largest proportion of gang members are African Canadian/Black (25%), First Nations (22%), and Caucasian/White (18%). The findings also indicate that a significant percentage (36%) of youth gangs across Canada cross cultural and racial lines and are comprised of two or more ethnic/racial groups. This appears most prevalent in Ontario (51%), British Columbia (46%), and Manitoba (24%). The most homogenous youth gangs are found in Nova Scotia with less than 1% and Saskatchewan with 7% of youth gangs reporting a mixture of ethnic/racial membership (Astwood Strategic Corporation, 2004).

WHY DO YOUTH JOIN GANGS?

Research indicates there exists no simple explanation why some young people are attracted to a gang lifestyle and other in similar circumstances do not become involved with gangs. Instead there appears to be a myriad of factors that may influence youth to join gangs. Michael Chettleburgh provides valuable insights into the complexity of this issue when he states:

> Talk to actual or reformed street gang members, and they'll give a wide variety of reasons for their involvement, including broken families, poverty, persistent discrimination, sibling or parental gang involvement, the sense of camaraderie and excitement of the gang, and a lack of positive role models and things to do. They'll also refer to the pull of the lucrative illicit drug trade and to dangerous housing communities, where oftentimes they are faced with a binary decision: either become a victim of gang violence or join a gang and victimize others (2008:2).

Much of the research focuses on the impact of social strain and disorganization on the lives and opportunities for success on the lives of youth. Strain theory, as its name suggests, has its focus on the relationships between individuals and social structures. According to strain theorists, all social structures exert pressures on individuals to conform to certain behavioral standards. These behaviors can either be socially sanctioned (conformist) or may be socially rejected (deviant). Modern western society encourages, or expects, youth to take on certain roles and to accept certain social expectations. These expectations include obedience, a successful completion of at least high school and the internalization of a strong, individualistic work ethic, all of which will lead to the successful entrance into adulthood. Criminal behavior results from the strain youth face between the goals sanctioned by society and legitimate opportunities to meet these goals. The fundamental argument put forward by strain theorists is that when youth are unable to legitimately meet the goals of society they experience strain because they do not fit in to society (Barak, 1998). Youth search for ways to fit in, and one of the ways may be to engage in illegitimate activities as a means to achieve certain goals. Using this interpretation gang membership provides individuals with a means of fulfilling their economic needs when they are excluded from the legitimate labor market (Fisher, Montgomery &Gardner, 2008). Robert K. Merton (1938) articulated several potential outcomes for young people exposed to strain. These outcomes ranged from an individual conforming to social norms and concentrating on developing legitimate means of goal attainment, to the complete rejection of socially acceptable behaviors and the acceptance of alternative and often illegal behaviors as a means of achieving their own defined goals.

Albert Cohen (1955) built upon and added to Merton's work in the area of juvenile delinquency. Cohen's research indicated that youth do not necessarily accept the culturally transmitted social goal of economic success and financial accumulation that appeared to motivate adult offenders. Cohen observed that much of the crime committed by youth appears to be aimless, malicious, and negative (Alvi, 2000). Cohen focused primarily on working-class boys and posited that instead of financial success, these youth were searching for the status and respect they were unable to command in their schools and communities. Cohen also posited that social institutions, including schools, are based on middle-class values and morals and incorporate what he referred to as "middle-class measuring rods" in order to judge youth. While middle-class children are able to meet these expectations which include achievement in both school and athletics, status frustration results when working-class youth are unable to meet the standards demanded of them by their teachers and community. The results of this strain could manifest itself in a number of ways. Some youth, according to Cohen, could strive to meet the expectations determined by the "middle-class measuring rods", while others could reject these standards and develop their own working-class expectations. Other youth could gravitate towards like-minded youth and form a delinquent sub-culture that allows the participant to achieve status he or she craved. Achieving status in a sub-culture might actually involve turning over middle-class values and expectations and doing the opposite of what is expected from successful middle-class youth.

Baron (1989) States

Youth subcultures represent the rebellion adaptation as the frustration over restricted opportunities leads lower-class youth to reject cultural goals and the legitimate means to achieve them. The cultural goals are replaced with those that can be more readily achieved. Subcultural formation takes place when there are a number of youth with similar problems of adjustment. The subculture addresses these problems of adjustment more effectively than any solutions offered by institutional means. It provides an environment where status can be achieved, and, furthermore, through the development of group norms and boundaries support the decision to reject the dominant ideology (291).

Mellor, MacRae, Pauls, & Hornick provide a further analysis of street gang identity when they state:

These groups of young adults come together as a semi-structured organization to engage in profit-driven criminal activity or organized violence against other gangs. Street gangs identify themselves as such through the adoption of a gang name, common brands, styles, colours of clothing, and/or jewelry; and tattoos to openly display gang membership to other gangs. These gangs are not part of a larger criminal organization and often have a definite territory or "turf" that they claim and defend as their own. Graffiti is often used as a form of marking a gang's territory and as a means of communication (2005:20).

Gang membership may be encouraged when the individual suffers low achievement in school (Hill, Howell, Hawkins, Battin-Pearson, 1999; Grekul, & LaBoucane-Benson, 2008; Le Blanc & Lanctot, 1998; Thornberry, Krohn, Lizotte, Smith, Tobin, 2003). Membership is also related to low academic aspirations, low commitment to school and teachers' negative labeling of struggling youth. Gottfredson and Gottfredson also posit that feeling unsafe at school may be a contributing factor to gang membership (2001). Sixteen year old Daniel who had extensive involvement with gang and gang activities discussed how school was not a particularly positive experience for him. Daniel stated:

School wasn't all that great. School, yeah, went back to my Reserve for a while. But in school, 'cause, kind of blamed me for stealing a T.V. or something, which I didn't but, I know who did, but school just accused me right away because I have a bad name or whatever, a bad reference. On my, a couple of us do, so I got mad at the principal and I...He's like, well I tried to go back to school the next day after the T.V. was missing but he's like "you can't come back here, you're not allowed here no more". So I got mad and I moved back to the city or whatever. Tried to start school but was like smoking weed in the bathroom or scrapping somebody out. Go high, half-snapped, or hung-over...I like to get high before I go to school. I can sit there and do my work and I feel relaxed....(Eisler, 2004: 161).

Cloward and Ohlin (1960) added a sub-cultural dimension to the works of Merton and Cohen with their theory of differential opportunity. They identified three types of gangs, and posited that criminal activities resulting from strain could actually be motivated by a drive for both financial success and for gaining status. Differential opportunity theory argued that while one could consider the potential legitimate opportunities for success, it was also important to consider the issue of access to illegitimate opportunities when considering motivations for criminal behaviors. Cloward and Ohlin posited that some individuals live in environments in which criminal behavior is the norm and these individuals have the opportunity to learn and internalize criminal values and norms as well as the techniques needed to engage in deviance. This would lead to the development of criminal subcultures. There was also the potential for violent or conflicting subcultures to emerge when there were neither legitimate nor illegitimate means of goal achievement or where youth could achieve status and relieve frustrations through participating in gang violence. This is evidenced in an excerpt from an article in the Globe and Mail which states:

Gangs are a fact of life on the Opaskwayak Cree Nation. The reserve, which sits just across the river from The Pas, a pulp-and-paper town 600 kilometers northwest of Winnipeg, is one of the most prosperous in Manitoba with a casino, hotel, shopping mall and a successful junior hockey team. Still, estimates of unemployment are close to 50 per cent, and for young people with few prospects, the allure of gang life is difficult to resist. Detective Jerry

Nutbrown of the local RCMP said it's quite common for young gang associates to earn $100 a day as drug mules, delivering packages by bicycle to customers who dial the number of a dealer's disposable cellphone... The RCMP say there are 15 to 20 senior Indian Posse members in The Pas and OCN, but each of these members has three or four prospective members, known as strikers, operating beneath him, trying to outdo one another with acts of violent bravado to earn membership in the gang. It's the strikers who hold the drugs and dish out most of the violence...Chief Glen Ross said a child on the reserve was recently caught carrying $20,000 worth of crack. Another band member who was trying to leave the gang was slain in Winnipeg last year, his Indian Posse tattoos carved from his skin (Friesen & O'Neill, 2008:3).

Retreatist subcultures develop when youth engage in alcohol and drug addictions as a result of being unable to create or participate in criminal or violent subcultures.

Agnew (1985) added to strain theories by positing that it is important to look past blocked opportunities and explore the strain that occurs when individuals attempt but fail to avoid stressful situations. Agnew drew attention to issues such as bullying, sexual harassment, and family violence and claims "adolescents located in aversive environments from which they cannot escape are more likely to be delinquent" (1985:163).

An extremely influential theory of crime, known as Differential Association Theory, has as its foundation in the idea that criminal activity is learned and the "role of parents, peers, and others from whom young people learn skills, norms, and values cannot be underestimated" (Alvi, 2000:95). Edwin Sutherland's original theory argued that all behavior is learned through interactions with others in a communication process. He also argued that the majority of this learning process happens in intimate groups and that this process includes learning the motivations and rationalizations for engaging in certain behaviors. These behaviors may be socially acceptable or they may be deviant or criminal in nature. Sutherland developed concepts to assist in understanding how differential associations vary in terms of quality and strength. Sutherland also argued that learning deviant behavior was like learning any socially acceptable behavior and that crime could not be explained in reference to the general needs and values of criminals as, for the most part, these appeared to be the same as non-criminal individuals. In this case, family and peers involved in gang activities appear to have a significant impact on the likelihood of a youth becoming involved in gang activities. Grekul and LaBoucane-Benson articulate:

> Damaged or weak family relationships contribute, then, to gang involvement. Invariably respondents indicate that the gang acts as, or promises to act as, a substitute family, filling the void left by family backgrounds marked by violence, substance abuse, and crime. Children longing for a sense of identity and belonging are pushed into the welcoming arms of gangs...(2008:68).

Sutherland also argued that if association with criminals could lead to the individual learning and engaging in criminal activities and behaviors, then associating with pro-social, non-criminal individuals or groups could provide individuals opportunities to learn socially acceptable and non-criminal behavior. Differential Association theory has been extremely influential in the study of crime and deviance. It has highlighted the role of learning and relationships with others in regards to criminal activities and has provided a way of exploring why, when facing similar situations (such as poverty or racism), some people engage in criminal activities while others do not. According to Vold, Bernard and Snipes (1998), Sutherland was aware that learning could be either inhibited or enhanced by the context in which it took place and that, therefore, communities had a role to play in an individual's learning process because communities either promoted or discouraged criminal associations.

Routine Activities Theory posits that potential for violent or delinquent activities increases with individual exposure to violent or delinquent activities. Sampson and Lauritsen (1990) refer to this concept as the "principle of homogamy." In other words:

> Individuals increase their likelihood of violence the more frequently they come into contact with, or associate with, members of demographic groups that contain a disproportionate share of violent offenders (Smandych, 2001: 160).

This theory also posits that individuals who experience violent environments and victimization will legitimate the use of violence as a viable solution to conflict much more readily than those who do not (Singer, 1986). Lauritsen, Sampson, and Laub (1991) also argue that subcultural expectations may exist that condone retaliation. In addition, theorists have claimed that there is a strong relationship between violence at home and future antisocial behavior (Elliott, 1994; Hotaling, Straus, and Lincon, 1989; Smith and Thornberry, 1995; Widom, 1989). Fagan and Jones (1984) claim that youth model the actions of their parents and internalize the idea that the use of violence is an acceptable interpersonal strategy to deal with conflict. Aggression is a viable means of problem solving and gaining compliance from others (Smandych, 2001: 165). Seventeen-year old incarcerated Muriel provides insight into a life where violence is a part of every-day family life when she says:

> I don't know, my mom is an alcoholic and she always drank so, I kind of – I don't know, she'd come home and she'd start getting mad at my dad and then they'd argue and stuff and you know, fight. But my dad never hit my mom. My mom always hit my dad. And all my brothers would be crying and tell mom to stop…I lived with my grandma until I was seven, my mom came and took me back when I was seven. And that's when all the violence started. I would have preferred to stay with my grandma because probably things would have been better, by maybe not…

> 'cause my grandma came and took me away from my reserve 'cause my brother did nothing but sex, drugs, alcohol, and gambling (Eisler, 2004: 157).

According to Regoli and Hewitt (1991), violent experiences sway youth to seek out and create violent situations. These situations may include joining other youth who approve and encourage the use of violence, while providing a sense of belonging (cited in Smandych, 2001:165). Siegel and Senna (1994) argue that the exposure to, and participation in, violence leaves youth more vulnerable to violence and victimization in the larger society. These youth are also more likely to be influenced by expectations and tolerance for violence.

Social Disorganization theories study the impact of social environment on communities, individuals and criminality. One of the most famous of the ecological theories developed at the University of Chicago in the1920s and came to be known as the Chicago School. The Chicago School focused on the "ways in which human societies resembled the organization and inter-relationship between plants and animals in nature" (Alvi, 2000:104). When applying this outlook to the study of youth crime, Shaw and McKay (1931, 1942) posit that crime was the corollary of the physical shape and character of neighborhoods. They argued that the shape and character of communities created conditions under which delinquent or criminal behavior could take place. Shaw and McKay focused their work on the concept of social disorganization and links to criminal activity. More recently, Sampson and Groves (1989)defined the links between neighborhood disorganization and criminal activity as; (1) low socio-economic status; (2) a mix of different ethnic groups; (3) high levels of social mobility; and (4) broken homes and family disruption (1989). The fundamental premise is that neighborhoods that exhibit high levels of these factors are more likely to generate crime than neighborhoods that do not because the social controls that prevent people from committing delinquent or criminal acts are weak or missing. Shaw and McKay further their explanation by postulating that the morals and values of the youth in these "disorganized" neighborhoods have been culturally transmitted by the greater number of individuals who have internalized criminal values (Alvi, 2000). Papachristos and Kirk argue that "the extension of social disorganization theory to gang behaviors is straightforward: gangs thus arise either to take the place of weak social institutions in socially disorganized areas, or because weak institutions fail to thwart the advent of unconventional value systems that often characterize street gangs (2005: 3). In the words of one young man who grew up in the inner city of Edmonton:

> When I look around [at the place I grew up] …this was the community league for the hood – this is where the gang members came, the drug dealers, the drunks, the drug addicts, the people from the street…[when I was 10] that was a hard thing to deal with…you get up in the morning, sometimes she would be there, sometimes she wouldn't. When she was there, she wouldn't be up to get us ready for school, to cook us breakfast. I would slap something together for me and my little brother, get my little brother dressed and away we went…[that's how I grew up], seeing my mother and stepfather fight a lot – that's how they handled their problems, by yelling, swearing, screaming, and physically assaulting one another. So I thought, Okay, that's how I deal with things (Campbell, 2005).

Research clearly indicates there are a myriad of factors that may contribute to the likelihood of certain youth to become involved in gang activities. These factors include dysfunctional families, broken homes, poverty and economic disadvantage, discrimination, low academic success, fear of personal safety, and peer involvement in gangs. The challenge then becomes how to deal with this issue. The next section provides discussion on Canadian-based programs and policies designed to tackle the issue of youth gangs in Canada.

DEALING WITH THE YOUTH GANG ISSUE

From a strain perspective, crime is not viewed as resulting from disturbed individuals acting in pathological manners. Instead, it is seen to be more of matter of 'normal' people engaged in 'abnormal' situations (White, Haines, & Eisler, 2008). The focus is on the social conditions and events that may influence individual and/or groups to participate in deviant or criminal behaviors and activities. Therefore solutions are addressed at the social and environmental levels in order to reduce strains felt by certain members of society.

In Canada, there has been a dual response to the issue of youth gangs and youth gang violence. On one hand we see an increased call for tougher laws and punishment for youth involved in violent activities as evidenced by recent proposals put forward by the Federal Government. The Canadian Government has proposed changes to the Youth Criminal Justice Act that would see youth 14-years and older sentenced to life in prison if convicted of first or second degree murder. Harsher sentences would also be leveled against other violent youth crime such as attempted murder, manslaughter, and aggravated assault.

Law enforcement agencies have been involved at projects that aim to disable and disband youth gangs in the Toronto area. Project Flicker, undertaken on September 15th, 2005 was aimed at dismantling the Ardwick Bloods in the Islington and Finch area, resulted in 1,350 charges being laid against 43 individuals ranging in age from 17-years to 49-years. More recently, in June of 2007, over 130 search warrants were executed and over 60 individuals were arrested in a series of raids on suspected members of the Driftwood Crips street gang, located in the Jane and Finch area of Toronto. Nearly 700 officers from across Ontario, including Toronto Police Services, and the Ontario Provincial Police participated in the project. Over 30 kilograms of cocaine, nine kilos of hashish oil, and several pounds of marijuana were confiscated. Dozens of weapons were also collected during the raids (Toronto Police Services, 2007).

Additionally, many researchers, law enforcement officers, politicians, community workers, and policy makers, while recognizing the need for enforcement, call for the development and implementation of strategies and programs aimed at both keeping kids from joining gangs and assisting those already involved in leaving. To quote Caroline Ross; "Talk to any gang investigator and you'll learn that enforcement is only part of the solution to any gang problem. Police and community partners must also focus on gang prevention – particularly among youth at risk for gang membership" (2008: 1).

This focus on gang prevention has resulted in the creation and implementation of programs across Canada aimed at gang prevention and re-integration into society for at-risk youth or youth involved in gang activities. Mellor, MacRae, Pauls, & Hornick undertook a comprehensive review of Canadian programs focused on youth involvement in gangs. They report that "gang prevention and intervention programs vary considerably in how they address the motivations and objectives that are at the root of why young people join gangs" (2005: 23). The review categorizes the programs into three levels of prevention. Primary prevention is the most basic form of prevention and link crime and victimization to broader social and cultural factors. Secondary prevention programs focus on at-risk individuals and situations in an attempt to target interventions more effectively pre-incident. Tertiary prevention provides a full range of responses post-crime or after an individual has joined a gang. The objectives are to repair some of the damages suffered by the victim, to rehabilitate and/or prevent recidivism, and the assist individuals in developing an exit strategy if they want to leave a gang (2005: 23).

Examples of primary prevention programs identified in the report include; Five Core Curriculum, created by the Toronto Police Services, 33 Division, which targets grade 8 and 9 students. As part of a five component crime prevent curriculum, a school liaison officer conducts a one-hour lecture series on youth gangs. "Gangs: Breaking News" was created by the British Columbia Safe Schools Program and Safe Communities in Abbotsford, British Columbia in 2003 to develop a video and facilitator's guide in order to teach youth how to avoid becoming involved in gang activity. Lighthouses is part of the Manitoba Justice

Neighbourhoods Alive initiative created in 2001 and targeted at youth at risk between the ages of 8 – 21. Lighthouses is a fund created to support recreational, educational and pro-social programs after hours for youth in communities across Manitoba (Mellor, MacRae, Pauls, & Hornick, 2005: 37-39).

Secondary prevention programs include; The Community Solution to Gang Violence, located in the greater Edmonton area. This program takes a community-wide approach to addressing the issue of gang violence. The overall goal of the program is to create and sustain a collaborative process between agencies and community members to engage and support citizens, agencies, institutions, and government to take collective and individual responsibility towards creating a community free of gang violence (40). The Clean Scene program was implemented in Alberta and the Northwest Territories in 2002 as an experimental drug prevention program aimed at students in grades 7 through 12. The program incorporates school forums, presentations, and web communications to connect with students and to reinforce the message of the program. The Choices Youth Program located in Winnipeg targets students in grades 6 through 8 at specific schools who have been identified as being at-risk of gang involvement, dropping out of school, and/or substance abuse. The program focuses on the development of basic cognitive skills, social and life skills with the goal of promoting social competency and resistance to peer pressure. Toi, pis ta gang (You, and your gang) is located in the Region of Cote de Baupre, Boischatel, Quebec and is targeted at latch key youth, at-risk youth aged 12 to 17, youth who have been expelled from school, and youth participating in anti-social behaviors. The main focus of this program is to provide aid, training, information, counseling, and support for youth dealing with difficulties. The difficulties may or may not be gang-related. Another goal of the program is to steer youth away from gang affiliation through the development of self-esteem and resiliency (2005: 40-48).

Tertiary prevention programs include the Adopt an Offender Program developed and implemented in Prince Albert, Saskatchewan by Prince Albert Police Services. This program targets young offenders who have been in contact with the criminal justice system and pairs members of the police force with young offenders. Most of the youth are either in gangs or are at risk of gang involvement. Officers develop a mentoring relationship with the youth, monitor their court orders, activities and contact with police. One goal is to provide the youth with options in order to deter and discourage them from crime and gang involvement. Officers also provide support to parents. The Gang and Violence Program is another tertiary prevention program located in Trenton, Ontario. The program is run by St. Leonard's Home, Young Offenders' Residential Services and provides young offenders with a life skills program aimed at informing them about gang life and violence, gang association and the effects of gangs, violence, and gang lifestyles. The program is comprised of four one-hour modules which provides youth with tools to set and accomplish positive goals and empowers them with the understanding that they have a choice. Youth who complete the program are granted a ¼ school credit (2005:60-63).

CONCLUSION

It is apparent that the issue of youth gang membership and activity is of growing concern to Canadian politicians, policy makers, law enforcement agencies, researchers, and community members. While there has been a lag between American-based research and Canadian research, it appears that researchers in Canada are now increasing their focus on this issue. Major challenges for researchers include the complexities of defining what a youth gang is, and the difficulty of collecting first-hand data on gang members and their activities due to the secretive organizational structure and the character of their criminal activities (Mellor, MacRae, Pauls, & Hornick, (2005), and creating and implementing programs aimed at prevention. Strain and disorganization theories with their focus on social and environmental factors have provided a means of analyzing and explaining why certain individuals or groups may join youth gangs. Programs and policies based on the principles embedded in strain and social disorganization theories have been developed and implemented in an attempt to mediate some of the challenged faced by disenfranchised and marginalized Canadian youth and to encourage youth to move away from gang membership and violent criminal activities. Whether these programs will be successful is yet to be determined.

REFERENCES

Agnew, R. (1985). A Revised Strain Theory of Delinquency. *Social Forces*, *64*, 151-167.

Alvi, S. (2000). *Youth and the Canadian Criminal Justice System*. Cincinnati: Anderson Publishing Company.

Barak, G. (1998). *Integrating Criminologies*. Boston: Allyn & Bacon.

Barron, S. W. (1989). The Canadian West Coast Punk Subculture: A Field Study. *Canadian Journal of Sociology*, *14*, *3*, 289-316.

Campbell, F. (Dir.) (2005). *Gang Aftermath*. Bearpaw Media productions. Native Counselling Services of Alberta.

Canada. (2006). Royal Canadian Mounted Police. *Environmental Scan: Features: Focus on Youth Gangs*. Ottawa: Royal Canadian Mounted Police.

Chettleburgh, M. (2008). 2002 *Canadian Police Survey on Youth Gangs*. Astwood Strategy Corporation. Ottawa: Public Safety and Emergency Preparedness Canada, 2004.

Clark, K. (2005). Increasing Violence of Gang Members a Concern. *Prince Albert Daily Herald. March, 16*.

Cloward, R. & Ohlin, L. (1960). *Delinquency and Opportunity: A Theory of Delinquent Gangs*. New York: Free Press.

Cohen, A. (1955). *Delinquent Boys*. New York: Free Press.

Eisler, L. D. (2004). *A Foucauldian Exploration of Youth At-Risk: The Adoption and Integration of Conventional Goals and Values*. Ph.D. Dissertation, Department of Sociology, University of Saskatchewan. Saskatoon, SK.

Elliott, D. S. (1994). Serious Violent Offenders: Onset, Developmental Course, and Termination. *Criminology, 32(1)*, 1-22.

Fagan, J. A. & Jones, S. (1984). Toward a Theoretical Model for Intervention with Violent Juvenile Offenders. In Robert Mathias, Paul DeMuro, & Richard S. Allinson (Eds.),

Violent Juvenile Offenders: An Anthology, 53-70. San Francisco: National Council on Crime and Delinquency.

Fasilio, R. & Leckie, S. (1993). *Canadian Media Coverage of Gangs: A Content Analysis*Users Report 1993-94. Ottawa: Ministry of the Solicitor General.

Fisher, H., Montgomery, P. & Gardner F. E. M. (2008). *Opportunities Provision for Preventing Youth Gang Involvement for Children and Young People (7-16)* (Review). The Cochrane Collaboration Issue, *4*.

Friesen, J. & O'Neil, K. (2008). Armed Posses Spreading Violence Across Prairie Communities. *The Globe and Mail*. Friday, May *9*.

Gordon, R. M., (1995). Street Gangs in Vancouver. In J. Creechan, & R. Silverman (Eds.), *Canadian Delinquency*. Scarborough: Prentice Hall.

Gordon, R. M., (1998). Street Gangs and Criminal Business Organizations: A Canadian Perspective. In K. Hazlehurst, & C. Hazlehurst (Eds.), *Gangs and Youth Subcultures: International Explorations*. New Brunswick, NJ: Transaction Books.

Gordon, R. M. (2000). Criminal Business Organization, Street Gangs, and "Wanna-be" Groups: A Vancouver Perspective. *Canadian Journal of Criminology* (January): 39-60.

Gordon, R. & Foley, S. (1998). Criminal Business Organizations, Street Gangs and Related Groups in Vancouver: The Report of the Greater Vancouver Gang Study, Ministry of Attorney-General, British Columbia.

Gottfredson, G. D. & Gottfredson, D. C. (2001). *Gang Problems and Gang Programs in a National Sample of Schools*. Ellicott City, MD: Gottfredson Associates.

Grekul, J. & LaBoucane-Benson, P. (2008). Aboriginal Gangs and Their (Dis)Placement: Contexualizing Recruitment, Membership, and Status. *Canadian Journal of Criminology and Criminal Justice* 50 (1): Need Page Numbers

Hebert, S., Hamel, S. & Savoie, G. (1997). *Youth and street gangs, phase I: Literature review*. Montreal, QC: l'Institut de recherché pour la developpement social des jeune (IRDS).

Hill, K. G., Howell, J. C., Hawkins, J. D. & Battin-Pearson, S. R. (1999). Childhood Risk Factors for Adolescent Gang Membership: Results from the Seattle Social Development Project. *Journal of Research in Crime and Delinquency, 36(3)*, 300-322.

Hotaling, G. T., Straus, M. A. & Lincoln, A. J. (1989). Intrafamily Violence, and Crime And Violence Outside the Family. In Michael Tonry, ed., *Crime and Justice: a Review of Research, vol.ll*, 315-75. Chicago: University of Chicago Press.

Joe, D. & Robinson, N. (1980). Chinatown's Immigrant Gangs. *Criminology, 18*, 337-345.

Kelly, K. & Caputo, T. (2005). The Linkages Between Street Gangs and Organized Crime: The Canadian Experience. *Journal of Gang Research, 13(1)*, 17-30.

Lauritsen, J. L., Sampson, R. J. & Laub, J. (1991). The Link Between Offending and Victimization among Adolescents. *Criminology, 29*, 265-91.

Le Blanc, M. & Lanctot, N. (1998). Social and Psychological Characteristics of Gang Members According to Gang Structure and its Subcultural and Ethnic Makeup. *Journal of Gang Research, 5(3)*, 15-28.

Mathews, F. (1993). *Youth Gangs on Youth Gangs*. Ottawa: Solicitor General Canada.

McLaren, S. (2004). A 10-year Nightmare: Authorities Struggle to Understand Indo-Canadian Youth Gangs, *Now*.

Mellor, B., MacRae, L., Paul, M. & Hornick, J. P. (2005). *Youth Gangs in Canada: A preliminary review of programs and services*. Ottawa, ON: Public Safety and Emergency Preparedness Canada.

Merton, R. (1938). Social Structure and Anomie. *American Sociological Review, 3*, 672-682.

Papachristos, A. V. & Kirk, D. S. (2005). *Neighborhood Effects of Street Gang Behavior*. A paper submitted for the 2005 Annual Conference of the American Sociological Association, Philadelphia, PA.

Regoli, R. M. & Hewitt, J. D. (1991). *Delinquency in Society*. New York: McGraw-Hill.

Sampson, R. J. & Lauristen, J. (1990). Deviant Lifestyles, Proximity to Crime, and the Offender-Victim Link in Personal Violence. *Journal of Research in Crime and Delinquency, 27*, 110-139.

Scott, N. (2005). Gangs Growing: Police. *Regina Leader Post*, March 15.

Shaw, C. & McKay, H. D. (1931). *Social Factors in Juvenile Delinquency.* Chicago: University of Chicago Press.

Shaw, C. & McKay, H. D. (1942). Juvenile Delinquency and Urban Areas. Chicago: University of Chicago Press.

Siegal, L. J. & Senna, J. J. (1994). *Juvenile Delinquency: Theory, Practice, and Law, 5th edition*. New York: West.

Singer, S. (1986). Victims of Serious Violence and Their Criminal Behavior: Subcultural Theory and Beyond. *Violence and Victims, 1*, 61-69.

Smandych, R. C. (2001). *Youth Justice: History, Legislation, and Reform*. Harcourt Canada: Toronto.

Smith, C. & Thornberry, T. P. (1995). The Relationship Between Childhood Maltreatment And Adolescent Involvement in Delinquency. *Criminology, 33(4)*, 451- 82.

Thornberry, T. P., Krohn, M. D., Lizotte, A. J., Smith, C. A. & Tobin, K. (2003). *Gangs and Delinquency in Developmental Perspective.* New York, NY: Cambridge University Press.

Toronto Police Services (2007). *Project Kryptic Marks End of Gang*. Toronto Police Service, Wednesday, June 13, 2007. Retrieved on November 15, 2008 at http://www. torontopolice.on.ca/modules.php?op=modload&name=News&file.

White, R., Haines, F. & Eisler, L. D. (2008). *Crime and Criminology: An Introduction, Canadian Edition*. Toronto,CA: Oxford University Press.

Widom, C. S. (1989). Child Abuse, Neglect, and Violent Criminal Behavior. *Criminology, 27*, 251-71.

Woods, A. (2004). Toronto and its Gangs. *National Post*. June 3.

In: Youth Violence and Juvenile Justice: Causes, Intervention... ISBN: 978-1-61668-011-4
Editor: Neil A. Ramsay et al., pp. 315-330 © 2010 Nova Science Publishers, Inc.

Chapter 14

RISK AND RESILIENCY AMONG JUVENILES AND YOUNG ADULTS[1]

Julie E. Sprinkle
Appalachian State University, Boone, North Carolina.

ABSTRACT

The Appalachian region of the United States extends from New York to Alabama. However, it is the central and southern Appalachians that seem to garner the most attention in television, magazines, and movies. This attention is often negative, with far-reaching implications for the members of the population. Using standardized risk and resiliency assessment tools, the current study investigates the risk and protective factors juveniles from the southern Appalachian region are exposed to and possess. In addition, comparisons to young adults residing outside of this region are explored to offer a thorough understanding of risk and resiliency among juveniles and young adults. There are numerous risk factors that increase the likelihood of an individual engaging in violent or aggressive acts, performing poorly in school, or falling victim to substance use and abuse. The current investigation also considers resiliency and seeks to examine the factors that allow some juveniles to emerge from neglectful families and drug-infested, poverty stricken neighborhoods without resorting to negative behaviors themselves. To conclude the chapter, implications for the prevention and treatment of juvenile crime both within and outside of Appalachia are presented.

INTRODUCTION

The central and southern Appalachian region stretches from West Virginia to Alabama, includes nine states and 267 counties, as well as seven independent cities in Virginia (ARC, 2007). This area has unjustly suffered from negative stereotypical portrays of its culture, people, and way of life. Commonly perceived as 'hicks', hillbillies, or rednecks by

---

[1] The author would like to thank Dr. Lisa Curtin and Dr. Sue Keefe for their assistance with this project

individuals outside of the area, television, movies, and print media seem to further this view; often depicting inbreeding, the lack of oral hygiene, poverty, illiteracy, unemployment, racism, and domestic violence as 'normal' in Appalachia. The true picture of this region and its inhabitants is a stark contrast to the one frequently accepted. The Appalachian people are proud, strong, accomplished, and deeply spiritual (Keefe, 2005). The purpose of this study is to investigate the risk and protective factors juveniles from the southern Appalachian region are exposed to and possess.

Literature

The literature on risk and resiliency is prevalent. There are numerous risk factors that increase the likelihood of an individual engaging in violent or aggressive acts, performing poorly in school, or falling victim to substance use and abuse. These factors can be divided into four categories; family, community, peer, and individual. First, family factors such as family structure (Valois, MacDonald, Bretous, Fischer, & Drane, 2002), poverty, poor supervision, physical and/or inconsistent discipline, poor parenting skills, and domestic violence (Bemak & Keys, 2000; Willimas, 2003; Fried & Fried, 2003) place individuals at risk. Community traits including poverty, access to drugs, alcohol, and firearms, inadequate housing, high unemployment, few community resources, and prevalence of violence further increase these risks (Bemak & Keys, 2000; Funk, Elliott, Urman, Flores, & Mock, 1999; Garbarino, Dubrow, Kostelny, & Pardo, 1992).

Peers can inhibit or encourage the negative or positive actions of one another. If individuals socialize with peers who display prosocial behaviors, the person's propensity to act negatively is reduced. Conversely, if individuals socialize with peers who have internalized antisocial norms, they are more likely to behave in non-positive ways (Eisenberg, Shell, Pasternack, Beller, Lennon, & Mathy, 1987; Eisenberg & Strayer, 1987; Eisenberg, Carlo, Murphy, & Van Court, 1995; Eisenberg, 1995). Certain individual factors such as lack of empathy, impulsivity, learning difficulties, low self-esteem, mental illness, and a history of victimization (Bemak & Keys, 2000; Fried & Fried, 2003) further increase the risks young adults experience. An additional risk factor individuals from the Appalachian region may suffer from or be exposed to is 'nerves' (Keefe, 2005); a combination of anxiety and depression not typically identified as mental illness by the region's inhabitants.

Resilience to childhood stressors and trauma has been the subject of intense investigation for the past two decades (Rutter, 2000). What factors allow some individuals to emerge from neglectful families and drug-infested, poverty stricken neighborhoods without resorting to negative behaviors themselves? According to the principle of cumulated risk (Garmezy, 1985; 1993), as the number of risk factors an individual has increases, so does his/her likelihood for engaging in negative behaviors. Garmezy (1993) asserts that there are three distinct types of protective factors that cushion stressors encountered by children and young adults. First are dispositional factors of the child, such as a positive temperament. Second are familial factors such as parent/child relationship, absence of parental mental illness, household stability, and adequate parenting skills. Finally, external support systems such as churches, schools, sports teams, and social service agencies can aid in protecting children from stressors. Falling into the third category are natural mentors such as teachers, older neighborhood peers, and sports coaches (Zimmerman, Bingenheimer, & Notaro, 2002). In the Appalachian culture, family, community, loyalty, independence, religion, and conflict avoidance are central values (Keefe, 1988; 2005). These numerous protective factors can increase the strength of individual resiliency beginning in childhood.

Demographics

The current study is concentrated in the North Carolina Appalachian region, which is part of the southern Appalachians. According to the 2000 US Census, this area contains 1,526,207 inhabitants, which indicates an increase of 16.8% from the 1990 Census (US Census, 2000). However, the average income in 2002 was around $26,000, or about $5,000 less than the US per capita income (ARC, 2002). Given the lower level of income, it is not surprising that persons in this geographic area are more likely to live in poverty than those residing outside of the region. Poverty, and the myriad of challenges it brings, contributes to the stigma and difficulties juveniles encounter on a daily basis.

The overall educational attainment of individuals in this area still falls below the US average; "in Maryland, North Carolina, and Virginia, the Appalachian counties had more adults with less than high-school education than college graduates, while the reverse was true for the rest of the states" (Haage, 2004). Only 75.8% of adults obtain a high school diploma in the North Carolina Appalachians and 19.1% of the population achieves a college degree, compared to roughly 25% of the general US population. However, the region is improving its ability to keep individuals in school; high school graduation rates have increased since the 1990's. Further, more women than men currently possess college degrees, dispelling the view of Appalachian women as consistently 'ignorant, barefoot, and pregnant' or mothers by their thirteenth birthday. With lower levels of income and less formal education, young adults from the southern Appalachians face daunting risks factors. However, the protective mechanisms of family and community may bolster their resiliency.

Purpose of the Study

The purpose of the current study is to determine the traits, characteristics, and events that lead to the development of risk and protective factors in juveniles and young adults. This project is a pilot study and foundation basis for a large scale examination of risk and resiliency in the Appalachian region. The instruments ask young adults from within and outside of the Appalachian region to consider both current behaviors and events and those that occurred when the respondent was a juvenile. The goal of the project is to discover the traits and attributes that comprise risk and protective factors in juveniles and young adults. The objectives are to determine (1) the effect of family on risk and resiliency (2) the effect of individual identity on risk and resiliency (3) the effect of community on risk and resiliency and (4) the effect of friendships on risk and resiliency.

The risk and resiliency measures used in this study were originally developed and tested with 18-24 year old young adults in Japan and China. While it may appear at first glance that Appalachian communities have little in common with those of Japan or China, this is not necessarily a valid assumption. All three communities highly value family, community, and loyalty (Keefe, 1988; Keefe, 2005; Lo & Bettinger, 2001).

Instruments

The instruments used in this study were developed and standardized by Dr. Julie Haddow. The two measures are the Haddow Ecological Protective Factors for Young Adults-Revised (HEPFYA-R) and the Life Events Survey for Youth (LESY) (with material adapted from the Teen Assessment Project (TAP) Survey written by Steven Small and the NLSY 79, 2000). The HEPFYA-R is an 84-item instrument with 26 subscales, while the LESY is a 102-item instrument with 31 subscales. After consultation with Dr. Susan Keefe, an expert in the Appalachian region, the researcher made several modifications in each questionnaire. As revised for the present study, the HEPFYA-R has 84 items and seventeen subscales, while the LESY has 102 items and seventeen subscales (sample items appear in Appendix A). Both instruments are divided into individual, family, and community measures of risk and resiliency. The individual sections include internal (e.g., faith, spirituality, self-esteem, etc.) and external (e.g., appearance, friends, social capital, etc.) determinants of protection and risk. For this study, the researcher reverse scored negatively worded questions and developed total risk and total resiliency scores. Risk scores could range from 84 to 420 while resiliency scores could range from 100 to 500. Higher scores indicate higher levels of risk and resiliency on the instruments and their individual subscales. The instruments were subjected to a factor analysis to determine the strength, reliability, validity, and loadings of each factor. The results were analyzed using the Statistical Package for the Social Sciences (SPSS) version 14.0.

Research Questions

Despite the exploratory nature of the study, several research questions were used to guide the investigation. The overarching research question was (I) what differences, if any, exist on measures of risk and resiliency between individuals who hail from the Appalachian region and those who do not? Based upon the literature review, the researcher predicted (1) persons from the Appalachian region will be more spiritual than those not from the region, (2) due to these spiritual beliefs and possible lower incomes, persons from the Appalachian region will be more fatalistic than those not from the region, (3) persons from the Appalachian region will have more trouble with depression and 'nerves' than those not from the region, (4) persons from the Appalachian region will be closer to their family than those not from the region, (5) persons from the Appalachian region will have less education than those not from the region, (6) persons from the Appalachian region will have more family support than those not from the region,

(7) persons from the Appalachian region will have more support from their friends than those not from the region, (8) persons from the Appalachian region will have closer community ties than those not from the region, (9) due to a strong belief in independence, persons from the Appalachian region will use social services and government programs less

than those not from the region, and (10) persons from the Appalachian region will have less social capital than those not from the region.

The Study Population

Study participants were recruited from students taking courses in the mid-sized University's psychology department. Completion of both questionnaires required 45-60 minutes of the participants' time. The main independent variable in the study was whether participants were from the Appalachian region or not, while the dependent variables were participants' scores on the risk (LESY) and resiliency (HEPFYA-R) measures. The initial goal of this exploratory study was to recruit an even number of individuals self-identified as from the Appalachian region and self-identified as non-Appalachian. Unfortunately, of the 58 participants who signed up for and completed the entire study, 30% percent were from the Appalachian region, while 70% identified themselves as non-Appalachian. The majority of participants hailed from mid-sized to small cities (44.8%) or small towns (24.1%), while 22.4% were from large urban areas and only 8.6% were raised in rural areas. The study population included 20 (35.5%) men and 38 (65.5%) women. The majority of study participants were 18 (24.1) and 19 (39.7) years old, while only 5 were older than 22 (8.6%). Similarly, most participants lived in a dorm (72.4%) or in an apartment with friends (20.7%), while only 5.2% lived by themselves and 1.7% lived with their families.

The Analysis

Each revised instrument, the LESY and the HEPFYA-R, was subjected to a factor analysis to determine the reliability, validity, and loadings of the instruments with the population under study. This process revealed several, strong subscales for each questionnaire. In addition, subscale scores were analyzed to determine their correlation with the total risk and resiliency scores. Finally, a multivariate analysis of variance or MANOVA was used to ascertain the differences and similarities across all measures between participants from the Appalachian region and those not from the region.

The Findings

The HEPFYA-R and LESY

Based upon the VARIMAX rotated component matrix, all of the items in each scale were retained because their item loadings were higher than the minimum of .30 (George & Mallery, 2003). The resiliency measure (HEPFYA-R), has a total of 84 items. While seventeen subscales were detected, the instrument itself has an overall alpha of .90, with item loadings ranging from .94 to .70. Together, these factors explain 75.6% of the variance in participants' scores on the instrument. The risk measure (LESY), has a total of 102 items, with an overall alpha of .65 and loadings ranging from .95 to .80. These factors explain 70.5% of the variance in participants' scores on the instrument. Based upon the alphas and loadings, it appears that each instrument measures its intended concept and each item logically and conceptually fits within its respective scale.

Table 1. Resiliency Subscale Alphas

Subscale	Alpha
Treatment by others	.61
Positive outlook	.80
Supportive friends	.70
Instructors at college	.74
Parental admiration	.82
Humor	.73
Success	.61
Self-efficacy	.50
Physical attractiveness	.78
Moral beliefs	.68
Spirituality	.95
Ask for assistance	.30
Partner support	.96
Neighborhood you grew up in	.86
Parent's protection	.73
Family finances	.85
Social Capital	.85

Table 2. Risk Subscale Alphas

Subscale	Alpha
Parental depression	.87
Parental assistance	.70
Parental awareness	.78
Corporal punishment	.82
Self depression	.89
Sexually and violently explicit movies	.71
Parental presence	.30
Parental alcohol use	.44
Siblings favored by parents	.73
Substance use	.67
Age of first sex/drugs	.45
Sexual abuse	.42
Exposure to physical violence	.45
Contact with the criminal justice system	.61
Perceptions of others substance use	.74
Perceptions of others sexual behaviors	.41
Perceptions of others enjoyment of life	.26

Subscales

After conducting a factor analysis on both instruments, several distinct subscales emerged. With regard to the measure of resiliency, seventeen subscales were present in the LESY. Each item had an eigenvalue between .92 and .32, indicating strong to adequate loadings with each subscale factor. The first subscale, *treatment by others*, includes three items (alpha=.61). Subscale two, *positive outlook*, has six items (alpha=.80). The third subscale, *supportive friends*, has four items (alpha=.70), while the fourth subscale, *instructors at college*, has seven items (alpha=.74). The fifth subscale, *parental admiration*, has six items (alpha=.82), the sixth subscale, *humor*, has three items (alpha=.73), the seventh subscale, *success*, has thirteen items (alpha= .61), the eighth subscale, *self-efficacy*, has six items (alpha=.50), the ninth subscale, *physical attractiveness*, has three items (alpha= .78), the tenth subscale, *moral beliefs*, has six items (alpha= .68), the eleventh subscale, *spirituality*, has four items (alpha=.95), the twelfth subscale, *ask for assistance*, has two items (alpha= .30), the thirteenth subscale, *partner support*, has two items (alpha= .96), the fourteenth subscale, *neighborhood you grew up in*, has six items (alpha=.86), the fifteenth subscale, *parent's protection*, has five items (alpha= .73), the sixteenth subscale, *family finances*, has two items (alpha= .85), and finally, the seventeenth subscale, *social capital*, has eleven items (alpha= .85) (Table 1; Appendix A).

With regard to the risk instrument, 17 subscales were detected through factor analysis of the 102 items. Each item had an eigenvalue of .95 to .30, once again indicating strong to adequate loadings of individual items with the instrument subscales. First, the subscale, *parental depression*, has eight items (alpha= .87), while the second subscale, *parental assistance*, has four items (alpha= .70). The third subscale, *parental awareness*, has two items (alpha= .78), the fourth subscale, *corporal punishment*, has four items (alpha=.82), the fifth subscale, *self depression*, has eleven items (alpha= .89), the sixth subscale, *sexually and violently explicit movies*, has two items (alpha= .71), the seventh subscale, *parental presence*, has six items (alpha= .30), the eighth subscale, *parental alcohol use*, has two items (alpha= .44), the ninth subscale, *siblings favored by parents*, has two items (alpha= .73), the tenth subscale, *substance use*, has nine items (alpha=.67), the eleventh subscale, *age of first sex/drugs*, has six items (alpha= .43), the twelfth subscale, *sexual abuse*, has four items (alpha= .42), the thirteenth subscale, *exposure to physical violence*, has five items (alpha= .40), the fourteenth subscale, *contact with the criminal justice system*, has six items (alpha= .61), the fifteenth subscale, *perceptions of others substance use*, has three items (alpha= .74), the sixteenth subscale, *perceptions of others sexual behaviors*, has three items (alpha= .32), and finally, the seventeenth subscale, *perceptions of others enjoyment of life*, has ten items (alpha= .26) (Table 2; Appendix A).

Total study population demographics

When examining the study population as a whole, 56.9% of the study population's mothers and 56.9% of their fathers had some college education. With regard to family contact, 48% of those surveyed stated they have daily contact with their mothers and 44% have weekly contact with their fathers. Only 6.9% and 27.6% of respondents admitted to having occasional to no contact with their mothers and fathers, respectively. Siblings were present in all but 5.2% of the study population, with the majority of participants having one (41.4%) or two siblings (36.2%). However, the range of sibling age was fairly equally distributed between one year younger/older (21%) to four years younger/older (29%) and the majority of respondents lived with their siblings constantly during their childhood and adolescence (75.9%). Not surprisingly, 69.9% of participants grew up living with their mother and father, while 6.9% lived exclusively with their mother, 3.4% lived solely with their father, and 8.6% lived with their parents and grandparents. Eighty-nine percent of respondents' families had never received social services during their lives. Finally, the total mean risk score was 280 (range=69), while the mean resiliency score was 320 (range=153). The mean risk score for the Appalachian population was 280 (range=57) and the resiliency mean was 314 (range=117). Similarly, the risk and resiliency means for the non-Appalachian population were 280 (range=69) and 322 (range=131), respectively.

Table 3. Risk and Resiliency Correlations for Appalachian and non-Appalachian Regions.

Variables	LESY Appalachian	HEPFYA-R Appalachian	LESY Non-Appalachian	HEPFYA-R Non-Appalachian
Parental awareness	-.57*	**	.39*	**
Self-depression	.54*	**	.57*	**
Corporal punishment	.54*	**	**	**
Substance abuse	.54*	**	.54*	**
Father's level of education	**	.56*	**	**
Support for parents	**	.66*	**	**
Parental presence	**	.60*	**	**
School interest	**	.58*	**	.32*
Parental admiration	**	.65*	**	
Spirituality	**	.57*	**	
Neighborhood environment	**	.83*	**	.71*
Parental finances	**	.60*	**	.45*
Social capital	**	.87*	**	.40*
Parental depression	**	**	.40*	.-35*
Parental substance abuse	**	**	.42*	**
Domestic Violence	**	**	.53*	**
Sex and Violence Movies	**	**	.38*	**
Beliefs about drugs	**	**	.58*	**
Beliefs about sex	**	**	.38*	**
Self-efficacy	**	**	-.40*	**
Moral beliefs	**	**	-.32*	**
Humor	**	**	**	.56*
Partner support	**	**	**	.38*
Parental divorce	**	**	**	-.45*
Positive outlook	**	.80*	**	.57*
Appearance	**	**	**	.57*
Parental beliefs	**	**	**	.60*

*Significant at P<.01
**Not significant

Correlations

Correlation analysis measures the strength and direction of the association between two variables (Hair, Anderson, Tatham, & Black, 1998). Correlations were determined for participants, using region as the control variable. Study participants from the Appalachian region exhibited stronger correlations across each demographic variable and subscale than participants from non-Appalachian regions. However, the subscale correlations are too numerous to list individually, resulting in only total score correlations presented for review. Appalachian region participants' total scores on the measure of risk (LESY) were negatively correlated with the following subscale: parental awareness

(r=.-57), and positively correlated with the corporal punishment (r=.54), self-depression (r=.54), and substance abuse subscales (r=.54). However, scores on the resiliency measure (HEPFYA-R) were positively correlated with the subscales father's level of education (r=.56), support for parents (r=.66), parental presence (r=.60), school interest (r=.58), parental admiration (r=.65), positive outlook (r=.80), spirituality (r=.57), neighborhood environment growing up (r=.83), parental finances (r=.60), and social capital (r=.87) (Table 3).

Non-Appalachian region participants' total scores on the LESY were positively correlated with the following subscales: parental depression (r=.40), parental awareness (r=.39), parental substance abuse (r=.42), self-depression (r=.57), domestic violence exposure (r=.53), exposure to sexually and violently explicit movies (r=.38), beliefs about drugs (r=.58), beliefs about sex (r=.38), and substance abuse (r=.54), yet negatively

correlated with self-efficacy (r=-.40) and moral beliefs subscales (r=-.32). However, scores on the HEPFYA-R were positively correlated with the subscales positive outlook (r=.57), school interest (r=.32), physical appearance (r=.57), humor (r=.56), partner support (r=.38), neighborhood environment growing up (r=.71), parental beliefs (r=.60), parental finances (r=.45), and social capital (r=.40), yet negatively correlated with the parental depression subscale (r=-.35) and having parents who are divorced (r=-.45) (Table 3).

Manova

A multivariate analysis of variance or MANOVA statistical analysis was used to assess the differences between group means on multiple dependent variables (Hair et al., 1998). MANOVA's require at minimum "two dependent variables and one independent variable with two levels" (George & Mallory, 2003, p. 295). Box's test of equality of covariance matrices and Levene's test of equality of error variances were not significant, indicating that the assumptions of MANOVA had not been violated. Three MANOVAS were conducted in the present investigation. In the first MANOVA, the impact of demographic variables on risk and resiliency scores for both the Appalachian region and non-Appalachian region was determined. The demographic variables had no significant impact on instrument scores in respondents from the Appalachian region. However, for participants from the non-Appalachian region, mother's level of education significantly impacted scores on the risk measure (F=5.1, p=.025). It appears that participants from the Appalachian region were less impacted by their mother's educational level due to the consistency of lower overall parental educational attainment in this population.

However, no significant differences were noted in the second MANOVA examining the independent variable of Appalachian versus non-Appalachian region and total scores on the risk and resiliency measures. Similarly, no significant differences were found in the third MANOVA examining region of origin and subscale scores on both instruments, indicating similar levels of risk and resiliency across all measures in both populations.

Discussion of the Findings

The overarching research question guiding the present study was to determine what differences, if any, exist between the risk and resiliency of those from the Appalachian region and those not from the region. The findings indicate there are subtle differences between these two groups. The first hypothesis, that persons from the Appalachian region will be more spiritual, was moderately supported. The maximum score on the spirituality subscale was 20. Only 14.3% of non-Appalachian respondents scored 20 compared to 27% of Appalachian respondents, indicating higher levels of spirituality. The second hypothesis, that Appalachian region respondents would be more fatalistic, was measured by the positive outlook subscale. The maximum score, indicating positive beliefs about the future, was 20. No Appalachian region respondent scored a 20, the highest was 17 (13.3%), while one non-Appalachian respondent scored a 20 and 21% scored 17. These scores indicate Appalachian region respondents were more fatalistic and had fewer positive beliefs about the future than non-Appalachian respondents, thus supporting the researcher's hypothesis. The third hypothesis, depression and 'nerves', was also supported. The mean score on the parental depression scale was 25 for Appalachian respondents and 12.5 for non-Appalachian respondents, indicating higher levels of depression and 'nerves' in the Appalachian population. The researcher's fourth hypothesis, familial closeness was also moderately supported. Fifty percent of participants from the Appalachian region had daily contact with both their mothers and fathers, while only 40% and 30% of non-Appalachian region participants had daily contact with their mothers and fathers, respectively, indicating a greater level of closeness between Appalachian regional participants and their families.

With regard to the fifth research hypothesis, that individuals from the Appalachian region will have less education than those not from the region, only 40% of both fathers and mothers of Appalachian respondents' were college graduates as opposed to 63% of non-Appalachian respondents' fathers and mothers, indicating lower levels of familial education in participants from the Appalachian region. The sixth hypothesis, greater family support, was also substantiated. Twenty-six percent of non-Appalachian respondents received frequent help from their mothers and fathers families and friends, while 38% of Appalachian respondents received frequent assistance from their families and friends, underscoring the importance and closeness of family ties in the region.

However, the seventh hypothesis, more supportive friends, was not sustained. Both Appalachian and non-Appalachian participants had equally supportive friends. The eighth hypothesis, community ties, also did not hold. There is no discernable difference between community ties from persons in the Appalachian region and those from the non–Appalachian region. Further, the ninth hypothesis, social services, was not supported. Approximately 90% of both respondent groups had never received social services, regardless of geographical region. This finding is likely due to the fact that mostly middle class college students were surveyed. The final hypothesis, participants from the Appalachian region will have less social capital, was not supported. Interestingly, participants from the Appalachian region reported greater social capital (x=43) than other respondents (x=40); possibly due to the presence of close family ties in the region.

Implications/Limitations

Although a MANOVA indicated no statistical difference between respondents from the Appalachian region and those not from the region, several statistically significant differences were exposed by correlation analysis. Father's level of education was moderately positively correlated with social capital in the Appalachian group, but not in the non-Appalachian group. This finding suggests father's level of education is a greater determinate of social capital for Appalachian respondents, possibly because of the central role father's play in the welfare of their families in the Appalachian region.

With regard to self-depression, Appalachian respondents exhibited a negative correlation with parental presence, displaying that as parental presence declines, depression increases. This trend was not detected in the non-Appalachian population, indicating that the non-Appalachian population appears less influenced by the presence or absence of parental figures and further underscores the importance of family in the Appalachian region.

Appalachian respondents' total scores on the risk measure were strongly positively correlated with parental awareness, corporal punishment, self-depression, and substance abuse, undergirding the contention that parents who are not aware of what their children are doing, who employ corporal punishment, who have individual depression, and who abuse drugs/alcohol pose the greatest risk to the Appalachian population. Conversely, total scores on the resiliency measure were strongly positively correlated with father's level of education, support for parents, parental presence, school interest, parental admiration, spirituality, neighborhood, parental finances, and social capital. Such results indicate that interested, financially well-off, admired parents, a good neighborhood, and a strong spiritual belief system produce the greatest resiliency in Appalachian region juveniles; a factor that carries over into adulthood. These variables are inclusive of school, family, community, and individual traits or all the items the literature suggests bolster resiliency.

In the non-Appalachian population, risk was strongly positively correlated with parental depression, parental awareness, parental substance abuse, domestic violence exposure, exposure to sexually and violently explicit movies, beliefs about drugs, beliefs about sex, and substance abuse, signifying a greater number of risk factors for non-Appalachian respondents during their juvenile years. Specifically, having depressed parents, uninterested, uninvolved, or unaware parents, parents who use/abuse drugs/alcohol, using substances oneself, parents who engage in domestic violence, being exposed to graphic movies, and having negative beliefs about drugs and sex increase risk for the non-Appalachian population. However, this population also revealed a number of protective factors, such as positive outlook, school interest, physical appearance, humor, partner support, neighborhood environment, parental beliefs, parental finances, and social capital, which are comparable to the resiliency factors evidenced by the Appalachian respondents. In sum, the greatest difference between the two groups appears to be the larger number of risk factors faced by the non-Appalachian population during their juvenile years.

The overall results of this study indicate (1) family acts as a buffer to decrease risk and increase resiliency in both respondent populations (2) a positive individual identity, with strong self-efficacy, decreases risk and furthers resiliency for all study participants (3) a strong community with feelings of closeness to the area and neighborhood pride reduce risk and bolsters resiliency in the Appalachian and non-Appalachian regions, and finally, (4) prosocial friendships deflect risk and aid resiliency for all respondents.

Regrettably, the study did have several limitations. First, the smaller number of Appalachian identified respondents and the inclusion of only University students reduce the number of conclusions that can be drawn from the study. However, the exploratory nature of the current investigation can accommodate and learn from such shortcomings. Second, a possible social desirability bias could have resulted in respondents from both regions answering questions in a manner that would reflect positively on their culture, region, and selves. Further investigations are needed to determine the consistency of findings. Third, given the sensitive nature of many questions asked on both questionnaires, it is possible some students provided socially acceptable responses, rather than admit their true experiences or feelings. However, the anonymous method of data collection should have prevented or curtailed this occurrence.

CONCLUSION

As the results of this study highlight the protective factors of family, community, individual traits, and friends, these natural barriers to risk should be bolstered through support programs and flexible policies that allow parents to spend more quality time with their children. Positive parental interaction would decrease the rate and occurrence of juvenile crime through supportive role modeling. The lessons learned through this interaction would help produce well-rounded adults who actively contribute to the betterment of society. Additionally, community action groups designed to make neighborhoods safe, secure, and welcoming should receive the necessary funding to ensure this becomes a reality rather than an elusive dream. The talents of all children and adolescents should be recognized, rewarded, and encouraged to promote resiliency and buffer risk. Children facing any number of risk factors should have options that include positive mentoring programs, sports programs, tutoring, problem solving skills, violence prevention, and leadership development opportunities. Finally, prosocial friendships should be encouraged by parents, teachers, neighbors, and peer groups. Many schools are now implementing prosocial skills programs that include components on peer pressure, how to avoid it, and why being part of the 'in' crowd should not necessitate participation in harmful and/or destructive activities.

Treatment programs for juvenile offenders should carefully examine the risk and protective factors present in the environment from which the individual hails. Programs should be aimed at increasing resiliency and decreasing risk by teaching positive skills and conflict resolution methods rather than sustain a punitive focus that merely serves to re-enforce negative behaviors.

In conclusion, this study underscores the impact juvenile experiences have in shaping who these individuals become as young adults. All juveniles should be given attention and recognition for their positive accomplishments and not be limited by the negative images society may have for them, regardless of their region of origin or residence.

REFERENCES

Appalachian Region Commission. (2002). *Economic overview of the Appalachian region.* Retrieved May 8, 2009 from http://www.arc.gov/index.do?nodeId=26.

Appalachian Region Commission. (2007). *Counties in Appalachia.* Retrieved May 8, 2009 from http://www.arc.gov/index.do?nodeId=27.

Bemak, F. & Keys, S. (2000). *Violent and aggressive youth: Intervention and prevention strategies for changing times.* Thousand Oaks, CA: Corwin Press, Inc.

Eisenberg, N. (1995). Prosocial development: A multifaceted model. In W. Kurtines & J. Geewirtz (Eds.), *Moral development.* Boston: Allyn and Bacon.

Eisenberg, N., Carlo, G., Murphy, B. & Van Court, P. (1995). Prosocial development in late adolescence: *A longitudinal study. Child Development, 66,* 1179-1197.

Eisenberg, N., Shell, R., Pasternack, J., Beller, R., Lennon. R. & Mathy, R. (1987). Prosocial development in middle childhood: A longitudinal study. *Developmental Psychology, 23(5),* 712-718.

Eisenberg, N. & Strayer, J. (Eds.), (1987). *Empathy and its development.* Cambridge: Cambridge University Press.

Fried, S. & Fried, P. (2003). *Bullies, targets, and witnesses: Helping children break the pain chain.* New York: M. Evans and Company, Inc.

Funk, J. B., Elliott, R., Urman, M., Flores, G. & Mock, R. (1999). The attitudes towards violence scale: A measure for adolescents. *Journal of Interpersonal Violence, 14(11),* 1123-1136.

Garbarino, J., Dubrow, N., Kostelny, K. & Pardo, C. (1992). *Children in danger: Coping with the consequences of community violence.* San Francisco: Jossey-Bass.

Garmezy, N. (1985). Stress resistant children: The search for protective factors. In: J. E., Stevenson, (Eds.), *Recent Research in Developmental Psychopathology* (213-233). *Journal of Child Psychology and Psychiatry Book Supplement.*

Garmezy, N. (1993). Children in poverty: Resilience despite risk. *Psychiatry, 56,* 127-136.

George, D. & Mallery, P. (2003). *SPSS for windows step by step: A simple guide and reference.* Boston, MA: Allyn and Bacon.

Haage, J. (2004). *Educational attainment in Appalachia.* Population reference bureau, Appalachian Region Commission, Retrieved May 8, 2009 from http://www.arc.gov/images.

Hair, J., Anderson, R., Tatham, R. & Black, W. (1998). *Multivariate data analysis.* Upper Saddle River, NJ: Prentice-Hall, Inc.

Keefe, S. E. (1988). (Eds.) *Appalachian mental health:* Lexington, KY: University of Kentucky Press.

Keefe, S. E. (2005). (Eds.) *Appalachian cultural competency. A guide for medical, mental health, and social services professionals.* Knoxville, TN: University of Tennessee Press.

Lo, M. & Bettinger, C. (2001). The historical emergence of a 'familial society' in Japan. *Theory & Society, 30,* 237-280.

Mather, M. (2004). *Housing and community patterns in Appalachia.* Regional report from the Appalachian Region Commission. Retrieved May 8, 2009 from http://www.arc.gov/images

Pollard, K. (2005). Defining sub regions in Appalachia: Are there better alternatives? Population reference bureau, Appalachian Region Commission, Retrieved May 8, 2009 from http://www.arc.gov/images.

Rutter, M. (2000). Children in substitute care: Some conceptual considerations and research implications. *Children and Youth Services Review, 22,* 685-703.

United States of American (2000). Census Data. Retrieved May 8, from www.census.gov

Valois, R. F., MacDonald, J. M., Bretous, L., Fischer, M. A. & Drane, J. W. (2002). Risk factors and behaviors associated with adolescent violence and aggression. *American Journal of Health Behavior, 26,* 454-464.

Williams, K. (2003). *The PEACE approach to violence prevention: A guide for administrators and teachers.* Lanham, MD: The Scarecrow Press, Inc.

Zimmerman, M., Bingenheimer, J. & Notaro, P. (2002). Natural mentors and adolescent resiliency: A study with urban youth. *American Journal of Community Psychology, 30,* 221-244.

APPENDIX A

Haddow Ecological Protective Factors for Young Adults-Revised (HEPFYA-R) Examples

Treatment by others
1. If family members are treating me poorly, I have the right to get away from them.
5=strongly agree, 4=agree, 3=neither disagree or agree, 2=disagree, 1=strongly
Positive outlook
2. I am always optimistic about my future.
Supportive friends
3. I feel that my friends would do anything to help me out.
Instructors at college
4. At school, there is an instructor that I like to talk to about my studies.
Parental admiration
5. I think highly of my father.
Humor
6. I feel that having a sense of humor helps me out.
Success
7. If I have been successful in the past, I am usually successful again.
Self-efficacy
8. If I put my mind to it, I can be successful.
Physical attractiveness
9. I consider myself to be attractive.
Moral Beliefs
10. I feel guilty if I do not do what I know is right.
Spirituality
11. My sense of spirituality gives me hope for the future.

> **Ask for assistance**
> 12. I feel that I should not ask for help from others.
> **Partner support**
> 13. Regarding your partner, how often does she/he encourage or help you to do things important to you.
> 5=strongly agree, 4=agree, 3=neither disagree or agree, 2=disagree, 1=strongly, 0=NA
> **Neighborhood you grew up in**
> 14.My neighborhood where I grew up was well maintained.
> **Parent's protection**
> 15. Growing up, I felt that my parent(s) could protect me from some of the bad things happening in the world.
> **Family finances**
> 16. I consider my family to be financially well off.
> **Social Capital**
> 17. I know ___ people that can help connect me to future jobs or careers.
> Reponses range from one (1) to four or more people (5)

Life Events Survey for Youth (LESY) Examples (with material adapted from the Teen Assessment Project (TAP) Survey written by Steven Small and the NLSY 79, 2000)

> How often did these things happen while you were growing up?
> 5=strongly agree, 4=agree, 3=neither disagree or agree, 2=disagree, 1=strongly
> Parental depression
> 1. My mom was very sad or depressed.
> Parental assistance
> 2. My mom had family help her out.
> Parental awareness
> 3. My mom was not aware of what I was doing.
> Corporal punishment
> 4. I was hit when I misbehaved.
> Self depression
> 5. I felt depressed.
> Sexually and violently explicit movies
> 6. I watched sexually explicit television shows or movies.
> Parental presence
> 7. My mom was home when I went to bed.
> Parental alcohol use
> 8. My mom drank alcohol to get drunk.
> Siblings favored by parents
> 9. My dad favored my sibling(s) over me. (If you have no siblings, do not answer).
> Substance use
> 10. I use marijuana.
> 5=daily, 4=weekly, 3=1-3 times per month, 2=once/twice this year, 1=never
> Age of first sex/drugs
> 11. The first time I had oral sex I was ___ years old.
> 1=never, 2=13 or younger, 3=14-15 years, 4=16-17 years, 5=18+years
> Sexual abuse
> 12. I was touched inappropriately by a stranger or adult I knew.
> 0=never, 1=1 time, 2=2 times, 3=3 times, 4=4 or more times
> Exposure to physical violence
> 13. I saw my father hit my mother.
> Contact with the criminal justice system

14. My dad was incarcerated.
What percentage of your peers do you believe does the following things?
1=Almost none (less than 10%), 2=About 25%, 3= About half (50%), 4=About 75%,
5=Almost all (more than 90%)
Perceptions of others substance use
15. Have used marijuana, inhalants, or other drugs.
Perceptions of others sexual behaviors
16. Have had more than ten sexual partners.
Perceptions of others enjoyment of life
17. Enjoy life.

In: Youth Violence and Juvenile Justice: Causes, Intervention…   ISBN: 978-1-61668-011-4
Editor: Neil A. Ramsay et al., pp. 331-346   © 2010 Nova Science Publishers, Inc.

Chapter 15

LEARNING FROM SUCCESS WITH AT RISK ADOLESCENTS

Helene S. Wallach[*1] *and Yafit Levi*[2]
[1]University of Haifa, Haifa, Israel
[2]Max Stern Academic College of Emek Yezreel, Israel

ABSTRACT

"I am reborn…and that will help me succeed" this sentence exemplifies the meaning of success among youth at risk. "Learning from success" is a system that advocates learning from clients who succeeded. This chapter reports on research that examined the parameters of success among youth at risk. Interviews were conducted with six youth living at the "House on Haim street" or the apartment belonging to the "Sachlav" project, as well as with the instructors and the manager of the "House". We chose adolescents who were identified as youth that succeeded in improving their condition. When we examined the data to determine what helped them make the change, several categories evolved: 1. Past behavior (anti-social behavior, low self esteem), 2. The change process (helping others without receiving compensation, listening understanding and accepting others, taking responsibility for ones behavior, a change in the social environment and degree of integration into a normative environment), 3. The change point (fear of alternatives, relationship to others). The important factors in the change process were: fear of the alternative such as going to jail or being kicked out of the "House", and the relationship with others in the "House". If these findings are replicated in further studies using additional populations, it will help to shape interventions with youth at risk.

Key Words: Learning from success, at risk adolescents, detached youth, parameters of success

---

[*] helenwa@yahoo.com

LEARNING FROM SUCCESS WITH AT RISK ADOLESCENTS

At Risk Adolescents

Many attempts were made over the years to define (and treat) youth who had left school, and all formal frameworks. For example: "gangs", "street corner group", "juvenile delinquents", "unattached youth", etc. (Lahav, 2000; Romi & Cohen, 1998). The definition, as well as the risk factors, changes according to the agent involved. The educational system relates to the risk for learning difficulties and low marks. Youth programs relate to the difficulties of youth at work and/or school which may result in them dropping out (Lahav, 2002). More stringent criteria relate to the risk the youth are exposed to in their family or environment. These criteria relate to neglect or abuse, lack of a connection to a normative framework, inability to fit into learning or work environment (Schmid, 2006).

This paper will use the term "at risk youth" to define youth who are still part of a formal setting and therefore not totally disconnected, which is the status of the youth who took part in this study. Although partially in a formal work or school setting, these youth suffered from neglect or abuse, attention disorders, and were not fully integrated into society.

Due to the varying definitions, and lacking a unified data base, it is difficult to know how many at risk youth exist. A rough estimate, based on children who came to the attention of social services as well as a national survey of nurses who routinely see babies during their first five years estimated that there are 330,000 at risk youth in Israel, which is 15% of the total number of youth (Schmid, 2006). This is similar to numbers found in the US. Muss & Porton, (1998) found that 50% of youth were classified as low risk (occasional drinking), 25% as medium risk (drug use or light crimes), 15% as high risk (two or three of the dangerous behaviors – drugs, alcohol, crimes, risky sex, but at low rate or low severity) and 10% in the very high risk group (two or three of the dangerous behaviors at high rate or high severity).

Interventions with at Risk Adolescents

In Israel, several programs that address at risk youth exist. Some are part of Governmental offices such as Ministry of Health, Ministry of Social Welfare, Israeli Defense Force, others are voluntary organizations (Romi & Cohen, 1998). As a result, participation in the programs is either mandatory or voluntary. Mandatory programs include Juvenile court, Juvenile remediation, etc. One example is the training schools that focus on helping the youth to change while detaching him from his problematic environment (Fleishman, 1999). Voluntary programs use outreach to find at risk youth. They also accept referrals from other organizations. Youth may choose to stay or leave these programs. These programs attempt to help the youth to change while detaching him from his problematic environment; however they usually have a stronger emphasis on enhancing their independence. One such example is the "Sachlav" program which is where we chose to examine success parameters. Sachlav is comprised of several components: day center, shelter and sheltered apartment.

Sachlav Program

Sachlav is a Haifa based program designed to provide short term solutions to at risk youth. It serves 12-19 year old boys and girls. Most of the youth come from low socio-economic status, with parents who have a hard time caring financially and psychologically for their children. Some of the parents suffer from drug or alcohol addiction, and the percentage of single mothers is larger than in the general population.

The program guidelines are: immediate response, availability, short-term interventions, crisis intervention and interventions in the community. The program offers both physical and psychological support and attempts to help the youth integrate back into society. There is a full range of interventions and they are tailored to each youth. Sachlav is an evolving program that continues to modify its interventions based on research findings. Interventions include individual and group interventions, work programs, etc.

How can We Determine What Works – Learning from Success

Treating at risk youth is a difficult endeavor. These adolescents have various needs, and usually suffer from severe deficits, as well as lack of basic trust which is a necessary component in helping them. In addition, they usually lack familial and community support networks. Existing programs rarely manage to meet the ever-growing need for help, and there is a general feeling of exasperation among those working with this population.

Sikes, Rosenfeld and Weiss (2006) suggest that organizations use ongoing study groups to evaluate their performance and make necessary adaptations in order to improve their service. They suggest that rather than learning from experience or from failures, one should learn from successes. Learning from success involves two main processes: 1. we cannot continue to use old approaches that have not been proven based only on their availability and 2. There is a need to constantly look for new and innovative approaches that will enable us to help those that we have not been able to help in the past. This is done by searching for new techniques as well as by concentrating on the interaction between our target population and our helpers, especially on interactions that we know have been successful (Rosenfeld, 1997).

There are three sources of learning (Rosenfeld, 1997): 1. Professionals speculate what they did that brought about success. 2. Learning from those that managed to get out of terrible situations without totally breaking down. 3. Analyzing interactions – based on the accumulated experience and the evidence gained from the helpers and the helped, speculating together on the ingredients of success. This chapter will report on a research study that used the third approach. We interviewed youth, which went through a successful process, as well their instructors. Success entails three criteria (Rosenfeld, 1997): 1. Looking back, those that were helped realize the process they underwent. 2. There is an objective basis to evaluate the success. 3. There are no negative side effects that can be seen.

This chapter reports on research undertaken to examine the ingredients in the successful change process that several at-risk youth underwent in the Sachlav project in Haifa, Israel. We hope that these results can help improve work with at-risk youth in other settings as well. The main research question was: what are the parameters of success that we can identify using the learning from success method when applied to at-risk youth.

METHOD

Setting – Sachlav Project – The House on Haim Street (The "House") and the Sheltered Apartment

Adolescents arrive at the House from their home, from the street or from a variety of residences. In most cases they derived secondary benefits from their anti-social act, and often became experts in anti-social behavior. Most of them come from a low socio-economic background. Sachlav provides short-term solutions and aims to integrate the youth back into society, and as such works in coordination with other municipal programs. Youth that suffer from psychosis or extreme behavior disorders are not accepted as they place others at risk.

The Sachlav project comprises several components. One is the House on Haim street. The "House" provides a temporary address for twenty youth who cannot or do not want to stay at home or at a residential placement and are therefore homeless. The house is open 24 hours a day, 365 days a year. Youth staying at the "House" gain a break that allows them to reorganize prior to reintegration into society. They can stay at the house for up to three months and then go on to a permanent residence. Often they stay at the House longer than three months if it is deemed necessary to enable them to advance enough so that they can be reintegrated successfully. In addition, some of the youth move on to a sheltered house owned by the project.

The "House" has a director who is there during the day, and counselors who are there 24 hours a day in eight hour shifts. The director is in charge of liaison between the youth, his parents and relevant various organizations (police, welfare, etc.). In addition, when necessary he is the one to set the youth straight. The counselors are in charge of the day to day performance of the youth – from making sure they get up in the morning through ensuring their participation in work/study/activities to making sure they go to sleep on time. They are also in charge of discipline, meals, medications as well as looking after personal effects belonging to the residents. Every day at 16:00 the director, counselors and youth convene to summarize each adolescent's daily behavior.

The sheltered apartment provides an interim solution for four adolescents who no longer need the intense program of the "House", but are not yet ready to integrate fully into society. In the apartment the adolescents live by themselves. They are responsible for all aspects of running the apartment. They generally work as well as volunteer in various organizations in the community, and/or serve as a guide to other youth. They can stay in the apartment for as long as they need to. However, they can be returned to the "House" if necessary.

Subjects

Six adolescents were interviewed for this study – five boys and one girl, aged 16-21. They were chosen by the director of the "House" and by the counselors as those who were successfully rehabilitated. Only those for whom there was agreement among the director and counselors were included in the project. The criteria used to define success were: integration into work or school, adherence to "House" or apartment rules, helping others, volunteering in the "House" and elsewhere.

The director and two counselors were interviewed as well. The counselors, who were chosen out of a pool of nine counselors, had the largest seniority and knew the youth well.

Measures

A semi-structured interview was used (Sikes and Rosenfeld, 2006). The interview involves nine stages: 1. Identifying a success we want to study by asking the youth what he identifies as his success. 2. Brief description of the success in terms of before and after. 3. Describing the positive (objective and subjective) results of the success. 4. Describing the negative (objective and subjective) byproducts of the success. 5. Asking ourselves if the success is worthy of examination. If not, we begin again from point 1 with a different success. 6. Identifying the "stations" and change points in the process. 7. Detailing the activities "knowledge directing action" that helped bring about the success at the change point. 8. Deriving action principles from the activities in stage 7. 9. Deriving unsolved issues for continued learning.

These stages comprise the retrospective format of learning from success (Sikes, Rosenfeld and Weiss, 2006). A detailed description of the stages follows:

- Step 1 - Identifying a success we want to study. The subjects are asked to briefly describe their successes and to choose one for joint study. The criteria for a success worthy of study are positive effects resulting from joint collaboration. Normally these are activities that helped overcome significant obstacles. This is a difficult step, since we are generally not used to focus on success.
- Step 2 - Brief description of the success in terms of before and after. Participants describe (briefly) the situation before and after the successful change. Here we need to differentiate between the fruits of the success and the activities that lead to the success. This is a difficult task, and therefore one needs to clearly describe the situation before and after the success, as well as avoid any attempt at explaining the change or describing how it came about.
- Step 3. Describing the positive (objective and subjective) results of the success. The group uses reflection to try and obtain a clear picture of the change process. They attempt to identify the objective and subjective indicators of success by examining it from various points of view: personal, interpersonal, functional, and systemic. Here we need to concentrate on the various outcomes, in order to identify those that are often hidden from the eye.
- Step 4 - Describing the negative (objective and subjective) byproducts of the success. The group examines both the effort involved as well as the negative byproducts of the success. The effort includes monetary expenditure, time and energy expended as well as other activities that were neglected due to this expenditure. Negative byproducts may include people who were hurt in the process or left behind, activities that are contrary to the value system of the performers, etc.

- Step 5 - Asking ourselves if the success is worthy of examination. If not, we begin again from point 1 with a different success. The success defined in step 1 is examined according to the information derived from steps 2-4. If there is any doubt as to the success, the members need to hold an open discussion while examining the cost and effectiveness of the success. If there is not general agreement as to the success chosen, then it should be discarded and a new one chosen.
- Step 6 - Identifying the "stations" and change points in the process. Here it is important to examine the various stations on the way to the success, in order to discover change points, points where the adolescent managed to successfully overcome obstacles.
- Step 7 - Detailing the activities "knowledge directing action" that helped bring about the success at the change point. Here we choose change points and examine the activities that helped bring them about. This is done by asking those who took part in the activity to recount the details that were essential for the success, so that others can learn from them. It is important to refrain from professional language which may hide important actions.
- Step 8 - Deriving action principles from the activities in stage 7. The target of this step is to define and simplify the actions that lead to success so that they may be used in other settings. One must take care not to make broad statements that cannot be interpreted into action. The key to developing good action principles is in rooting them in specific activities, as described in step 7, while keeping them general enough so that they can be generalized to other settings and situations.
- Step 9 - Deriving unresolved issues for continued learning. Important unresolved issues came up during the previous stages and were not dealt with since they are not crucial for understanding the success. These issues are discussed in this stage.

Procedure

This chapter reports on a qualitative research performed at the "House" and the sheltered apartment. The adolescents were interviewed during the evening. Originally we planned to interview 15 adolescents who were chosen by the counselors and director as good examples of a successful process. However, prior to interviewing, we needed to exclude seven and two more during the interview process, leaving us with six youth. Exclusion was due to their behavior, such as hiding liquor, attempted suicide, etc. These behaviors indicated to us that the adolescents had not internalized the change process. They hoped to impress their counselors, or tried to gain secondary benefits such as early release from parole, etc. Therefore, they could not serve as good examples for a successful change process.

The counselors and director were interviewed after we completed the interviews with the adolescents. This was done in order to maintain objectivity in our interviews with the youth.

Due to the transient nature of the stay at the "House", an added difficulty in choosing adolescents for this research lies in the fact that many leave the "House" in the early stages of the change process, before we can be sure that they have made a successful change. Therefore, the adolescents chosen for this research project ended up being those who stayed at the "House" over six months, or were in the sheltered apartment.

Adolescents who agreed to take part in the research were guaranteed anonymity. Their responses were coded and the results are reported without their names.

The interviews were semi structured. The questions were derived from the nine steps outlined above. Adolescents, counselors and director were asked to: 1. Adolescents were asked to describe a behavior or habit that changed as a result of their stay in the House/Apartment, describe other's behavior or a conversation that helped them make the change; 2. The director and counselors were asked to briefly describe the adolescents behavior before and after the change; 3. All subjects were asked to describe the positive outcomes of the change; 4. All subjects were asked to describe the costs of the change as well as the negative outcomes. For the director and counselors, these costs and negative outcomes were not limited to the youth, rather were seen on a larger scale; 5. All subjects were asked if they can identify change points in the process; 6. All subjects were asked to recount the details that helped them make the changes outlined previously.

RESULTS

Analyzing the Results

First, we looked for common elements in the answers we received from the adolescents. Elements that were found in answers from several youth were viewed as more important than those that appeared in the answers of just one or two adolescents. Next, we grouped these elements together and created categories and sub-categories. And finally, we looked for these categories and sub-categories in the answers we received from the director and the counselors (Gibton, 2001). Looking at the interviews from those who helped the change process to occur (in our case the director and counselors) is seen by Rosenfeld (1997) as the "objective basis" to prove that they in fact were successful in making the change. In the final stage we created the link between the categories derived from this research and existing theories regarding at-risk youth.

Categories Derived

Despite the large difference in the youth's backgrounds, ranging from being sexually assaulted to having committed a crime and being at the House instead of jail, we were able to find similar patterns in their responses. The first category includes past behavior, the second the change process and the third the factors which helped the change process to occur.

1. Past behavior
    - Anti social behavior
    - Low self esteem
2. The change
    - Helping others without expecting compensation

- Listening, understanding and accepting others
- Accepting responsibility for behaviors
- New social environment
- Integrating into the normative society
3. What made the change
  - Fear of the alternatives
  - Relationship with significant others in the House
  - Support of and belief in the youth
  - Having basic needs met
  - Having limits put on one's behavior
  - Being emotionally contained

1. Past Behavior

Anti-Social Behavior

Several behaviors fit into this category, the main one being illegal behavior, as one boy said: "we used to break into houses. Drink alcohol, do drugs." An additional anti - social behavior we found was verbal and/or physical violence, as one girl said: "once I was very violent, a lot of verbal violence, I was cheeky". Similarly, low frustration tolerance was articulated by one boy who said "I never listened to others and I always did what I wanted to and I didn't care what others thought so I didn't listen to them, I only wanted to hear my own opinion". The director and counselors were in agreement regarding the anti-social behavior that typified the youth upon entering the "House", as the director said about one of the boys: "in the past he was without boundaries, he used drugs…"

Low Self Esteem

Five of the six youth admitted to having low self esteem. They said they ran away from their homes because they felt that their parents paid more attention to their siblings. One boy said: "I am very happy that I made the change since it helps me value myself more and I see that I can work at things that I like". Another example is a boy that said: "It helped me understand that with the help of the counselors I can…it gave me a lot of confidence". The director and counselors also found this to be an important parameter as they said about one girl: "she is very intimidated by people".

2. The Change

Helping Others without Expecting Compensation

The adolescents understood the importance of helping and being part of the group, as one boy said: "I began to help in the kitchen, I like cutting up vegetables, I like helping the other boys and I feel connected to them. In the past I never did this, I preferred not to". Another boy said: "I started helping boys with the chores in the "House"". The director and counselors also stated that there was a major change in helping and stated as an example the fact that four of the six youth volunteered in an outreach project directed towards other at-risk youth who are not in the "House". They saw this as a meaningful accomplishment.

Listening, Understanding and Accepting Others

The adolescents understand that they need to listen, understand and accept others in order to form good interpersonal relationships, as one boy said: "today I am able to restrain myself, I keep quiet, I don't get upset, and I keep to myself on the side". And another boy said: "I accept everyone, I don't judge anyone. I am grateful for what I receive".

Accepting Responsibility For Behaviors

When they first came to the "House" they felt that they were under investigation, similar to a police interrogation, and were afraid to take responsibility for their acts as they were afraid of the consequences. Hence, they used all kinds of excuses for their behavior. One boy said: "If I am to blame I can say it is me and admit to my mistake". With time the youth understood that even if they admitted to wrongful behavior, they will not be sent to jail. Furthermore, they realized that taking responsibility reflects maturity, and that their punishment will be related to their acts, and not beyond that. One boy said: "I began to admit to mistakes I made and to ask for help, in the past I was not able to admit to this". The director and counselors agreed that the youth tended to blame others rather than admit to their behavior and difficulties as a counselor said about one boy: "he blames the whole world for his behavior and not himself". And the director added about another boy: "tends to minimalize his behavior and generally uses a lot of denial".

New Social Environment

The adolescents arrived from broken homes or from residential settings, as one counselor said: "he was in a residence where they tended to hit anyone who cried". After going through the change process in the "House", they realized that their previous environment was detrimental to them, as one said: "I have a lot of positive friends, I can always ask them for help, they will always help me". And another boy said: "the people around me are for me, they are better."

Integrating into the Normative Society

Most of the youth interviewed for this study managed to integrate into the normative society – they rented an apartment, found a job or volunteered in civil service (an alternative in Israel to compulsory army service) or studied. As one counselor said about a boy in the sheltered apartment: "originally he wasn't able to stick to a job longer than a month, after that he managed to last six months and now he is working steadily in one place". One boy that started to work said: "today I work as...and they even leave me alone in the lab". And another boy who came from a drug and alcohol program to the "House" was happy to be in civil service.

3. What Made the Change

This is the most important point, and the focus of this research and chapter. We started out on this project to discover the change and support elements that helped bring about the change. We found two main points that seemed to be the most important influences on the youth, of them, the relationship with significant others was the most important.

Fear of the Alternatives
Four boys feared abandonment and being left alone, as one boy stated: "being expelled from the "House" helped me a lot". The director added that one boy's changing point was when he was expelled for violence. The boys knew that once they leave the "House", they have nowhere else to go, therefore they stayed and underwent change. In addition for one boy there was the fear of punishment as he said: "they wanted to expel me from the "House"...since then I started to change because I didn't want to go back to jail and that was the only option I had if I was expelled".

Relationship with Significant Others in the House
As previously stated this point was the most important one in the change process. Several elements comprised this relationship as follows.

Support of and Belief in the Youth
When the family does not provide support and love, the adolescent will look for it elsewhere, as one youth said: "the talks with the counselors helped a lot. They told me that they care about me and want me to succeed." Another youth said: "I am happy that they trust me and give me so much responsibility at work".

The counselors lend extra support to this. They all felt that it was a very important point in the change process, and that it helps to continue on. One counselor said: "The "house" knows how to give the feeling that you are somebody, to care. Some of the youth never felt this before; no one cared if they were at home or on the street."

Having Basic Needs Met
Basic needs of food and shelter as one youth said: "the security is what helped make the change".

The counselors and house manager agreed that it is important to meet basic needs. Some of the youth arrive in the "house" looking for a roof over their heads. A counselor said: "He felt more secure, more protected".

Having Limits Put on Ones Behavior
Teaching values requires limit setting. The limits in the "house" are very clear and range from prohibiting drugs and alcohol to keeping a distance between girls and boys. One youth said: "the setting and the limits in the "house" helped change me". Another one said: "My success is due to the clear limits in the "house".

The manager of the "house" and the counselors agree on limit setting, for each adolescent, as the manager said: "he needs a father figure, therefore he needs limits". This saying ties in limit setting and the need for an authoritative figure.

Being Emotionally Contained

The counselors and the manager felt that this is a very important point in the change process. They felt that the other needs can be met at a variety of other settings, but that this containment – being flooded with love – can be received only at the "house". They felt that this is what keeps the youth at the "house" and helps them change. Proof for that is what the manager said about the success of one girl: "instill trust and security and give her the feeling that she is loved". And about the change point of one boy: "endless love, to fight and not give up on him".

The youth agree with this. They all pointed out emotional containment as a significant point in the change process. One boy said: "when the counselor gave me a hug and told me he loves me it helped me". Another youth, when trying to point out the factors that helped her change said: "the setting, the listening, and the understanding".

DISCUSSION

Lately we note a change in the treatment of at-risk youth. Still, it is important to be on the lookout for new methods to help them and not to stick to theories and methods that are no longer helpful. Learning from success is built on continual learning and research with those who have succeeded so that we can learn from their success. The "Sachlav" project, adopted this approach.

The "house" shelters boys and girls with a wide range of behavior problems, all of whom are at-risk youth. Most of them arrived at the "house" after committing an anti-social or criminal act.

The Change Process

The youth underwent many changes while staying at the "house". One of the changes was their ability to take responsibility for their behavior. According to neutralization theory youth who behave in an anti-social manner use various techniques to explain and rationalize their behavior. These rationalizations and explanations protect them from self blame and from others blaming them (Cromwell & Thurman, 2003). The counselors in the "house" agree that some of the youth use these neutralization processes. Therefore, taking responsibility for their behavior arrives at a later stage when they are able to understand their difficulties and accept their shortcomings.

This change may have occurred due to the social environment in the "house". The youth in this study had few social contacts prior to entering the "house". In addition, they all came from disadvantaged neighborhoods and from low socio-economic status. Social control theory states that various factors such as modernization, dual career families, lead to a lessening in parental and societal control over adolescents. A lessening of control leads to a rift between the youth and normative behavior. Thus the youth tend to overtake the boundaries and to turn to anti-social behavior. This in turn leads to an increase in crime (Agnew, 2003). This is a good description of the youth at the "house". They dropped out of school, roamed the streets and befriended delinquent youth.

Sutherland's social learning theory (Agnew, 2003) claims that anti-social behavior is learnt like any other behavior. We can assume that the youth in our study learned this behavior from their surrounding environment.

Maslow claims that social needs such as the need to be accepted and respected and the need to love and be loved are higher in the hierarchy and therefore can be fulfilled only after basic needs are looked after. In the "house" the youth received food and shelter and thus were able to turn to fulfill social needs. They helped others without expecting any return, listened to other youth, and displayed acceptance and understanding of them (Nadler, 1994).

The Change Point

We found several factors which encouraged the adolescents to make the change. One was the fear of the alternative such as return to jail, return to an abusive family or return to the street. Some were afraid of leaving the warm environment of the "house".

Abuse, neglect or other early life crises may lead to an insecure attachment in later life. Insecurely attached youth have a difficult time in dealing with stressful situations, and are at risk for developing adjustment disorders. They learned early on that they cannot depend on their attachment figure for help (Mikulincer & Florian, 1998). Most of the youth in the "house" and those that took part in this research suffered these crises in early life, and thus were probably insecurely attached. Their experience in the "house" served to counter these early experiences. They received empathy and were emotionally contained. Youth and their counselors felt that this containment was a crucial ingredient in their success. This containment helped the youth search for a job, return to school, and/or move to a permanent residence.

A related factor in the change process was the trust and support they received from the counselors. This helped to make up for their early deprivation. Initially they looked for this support from peers, often anti-social peers, and this lead them to anti-social and illegal activities. In the "house" they received love, security and caring from the counselors and this helped them begin the change process.

Limit setting was another important factor. Children, who grow up without limits, are afraid of their impulses. They fear that they may lose control over their aggression, jealousy or need for immediate reinforcement and as a consequence will be overwhelmed by these needs (Fuchs-Shabtai & Blank, 2004). The limits in the "house" are strictly kept, and help the youth regain inner control over their needs and impulses.

SUMMARY

In order to be able to reinforce and generalize these findings, it is important to replicate this research with a larger number of youth in various settings. In addition, it is important to examine the change process over time to ensure that the youth manage to maintain their gains. At this point in time, we can tentatively say that providing basic needs together with limit setting and emotional containment are the main ingredients in the important change process from an at-risk adolescent to a normative, productive youth.

At risk youth are a major concern in Israeli society, as they are in other countries as well. It is imperative to find ways to help them. The main theoretical and practical contribution of this research is in applying the learning from success model to the topic of at-risk youth.

REFERENCES

Agnew, Robert. (2003). An integrated theory of the adolescent peak in offending. *Youth and Society, 34,* 263-299.

Cromwell, P. & Thurman, Q. (2003). The devil made me do it: Use of neutralizations by shoplifters. *Deviant Behavior, 24*, 535-550.

Fleishman, R. (1999). *Survey of Residential Solutions for At-Risk Youth.* Jerusalem: Joint-Brookdale Institution.

Fuchs-Shabtai, A. & Blank, S. (2004). *Parents Who Are Too Good*. Or Yehuda: Kineret. (In Hebrew).

Gibton, D. (2001). Theory anchored in reality: The importance of analyzing the results and building a theory in qualitative research. In N. T. Ben-Yehoshua (ed.). *Tradition and . .Change in Qualitative Research (p. 195-228).* Tel-Aviv: Dvir. (In Hebrew).

Lahav, C. (2000). A perspective on at-risk youth. In A. Shemesh (ed.). *From Displacement to Integration, 10*, (p. 8-17). Jerusalem: Ministry of Education, Youth Division (in Hebrew).

Lahav, C. (2002). *Helping At-Risk and Disconnected Youth in Israel.* Jerusalem: Ministry of Education, Youth Division (in Hebrew).

Mikulincer, M & Florian, V. (1998). The relationship between adult attachment styles and emotional and cognitive reactions to stressful events. In: A.J. Simpson, & W.S. Rholes (Eds). *Attachment Theory and Close Relationships*. (143-165). New York: Guilford press.

Muss ,R. & Porton, H. (1998), *Adolescent Behavior and Society: A Book of Readings* (5ed). New York: McGraw-Hill College.

Nadler, A. (1994). *Social Psychology.* Tel-Aviv: Open University (In Hebrew).

Romi, S. and Cohen, Y. (1998). *The Influence of Survival Trips on Disconected Youth's Personality in Israel.* Ramat-Gan: Bar-Ilan University (in Hebrew).

Rosenfeld, M. (1997). Learning from success – how to model social work to respond to its clients? *Society and Welfare, 17,* 361-377. (in Hebrew).

Schmid, H. (2006). *Public Committee Report on the Condition of At-Risk Children and Youth.* Jerusalem: Government report.

Sikes, Y., Rosenfeld M., and Weiss S. (2006). *Learning from Success as an Impetus for School Learning: 2002-2005 Pilot Program: the Retrospective Method.* Jerusalem: Maiers-Joint, Brookdale Institute and Minsitry of Education.

In: Youth Violence and Juvenile Justice: Causes, Intervention...   ISBN: 978-1-61668-011-4
Editor: Neil A. Ramsay et al., pp. 347-354   © 2010 Nova Science Publishers, Inc.

Chapter 16

THE INFLUENCE OF NORMATIVE BELIEFS ABOUT AGGRESSION ON BEHAVIOR IN CHILDREN

Julie E. Sprinkle
Appalachian State University, Boone, North Carolina, USA

ABSTRACT

Beliefs and attitudes have each been shown to exert an indirect influence on behaviors – including but not limited to violent and aggressive behaviors. Beliefs about whether or not the consequences of the behavior outweigh the benefits mediate the relationship. However, positive associations between proviolence attitudes and violent behavior have been documented by several research studies (Tolan, Guerra, & Kendall, 1995). Similar associations have been acknowledged between normative beliefs about aggression and actual violent and aggressive behaviors. While behavioral beliefs are based upon an individual's weighing of the cost versus benefit of an action, normative beliefs are an individual's schema for viewing behaviors as good or bad, right or wrong. The current study investigates the relationship between normative beliefs about aggression and subsequent aggressive behaviors of school-aged children using two standardized instruments. The results of the present study are examined using inter-item correlation analysis. Recommendations for extinguishing violent and aggressive beliefs and behaviors in children are presented.

INTRODUCTION

Beliefs and attitudes have each been shown to exert an indirect influence on behavior – including but not limited to violent and aggressive behavior. Since beliefs and attitudes can influence behavior, it follows that changing beliefs and attitudes about violence and aggression can produce a change in behavior. The current study examines self-reported normative beliefs about aggression and teacher observed aggressive behaviors in school-aged children from three counties in one state. The over-arching goal of the present investigation is to determine the impact student-held beliefs about aggression have on behaviors. Two standardized instruments, the Normative Beliefs about Aggression Scale (NOBAGS) (Huessman & Guerra, 1997) and the Aggressive Behavior Teacher Checklist (ABTC) (Dodge & Coie, 1987), are used as analytical tools in the current study.

BELIEFS AND BEHAVIORS

The debate surrounding the connection between beliefs, attitudes, and behaviors began as early as 1862 (Ajzen & Fishbein, 1980). Huesmann and Guerra (1997) established a direct correlation between normative beliefs and behaviors while Funk, Eilliott, Urman, Flores, & Mock (1999) postulate that a change in attitude produces a change in behavior. Conversely, Ajzen and Fishbein (1980) assert that beliefs, which can be behavioral or normative, and attitudes are only two components affecting behavior. A third component, intent, is also necessary for the prediction of behavior. This process is known as the theory of reasoned action (TRA) (Ajzen & Fishbein, 1980; Fishbein & Ajzen, 1975). Figure 1 provides a pictorial diagram of the theory of reasoned action.

Behavioral beliefs are based upon an individual's weighing of the cost versus benefit of an action. For example, if an individual would like to steal a watch, but thinks he/she may be caught, the behavioral belief serves as a deterrent. Normative beliefs however, are the focus of the present study. Normative beliefs are an individual's schema for viewing behaviors as good or bad, right or wrong. These beliefs are grounded in socially sanctioned and approved mores of behavior. Even though normative beliefs are socially sanctioned, this does not mean that they are sanctioned by the dominant society. Children raised in homes where theft and physical violence are accepted mechanisms of obtaining wanted goods incorporate the normative belief that theft and physical violence are 'okay.' Governed by normative beliefs, the same individual who pondered stealing the watch is deterred if his/her reference group would disapprove and encouraged if his/her reference group would find nothing offensive about his/her actions. Reference groups can conflict, such as a child with a deviant peer group and a law abiding family. In this situation, the child is likely to revert to behavioral beliefs in order to determine whether or not to commit the crime.

The normative and behavioral beliefs of an individual influence attitudes. Attitudes are hypothetical constructs created by the internal value system of the individual (Fishbein & Ajzen, 1975; Roth & Upmeyer, 1989; Funk et al., 1999; Funk, Elliott, Bechtoldt, Pasold, & Tsavoussis, 2003) that predispose an individual to view behaviors, people, places, or objects favorably or negatively. According to Ajzen (1988) and Eiser and van der Plight (1988), attitudes are the outgrowth of an individual's cognitive and affective reactions to life experiences. Whether these reactions are positive or negative shape whether an individual has favorable or disdainful attitudes toward a person, place, event, idea, or object. Therefore, beliefs about the consequences and social acceptability of an action couple with past experiences to shape the attitude system of an individual.

A major shortcoming of the theory of reasoned action is that it fails to take into account factors such as opportunities, resources, and skills. Realizing this omission, Ajzen (1985) expanded the theory to include these critical determinants of beliefs, attitudes, intentions, and behaviors. The reformulated theory was dubbed the theory of planned behavior (TPB). Figure 2 provides a pictorial diagram of the theory of planned behavior.

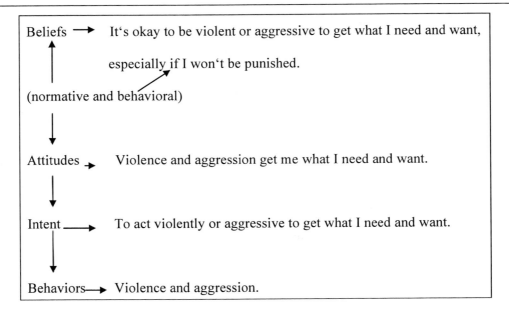

Figure 1. The relationship of beliefs, attitudes, intent, and behaviors according to TRA.

The theory of planned behavior asserts that the amount of behavioral control an individual perceives him/herself to have is strongly associated with the opportunities, resources, and skills available to him/her (Ajzen, 1991; Zint, 2002). If an individual has access to many opportunities and resources, he/she is likely to have a high level of perceived behavioral control. The converse is also true. Perceived behavioral control has a reciprocally influential relationship with attitudes and beliefs. For example, if a violence prevention program teaches students new skills of conflict resolution, empathy, and anger management, (1) their attitudes toward violence and beliefs about aggression are positively altered and (2) their perception of behavioral control increases because they have new mechanisms with which to respond to confrontational situations. This increased sense of control further modifies attitudes and beliefs about the acceptability of violent and aggressive behaviors.

COGNITIVE AND MORAL DEVELOPMENT

Cognitive and moral developmental theorists assert that progression through developmental stages makes prosocial behavior and empathic reasoning possible (Kohlberg, 1969; Eisenberg, Carlo, Murphy, & Van Court, 1995). Moral behavior encompasses the actions sanctioned by the social ruling class or dominant members of the society under investigation. Societal views of 'right' and 'wrong' are primarily determined by these dominant or majority group members. Ideally, children are taught or learn positive character-related behaviors from family, friends, schools, and communities.

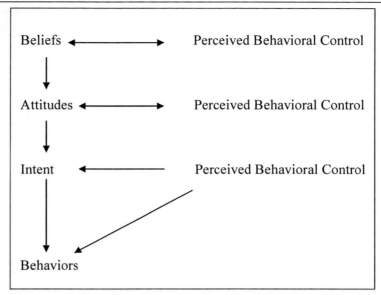

Figure 2: The relationship of beliefs, attitudes, perceived control, intent, and behaviors according to the TPB

Kohlberg (1969; 1976; 1981) conceptualized six stages of moral development. The first four are applicable to the current study. Stages one and two comprise the preconventional level, spanning from birth to age nine. During stage one, the child is concerned with avoiding punishment. Conversely, during stage two moral reasoning is dictated by obtaining rewards. Between the ages of nine and fifteen, children are in the conventional level of moral development. Stage three of this level is governed by a desire to gain approval while stage four signifies internalization of social rules through conformity to norms. The postconventional level, including stages five and six, extends from age sixteen until death.

Kohlberg's (1969; 1976) failure to investigate gender differences led Carol Gilligan (1982) to examine moral development in women. According to Gilligan, women are less concerned with rules and abstract principles than men. Instead of relying on such abstractions, women tend to make moral judgments based upon relationship and responsibilities. While Kohlberg explores the way people think about moral dilemmas, Gilligan expands her theoretical formulation to include the manner in which people define moral problems. Additionally, Gilligan suggests that gender may mediate the individual view of moral conflicts.

A second important distinction between Kohlberg (1969; 1976) and Gilligan (1982) are the actual stages of each theory. Unlike Kohlberg, Gilligan did not assign age categories to the stages of moral development. Similarly, Gilligan's model consists of three rather six stages: self-survival (solely concerned with one's self), caring for others (solely concerned with the care and nurture of others), and interdependence (balancing the needs of self and others). Despite Gilligan's attempt to give feminist voice to moral development, critics have faulted Gilligan for failing to account for structural differences, such as opportunity and individual psychology, in the development of moral reasoning (Hussey, 1998).

Given the differential effects of gender on the internalization or externalization of violent and aggressive behaviors (Galen & Underwood, 1997), Gilligan's theory of moral development is helpful in explaining why females tend to be socially aggressive and boys tend to be physically aggressive. Through the lens of this theory, female moral development is tied to interpersonal relationships. Therefore, relationships are the target of antisocial as well as prosocial behaviors while females are moving through the developmental process.

HYPOTHESES

After reviewing the literature, several hypotheses were developed by the researcher for investigation in the current study. First, students' normative beliefs about aggression will positively correlate with their teacher-observed aggressive behaviors. Second, female participants will have fewer normative beliefs sanctioning aggression than male participants. Third, female participants will have lower teacher-observed aggressive behaviors than male participants. Fourth, age will be positively correlated with scores on both instruments, indicating more aggressive beliefs and higher levels of displayed aggression. Fifth, students who reside in counties with high rates of juvenile crime will have higher scores on both instruments, indicating more aggressive beliefs and higher levels of displayed aggression.

INSTRUMENTS

Normative Beliefs about Aggression Scale (NOBAGS)

The Normative Beliefs About Aggression Scale (NOBAGS) is a 20-item scale designed to measure individuals' perceptions of the acceptability of aggressive behavior when provoked and under normal circumstances (Huesmann & Guerra, 1997). The scale has been tested on participants from age 6-30 in several countries. Different wording is used with various age groups and reliability can be assessed by using two versions of the scale with respondents where the words "wrong" and "okay" are interchanged.

NOBAGS is a revision of the previous 35-item Aggression Approval Scale (AGGAPS) (Huesmann, Guerra, Miller, & Zelli, 1992). The instrument consists of 12-items that measure approval of aggression when provoked (retaliation aggression) and 8-items assessing approval of general aggression. Each item has a likert-type 4-point response choice in which participants are asked to indicate their level of agreement with the statement presented. Response choices range from 1= It's perfectly ok, 2= It's sort of ok, 3= It's sort of wrong, and 4= It's really wrong. Negatively worded items reverse the order of the response choices so that 1= It's really wrong, 2= It's sort of wrong, 3= It's sort of ok, and 4= It's perfectly ok. A higher score indicates greater acceptance of total, general, and retaliation aggression.

When developing NOBAGS for use with elementary school children, Huesmann, Guerra, Miller, and Zelli (1992) recruited an initial sample of 1,550 first (n= 784) and fourth (n= 766) grade students. The participants were drawn from 16 schools in two Midwestern cities with low socioeconomic status and high crime neighborhoods. The sample was ethnically diverse with African American (38.3%), Caucasian (18.1%), and Hispanic (36.6%) respondents. Similarly, the sample was inclusive of both genders with 48% of the sample being male and 52% being female. Data was collected from the sample three times; during the spring of 1991, the fall of 1991, and the spring of 1992. After finding the stability of test-retest scores to be weak (.36-.74), a revised 20-item scale was developed. This scale consisted of 12-items from the original scale that were highly correlated with retaliation aggression, plus 8-items designed to measure general aggression.

Actual aggressive behaviors were measured to assess the construct validity of the revised NOBAGS. Students were asked to complete the Peer-Nominated Index of Aggression (Eron, Walder, & Letkowitz, 1978) and teachers rated all study participants by completing the Child Behavior Checklist (CBCL) (Achenbach, 1978). Both instruments have a documented history of good reliability and validity (Huesmann & Guerra, 1997). The Peer-Nominated Index of Aggression was significantly positively correlated across all dimensions of the NOBAGS at $p < .001$. Similarly, the CBCL was significantly positively correlated with NOBAGS at $p < .05$. These results indicate NOBAGS adequately measures the construct aggression.

A factor analysis yielded a total scale, two major subscales, and four minor subscales on the NOBAGS. However, only the total scale and two major subscales are relevant to the current study. The total approval of aggression score is obtained by summing responses to each item. The total aggression scale has an alpha of .86. The first major subscale, general approval of aggression, has an alpha of .80. The following items comprise this factor – 13.) In general it is OK to hit other people. 14.) If you are angry, it is wrong to say mean things to other people. 15.) In general, it is wrong to yell at others and say bad things. 16.) It is usually wrong to push or shove other people around if you're mad. 17.) It is OK to insult other people. 18.) It is OK to take it out on others by saying mean things when you are mad. 19.) It is generally OK to get into physical fights with others. 20.) In general, it is wrong to take your anger out on others by using physical force.

The second subscale, approval of retaliation, is inclusive of all four minor subscales and has an alpha of .82. The first minor subscale, approval of retaliation, weak provocation has an overall alpha of .75 and includes the following items – Suppose a boy says something bad to another boy, John. 1.) Do you think it's OK for John to scream at him? 2.) Do you think it's OK for John to hit him? Suppose a boy says something bad to a girl. 3.) Do you think it's wrong for the girl to scream at him? 4.) Do you think it's wrong for the girl to hit him? Suppose a girl says something bad to another girl, Mary. 5.) Do you think it's OK for Mary to scream at her? 6.) Do you think it's OK for Mary to hit her? Suppose a girl says something bad to a boy. 7.) Do you think it's wrong for the boy to scream at her? 8.) Do you think it's wrong for the boy to hit her?

The second minor subscale, approval of retaliation, strong provocation, has an alpha of .71 and includes the following items – 9.) Suppose a boy hits another boy, John. Do you think it's wrong for John to hit him back? 10.) Suppose a boy hits a girl. Do you think it's OK for the girl to hit him back? 11.) Suppose a girl hits Mary. Do you think it's wrong for Mary to hit her back? 12.) Suppose a girl hits a boy. Do you think it's wrong for the boy to hit her back? The third minor subscale, approval of retaliation against males has an alpha of .70 and includes items 1-4, 9, and 10. The fourth minor subscale, approval of retaliation against females has an alpha of .70 and includes items 5-8, 11, and 12.

In a follow-up longitudinal study designed to increase the reliability and validity of NOBAGS, Huesmann and Guerra (1997) selected a sample of 1,015 inner-city school children in second (n= 317), third (n= 323), and fifth (n= 375) grades. A MANOVA revealed significant gender effects, $F(1, 1009) = 80.5$, $p < .001$, significant cohort effects, $F(2, 1009) = 33.3$, $p < .001$, and a significant cohort by grade interaction, $F(4, 2016) = 4.89$, $p < .001$. The gender and age effects indicate that children who are male have more approving beliefs about

The Influence of Normative Beliefs about Aggression on Behavior in Children   323

aggression, while general and retaliation approval increase steadily with age. The results of the second study also support initial findings that normative beliefs about aggression are directly, positively correlated to actual aggressive behaviors.

Aggressive Behavior Teacher Checklist (ABTC)

The Aggressive Behavior Teacher Checklist (ABTC) is a 6-item instrument designed to measure proactive and reactive aggression in elementary school children (Dodge & Coie, 1987). The ABTC consists of five point Likert-type response categories ranging from 1= never to 5= almost always. A higher score is indicative of greater levels of aggressive behavior. In developing the ABTC, Dodge and Coie (1987) initially sampled 12 public school teachers with a total of 259 third through sixth grade students. Teachers were asked to complete a 24-item instrument for each of their students. The 6 aggression items loaded strongly on one factor with an Eigenvalue of 8.26. The internal consistency of the instrument is .90.

In a follow-up study conducted to assess the validity of the ABTC, students rated by teachers were observed in free-play interactions with their fellow students. There was a statistically significant positive correlation between teacher ratings and direct observer ratings; $r = .27$, $p < .004$. This finding supports construct validity of the ABTC.

METHODOLOGY

The study population was comprised of students from three separate counties in one state (N= 310). The sample respondents ranged from grades three through six, included an equal numbers of male and female participants, and an almost equal number of minority (47%) and non-minority (53%) students. Two counties were rated high in levels of juvenile committed crimes (44%), while the third county was rated low on levels of youth crimes (56%). These ratings were obtained through the state's Department of Juvenile Justice. While this measure does not provide individual information about the sample participants, it lends another dimension to the data analysis as the researcher is able to examine the correlation of youth crime rates with student beliefs and behaviors.

Students were given the NOBAGS to complete, while teachers (N=12) were asked to rate students' aggressive behaviors using the ABTC. Student subscale and total scale scores from the NOBAGS were correlated with teacher ratings from the ABTC to determine the strength, direction, and degree of the relationship between students' attitudes about aggression and their observed behaviors. In addition, student demographic variables were analyzed to explore their impact on beliefs and behaviors. Finally, the county in which participants reside (high or low levels of juvenile crime) was correlated with student and teacher scores to discern the relationship between rates of youth crime and aggressive beliefs and behaviors in the county's children.

FINDINGS

Nobags

Participant scores on the Normative Beliefs about Aggression Scale (NOBAGS) indicated moderate levels of aggressive beliefs. The NOBAGS has two subscales – retaliation aggression (questions 1-12) and general aggression (questions 13-20) and one large scale – total aggression (questions 1-20). Lower scores are indicative of less acceptance of aggression while higher scores indicate greater levels of aggression acceptance. Since each question is scored on a four point scale, the lowest possible score on the retaliation subscale is 12, while the highest is 48. The lowest possible score on the general aggression subscale is 8, while the highest possible score is 32. For total aggression, the lowest possible score is 20, while the highest possible score is 80.

Retaliation aggression

Only 4.5% (n=14) of the study population received a score of 12 on the retaliation aggression subscale indicating no sanctioning of retaliation aggression. The mean score on the retaliation aggression dimension was 24 (SD= 7.6) while the mode score was 16. The maximum score on the retaliation measure, 48, was attained by .6% (n=2) of the study population. The distribution is almost symmetrical (skew= .38, kurtosis= -.33) around the mean, indicating that the majority of students have low to moderate levels of retaliation aggression beliefs.

General Aggression

Only 11.3% (n=35) of the sample received a score of 8 on the general aggression scale, indicating no sanctioning of general aggression. The mean score on the general aggression dimension was 14 (SD= 5.7) while the mode score was 13. The maximum score on the general aggression measure, 32, was attained by .6% (n=2) of the study population. The frequency distribution is slightly positively skewed (skew= .65, kurtosis= -.27), indicating that students have low overall levels of general aggressive beliefs.

Total Aggression

Only 4% (n=12) of the study population received a score of 20 on total aggression, indicating no aggression. The mean score on the total aggression dimension was 37 (SD= 12.2) while the mode score was 25. The maximum score on the total measure, 80, was attained by .6% (n=2) of the study population. The distribution indicates (skew= .53, kurtosis= -.03) study participants had low total aggressive belief levels, thus slightly positively skewing the distribution.

ABTC

Participant scores on the Aggressive Behavior Teacher Checklist (ABTC) were consistent with respondents' scores on the NOBAGS. The ABTC has one scale (items 1-6), with a minimum score of 6 and a maximum score of 30. A higher score indicates high levels of aggression, while a lower score indicates low levels of aggression. Twenty-three point two percent (n=72) of the sample received a minimum score of 6, while 2.3% (n=7) of participants received a maximum score of 30. The mean score on the ABTC pre-test was 12.7 (SD= 6.6) while the mode was 6. The frequency distribution indicates teachers in the study population had low overall perceptions of students' aggressive behaviors, thus positively skewing the results (skew= .87, kurtosis= -.21).

CORRELATIONS

An analysis of the NOBAGS produced expected correlations between each dimension of the scale. Using Pearson's correlation (r) two-tailed test for significance, the retaliation aggression dimension was strongly positively correlated with both the general aggression dimension (r=.69, p<.01) and the total aggression score (r=.94, p<.01). Similarly, the general aggression dimension and the total aggression score were also positively correlated (r=.90, p<.01) (Table 1). These results indicate good reliability and validity in measuring the construct beliefs about aggression.

Each dimension of the NOBAGS was positively correlated with the ABTC using Pearson's correlation two-tailed test of significance. With regard to the retaliation aggression dimension, it was moderately positively correlated with the ABTC (r=.48, p<.01). Likewise, the general aggression dimension (r=.43, p<.01) and the total aggression score (r=.50, p<.01) showed a medium strength positive correlation with the total ABTC score of study participants (Table 2). These results indicate that student self-reports of aggressive beliefs are congruent with teachers' perceptions of the students' outwardly aggressive behaviors.

Demographic variable correlation indicated females have fewer normative beliefs sanctioning aggression and lower levels of teacher observed aggressive behaviors, while the converse is true for males. This finding held constant for age, with older students expressing more normative beliefs about aggression and exhibiting higher levels of aggressive behavior across gender lines. Further analysis indicates that respondents from counties with higher rates of juvenile crime have more normative beliefs sanctioning aggression and higher levels of displayed aggression while the participants from the county with lower rates of juvenile crime have lower scores across both instruments.

Table 1. Correlations Between Dimensions of the NOBAGS.

	Retaliation Aggression	General Aggression	Total Aggression
Retaliation	1*	.69*	.94*
General	.69*	1*	.90*
Total	.94*	.90*	1*

* Pearson's correlation is significant at the p<.01 level (two-tailed)

Table 2. Correlations Between the NOBAGS and the ABTC.

	Retaliation Aggression	General Aggression	Total Aggression
ABTC	.48*	.43*	.50*

* Pearson's correlation is significant at the p<.01 level (two-tailed)

DISCUSSION

As hypothesized, students normative beliefs about aggression are positively correlated with their displays of outwardly aggressive behaviors. Even though the relationship was not as strong as the researcher initially predicted, a positive correlation signifies an association between these two variables and strengthens the assertion that the instruments used in the investigation accurately detect the concepts under study. The moderate scores on the NOBAGS and ABTC by the majority of participants could be influenced by several factors. Since the ABTC relies on teacher observation, it is possible that teachers did not observe or accurately rate the aggressive behaviors of some participants. Further, teachers may have been more likely to rate male students as outwardly aggressive than female students due to the societal norm that girls should be lady-like while boys are expected to be more physical. As with any self report, student responses on the NOBAGS may be biased or exhibit a socially desirable skew. In addition, simply because a child knows right from wrong does not mean he/she will act accordingly. Situational variables and contexts often influence behaviors, regardless of beliefs.

The second and third hypotheses, female participants will have fewer normative beliefs sanctioning aggression and lower teacher observed aggressive behaviors than male participants, were moderately supported. Study findings indicate females are more likely to have low levels of aggressive beliefs and demonstrate outwardly aggressive behaviors than their male counterparts. As previously mentioned, teacher/student bias could influence instrument scores; however, the socialization of males and females tends to encourage the type of dichotomy detected in this investigation.

The fourth hypothesis, age will be positively correlated with scores on both instruments, indicating more aggressive beliefs and higher levels of displayed aggression, was strongly supported. Older study participants were more likely than younger study participants to indicate normative beliefs sanctioning aggression and to display outwardly aggressive behaviors as indicated by self report and teacher ratings. Since younger study participants are in Kohlberg's pleasing others/gaining approval stage, it is possible they responded in a manner consistent with what they believed would gain approval, rather than sharing their true beliefs. However, the validation provided by teacher ratings on the ABTC helps to dispel this assertion.

The fifth hypothesis, students who reside in counties with high rates of juvenile crime will have higher scores on both instruments, indicating more aggressive beliefs and higher levels of displayed aggression, was moderately supported. Children who are exposed to crime are more likely to develop normative beliefs that sanction such activities, often resulting in participation in criminal behaviors. It is important to note that the county rates of juvenile crime were not specific to participants and were inclusive of non-violent crime as well as violent crime. In future investigations, a more robust and accurate measure of youth violence is needed. However, for an initial investigation, the juvenile crime index added depth and an additional method of comparison for student and teacher scores on the instruments.

CONCLUSION

The present investigation indicates a clear positive relationship between the normative aggressive beliefs and aggressive behaviors of school-aged children. The relationship necessitates that violence/aggression prevention programs target the beliefs of participants, rather than focus primarily on behaviors. As the ability to relate empathically to others inhibits antisocial behavior (Eisenberg-Berg, 1979; Eisenberg et al., 1995; Eisenberg, 1986, Eisenberg, 1995), fostering the development of empathy is an objective in many school-based violence prevention programs (Cooper, Lutenbacher, & Faccia, 2000; Mytton, DiGuiseppi, Gough, Taylor, & Logan, 2002; Daiute, Stern, & Lelutiu-Weinberger, 2003). Examples of such programs include I Have a Future (Greene, Smith, & Peters, 1995), Smart Talk (Bosworth, Espelage, & Dubsy, 1998), Peace Builders (Krug, Brner, Dahlber, Ryan, & Powell, 1997), and Second Step (Grossman, Neckerman, Koepsell, Liu, Asher, Beland, Fry, & Rivara, 1997; Orpinas, Kelder, Frankowski, Murray, Zhang, & McAlister, 2000).

While empathy is often a key variable in school-based violence prevention programs, the actual social skills taught in many violence prevention programs are conflict resolution, anger management, and peer mediation. In order to resolve conflicts, control anger, or mediate among peers, individuals must be capable of perspective-taking. Without being able to see the situation through someone else's eyes, there is a disjoint between cognition and emotion, leading children to act impulsively. Therefore, cognitive and affective aspects of violence prevention programs must be given equal attention to ensure that skills are being appropriately developed and applied. By instilling prosocial and empathic attitudes and beliefs in children, rates of youth violence and aggression can be significantly decreased and perhaps even eradicated. Current and future generations of our society deserve no less.

REFERENCES

Achenbach, T. M. (1978). The child behavior Profile: I. Boys aged 6-11. *Journal of Consulting and Clinical Psychology, 46,* 478-488.

Ajzen, I. (1985). From intentions to actions: A theory of planned behavior. In J. Kuhl & J. Bechmann (Eds.), *Action-control: From cognition to behavior* (11-39). Heidelberg: Springer.

Ajzen, I. (1988). *Attitudes, personality, and behavior.* Chicago: Dorsey.

Ajzen, I. (1991). The theory of planned behavior. *Organizational Behavior and Human Decision Processes, 50,* 179-211.

Ajzen, I. & Fishbein, M. (1980). *Understanding attitudes and predicting social behavior.* Upper Saddle River, NJ: Prentice-Hall, Inc.

Bosworth, K., Espelage, D. & DuBay, T. (1998). A computer-based violence prevention intervention for young adolescents: Pilot study. *Adolescence, 33,* 785-795.

Cooper, W., Lutenbacher, M. & Faccia, K. (2000). Components of effective youth violence prevention programs for 7-to 14-year olds. *Archives of Pediatrics and Adolescent Medicine, 11,* 1134-1139.

Daiute, C., Stern, R. & Lelutiu-Weinberger, C. (2003). Negotiating violence prevention. *Journal of Social Issues, 59(1),* 83-101.

Dodge, K. & Coie, J. D. (1987). Social-information-processing factors in reactive and proactive aggression in children's peer groups. *Journal of Personality and SocialPsychology, 53(6),* 1146-1158.

Eisenberg, N. (1986). *Altruistic emotion, cognition, and behavior.* Hillsdale, NJ: Erlbaum.

Eisenberg, N. (1995). Prosocial development: A multifaceted model. In: W., Kurtines, & J., Geewirtz, (Eds.), *Moral development.* Boston: Allyn and Bacon.

Eisenberg, N., Carlo, G., Murphy, B. & Van Court, P. (1995). Prosocial development in late adolescence: *A longitudinal study. Child Development, 66,* 1179-1197.

Eisenberg-Berg, N. (1979). Development of children's prosocial moral judgment. *Developmental Psychology, 23(15),* 128-137.

Eiser, J. R. & van der Plight, J. (1988). *Attitudes and decisions.* New York: Routledge.

Eron, L. D., Walder, L. O. & Lefkowitz, M. M. (1978). *The learning of aggression in children.* Boston: Little-Brown.

Fishbein, M. & Ajzen, I. (1975). *Belief, attitude, and behavior.* Reading, MA: Addison-Wesley.

Funk, J. B., Elliott, R., Bechtoldt, H., Pasold, T. & Tsavoussis, A (2003). The Attitudes Towards Violence Scale - Child Version. *Journal of Interpersonal Violence, 18,* 186-196.

Funk, J. B., Elliott, R., Urman, M., Flores, G. & Mock, R. (1999). The attitudes towards violence scale: A measure for adolescents. *Journal of Interpersonal Violence, 14(11),* 1123-1136.

Furlong, M. J. & Smith, D. C. (Eds.) (1994). *Anger, hostility, and aggression: Assessment, prevention, and intervention strategies for youth.* Brandon, VT: Clinical Psychology.

Galen, B. R. & Underwood, M. K. (1997). A developmental investigation of social aggression among children. *American Psychological Association, 33(4),* 589-600.

Gilligan, C. (1982). *In a different voice: Psychological theory and women's development.* Cambridge, MA: Harvard University Press.

Greene, L. W., Smith, M., S. & Peters, S. R., (1995). "I have a future" comprehensive adolescent health promotion: cultural considerations in program implementation and design. *Journal of Health Care of the Poor and Underserved, 6,* 267-281.

Grossman, D. C., Neckerman, H. J., Koepsell, T. D., Liu, P. Y., Asher, K. N., Beland, K., Frey, K. & Rivara, F. P. (1997). Effectiveness of violence prevention curriculum among children in elementary school: A randomized controlled trial. *Journal of the American Medical Association, 277,* 1605-1611.

Huesmann, L. R. & Guerra, N. G. (1997). Children's normative beliefs about aggression and aggressive behavior. *Journal of Personality and Social Psychology, 72(2),* 408-419.

Huesmann, L. R., Guerra, N. G., Miller, L. & Zelli, A. (1992). The role of social norms in the development of aggression. In: H., Zumkley & A., Fraczek, (Eds.), *Socialization and aggression.* New York: Springer.

Hussey, D. (1998). Theories of cognitive and moral development. In: S., Robbins, P. Chatterjee, & E. Canda, (Eds.), *Contemporary human behavior theory: A critical perspective for social work.* Needham Heights, MA: Allyn and Bacon.

Kohlberg, L. (1969). *Stages in the development of moral thought and action.* New York: Holt.

Kohlberg, L. (1976). The cognitive-developmental approach to moral education. In: P. H., Martorell, (Eds.), *Social studies strategies: Theories into practice.* New York: Harper and Row.

Kohlberg, L. (1981). *Essays on moral development (Vol. I). The philosophy of moral development.* San Francisco: Harper & Row.

Krug, E. G., Brener, N. D., Dahlberg, L.L., Ryan, G. W. & Powell, K. E. (1997). The impact of an elementary school-based violence prevention program on visits to the school nurse. *American Journal of Preventive Medicine, 13,* 459-463.

Mytton, J., DiGuiseppi, C., Gough, D., Taylor, R. & Logan, S. (2002). School-based violence prevention programs: A systematic review of secondary prevention trials. *Archives of Pediatric and Adolescent Medicine, 156,* 752-762.

Orpinas, P., Kelder, S., Frankowski, R., Murray, N., Zhang, Q. & McAlister, A. (2000). Students for Peace Project program evaluation. *Health Education Research, 15(1),* 45-58.

Roth, H. G. & Upmeyer, A. (1989). Behavior as an expressive function of attitudes. In A. Upmeyer (Eds.), *Attitudes and behavior decisions* (217-254). New York: Springer-Verlag.

Tolan, P., Guerra, N. & Kendall, D. C. (1995). A developmental-ecological perspective on antisocial behavior in children and adolescents: Towards a unified risk and intervention framework. *Journal of Consulting and Clinical Psychology, 63,* 579-584.

Zint, M. (2002). Comparing three attitude behavior theories for predicting science teachers' intentions. *Journal of Research in Science Teaching, 39,* 819-844.

In: Youth Violence and Juvenile Justice: Causes, Intervention... ISBN: 978-1-61668-011-4
Editor: Neil A. Ramsay et al., pp. 361-365 © 2010 Nova Science Publishers, Inc.

Chapter 17

PUBLIC PERCEPTIONS OF REGISTRY LAWS FOR JUVENILE SEX OFFENDERS

Carrie E. Reynolds[1], Cynthia J. Najdowski[1], Jessica M. Salerno[1], Margaret C. Stevenson[2], Tisha R. A. Wiley[3] and Bette L. Bottoms[3]
[1]University of Illinois at Chicago, IL, USA
[2]University of Evansville, IL, USA
[3]University of Illinois at Chicago, IL, USA

INTRODUCTION

The first federal sex offender registry law was established in 1994 with the creation of the Jacob Wetterling Crimes Against Children Sexually Violent Offender Registration Act (1994). This law requires that sex offenders register personal information (e.g., name, address, photograph, etc.) with law enforcement after serving their sentences. Megan's Law amended the Wetterling Act, further requiring that all states have procedures in place to notify communities of local sex offenders.

These laws were created to prevent sex offender recidivism. Specifically, the goals of these laws are to (a) facilitate the quick and efficient apprehension of offenders, (b) deter offenders from re-offending by letting them know that they are being watched, and (c) make the public more aware of offenders living nearby. In 2006, the Sex Offender Registration and Notification Act (SORNA; 42 U.S.C. § 16911), also known as the Adam Walsh Act, extended adult sex offender registry laws to include juveniles convicted in adult court of sex offenses and juveniles 14 years of age and older adjudicated in juvenile court for sex offenses involving aggravating circumstances. SORNA established these minimum registration guidelines for juveniles, but many states have stricter, more inclusive laws. For example, in some states, juveniles as young as 7 years of age can be required to register.

As reviewed by Salerno and colleagues (in press), 33 states require juveniles adjudicated in juvenile court to register as sex offenders under certain circumstances. In 26 of those states, registration is mandatory for juvenile sex offenders. That is, if juveniles are found guilty of certain sex offenses, they are required to register—judges are unable to exercise discretion on a case-by-case basis. Twenty-two states require that juvenile offenders remain on the registry for at least 10 years; other states require that juveniles remain on the registry for their entire lives.

States also vary on the types of offenses for which juvenile offenders are required to register. Some states require that juveniles register for only more severe offenses that involve threats, use of force, or incapacitation. Others, however, require juveniles to register after being adjudicated of any sex offense, even for acts such as sending naked pictures of themselves to peers (*A. H. v. Florida,* 2007), having consensual sexual relationships with peers ("No Easy Answers," 2007; *Wilson v. State of Georgia,* 2006), and puerile acts such as mooning and grabbing buttocks (Trivitts & Reppucci, 2002). Thus, many juveniles on the registry might not fit the prototype of a sex offender (e.g., a rapist) that is commonly envisioned by proponents of the sex offender registry.

Sex offender registration laws are implemented under the presumption that they decrease the otherwise high rates of sex offender recidivism. These assumptions, however, might be false. Sandler, Freeman, and Socia (2008) found no evidence that sex offenses have decreased since registry laws were implemented, for either first-time adult offenders or re-offenders. Others found no differences between recidivism rates for registered and nonregistered juvenile and adult sex offenders (e.g., Adkins, Huff, & Stageberg, 2000; Letourneau & Armstrong, 2008; Schram & Millov, 1995). Furthermore, the assumption that juvenile offenders have recidivism rates similar to that of adult offenders is not supported: Compared to adult offenders who re-offend at rates of 20-40% (Trivits & Reppucci, 2002), only 5-15% of juvenile sex offenders re-offend (Chaffin, 2008; Trivits & Reppucci, 2002). Juveniles 12 years old and younger have an even lower recidivism rate (2 to 7% over 10 years) (Carpentier, Silovsky, & Chaffin, 2006). Finally, in terms of rehabilitation, juvenile offenders are more similar to juveniles who commit nonsexual crimes than adults who commit sexual offenses (St. Amand, Bard, & Silovsky, 2008). Thus, the reasons for including juveniles on the registry in the first place are unsupported by extant research.

Requiring sex offenders to register can have negative outcomes. Research on sex offenders shows that registration can lead to job loss, harassment, and physical assault (Levenson & Cotter, 2005; Levenson, D'Amora, & Hern, 2007; Tewksbury, 2005). Some have suggested that these negative outcomes might actually make offenders *more* likely to re-offend (Letourneau & Miner, 2005; Trivits & Reppucci, 2002). Juveniles also may be at risk for experiencing these iatrogenic effects.

Registry laws are implemented because politicians and policymakers believe that the public supports them, but this assumption may not be true. Research on public perceptions of sex offender registry laws for *adult* offenders reveals generally strong support (Levenson, Brannon, Fortney, & Baker, 2007; Phillips, 1998; Caputo & Brodsky, 2004). Such support probably deters politicians from attempting to redefine these laws in line with research findings (Chaffin, 2008; Brenton, 2008).

How much public support is there for registry laws applied to *juvenile* offenders? To date, few studies have assessed perceptions of registry laws for juvenile offenders (but see Salerno et al., in press; Stevenson, Sorenson, Smith, Sekely, & Dzwairo, in press). Salerno and colleagues (in press) found that family law attorneys, but not undergraduates or prosecuting attorneys, supported registry laws for juvenile sex offenders less than for adult sex offenders when asked in the abstract about their support for laws. This effect might be explained by the fact that family law attorneys were the only group to recognize that juvenile sex offenders are less likely to recidivate than are adult sex offenders. In a follow-up study, Salerno et al. asked about laws applied to specific offenders in scenarios. Undergraduates read about either a 12- or 16-year-old juvenile, who was involved in pornography (i.e., was caught looking at naked pictures of underage girlfriend), harassment (i.e., ran through school hallways slapping girls' buttocks), statutory rape (i.e., had consensual oral sex with an under-aged girl), or rape. Participants supported registry laws more for (a) the 16-year-old than for the 12-year-old, and (b) the rape offense than for the statutory rape and harassment cases, and more for these cases than for the pornography case. Participants estimated similar recidivism rates for the 12- and 16-year-old, but different recidivism rates depending on offense severity, echoing the pattern describe above for registry support.

In another similar study, Stevenson and colleagues (in press) experimentally manipulated the ethnicity of the juvenile sex offender and the victim (African American or White) in the context of the same statutory rape case described above. Community members were more supportive of registration when the defendant and the victim were of different races than when they were of the same race—an effect likely driven by societal lack of acceptance of interracial relationships. In addition, women (but not men) recommended registration more when the victim was White than African American, illustrating evidence of racial bias in these types of cases. Finally, these effects were driven by desire for retribution rather than by utilitarian goals to protect society.

Based on this preliminary evidence, the public actually does *not* appear to support mandatory registry laws for juveniles: Participants' support for registry laws depended on offender age and offense severity, and it was influenced by extralegal factors like race. Thus, registry laws that do not allow the judge discretion based on offender age or offense severity are not in line with public sentiment. At the same time, precautions must be taken to ensure that extralegal factors do not influence which juveniles are required to register. Although it is important to protect children from future abuse by potential offenders, it may also be prudent to protect juveniles, especially young juveniles, from being placed on the registry for acts that the public does not deem worthy of such punishment, especially since the registry might have negative consequences for youthful offenders. Future research should continue to assess the public's perceptions of these juveniles and the constraints on their support for these laws.

REFERENCES

A. H. v. Florida, 949 So. 2d 234 (Fla. 1st Dist. 2007).

The Adam Walsh Child Protection and Child Safety Act of 2006, 42 U.S.C. § 16911 (2006), Pub. L. No. 109-248, 120 Stat. 587 (codified in various sections of 42 U.S.C.).

Adkins, G., Huff, D. & Stageberg, P. (2000). *The Iowa sex offender registry and recidivism.* Des Moines: Iowa Department of Human Rights.

Brenton, S. (2008, May 28). *Fallon Campaign: Sex offender law makes children less safe – Fallon was right!* [Press release]. Retrieved on March 9, 2009 from www.iowapolitics.com.

Caputo, A. A. & Brodsky, S. L. (2004). Citizen coping with community notification of released sex offenders. *Behavioral Sciences and the Law, 22,* 239-252.

Carpentier, M., Silovsky, J. F. & Chaffin, M. (2006). Randomized trial of treatment for children with sexual behavior problems: Ten-year follow-up. *Journal of Consulting and Clinical Psychology, 74*, 482-388.

Chaffin, M. (2008). Our minds are made up-- Don't confuse us with the facts: Commentary on policies concerning children with sexual behavior problems and juvenile sex offenders. *Child Maltreatment, 13*, 110-121.

Jacob Wetterling Crimes Against Children and Sexually Violent Offender Registration Act, *42*, U.S.C. § 14071 (1994).

Letourneau, E. J. & Armstrong, K. S. (2008). Recidivism rates for registered and nonregistered juvenile sexual offenders. Sexual Abuse: *A Journal of Research and Treatment, 20*, 393-408.

Letourneau, E. J. & Miner, M. (2005). Juvenile sex offenders: A case against the legal and clinical status quo. *Sexual Abuse: Journal of Research and Treatment, 17*, 293-312.

Levenson, J., Brannon, Y., Fortney, T. & Baker, J. (2007). Public perceptions about sex offenders and community protection policies. *Analyses of Social Issues and Public Policy, 7*, 1-25.

Levenson, J. & Cotter, L. (2005). The effect of Megan's law on sex offender reintegration. *Journal of Contemporary Criminal Justice, 21*, 49-66.

Levenson, J., D'Amora, D. & Hern, A. (2007). Megan's Law and its impact on community re-entry for sex offenders. *Behavioral Sciences & the Law, 25*, 587-602.

No Easy Answers: Sex Offender Laws in the US. (2007, September). *Human Rights Watch*, 19. Retrieved on January 7th, from http://www.hrw.org/en/reports/2007/09/11/no-easy-answers.

Phillips, D. (1998). *Community notification as viewed by Washington's citizens*. Olympia, WA: Washington State Institute for Public Policy.

Salerno, J. M., Stevenson, M. C., Wiley, T. R. A., Najdowski, C. J., Bottoms, B. L., Schmillen, R. A. (in press). *Public Attitudes toward Applying Sex Offender Registration Laws to Juvenile Offenders.*

Sandler, J. C., Freeman, N. J. & Socia, K. M. (2008). Does a watched pot boil? A time-series analysis of New York State's sex offender registration and notification law. *Psychology, Public Policy, and Law, 14*, 284-302.

Schram, D. D. & Milloy, C. D. (1995). *Community notification: A study of offender characteristics and recidivism*. Olympia, WA: Washington State Institute for Public Policy.

St. Amand, A., Bard, D. B. & Silovsky, J. F. (2008). Meta-analysis of treatment for child sexual behavior problems: Practice elements and outcomes. *Child Maltreatment, 13*, 145-166.

Stevenson, M. C., Sorenson, K. M., Smith, A. C., Sekely, A. & Dzwairo, R. A. (in press). Effects of defendant and victim race on perceptiosn of juvenile sex offenders. *Behavioral Sciences and the Law*.

Tewksbury, R. (2005). Collateral consequences of sex offender registration. *Journal of Contemporary Criminal Justice, 21,* 67-81.

Trivits, L. & Reppucci, N. (2002). Application of Megan's Law to juveniles. *American Psychologist, 57,* 690-704.

Wilson v. State of Georgia, 279 Ga. App. 459 (2006).

INDEX

A

aboriginal, 285
abusive, 45, 102, 104, 314
academic performance, 103, 126, 186, 200, 250
academic success, 281
academics, 145, 155
accidental, 246
accommodation, 11
accountability, 253
accounting, 232, 262, 265
acculturation, x, xii, xiii, 1, 2, 3, 4, 5, 6, 7, 8, 9, 10, 11, 12, 13, 17, 24, 25, 27, 29, 30, 31, 32, 33, 205, 206, 207, 208, 209, 210, 211, 213, 214, 215, 218, 219, 220, 221, 222, 223, 224
acculturation level, 17, 206
achievement, 7, 31, 40, 42, 43, 44, 69, 95, 101, 110, 119, 126, 146, 184, 186, 191, 196, 197, 198, 199, 201, 203, 277, 278
acid, 69, 71
acute, 237
adaptability, ix, 1, 2, 8, 18, 20, 22, 24, 27, 30
adaptation, 5, 29, 56, 137, 256, 277
addiction, 305
ADHD, 21, 41, 69, 89
adjustment, 4, 28, 29, 32, 47, 74, 79, 84, 85, 87, 88, 113, 118, 119, 120, 122, 127, 135, 137, 155, 161, 200, 202, 222, 224, 234, 240, 277
administration, xii, 17, 163, 169, 210, 254, 255
administrative, x, 65
administrators, 120, 250, 300
adolescent behavior, 22, 32, 54, 61, 87, 208, 232
adolescent boys, 29, 74, 108, 222
adolescent female, 198
adolescent problem behavior, 6, 53, 87
adult, xii, xv, 37, 38, 78, 105, 112, 113, 119, 121, 137, 147, 148, 163, 164, 165, 169, 172, 174, 176, 181, 226, 244, 246, 252, 253, 255, 257, 274, 277, 301, 315, 331, 332

adult population, 147
adulthood, 54, 67, 74, 86, 88, 94, 100, 126, 169, 180, 233, 235, 276, 297
affective reactions, 264, 265, 269, 271
African American, 5, 12, 28, 31, 51, 58, 60, 76, 77, 85, 87, 88, 89, 129, 130, 131, 136, 160, 187, 220, 222, 223, 224, 239, 245, 246, 255, 258, 321, 333
African Americans, 129
after-school, 94, 114, 131, 166, 202, 247
Ag, 225
agent, 304
agents, 140, 151, 157, 158, 232
aggressiveness, 95, 112, 113
aging, 249
aid, 44, 105, 283, 288, 298
AIDS, 264, 271
air, 295
alcohol, xi, 2, 3, 4, 5, 7, 37, 40, 53, 54, 57, 60, 61, 86, 89, 93, 109, 110, 111, 113, 125, 136, 167, 173, 206, 212, 222, 223, 236, 266, 279, 280, 288, 292, 293, 297, 301, 304, 305
alcohol abuse, 61, 89, 236
alcohol consumption, xi, 93, 109, 111
alcohol problems, 61
alcohol use, 3, 4, 53, 110, 113, 222, 223, 292, 293, 301
alcoholism, 5, 57
alienation, 3, 155, 156
alpha, 188, 211, 212, 213, 267, 291, 293, 322
alternative, xv, 5, 7, 22, 24, 26, 51, 55, 83, 98, 101, 130, 132, 173, 176, 219, 238, 244, 277, 303
alternative behaviors, 51, 83
alternative hypothesis, 22
alternatives, xv, 133, 134, 223, 300, 303
ambiguity, 267
ambivalence, 170
American culture, 18, 28, 222

American Indian, 30
American Psychiatric Association, 28, 31, 51, 95, 105
American Psychological Association, 28, 30, 41, 58, 73, 83, 107, 113, 258
American Society of Criminology, 54
amphetamines, 40
analysis of variance, 291, 295
analytical tools, 318
anatomy, 110
androgen, 69, 71, 84
anger, 127, 130, 132, 176, 237, 319, 322, 327
anger management, 319, 327
animals, 41, 280
antagonistic, 247
antecedent variables, 14
antecedents, 28, 135, 164, 260, 262, 263, 265
antisocial behavior, xi, 2, 42, 45, 48, 51, 52, 54, 55, 57, 58, 80, 86, 87, 93, 102, 108, 110, 111, 114, 119, 123, 166, 181, 185, 202, 203, 222, 226, 227, 228, 229, 230, 231, 232, 233, 280
antisocial behaviour, xiii, 147, 148, 225, 229, 233, 241
antisocial children, 231
antisocial personality, 41, 45, 174
antisocial personality disorder, 41, 45, 174
anxiety, 4, 6, 7, 9, 41, 69, 76, 85, 95, 103, 106, 121, 122, 126, 127, 165, 186, 203, 210, 212, 227, 237, 247, 288
anxiety disorder, 41
APA, 41
application, xiii, 30, 61, 104, 118, 165, 169, 172, 177, 179, 234, 259, 264, 270
ARC, 287, 289
argument, 238, 265, 277
arousal, 165, 173
arrest, 236, 254, 266
arson, 168
articulation, 252
assault, ix, x, 35, 67, 73, 110, 111, 113, 124, 168, 254, 282
assaults, 41, 74, 101, 251
assertiveness, 5, 166
assessment, xiv, 17, 36, 50, 55, 58, 83, 106, 128, 133, 169, 179, 181, 207, 229, 235, 251, 252, 257, 263, 265, 269, 287
assessment tools, xiv, 287
assets, 4, 31, 32, 209, 219, 220, 224, 255
assignment, 14, 17
assimilation, xiii, 2, 3, 4, 5, 7, 11, 17, 205, 206, 207, 209, 218, 219, 221
association theory, 236
assumptions, 20, 48, 80, 295

athletes, 102, 111, 114
athletic competence, 135
atmosphere, 226, 274
attachment, xi, 40, 44, 46, 66, 69, 70, 76, 79, 85, 144, 165, 174, 179, 188, 199, 200, 230, 235, 238, 239
attachment theory, 165, 179, 188, 239
attacks, 254
attempted murder, 282
attention problems, 19, 20, 22, 24, 25, 27, 71, 167, 168
attractiveness, 292, 300
attribution, 94, 138, 240
attribution bias, 94
authority, 119, 121, 140, 141, 142, 143, 144, 145, 146, 147, 148, 149, 150, 151, 152, 155, 157, 158, 159, 160, 161, 165, 244, 248, 249, 256
autonomic nervous system, 91
autonomy, 50, 83, 209, 256
availability, 158, 170, 245, 305
averaging, 267
avoidance, 120, 134, 168, 175, 176, 289
awareness, 102, 246, 251, 292, 293, 294, 295, 297, 301

B

babies, 304
barbiturates, 40
bargaining, 123
barriers, 2, 158, 298
basic trust, 305
basketball, 108
beating, 73
behavior modification, 177
behavior therapy, 58, 62, 165
behavioral change, 10, 170, 173
behavioral difficulties, 51
behavioral disorders, 248
behavioral dispositions, 260, 261
behavioral dysregulation, 202
behavioral intentions, 260, 261, 262, 265, 267, 268, 269
behavioral manifestations, 234
behavioral problems, 4, 7, 47, 71, 72, 79, 95, 96, 104, 167, 185, 239
behaviours, xii, 139, 140, 144, 151, 157, 234
beliefs, ix, x, xv, 2, 39, 40, 41, 42, 65, 69, 155, 159, 174, 188, 211, 260, 261, 262, 263, 264, 265, 269, 290, 292, 293, 294, 295, 296, 297, 317, 318, 319, 320, 321, 322, 323, 324, 325, 326, 327, 328
belongingness, 74
beneficial effect, 95, 100

Index

benefits, xv, 25, 29, 47, 80, 95, 98, 99, 100, 102, 103, 109, 111, 129, 219, 264, 268, 306, 308, 317
Best Practice, 171, 172
bias, 16, 174, 234, 236, 266, 298
bilingual, 4, 15, 210
binary decision, 276
biological parents, 47, 233
biopsychosocial model, 108, 200
bipolar illness, 201
BIQ, 211, 216
birds, 85
birth, 54, 71, 100, 140, 168, 187, 228
blacks, 142, 143, 146, 150, 157
blame, 6, 126, 173, 240
blaming, 313
bonding, 7, 37, 43, 50, 67, 69, 76, 82
bonds, 37, 67, 75, 96, 113, 160, 174, 239, 244, 248
boot camps, 171
borderline, 174, 178
borderline personality disorder, 174, 178
boredom, 128, 172, 247
boxer, 101
brain, 100
brain damage, 100
breakdown, x, 35, 255
breakfast, 281
breeding, 247, 250
Bronfenbrenner, 117, 134, 199, 200, 234, 239, 252, 256
brothers, 227, 280
bubble, 255
buffer, 78, 237, 298
bullies, xii, 120, 121, 122, 124, 125, 126, 127, 129, 131, 132, 133, 136, 137, 183, 184, 185, 186, 189, 190, 191, 196, 197
burglary, 37, 168

C

cannabis, 113
capitalism, 258
caregiver, 70, 246, 247, 248
caregivers, 246, 247, 249, 250
caregiving, 47, 79
cast, 131, 133
category a, 288
catharsis, 12
Caucasian, 276, 321
Caucasians, 129
causal antecedent, 230
causal inference, 14
causal model, 107
causal relationship, 142, 201

cave, 113
Census, 2, 33, 289, 300
Census Bureau, 2, 33
Centers for Disease Control, 2, 13, 29, 212, 222
cerebrospinal fluid, 69, 71
CFI, 189, 190, 191, 193, 194, 213, 214
child abuse, x, 65, 254
Child Behavior Checklist, 18
child development, ix, xi, 117, 118, 124, 137, 256
child maltreatment, 88, 200, 239
child molesters, 162
child rearing, xiii, 225, 238, 239
childcare, 160
childhood aggression, 78, 123, 135, 202
childrearing, 79, 88
child-rearing practices, xiii, 225, 226, 228, 229, 232, 234, 235, 236
Chi-square, 189
chronic stress, 237
cigarettes, 36, 40, 212
citizens, 141, 143, 146, 150, 153, 157, 283, 334
civil rights, 251
civilian, 246
classes, 158
classical conditioning, 165
classification, 119, 120, 164, 177
classroom, xi, 44, 75, 79, 117, 119, 123, 126, 127, 133, 162
classroom environment, 75
classrooms, 89, 118, 128, 202
clients, xiv, 28, 50, 82, 112, 170, 303
clinical assessment, 89
clinical psychology, 84
clinical trial, 7, 14, 48, 49, 55, 57, 81, 87, 252
clinical trials, 14, 48, 49, 81, 252
closure, 10, 12
clustering, 15
Co, 58, 100, 103, 141, 143, 145, 146
coaches, 102, 111, 112, 113, 250, 289
coalitions, 48, 80
cocaine, 3, 27, 54, 206, 244, 245, 251, 282
cocaine use, 27, 54, 206
coercion, 109, 231, 236
cognition, 76, 173
cognitive behavioral therapy, 170
cognitive development, 229
cognitive function, 11, 69, 71, 86
cognitive process, 29, 71, 166
cognitive representations, 240, 263, 265
coherence, 7
cohesion, 4, 30, 48, 50, 79, 81, 82, 184
cohesiveness, xi, 66, 250
cohort, 168, 228, 322

collaboration, 187, 275, 285, 307
college students, 297
combined effect, 264
commodity, 255
commodity markets, 255
communication, x, 5, 10, 13, 18, 25, 35, 125, 144,
    151, 157, 159, 167, 170, 251, 278, 279
communication skills, 5, 167
communities, xi, xiv, xv, 14, 44, 55, 63, 66, 76, 77,
    86, 87, 97, 123, 170, 182, 220, 244, 246, 247,
    248, 249, 250, 251, 253, 254, 255, 256, 273, 275,
    276, 277, 280, 283, 289, 319, 331
community psychology, 58, 63, 89
community relations, 141
community service, 48, 59, 69, 77, 81
community support, 247, 305
comorbidity, 187, 197, 221
Comparative Fit Index, 189
compassion, 129
compensation, xiv, 303, 309
competence, 4, 5, 30, 31, 50, 62, 63, 82, 91, 106,
    109, 114, 119, 121, 134, 160, 172, 208
competency, 283, 299
competition, 95, 103, 110, 245
competitive sport, 98
competitiveness, 104
complement, 26, 253
complex systems, 48, 80
complexity, 36, 263, 276
compliance, xii, 139, 140, 141, 145, 146, 151, 152,
    153, 154, 155, 156, 157, 158, 161, 280
complications, 69, 71, 100, 167
components, 130, 170, 171, 172, 176, 230, 264, 265,
    267, 298, 304, 306
composition, 260
comprehension, 37, 103
concentration, 5, 69, 127, 186, 275
conceptual model, 8
concrete, 231
condom, 264
conduct disorder, 36, 41, 43, 48, 49, 51, 80, 81, 108,
    110, 111, 125, 127, 136, 159, 231, 250, 241
conduct problems, 6, 7, 9, 47, 49, 72, 75, 78, 80, 82,
    84, 85, 87, 91, 108, 180, 200, 207, 208, 219
confidence, 121, 157, 160, 213, 228, 233, 267
confidence interval, 213
confidentiality, 253
confinement, 164, 171
conflict avoidance, 289
conflict resolution, 106, 157, 165, 298
conformity, 98
confounding variables, 228
confrontation, 78

congenital adrenal hyperplasia, 84
consensus, 165, 223, 275
consent, 130, 210
constraints, 333
construct validity, 161
consulting, 114
consumption, xi, 3, 58, 93, 109, 111
contamination, 15
continuity, 122, 181, 226, 227
control condition, 7, 49, 81, 100
control group, 5, 6, 7, 100, 129, 130, 173, 229
controlled trials, 50, 82, 108
conviction, 125
coping, 56, 63, 87, 159, 202, 241, 299
coping strategies, 158, 220
coping strategy, 158
corporal punishment, xi, 66, 292, 293, 294, 295, 297,
    301
correlation, xv, 87, 208, 213, 250, 264, 267, 291, 297
correlation analysis, xv, 297
correlations, 194, 198, 213, 234, 260, 267, 295
cortisol, 69, 71, 88, 89
cost benefit analysis, 182
cost effectiveness, 252
cost-effective, 175, 238
costs, 28, 48, 81, 103, 264, 309
counsel, 104
counseling, 15, 28, 49, 55, 82, 87, 283
couples, 90
courts, 37, 251, 252, 253, 254
covariate, 186
crack, 244, 245, 251, 279
creative thinking, 173
credit, 283
crimes, 43, 73, 94, 100, 104, 106, 167, 168, 169,
    246, 251, 253, 304, 323, 332
criminal activity, 37, 48, 81, 168, 275, 278, 279, 281
criminal acts, 94, 281
criminal behavior, xi, 37, 93, 94, 103, 106, 169, 181,
    274, 278, 279, 281
criminal justice, 159, 275, 283, 292, 293, 301
criminal justice system, 275, 283, 292, 293, 301
criminality, ix, x, 35, 52, 65, 70, 104, 109, 226, 228,
    231, 233, 236, 280
criminals, 173, 253, 256, 279
criminology, 172, 235, 241
crisis intervention, 305
critical value, 217
criticism, 122, 173, 206, 262, 264
cross-sectional, 95, 185, 196, 197, 206, 207, 209,
    218, 219
crying, 280
cultivation, 255

cultural differences, 12
cultural factors, 282
cultural heritage, 240
cultural identities, 28
cultural risk factors, 31, 32, 224
culture, xiii, 2, 5, 6, 10, 11, 12, 29, 44, 85, 98, 101, 103, 205, 207, 209, 211, 218, 219, 239, 277, 287, 289, 298
culture conflict, 207
curiosity, 165
current limit, 176
curriculum, 6, 10, 11, 22, 24, 27, 282, 328
customers, 279
cynicism, 102, 159

D

danger, 165, 247, 299
data analysis, 203, 299
data collection, 14, 131, 212, 298
data set, 187, 235
database, 171
dating, 26, 67, 117
death, 246, 247
decision making, 94, 99, 264
decisions, 173, 246, 253, 261, 263, 264, 268, 269
decomposition, 215
defense, 123, 124
deficit, x, 19, 20, 22, 24, 25, 27, 65, 110, 125, 126, 127, 164
deficits, xii, 74, 103, 121, 122, 129, 163, 166, 172, 232, 305
definition, 163, 260, 263, 274, 275, 304
delinquent acts, 43, 73, 101, 148
delinquent adolescents, 48, 99, 106, 223
delinquent behavior, ix, x, 33, 35, 37, 38, 40, 42, 43, 44, 45, 48, 49, 50, 51, 53, 62, 73, 75, 96, 97, 100, 102, 104, 108, 111, 166, 167, 168, 201, 207, 224, 227, 228, 230, 232, 233, 234, 235, 236, 241, 250
delinquent friends, 84
delinquent group, 39
delinquents, vi, 37, 41, 42, 47, 52, 53, 55, 87, 100, 101, 104, 108, 146, 147, 148, 160, 165, 171, 175, 179, 180, 227, 235, 253, 304
delivery, ix, xii, 1, 13, 23, 24, 25, 27, 53, 71, 163, 167, 170, 172, 269
democracy, 258
demographic characteristics, 234
demographic factors, 61
demographics, 187, 293
denial, 166
Department of Education, 259

Department of Health and Human Services, 56, 75, 85
Department of Justice, 59, 87, 257, 274
dependent variable, 14, 19, 22, 291, 295
depressed, 19, 24, 25, 220, 297, 301
depression, ix, xiii, 1, 4, 7, 9, 14, 22, 24, 25, 27, 69, 70, 76, 77, 91, 103, 125, 126, 127, 154, 201, 203, 205, 207, 208, 210, 223, 227, 237, 288, 290, 292, 293, 294, 295, 296, 297, 301
depressive disorder, 41
depressive symptoms, 126, 127, 208, 223
deprivation, 164, 228, 237, 314
destruction, 41
detainees, 53
detention, x, 35, 41, 51, 53, 61, 142
deterrence, 106
developmental change, 201
developmental psychopathology, 110, 137
developmental theories, 167
deviant behaviour, 160, 229
deviation, 17
Diagnostic and Statistical Manual of Mental Disorders, 41
dichotomy, 326
differentiation, 260
dignity, 141, 157
dimensionality, 265
direct measure, 265, 266
directionality, 186
disability, 114, 121
disabled, 249
discipline, x, 36, 39, 46, 65, 77, 78, 85, 87, 97, 105, 201, 219, 227, 231, 235, 236, 237, 248, 249, 288, 306
discontinuity, 226
discretionary, 5
discrimination, 2, 9, 10, 12, 150, 207, 208, 210, 211, 214, 215, 217, 218, 219, 220, 221, 229, 276, 281
disorder, 20, 27, 41, 60, 88, 95, 100, 105, 108, 110, 111, 125, 126, 127, 135, 136, 164, 175, 178, 179, 231, 247, 257
disposition, 147
distortions, 69, 166
distraction, 42
distress, 74, 107, 154, 184, 239
distribution, 37, 254, 324, 325
diversity, 29
divorce, 46, 294
divorce rates, 46
dizygotic, 233
dizygotic twins, 233
domestic violence, ix, x, 35, 288, 295, 297
dominance, 90, 124

340 Index

dosage, ix, 1, 13, 17, 21, 22, 24, 25, 170
dream, 298
drinking, 33, 37, 40, 112, 125, 127, 228, 304
dropouts, 75
drug abuse, 32, 55, 57, 58, 60, 61, 90, 111, 114, 171, 254
drug abusers, 61
drug addict, 279, 281
drug addiction, 279
drug dealing, 268
drug trafficking, xiii, 76, 168, 243, 244, 257
drug treatment, 52
drug use, 2, 28, 38, 40, 44, 48, 53, 54, 55, 56, 58, 74, 81, 86, 97, 107, 114, 167, 168, 222, 223, 224, 304
drug-related, 48, 81
drugs, 39, 43, 55, 70, 73, 76, 97, 103, 212, 251, 257, 266, 279, 280, 288, 292, 293, 294, 295, 297, 301, 304
DSM-II, 33
DSM-III, 33
DSM-IV, 41
duration, 171, 173
duties, 149
dynamic risk factors, 176
dysphoria, 237
dysregulation, 90, 202

E

eating disorders, 126, 127
ecological, 4, 7, 29, 50, 56, 57, 82, 88, 135, 200, 201, 209, 219, 222, 234, 237, 252, 280, 329
ecological systems, 7, 222, 234, 252
ecology, 54, 56, 113, 251, 256
economic disadvantage, 86, 236, 237, 247, 281
economic growth, 254, 255
economic status, 102, 167, 228, 234, 236, 281, 305
economic transformation, 244
economically disadvantaged, 83
economics, 76, 77
education, 16, 21, 23, 31, 32, 98, 107, 109, 110, 111, 159, 160, 162, 200, 201, 241
educational attainment, 289, 295
educational policy, 224
educational programs, xi, 93, 105, 255
educational system, 304
educators, 120
ego, 62, 91, 136, 178
elderly, 255
elders, 249
elementary school, 17, 75, 76, 78, 90, 91, 118, 126, 135, 184, 185, 197, 198, 200, 201
eligibility criteria, 14

emotion, 90, 106, 327, 328
emotion regulation, 90
emotional, 4, 7, 18, 47, 49, 69, 71, 79, 81, 94, 95, 98, 103, 104, 108, 114, 120, 160, 161, 164, 170, 173, 201, 230, 237, 239, 246, 248, 313, 314, 315
emotional experience, 164
emotional health, 98
emotional responses, 71
emotional stability, 201
emotional well-being, 95, 108, 114
emotions, 151, 152, 161, 173, 264
empathy, xii, 50, 82, 133, 152, 153, 155, 156, 157, 161, 162, 163, 166, 172, 173, 175, 248, 249, 288, 314, 319, 327
employment, 16, 41, 103, 170, 248, 255
empowered, 51, 252
encouragement, 102, 173
energy, 263, 307
engagement, 42, 49, 52, 60, 82, 121, 123, 187, 189, 246, 247
enrollment, 213
entertainment, 42, 101, 211
enthusiasm, 165
environment, xv, 11, 30, 42, 44, 47, 50, 75, 78, 79, 82, 101, 118, 120, 133, 158, 165, 170, 197, 220, 226, 227, 233, 234, 237, 247, 255, 260, 277, 294, 295, 297, 298, 303, 304
environmental factors, 72, 229, 233, 261, 284
epidemiology, 202
equality, 295
ethical standards, 187
ethnic groups, 220, 281
ethnicity, 28, 29, 129, 142, 143, 151, 167, 187, 203, 222, 223, 235, 236, 244
etiology, 52, 182
evolution, 7, 12
examinations, 248
exclusion, 159
execution, xiv, 259, 261, 264, 265
exercise, 11, 95, 96, 106, 107, 108, 112
experimental design, 6, 14, 22, 28, 48, 81
explosions, 231
exposure, x, 13, 29, 35,39, 40, 51, 69, 71, 73, 74, 76, 86, 90, 237, 247, 280, 292, 293, 295, 297, 301
expulsion, xi, 66
external validity, 14
externalizing, 3, 19, 31, 38, 54, 63, 73, 74, 77, 78, 79, 84, 85, 89, 95, 120, 125, 189, 200, 202, 208, 209, 223, 224, 227, 232, 237, 257
externalizing behavior, 3, 54, 63, 73, 74, 77, 78, 79, 84, 85, 125, 223, 232, 257
externalizing problems, 3, 120, 208, 209

F

facilitators, 13, 15
factor analysis, 290, 291, 293
failure, x, 8, 39, 41, 43, 65, 69, 75, 98, 103, 164, 179, 231, 249, 250, 260
fairness, 102, 141, 143, 144, 149, 150, 151
faith, 290
familial, 79, 113, 227, 236, 247, 253, 288, 296, 300, 305
family conflict, x, 6, 46, 65, 207, 208, 219
family environment, xii, xiii, 70, 77, 79, 205, 221, 225, 227, 229, 233, 234, 238
family factors, 231, 288
family functioning, xiii, 6, 7, 49, 50, 56, 59, 81, 82, 225, 226, 227, 234, 235, 238, 252
family history, 57
family income, 17, 19, 20, 22, 24, 255
family interactions, 77, 78
family life, 48, 49, 80, 81, 228, 256, 280
family members, x, 3, 6, 10, 25, 41, 49, 65, 70, 77, 79, 81, 82, 97, 120, 229, 231, 300
family relationships, x, 36, 40, 48, 51, 70, 81, 100, 206, 209, 211, 257, 279
family structure, 91, 255, 288
family studies, 230
family support, 47, 62, 63, 79, 91, 229, 230, 237, 290, 296
family system, 3, 25, 28, 31, 42, 44, 45, 46, 47, 51, 80, 83, 209, 218, 223, 251
family therapy, x, 6, 10, 26, 32, 36, 48, 50, 52, 53, 57, 58, 59, 60, 61, 80, 81, 82, 84, 89, 258
family violence, 56, 279
fatalistic, 290, 296
fear, xv, 3, 101, 121, 128, 184, 274, 281, 303
fears, 19
feedback, 98, 170, 173
feelings, 46, 107, 123, 124, 127, 129, 130, 141, 151, 173, 174, 188, 247, 265, 298
females, 42, 45, 71, 147, 198, 320, 322, 325, 326
feminist, 320
FFT, 50, 82
fidelity, 14, 15, 55, 87, 171, 252
finance, 258
financial support, 248
firearm, 245, 246
firearms, 244, 246, 288
flexibility, xii, 104, 163, 199, 253
focusing, xii, 31, 98, 99, 101, 139, 148, 157, 224
food, 36, 211, 247, 270, 312, 314
forensic, 140, 164, 172, 173, 176, 177, 179, 182
forensic psychology, 172
formal education, 289

fraud, 228
freedoms, 155
friendship, 43, 74, 84, 89, 97, 136
friendship networks, 97
fruits, 307
frustration, 67, 125, 236, 277
fuel, 3, 254
funding, 97, 254, 255, 298
futures, 245

G

gambling, 280
games, 173
gang crimes, 246
gangs, ix, xiii, xiv, 54, 67, 73, 76, 86, 87, 101, 220, 243, 244, 245, 246, 247, 250, 252, 254, 256, 257, 258, 273, 274, 275, 276, 278, 279, 281, 282, 283, 284, 285, 304
gender, 6, 28, 40, 51, 52, 57, 62, 67, 69, 84, 85, 88, 106, 111, 129, 130, 142, 143, 144, 145, 146, 147, 148, 150, 151, 159, 160, 161, 186, 187, 194, 198, 201, 203, 222, 223, 248, 320, 322, 325
gender differences, 52, 62, 67, 84, 147, 186, 198
gender effects, 144, 145, 146, 148, 150
gene, 233
general intelligence, 235, 236
generalizability, 15, 26, 210
generation, 140, 206, 223
generational status, 3, 206, 219
genes, 70
genetic factors, 227
genetics, 47
girls, 41, 67, 71, 73, 74, 75, 79, 87, 94, 121, 122, 124, 127, 130, 131, 135, 154, 157, 186, 194, 198, 201, 224, 228, 257, 305
globalization, 54
goal attainment, 98, 277
goal setting, 98, 99, 114
goal-directed, 72, 176
goal-directed behavior, 176
goals, xv, 5, 50, 82, 83, 98, 103, 109, 123, 130, 174, 176, 276, 277, 283, 331, 333
going to school, 19
good behavior, 44, 46
goodness of fit, 213
gossip, 127
government, 275, 283, 290
grades, 7, 31, 75, 77, 144, 150, 154, 157, 186, 187, 188, 190, 194, 198, 224, 250, 283
graduate students, 130, 210
graffiti, 275
grandparents, 294

342 Index

grounding, 36
group activities, 173
group interactions, 121
group involvement, 274
group membership, 100, 101, 228
group processes, 118, 132
group work, 30, 115
growth, xi, 95, 117, 188, 189, 190, 191, 192, 193, 198, 244, 254, 255
growth factors, 188
guidance, 43, 165, 228, 246, 247, 248, 249
guidelines, xv, 99, 179, 257, 305
guilt, 46, 69, 265, 269
guilty, 37, 100, 267, 269, 300
guns, 245, 257

H

handicapped, 235
handling, 9, 98, 132
happiness, 154
harassment, 101, 138, 203
hardships, 237
harm, 43, 67, 71, 72, 107, 124, 126, 140, 175, 184
hate, 127, 274
Head Start, 55
health, 2, 4, 26, 29, 32, 71, 85, 87, 94, 95, 99, 102, 105, 111, 112, 114, 125, 127, 209, 223, 252
Health and Human Services, 56, 75, 85
health problems, 94
health psychology, 29
health services, 28, 136
health-promoting behaviors, 99
heart, 69, 97t, 160
heart rate, 69
heavy drinking, 33
hegemony, 98
helplessness, 247
heroin, 40
heterogeneous, 122, 275
high risk, 40, 53, 55, 86, 121, 170, 197, 247, 304
high school, 17, 32, 40, 75, 99, 109, 112, 138, 187, 220, 276, 289
higher education, 110
higher quality, 4, 74
high-level, 169
high-risk, x, 6, 35, 47, 48, 50, 57, 80, 82, 88, 105, 115, 169, 171, 173, 253
hip, 230, 243
hips, 156
hiring, 250
Hispanic, 4, 28, 29, 30, 31, 32, 33, 49, 56, 57, 58, 59, 61, 81, 90, 187, 206, 208, 222, 223, 224, 321

Hispanic population, 31, 33
Hispanics, 30, 31, 223
HIV, 49, 58, 82
HIV/AIDS, 49, 82
hockey, 107, 112, 113, 114, 278
homeless, 52, 58, 62, 63, 84, 89, 306
homeostasis, 128
homework, 9
homicide, 67, 153, 245, 254, 257
homicide rate, 254
homicide rates, 254
homogenous, 276
hospitals, 187
host, 2, 3, 10, 11, 12, 218
hostility, 94, 95, 107, 155, 184, 185, 231
household, 6, 17, 18, 70, 78, 79, 197, 248, 288
household composition, 6
household income, 17
households, 77, 78, 79
housing, 70, 254, 255, 276, 288, 300
human, 32, 37, 54, 88, 95, 97, 137, 176, 200, 251, 256, 263, 280, 328
human behavior, 263
human development, 200, 256
Human Kinetics, 108, 110, 111, 113
humans, 174, 176
humiliation, 45, 132
hygiene, 288
hyperactivity, x, 19, 20, 22, 24, 25, 27, 65, 110, 121, 125, 167, 168, 233
hyperplasia, 84
hypersensitive, 122
hypothalamic, 69, 71
hypothalamic-pituitary-adrenal axis, 69, 71, 91
hypothesis, 22, 24, 106, 154, 209, 218, 219, 236, 237, 296, 326

I

id, 7, 13, 193
identification, 98, 108, 188, 234, 235, 263, 269
identity, ix, 1, 6, 11, 18, 20, 22, 24, 25, 27, 31, 98, 100, 101, 103, 105, 131, 208, 209, 211, 220, 223, 224, 244, 246, 250, 254, 277, 279, 289, 298
ideology, 113, 274, 277
idiosyncratic, 167, 263
illiteracy, 288
illumination, 51
images, 299, 300
imagination, 165
immediate gratification, 164
immigrants, xiii, 2, 205, 212
immigration, 3, 17, 20, 24, 27, 28, 222

Index
343

implementation, ix, 1, 12, 14, 15, 25, 51, 70, 83, 101, 102, 104, 169, 171, 252, 282, 328
imprisonment, 45, 58
impulsive, 19, 42, 122, 125, 249
impulsivity, xii, 41, 69, 121, 124, 130, 163, 167, 168, 172, 288
in situ, 71
inbreeding, 288
incarceration, xi, 48, 59, 66, 81, 253, 268
incidence, xiii, 94, 205, 206, 220
Incidents, 162
inclusion, x, 8, 14, 35, 43, 47, 80, 159, 176, 177, 186, 213, 265, 269, 298
income, 15, 17, 19, 20, 22, 24, 70, 76, 77, 79, 85, 235, 236, 244, 254, 255, 289
incomes, 290
independence, 20, 289, 290, 304
independent variable, 14, 20, 291, 295, 296
indication, 218
indicators, 12, 16, 26, 206, 209, 214, 215, 216, 220, 235, 236, 307
indices, 201, 228
indigenous, 252
indirect effect, 215, 217, 261, 262, 265
individual development, 105, 167
individual differences, x, 65, 100, 113
individual rights, 155
inequality, 32
infancy, 44, 67, 79, 237
infants, 228
inferences, 237
inflation, 19
information processing, 135, 261
inhibition, 230
initiation, 60, 77, 105, 232, 238
injuries, 246
injury, ix, x, 35, 177
injustice, 159, 162
inmates, 150
insight, 12, 129, 155, 262, 280
inspection, 193
instability, 16, 70, 77, 83, 228, 238
institutionalisation, 166
institutions, 37, 48, 67, 80, 147, 148, 156, 160, 170, 230, 270, 281, 283
instruction, 44
instructors, xiv, 96, 293, 303, 305
instruments, xv, 3, 17, 95, 169, 289, 290, 291, 293, 296
integration, ix, xv, 1, 10, 11, 20, 22, 24, 27, 29, 49, 81, 82, 95, 223, 282, 303, 306
integrity, 165, 174, 175
intelligence, 69, 71, 119, 121, 135, 234

intentions, 100, 138, 142, 143, 151, 155, 157, 260, 261, 262, 263, 264, 265, 267, 268, 269
interaction, xi, 19, 38, 54, 66, 69, 75, 87, 110, 129, 130, 134, 137, 158, 219, 230, 231, 234, 246, 248, 249, 251, 298, 305
interaction effect, 230
interaction effects, 230
interactional perspective, 181, 231
interactions, 2, 6, 18, 19, 47, 49, 70, 73, 77, 78, 79, 81, 119, 121, 122, 130, 133, 233, 234, 247, 248, 249, 250, 257, 279, 305, 323
interface, 29
intergenerational, 6, 9, 32, 33, 61
internal consistency, 18, 19
internal validity, 14, 28
internal value, 318
internalization, 276
internalizing, xiii, 19, 31, 38, 54, 63, 85, 89, 103, 122, 189, 200, 202, 205, 207, 209, 210, 212, 213, 215, 217, 218, 219, 220, 221, 223, 224, 227, 237
interpersonal conflict, 175
interpersonal relations, 49, 81, 94, 161, 174
interpersonal relationships, 49, 81, 94, 161, 174, 311, 321
interpersonal skills, 160, 170
interpersonal support, 13
interrelations, 137
interrelationships, 119, 267
intervention strategies, x, 35, 37, 47, 105, 106
interview, 15, 17, 187, 210, 266, 307
interviews, 14, 170, 210, 308, 309
intimacy, 166
intimidation, 138, 184, 274
intrinsic, 14, 170
intrinsic motivation, 170
inventories, 30
investment, 7, 8, 24, 30, 75, 207, 208, 219
IQ, 39, 40, 42, 43, 69
irritability, 237
isolation, 69, 72, 73, 74, 118

J

jails, 142
jewelry, 278
job loss, 332
jobs, 244, 247, 255, 300
judge, 277, 311, 333
judges, 252, 253, 331
judgment, 71, 245
jurisdiction, 274
jurisdictions, 163

344 Index

justice, 37, 38, 40, 43, 45, 50, 51, 53, 55, 59, 82, 83, 85, 141, 142, 143, 149, 150, 157, 159, 160, 161, 162, 171, 252, 253, 255, 256, 257
justification, 247
juvenile crime, ix, xiv, 104, 111, 247, 254, 258, 287, 298
juvenile delinquency, ix, x, xiii, 35, 36, 37, 40, 41, 43, 44, 47, 48, 55, 56, 59, 61, 80, 87, 89, 94, 96, 104, 108, 109, 111, 114, 171, 179, 225, 226, 228, 229, 230, 234, 235, 236, 237, 238, 240, 253, 277
juvenile delinquents, 37, 41, 42, 47, 52, 100, 108, 175, 179, 227, 304
juvenile justice, vi, 37, 38, 40, 43, 45, 50, 51, 59, 82, 83, 171, 252, 253, 255, 257
juveniles, ix, x, xiv, xv, 35, 37, 51, 67, 100, 104, 159, 160, 161, 163, 168, 169, 172, 181, 227, 236, 245, 253, 275, 287, 288, 289, 297, 299

K

kidnapping, 168
kindergarten, 114

L

labeling, 278
labor, 277
lack of confidence, 121
language, 2, 3, 4, 15, 31, 32, 105, 206, 207, 208, 210, 211, 213, 215, 218, 308
language barrier, 2
language impairment, 105
language skills, 32
large-scale, 171, 174
later life, 75, 94, 314
Latino, vii, viii, ix, xii, 1, 2, 3, 4, 5, 7, 8, 10, 11, 12, 13, 14, 15, 17, 18, 25, 26, 27, 28, 29, 30, 31, 32, 33, 58, 205, 206, 207, 208, 209, 210, 211, 214, 215, 216, 218, 219, 220, 221, 222, 223, 224
Latinos, x, xiii, 1, 2, 3, 4, 14, 29, 30, 205, 206
law, xv, 59, 97, 101, 145, 146, 147, 148, 162, 164, 229, 251, 255, 265, 274, 275, 282, 284, 318, 331, 332, 333, 334
law enforcement, xv, 101, 162, 251, 255, 274, 275, 282, 284
laws, xv, 2, 37, 41, 69, 141, 145, 155, 171, 253, 282, 331, 332, 333
leadership, 44, 104, 119, 121, 298
learning, x, xiv, 12, 24, 25, 44, 65, 71, 103, 105, 106, 111, 114, 129, 133, 157, 158, 165, 173, 231, 232, 279, 288, 303, 304, 305, 307
learning difficulties, 105, 288, 304

learning disabilities, x, 65
learning environment, 44, 157, 158
learning process, 133, 279, 280
legal systems, 163
leisure, 96, 97, 101, 106, 109
leisure time, 96, 106
life course, 113
life experiences, 158
life span, 178, 229, 232
lifestyle, 52, 161, 199, 248, 276
lifestyles, 283
lifetime, 212
likelihood, xiv, 38, 40, 43, 44, 45, 46, 66, 74, 76, 77, 197, 198, 208, 213, 220, 222, 235, 245, 250, 279, 280, 281, 287, 288
Likert scale, 18, 19, 119, 211, 212, 213
limitation, 27, 269
limitations, xiii, 26, 176, 205, 233, 298
linear, 11, 30, 60, 191, 193, 194
linear regression, 30
linguistic, 207, 208, 219
links, xi, 93, 186, 206, 207, 209, 281
liquor, 308
listening, xiv, 303
literacy, 17, 105, 210
living conditions, 247
locus, 201
loneliness, 123, 126, 135, 137, 158
longitudinal studies, x, 65, 66, 168, 169, 178, 179, 180, 181, 218, 229, 258
longitudinal study, 28, 42, 53, 71, 73, 91, 96, 102, 106, 113, 123, 134, 136, 207, 208, 219, 222, 227, 228, 235, 299
long-term impact, 99, 104
love, 135, 253
low risk, 170, 171, 304
low-income, 76, 77, 85, 235
low-level, 169
loyalty, 289, 290
lying, 41

M

magazines, xiv, 287
mainstream, 89
maintenance, 37, 62, 67, 170, 229, 232
major cities, 250
major depressive disorder, 41
maladaptive, 118, 155, 218, 219
males, xiii, 39, 42, 45, 71, 76, 89, 106, 135, 145, 150, 153, 160, 168, 169, 198, 222, 235, 243, 244, 257, 265, 322, 325, 326
malicious, 149, 277

maltreatment, 61, 70, 78, 240, 241
management, x, 27, 35, 44, 47, 49, 70, 79, 82, 95, 97, 165, 169, 173, 228, 229, 236
management practices, 70
mandatory sentencing, 253
manipulation, 72, 101
manners, 281
MANOVA, 291, 295, 296, 297
manslaughter, 168, 282
manufacturing, 244
marginalization, 123
marijuana, 3, 5, 27, 49, 53, 69, 75, 82, 206, 212, 282, 301
marital discord, 87, 88
marital status, 19, 22, 24, 187
market, 244, 245, 251, 277
markets, 76, 245, 246, 255
maternal, 77, 185, 201, 226, 231, 235, 237
matrix, 267, 291
maturation, 14, 96
meals, 3, 306
meanings, 37, 241
measurement, 119, 186, 188, 190, 198, 213, 214, 227, 229, 260, 265, 269
measures, xiii, 3, 5, 6, 7, 13, 16, 17, 20, 22, 26, 31, 99, 105, 123, 130, 136, 161, 187, 205, 206, 207, 210, 211, 226, 236, 260, 267, 274, 289, 290, 291, 292, 295, 296, 322
media, x, xiv, 65, 66, 69, 112, 135, 245, 273, 274, 288
mediation, xiii, 20, 24, 29, 133, 205, 208, 215, 217, 218, 219, 220, 221, 222, 237
mediators, xii, 31, 50, 82, 85, 205, 209, 210, 215, 218, 219, 221, 223, 224, 234, 236, 239, 261
medical care, x, 35
medications, 306
membership, 39, 72, 73, 84, 97, 101, 189, 275, 276, 277, 278, 279, 282, 284
memory, 103, 105, 113, 263
men, 109, 111, 123, 137, 289, 291, 320, 333
mental disorder, 41, 51, 57, 105, 112, 136, 201, 239
mental health professionals, 61
mental illness, 40, 41, 42, 162, 288
mental states, 175
mentor, 237
mentoring, 171, 283, 298
mentoring program, 298
messages, 235
meta-analysis, 26, 29, 48, 53, 60, 81, 90, 118, 136, 160, 171, 172, 173, 175, 178, 179, 180, 181, 182, 256
metaphor, 48, 80
metropolitan area, 209

middle class, 236, 254, 297
middle schools, 7
migrant, 33
military, 246, 257
mimicking, 43
minorities, 110, 142
minority, 2, 31, 32, 91, 100, 126, 155, 159, 187, 191, 223, 224, 244, 323
minority groups, 187
minority students, 31
minors, 37
mirror, 131, 133, 212, 255
misconceptions, 88
misleading, 196
missions, 247
mobile phone, 101
mobility, 70, 102, 235, 254, 281
modalities, 48, 80
modality, 6, 26, 29, 32, 61
modeling, 6, 8, 98, 100, 102, 118, 188, 189, 191, 193, 201, 213, 298
modeling therapy, 6
moderators, 239
modules, 130, 173, 176, 177, 283, 286
money, 73, 103, 258, 275
monozygotic, 233
monozygotic twins, 233
mood, 96, 248
moral beliefs, 40, 293, 295
moral development, 95
moral reasoning, xii, 98, 102, 112, 162, 163, 172
morals, xi, 66, 140, 277, 281
morning, 281, 306
motherhood, 57, 78
mothers, xii, 6, 15, 183, 185, 186, 187, 188, 191, 193, 194, 197, 198, 199, 200, 201, 207, 226, 255, 289, 293, 296, 305
motion, 131, 133, 231
motivation, 100, 101, 102, 120, 170, 199, 261
motor skills, 103
motor vehicle theft, 168
movement, 11, 12, 28, 103, 111, 120
multicultural, 209
multidimensional, 3, 58, 260, 274
multi-ethnic, 56
multimedia, 49, 82
multiple factors, 51
multiple regression, 19, 20, 22, 24
multiple regression analyses, 19, 20
multivariate, 32, 235, 291, 295
multivariate data analysis, 235
multivariate statistics, 32
murder, 73, 126, 168, 254, 256, 282

N

narcissistic, 164, 165
nation, 2, 253
National Institutes of Health, 56
Native American, 5
NATO, 134
natural, 170, 226, 288, 298
negative attitudes, xii, 102, 139, 145, 147, 148, 149, 150, 151, 155, 156, 158
negative emotions, xi, 93
negative experiences, xii, 2, 139, 142, 143, 144, 145, 150, 151, 152, 157
negative life events, 78, 237
negative outcomes, 37, 67, 99, 207
negative relation, 156, 230
neglect, ix, x, xi, 45, 65, 70, 78, 117, 239, 248, 304
negotiating, 133, 173
negotiation, 123, 173
nerves, 288, 290, 296
network, 97, 110, 123, 177
neuroendocrine, 234, 239
neurological disorder, 100
neuropsychological tests, 71
neurotic, 127
neutralization, 160, 313
New York Times, 256
news coverage, xiv, 273
next generation, 8, 208
nightmares, 36, 126
NNFI, 157
non-clinical, 250
non-institutionalized, 147, 148
non-violent, 153, 166, 168, 182, 326
normal, 20, 43, 100, 230, 238, 281, 288, 321
normal development, 230
norms, xii, 2, 3, 37, 41, 67, 76, 98, 101, 139, 140, 141, 145, 151, 152, 154, 155, 156, 157, 158, 162, 164, 177, 206, 218, 233, 245, 260, 261, 263, 277, 278, 279, 288, 320, 328
nurse, 329
nurses, 304
nurturance, 248, 249
nurturing parent, 185

O

obedience, 145, 249, 276
objectivity, 308
observations, 130, 199
odds ratio, 206
Office of Justice Programs, 87

Office of Juvenile Justice and Delinquency Prevention (OJJDP), 62, 87, 111, 166, 257
olfactory, 165
online, 32, 108
opiates, 40
opposition, 22, 185
optimism, 50, 82
oral, 288, 301, 333
oral hygiene, 288
organized crime, xiv, 273
orientation, 12, 39, 42, 69, 146, 161, 229
outliers, 20
outpatient, 53, 175
oversight, 97

P

pain, 299
pairing, xi, 117, 129, 130, 133, 137
parameter, 213, 310
parameter estimation, 213
parental authority, 161, 256
parental care, 240
parental influence, 7, 232
parental involvement, x, 39, 65, 70, 102
parental support, 232
parent-child, xii, 4, 7, 39, 46, 70, 78, 177, 183, 184, 185, 187, 188, 189, 196, 197, 198, 199, 200, 202, 207, 212, 214, 215, 228, 231, 232, 237, 248, 249
parenthood, 46
parenting, xiii, 7, 45, 46, 47, 55, 60, 63, 70, 76, 77, 78, 79, 80, 87, 91, 122, 123, 167, 168, 185, 198, 199, 201, 202, 225, 226, 227, 229, 230, 231, 232, 235, 237, 238, 239, 248, 249, 250, 252, 288
parenting styles, 46, 78, 122, 123, 249, 250
parole, 251, 308
passive, 24, 125, 184, 227
paternal, 89, 228, 236
path analysis, 189, 213
path model, 219
pathology, 251
pathways, x, xii, 8, 65, 66, 91, 112, 205, 208, 209, 214, 217, 219, 220, 221, 229, 234, 254
patients, 58, 63, 89, 164, 165, 174, 178
PBC, 261, 262, 263, 265, 266, 268
pediatrician, 41
peer conflict, 250
peer group, 67, 69, 72, 73, 90, 118, 120, 121, 123, 127, 128, 137, 166, 172, 202, 231, 236, 247, 249, 250, 251, 255, 298
peer influence, 40, 256
peer rejection, 43, 62, 69, 74, 88, 109, 119, 123, 134, 135, 250

peer relationship, 74, 85, 118, 120, 134, 136, 138, 208, 209, 218, 220, 233
peer support, 250
penalties, 251
penalty, 177
per capita, 236, 289
per capita income, 289
perceived control, 269
perceived norms, 261
perception, xiv, 44, 113, 127, 140, 158, 201, 273, 319
perceptions, 18, 91, 102, 103, 111, 127, 145, 151, 158, 161, 199, 211, 223, 263, 293
performers, 307
Permissive, 249
perpetration, 3, 74, 207
personal goals, 103
personality, 29, 41, 89, 106, 137, 174, 199, 249, 257
personality dimensions, 137
personality disorder, 41, 174
personality traits, 41
philosophers, 140
philosophical, 95, 96
philosophy, 329
phone, 36, 117, 183, 249
physical abuse, 45, 78
physical activity, 99, 104, 109, 110, 112, 113
physical aggression, 90, 152
physical attractiveness, 293
physical education, 109
physical exercise, 170
physical force, 97, 322
physical health, 177
physiological, 69
physiological factors, 69
pilot study, 289
placebo, 100
planning, 262, 264
plants, 280
play, 6, 12, 36, 44, 73, 98, 109, 120, 121, 122, 129, 130, 131, 132, 140, 152, 156, 158, 174, 280, 297, 323
pleasure principle, 164
pluralistic, 275
police, 36, 97, 140, 141, 142, 143, 144, 145, 146, 147, 148, 149, 150, 151, 155, 157, 158, 159, 160, 161, 162, 227, 236, 251, 255, 274, 275, 283, 306, 311
policy makers, 282, 284, 332
politicians, 282, 284, 332
politics, 109, 251, 258
polynomial, 188, 189

poor, x, xi, xii, xiii, 42, 43, 46, 65, 66, 69, 75, 78, 94, 103, 110, 123, 125, 126, 136, 163, 164, 167, 172, 186, 201, 225, 226, 227, 228, 231, 233, 234, 235, 247, 249, 250, 251, 254, 258, 288
poor performance, 69
population, xiv, 2, 31, 33, 40, 41, 72, 109, 112, 154, 181, 209, 226, 233, 234, 239, 244, 251, 254, 267, 287, 289, 291, 293, 295, 296, 297, 305, 323, 324, 325
pornography, 333
positive attitudes, 97, 101, 145, 146, 147, 148, 149, 150, 151
positive emotions, 146, 150, 173
positive interactions, 248
positive mood, 248
positive regard, 165
positive reinforcement, 51, 165, 170, 173
positive relation, 4, 44, 47, 75, 79, 97, 101, 119, 153, 158, 220
positive relationship, 4, 44, 47, 69, 75, 79, 97, 101, 119, 153, 158, 220
posttraumatic stress disorder (PTSD), 36, 58, 63, 89, 257
poverty, xiv, 15, 39, 45, 70, 78, 167, 168, 247, 254, 255, 276, 279, 281, 287, 288, 289, 299
poverty line, 254
poverty rate, 255
poverty threshold, 15
power, 48, 51, 80, 83, 85, 96, 108, 124, 151, 155, 184, 186, 200, 247, 252, 253, 254
pragmatic, 251
preadolescents, 118
prediction, xiv, 108, 110, 180, 198, 223, 228, 229, 257, 259, 260, 261, 262, 263, 264, 265, 268, 269
predictive validity, 3
predictor variables, 228
predictors, 57, 58, 59, 77, 78, 85, 102, 136, 162, 167, 207, 223, 226, 227, 228, 235, 236, 262, 268
preference, 118, 119, 121, 137, 244
pregnancy, ix, x, 31, 35, 69, 71, 76, 167, 177
pregnant, 289
preschool, 5, 28, 107, 167, 231, 237
preschool children, 5, 28, 107
preschoolers, 85
prescription drug, 40
pressure, 5, 33, 98, 208, 221, 239, 247, 283, 298
prestige, 73
preventive, xiii, 52, 55, 57, 60, 88, 225, 228
primary care, 70, 78, 237, 238
primary caregivers, 237
primary school, 203
prisoners, 155
prisons, 253

privacy, 247
private, 106
proactive, xi, 66, 72, 91, 109, 120, 323, 328
probability, 10, 20, 37, 38, 67, 71, 123, 170, 207, 220, 230, 247, 260
probation, 97, 170, 171, 251
probation officers, 170, 251
problem behavior, 3, 17, 29, 32, 33, 37, 38, 49, 53, 54, 67, 73, 81, 82, 83, 94, 106, 107, 122, 125, 136, 200, 201, 202, 207, 208, 209, 219, 222, 224, 252
problem behaviors, 17, 33, 37, 38, 49, 54, 67, 73, 81, 82, 83, 94, 122, 125, 209, 224
problem children, 61
problem solving, 99, 112, 114, 123, 127, 130, 173, 176, 280, 298
problem-solving, xii, 45, 74, 98, 109, 125, 163, 172
problem-solving skills, xii, 74, 109, 125, 163, 172
procedural fairness, 143, 159
procedural justice, 141, 142, 143, 150, 157, 160, 162
professionalization, 114
profit, 177, 278
profits, 245
program outcomes, 99
programming, xii, 15, 17, 163, 168, 172, 220
proliferation, 246
property, 37, 41, 42, 53, 94, 96, 101, 126, 167, 173, 226, 245
property crimes, 167
proposition, 229, 238, 263
prosocial behavior, 31, 97, 98, 102, 111, 113, 119, 130, 165, 224, 288
prosocial children, 74
prostitution, 45
protection, 37, 40, 67, 102, 121, 140, 155, 156, 247, 252, 258, 290, 292, 293, 300, 334
protective mechanisms, 244, 289
protective role, xiii, 225, 238
protocol, 180, 210
protocols, 131, 169, 210
provocation, 72, 322
proxy, 3, 17, 206
psychiatric diagnosis, 203
psychiatric disorders, 30, 33, 41, 48, 54, 81, 233
psychiatric illness, 41
psychiatrist, 36, 41, 164, 253
psychological distress, 154, 155, 160
psychological health, 95, 103, 111
psychological problems, 234
psychological processes, 263
psychological stress, 86, 112
psychological well-being, 30, 176

psychology, xii, 28, 62, 105, 107, 111, 113, 114, 130, 139, 140, 180, 221, 257, 258, 291
psychometric properties, 17
psychopathic, 153, 159
psychopathology, 2, 27, 32, 53, 59, 83, 89, 109, 110, 137, 159, 206, 223, 239, 241
psychosis, 306
psychosocial development, xiii, 225, 227, 237, 238
psychosocial functioning, 234
psychosomatic, 89, 112, 127
psychotherapeutic, 165, 170
psychotherapy, 15, 26, 28, 30, 59, 89, 146, 175, 176, 178, 179, 182
psychotic, 127
pubertal development, 89
puberty, 100, 202
public, xiv, xv, 60, 78, 129, 135, 150, 159, 162, 210, 246, 254, 273, 274, 323, 331, 332, 333
public health, 60, 135, 210
public housing, 254
public opinion, 162
public support, 162
punishment, xi, 66, 125, 164, 171, 231, 249, 252, 253, 255, 282, 292, 293, 294, 295, 297, 301
punitive, xi, 66, 237, 253, 298
pupils, 203
purchasing power, 254

Q

quality of life, 30, 254
quality of service, 171
questioning, 170
questionnaire, 18, 97, 290, 291
questionnaires, 291, 298

R

race, 28, 109, 129, 142, 150, 222, 235, 236, 248, 256
racial groups, 131, 276
racism, 279, 288
random, 6, 14, 15, 229, 244, 246
random assignment, 6, 14, 15, 229
range, 5, 10, 15, 17, 18, 19, 26, 41, 66, 94, 95, 104, 121, 166, 210, 212, 233, 234, 237, 248, 282, 290, 293, 300, 305, 312, 313, 321
rape, 67, 110, 254
rating scale, 266, 267
ratings, 5, 118, 119, 130, 143, 150, 227, 228
rationality, 263
reading skills, 103
reality, 164, 247, 298

reasoning, xii, 42, 71, 98, 102, 103, 112, 162, 163, 172, 173, 263, 319, 320
reasoning skills, 42, 103
rebel, 46
recidivate, 333
recidivism, xv, 48, 52, 53, 58, 81, 94, 99, 103, 105, 164, 166, 170, 171, 173, 175, 176, 179, 181, 270, 282, 331, 332, 333, 334
recidivism rate, 170
recognition, x, 44, 65, 66, 74, 231, 232, 299
reconditioning, 165
recovery, 53
recreation, 109, 111, 171
recreational, 110, 250, 283
recruiting, 14, 15
reflection, 42, 76, 95, 174, 307
regional, 296
regression, 19, 20, 23, 30, 135, 206, 261, 268
regression analysis, 135, 268
regression equation, 19, 268
regular, 95, 129, 147, 170
regulation, 7, 69, 90, 166, 174, 181, 182, 261, 264
rehabilitate, 282
rehabilitation, xi, 93, 94, 96, 98, 99, 100, 105, 112, 180, 182, 251, 253
rehabilitation program, 112
reinforcement, 51, 70, 134, 165, 170, 173, 260, 314
rejection, ix, x, xi, 39, 43, 53, 62, 65, 69, 72, 74, 76, 88, 103, 106, 109, 117, 118, 119, 122, 123, 130, 134, 135, 136, 137, 173, 230, 231, 235, 248, 250, 277
relapse, 166, 178, 179
relapses, 50, 82
relationship quality, 189, 199, 200
relatives, 249
relevance, xii, 139, 140
reliability, 18, 19, 188, 199, 211, 212, 213, 221, 267, 290, 291, 321, 322, 325
religion, 289
religions, 2
religiosity, 42
remediation, 304
repair, 282
replication, 8, 98, 110, 178, 202, 221, 239
reporters, 26
reproduction, 32
reputation, 152, 154, 155, 156, 157, 158, 159, 160
reputation enhancement, 158, 159, 160
research design, ix, 1, 5, 13, 14, 233
resentment, 155
residential, 59, 70, 172, 246, 306, 311
residuals, 20

resilience, 38, 56, 62, 68, 74, 88, 121, 135, 235, 237, 255, 258
resistance, 61, 106, 165, 209, 221, 283
resolution, 106, 157, 165, 175, 298, 319, 327
resources, xii, 4, 44, 50, 51, 77, 83, 103, 139, 220, 247, 253, 255, 268, 288, 318, 319
response format, 18
responsibilities, 18, 41, 102, 103, 246, 248, 249, 320
restitution, 171
retaliation, x, 65, 121, 245, 280, 321, 322, 323, 324, 325
retention, 10, 16, 53, 54, 55, 60, 84
retribution, 126
rewards, 260
rhetoric, xiv, 273
rigidity, 173
risk behaviors, 30, 38, 53, 85, 112, 114, 223
risks, 7, 37, 67, 112, 121, 134, 288, 289
risk-taking, x, xii, 42, 65, 109, 205, 219
RMSEA, 157, 189, 190, 191, 193, 194, 213, 214
robbery, 67, 168
role-playing, 131, 173
rolling, 253
Rosenberg Self-Esteem Scale, 212
rugby, 97
runaway, 41, 58, 63, 89
rural, 14, 15, 26, 33, 56, 209, 210, 291
rural areas, 210, 291
rural communities, 26

S

safety, xi, 41, 98, 105, 117, 133, 135, 220, 247, 250, 281
salaries, 248
sampling, 15, 187, 210
sanctions, xiii, xiv, 39, 42, 69, 113, 180, 253, 259, 265, 268, 269
satisfaction, 16, 72, 141, 152, 154, 155, 156, 158, 160
scavenger, 244
schema, xv
schizophrenia, 41
school achievement, 184, 197, 229
school activities, 69, 108
school adjustment, 186, 201
school authority, 150
school climate, xi, 117
school failure, 38, 177, 232
school performance, xii, 52, 183, 184, 186, 187, 188, 189, 191, 192, 194, 195, 196, 197, 198, 248, 250
school work, 186
schooling, 17, 172

scores, 6, 17, 18, 19, 20, 22, 24, 71, 74, 118, 119, 120, 130, 153, 188, 211, 212, 213, 267, 290, 291, 295, 296, 297
search, 94, 237, 277, 282, 299
searching, 277, 305
secondary school students, 144, 146, 148, 149, 150, 153, 154, 157
secondary schools, 147
security, xi, 85, 117, 133, 165, 179, 199, 238, 312, 313, 314
sedatives, 40
sedentary, 112, 113
sedentary behavior, 112
selecting, 261
self esteem, xiv, 303
self-concept, 6, 7, 130, 160, 201
self-confidence, 103
self-control, 5, 122, 173, 235
self-efficacy, 50, 69, 83, 103, 177, 271, 293, 295, 298
self-esteem, xiii, 7, 31, 69, 71, 76, 95, 101, 102, 103, 108, 109, 125, 126, 127, 129, 159, 166, 203, 205, 208, 209, 210, 212, 213, 214, 217, 218, 219, 220, 221, 223, 224, 231, 283, 288, 290
self-image, 224
self-improvement, 250
self-monitoring, 71
self-perceptions, 127
self-regulation, 7, 69, 166, 182, 261, 264
self-report, 28, 48, 54, 71, 75, 81, 108, 161, 168, 222, 227, 232, 233, 237, 317, 325
self-worth, 89, 247
semantic, 239, 266, 267
sensitivity, 45, 56, 213, 238
sentences, xii, xv, 163, 266, 282, 331
sentencing, 253
separation, 46, 70, 227, 237, 247
sequelae, 53
series, 17, 47, 79, 98, 134, 180, 253, 282, 334
serotonin, 69, 71, 84
service provider, x, 36, 37, 39, 68, 97
services, vi, x, 2, 26, 32, 35, 41, 47, 48, 50, 52, 53, 69, 77, 80, 81, 82, 97, 170, 171, 177, 251, 252, 286, 290, 294, 296, 299, 304
SES, 79, 212
severity, 18, 19, 53, 66, 67, 84, 88, 101, 103, 122, 136, 253, 304, 333
sex, xv, 38, 171, 173, 179, 280, 292, 293, 294, 295, 297, 301, 304, 331, 332, 333, 334
sex offenders, xv, 173, 179
sexual abuse, 45, 293
sexual assault, ix, x, 35, 110, 111, 168

sexual behavior, 49, 57, 81, 102, 264, 292, 293, 301, 334
sexual harassment, 279
sexual intercourse, 264
sexual offending, 155
sexual risk behavior, 201
sexuality, 166
sexually abused, 36, 45
SFT, x, 6, 36, 48, 49, 80, 81
shame, 265, 269
shape, xv, 140, 143, 145, 156, 158, 189, 248, 249, 281, 303
shaping, 142, 162, 233, 299
sharing, 100, 133, 236, 326
shelter, 304
shocks, 165
short-term, 50, 51, 82, 83, 100, 183, 305, 306
shy, 95, 120
shyness, 135
sibling, 79, 85, 233, 276, 293, 301
siblings, 15, 70, 79, 201, 293, 301
side effects, 305
sign, 16, 274
signals, 238
signs, xii, 67, 72, 139, 140, 151, 152, 155, 156
similarity, 145
sites, 14, 15, 221
skills training, ix, x, 1, 5, 6, 7, 8, 10, 13, 14, 23, 24, 25, 28, 35, 51, 56, 99, 109, 129, 130, 221
skin, 279
sleep, 36, 306
slums, 258
SMA, 62
smoking, 38, 40, 125, 278
soccer, 97, 113
sociability, 42
social activities, 39, 250, 253
social adjustment, 90, 137
social behavior, xiv, 104, 108, 160, 245, 249, 251, 252, 253, 257, 283, 303, 306
social behaviour, 141, 151, 153
social capital, 290, 291, 293, 295, 297
social class, 228, 236
social cognition, 90
social competence, 7, 106, 109, 121
social context, 98, 134, 199, 200, 202
social control, 44, 236, 281
social desirability, 298
social development, 52, 136, 141, 160, 257
social environment, xv, 120, 280, 303, 310, 313
social exchange, 231
social exclusion, 152, 159
social factors, 42

social group, xiii, 115, 243, 244, 274
social identity, 244
social influence, 222
social institutions, 277, 281
social integration, 95
social isolation, 72, 73
social learning, 106, 202
social life, 118
social maladjustment, 6, 206
social network, 13, 25, 85, 123
social norms, xii, 41, 139, 140, 141, 145, 151, 152, 154, 155, 156, 157, 158, 177, 262, 277
social order, 155
social participation, 123
social performance, xi, 66
social problems, 18, 97, 103
social psychology, 140, 159
social relations, 3, 73, 130, 201, 202
social relationships, 3, 73
social responsibility, xi, 93, 104
social sciences, 29, 134
social services, 26, 97, 251, 290, 294, 296, 299, 304
social situations, 122, 173
social skills, x, xii, 5, 30, 40, 42, 65, 69, 75, 121, 129, 130, 163, 166, 173, 177, 231, 248, 249
social skills training, 5, 130
social status, 118, 128, 134, 135
social structure, 236, 276
social support, 9, 10, 99, 109, 114, 121, 129, 244, 247, 251, 252, 254, 255
social support network, 9, 10
social systems, 182
social welfare, 236
social withdrawal, 134
social work, 15, 55, 61, 90, 119, 128, 129, 131, 133, 210, 250, 251, 315, 328
social workers, 119, 128, 133, 250, 251
socialization, 62, 95, 110, 155, 160
socializing agent, 140, 151, 157, 158
socially acceptable behavior, 277, 279
socially responsible, xi, 93
socioeconomic, 15, 16, 39, 44, 45, 46, 69, 70, 77, 85, 89, 94, 104, 321
socioeconomic background, 44
socioeconomic status, 15, 45, 46, 69, 70, 77, 85, 89, 94, 104
socio-emotional, xiii, 225, 226, 229, 237, 238
sociological, 206, 236, 250
solidarity, 142, 143, 247
somatic complaints, 103
special education, 105, 113
specificity, 261
spectrum, 173

speed, 12, 36
spiritual, 288, 290, 296, 297
spirituality, 290, 293, 295, 296, 297, 300
sport psychologists, 107
sports, 96, 97, 98, 100, 101, 102, 104, 106, 107, 108, 109, 110, 111, 113, 114, 288, 298
spouse, 173
SPSS, 19, 190, 290, 299
stability, 45, 78, 118, 122, 137, 195, 198, 201, 203, 227, 228, 229, 247, 288, 321
staff development, 252
stages, 12, 30, 67, 105, 167, 307, 308, 319, 320
standard deviation, 17, 20, 21, 22, 190, 213
standard error, 214, 217
standards, xiii, 43, 187, 243, 276, 277
stars, 131
statistical analysis, 235, 295
Statistical Package for the Social Sciences, 290
statistics, x, 32, 65, 66, 206, 213
status of children, 120
statutory, 333
stereotypes, 220
stereotypical, 287
stigma, 253, 289
stock, 178, 179, 180, 181, 258
strain, xiv, 6, 236, 241, 273, 276, 277, 278, 279, 281, 284
strains, 2, 3, 5, 8, 281
strategies, ix, x, xi, 1, 10, 26, 29, 35, 37, 47, 49, 66, 75, 77, 81, 99, 104, 105, 106, 109, 127, 132, 158, 173, 176, 177, 202, 220, 274, 282, 299, 328, 329
streams, 8
strength, xi, 26, 65, 67, 96, 184, 231, 261, 279, 289, 290, 295, 323, 325
stress, xi, xii, 2, 3, 4, 5, 8, 9, 24, 28, 29, 46, 66, 69, 71, 76, 78, 86, 91, 95, 105, 112, 121, 205, 206, 207, 208, 209, 211, 213, 214, 215, 216, 218, 219, 220, 221, 222, 223, 237, 239, 257
stressors, xii, 2, 4, 9, 89, 205, 207, 208, 209, 218, 219, 221, 231, 235, 237, 239, 288
structural equation model, 118, 198, 201, 213, 219, 220, 222, 223, 232
structural equation modeling, 118, 201, 213, 223, 232
Structural Equation Modeling, 222, 223
Structural Family Therapy, 48, 80
student populations, 26
subgroups, 119, 121, 122, 123
subjective, xiv, 162, 252, 259, 260, 261, 263, 265, 266, 267, 268, 269, 307
substance abuse, ix, x, 31, 35, 40, 41, 43, 45, 50, 51, 52, 54, 55, 56, 57, 58, 59, 62, 63, 69, 70, 76, 82,

84, 86, 88, 89, 94, 111, 167, 180, 226, 231, 232, 262, 279, 283, 294, 295, 297

substances, 37, 40, 42, 45, 51, 77, 153, 297

substitutes, 248

suburban, 73

suicidal, 32, 207, 223, 224

suicidal behavior, 32, 224

suicidal ideation, 207, 223

suicide, 126, 210, 224

summaries, 29

summer, 87, 247

superego, 164

supervision, 15, 39, 46, 70, 77, 78, 164, 167, 169, 171, 201, 210, 226, 227, 228, 235, 240, 247, 252, 275, 288

suppression, 166

survival, xii, 139, 140, 320

symbiotic, 199

symbols, xiii, 243

sympathy, 131

symptom, 44, 53, 84, 166, 255

symptoms, 31, 41, 44, 51, 74, 114, 126, 127, 136, 165, 200, 208, 223, 224, 227, 232, 257

synthesis, 180, 206

systemic change, 51, 59, 63, 90

T

tactics, 124, 128

tangible, 248

target behavior, 104

target population, 305

targets, 104, 121, 123, 125, 170, 173, 247, 282, 283, 299

taxonomy, 181

teachers, 10, 41, 44, 72, 75, 119, 130, 140, 141, 144, 146, 147, 148, 149, 150, 155, 157, 158, 160, 161, 162, 169, 227, 230, 250, 277, 278, 288, 298, 300

teacher-student relationship, 87

teaching, 5, 96, 98, 112, 140, 176, 181, 238, 298

technology, 128

teenagers, 5, 58

teens, 41, 50, 82

telephone, 127, 205

television, xiv, 39, 287, 288, 301

temperament, 39, 42, 69, 167, 231, 288

temporal, 87

territorial, 244, 245

territory, xiii, 159, 243, 244, 246, 250, 254, 275, 278

testosterone, 69, 71, 84, 89, 90

testosterone levels, 89

text messaging, 128

theft, 41, 51, 94, 97, 168, 180, 224, 228

Theory of Planned Behavior, 260, 270, 271

therapeutic interventions, 58

therapeutic relationship, 165

therapists, 6, 41, 49, 51, 82, 83, 165, 174

therapy, x, 6, 8, 28, 29, 30, 36, 37, 48, 50, 54, 55, 58, 59, 61, 63, 80, 82, 87, 90, 112, 165, 166, 170, 171, 173, 176, 177, 257, 258

thinking, 4, 19, 132, 173

threat, xi, 72, 117, 124, 133, 140, 175, 247

threatened, 246

threatening, 244

threats, 14, 128, 152, 231, 244, 332

three-dimensional, 180

threshold, 15, 24

time frame, 167

time periods, 251

timing, 241

tobacco, 5, 113, 167

tolerance, 20, 125, 248, 280, 310

toughness, 247

traction, 251

trade, xiv, 273, 276

tradition, 166, 174

traditional views, 164

traffic, 125

traffic violations, 125

training, ix, x, 1, 5, 6, 7, 8, 10, 13, 14, 23, 24, 25, 28, 30, 32, 35, 46, 51, 56, 61, 95, 99, 107, 109, 112, 113, 114, 129, 130, 157, 170, 171, 172, 210, 221, 229, 231, 283, 304

training programs, 6, 7, 8, 25, 157

traits, 41, 42, 159, 200, 261, 288, 289, 297, 298

trajectory, 72, 168, 189

tranquilizers, 40

transfer, 97, 99, 253

transference, 165

transformation, ix, xiii, 198, 243, 244

transition, 60, 198

transitions, 69

transmission, 228

transnational, 257

transparent, 102

transportation, 15

transracial, 30

trauma, 257, 288

traumatic events, 104

treatment programs, xii, 37, 163, 166, 170, 171, 174, 175, 176, 180

trial, 7, 12, 55, 57, 60, 87, 109

truancy, 37, 43

true/false, 212

trust, 141, 151, 157, 158, 159, 160, 211, 250

T-test, 16

Index

tutoring, 298
twin studies, 233
twins, 233, 234
typology, 245

U

underemployment, 244
undergraduate, 143
undergraduates, 332
underlying mechanisms, 110
unemployment, 70, 76, 94, 244, 255, 278, 288
unemployment rate, 255
university students, 142, 143, 146, 150, 153, 157
upward mobility, 254
urban areas, 107, 244, 251, 291

V

validity, 3, 14, 28, 137, 156, 161, 221, 290, 291, 322, 323, 325
values, xi, xiii, 3, 12, 18, 44, 66, 99, 106, 110, 162, 172, 173, 190, 206, 211, 217, 218, 234, 236, 243, 249, 268, 277, 278, 279, 281, 289, 312
vandalism, 224
variability, 37, 160, 188, 189, 191, 193, 230, 234, 265
variables, xiii, 14, 20, 24, 59, 103, 156, 185, 186, 188, 194, 195, 197, 199, 207, 208, 213, 215, 218, 219, 225, 226, 227, 228, 234, 235, 237, 258, 262, 264, 265, 267, 268, 295, 297
variance, 19, 20, 24, 25, 189, 226, 227, 228, 262, 265, 268, 269, 291, 295
variation, 11, 19, 22, 36, 37, 85, 171
variety of domains, 238
vegetables, 310
vein, 101
verbalizations, 78
victims, xi, xii, 37, 76, 94, 101, 117, 121, 122, 123, 124, 125, 126, 127, 129, 131, 133, 137, 138, 141, 153, 159, 175, 177, 183, 184, 185, 186, 189, 190, 191, 194, 196, 197, 202, 203, 246
violent behavior, x, xi, xv, 49, 65, 66, 67, 68, 71, 72, 73, 74, 75, 76, 77, 78, 79, 80, 81, 83, 86, 89, 94, 101, 107, 164, 168, 255, 317
violent behaviour, xii, 139, 140, 142, 144, 145, 146, 147, 155, 159, 161, 178

violent crime, 73, 103, 104, 167, 244, 254, 327
violent crimes, 73, 104, 244
violent offences, 167, 168
violent offenders, 160, 169, 173, 280
visible, 172, 251
vocabulary, 42
vocational, 102, 171, 172, 236, 252
vocational performance, 252
vocational training, 171, 172
volleyball, 97
voluntary organizations, 304
vulnerability, 37, 47, 51, 62, 63, 67, 70, 79, 91

W

wages, 248
walking, 12
war, 246, 247, 251, 254, 257
warfare, 244
warrants, 102, 282
wealth, 244, 254
weapons, 39, 67, 70, 126, 244, 245, 246, 282
Wechsler Intelligence Scale, 6
welfare, 78, 257, 297, 306
well-being, 30, 38, 68, 95, 108, 112, 114, 133, 176, 223
winning, 103, 244
wisdom, 62, 91
withdrawal, 122, 136, 227, 231, 237
witnesses, 76, 128, 299
women, 98, 106, 187, 289, 291
woods, 131
work environment, 304
work ethic, 276
workers, 10, 41, 119, 128, 170, 172, 175, 176, 250, 282
working memory, 103, 105, 113
worldview, 6

Y

young adults, xiii, xiv, 123, 126, 226, 238, 243, 245, 274, 278, 287, 288, 289, 299
young men, 123
younger children, 104, 118, 231, 249